Great Strategic Rivalries

EDITED BY
JAMES LACEY

Great Strategic Rivalries

From the Classical World to the Cold War

OXFORD
UNIVERSITY PRESS

Oxford University Press is a department of the University of Oxford. It furthers the University's objective of excellence in research, scholarship, and education by publishing worldwide. Oxford is a registered trade mark of Oxford University Press in the UK and certain other countries.

Published in the United States of America by Oxford University Press
198 Madison Avenue, New York, NY 10016, United States of America.

© Oxford University Press 2016

First issued as an Oxford University Press paperback, 2020

Library of Congress Cataloging-in-Publication Data
Names: Lacey, James, 1958- editor.
Title: Great strategic rivalries : from the classical world to the Cold War /
   edited by James Lacey.
Description: New York, NY : Oxford University Press, 2016. | Includes index.
Identifiers: LCCN 2016008635 (print) | LCCN 2016039666 (ebook) |
ISBN 9780190620462 (hardback) | ISBN 9780190053192 (paperback) |
ISBN 9780190620479 | ISBN 9780190620486
Subjects: LCSH: Strategic rivalries (World politics)—History. | Strategic
   rivalries (World politics)—Case studies. | BISAC: HISTORY / World. |
   HISTORY / Military / General. | POLITICAL SCIENCE / International
   Relations / General.
Classification: LCC JZ5595 .G74 2016 (print) | LCC JZ5595 (ebook) | DDC 327.1—dc23
LC record available at https://lccn.loc.gov/2016008635

9 8 7 6 5 4 3 2 1

Printed by Sheridan Books, Inc., United States of America

CONTENTS

MAPS

CONTRIBUTORS

James H. Anderson serves as the Vice President for Academic Affairs, Marine Corps University. He is currently coauthoring a book on US policy toward China. Dr. Anderson earned his doctorate in international relations from the Fletcher School of Law and Diplomacy, Tufts University.

Kathleen M. Burk was educated at Berkeley and Oxford, where she was also the Rhodes Fellow for North America and the Caribbean. She is Professor Emerita of Modern and Contemporary History at University College London. The author or editor of nearly a dozen books, including *Old World, New World: Britain and America from the Beginning* (Little Brown, 2007), she is currently writing a book on the interaction of the British and American empires from 1783 to 1972. She also writes on wine.

Robert M. Citino is a Professor of Military History at the University of North Texas. He is the author of nine books, including the award-winning *The Wehrmacht Retreats: Fighting a Lost War, 1943* (University Press of Kansas, 2012). He has taught at the US Military Academy and the US Army War College.

Kelly DeVries is Professor of History at Loyola University Maryland and Honorary Historical Consultant of the Royal Armouries, UK. He is the author, coauthor, or editor of twenty-two books and more than eighty articles on medieval military history and technology.

Kenneth W. Harl is Professor of Classical and Byzantine History at Tulane University in New Orleans, where he teaches courses in Greek, Roman, Byzantine, and Crusader history. He is the author of *Civic Coins and Civic*

Politics in the Roman East, 180–275 A.D. (University of California Press, 1987) and *Coinage in Roman Economy, 300* B.C.–*700* A.D. (Johns Hopkins Press, 1996).

James Lacey is the Professor of Strategy at the Marine Corps War College. He is the author of numerous books, most recently *The First Clash* (Bantam, 2013), *Pershing* (Palgrave, 2012), and *The Moment of Battle* (Bantam, 2015). His book on political, military, and economic disputes in Washington, DC, during World War II is forthcoming.

Michael V. Leggiere is Assistant Professor and Deputy Director, Military History Center, University of North Texas, and author of *Napoleon and Berlin: The Franco-Prussian War in North Germany, 1813* (Oxford University Press, 2002); *The Fall of Napoleon*, Vol. I: *The Allied Invasion of France, 1813–1814* (Cambridge, 2007); and *Blücher: Scourge of Napoleon* (University of Oklahoma Press, 2014).

William M. Morgan is the Professor of Diplomacey and Statecraft at the Marine Corps War College. Previously, he earned a PhD in diplomatic history from the Claremont Graduate University in California, then served over thirty years in the Foreign Service of the US Department of State. He is the author of *Pacific Gibraltar: U.S.-Japanese Rivalry over the Annexation of Hawaii, 1885–1898* (Naval Institute Press, 2011).

Williamson Murray is a Professor Emeritus of History from Ohio State University. He has written a wide selection of articles and books, most recently *Making of Peace: Rulers, States, and the Aftermath of War*, which he edited with James Lacey (Cambridge University Press, 2009); *The Shaping of Grand Strategy, Policy, Diplomacy, and War*, which he edited with Richard Sinnreich and James Lacey (Cambridge University Press, 2011); and *Hybrid Warfare*, coedited with Peter Mansoor (Cambridge University Press, 2012). At present he has the following completed manuscripts: *A Savage War, A Military History of the Civil War*, coauthored with Wayne Hsieh (scheduled for publication by Princeton University Press in 2016); *When Great Captains Fight*, coauthored with James Lacey (scheduled for publication by Random House in 2017); and *Grand Strategy and Coalition Warfare* (scheduled for publication by Cambridge University Press in 2016).

S. C. M. Paine is the William S. Sims Professor of History and Grand Strategy at the US Naval War College. She has authored *The Wars for Asia 1911–1949* (Leopold prize and PROSE award) (Cambridge University Press, 2012), *The Sino-Japanese War of 1894–1895* (Cambridge University Press, 2003), and

Imperial Rivals: China, Russia, and Their Disputed Frontier (Jelavich prize) (M. E. Sharpe, 1996); coedited with Bruce A. Elleman a series of books on naval operations, including blockades, commerce raiding, peripheral operations, coalitions, and non-military missions; and cowritten with him *Modern China: Continuity and Change 1644 to the Present* (Prentice Hall, 2010). She is working on a history of the Cold War.

Geoffrey Parker is the Andreas Dorpalen Professor of European History and an Associate of the Mershon Center at The Ohio State University, was born in Nottingham, and has written or cowritten thirty-nine books, including *The Grand Strategy of Philip II* (Yale University Press, 1998); *The Spanish Armada* (with Colin Martin, Manchester University Press, 1999); and *Imprudent King: A New Biography of Philip II* (Yale University Press, 2014).

Paul A. Rahe holds The Charles O. Lee and Louise K. Lee Chair in the Western Heritage at Hillsdale College, where he is Professor of History. He is the author of *Republics Ancient and Modern: Classical Republicanism and the American Revolution* (University of North Carolina Press, 1992); *Against Throne and Altar: Machiavelli and Political Theory under the English Republic* (Cambridge Universitry Press, 2008); *Montesquieu and the Logic of Liberty: War, Religion, Commerce, Climate, Terrain, Technology, Uneasiness of Mind, the Spirit of Political Vigilance and the Foundations of the Modern Republic,* and *Soft Despotism, Democracy's Drift: Montesquieu, Rousseau, Tocqueville and the Modern Prospect* (Yale University Press, 2009); *The Grand Strategy of Classical Sparta: The Athenian Challenge* (2015); and *The Spartan Regime: Its Character, Origins, and Grand Strategy* (Yale University Press, 2016).

Matt J. Schumann received his doctorate in history from the University of Exeter (UK) in 2005, and now teaches at Eastern Michigan University. His publications include *The Seven Years War: A Transatlantic History* (Routledge, 2008), coauthored with Karl W. Schweizer, and several articles on war and foreign relations in the eighteenth-century Atlantic world. He is currently working on a book entitled *Under the Shadow of War: Cultural Change and the Diplomatic Revolution, 1748–1756.*

Christine Shaw has been a Research Officer at the London School of Economics, Senior Research Fellow at the University of Warwick, Senior Research Associate at the University of Cambridge, and a Visiting Professor at Villa I Tatti. She is an Associate Member of the Faculty of History of the University of Oxford. Her major publications include *Julius II: The Warrior Pope* (Blackwell, 1993); *The Politics of Exile in Renaissance Italy* (Cambridge University Press, 2000); *Popular Government and Oligarchy in Renaissance*

Italy (Brill, 2006); *The Italian Wars 1494–1559: War, State and Society in Early Modern Europe* (with Michael Mallett, Pearson, 2012); and *Barons and Castellans: The Military Nobility of Renaissance Italy* (Brill, 2015).

Barry S. Strauss is the Bryce and Edith Bowmay Professor in Humanistic Studies and Chair of the Department of History at Cornell University. He is currently the director of Cornell's Program on Freedom and Free Societies. His book *Battle of Salamis: The Naval Encounter That Saved Greece—and Western Civilization* was named one of the best books of 2004 by the *Washington Post*. His books have been translated into nine languages. His latest book, *Masters of Command: Alexander, Hannibal, Caesar and the Genius of Leadership* (Simon & Schuster, 2012), was named one of the best books of 2012 by Bloomberg.

Geoffrey Wawro is Professor of History and Director of the Military History Center at the University of North Texas. He studied at Brown and Yale and is the author of five books, including *The Franco-Prussian War, Quicksand: America's Pursuit of Power in the Middle East* (The Penguin Press, 2010), and *A Mad Catastrophe: The Outbreak of World War I and the Collapse of the Habsburg Empire* (Basic Books, 2014).

Andrew Wheatcroft is Professor of International Publishing and Communication and Director of the Centre for Publishing Studies at the University of Stirling. He is the author of *Infidels* (Random House, 2005), *The Habsburgs* (Penguin Books, 1996), *The Ottomans* (Penguin Books, 1995), and *The Enemy at the Gate* (Basic Books, 2010).

Great Strategic Rivalries

Introduction
James Lacey

M ORE THAN HALF OF all wars since 1816 have taken place among enduring strategic rivals, while less than a fifth have been between states without any established rivalry. Surprisingly, given such a remarkable correlation, there are very few studies on the topic of enduring strategic rivalries. Though they have dug deep into the histories of particular rivalries, historians have not approached the topic in a thematic way to create a body of historiographical literature that allows one to compare and contrast rivalries across the ages. Political scientists have done little better. Until the late 1980s, they had not addressed the topic at all.[1] But from the mid-1990s until approximately 2002, a small group of political scientists did conduct mostly statistical-based examinations of "intra-state enduring rivalries." Then they went silent. For more than a decade now, the field of political science has offered little on the topic of enduring strategic rivalries.

If one were to surmise a reason for the rapid passing of what at first appeared a fruitful field of research, the only apparent reason was that political scientists had exploited all of the available data. Given their approach, which mostly amounted to counting conflicts and determining the dates between them, there were only a limited number of variables to explore and a relatively small data set with which to work. Political scientists quite literally ran out of inferences that they could make, based on the data available to them. In short, they had exhausted all the possibilities for further research, at least with quantitative data capable of being gathered and modeled.

Thankfully, those political scientists addressing this issue did not quit the field without first leaving us with a number of observations that clearly make a case for the central importance of enduring rivalries in international affairs, particularly those among great powers.[2] Such observations provide an essential steppingstone for a deeper, historically based analysis of enduring rivalries, aimed at drawing out commonalties and possible lessons that endure across the centuries.

Characteristics of Enduring Rivalries: What the Data Tell Us

Enduring rivalries do not suddenly appear. Rather, they are the result of a series of previous interactions that appear to lock in future behavior.

1. As states interact and crises develop, one side invariably retreats.
2. Typically, states do not learn how to avoid future crises or methods of peacefully edging away from calamity. Rather, after each successive encounter, both parties tend to become more belligerent.[3]
3. Moreover, the perceived winner of a previous dispute usually sees no reason to change its strategy during the next encounter, as it believes it can continue to get what it wants by continuing to hold to a firm line.
4. The loser, on the other hand, sees defeat as a matter of not having acted with sufficient strength or resolve. It, therefore, adopts a more coercive position in the future.[4]
5. This apparently holds true even after a military defeat, where one might expect the losing state to behave with greater caution during a future dispute. The opposite is the case: *the loser of a previous contest is almost always more belligerent in any future crisis.*

Pushing such data further demonstrates the profound effect that *bullying* has on future relations. In every data set examined by political scientists, save one, the third instance of bullying (threatening military conflict) led to war. Probably for reasons of "reputation," a major power could not allow itself to be seen as repeatedly backing down in the face of threats. The only example of states avoiding war in this situation was the Cuban missile crisis, where the threat of an impending nuclear holocaust hung over the proceedings. Unfortunately (or more probably, fortunately) there are insufficient data to determine the overall effect of nuclear weapons on enduring state rivalries: it is impossible to build patterns out of a single data set containing a single example (the Cold War).

Despite a few instances where one side replaced its strategic assessment with "hope" (e.g., Japan vs. United States), it is worth noting that the crises under study almost always occurred when both sides viewed the net balance of power between them as roughly equal, giving each a perceived chance of winning a conflict. Many therefore assume, based on the record, that weaker states are unlikely to provoke a crisis with a more powerful one.

The historical record is likely more mixed then the data sets allow, particularly in the modern era. For instance, the data do not adequately capture the effect of a superpower standoff. During the Cold War, Cuba was capable of provoking any number of crises situations with the far more powerful United States, on the assumption that US policymakers would draw back rather than allow a localized crisis to create a wider dispute with the Soviet Union. Moreover, the data fail to capture the effects of the "edge of empire" or the "edge of power." For instance, during World War II, Japan, with only 10 percent of America's industrial capacity, was able to withstand four years of total war before its collapse. The length of this struggle reflects the fact that as the war grew closer to Japan, its relative strength grew, as the United States was forced to project forces over greater distances. Similarly, 2,500 years ago, tiny Athens was able to resist the might of Persia because the Persians were capable of projecting only a fraction of their total power at the edges of their vast empire. In the future, even if the United States remains vastly superior to any other state in total military power, it may find it progressively more difficult to win in the immediate vicinity of a near-peer competitor.

Further revelations from the study of the data sets include the following:

- Most enduring rivalries do not start out as long-term "hate affairs." States often do not even perceive themselves as involved in an enduring rivalry for many years after its initiation or after multiple militarized disputes.
- In the early years of a developing rivalry, the single most crucial factor in its continuance and militarization is domestic politics. In almost every case, hardening attitudes and increased belligerence correlate very closely to a rapid rise in the level of agitation not to retreat from a perceived provocation.
- Power shifts (real or perceived) double the chance of war. In this regard, shifts toward parity are most likely to start wars. For instance, a doubling of the US nuclear arsenal is unlikely (according to the data) to inflame the US-Sino proto-rivalry, as increasing an already overwhelming US nuclear preponderance does little to affect the

current strategic calculus. On the other hand, a dramatic rise in Chinese nuclear weaponry, aimed at achieving parity with the United States, would radically alter each side's strategic calculus and would have a much higher probability of leading to conflict. A clear historical example of this effect was Germany's drive to build a fleet the equal of Great Britain's at the start of the twentieth century.

- The course and consequences of each successive conflict within an enduring rivalry profoundly affect subsequent conflicts. For instance, the reasons for the French military defeat in the Franco-Prussian War (1870–1871) directly affected its military approach in World War I, while the consequences of that earlier war provided the rationale for France's later war aims.

- All enduring rivalries appear to have certain strategic commonalities:
  - an outstanding set of unresolved issues,
  - strategic interdependence,
  - a psychological manifestation of enmity, and
  - repeated militarized conflicts (not necessarily war).

- Changes in preference and perception often affect the course of rivalries. For instance, when the United States no longer appeared interested in absorbing Canada, coupled with US perception that it faced greater threats than those posed by Great Britain, it became much easier to manage both nations' commercial competition without militarizing disputes.

- Major shocks to the global system are a necessary catalyst and a key ingredient in the development of an enduring strategic rivalry. For instance, there was little room for a new strategic-level rivalry to take hold during the Cold War. Only after the demise of the Soviet Union was it possible for new rivalries to emerge. Similarly, it was the collapse of German power, as well as the fall of two other empires (Russian and Austro-Hungarian), in the wake of World War I that opened the door for the emergence of new rivalries.

- Disputes among recognized enduring rivalries are two times more likely to end in war than isolated, one-time disputes. Moreover, in the modern era (post-1815, or the Treaty of Versailles), 45 percent of all wars have been between enduring rivals. If one includes proto-rivalries, that total rises above 80 percent.[5] Moreover, 90 percent of all enduring rivalries end with a shock to the global system. For instance, the Persian-Roman rivalry in the East abruptly ended with the rise of Islam, as both powers were eventually subsumed by the rising power.

As we see from the preceding, the data collected and utilized by political scientists provide a number of crucial points for consideration. However, from the point of view of policymakers, there are several major problems with such an approach to examining enduring rivalries. This first becomes obvious in the widely accepted definition that political scientists have given to rivalries, which in their conception *must always be militarized.*

Moreover, to be considered a rivalry, a certain number of disputes must be concentrated within a specific time span. Typically, if two rivals go twenty years without a militarized dispute (not necessarily a war), political scientists deem the rivalry at an end. The historical record, however, demonstrates that disputes can lie dormant for many decades before erupting once again into major intra-state conflict. Therefore, one must question the appropriateness of such an arbitrary number of "twenty years." By applying such an artificial construct, all analysis of the decisions and events that keep the rivalry simmering go unexamined.

Further, political scientists in simplifying the data do not make room for enduring rivalries that do not end up in a series of violent conflicts. In this formulation, *competition is not rivalry.* For the policymaker, the analytical exclusion of competitions that fall short of war presents a clear problem: How does one examine methods for keeping a competition—let us say a hard-fought global commercial rivalry—from turning into a shooting war? As a number of violent enduring rivalries arose only after a prolonged period of commercial (that is, economic) competition, the political science approach neglects any examination of how to keep competitive interactions from creating the conditions for militarized hostility. Such disregard of *enduring commercial rivalries* that never become violent conflicts deprives policymakers of evidence-based guidance on how one might compete for economic predominance without causing a war.

In establishing a complete set of guideposts for strategists and policymakers, it is, therefore, essential to scrutinize both (1) commercial rivalries that have turned violent and (2) those that remain peaceful. The first may illuminate untaken opportunities that could have avoided war, while the second may present lessons on the accommodations necessary for extending peace during periods of intense competition. Unfortunately, in this regard, the data underpinning political science research have little to offer. For commercial rivalries turned violent, the data tell us a lot about the number of disputes and their intervals, but present little in the way of explanation. In the latter—a nonviolent competition—the data are silent, as these conditions are not included in their data collections.

The inability to explain events has always haunted political scientists. Though their data demonstrate that the militarized disputes are twice as likely to lead to war if there had been two previous such disputes, that finding alone does little to explain how such disputes got started, how they remain alive, or how one might avoid them. Explanations such as "each dispute caused both parties to harden their positions so that war remained the only viable option" remain merely *suppositions*, as data sets contain no evidence of actual hardening. Moreover, to make sense of the volumes of data typically employed by political scientists, they have developed techniques that tend in many ways to distort actual events. This is most often done by selecting one or two variables to test, while either ignoring or "controlling" for all of the other variables affecting a solution. In short, political scientists remove both the context and messiness of real-world situations. Policymakers and strategists, on the other hand, always work in *a world filled with context and where messiness prevails*. And, in reality, extraneous variables are rarely controlled, as they wreak havoc on the best-laid plans.

Grasping all of this contextual messiness requires one to go far beyond a reliance on data sets and to delve deeply into all of the factors and conditions that propelled history's various enduring strategic rivalries forward. Only by doing so can one draw out vital lessons on *rivalry management* that will assist policymakers in navigating the dangerous shoals of new or re-emerging rivalries already becoming visible on the global horizon. The essays used to underpin the observations presented here are not meant to replace the work of political scientists. Rather, they are the next logical step in developing a deep understanding of the character and nature of enduring strategic rivalries, a step that explains not only what happened but why.

Historical Observations

ROOT CAUSES

The existing literature on enduring strategic rivalries commonly breaks such rivalries into three main types. (Unfortunately, the strategic pairs of rivalries examined for this project fail to bear out the existence of these simple categories.)

- Spatial: Rivals contest exclusive control of a region.
- Ideological: Rivals contest the superiority of their particular belief systems, whether they are religious, economic, or political.
- Positional: A contest over relative influence and prestige within a system.[6]

Few of the great rivalries in history are centered on controlling a region. True, the military actions that go hand in hand with a strategic rivalry are often fought out in a certain, often small, region, but this typically reflects the fact that either the geographic area is typically the point where two rivals can most easily get at one another, or contesting control of this region is acting as a trigger point for larger issues.

Similarly, the evidence that enduring rivalries are maintained by deep ideological difference is, at best, not proven. Though ideological differences are often present in some of the rivalries, particularly in the modern era, in every case where a choice is required between ideology or advancing geopolitical interests, ideology is thrown away. Though ideology colors attitudes and, as a result, becomes a prism through which rivals evaluate each other's actions, it rarely, if ever, plays a dominant role in determining state actions. *Prestige* and *garnering influence*, on the other hand, come with a specific problem: they are part of the reason behind every action of every state in existence, making it impossible to separate out the *positional* concerns of strategic rivals from the concerns they would have if the state had no rival. The evidence demonstrates that *positional* concerns mount once a rivalry is underway, with each party casting around for allies and other support from within the current state system. In fact, once a rivalry is underway, *prestige* becomes the dominant factor in pushing diplomatic crises toward war.

Dismissing the current explanatory paradigm for strategic rivalries begs the question: *What will replace it?* As one reviews the historical examples, however, it becomes clear that there was no need to establish a new paradigm, as one already exists. What Thucydides wrote 2,500 years ago, as he elucidated the reasons for the Athenian-Spartan rivalry, still suffices to explain state motivations and actions in every rivalry under consideration in this work:

> And the nature of the case first compelled us to advance our empire to its present height; fear being our principal motive, though honor and interest afterwards came in. . . . And no one can quarrel with a people for making in matters of tremendous risk, the best provision that it can for its interest. . . . It follows that it was not very remarkable action or contrary to the common practice of mankind, if we did not accept an empire that was offered to us, and refused to give it up under the pressure of the three strongest motives, fear, honor, and interest.[7]

For the next 2,500 years, the idea of fear, honor, and interest has remained the best paradigm for explaining both the arrival and course of strategic rivalries. Where one can interchange the words *prestige* and *honor*, it is clear that, in this regard, theorists have identified a long recognized factor but, for reasons unknown, have considered it important to rename it. As the classical scholar Donald Kagan has noted, where one nation seeking to improve its honor or prestige tramples on another state's interests, conflict becomes nearly inevitable.

In this collection of essays, both Geoffrey Wawro (Chapter 10) and Williamson Murray (Chapter 12) illustrate that many of Germany's pre–World War I actions were motivated by its desire to gain prestige in a European environment where it was viewed as the new kid on the block, having only become a unified nation in 1870. One would have to peer deep indeed to see any motivation besides attempting to increase its prestige (honor) for Germany to be provoking successive crises in Bosnia and Morocco between 1906 and 1911. Moreover, it is easy to see how the "fear" engendered by Germany's actions propelled the spate of alliance making that aligned the great powers—England, France, Russia—against the German state. In defending this alignment, David Lloyd George, in his famous Mansion House Speech, stated,

> I believe it is essential that Britain should at all hazards maintain her prestige among the great world powers.... I say emphatically that peace at that price [abandoning France] would be a humiliation intolerable for a great country like ours to endure.[8]

When war finally did break out, Great Britain, despite having clear economic interest in steering clear of the conflict, felt honor bound to come to the aid of Belgium once it was under German assault. British citizens were given the practical reason that German conquest of the Channel ports put British trade and possibly the survival of the country at intolerable risk. This is not a trivial reason, but one can doubt the continuing strategic threat that control of the Channel ports presented after the end of the Age of Sail. But as Donald Kagan demonstrates by quoting British Foreign Secretary Sir Edward Grey, "honor" provided a deeper motivation: "Britain could keep out of the war by issuing a proclamation of unconditional neutrality.... If we did take that line by saying we will have nothing to do with the matter ..., we should, I believe, sacrifice our respect and good name and reputation before the world." Years later, Grey wrote that

> the real reason for going into the war was that, if we did not stand by France and stand up for Belgium against [German] aggression, we should be isolated, discredited, and hated; and there would be nothing for us but a miserable and ignoble future.[9]

Britain could clearly see the risks to the standing national order presented by an aggressive German state, but it still felt the need to clothe the decisions that led it into war as acts of honor without ever spending much time making a case for war based on its own interests. How much different it was two decades later, when Sir Neville Chamberlain defended his dooming Czechoslovakia, by appeasing Hitler at Munich, by explaining the lack of British interests in the region. Demonstrating, however, that honor remained a crucial ingredient in geopolitics, Churchill said of the Munich agreement, "The government had to choose between war and shame. They chose shame. They will get war." Despite having as few practical interests in Poland as they had in Czechoslovakia, both Britain and France, after the humiliation of Munich, felt honor bound to go to war when Poland's sovereignty was threatened.

It did not have to be this way. After the unification of the German state, Chancellor Bismarck clearly saw that both Russia and France perceived a unified Germany as a threat. To counter this, Bismarck undertook a charm offensive aimed at keeping France isolated from any power that could help it gain revenge for its defeat in the Franco-Prussian War (1870). During his travels, Bismarck constantly repeated the phrase "*Wir sind satt*!" ("We are full!"), trying to convince Russia and others that Germany was now a satisfied power, with no further territorial ambitions. Such protestations came with reminders of the long friendship between Russia and Prussia, which were both part of the coalition that defeated Napoleon and maintained the "Concert of Europe" for the better part of a century. But as Henry Kissinger points out, honeyed words about conservative solidarity and the traditional friendship between Prussia and Russia meant nothing in the face of national self-interest.[10] All Russia was able to see was a large and growing power on its border.

Similarly, we will see, at the nexus of honor and interest is war. By any measure, the German decision at the beginning of the twentieth century to build a fleet capable of challenging Britain on the high seas was a foolish measure. In practical strategic terms, the effort consumed vast resources that Germany desperately missed when war erupted in 1914. Moreover, it did so with almost no practical gain, as the bulk of the German High Seas Fleet spent almost the entire war in port, taking no part in disrupting British commerce or even attempting to break the blockade that was strangling the German economy. Except for one brief foray out to Jutland, which ended in ignominious retreat as the British fleet approached, the German navy was not heard from for the remainder of the war. What is remarkable in this entire episode is that with France and Russia already allied against her, Germany undertook the one measure that was sure to alarm Britain. By deciding to build a fleet that could contest the British Royal Navy on the high seas, Germany, in a single stroke, ended hundreds of years of Anglo-French hostility, as both former historic rivals found more to "fear" from the growth of German economic and military power then they did from each other. For the Germans, the building of a great fleet was a matter of honor, but for the British, the German fleet was a sword pointed at its heart.

The German example of the relevance of "fear, honor, and interest" in creating and propelling a strategic rivalry is not a stand-alone instance. Similar concerns and motivations can be extrapolated from every enduring rivalry covered in this work. For instance, the competition between Rome and Carthage was about security [fear], greed [interest], and ambition [honor]. Rome intervened in Sicily against Carthage because it *feared* the Carthaginian threat to the trading interests of its southern Italian allies, because it coveted Sicilian wealth, and also because ambitious Romans sought a new arena for winning glory. On the other side of the rivalry ledger, Hannibal invaded Italy because he inherited a *fear* and hatred of Rome from the First Punic War, while also considering Rome a threat to his country's—and his family's—empire in Spain.

Later, led by Cato, Rome attacked Carthage in the Third Punic War because it feared a Carthaginian military revival, disliked Carthaginian commercial competition in the western Mediterranean, and coveted Carthage's wealth. Because of this combination of concerns, we have Cato picking up some figs that had just arrived from Carthage to remind his fellow citizens that their most feared foe was growing stronger daily, and were only three sailing days from their shores. In every speech after that staged event, Cato played on Roman fears and their interest in their own expansion by ending with the statement, *"ceterum censeo Carthaginem esse delendam"* ("Furthermore I consider that Carthage must be destroyed.") Eventually, the combination of *fear* (Roman mothers still used Hannibal as the bogeyman in children's dreams), *honor* (supporting their Numidian allies then under attack by Carthage), and *interest* (Rome needed the highly productive Carthaginian agricultural system to feed its burgeoning population) led to war and Carthage's utter destruction.[11] Thus ended one strategic rivalry.

A similar tale is found in every enduring strategic rivalry from antiquity to the late twentieth century. Such concerns are so common that political scientists have coined the term "Thucydidean trap" as a way of describing current international tensions that might lead to war.[12] While fear, honor, and interest might explain the crucial motivations behind an enduring rivalry, they remain only part of the story. They do not, for instance, explain the conditions required for a rivalry to form. For states are not born fearing each other, and if a state plans to defend certain specific interests, it must perceive another state's threat to them.

MACRO-EVENTS ESTABLISH BASE CONDITIONS

One of the observations that political scientists drew from their data is that *rivalry ignitions require a major shock to the established global system or order.* Historical analysis bears this out. Moreover, it appears that it requires *a similar huge international disruption to end a rivalry*, though the traumatic end of the rivalry could be the shock that both ends one rivalry and opens the door for the next (e.g., Rome vs. Carthage).

Paul Rahe in Chapter 1 concludes that while the Spartan-Athenian alliance against Persia was often uneasy, as alliances nearly always are, it was a genuine alliance. It had been summoned into existence by the Persian threat, and it was not apt to dissolve as long as it seemed possible that Persia might attempt to conquer Greece. Only after the battles of Marathon, Salamis, and Plataea, coupled with the Athenian-led counterattack across the Aegean, did the Persian menace retreat—but in doing so, it opened the door to a split in the alliance and a growing rivalry.

It was perhaps inevitable that two such *polities* would come to blows. The difference in their respective *ethos* inevitably gave rise to misunderstandings and a measure of mutual dislike. Moreover, despite the best efforts of leaders in each city-state who were sympathetic to the concerns of the other, there were citizens in both Athens and Sparta who were suspicious of or resentful toward the other polity: in Sparta, those who found the growth in Athenian power daunting and, as a result, argued that Athens was the new Persia; and those at Athens who feared that sooner or later the Spartans would intervene in their affairs, as they had done in the past.

Still, those propensities were held in check as long as a Persian resurgence was expected. Persia, until the advent of the Roman Empire, was the greatest empire in antiquity. Held together for 200 years by a huge and efficient military force, it had for most of that time been an overawing threat to Greece. The sudden removal of that threat was, by any measure, a tectonic shift in power arrangements that had dominated the eastern Mediterranean for centuries. Were it not for the demise of Persian power and influence in the region, neither Sparta nor Athens, the bulwarks of the anti-Persian coalition, would have dared allow their mutual antagonisms to dominate their relations.

Similar shocks are found both at the start and end of the enduring strategic rivalries studied (see Table 0.1 on international shocks). Moreover, the historical record clearly shows that the formation of a major interstate rivalry tends to limit or tamp the formation of other rivalries within the system. The reasons for this remain uncertain, but probably include the following:

- Other states do not possess the power to undertake a rivalry that may become militarized.
- Other states are able to conduct their own rivalries within the structure of the enduring strategic rivalry by choosing to join with opposing sides of the dominant rivalry.
- The great powers involved in an enduring strategic rivalry forbid the lesser powers from acting in a manner that could draw them into conflicts not of the dominant powers' time and choosing.
- Some combination of the preceding, coupled with the fact that historians focus on conflicts between the great powers, leaving the causes and progress of other rivalries relatively understudied and unnoticed.

But do such shocks kick off enduring rivalries? Here the evidence is difficult to unravel, but it appears that systemic shocks are not the cause of a new rivalry starting. Rather, they set the condition that makes a rivalry possible. They do not, however, guarantee that a rivalry will develop. For that, a number of other factors must be present.

For instance, as Kelly Devries points out in Chapter 4, before 1066, the English and the French had traveled in completely different orbits. William the Conqueror's invasion forced the English to deal with France substantially for the first time. Likewise, the Ottomans and the Hapsburgs were rarely in contact, until Constantinople's fall in 1453 gave them a mutual border. Similarly, other shocks placed major powers in close proximity to each other for the first time (e.g., the unification of Germany placed a powerful state—Germany—up against France's borders; and Poland failed to become a stable state for much of the twentieth century because German unification pressed Poland against Russian territory). Slightly more puzzling are those rivalries that are maintained between powers distant from one another (Japan-US, Russia-US, and to some extent Genoa-Venice). Largely this is explainable by the march of technology that has gone a long way toward conquering the tyranny of distance, and in some cases (e.g., the movement of information) has eliminated it. The near eradication of distance, from at least the start of the Age of Sail and the Industrial Revolution, has expanded the interests of great states. In short,

TABLE O.I International Shocks: The Advent and the End of Rivalries

The Rivalry	Shock: Start of Rivalries	Shock: End of Rivalries
Athens vs. Sparta (465–404 BCE)	The end of the Persian military threat	As Athens rebuilt much of its power after its defeat in the Peloponnesian War, the true shock to the system was first the rise of Thebes and then Macedon under Philip II and his son Alexander.
Rome vs. Carthage (264–146 BCE)	The temporary elimination of the threat to Rome from the Gauls and from Pyrrhus Greek invasion, leading to Rome's emergence as a major military and economic power	The destruction of Carthage
Rome-Byzantium vs. Persia (69 BCE– 636 CE)	The destruction of the Western Roman Empire, and the rise of the Sassanid Dynasty in Persia	The Islamic invasion
England vs. France (1066–1453, the Middle Ages)	The 1066 Norman conquest of France	English defeat that saw their military forces and political structures eliminated on the Continent; and political upheaval in England (but the barons got their Magna Carta)
Genoa vs. Venice (13th and 14th centuries)	The end of the medieval era in Italy, the development of new methods of finance, the destruction of the Crusader states, Ottoman power expansion	Political, financial, and military revolution in Europe that reduced the Italian city-states to insignificance within the European power system
Hapsburgs vs. Europe (1516–1713)	The creation of a powerful Hapsburg Empire	The destruction of a sizable portion of Hapsburg power, and the rise of France as a European superpower

(continued)

The Rivalry	Shock: Start of Rivalries	Shock: End of Rivalries
Ottomans vs. Hapsburgs	The fall of Constantinople (1453)	The Ottoman Empire ceased to be a threat when it failed to modernize to keep up with technological and organizational developments in the West.
England vs. France (1337–1453)	The creation of powerful centralized proto-states (as in the Hundred Years War)	Total English defeat
England vs. France (1792–1815, the "Napoleonic Era")	The French Revolution (1789) and the destruction of the old political order, the *ancien régime*	The final and total defeat of Napoleon and the establishment of the Concert of Europe
Germany vs. France (1866–1945)	The creation of a new unified power within the European order and the Industrial Revolution	German defeat in two world wars
Germany vs. Europe (1815–1945)	The threat posed by a strong, industrialized, and unified Germany in the heart of Europe	German defeat in two world wars
United States vs. United Kingdom (ca. 1812–ca. 1940)	The entry of a new economic superpower into the global order	The recognition of common enemies, first Germany and then Germany coupled with Japan
United States vs. Japan (1897 to 1941)	The sudden forced opening of Japan and its subsequent rapid modernization, and its entry as a new power in the global system	The complete military defeat of Japan
United States vs. USSR[a] (1945–1991)	End of World War II (1945)	The collapse of the Soviet Empire (1991)

[a] *USSR: Union of Soviet Socialist Republics*

early rivalries, limited by the inability to overcome geography, could only be against states in relatively close proximity. In the modern era, states are not nearly as bound by such restrictions.

Systemic shocks not only provide the conditions for starting a rivalry, they are also required for ending one. In some cases, the required systemic shocks are a result of the climactic ending of a prior rivalry. For instance, the Carthage-Rome rivalry ended when one power (Rome) annihilated the other in 146 BCE. Similarly, the German-European powers set of rivalries terminated when the other European powers (assisted by the United States) overran, occupied, and remade the German political system. Other rivalries ended because a new and more lethal danger arose. This is clearly visible in the ending of the Roman (Byzantine)–Persian rivalry, which was accomplished by Arab raiders, propelled by the driving force of Islam, threatening the destruction of both empires. The same is true of the Anglo-French rivalry, which was put aside when both sides began to perceive Germany as the greater threat.

What is the importance of this observation in today's world? In recent decades, the globe has undergone a series of systemic shocks to the global order, any one of which could establish the conditions for the emergence of a new rivalry, or possibly (in the case of a revived Russia) the extension of a previous one. These shocks include but unfortunately may not be limited to the following:

- The collapse of the Soviet Union, ending the Cold War and assumedly ending the US-Russian rivalry (though recent events leave this conclusion open to question);
- The rise of another great power (China) within the global system;
- The impending collapse of Arab civilization;
- An ongoing remaking of the global economy, in ways that will rival the effects of the Industrial Revolution.

Many researchers assume that if a new enduring rivalry is going to develop, it is likely to be between the United States and China. But a word of caution is in order. The globe is in a period of uncertainty, with the current international order facing a number of threats to its stability. Such periods have occurred before in history, and those experiences cast doubt on our ability to forecast what the political order will look like in a few decades. It is possible that the United States is on the cusp of a new enduring rivalry with China, but that is far from preordained. Moreover, even if a rivalry does develop, it remains possible to keep it from becoming overly militarized or marked by periods of direct military conflict.

Even if a China-US rivalry fails to develop, a different rivalry pair is almost certain. In more than 2,500 years of recorded history, the international system has rarely been without a pair of rival states contending for power and influence. The exceptions are marked by one of three phenomena:

- A hegemon that no other power can contest, such as China for most of its history prior to the great European commercial empires establishing themselves in Asia;
- A stark period of widespread disorder (consider the Dark Ages in Western Europe);
- A number of smaller but just as intense regional rivalries develop, as there is no overarching rivalry to tamp down or subsume them. This may arguably have been the case in the post-Napoleonic world, where simultaneous rivalries were starting or ongoing (Anglo-American, Japan-China, Japan-Russia, and various German rivalries with its neighbors).

Given these choices, what is the most likely? Looking at the current global environment, one is tempted to say "all of them." Still, even as we witness increasing chaos in huge swaths of the world (the so-called "Arch of Crisis"), there remains a strong likelihood that the major powers can contain the spread of disorder within their current region(s). If one accepts that geopolitics is remerging after a temporary post–Cold War hiatus, coupling this with the observed pattern of rising regional powers (often multiple powers in a single region), then we have the making of a powerful, and in many ways, unique future—a *system of rivalries*.

Consider for a moment the strategic implications of a world in which the United States remains the predominant economic and military power, but is locked in multiple enduring rivalries with near-peer competitors—China, a resurgent Russia (assuming it overcomes its crippling economic and demographic challenges), and possibly even the European Union (particularly on the commercial level). Simultaneously, a number of regional rivalries may be able to sustain themselves, as the rivalries between those powers with global reach never would achieve the red-hot intensity that would force the rest of the world to pick a side. Or conditions do not form where every act of other states is seen through the prism of the overarching "great rivalry." Such a world would be prone to periodic dangerous flare-ups in widely disseminated locations. Sustaining order in this world would require the United States (as the remaining dominant power) to undertake a very delicate balancing game between multiple powers. Unfortunately, within such a global order the United States may be unable to dictate every solution. Still, it may be one where the United States can still have a strong influence in most affairs—something similar to that of the United Kingdom from 1815 to at least 1914.

The other alternative is a US retreat from hegemonic power (no longer accepting the role of global policeman), perhaps with the specific intent of avoiding a possibly draining rivalry—assuming that avoiding a rivalry is even possible, as rivalries have an internal dynamic that makes them difficult, if not impossible, to avoid. In this case, a US retreat opens the door to a selection of not mutually exclusive options:

- Another hegemon will step into the vacuum, inserting a new paradigm in place of the current liberal global order—one that may be inimical to the interests of the United States and the West.
- Multiple rivalries will coexist without a powerful balancing force to tamp down their excesses (e.g., a situation similar to what existed during the rise of Germany and Japan in the 1930s).
- No rivalries take hold as global disorder increases in a world where less powerful states (the regional powers), with a limited perception of their stake in an established world order, are incapable of containing violent excesses.

An American retreat from hegemony is extremely unlikely to lead to a universal utopia. As the alternatives to US engagement all imperil the liberal world order from which the United States has benefited, one is forced to accept continuing US engagement as the one remaining viable action. Such a choice not only risks the formation (or continuation) of a strategic enduring rivalry, it is, historically speaking, a foregone conclusion. This leads to several important questions that are addressed in the chapters of this volume:

- How have enduring rivalries maintained themselves over time?
- Can the competitions between rivals be carried out without turning into an enduring series of wars?
- Do enduring rivalries always enervate (i.e., weaken) the participating powers? If not, how does a nation avoid the inevitable exhaustion?

Starting an Enduring Rivalry

Systemic shocks and "fear, honor, interest" can go far toward explaining the macro conditions for the start of a rivalry. But one can also examine the historical record to determine if there are any specific circumstances common to the start of an enduring rivalry. Here the record appears mixed (see Table 0.2).

In some cases, the rivalry gets underway immediately after the shock that preceded it (the Franco-German rivalry began immediately upon German unification in 1870). In these cases, however, the groundwork for the rivalry (national or ethnic animosity, previous periods of rivalry) was established

TABLE 0.2 Rivalries and the Advent of Armed Conflict

Rivalry	Precipitating Event
Athens vs. Sparta	Revolt in Corcyra
Rome vs. Carthage	Intervention in Messana
Rome-Byzantium vs. Persia	Sassanid raids into Mesopotamian border regions (Rome's economic sphere)
England vs. France (the Middle Ages)	General medieval military chaos; French fleet threatens England; Battle of Sluys
Genoa vs. Venice	Sack of the Genoese quarter in Byzantium by the Pisians (supported by Venice).
Hapsburgs vs. Europe	The Italian Wars, which began with a plea from Milan for support against Naples
Ottomans vs. Hapsburgs	Ottoman victory over the Hungarians at the Battle of Mohács
England vs. France (18th century)	Prussian invasion of Silesia and France building forts in the Ohio Valley
England vs. France (Napoleonic Era)	Prussian-Austrian announcing their interest in protecting Louis XVI (Declaration of Pilnitz), which led directly to France declaring war
Germany vs. France	Defeat of the Austrians in 1866
United States vs. United Kingdom	Embargo Act of 1807
Germany vs. Europe	Moroccan Crisis of 1905
United States vs. Japan	First Sino-Japanese War (1894–1895)
United States vs. USSR	Soviet establishment of a communist-dominated government for Poland (the Lubin Government) in 1944.

decades or even centuries before. In most historical cases, however, there was a substantial period—in some cases, stretching decades—from when the preconditions for a rivalry were established and when the rivalry actually began.

Furthermore, many rivalries are well underway long before both sides elevate their competition to war, though, particularly in the modern era, there tends to be a number of militarized conflicts prior to the outbreak of hostilities (e.g., the successive international crises prior to August 1914). *Interestingly, the event that starts a major period of armed hostility is, more often than not, located some distance from where the rivals are geographically adjacent, and typically remains far removed from the central theater(s) of conflict once war erupts.*

Of the rivalries included in this work, as well as many of those surveyed for background information, an overwhelming number started out as commercial and/or economic rivalries. This is true even when economics appeared to be a secondary factor. For instance, while there are many factors in the Cold War rivalry between the United States and the Soviet Union, it was always a conflict between two antagonistic and largely mutually exclusive economic systems. The rivalry was eventually ended when one side collapsed from economic exhaustion engendered by the purposeful actions of the other.

The end of a period of conflict, short of the utter subjugation or destruction of one side, rarely means the end of a rivalry. Most rivalries are sustained over long periods of intermittent violent conflict in which each successive round of fighting increases the intensity of the conflict. Between these wars, passions rarely subside, and the competition continues. *In virtually every case, particularly in the modern era, this ongoing "peacetime" competition is fought out primarily in the communications and commercial-economic sphere.* Moreover, even during periods of peace, rival states often employ proxies to continue armed conflicts. It is in this period, recently referred to by Nadia Shadlow as the "space between," that both sides continue the struggle through other means to set the conditions for the next round of direct warfare.[13]

Somewhat perplexingly, in many cases, one side or the other vacates the "space between" for long periods. Typically, this space is vacated by the winner of the last conflict, but not always. For instance, Carthage did little to resurrect its military power after the Second Punic War, preferring instead to focus almost exclusively on winning the economic competition. Carthaginians were, as a result, ill prepared when Rome, realizing it was losing on an economic level, sent its legions to crush finally the city-state.

More recently, we can see the difference in the level of preparations each side took prior to World War I, in contrast to the interwar years (1919–1939), when the Allied powers only began their mobilization process at the eleventh hour. Similarly, the Western nations, included the United States, tend to pull back from risky engagements in the wake of Cold War conflicts, vacating a space that their previous foes were quick to fill. Where this happened (South Vietnam), the results were often negative for the nation or region previously under US protection. Where the United States remained involved (South Korea), a political and military standoff was the most likely result. In the Cold War's big picture, the containment policy was just barely sufficient to maintain an expensive global competition, despite many setbacks, until the Soviet Union imploded because of its wasteful economic system.

Conflicts that end short of the total defeat of one side or the other rarely affect the underlying causes of a strategic rivalry; hence, it is difficult to fathom why one side of a rivalry all but vacates the "space between," even after it is clear that the other side is remaining active. The most likely answer is that—as this is typically the course taken by the winner of the previous conflict—power is now "satisfied." The loser of that conflict, however, is far from satisfied, and through the prism with which its policymakers view the world, the post-conflict status quo has turned against its interests. Victory is, therefore, seen by one side as an opportunity to demobilize, return to peaceful pursuits, and either reduce or redirect government expenditures.

For the loser, however, the advent of peace is a period in which to recoup lost strength, rebuild its finances, and otherwise prepare for a future opportunity to overturn the status quo (e.g., Germany in the post-Versailles era). Circumstances may dictate that the losing side of a conflict will have to eschew another war, or an overly militarized direct confrontation, for a possibly prolonged period. Still, the need to redress the humiliation of defeat and to gain an acceptable long-term status quo means that the defeated and "temporarily" weaker rival almost always undertakes actions designed to weaken its foe, as it prepares for the next major effort. The "space between" can easily become a period of military, diplomatic, and economic contests designed to both weaken and test the resolve of a rival, even as it works to avoid a direct confrontation. As Geoffrey Wawro indicates in Chapter 10,

> The timeless lesson is clear. A power eclipsed by another is not disarmed; on the contrary, it can use military deterrents, alliances, finances, trade, and levers of the media and public opinion (soft power) to improve its relative situation and thwart the "winner."

All of this is done for one purpose: to improve the weaker rival's position relative to the stronger, for the next great contest (i.e., war).

James Anderson details the many examples of how rivals can and do contest the "space between," short of taking each other on in a direct confrontation. In Chapter 16 on the long Cold War rivalry, Anderson outlines how the US-USSR enmity was undertaken across the full spectrum of state interactions, for example, proxy wars, terror, diplomacy, economics, trade, intelligence, and communications. Where the Cold War differs from many previous historic examples is that both sides strongly contested the "space between." Typically, one side (the stronger) vacates much of this space to its later detriment. More typically, only when one side of the rivalry overreaches does it become possible for the other side to mobilize its population and expand its military resources to counter the moves of the other. By this time, the crisis is usually so far advanced that another war is already on the immediate horizon. Examples in the modern era include the following:

- The Japanese advances in East Asia were mostly uncontested by the United States until midway into 1941 when an oil embargo was established.
- During the interwar years, Germany's military, diplomatic, and economic moves went uncountered until after the Munich crisis.
- At the beginning of the twentieth century, Germany was not perceived as overreaching by the United Kingdom until after Kaiser Wilhelm II began to build a high-seas fleet. And the French did not begin to counter Germany's increasing aggressiveness until after the 1908 Moroccan crisis.

More recently, as Nadia Schadlow points out, our current difficulties with the Islamic State reflect the dangers of declaring victory (Iraq) and then mostly vacating the "space between."

Maintaining the Enduring Strategic Rivalries

Why rivalries start is often easier to grasp than the reasons that they continue, often for decades or centuries. The historical examples examined in this report reveal a simple answer: throughout the period of the rivalry, the two rivals remain dominant powers, are still in close proximity, and concerns about "fear, honor, and interest" rarely abate. Moreover, each collision, whether militarized or not, hardens attitudes not only among a state's elite but also, and more dangerously, among the vast majority of the general population. At times such attitudes can be overcome by a state leader willing to take the political risk necessary to break the paradigm. But that takes a statesman of unusual ability who is also previously identified as a foe of the rival. For instance, only Churchill, a well-known staunch enemy of the Soviet Union, could have welcomed it into the Allied coalition in June 1941 ("If Hitler invaded hell I would at least make a favorable reference to the devil in the House of Commons"[14]). Similarly, "Only Nixon could have gone to China." Both of these budding enduring rivalries were halted because each side recognized that they faced a larger threat, one whose defeat required the cooperation of the other.

Despite the ongoing underlying reasons for the continuance of rivalries, at some point, one would assume the rival states would take note of the costs. The standard assumption is that each conflict between rival states becomes progressively more ruinous, particularly in financial terms. The problem is that, in most cases, the standard assumption is wrong. Take the multiple Anglo-French rivalries. With the exception of the years of the Black Death and the English Civil War, British gross domestic product (GDP) rose, including substantial increases during periods of military conflict and in the decades thereafter.[15] The statistical evidence for France during this period has not been accumulated or studied to the degree that the same type of evidence has been for Great Britain. However, from the extant evidence, French growth rates follow a similar pattern, and this pattern repeats itself throughout the ancient and pre-modern era. As long as a state was able to avoid total defeat, and to the extent it could keep the fighting off its own territory, a rivalry and even a war were almost always an economic boom.

The reality was that wars were, at least until the modern era, ruinous for a government's finances, with many governments going bankrupt because of extended conflicts. But as these governments were rarely able to tax away much more than a few percentages of the wealth of a state, one could see what would be a paradox in the modern world: bankrupt governments sitting on top of a burgeoning economy. If we were to examine Angus Madison's statistics for the period after the Industrial Revolution, major rivalries are clearly good for economic growth.[16] Figure 0.1 shows the growth trajectories of the major European powers since 1830. Though many factors are involved, we see that the states with the most intense rivalries during the period also had the fastest growth rates. It may be going too far to say that a strategic rivalry is one of the crucial factors in this rapid growth; however, we can state that a major interstate rivalry is not retarding growth.

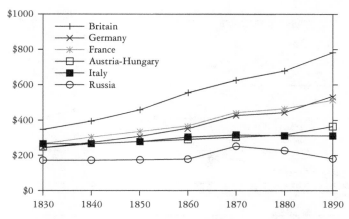

FIGURE 0.1 Growth trajectories of the major European powers since 1830

GROWTH TRAJECTORIES OF THE MAJOR
EUROPEAN POWERS SINCE 1830

Figure 0.2 is also taken from Angus Maddison's data. It shows two important details: this relationship extends back into the pre-modern era, and there is a substantial net gain to the nation that becomes the global hegemon—even if that means having to face a strategic rival.

Only in the last century did this pattern begin to break down. This coincides with a period when the state apparatus became capable of taking and using for its own purposes a much larger slice of a nation's wealth. An example may help get the point across. At the end of the Napoleonic wars, Britain had been at war for fifty of the previous hundred years, and on a war footing for much of the time between wars. The total cost of all of this conflict was nearly double the GDP of Britain. In other words, on average, *fifty years of war consumed about 2 percent of GDP per year*. Even if we concentrate an overwhelming share of that spending into the actual years fighting Napoleon, we can barely get to 6 percent of GDP per year. This is only a tenth of the percentage of GDP consumed by the United States and Great Britain for each year of World War II.

COUNTRY GDP PER CAPITA AS A RATIO
TO WORLD GDP PER CAPITA

What does this mean? In the years prior to the Industrial Revolution and its coinciding financial revolution, the financial damage of a rivalry was mostly inflicted on state finances. The bankruptcy of the central government could

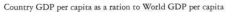

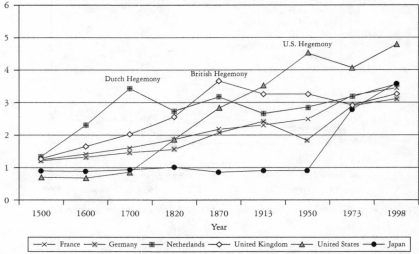

FIGURE 0.2 Country GDP per capita as a ratio to world GDP per capita

slow a state's economic growth for a time: for example, the Bardi-Peruzzi collapse when England defaulted on debts incurred in the Hundred Years War plunged Europe into an economic depression. But it was rarely sufficient to damage the underlying economy or even hold it back for long.

This phenomenon puts a new twist on what Paul Kennedy termed "imperial overstretch." Government finances might, and often did, become overstretched, but such an event appears to have had only a temporary effect on the broader economy. This changed when governments gained the capacity to access huge portions of a state's income and wealth to support a rivalry or conflict. This had two results:

- First, there was typically a huge upsurge in economic performance, as the economy reacted to what amounted to a sustained bout of Keynesian spending.
- Second, as this spending typically went toward sectors incapable of generating a self-sustaining virtuous cycle of economic growth, it inevitably damaged the real economy. In time, such damage made it impossible to maintain spending aimed at winning an enduring rivalry (one example is the Soviet Union's collapse in 1991).

Such spending in a concentrated period (war) could fundamentally wreck a nation's economy and finances in a relatively short time. Great Britain, for instance, was close to financial ruin before the United States tipped World

War II's financial scales for the better. Despite the US financial aid, the war's cost so damaged the British economy that postwar ruin was only averted through a huge low-interest loan from the United States. In contrast, when such spending ended with military defeat, as it did for Germany and Japan at the end of World War II, the economic damage was devastating. Only large amounts of American postwar financial assistance, coupled with American spending for its next rivalry, now with the Soviet Union, made the recovery of these vanquished nations possible.

For future rivalries, the implications of these economic and financial changes are possibly enormous. First, the cost of sustaining a prolonged militarized rivalry is going to absorb vastly larger sums as a percentage of a state's GDP than historically has been the case. As such, the effect on the underlying economy of both rivals will be much broader, putting at risk the broad public support the states had previously enjoyed in historic rivalries. The question remains: If a rivalry is going to be sustained over decades, what percentage of GDP can be employed without damaging the host economy and thus removing public support? Here, the jury remains out. The United States was able to sustain military spending in excess of 6 percent of GDP during much of the Cold War, while the Soviet Union, by spending in the vicinity of 17 percent during the same period, wrecked its economy. As S. C. M. Paine states in Chapter 13,

> Leonid Brezhnev overextended Russia financially and territorially by failing to fix the economy, whose growth had stagnated, while still funding an expanding list of expensive adventures in the Third World and missile deployments in Europe. The [Soviet Union's] assisted suicide included the militarization of the Russo-Chinese frontier, which was far more expensive for Russia than for China, whose population density formed a powerful defense. Russia, whose eastern periphery had hardly any Russian population, relied on expensive mechanized forces. These expenses in combination with Russian military expenses garrisoning Eastern Europe and defending against NATO constituted an enormous financial burden on a not particularly productive economy.

Though the United States committed only a third as much of its economy, as a percentage of GDP, to winning the Cold War, it did not escape economic strain, particularly when the nation later launched its simultaneous "Great Society" initiatives. As James Anderson reminds us,

> Over time, the costs of maintaining such large forces at home and overseas—though never as crippling as what the Soviets endured—left a deep imprint on the U.S. economy. The military-industrial complex

that Eisenhower warned America about in his Farewell Address (January 17, 1961) came into existence and continued growing. Large, and by U.S. historical standards, *unprecedented peacetime military spending distorted the economy*: the government soaked up research dollars at the expense of the private sector, and the practice of spreading procurement dollars across a large number of congressional districts made defense spending more responsive to political interests than to strategic ones.

In the immediate future though, there may be complications that are worth contemplating. For instance, the historical evidence appears to show *that sustaining support for even a modest expenditure of GDP on a state's military often requires a rapidly growing economy*. Support for such expenditures rapidly ebbs as an economy stagnates or enters a period of slow growth.

Further, while the evidence for this is not as clear, as states undertake large social commitments, there appears to be a pronounced tendency to forgo military spending in favor of entitlement spending. In the past, rivalries ended or more often went into hibernation when its costs were sufficient to bring about Kennedy's "imperial overstretch." In the future, rivalries may end because of "entitlement overstretch." At the moment, this is speculative, but it is worth noting that the rivalries that ended with World War II required the victors to incur debt loads in excess of 100 percent of GDP. Historically, nations have been able to sustain, for a short period, debts in excess of 200 percent (e.g., Great Britain in 1815, and Japan in the present day).

However, it is worth asking this: *Can a nation sustain a rivalry if its debt load is already in excess of 100 percent of GDP before said rivalry even begins? Moreover, can it finance a conflict if its debt exceeds 200 percent before the conflict erupts?*

No one knows if a modern nation, particularly one that cannot finance its debt in its own currency, will break at debt loads of 250 percent or 300 percent of GDP. What is certain is that there is a number where financial collapse becomes inevitable. At the moment, this is unchartered territory, but the answer will have large implications for establishing and sustaining any future rivalry.

Still, nationalism and other factors can motivate populations and rekindle even a waning rivalry. While the underlying economics may dictate how long a strategic rivalry can continue, such planning is often overrun by flashes of national passions, particularly if they are being stoked by internal politics. *Often a rivalry is continued purely because it is fed by the internal posturing of one state or another.* For instance, as Geoffrey Wawro points out in Chapter 10, by 1911 the Franco-German rivalry had been brought down to a lower temperature. L'affaire Dreyfus caused French politicians to look inward for explanations of who and what were undermining the republic. Moreover, most Frenchmen had come to terms with the loss of Alsace and Lorraine after their annexation in 1871 by Germany, which they did not see as worthy of risking a major industrial war. Besides, French politicians were able to point to their rapidly expanding colonial empire as more than sufficient recompense for the loss of a province or two. But as suddenly as the rivalry had waned, it sparked to life again in 1911. The lost provinces again became an unhealthy obsession, not for strategic reasons—the lost frontier had been sealed with a belt of new fortresses from Verdun to Belfort in the 1870s—but for opportunistic political ones. French politicians intoxicated voters with fairy tales about resurgent French pride and power. From that point forward, the French army entered a period of rapid expansion that soon caught the attention of the Germans. Hence, a rivalry that had been tamped down in favor of pursuing other interests roared back to life as a result of a political enthusiasm of the moment.

Geoffrey Parker, in Chapter 6, posits another theory for the longevity of enduring rivalries long past the time when it was in the interest of one or both states to conclude them. In Parker's example, the Spanish King Philip IV's ministers constructed an elaborate "domino theory" to justify the fighting. In 1624, they warned that "once the Netherlands are lost, America and other kingdoms of Your Majesty will also immediately be lost with no hope of recovering them." Four years later, a Spanish official in Brussels repeated the point: "If we lose the Netherlands, we will not be able to defend America, Spain, or Italy." A few years later, a veteran diplomat extended the argument yet further: "We cannot defend the Netherlands if we lose Germany." *Like the Spanish Hapsburgs, political leaders always seem more disposed to take risks in order to avoid losses than to make gains.*

Obviously, this is not a stance limited to a particular era. It is a recurring theme in many historical rivalries; most famously, it was used as a justification for US involvement in Southeast Asia during the Cold War. While the *domino theory of risk avoidance* has been discredited in the popular imagination, it still has much of its historic credibility. Events acquire momentum: one defeat or withdrawal has historically led to a series of such incidents.

Within the United States, Vietnam may have created a backlash against using the domino theory to support intervention, but that does not negate its practical reality. *The nature of a rivalry is that it is a contest. If one side retreats, the other will fill the void, either on its own or through proxies.* Without commenting on the rights or wrongs of the US withdrawal from Iraq, we are likely witnessing this process now as the Islamic State projects itself to wherever it detects a vacuum of power. Historically, this process continues until the expansion is checked by military force or until the expanding power pauses to consolidate its gains.

Endless Streams of Money Equals Victory

As stated previously, until the modern era the cost of sustaining a rivalry was never in and of itself sufficient to end a rivalry. This does not mean that rivalries were without cost; though the long-term effects of a rivalry might actually add to a nation's economic growth, in the short term a lack of funds could be catastrophic. When a state ran out of funds, particularly if it was in the midst of a conflict, it needed to end hostilities on any terms the rival wished to offer. Because of this, a state's economic infrastructure and capacity to generate wealth often became a rival's primary target. In this regard, Michael Leggiere notes the following in Chapter 9 of this volume:

> Acknowledging that British gold had financed the three previous coalition wars, Napoleon targeted the heart of Britain's power: its maritime economy. Lacking the resources either to invade Britain or decisively defeat the Royal Navy at sea and unable to compete with Britain's maritime policy in a conventional manner, Napoleon developed an alternate maritime economic strategy: the Continental system. As a result of the Industrial Revolution, Britain emerged as Europe's manufacturing and industrial center. To ruin its economy by causing inflation and debt, Napoleon implemented an embargo against British trade with the European nations under his control. Without the European market to buy its manufactured goods and the re-export of colonial goods, he expected Britain to experience a severe depression, hurting the nation's economy and its ability to maintain its global colonial empire. Knowing that public opinion could unseat a British Cabinet, he hoped a depression would usher in a new government that would be willing to accept French dominance of the Continent. Moreover, Napoleon believed his new system would not only cause the British grave problems, but would open the door to a tremendous expansion of French trade, which would rush in to fill the void. His hope was that France would soon replace Britain as the economic engine of Europe.

But Napoleon miscalculated. Britain found new markets, and the Continental system leaked like a sieve. Rather than weaken Britain,

Napoleon's blockade actually strengthened the British economy. Worse, the blockade had a crippling effect on the rest of Europe, which was thrown into an economic depression when the Royal Navy brought overseas European trade to a near standstill. Napoleon had discovered the one strategy that made his enemy stronger while increasingly weakening the French economy, which was progressively undermined by his economic warfare aimed at Britain. Leggiere continues:

> As a result of the crippling effects of the Continental system, Czar Alexander issued a decree on December 31, 1810, to tax luxury goods and wines, some of France's largest exports. Moreover, the decree opened Russian ports to neutral ships carrying British exports. British goods soon flooded the markets of Eastern and Central Europe. Napoleon had few choices other than to force Alexander's continued participation in the Continental system. Thus, in 1811, both emperors started preparing for war.

In other words, rather than suspend execution of a strategy that was damaging his own interests and helping his rival, Napoleon doubled down. The result was the annihilation of the French army in the Russian snows, setting Napoleon on the path of irreversible ruin. Napoleon had picked the right target—he just applied the wrong strategy. He may have been better off emulating Britain's internal economic policies, which allowed a state with only a third of France's population and landmass to punch far above its apparent weight.

How important was Britain's economic contribution to ultimate victory? As Leggiere points out in his Chapter 9,[17]

> On March 3, 1813, the British formed the Sixth Coalition with Russia and Sweden against France. The Anglo-Swedish portion of the alliance obligated London to provide the Swedes £1,000,000 by October 1813. In mid-March, Prussia joined the coalition by signing a bilateral alliance with Russia and declaring war on Napoleon. London restored official diplomatic relations with the Prussians after they formally declared the end of the Continental system in North Germany on March 20. The British bolstered the alliance by dispatching a convoy to the Baltic carrying 54 cannon as well 23,000 stands of arms to be shared by the Russians and Prussians.[18] Despite its commitments to Iberia, North America, and now Sweden, London offered a subsidy of £2,000,000 to be shared by the Russians and Prussians, with the former taking £1,333,334, or two-thirds, and the latter £666,666.[19]

Negotiations ensued until the Prussian and Russian foreign ministers officially signed the subsidy treaties on June 14 and 15, 1813, respectively. In addition, the Russians received £500,000 for the support of their Baltic Fleet.[20] On August 11, the British government accepted an Allied proposal to issue £2,500,000 of paper money to cover the cost of military expenditure, with London accepting responsibility for the full amount of the capital and interest.[21] Signed on October 3, 1813, an Anglo-Austrian subsidy treaty granted the Austrians a subvention in the amount of £1,000,000.[22] All four subsidy treaties obligated the signatories not to make a separate peace with Napoleon. Although no British ground forces would be committed to Central Europe, the British ambassadors to all four recipients of British aid would accompany the Allied armies, with the authority to withhold subsidy payments if any coalition partner failed to give its all for the general cause of liberating Germany from French control.

These costs, while enormous, are typical of any period where an enduring rivalry turns into a conflict, which often is just as much about obtaining endless streams of money as it is about winning on the battlefield. One remembers that Sparta finally won the Peloponnesian War when it blockaded the Athenian silver mines; that Rome finally turned the tide against Carthage by using debt financing to maintain a war effort (the first historical evidence of using such an approach to making war); and that Rome's final collapse was the result of invaders breaking its tax spine.[23] So it continues through more than two millennia of history.

In Chapter 6, Geoffrey Parker presents us with an example of the results of extending rivalry commitments beyond the state's capacity to meet the financial obligations required by its strategy:

The central government ran up a sovereign debt far beyond Spain's capacity to service: 85 million ducats by 1598, over 112 million by 1623, almost 182 million by 1667, and almost 223 million by 1687. Public sector borrowing on this scale—ten times total revenues, if not more—drained capital and raw materials from Spain, undercut local manufactures, and encouraged a "rentier" mentality among those sectors of the population with the potential to be entrepreneurs, while the need to create and increase taxes to repay lenders led to onerous fiscal expedients (especially duties on sales and on manufactures) with high social and economic costs. Worst of all, most tax revenues were remitted abroad, to fund armies and navies fighting to achieve international goals that mattered to the dynasty but not to most Spaniards. The government of Philip IV exported at least 150 million ducats to fund his foreign wars.

As a result, Spain became a serial defaulter, which had vast negative consequences for its capacity to sustain a rivalry, as well as the economy that underpinned it. This is one of the few cases where the economic effects of a rivalry (or in Spain's case, rivalries) did substantial damage to the underlying economy. As a result, it eventually undermined public support for continuing the rivalry (particularly among the elites, who became liable for taxes they had been previously been excused from paying). Why this happened is probably a result of circumstances particular to Spain and its Hapsburgs. While other rivalries were marked by long periods of peace between periodic wars, Spain and the Hapsburgs were usually at war on multiple fronts. Just one conflict, the Eighty Years War against the Netherlands, cost more silver than was being shipped from the lucrative mines of the New World. Add this to Spain's inability or refusal to modernize its financial and administrative system, and collapse was unavoidable. The miracle was that it endured for as long as it did.

France, under the influence of a reforming Cardinal Richelieu and the modernizing minister Jean-Batiste Colbert, had learned the lessons the Spanish refused to heed. Their remaking of French financial institutions financed a vast expansion of French military power in the eighteenth century. According to Matt Schumann in Chapter 8, this transformation consisted of

high tariffs and regulated industry making it one of the richest countries in Europe. Subsequent military expansion and reforms under Michel le Tellier and his son the Marquis de Louvois enabled France to field over 400,000 troops by the early 1690s. William and Leopold formed the League of Augsburg—titled the Grand Alliance as Spain and Britain joined at the end of the 1680s—in order to contain this power, and they gained enormously from turns of fate far away from the battlefield. Louvois's unexpected death in 1691 and a major crop failure in 1693 harmed Louis's finances, forcing him to choose by 1695 between army and naval priorities. Unable to keep up the arms race with England, France maintained a respectable fleet but largely abandoned the *guerre d'escadre* philosophy of fleet-to-fleet combat. Seeking to save money from his naval budget, Louis turned instead to *guerre de course*, or commerce raiding, based largely on privateers.

. . .

In sum, although dynastic and religious issues were clearly at play, the Anglo-French rivalry ultimately hinged on land claims and state finances. Nationalized industry and trade enabled Louis XIV to seek dynastic glory with an oversized military—and to keep Europe in awe—through most of his long reign. Though allied with the Stuart kings, Louis's dominance in European affairs put the English people on edge, sparking the Glorious Revolution. With substantial Dutch help, Britain soon emerged as a major financier for France's enemies, and set France on the defensive in the colonies, at sea, on land, and at the negotiating table.

Britain was able to finance its rivalry against France and subsidize numerous European allies because it undertook a financial revolution to coincide with its 1688 political revolution. Schumann continues:

> Built up initially by Dutch investments and financial know-how, England turned itself into a worthy rival for a France whose internal wealth had grown considerably under Cardinal Richelieu, Cardinal Mazarin, Colbert, and Louvois. Despite having only one-third of the population, far fewer resources, and less-well-developed internal communications than France, Britain greatly benefited from much more sophisticated financial systems, supporting a huge fleet and large subsidies for Continental allies. By 1748, British superiority was clear enough to prompt a major shift in French strategic thinking, marked by the rise of the Gournay circle and ambitious projects in several colonial theatres. The pace of these reforms was too slow to be effective, yet fast enough to pique British ire and lead to a catastrophic French defeat in the Seven Years' War. After 1763, political turmoil in London made peace a vital interest for the British, while Choiseul turned France away from its former dynastic concerns on the continent to concentrate more fully on its major financial and strategic rival.

The crucial lesson to draw from this rivalry, one that is on display in every rivalry in the past 300 years, is that the size of an economy is not nearly as important as is a state's capacity to draw resources from that economy. This reverses Paul Kennedy's famous observation, "Victory has always gone to the side with the more flourishing production base."[24] Victory has not always gone to the side with the greatest materiel resources, although that often remains the best wager. Rather, it has gone to the side best able to mobilize its resources for the decisive effort of war.[25]

IS IDEOLOGY A MASK FOR WHAT A STATE
WOULD OTHERWISE DO IN ANY EVENT?

Our historical survey has drawn mixed conclusions on the importance of ideology for starting and sustaining a rivalry. For most of recorded history, religion provided the ideological underpinning for state actions. Just as Pope Urban II's blessing of "God wills it" (*Deus volt*) sent tens of thousands of Crusaders into the Levant, religion was always able to motivate the masses to action. In the modern era, religion as a motivating force was largely replaced by the ideology of the "-isms"—communism, fascism, Nazism. If, as is clearly visible in the historical record, ideology plays a crucial rule in strategic rivalries, what makes this conclusion uncertain? Doubt prevails mostly as a result of the observation that religion is often a mask for what rulers were already inclined to do. This does not negate the considerable influence of religion as a motivating factor, but our historical analyses have found that removing religion as a consideration for starting and sustaining a rivalry does not change how states conducted their affairs.

Geoffrey Parker, in Chapter 6, notes that "[a]s early as 1574, an English observer in the Netherlands discerned two motives for Philip II's refusal to negotiate with his enemies: 'The pride of the Spanish government and the cause of religion'—a combination that the Hapsburgs called 'religion and reputation.'" Perhaps there is little difference between the concept of "religion and reputation" and the Thucydidean idea of "honor." But faith in an ideology (religion or an "-ism") often has a tendency to replace reason and calculation with faith, the outcome being a negative effect that is rarely seen in state actions grounded in concerns of "fear, honor, interest." So we see Philip II sending the Spanish Armada to England despite numerous warnings that it would fail. As one Spanish captain warned,

> Unless God helps us by a miracle the English, who have faster and hardier ships than ours, and many more long range guns, and know their advantages as well as we do, will never close with us at all, but stand aloof and knock us to pieces with their culverins, without our being able to do them any serious harm.[26]

Still the Armada sailed, with doubters silenced by Philip II's "confident hope of a miracle."[27] As Geoffrey Parker concludes, the Spanish, because they perceived themselves to be on the path of righteousness, always expected such miracles to bridge any gap between ends and means.

In many cases, ideology infringes on a state's ability to conduct an *accurate net assessment* of its rival. Worse, even when an accurate assessment is made, ideology often allows a state to ignore the math so it can undertake policies that by any reasonable calculation will lead to disaster. In Chapter 15, William Morgan shows how this worked in the US-Japan rivalry starting in 1897:

> The two nations made accurate net assessments of material factors. They understood each other's resource base, trade flows, productive capability, and existing and planned force structure. Virtually all American and most Japanese policymakers knew intellectually that Japan would lose a total war.
>
> But war came anyway. Why? Because national goals and policy positions were defined by ideology, by ideas and beliefs and values. Japan chose to define its future as a powerful, autonomous empire, an Asian hegemon. The United States chose to overvalue its national interests in Asia and to hold tightly to Open Door principles. Rather than accept the certain loss of compromising, Japan gambled on war with little chance of victory [an example of a point made earlier; a state will risk much to avoid an otherwise certain loss]. By standing pat on its Open Door principles, the United States too avoided the certain loss a compromise would entail, confident that its obvious material superiority would bring Japanese compliance and American "victory" without a war.

Morgan found that

> [a]s a group, Japanese leaders increasingly tended toward stronger positions, rather than caution and moderation. This was partly because those positions came from ultra-nationalists, whose mindset prized boldness, a pure spirit that foreswore compromise, and *a belief that will and commitment could prevail over material reality*. [emphasis added] The inner circle performed no analysis that resolved policy contradictions and conflicts. Platitudes—such as "We must work hard to prepare"—glossed over serious planning flaws and wrong-headed assumptions.

The Japanese military purposely excluded the finance minister, as well as representatives from his ministry, from all high-level government meetings. As Morgan points out, with this exclusion the military ignored the mortal economic effects of its preferred strategy that rested increasingly on wishful thinking rather than on a hardheaded assessment of capabilities and goals. Japan's leaders forgot the roots of their prosperity, which lay in trade, not warfare.

Ideology also plays a major role in state governance that may have a profound impact on the capacity of a state to sustain a rivalry. For instance, the Soviet Union's capacity to support a long economic competition with the United States was directly tied to a communist ideology that dictated the Soviet economic system. James Anderson, in Chapter 16 of this volume, indicates that, though the communist model proved effective at imposing and maintaining one-party rule and installing a dictator for life, it was ill suited for creating prosperity thereafter. So they executed the very categories of people necessary to run a modern economy. Likewise, they eliminated the very institutions and laws necessary to promote economic growth—most notably private property and free markets. Moreover, if one views capitalism as an ideology, then the United States had adopted an economic system uniquely capable of generating the massive amounts of wealth necessary for sustaining a strategic rivalry for a prolonged period.

Today, it is worth examining the ideologies of potential rivals to the United States—and making a realistic assessment of their capacity to endure in a prolonged contest (assuming no collapse of will within the United States and/or the West).

For instance, in what is increasingly looking like a "long war" with Islamists, one fails to see how their ideology can implement an economic program that has any hope of creating wealth in the modern world. Even if a group like the Islamic State occupied all twenty-two Arab nations, they would start with an economic base (including oil) not quite equal to Spain's. Given their ideological antagonisms toward everyone, they are unlikely to attract much-needed foreign investment or to integrate a collapsing economic system into a globalized world. In short, the Islamic State is following an ideology that should lead to an economic collapse, much the way the Soviet Union's did (this does not mean that they are incapable of creating widespread destruction and misery before their ultimate collapse).

China has adopted a capitalist-based economic system within an otherwise stifling political system, which has created huge amounts of wealth over the past two decades. The question remains, however, as to whether a capitalist economic model can survive within a communist political system, but history demonstrates that states forced to make a final choice between political ideology and economics *typically favor their political system.* Though China may be able to generate sufficient wealth to sustain an enduring rivalry, the case is unproven.

* * * * *

Is ideology a mask for what a state would otherwise do in any event?

The answer is unclear in terms of religion, particularly in the premodern age. Though some economic benefits came out of the Crusades, one must judge it highly doubtful that so vast an enterprise would have been attempted if not for the pull of religion. It surely could not have been sustained for over a century without religious motivations. Still, as Western rulers became more focused on concerns nearer home, their religious duties were set aside, and the Crusading states were allowed to wither until their final extermination.

This pattern is repeated in many of the historical studies in this work. *Whenever a state was forced to choose between ideology and a geopolitical imperative, ideology was cast aside.* As S. C. M. Paine points out in Chapter 13, when a Manchurian warlord in 1929 demanded that the Soviet Union give up its railway concessions as a good communist should, the Soviet Union deployed its army and China lost the ensuing Railway War. Thus, despite the communist propaganda, the Soviet Union continued to follow the foreign policy of a traditional land power aimed at territorial maximization. In geopolitical terms, very little differentiates the ambitions of the czars from those of the Politburo.

James Anderson reminds us in Chapter 16 that for the Soviet Union, communist ideology was rarely the determining factor in the Kremlin's overall strategic considerations:

> "At the bottom of the Kremlin's neurotic view of world affairs is traditional and instinctive Russian sense of insecurity," observed George Kennan, the architect of containment, in his famous long telegram to George C. Marshall, then secretary of state, in 1946.[28] Echoing English geographer Sir Halford Mackinder's argument made nearly a half century earlier, Kennan added: "Originally, this was insecurity of a peaceful agricultural people trying to live on vast exposed plain in neighborhood of fierce nomadic people."[29] At the Yalta Conference, February 4–11, 1945, these ancestral fears reinforced the Soviet determination to prevent a resurgent, postwar Germany.

Obviously, geopolitics trumped ideology during World War II, as Roosevelt, Churchill, and Stalin made common cause despite two previous decades of ideological antipathy. As long as both sides were locked in a desperate struggle for survival, ideological tensions remained muted. Unfortunately, goodwill engendered by wartime cooperation soon dissipated. By the time of the Potsdam Conference (1945), if not earlier, ideological differences were reasserting themselves. Still, Soviet demands in the years after World War II were rarely based in ideology. Rather, they took the form of securing itself from another invasion from the West, which would have been the third in as many decades.

The Reach of States and Empires

In the past, the extent of a state or empire not only determined much of its power, it also placed severe limits as to how much power could be expanded at the edges of its domains or any great distance from that state's center of power. This was first recognized by the Romans, who found it increasingly difficult to project sufficient power from the political and economic center (Rome) to contest Parthian and later Sassanid (Persians) encroachments. Rome's solution was both novel and quite possibly unrepeatable by any other state (though Charles V tried something similar with the Hapsburg state): they created a second center of power in Constantinople, on the very edge of Parthian domains. The Roman Empire's new Eastern capital became so powerful that it outlasted the fall of Rome by almost a thousand years. But the creation of a new power center and the eventual defeat of the Parthians had unforeseen consequences. As Kenneth Harl points out in Chapter 3,

> Rome defeated Parthia (even if diplomacy rather than Roman arms avenged Carrhae), but the result was the creation of a far more formidable rival. Sassanid Persia forced Rome to reorganize army and bureaucracy to defend the vital provinces of the eastern Mediterranean. This unseen consequence of victory over Persia in the third century was to transform Rome into a significantly weaker power in the fourth century. The defeat of Julian in 363 put Rome and the imperial army on the defensive. The court of Constantinople thus could not lend significant aid to prevent the collapse of the Western Roman Empire in the fifth century.

Geoffrey Parker reminds us in Chapter 6 that the extensive Hapsburg Empire faced a number of the same challenges as Rome. Many of the Hapsburg territories were far from the center of government and therefore proved difficult to defend, leading to prolonged wars that exacted a high economic and human toll from the empire as a whole. The "empire on which the sun never set" became in the seventeenth century the "target" on which the sun never set. Beset by enemies on every border, Charles V blamed his inability to deal with them on "the distance that separates one state from another." As he viewed it, the central issue was the slow speed at which information traveled, which doomed him. Small problems at the edge of empire would turn into a crisis before he was even aware of trouble. His courtiers joked, "If we have to wait for death, let us hope that it comes from Spain, for then it would never arrive."[30]

To counter this danger, powerful states have spent enormous portions of their revenues improving their communications systems. The early Persian Empire, for example, built the Royal Road System, where special couriers, whose motto was adopted by the US Postal Service, linked the crucial centers of the empire. Unfortunately, this same road system proved of inestimable value as an invasion corridor for Alexander the Great. In another example, the Roman Empire put so much effort into its transportation networks that much of the system survives today. For those who doubt these roads were arteries for information and military forces rather than trade, it is worth noting that no Roman road was ever large enough for two carts to pass side by side. Similarly, and centuries later, the British expended huge sums maintaining and defending the sea lanes that linked its vast global empire.

Historically, great powers with extensive interests have had to contend with two crucial problems:

- They offer many points for foes to threaten and attack.
- Their capacity to project power to the edges of their empire (or zone of interest) is greatly diminished the further the contested area is from the core of a state's power, though local allies can hugely alleviate this problem.

What is notable is that the relative amount of power a state can sustain far from its economic core is little changed over the past two thousand years. Remarkably, great powers, though capable of huge surges of power, have found it nearly impossible to maintain more than 50,000 combat troops at the margin of empire or their zone of interest. Anything much beyond that, unless allies are picking up much of the cost, rapidly becomes economically crippling. For instance, though the Persians were capable of launching a massive offensive against Greece, it proved unsustainable. Within a year, the Persian king Xerxes was forced to take most of his army back to Persia, leaving only about 50,000 troops in Greece, where they were defeated the following campaigning season. Similarly, Rome found it difficult to sustain more than a few legions to defend its political interests in Armenia against the Persians, and were never able to keep much more than that on the other side of the Rhine or Danube rivers. Only when rival states are close to each other's core can they sustain huge forces over a prolonged period.

Even now in the modern era, it is interesting to see how difficult it is for even a modern state to sustain forces far from its core.

- The Germans, for instance, were capable of sustaining only a small fraction of their army at Stalingrad, or in North Africa.
- During the World War II era, even mighty America was straining every logistical sinew to sustain just a few tens of thousands of infantrymen on Okinawa. Of course, the United States was surging 4 million military personnel overseas during this war, but such a tremendous effort could not be sustained for many more years.
- Also consider that the buildup for the Normandy invasion took well over a year, and the invasion ran out of logistical steam before the assault could reach the Rhine. Toward the end, the Allies were moving forward with just a few divisions at a time, while the rest stalled for lack of fuel.
- The Russians, just a few hundred miles from their borders, required many months to bring up supplies and position forces for the final surge to Berlin.
- Later, throughout the Cold War, both the Russians and Americans kept sizable forces forward deployed, but only by drawing support from allies.
- In the final analysis, one state was unable to bear the cost; it is worth noting that soon after the Soviet Union's collapse, the United States immediately began reducing its overseas forces.

In any event, though exceptions to the preceding come readily to mind, the general point—that *a state can sustain only a fraction of its overall power far from its economic core*—is indisputable. Moreover, almost all of the exceptions were sustained for only a brief period, a few years at most. No state can sustain an effort equal (as a percentage of GDP) to what the United States accomplished from 1941 to 1945 for anything approximating the average length of an enduring rivalry. This observation has large implications for the United States:

- If our commercial rivalry with China is permitted to turn into an enduring militarized rivalry, the nation will often have to project substantial power into East Asia. The cost of projecting sufficient power to deter or win a militarized encounter is always going to be massive, while China, which needs only to project power into areas immediately adjacent to its economic core, will always have a tremendous cost advantage.

- Much of the cost of US deployments can be offset by the deployment of power by local allies, or using an allied infrastructure to support a US deployment. For that reason, the United States may expect to see China making serious efforts to disrupt US alliances throughout Asia, as one of the early moves of a budding enduring rivalry (Shadlow's "Space Between" again).

Allies and Enduring Rivalries

Allies can play a crucial role in lowering the overall cost of sustaining a rivalry, as well as providing invaluable assistance when the rivalry turns into a violent confrontation (war). Of course, this is not true in all cases, as some allies can end up costing more than they ever contribute (e.g., Italy as a burden to Germany in World War II).

In some cases, allies can become such a burden that they cripple the dominant state's economy. The Soviet Union, as James Anderson points out in Chapter 16, realized this much too late to save itself from financial collapse:

> Moscow's economic burdens, at this time, were also growing, as the Soviets discovered what previous empires had all endured: at some point, client-states stop providing net economic gains, and, instead, become a resource drain. As a result, the Soviet Union's efforts to update its own economy were greatly hampered by the fiscal and resource drain imposed by Moscow's Eastern European clients. For a time, the Soviet Union's abundant natural resources and growing populations could compensate for these disadvantages, but stated GDP growth was masking the system's pervasive structural weaknesses.

Still, most states in a rivalry consider it crucial to have allies whose support can be relied on at crucial moments. Given this, what does historical experience tell us about the role of rivals in an enduring rivalry?

First, we learn that *allies require substantial care and feeding, particularly in the years before their aid is actually needed.* As Geoffrey Wawro reminds us in Chapter 10 of this volume,

> By July 1870, the French were well aware that they were on the verge of a major war with Prussia, yet the French foreign ministry under the Duc de Gramont made no effort to pursue alliance strategies that

might have given France an overpowering hand. Gramont merely assumed that the Austrians would intervene in any Franco-Prussian conflict "to erase the memories of 1866." He also assumed that the Italians would join the war to show their gratitude for French assistance in the war of 1859 (and he assumed that the Austrians would permit an Italian army to cross their territory to join the war against Prussia). Further, he was convinced that the Danes would join the war to take back Schleswig, seized by the Prussians in 1864.[31] Had Gramont breathed life into these assumptions with an active foreign policy, they might have resulted in sturdy alliances, a "revenge coalition" against Berlin. Instead, he merely took for granted that Prussia's old victims and France's old protégé would join the war spontaneously. For a nation locked in a harrowing strategic rivalry, this was gross negligence, and a real contrast with Bismarck's careful management of any off-stage actors who might have been expected to intervene.

Second, *during a rivalry, an assortment of strong, generally self-supporting allies is always important, but during a conflict they are crucial.* At times, however, the dominant power is tempted to push too much of the burden onto allies. This is particularly dangerous during a conflict where the leading power is tempted to conserve its strength or more often substitute cash for "boots on the ground." As Michael Leggiere states in Chapter 9,

Before 1808, the British mainly contributed to the successive coalition wars against France by funding in the form of loans, subsidies, and credits to allies such as Austria and Russia, whose armies would shoulder the main burden of fighting the French. Total domination of the seas then allowed the British to conduct limited military operations against secondary targets such as the Netherlands and Naples, either unilaterally or in conjunction with the Russians. However, London's 1808 decision to commit the British army to the Iberian Peninsula marked a monumental policy change for the maritime economic power. Yet this was not enough. Although the British distracted Napoleon and tied down vital imperial resources in Iberia and the Mediterranean, they realized that Napoleon's hegemony over the Continent could only be broken in Central Europe. For this reason, the British could not turn their backs on Austria, Prussia, and Russia, even after all three were counted among Napoleon's allies following the failed Franco-Austrian War of 1809. The British understood that when the time came for Europe to rise against France, Britain would be expected to support it with both arms and money.

As the United States first discovered in World War I and later in World War II, a generous disbursement of cash is important but rarely enough to ensure victory, or to have much influence in the post-conflict order. That this lesson was absorbed by decision-makers is made clear by US actions during the Cold War, where sufficient military force was maintained at potential hot-spots to assure allies of America's commitment to join in any fighting from the earliest point in a conflict. *The historical record is clear: if the dominant nation is unwilling to place its ground troops in harm's way, it is difficult to convince allies of the seriousness of its intent.*

Finally, when it comes to allies, the historical record bears out Lord Palmerston's warning: "Nations have no permanent friends, they only have permanent interests." Generally, an alliance structure held together only for as long as the allies shared a common interest. Typically, this meant that your allies had more to fear from your rival than they did from you.

Complexity, Information, and Strategy

As rivalries move from one crisis to the next, they are beset with problems of differing complexity and importance. Each of these problems comes with its own flow of information that competes for policymakers' attention with huge amounts of informational white noise. Of course, this is true of any major power, whether it is engaged in a strategic rivalry or not. But nations engaged in an *enduring rivalry* exhibit two common characteristics when dealing with information overload: (1) a tendency to overly focus on minor issues and problems; and (2) to examine every international event through the prism of the ongoing rivalry.

Geoffrey Parker in Chapter 6 identifies this difficulty as a major cause of a Spanish collapse in the sixteenth century:

> The Spanish Hapsburgs' . . . reaction to the information overload they had created was to focus on minor problems (*menudencias*, or "trivia," . . .) instead of wrestling with the crucial decisions on which the fate of the monarchy depended. In 1584, Cardinal Granvelle (Philip II's senior adviser) complained bitterly: "I see in all matters delays, so pernicious and in so many ways prejudicial to our own affairs, including the most important ones, which become lost to view . . . with so many petty details that . . . no time [is] left to resolve what matters most."

It has forever been so. Consider the Athenians even as they went forward with their invasion of Sicily—the largest military endeavor the ancient

Greeks attempted before the Age of Alexander—they became obsessed with calling back their commander, Alcibiades, to stand trial for what was, in relation to what was at stake, a minor matter. This cost them the services of the one general who could have assured the expedition's victory, and arguably set Athens on the path to final defeat, as Alcibiades sought refuge in Sparta, where he gave the Spartans the key to defeating Athens.

Even Rome, which was far better than most at keeping a firm focus on the main effort, finally succumbed when its leaders failed to recognize that the crucial threat was not the one on which they were focused. In the western part of the empire, Rome was so preoccupied by the Huns that they took little note of a relatively small force of other barbarians—the Vandals—breaking their tax spine in North Africa. Later, in the eastern empire, the Byzantines were so focused on the Persian threat that they took little notice—until it was too late—of the Arab raiders flying the flag of Islam.

Interestingly, the capability to accumulate and process large amounts of information, even if your capacity to do so is superior to that of a rival, provides no assurance of ultimate strategic success. Geoffrey Parker again reminds us of the historical fact that

> the king [Philip II] himself blamed many of the problems he had faced on "the distance that separates one state from another," and in the course of his reign he repeatedly complained about delays in the transmission of important information.[32]
>
> Nevertheless, as Braudel recognized, the same was true of all empires: "Although much criticized, the Spanish empire was equal or indeed superior to other leading states for transport, transfer and communications." Throughout the sixteenth century, he added, "over equal distances Spanish communications were on the whole a match for anyone's." Contemporaries agreed. In the awed phrase of an observer at the Court of Spain in 1566, writing to his master in the Netherlands: "As Your Lordship knows, nothing happens there that is not immediately known here." Five years later, when the ambassador of the Venetian republic (which prided itself on the speed and efficiency of its communications network) hurried to the royal palace to inform Philip II of the great victory of Lepanto, he found that the king had already received the news from one of his own couriers. The same ambassador later complained ruefully that the information at Philip's disposal "was such that there is nothing he does not know."[33]

In this regard, the ability to gather vast amounts of information pales in comparison to deciding (1) what is of crucial importance, and (2) what can be turned into knowledge that can drive decisions. In other words, *what information was vital to making an accurate net assessment of one's rival?* Focusing on the right information is still only half the battle. Often a state has conducted a thorough net assessment and then either has drawn outstandingly wrong conclusions or has found reasons to dismiss the assessment. For instance, though Spain's Philip II was warned repeatedly that his policies were leading to disaster—an assessment he acknowledged—he chose to ignore such warnings for reasons that Geoffrey Parker says were correct given Philip's worldview. This is evidenced by Philip II's reply to an adviser who wished him to pull back from some of his commitments:

> But you must also understand that these are not matters that can be abandoned by a person who is as conscientious about his responsibilities as you know me to be, because they depress me and matter to me more than to anyone. Taken together, they involve far more problems than people think. . . . Moreover, these issues involve religion, which must take precedence over everything.

According to Parker, Philip thus did not dispute the material evidence of impending disaster—but his faith-based political vision led him to ignore it. Similarly, the Austrian branch of the Hapsburg Empire continued building huge fortresses to ward off Ottoman assaults long after any realistic net assessment would have deemed such a strategy expensive and foolish. The last of these great fortresses (Karlstadt) was not completed until the eve of the American revolution and long after the Ottomans were a viable threat to the empire.

The Hapsburgs were not blind to the strategic threat posed by Prussia and later France, but it was irrelevant. A kind of strategic myopia had set in, where the searing emotional memories of the past dominated planning for a radically different future. This is something that strategic rivals in many historical examples given in this report were prone to at one time or another, often with disastrous results. William Morgan in Chapter 15 clearly identifies this same myopia on both sides of the US-Japan rivalry:

> Knowing that Japan's military and economic strength, though sizable, could not defeat the United States in a long war, American officials reasoned that Japan would not start a war that it was certain to lose. Realism prevented them from imagining that Japan might, if pushed to the limit, go to war for non-realist ideological and emotional

reasons. Hence the primary American misjudgments were assuming that Japan would behave according to an American vision of rationality and that the United States had enough leverage to change Japan's policy.

. . .

The Navy and Army leaders never directly and comprehensively analyzed whether Japan could win the war. When they got past the opening stages of the war, they said there were too many variables to make an accurate assessment. More prudent and realistic leaders might have declined to go to war until the variables became clearer. Essentially, Japanese leaders rolled the dice. They counted on favorable future political and diplomatic developments, such as a German defeat of Britain. They assumed a bloodied, timid America would negotiate an early peace rather than fight a long war. They hoped a devastating strike at the beginning of the conflict would lead to an early peace, as had happened at the outset of the 1894–1895 war against China and the 1904 Russo-Japanese war. They made wildly unrealistic estimates about resource consumption and supply from conquered territories. They blundered ahead, avoiding hard realities and comforting themselves by stringing out pointless negotiations.

In every case of a strategic rival meeting with some debacle, all of the warning signs were present long before disaster became inevitable. In these cases, the problem was not lack of information, but always one of miscalculation or even a reluctance to make a calculation. Captured by ideology, past history, or wishful thinking, time and again states make incorrect assessments of their rivals.

Strategic rivals suffer from another kind of myopia that we have mentioned several times previously (e.g., the Vandals attacking Rome, or the Arabs versus the Byzantines and the Persians), but it bears careful noting. The state that is the largest and most ostentatious might not be the one the hegemonic state need fear. Rather, what may seem to be a small, frontier state with a small population and economy might be the greater threat. The determination to have a world identity is a strong strategic driving force. Often in a quiet, small-scale, but persistent way this determination, given enough patience, can build a small frontier state into a large superpower. Historical examples for this are numerous: the Persians, the Macedonians, the Romans, the Huns, the Arabs, the Mongols, the Seljuk Turks, the Ottoman Turks, the list could go on. All of these started out as small frontier states and, by historical logic, they should have stayed that way. But all of them grew to threaten the world. One cannot help but wonder what future world power is currently sitting on the global margins, patiently waiting to exploit its opportunity. The Islamic State probably views itself as filling such a role, but strategists must remain vigilant lest a state or other entity not yet even on our radar begins a drive to power that we are unprepared to stop.

Concluding Thoughts

Early in this effort, I listed a number of items that the various chapter authors were to use as a guide as they approached writing their essays. In that regard, each author did a commendable job in including those items. I believe it is worth examining those original questions to determine what overarching observations history provides to our understanding of the development, management, and conclusion of rivalries. Where a topic has been adequately covered in the preceding, I will not rehash it in this conclusion.

WHAT WERE THE IMPORTANT ASYMMETRIES IN THE COMPETITION?

Every single one of the rivalries examined is littered with various asymmetries, most of them real and easily visible, others imagined but no less potent in their effects on decision-making. The crucial point, however, is not that asymmetries existed but in how they were used. In almost every case examined, an asymmetry played more of a role as a propaganda tool than as a method of determining military conflict. In other words, rivals spent considerable effort pointing out asymmetries in each other as a method of rallying support for continuing the rivalry. Still, except for economic differences, it is not clear that the types of asymmetries in "the others" made any profound difference in a conflict.

Most often, asymmetries are used to play up one rival's difference from the others (themselves) in propaganda, or to rally one's own side through fear. The asymmetry itself is often pointed out as something that makes that rival state different and detestable. So, in Napoleon's formulation, Britain's maritime trade-based power turns into "perfidious Albion" and a "nation of shopkeepers." Similarly, the Bismarck and the kaiser built up a popular idea—German martial superiority—by demeaning maritime Britain's "contemptible little army." This is reflected in Bismarck's famous quote, "If Lord Palmerston sends the British Army to Germany, I shall have a policeman arrest them" (Viscount Palmerston, Speech before the House of Commons, March 1848). The true danger of an asymmetry, therefore, is that deepens the notion of "otherness" between rivals. This "otherness" is often based on religion, ethnicity, or ideology; but it can also result from a difference in power or types of power—economic and/or military.

Paradoxically, a power asymmetry does not typically destabilize a rivalry system or push it toward conflict. Rather, the international equilibrium is most often upset when one side attempts to close a perceived gap in certain asymmetries. Such acts not only threaten the established order, they hugely increase the propensity for the rivals to opt for restarting militarized conflicts. For instance, the great asymmetry between Germany and Britain was that one was a maritime power with a fleet that dominated the high seas, and the other was mostly a continental, that is, a land-based power. Only when Germany began building a high-seas fleet that threatened Britain's primacy did Britain find common cause with its long-term strategic rival France to counter growing German power. Similarly, rapid Russian economic growth from 1908 on so threatened Germany's position as the mightiest economic power in Europe that Germany began actively seeking an excuse for war.

WHAT WAS THE COMPETITION REALLY ABOUT?

This question has been answered substantially in the early pages of this Introduction in discussing three of the reasons for starting and maintaining a strategic rivalry: "fear, honor, and interest." However, two more points are worth pointing out.

- First, in almost every examined case, these rivalries were, at their base, *power contests* to determine who would dominate a specific sphere of interest and establish the rule-set that underpinned the global order. Such rule-sets could be based on various factors such as religion (Islam vs. Christian) or economics (communism vs. capitalism).
- Second, with few exceptions, one rival is already the dominant power (happy with the status quo), and the other is a rising power (unhappy with the status quo) looking to establish its primacy.

Table 0.3 presents a brief summary of the overall causes.

TABLE 0.3 What Was the Rivalry About?

Rivalry	Causes and Goals of Rivalry
Athens vs. Sparta (465–404 BCE)	Who would be the dominant power in Greece? *Rising Power: Athens*
Rome vs. Carthage (264–146 BCE)	Who would be the dominant power in the Mediterranean? *Rising Power: Rome*
Rome-Byzantium vs. Persia (69 BCE–636 CE)	Changed over time—but generally one sought the destruction of the other and a new global order, particularly in the Eastern Mediterranean and Mesopotamia *Rising Power: Persia*
England vs. France (1066–1453, the Middle Ages)	To overthrow and replace the government of the other with its own *Rising Power: England*
Genoa vs. Venice (13th and 14th centuries)	Commercial dominance in the Mediterranean, though neither would have missed an opportunity to destroy the other *Rising Power: Genoa*
Hapsburgs vs. Europe (1516–1713)	The Hapsburgs sought European dominance, while various other states either sought to survive outside Hapsburg control or to destroy the Hapsburg Empire. *Rising Power: Disputed . . . varies over time*
Ottomans vs. Hapsburgs	The destruction of the other as a political entity within Eastern Europe. This was a contest to decide the world order over much of Europe. *Rising Power: NA*
England vs. France (1658–1783)	Global commercial dominance, as each sought to limit the other's power both within Europe and on a global scale. *Rising Power: England (with some dispute according to viewpoint)*
England vs. France (1792–1815, the Napoleonic Era)	France was seeking a European Empire, while Britain and her allies sought the destruction of Napoleonic power and a return to the political status quo prior to the French Revolution. *Rising Power: France*

TABLE 0.3 Continued

Rivalry	Causes and Goals of Rivalry
Germany vs. France (1866–1945)	Political, economic, and military supremacy within Europe *Rising Power: Germany*
Germany vs. Europe (1815–1945)	Establishment of a German-led order within Europe, which would eventually spread on a global scale. The rival powers were set on destroying German military power and thwarting her ambitions. *Rising Power: Germany*
United States vs. United Kingdom (ca. 1812–ca. 1940)	Commercial dominance *Rising Power: United States*
United States vs. Japan (1897 to 1941)	Establishment of and resistance to a Japanese imperial world order throughout Asia *Rising Power: Japan*
United States vs. USSR (1945–1991)	Establishment of a dominant global world order *Rising Power: Simultaneous post–World War II rise to potential global dominance*

NA: Not applicable.

WHAT FACTORS CAUSED AN ESCALATION OF THE RIVALRY? FOR THOSE RIVALRIES THAT DE-ESCALATED OVER TIME, WHAT FACTORS WERE INVOLVED?

As stated previously, rivalries were a result of a major systemic shock to the global order that created the conditions for the establishment of a rivalry. As rivalries continue, there is always a strong tendency to escalate their intensity. This is typically a result of a succession of militarized engagements (this, however, does not always mean war). In each of these engagements, there is one winner, who learns that it can achieve its objectives by standing firm or through a military victory. There is also a loser, who has spent the intervening years preparing itself for a militarized future where it can redress the past defeat and possibly make gains of its own. In each succeeding conflict, national popular attitudes harden, limiting the number of alternatives to war available to policymakers. At the same time, each new conflict is typically of greater scope and passion, as wars tend to head toward a Clausewitz absolute.

The rivalries studied in this work that de-escalated over time did so as a result of the rise of a more dangerous threat, exempting, of course, those rivalries where one side was totally defeated or eradicated. It helped if the rivals shared a common outlook as to the nature of the world order and its political order. For instance, it was much easier for Britain to put aside its rivalries with France and the United States as the German threat arose, for all three nations—Britain, France, the United States—shared civilizational bonds dating back to their Greco-Roman heritage, as well as a collective Judeo-Christian outlook. On the other side stood the Hapsburgs. Long after the Ottomans had ceased to be a serious military danger, the Hapsburgs found it difficult to refocus their attention toward the perils in the West, the far more serious threats from Prussia and France. At least some measure of this reluctance must be based in the profound cultural and civilizational differences between the Hapsburgs and the Ottomans.

WHAT ASSESSMENT METHODS DID THE RIVAL STRATEGIC STATES DEVELOP TO DETERMINE WHERE THEY STOOD? HOW DID THEY PERCEIVE THEIR PERFORMANCE IN THE COMPETITION? HOW GOOD WAS THEIR SENSE OF THEIR RELATIVE STRENGTHS AND WEAKNESSES?

The most profound observation dealing with how rivals assessed each other is that they *almost always* got it right. Rivals always appeared to have a good understanding of each other's strengths and weaknesses. Moreover, they typically were able to amass significant data on each other, to the point where each rival's capabilities were an open book to the other.

Where they failed was in *interpretation and imagination*. Rarely was one state able to turn its deep knowledge of a rival's capacity and capabilities into an accurate assessment of its intentions or future strategic actions. Repeatedly, one rival would endure a moment of strategic surprise, despite a precise net assessment of its competitor's capacity to undertake such a "surprising" action. Almost as often, a rival that finds itself at a power disadvantage will replace an accurate assessment of its competitor with wishful thinking (Japan vs. United States).

In summary, the problem was rarely with collecting intelligence and assessing it; repeated strategic failure was a result of an inability to fathom how a competitor would employ the power at its disposal.

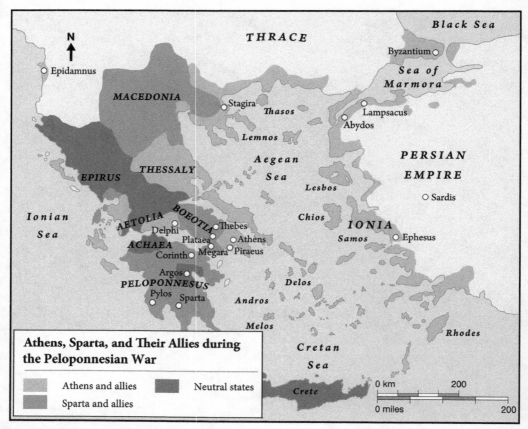

Athens, Sparta, and Their Allies during
the Peloponnesian War

Athens and allies
Sparta and allies
Neutral states

N

Black Sea

THRACE

Byzantium

Sea of
Marmora

Epidamnus

MACEDONIA

Stagira

Thasos

Lampsacus

Abydos

PERSIAN
EMPIRE

Lemnos

Aegean
Sea

EPIRUS

THESSALY

Ionian
Sea

AETOLIA

BOEOTIA

Delphi

Plataea

Thebes

Athens

Lesbos

Sardis

Chios

IONIA

Samos

Ephesus

ACHAEA

Corinth

Megara

Piraeus

PELOPONNESUS

Argos

Pylos

Sparta

Andros

Delos

Melos

Cretan
Sea

Crete

Rhodes

0 km   200

0 miles   200

Eastern Mediterranean on the eve of war.

CHAPTER I

The Primacy of Greece

Athens and Sparta

Paul A. Rahe

I T WOULD BE AN error to suppose that there was a strategic rivalry between Athens and Sparta before the Hellenic victory at the battle of Salamis. The two polities had clashed in the late sixth century when the Lacedaemonians had intervened at Athens—initially for the purpose of overthrowing the Peisistratid tyranny, and twice again later to install a satellite regime.[1] But no one at the time had thought Athens in the same league as Sparta, which had already been recognized as a power of consequence by Lydia and Egypt four decades before. No strategic rivalry was, in fact, imaginable before the Hellenic victory at the battle of Salamis in 480 BC—when Athens, which had provided nearly half of the ships in the Hellenic fleet, first emerged as a great power in its own right. Indeed, none was possible until after the Hellenic victory at Plataea and the expulsion of Persia from the Balkans.

Even then, it would have been a mistake to think of Athens and Sparta as rivals. Their alliance against Persia was uneasy, as alliances nearly always are. But it was a genuine alliance, nonetheless. It had been summoned into existence by the Persian peril, and it was not apt to dissolve as long as it seemed possible that Persia might try again to conquer Greece.

There were, to be sure, Lacedaemonians who dreamed of empire in the wake of the battles of Plataea and Mycale in 479 BC. The regent Pausanias, who led the Spartans to victory in the former battle, appears to have had something of the sort in mind, and he commanded considerable support in Lacedaemon.[2] But such aspirations had little in the way of staying power.

Sparta was a satisfied power. It ruled two-fifths of the Peloponnesus, and it had long before come to recognize that, in subjecting Messenia and reducing the inhabitants of that region to a servile status as helots, it had taken on a strategic burden that virtually precluded further expansion.

Sparta's world was constituted by the Peloponnesus. The formation and maintenance of its alliance system within that great peninsula—a system aimed at keeping the helots down, the Arcadians in, and the Argives out—constituted for Lacedaemon a long-term grand strategy. Sparta overthrew tyrannies and sponsored oligarchies in the Peloponnesian *póleis* with an eye to containing Argos and commanding the support needed to crush any uprising the helots might attempt. Outside the Peloponnesus, it might cautiously intervene to fend off a threat and shore up its position, but it was not prepared to make a long-term commitment. Sparta lacked the necessary manpower. The city never had more than nine or ten thousand adult male citizens, and sustaining the regimen and the singular institutions that enabled it to dominate the helots of Laconia and Messenia required on the part of Lacedaemon a measure of cultural and political isolation.[3] In consequence, despite grave misgivings in certain quarters, Sparta stood aside while the Athenians took the lead in founding the Delian League and in continuing the war at sea against the Persians during and after 477.[4]

As the Lacedaemonians understood at the time, that war was by no means over. The defeats inflicted by the Hellenes on the forces deployed by Xerxes at Salamis in 480 and at Plataea and Mycale in 479 had been a considerable shock, but they had not brought the Mede to his knees. Persia's monarch styled himself the "king of kings," and that is what he was. Salamis and Plataea had done nothing to alter that fact. Achaemenid Persia cannot now be judged the greatest power in human history. There were, in later ages, dominions that governed more individuals and a larger territory. Moreover, in modern times, technology has profoundly altered the strategic playing field and opened up the possibility of a global hegemony. But if one were to assess the power of polities solely in relative terms, as perhaps one should, one would have to award this ancient Near Eastern kingdom the crown. The empire ruled by Darius and his son Xerxes commanded a greater proportion of the world's population and of the world's resources than any dominion that preceded or followed it, and it dwarfed all conceivable rivals. The ancient world was lightly populated. The only regions of any size in which population density was considerable were the four great river valleys where irrigation made possible the production of grain or rice on a grand scale. In the early fifth century, only one of these four—the Yellow River in China—lay outside Darius's and Xerxes' control. The Indus, the Nile, and the Tigris and Euphrates—over these mighty rivers, the fertile and well-watered valleys through which they ran, and the great civilizations to which they had given rise, the first two Achaemenid monarchs held sway, and the resources that this great empire afforded him were more than sufficient to allow Xerxes to renew the war.[5]

Of course, the Persian army had departed from Hellas, and it was not likely to return any time soon. The Hellenes' control of the sea precluded that. To enable his army to march from Sardis in Anatolia to and across the Hellespont, then through Thrace and Macedonia to Thessaly in Hellas and points south within the Balkan peninsula, Xerxes had had to ship foodstuffs in massive quantities well in advance by sea to depots established at regular intervals along the Aegean coast of Thrace and Macedonia. He also had to dispatch a great fleet and a host of merchant ships to accompany his army. He could not ignore the logistical imperatives.[6] He could not even begin contemplating a second invasion of Greece by land until he had first regained the maritime dominance Persia had once possessed.

This the Spartans understood. They also knew that the Athenians—and no other city—had the ships needed for fending off the Mede. They recognized that Athens was more than willing to shoulder the responsibility;[7] and, as in the past, the Lacedaemonians were perfectly happy to stand by while others did their fighting for them. Athens's assumption of the hegemony at sea made perfect sense from their point of view.

Triremes and Hoplites

If Athens's emergence as a major maritime power was nonetheless unsettling, it was because it was a development sudden, quite recent, and unforeseen. Just a few years before Xerxes' invasion, that city's navy had been a negligible force—inferior to the fleet deployed by its local rival, the little island of Aegina, situated nearby in the Saronic Gulf. To counter the Aeginetan fleet, Athens had had to buy used triremes from a friendly power willing to sell them for a pittance. At this point, the Athenians had been, nearly all of them, landlubbers; and landlubbers they certainly would have remained—given the stupendous cost of building, maintaining, and staffing such ships—had the city not profited from a spectacular silver strike just a few years after its unexpected victory on land over a Persian expeditionary force at the battle of Marathon.[8]

The trireme, which appears to have been introduced in the sixth century BCE, was a triple-banked shell, shaped like a wine glass; in the manner of the double-banked penteconters that had preceded it, this vessel sported a prow equipped with a bronze-sheathed ram. Its ram, however, had not one, but three horizontal cutting blades capable of slicing through the hull of virtually any vessel equal or smaller in mass that it struck amidships or in the stern. Triremes varied in size—from about 120 to 130 feet long and from about 15 to 18 feet wide. When fully manned, each was powered by 170 oarsmen facing the stern, each plying a single oar 14 feet in length, using as a fulcrum a tholepin to which the oar was tied by a well-greased leather oar loop. These rowers, who slid back and forth on cushions of fleece so that they could leverage the muscles in their legs as they pulled the oars, were organized on three levels—with at least two-thirds of them enclosed within the hull and unable to see their own oars.

Within a trireme, there were officers on deck to decide and direct the ship's course, to dictate and sustain the tempo of the oarsmen's strokes, and to convey to them the orders of the trierarch in command. There was also a shipwright on board and a purser, and there were specialists trained in handling the sails, as well as archers and marines fully equipped for combat— enough to bring the boat's full complement to 200 men at a minimum; its weight, when loaded with all of the pertinent equipment and personnel, to something on the order of 50 tons. When fully manned—as it had to be if it was not to be underpowered, slow, hard to maneuver, and unlikely to survive a contest—this newfangled ship was a formidable fighting machine.

Rowing such a vessel required, as one commander reportedly put it, that one embrace "hardship" and "toil." It, in fact, took extraordinary grit, determination, discernment, and discipline on the part of a great many men for a trireme to be operated in battle to advantage. The trierarch in command had to be a man of fine judgment—quick to sense danger, and no less quick in recognizing opportunity—and he had to have an intimate knowledge of the capacity of his ship and crew and of their limits. The helmsman (*kubernétēs*) stationed immediately below the trierarch's perch at the stern was in charge in the trierarch's absence and had to possess the same capacities. He also had to be skilled and precise in his use of the vessel's two steering oars. Everything depended on his ability to maneuver the galley into a position from which it could strike and not be struck in return, and an error or even a measure of imprecision on his part could quite easily be fatal to all concerned. When the trireme was in motion, the archers and marines on deck had to remain seated lest they destabilize the vessel. In consequence, they had to be able to shoot or hurl projectiles with great accuracy from an uncomfortable, sedentary position. With the help of a flutist (*aulétēs*) located amidships keeping time with his instrument, the exhorter (*keleustēs*) situated on the gangway near the stern and his colleague, the bow-master (*prōrátēs*) stationed near the prow, had to drill the oarsmen in synchronizing their strokes and in rowing forward now at this pace, now at that. These two also had to teach them how to reverse themselves on the benches and back water without missing a beat; they had to instruct them how to partially ship their oars on command when a few seconds delay could result in the oars on one side being sheared off, in some of the oarsmen being killed by whiplash, and in the galley itself being disabled. In time of battle, moreover, these two officers had to convey the helmsman's orders quickly and accurately, and throughout, they had to sustain the morale of men whom they were driving quite hard.

The oarsmen themselves had to learn endurance and close coordination. This was no small thing, as scholars first came fully to appreciate in the late 1980s and early 1990s, when, under the guidance of an intrepid group of British classicists and naval experts, a Greek shipyard built a replica of a trireme, and every other summer volunteers gathered from far and near to take the *Olympias*, as it was called, to sea and put it through a series of trials. There was, these scholars discovered, a great deal to endure, and everything depended on a precise synchronization of the rowers' strokes.

On journeys, for example—when the sea was becalmed, when the wind blew from the wrong quarter or was insufficient—it became clear that the oarsmen of ancient times had to row steadily for hours and hours. When the fleet was arranged for battle in line abreast, they had to row gently forward and then back water and do this again and again to maintain their galley's position in the formation. In the battle itself, when maneuvering for advantage, they had to be able to turn the vessel on a dime; and, when closing in for a kill or fleeing attack, they had to drive the vessel forward at maximum speed. If, at the end of such a sprint, their ship succeeded in ramming at high speed an enemy trireme, they had to back water at a moment's notice to prevent the two vessels from being locked together in such a manner that the infantrymen seated on board the damaged ship could attempt to board and seize their own. Alternatively, if the trierarch's aim was to approach an enemy vessel head-on at full tilt, then narrowly dodge a collision and coast along the enemy boat's starboard or port side with an eye to shearing off half of its oars and rendering it defenseless and incapable of maneuver, the oarsmen on the vulnerable side of his own trireme had to be able to partially ship their oars at a moment's notice while their colleagues on the other side of the vessel simultaneously lifted theirs out of the water. For the rowers to be able to do all of this with maximum effectiveness, those who conducted *Olympias's* sea trials discovered, they had to drill and drill and drill once more. Following orders and close coordination had to become second nature for each and every one of them.[9]

Themistocles was the architect of Athens's emergence as a power at sea. He it was who persuaded his compatriots to devote the city's income from its great silver strike to the construction of triremes.[10] In doing so, he saddled them with the unenviable task of mastering the art of war at sea. It was, moreover, the astonishing victory that he engineered in 480 by luring Xerxes' fleet into the narrows at Salamis, where its superiority in size and maneuverability produced no advantage, that gave his compatriots the confidence to sustain the effort thereafter. To be precise, it enabled Themistocles' erstwhile rival Aristeides to organize the newly liberated island polities of the Aegean and the Greek cities scattered along the coasts of Thrace, the Hellespont, the sea of Marmara, the Bosphorus, western Anatolia, and Lycia in the south into an alliance capable of extracting from its members the quite substantial resources necessary for it to field year in and year out a navy sufficient to keep the Mede at bay.[11]

From the outset, when it came to warfare at sea, money was the sinews of war.[12] At the time of the great conflict with Persia, however, this was not the case in Hellas with regard to warfare on land. The hoplite army that defeated the expeditionary force that Darius of Persia sent to Marathon was a civic militia—made up almost entirely of men who farmed the land themselves or employed slaves to work under their direction. Of course, the citizens who served in Athens's phalanx were formidable practitioners of hand-to-hand combat. When Darius's commanders initiated a withdrawal from Marathon by loading their cavalry back on the horse transports that had conveyed them to Marathon from Asia Minor, the infantrymen of Athens and its ally Plataea, though greatly outnumbered, had the presence of mind to seize the opportunity. In close formation, they charged the archers, doubling as spearmen, who constituted the foot soldiers of the Great King. They shoved aside the wall of wicker shields that had been set up to protect the shield-less bowmen, and then they massacred the Persian host.[13] But, competent and effective though they were, the hoplites who did this were not professional soldiers. At best, they could be described as weekend warriors. They were not all that numerous, and they were unpaid.

The Spartans who, at Plataea, did the same to the infantrymen brought to Hellas by Xerxes might, of course, be described as professionals. They were rentiers supported by servile labor, and they were graced with leisure in abundance—much of which they devoted to the preparation for war. They put great effort into gymnastic training, and they learned how to wield to good effect the heavy hoplite shield and the thrusting spear that served as the

Greek infantrymen's chief offensive weapon, as well as the sword that each fell back on when that spear had been wrenched from his grasp or shattered. They practiced forming, via a phalanx eight men deep, an almost impenetrable wall of shields—and all of this effort gave them a decided edge when thrown into combat with their fellow Hellenes. But it did not alter in any marked way the nature of hoplite warfare, and supporting a force of this sort did not at this time require any particular financial acumen. In fact, Lacedaemon, the only classical Greek city with a quasi-professional infantry force, managed to field a hoplite army without ever having to coin any silver at all.[14]

The Emergence of Rivalry

Even at this time, there were Athenians who regarded Sparta as a threat. What had happened in the late sixth century had not been forgotten at Athens; and when, after the battle of Plataea, the Lacedaemonians urged the Athenians not to rebuild their walls, the latter warily ignored the request,[15] and they soon thereafter went on to fortify Peiraeus as a port.[16] Moreover, Themistocles, whom Thucydides depicts as a man of unparalleled strategic foresight, appears to have been ready to turn on Lacedaemon and its allies once the Persians had been sent packing.

At Athens, however, as one would expect, Panhellenic sentiment was at this time strong. Persia still inspired fear, the desire for revenge was great, and Cimon, son of the Miltiades who defeated the Persians at Marathon, bested Themistocles in the political struggles that took place in the 470s, secured his ostracism for a ten-year term in 471,[17] and pursued a policy of accommodating Sparta in the Balkans and of harrying the Persians in the eastern Mediterranean. This suited nearly everyone at the time. The Spartans recognized that, as long as the Greeks controlled the sea, logistical difficulties would prevent the Persians from returning by land, and Cimon understood the reasons for Sparta's reluctance to venture beyond its Peloponnesian stronghold.

Political communities are, however, prickly—and this was especially true in antiquity, when commerce for the most part played a marginal role and economic interdependence was not even a dream. Potential rivals who are close trading partners have something to lose from war. Potential rivals operating in a technologically stagnant world in which war is a far more promising outlet for man's acquisitive instincts than is trade know no such restraints.[18] Athens relied on commerce for the import of grain, which was for that community a strategic substance,[19] but it was a martial, not a mercantile, polity.

Most of its commerce with the outside world was conducted by foreigners. Insofar as the political community drew sustenance from the international arena, it was by way of the contributions made by its allies for the support of the Delian League's fleet—and these contributions, which in time came to be regarded as tribute by the contributors and the recipients alike, soon also came to be thought vital to the well-being of Athens. For the host of officials who managed the dominion and for the impoverished thetes who rowed in its fleet, the Delian League provided a livelihood.[20]

If Athens was not just warlike but exceedingly aggressive and sometimes bold beyond reason, it was in part because it was a democracy in which land-less men, desperate for acquisition and with little to lose, had a considerable say. If Sparta, though martial, was nonetheless averse to armed conflict, it was in part because its citizenry was by ancient standards well-to-do and had a great deal to lose. Laconia was geographically isolated and relatively easy to defend—cut off, as it was, from the outside world by mountains and hill country. Messenia was in similar fashion a world unto itself. As a polity, Lacedaemon was virtually an autarchy. Economically, it was inward-looking. Its citizens were gentlemen farmers. They relied on the land and the helots the city owned for nearly everything that they needed. They had no trading relations worth mentioning, which helps explain why the city never had any coinage of its own.

It was perhaps inevitable that two such polities come to blows. The dif-ference in ethos inevitably gave rise to misunderstanding and a measure of mutual dislike. Moreover, despite the best efforts of Cimon and his counter-parts in Lacedaemon, there were citizens in both Athens and Sparta who were suspicious of or resentful toward the other polity. At Lacedaemon, there were those who found the growth in Athenian power daunting and who argued that Athens was the new Persia; and there were those at Athens who feared that sooner or later the Spartans would intervene, as they had done in the past.

These propensities were held in check as long as a Persian resurgence was expected—and eventually just such a resurgence did take place. The precise date is unclear, but the odds are good that Xerxes ordered the construction of a great fleet in the late 470s, and there is reason to date to the summer of 469 the momentous clash that ultimately took place at the mouth of the Eurymedon River in southern Anatolia—where, on a single day, Cimon both annihilated the Persian fleet and massacred the army posted to support it.[21] It is by no means certain that it was in the aftermath of this battle that Cimon's brother-in-law Callias first negotiated a formal peace with Persia. But it seems highly likely that some sort of understanding was worked out. For Cimon did not at this time capitalize on his victory by seizing Cyprus, where there was a number of Greek cities; and, with regard to the years immediately following, we have no more reports mentioning a clash of arms between Persian and Greek.[22]

The tensions that quite naturally emerged between Athens and Sparta once the Persians decided to back off appear to have been aggravated by the activities of Themistocles in the early 460s. After his ostracism, he resided for some years at Argos, Sparta's age-old strategic rival within the Peloponnesus. From there, we are told, he traveled throughout that great peninsula. It was in these years that Sparta found itself politically isolated there and fought a great battle not only with Argos but also with Tegea, the most strategically important of its Peloponnesian allies. It is a reasonable guess that the exiled Athenian bore some of the responsibility for Sparta's travails at this time,[23] and there is evidence suggesting the presence of Athenian volunteers in the Argive-Tegean army that battled with Lacedaemon (Simonides F122–123 [Diehl]). Themistocles may even have conspired with the renegade Spartan regent Pausanias to bring Lacedaemon down. For Pausanias, who had long been suspected of Medism, was discovered at this time not only to be intriguing with the Persians but also to be stirring up a rebellion on the part of Lacedaemon's helots, and he is said to have divulged his plans to the Athenian. This, in any case, was the accusation that the Spartans advanced against Themistocles at Athens—and when recalled for trial on a charge of Medism, the architect of the Hellenic victory at Salamis did not even bother to return home to defend himself. Instead, he fled to Corcyra, then via the Molossian kingdom to Macedon, and ultimately on to Persia, where he was graciously received, feted, and rewarded by Xerxes' son and heir Artaxerxes.[24]

Taken together, Athens's victory at Eurymedon, its reaching an accommodation with Persia, and Themistocles' machinations in the Peloponnesus appear to have worked a transformation in Spartan attitudes. For we are told that in 465, when the *pólis* on the island of Thasos, infuriated at Athenian encroachment on the gold mines it controlled in Thrace, tried to withdraw from the Delian League and was defeated at sea, the authorities at Lacedaemon secretly offered Spartan support to the Thasians.[25]

It is difficult to say whether the Spartans would have made good on the pledge issued by those in authority at this time had they been able to do so. Ordinarily, they were anything but venturesome, as we have seen. In the event, even had they been fiercely resolute, they would not have been able to field an army on Thasos's behalf—for, in 465, a series of earthquakes struck Laconia.[26] The epicenter appears to have been near the constitutive villages of Sparta. We are told that these earthquakes left only five houses standing,[27] that 20,000 Lacedaemonians died, and that more than half of the Spartiates (the full citizens of Lacedaemon) were killed. There is also reason to suspect that many more Spartiates died in the helot revolt that followed fast on this event,[28] and some were no doubt killed shortly thereafter when the survivors of the earthquake found themselves forced to fight Tegea and all of the other Arcadians, apart from the Mantineians, at a place called Dipaea in a battle in which the Lacedaemonians' dearth of manpower is said to have left them capable of fielding a phalanx only one shield in depth.

Some scholars regard the ancient testimony concerning these events as exaggerated. There is one sign, however, that this was not the case. The authorities at Lacedaemon, who had been ready to go to war with Athens just a few months before, in desperation actually asked the Athenians for military aid.[29] It was the provision of this assistance at Cimon's urging and the Lacedaemonian reaction to anti-Spartan grumbling within the Athenian army that occasioned the fatal breach between the two chief members of the Hellenic League. When, at Spartan insistence, Cimon led the Athenian army on the long, dreary march back home,[30] his enemies Ephialtes and Pericles— the erstwhile admirers and allies of Themistocles—pounced. By then, Thasos had fallen. By then, we must presume, the Athenians had learned that the Spartan authorities had promised the islanders help.

Given what the Spartans were then known to have done, Cimon did not have a leg to stand on. In 461, he was ostracized for a term of ten years,[31] and the Athenians soon formed an alliance with Lacedaemon's rival Argos and with the Thessalians. Then, when the Spartans refused an appeal on the part of their Megarian ally that they act to prevent Corinth from bullying its neighbor in the matter of a territorial dispute and the Megarians turned to Athens to ask for help, the Athenians accepted Megara into an alliance, knowing full well that this would enrage the Corinthians and produce a war with Lacedaemon.

Recurrent War

From this time onward until the end of the great Peloponnesian War and the surrender of Athens in 404, there was an enduring strategic rivalry between the Athenians and the Spartans. The contest was, however, an exceedingly awkward one. In 461, when their first armed conflict began, the rebellious helots in Messenia were holed up on Mount Ithome, and the Lacedaemonians were unable to dislodge them. As long as this was the case, the Spartans, whose numbers were in any case depleted, could not afford to send an army of any size far afield. Even after 455, when a withdrawal of the Messenians was negotiated, they were constrained. As long as Athens held Megara and could fortify the passes leading from the Megarid to the Isthmus of Corinth, it could greatly hinder, if not block, egress by land from the Peloponnesus; and there was little that Sparta—lacking, as it did, the financial resources needed for the construction of a great fleet—could do to strike at its enemy. The same would be true in some measure even after the Athenians lost control of Megara. For, in 457, the Athenians began, in earnest, building "Long Walls" to link the fortifications at Athens with those surrounding its port-town at Peiraeus. Once these were complete, the citizens could, in an emergency, withdraw from the countryside, take refuge behind their walls, and import food by sea.[32]

It was similarly difficult for Athens, which was a sea power, to strike a blow directly at Lacedaemon. It could raid the subject towns of Sparta's *períoikoi* situated on the mountainous Laconian coast and burn the city's dockyards at Gutheion. It could seize islands such as Aegina, Zacynthus, and Cephallenia, which were allied with Lacedaemon or Corinth. It could also strike at those of Sparta's allies situated along the coasts of the Peloponnesus, and some of them it could seize or pry loose from that alliance.[33] The Athenians could even mount a blockade of sorts against the Corinthians by basing a small fleet at Salamis in the Saronic Gulf and another at the Megarian port of Pegae on the Corinthian Gulf. Moreover, after 455, they were in a position to tighten this blockade by stationing a third fleet at Naupactus near the narrows just inside the entrance to the latter gulf, for it was there in that year that they settled the surviving Messenian rebels given safe conduct to leave the Peloponnesus by the Spartans.[34]

All of this the Athenians could do, but they did not have infantry forces adequate to strike at the holdings of the Spartiates in the heart of Laconia or Messenia, and, thanks in part to the role played by the thetes in the Athenian assembly, they were prone to foolhardy adventures apt to deplete their power. In the late 460s, when Artaxerxes refused to renew the peace his father had negotiated,[35] the Athenians restarted their war with the Mede, attacked Cyprus, and intervened in Egypt with a fleet of 200 triremes to support that satrapy's revolt against Persia. Five years later, upstream along the Nile, they lost hundreds of triremes and something like 40,000–50,000 men—among them perhaps as many as 10,000–15,000 of Athens' poorer citizens.[36] For a community made up at the time of no more than 50,000 adult male citizens, if even that, such a loss was a terrible blow.[37]

At one point, in 457, the Lacedaemonians did manage to elude the Athenian blockade and ship across the Corinthian Gulf a small corps of Spartiates and a much larger body of their *períoikoi* and Peloponnesian allies for the purpose of defending Doris against its Phocian neighbors; on its return overland to the Peloponnesus, this army did fight a battle at Tanagra in Boeotia against the Argives and the Athenians, who subsequently allowed it to pass unopposed through the Megarid to the Peloponnesus. But, even though the losses were heavy on both sides at Tanagra and the Peloponnesians were victorious,[38] theirs was a victory without consequence. And, although the Athenians soon thereafter seized Boeotia, that, too, was without consequence for the struggle with Sparta; the same can be said for their attempts to lure the coastal communities of the Peloponnesus into their alliance. Though largely successful, this effort seems to have had little impact on Lacedaemon.

More than half a century later, a Corinthian leader is said to have summed up Sparta's strategic position by comparing Lacedaemon to a mighty stream. "At their sources," he noted, "rivers are not great and they are easily forded, but the farther on they go, the greater they get—for other rivers empty into them and make the current stronger." So it is with the Spartans, he continued. "There, in the place where they emerge, they are alone; but as they continue and gather cities under their control, they become more numerous and harder to fight." The prudent general, he concluded, would seek battle with the Spartans in or near Lacedaemon, where they are few in number and relatively weak.

This is, of course, precisely what Themistocles had done, and it had very nearly worked. If Athens's aim after 461 was to duplicate his achievement, it would have to subvert Sparta's alliance, rally the Argives, draw a great many of the Arcadians and perhaps the Eleans as well into a league with Argos, and stage a decisive hoplite battle in the vicinity of Laconia or Messenia, as he had done. But this, despite a valiant effort, the Athenians failed in the 450s to accomplish. The moment of opportunity exploited by Themistocles had passed. By the late 460s, Sparta had brought its most recalcitrant allies back into line. In the first few decades that followed, they remained doggedly loyal. In consequence, Lacedaemon was able to compensate for the sudden and dramatic decline in Spartan manpower by marshalling infantry from its allies; in these circumstances, Argos had no allies in the Peloponnesus capable of helping it to field a hoplite force adequate to the task.

The Athenians were hyperactive in this period, as was their wont. The Spartans did next to nothing.[39] As long as the Messenian rebels were holed up on Mount Ithome, they were preoccupied. Even thereafter, however, in part because of the severe losses that they had incurred at the time of the earthquake and in part because of their instinctive inclinations, they were, as adversaries, inactive. Insofar as there was fighting, the Aeginetans and the

Corinthians bore the brunt of it. The Lacedaemonians no doubt looked on with interest, anxiety, and more than a trace of schadenfreude as the Athenians got themselves into deep trouble; as they lost one, then two fleets in Egypt; and as the Persians built a navy, recovered their hold on the Nile valley, and once again took to the sea. Finally, however, after Pericles induced the assembly to recall Cimon from exile,[40] the latter returned and in due course journeyed to Lacedaemon to negotiate a five-year truce; and, in 451, the Spartans gave him what he asked. All that it took at this time to persuade the Lacedaemonians that Athens's maritime hegemony really was to their advantage was a sharp reminder that, just over the horizon, the Persians were girding their loins, poised and ready to renew their quest to conquer Greece.

Of course—in 446, when those five years had passed, when Cimon had died, when the Athenians had won a great battle on both land and sea at Cypriot Salamis against the Mede and the peace with Persia had been renewed—the Spartans did act. The events seem in part to have been carefully choreographed. First, the Boeotians rebelled against Athens's dominion. Then, when they had secured their liberty by ambushing and annihilating an Athenian army at Coronea, the Euboeans followed suit; and, when Pericles left for that island with Athens's remaining hoplites, the Megarians opened their gates to the Corinthians, Sicyonians, and Epidaurians and massacred the Athenian garrison. Finally, when Pericles crossed back over to Attica with Athens's hoplites, invaded the Megarid, ravaged the territory of the Megarians, and defeated a Megarian force, Sparta's Agiad king Pleistoanax, son of Pausanias, led an army of Peloponnesians through the Megarid into Attica.

This turn of events caught the Athenians flat-footed. Eleven years prior, the Athenians had begun building "Long Walls" to link the city of Athens with the Peiraeus, and they are said to have finished them in short order. In principle, at the time of Pleistoanax's invasion, the Athenians could have found refuge behind these walls and could have imported food by sea, as we have seen. But this, in 446, they did not do—perhaps because their hoplite army was already exposed and in the field.

Had Pleistoanax been intent on Athens's defeat and subjection or even on its destruction, he might well have been able to achieve that on this occasion. But to the surprise and consternation of many of his fellow Spartans, a negotiation, rather than a battle, ensued.[41] The Athenians indicated a willingness to relinquish everything, apart from Aegina and Naupactus, that they had gained in the course of their war with Lacedaemon; the Spartans pledged in effect to respect Athens's rule over the members of the Delian League; and both sides agreed that neither would infringe on the other's alliance, that neither would accept into its league the other's allies, that neutrals could join either alliance, and that disputes would be arbitrated.[42] Although Pleistoanax and Cleandridas, the ephor who had assisted him in the negotiations, were soon thereafter charged with treason and an acceptance of bribes and the former was fined and both fled the scene,[43] the Spartans ratified the agreement they had negotiated. It was supposed to last for thirty years.

The deep ambivalence on Lacedaemon's part, evident in these proceedings, was not an aberration. It was there from the beginning, and it was a natural concomitant of its strategic situation. Athens's rise to preeminence and its brashness were a source of resentment from the outset, but at the same time, its contribution in fending off the Mede was deeply appreciated. Some were furious that, when Pleistoanax had the Athenians at his mercy, he had failed to annihilate Athens's army. Others were relieved that Lacedaemon was spared the responsibility of keeping the Persians at bay, as well as the danger to its way of life apt to be attendant on an acceptance of that responsibility. It is no surprise that—six years after the peace of 446 was signed, when the Samians and Byzantines bolted from the Delian League and staged a rebellion—the authorities at Sparta were once again willing to contemplate war. We can also be confident that many at Lacedaemon were relieved when the Corinthians—who had suffered grievously in the previous war and who, as the only Peloponnesian power with a navy of any size, would have borne the brunt of any struggle aimed at breaking up the Delian League—blocked the enterprise.[44]

In 446, the Athenians had been exhausted, chastened, and ready to agree to a peace thirty years in duration. But it would be a mistake to accuse them of ambivalence. They had been caught napping, and they had made the best deal they could. Moreover, after the grievous loss of life at Tanagra, the catastrophe in Egypt, and the massacre at Coronea, they needed breathing space—time for their population to recover, time for reflection, and time for the Delian League treasury to recoup the losses it had suffered when the fleets sent to Egypt were destroyed, the reserves were deployed, and hundreds of new triremes had to be built.

There are some who believe that Pericles, who was now fully in charge, had learned a lesson and that he was now committed to a permanent posture of peaceful coexistence with Sparta, similar to the policy that Cimon had once so resolutely pursued. He had certainly learned something. He had learned that, if the Peloponnesians were to invade again, it was essential that the Athenians seek refuge behind the "Long Walls," and he had reached another conclusion as well. When war clouds once again hovered on the horizon, Pericles repeatedly warned his compatriots against adventurism of the sort that they had engaged in when, in the midst of a struggle with Lacedaemon, they had lent support to the Egyptian revolt against the Mede. But it would be an error to think that Pericles ever imagined it possible for Athens and Sparta to live in peace and amity for any great length of time. If he ever even entertained such a possibility, the news that the authorities at Lacedaemon had attempted to rally their allies against Athens in 440 at the time of the Samian and Byzantine revolts would have disabused him of the notion.

"War is," as Thucydides tells us, "a violent teacher." At an exorbitant price, it dispels illusions. Athens had an Achilles heel. So did Sparta. The war that was brought to an end in 446 illuminated both of these. In neither case, as it happens, was this point of vulnerability easy for the other power to approach. To defeat a maritime power such as Athens, one would have to take to the sea and raise up a rebellion in its empire. Once the Athenians had completed the "Long Walls" linking the city with its port and turning Athens into an artificial island virtually impervious to invasion by land, nothing else would do. To defeat Sparta, as we have seen, one would have to master the land and field a hoplite army superior to its own. This one could do, as Themistocles had demonstrated, solely by rallying Argos, subverting the Spartan alliance, and using Lacedaemon's erstwhile allies to bring it down. The requisite manpower was available nowhere else.

Pericles' Calculated Risk

As the Athenians had learned in the course of their first war with the Peloponnesians, it would not be easy to duplicate what Themistocles had done. For such an enterprise, circumstances in the 440s and the early 430s were not at all propitious. In 451, when Cimon negotiated a five-year truce between Athens and Sparta, Argos, fearing what Lacedaemon would do in the interim, agreed to a peace of thirty years duration with its ancestral foe. When the limited term stipulated in that agreement came to an end in 421, the Argives might well be willing to make another attempt to bring Sparta's hegemony within the Peloponnesus to an end. Prior to that time, however, they would be highly reluctant to do anything of the sort.

The logic of Athens's situation and everything that the Athenians had learned the hard way in the 450s and the early 440s argued for peace. In the short run, the city had little, if anything, to gain from a major war. Pericles and his compatriots had come to appreciate the virtues of Cimon's Persian policy. One might disagree as to whether there ever had been or ever could be any point in Athens's attempting to extend its empire into the Levant. But it was clear enough to everyone who had witnessed the debacle in Egypt that mounting such a venture while Lacedaemon remained a threat was madness in the extreme. If Pericles and others continued to think Cimon's posture with regard to Sparta unpalatable, they were nonetheless forced to acknowledge that for the time being, as an expedient, it made excellent sense. In the long run, it might well be inevitable that there be a showdown with Lacedaemon. But the only such war worth fighting was a war likely to eventuate in a hoplite battle deep within the Peloponnesus in which Sparta's most important allies were ranged against their hegemon. There are times when a statesman must watch and wait.

In the late 430s, as I have argued in detail elsewhere, an opportunity unexpectedly presented itself, and Pericles moved deliberately with consummate skill to seize it.[45] There was one city within Sparta's Peloponnesian League that was a profoundly unsatisfied power, and it was of vital importance to Lacedaemon. Corinth was strategically located. It controlled the isthmus linking the Peloponnesus to the Greek mainland and guarded the entrance to that peninsula. It occupied a narrow neck of land separating the Corinthian from the Saronic Gulf; it had ports on both bodies of water; and it maintained a drag-way, which made it possible to convey vessels of some magnitude from one gulf to the other. Corinth was, in consequence, the chief commercial center in the Peloponnesus and, as such, had considerable leverage over its Peloponnesian neighbors. It was also, now that Aegina had come under Athens's control, the sole significant ally of Lacedaemon in possession of a sizable fleet. It was, in short, indispensable.

In the archaic period, Corinth had been a great colonizer; and, unlike most Greek cities, it maintained exceedingly close relations with these colonies. Most of the maritime cities on the Greek mainland were agricultural in character and eastern in orientation. Corinth was an anomaly. Its farmland was sparse; it was more dependent on trade than any other Greek city; and it looked first and foremost to the west—to and beyond the aptly named Corinthian Gulf. All of its colonies lay in that direction, with the single exception of Potideia in the Thracian Chalcidice. Corinth drew sustenance chiefly from the Adriatic, from southern Italy, and from Sicily.[46]

When the Athenians took Megara under their wing in 461, then defeated Corinth on land and at sea, and instituted a blockade of its trade from both the Saronic and the Corinthian Gulf, they struck at the city's livelihood and threatened its very existence. This was not done by the Athenians out of any particular solicitude for the welfare of the Megarians. Nor did they act in consequence of a hostility to Corinth as such. As the Corinthians clearly recognized, Athens's aim was to guarantee its own security by bottling up the Spartans and their allies within the Peloponnesus, and it also wanted to dismantle Sparta's Peloponnesian League.

In the aftermath of this war, when Megara was once again a member of the Spartan alliance, the Corinthians, who had been made to suffer for their connection with Lacedaemon, were, naturally enough, intent on preventing a repeat of that bitter experience. To this end, they did everything that they could to shore up their position in the west. Their aim was to build up an empire of sorts with resources sufficient to enable them once again to be the dominant power in the Corinthian Gulf and along the trade route that ran up the Adriatic coast of the Balkans and across the sea to Italy and Sicily. Their goal was to render it impossible for the Athenians ever to impose another blockade. Behind their pursuit of this end, there was a pent-up fury, fueled by bitterness and driven by dread.

Corinth faced two obstacles. The Messenians, whom the Athenians had settled at Naupactus on the northern shore of the Corinthian Gulf near its entrance, were still there, firmly ensconced—and they were still allied with the Athenians. Should war again erupt between Athens and Sparta, Naupactus would once again function as an Athenian base. This the Corinthians knew. The other obstacle to their aspirations was Corcyra—an island polity in the Adriatic, founded as a colony by Corinth centuries before, which had come into conflict with its mother city and which treated the Corinthians with a measure of contempt. To add injury to insult, Corcyra maintained a fleet second only to that of Athens, and the island was strategically located athwart the trade route to Italy.

In the 430s, opportunity knocked. Epidamnus, a city situated in the Adriatic on the Balkan coast where the Albanian city of Durazzo is now located, was wracked by civil strife. One faction sought Corinth's aid, and the Corinthians leapt at the opportunity to take control of the town—which lay north of Corcyra at the jumping-off point for the voyage from the Balkans to Italy and Sicily. Then, when the Corcyraeans, who had founded Epidamnus, objected to Corinth's interference in their sphere of influence and came to the defense of the other Epidamnian faction, war broke out between the two naval powers. Corcyra won the first great battle at sea. But this did not stop the Corinthians, who immediately began building a second and much larger fleet and, in their fury, flatly refused an offer of arbitration on the part of the Corcyraeans that was tantamount to a surrender of their claims.[47] It was at this point that the Athenians became involved.

Pericles handled the situation with a cunning worthy of comparison with that later displayed by Otto von Bismarck. As he and his compatriots recognized, were the Corinthians to conquer Corcyra and pool their ample resources with those of the Corcyraeans, they would become a threat to Athens's maritime hegemony. This the Athenians could not allow. But it was also to their advantage that responsibility for the conflict be pinned on the Corinthians alone—for this might obviate war, and it would certainly produce strains within the Spartan alliance.

To this end, Pericles persuaded his compatriots to form a defensive, rather than an offensive, alliance with the islanders. He put pressure on the cities within the Peloponnesus that had joined Corinth's first expedition, demanding that they deny it further support. Apart from Megara, all of the communities on the Saronic Gulf complied, and in short order the outlier was made to pay a price.[48] The Megarians had a long-standing border dispute with Athens and had purportedly been providing refuge to its runaway slaves. With this as an excuse,[49] a decree was passed at Athens denying Megarian citizens access to the markets and harbors of the members of the Delian League.[50]

When it became clear that the Corinthians had not been deterred and that a battle was in the offing and the Corcyraeans invoked the alliance and asked for Athenian aid, Pericles saw to it that his compatriots dispatched only ten ships. These he put under the command of a *próxenos* of the Spartans at Athens, who just happened to be a son of Cimon. Tellingly, the man bore the name Lacedaemonius, and he was told to enter the battle if and only if the Corcyraeans were on the verge of defeat. It was, it appears, only as an afterthought that the Athenians pressed Pericles to dispatch to Sybota twenty additional ships to reinforce the original ten.[51]

Almost everything that Athens did in the course of thwarting Corinth's assault on Corcyra, which took place in August 433 (ML no. 61), could be defended as a dictate of necessity, and none of it afforded grounds for claiming that the terms of the Thirty Years Peace had been broken. That agreement had specified that neutral powers, such as Corcyra, could be accepted into either alliance. Nowhere did it stipulate that one could not cut off all contact with a member of the opposing league.[52] Nowhere did it specify that the members of either league would be autonomous.[53] To both Sparta and Athens, each within its sphere, the treaty left considerable leeway. There was, however, provision within that instrument for the peaceful settlement of disputes between the two great powers. They were supposed to be submitted to arbitration. If the battle of Sybota and the Megarian Decree were to be made a *casus belli* and the arbitration clause ignored, the onus would fall on Lacedaemon.

That was one dimension of the bind that Athens put Sparta in. There was another—for everything that Athens did was also brilliantly designed for the purpose of enraging the Corinthians and encouraging them to direct their anger at the Spartans. Being denied their prize in the Adriatic was a painful blow, and it was rendered doubly painful by the fact that, on that fateful day at Sybota, victory had been within Corinth's grasp. This was bad enough. But to it was added the embargo the Athenians directed at Megara and the suffering it produced (Ar. *Ach.* 495–556, 729–764; *Pax* 246–249, 605–614). Given what the Corinthians had undergone in the earlier war with Athens, Megara was for them a sore point. If the Lacedaemonians were unwilling to go to war to prevent Athens from bullying Megara, if they were to allow the former to force the latter into submission, the Corinthians could not see the point of the Peloponnesian alliance to which they had so long belonged.

The embassy that the Corinthians sent to Lacedaemon on this occasion to press their grievances pulled no punches. They held the Spartans responsible for their suffering during the previous war, and they blamed them for the predicament in which they now found themselves. The picture they painted of the Athenians and the Lacedaemonians is a lively one:

The Athenians are innovators, keen in forming plans, and quick to accomplish in deed what they have contrived in thought. You Spartans are intent on saving what you now possess; you are always indecisive, and you leave even what is needed undone. They are daring beyond their strength, they are risk-takers against all judgment, and in the midst of terrors they remain of good hope—while you accomplish less than is in your power, mistrust your judgment in matters most firm, and think not how to release yourselves from the terrors you face. In addition, they are unhesitant where you are inclined to delay, and they are always out and about in the larger world while you stay at home. For they think to acquire something by being away while you think that by proceeding abroad you will harm what lies ready to hand. In victory over the enemy, they sally farthest forth; in defeat, they give the least ground. For their city's sake, they use their bodies as if they were not their own; their intelligence they dedicate to political action on her behalf. And if they fail to accomplish what they have resolved to do, they suppose themselves deprived of that which is their own—while what they have accomplished and have now acquired they judge to be little in comparison with what they will do in the time to come. If they trip up in an endeavor, they are soon full of hope with regard to yet another goal. For they alone possess something at the moment at which they come to hope for it: So swiftly do they contrive to attempt what has been resolved. And on all these things they exert themselves in toil and danger through all the days of their lives, enjoying least of all what they already possess because they are ever intent on further acquisition. They look on a holiday as nothing but an opportunity to do what needs doing, and they regard peace and quiet free from political business as a greater misfortune than a laborious want of leisure. So that, if someone were to sum them up by saying that they are by nature capable neither of being at rest nor of allowing other human beings to be so, he would speak the truth (Thuc. 1.70).

This depiction, which is borne out by the facts, helps explain why, in their fury, the Corinthians threatened to leave the Peloponnesian League and take others with them.

Pericles' gambit had worked. The Spartans were trapped. Arbitration was not an option. They knew that, under the terms of the treaty, they would lose. In the circumstances, therefore, they were faced with only two choices—neither of them palatable. They could stand idly by while the Corinthians bolted from their alliance; sidled up to the Argives, the Athenians, or both; and sought to lure away their other allies. Or this exceptionally pious people could go to war, knowing full well that, in doing so, they were incurring the wrath of the gods in breaking their oaths.

As in the past, there were those at Sparta who welcomed the prospect of such a war, and on this occasion they had such strong support from the Corinthians that they had little trouble in winning over the Lacedaemonian assembly. There were others, however, who were appalled—among them Archidamus, Sparta's Eurypontid king. He recognized that Athens would not quickly fold; that the Long Walls, now complete, rendered invasion by land futile; and that Sparta, which lacked the wherewithal with which to fund a great fleet, had no obvious path to victory—and he predicted that the war might last a generation or more.[54]

Pericles, in contrast, had the Spartans precisely where he wanted them. If they chose not to go to war, their alliance would come apart and there would very likely be an opening of the sort that Themistocles had exploited in the 460s. If they opted for war, they would only demonstrate to all and sundry their fecklessness; and in time, when they wearied of war and proposed peace, the Corinthians would bolt, others would leave the Spartan alliance, and the same sort of opening would present itself to the Athenians. It is telling that in 431 on the eve of the first Spartan invasion of Attica—when, almost certainly at Archidamus's instigation, Sparta's ambassadors intimated that a repeal of the Megarian Decree would be sufficient for the avoidance of war—Pericles refused to even consider that measure's repeal.[55] In his eagerness to take advantage of the situation, the Athenian statesman left nothing to chance. Or so he supposed.

The Road to Mantineia

Statesmanship notwithstanding, international affairs rarely, if ever, escape the vagaries of fortune. The plague was to Athens what the earthquake had been to Sparta—a bolt from the blue that turned everything upside down. Had Athens not been struck early in the war by the plague and had Pericles lived, the intricate scheme that he had devised might well have worked. In the beginning, things went precisely as planned. The Peloponnesian invasion was without consequence. The Athenians withdrew to their fortifications. Certain parts of Attica were ravaged, and the Peloponnesians went home. Then, the Athenians invaded and ravaged the Megarid, and the marines accompanying their fleet wreaked havoc on the coastal communities of the Peloponnesus. In time, they placed a small fleet at Naupactus to harry the traders of the Corinthian Gulf; and, on one occasion, they very nearly stormed the Peloponnesian city Epidaurus.[56]

Step by step, had the plague not intervened, the Athenians would have recovered most, if not all, of what they had given up in 446, and there is no reason that they should not have seized Cythera off the coast of Lacedaemon and established a base on the coast of Messenia, as, in time, they did. As the semiannual attacks on the Megarid and the massive expedition that attempted to seize Epidaurus suggest, Pericles' strategy was not, as is often claimed, defensive. Its purpose was to sap the vitality of the Spartan alliance, to strike at Peloponnesian morale, and to lure Argos into the war.[57] If, in the speech he gave on the eve of the war, Pericles did not spell out his larger purpose, it was because he did not want to advertise to the Spartans and the Corinthians just how insidious his strategy was. War leaders very rarely favor their opponents (or even their compatriots) with a full publication of their plans.

The plague upset Pericles' scheme. There is reason to believe that it killed between one in four and one in three Athenians.[58] In its immediate demographic impact, it was at least as important as and probably more significant than the losses that Athens suffered during the Egyptian expedition. In its impact on morale, it may have been worse. The Athenian response to their predicament was as predictable as it was foolish. After enduring two Spartan invasions and the plague, they briefly sidelined Pericles and sued for peace. But, of course, they did this to no avail—for their display of weakness served only to encourage those in Sparta intent on depriving Athens of its dominion altogether, and no one in Athens could contemplate abandoning the city's mastery over the sea. Even worse for the Athenians, however, was the fact that, in the end, after they had fined and re-elected Pericles as general, the plague killed the mastermind himself, leaving Athens adrift, without a coherent strategy or even a strategist, and what is worse, with no one in charge, able to guide, rather than follow, the vagaries of public opinion.

None of this was of much use to the Spartans. Apart from invading Attica once a year, they did little, and nothing that they did was of consequence. With the help of their allies, they could besiege and conquer Plataea, field an ineffective fleet in the Corinthian Gulf, plan an abortive raid on Peiraeus, and even dispatch a flotilla on a hasty tour through Ionia.[59] But they were not prepared to raise the resources, build the ships, find experienced officers, and hire the rowers requisite for a concerted attempt to wrest the maritime hegemony from the Athenians.

So the war dragged on and on—until an enterprising Athenian general named Demosthenes developed an ingenious scheme to fortify a headland in the natural harbor at Pylos on the west coast of Messenia and post there a handful of triremes and a garrison of Messenians who might make incursions into the heartland of Messenia and threaten the Spartans where it mattered most. The effect of this on the Spartans was electric. Archidamus's son and successor Agis immediately withdrew the Peloponnesian army from Attica, and the Spartans and Peloponnesians gathered at Pylos. The details of the struggle that then ensued need not detain us.[60] It should suffice to say that it eventuated in the isolation and capture of a small host of Spartiates, in the surrender of sixty Peloponnesian triremes, and in an offer of peace on Sparta's part.

Had Pericles been alive, he might have negotiated an agreement at this time. Prestige is, he knew, a force-multiplier. Quite often, it enables one to work one's will without deploying one's forces at all. By the same token, a dramatic loss of prestige can trigger the collapse of one's position. For the Spartans to make peace on such an occasion would have shattered the confidence of their allies. They had gained immensely in prestige when they had sacrificed the 300 with Leonidas at Thermopylae. To have made peace over a like number of Spartiates trapped, then captured on the island of Sphacteria in Navarino bay, would have cost them dearly.[61]

Pericles might also have delayed. The simple fact that the Spartans had sought peace might have been considered a sufficient blow to their prestige.

There was also another consideration. Time was on Athens's side. In four years the peace treaty negotiated by the Spartans and the Argives would lapse. In the interim, if the Athenians pressed on, mounting raids into Messenia; if they seized Cythera and used it as a base from which to raid Laconia; if they managed to seize Troezen, Hermione, Halieis, Epidaurus, or territory nearby lying on the overland route from the Saronic Gulf to Argos, Sparta's strategic situation would further deteriorate.

In this instance, the Athenians did choose to delay. But they did not profit from their choice. The city was divided. There was no leader with the authority Pericles had possessed, and the Spartans were driven by desperation to allow Brasidas, their most enterprising commander, to mount an audacious attempt to wrest the Greek cities in Thrace from the Athenians. His successes in that strategically vital region of gold and silver mines were sufficient to alarm the Athenians and cause the two sides to negotiate a truce; and the stalemate that he produced eventuated in 421 in the ratification of a peace fully satisfactory to neither, which left the Corinthians enraged.[62]

Had the Athenians had a leader at this time of Pericles' stature and understanding, this peace would in all likelihood have been a prelude to Sparta's demise. For, in their anger, the Corinthians made good on their earlier threats and sought an alliance with Argos, and into this new alliance they lured the Eleans and the Mantineians as well. There was at Athens one man blessed with the strategic insight necessary for grasping the situation. His name was Alcibiades. He was Pericles' ward. He possessed courage and a great deal of charm, but he was also notoriously dissolute, and he was young. Nicias, an older and more respectable man with ample experience as a general, had more influence. He had sponsored the peace, and he believed in his handiwork. Indeed, he shared Cimon's conviction that things would go well if Athens and Sparta operated once again as yokefellows.

In pulling together the anti-Spartan coalition deep within the Peloponnesus, Alcibiades performed something like the role of Themistocles. He had the vision, and he had the charisma to make it work. He was also like Themistocles in one other particular. In his fatherland, his conduct did not inspire trust, and he could not carry his compatriots with him. When the crucial battle took place in the plain between Mantineia and Tegea, he was able to rally as volunteers willing to fight alongside the Argives, Mantineians, and Eleans only 1,000 Athenian hoplites and 300 cavalrymen.[63] Had there been 5,000 Athenians present, the Lacedaemonians would almost certainly have lost the battle; and, given the precariousness of the Spartiates' hold on their subordinates, a helot uprising, the liberation of Messenia, and the elimination of Sparta as a great power would in all likelihood soon thereafter have taken place. In the fifth century, the Athenians had two splendid opportunities in which they might have brought Lacedaemon down; and, despite their predilection for audacity and aggression, they absented themselves on these two crucial occasions.

Sparta's Eventual Victory

Had Alcibiades prevailed in the debates that took place at Athens in 418, the Athenians might well have eliminated Sparta as a great power. The fact that he did prevail in 415 opened up a serious possibility that Athens might be eliminated from the fray. Pericles, with an eye on the Egyptian debacle, had repeatedly warned the Athenians that adventurism might be their downfall. But, at the same time, he had encouraged them to think big. Once Lacedaemon was out of the way, he implied, almost anything was possible. Alcibiades capitalized on the latter of Pericles' two exhortations when he proposed an expedition to Sicily, and he managed to make his compatriots forget the catastrophe that had taken place four decades before. Moreover, in warning against this enterprise, Nicias magnified the dangers in a fashion that stirred up ambitions and backfired, and the Athenians ended up sending a much larger expedition to Sicily than Alcibiades had intended. Although the defeat of Syracusa, the largest Greek city on the island, was not out of the question, the risks were nonetheless considerable, and the Athenians ended up losing not only the fleet originally sent out but also the rescue force dispatched as a reinforcement.[64] Athens' losses in 413 rivaled those associated with the Egyptian expedition more than forty years before.

This time, however, the Spartans were less accommodating. The Peace of Nicias had very nearly been their undoing. This they knew. To the battle of Mantineia and to the presence of large numbers of Athenian volunteers in the enemy phalanx, they responded with a fury reminiscent of their reaction to the battle of Tegea and the presence of large numbers of Athenian volunteers alongside the Argives and Tegeans. Athens they now looked on as a clear and present danger to Lacedaemon. Achaemenid Persia—which had, tellingly, demonstrated no propensity to reassert itself at sea in nearly forty years—seemed no longer a threat; and, as Thermopylae, Salamis, Plataea, and Mycale became distant memories, Spartan hostility to the Great King waned.

In consequence, the Spartans lent aid to the Syracusans in their battle against Athens, and they seized on an Athenian breach of the terms of the Peace of Nicias, renewed the war with the Athenians, marched into Attica, and established a permanent fort within sight of the city of Athens. By this last act, they denied the Athenians access to their silver mines and farms throughout the year. Then, when Athens' principal allies within the Delian League seized on its defeat in Sicily as an opportunity to rebel and sought Spartan assistance, and when Tissaphernes and Pharnabazus, the Persian satraps in western Asia Minor, offered financial support, the Lacedaemonians leapt into the fray.[65] In all of this, Alcibiades played a role. Shortly after the departure of the Sicilian expedition, he had been recalled to Athens to be tried on a charge of impiety. Instead of returning to face charges, he fled to Lacedaemon. There he had encouraged the dispatch of a lone Spartiate to serve as an advisor to the Syracusans; and later he had reinforced the counsels of those at Lacedaemon who favored renewing the war with Athens, establishing a permanent fort on its territory, and striking at its center of gravity in the Aegean.[66] For the first time in its history, Sparta fielded a sizable fleet. For the first time, it committed itself to an imperial venture outside the Peloponnesus.

The Athenians were undaunted. Against formidable odds, they fought on and on and on, exploiting their long experience in maritime affairs and justifying by their courage, audacity, and determination the portrait of them limned by the Corinthians on the eve of the Peloponnesian War. The Sicilian debacle had sapped Athenian morale, and the city succumbed to severe civil strife in 411. But the Athenians weathered the crisis, their democracy was restored, and in the Aegean they regained much lost ground. Had it not been for resoluteness on the part of the Mede, they would in time have recouped their losses.

Alcibiades, who had run into trouble with the Lacedaemonians, soon found favor with Tissaphernes, and, as the satrap quickly came to recognize, the advice that the renegade Athenian gave—that it was in Persia's interest that neither Greek power emerge triumphant and that the servants of the Great King should play the two off against one another—was sound. Had it been followed, however, the odds are good that the Spartans would have lost heart long before the Athenians did. For the Athenians were almost as one in their commitment to empire, and there were those at Lacedaemon who detested their alliance with the Mede, who feared what Sparta might become should it win, and who looked back on the dual hegemony with a measure of nostalgia.

In the end, however, domestic Persian politics determined the fate of Hellas. Darius II, a bastard son of Artaxerxes, had fought his way to the Persian throne in 423 after his father's death. By 408, it was clear that this usurper's days were numbered; and his wife Parysates, who hated her elder son's wife, favored for the succession her second son Cyrus. The following year, at her instigation, this young man—hardly more than a boy—was dispatched to Anatolia and put in charge of the Greek war. His purpose was to acquire a mercenary army of Greek hoplites. If he could get such a force to work in close coordination with Persian cavalry, he believed that, when his father died, he could oust his older brother from the throne and take it for himself.

In pursuit of this end, Cyrus sought to form a lasting friendship with a leading Spartan, to promote the man's fortunes at Lacedaemon, and to settle the war in Sparta's favor—which is what he did. The man in question was a Spartiate named Lysander, and Cyrus supported him through thick and thin until he won the war. In the circumstances, the Athenian cause was very nearly hopeless. They could win and win and win again, and each time that they won Cyrus had a new fleet built for the Spartans. His resources were boundless; those of the Athenians were finite. Their only hope was that, before it was too late, Darius II would die and that his older brother would shunt Cyrus aside or that the Lacedaemonians would turn with a vengeance on Cyrus's Spartan favorite. In the end, however, they had no such luck. In 405, Lysander caught the Athenians off guard and annihilated their fleet at Aegospotami. In 404, after a lengthy siege, Athens surrendered.[67]

Aftermath

The Spartans were urged by their allies to destroy Athens. Instead, they installed a narrow oligarchy and made of it a satellite; for a time, that was its status—but not for long. The Athenians cannily exploited the divisions at Sparta, took advantage of the conflict that grew up between Lacedaemon and Achaemenid Persia and of the dissatisfaction of Sparta's allies—and, step by step, they regained their autonomy, then their freedom of action. Alongside Argos, Corinth, and Thebes, Athens labored to rein in the Spartans, and eventually managed to found a second Athenian confederacy. But the strategic rivalry with Lacedaemon was never revived. The most that Athens and its new allies could do was to engineer a collapse of the Lacedaemonian empire—and this largely accrued to the benefit of the Great King.[68] For a brief time thereafter, the Athenians once again formed an alliance with Lacedaemon—this time against Thebes, which nonetheless managed to defeat the Spartans, invade Laconia, liberate the Messenians, found in southwestern Arcadia a city called Megalopolis, and organize the Arcadians into a confederacy capable of joining with the Messenians in containing Lacedaemon.[69] In the end, neither of the old rivals was able to dominate Greece, and the Thebans fell short as well. Philip of Macedon and his son Alexander would succeed where the various Hellenic powers had all failed.

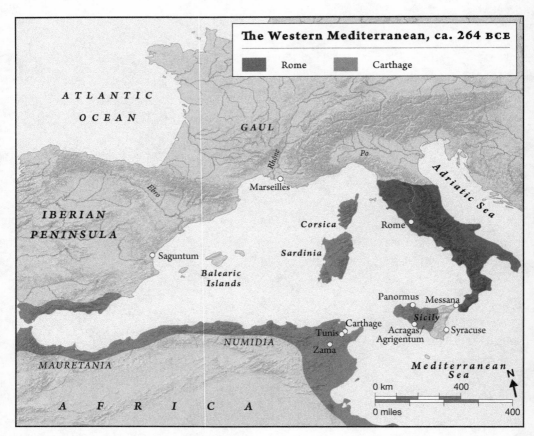

ATLANTIC
OCEAN

GAUL

Rhône

Po

Adriatic Sea

Marseilles

Ebro

Corsica

Rome

IBERIAN
PENINSULA

Sardinia

Saguntum

*Balearic
Islands*

Panormus   Messana

Sicily

Carthage   Acragas/   Syracuse
         Agrigentum

NUMIDIA   Tunis

Zama

MAURETANIA

*Mediterranean
Sea*

N

A   F   R   I   C   A

0 km   400

0 miles   400

The Western Mediterranean, ca. 264 BCE.

CHAPTER 2

The War for Empire
Rome versus Carthage
Barry S. Strauss

T HIS IS THE STORY of two countries that had long enjoyed peaceable
and sometimes friendly relations, then turned on each other and fought
the most destructive series of wars of the ancient world (the Punic Wars,
264–146 BCE).[1] The end saw such a complete victory that the losing state
was wiped out as a political unit. In fact, the Roman destruction of Carthage
was the closest to genocide that antiquity got. Before that, however, Carthage
inflicted the most humiliating battlefield defeat the Roman republic ever
endured (Cannae, 216 BCE), and it gave the ancient world one of its most
glamorous and tactically brilliant commanders—Hannibal. How and why
did this roller-coaster ride of a conflict end as it did? Why did it happen in
the first place?

Rome and Carthage fought three wars: 264–241 BCE, 218–201 BCE, and
149–146 BCE. The three conflicts are generally known by their Latin name,
the Punic Wars; if Carthage had won, we might call them the Roman Wars.
The name originated from the origins of Carthage, a colony of the Phoenician
city Tyre (in present-day Lebanon). Carthaginians spoke Phoenician and the
Romans sometimes referred to them as Phoenicians. The adjective *Phoenician*
is *Punicus* in Latin, hence the term *Punic*.

Not only is the name of the conflict Romano-centric, so are the sources
of information. Almost no Carthaginian sources have survived, which leaves
us at the mercy of Greco-Roman sources. Fortunately, they include two
great historians, Livy (59 BCE–17 CE) and Polybius (ca. 200–ca. 118 BCE).
Polybius, a Greek living in Rome, wrote the best surviving account of the

Punic Wars. Still, discussions of Carthaginian motivation involve an element of guesswork.

Background

In the beginning, geography and military culture kept the two states apart. Although they were both great powers, as a result of Carthage being primarily a sea power, and Rome primarily a land power, their interests rarely overlapped. Founded circa 750 BCE by Phoenicians from Tyre, Carthage acquired a maritime empire by expanding into the islands and coastal harbors of the central and western Mediterranean, from Sicily to Atlantic Spain. Rome, also founded in the eighth century BCE, expanded on the Italian peninsula. Between about 509 and 265 BCE, Rome became the ruler of all Italy south of a line running from the Arno to the Rubicon rivers, that is, from the Tyrrhenian Sea at Pisae (present-day Pisa) eastward to Ariminium (present-day Rimini) on the Adriatic. In the 220s Rome conquered the Po Valley and the Alpine foothills and began their incorporation into the Republic's polity. At the start of the Punic Wars, Roman Italy was a piecemeal collection of Roman territory and colonies, close allies who spoke Latin like the Romans, and other, more diverse cities and territories speaking such languages as Etruscan, Oscan, and Greek.

By the mid-third century BCE, Rome and Carthage were both great powers and were beginning to bump into each other. A series of treaties between 509 and 279 BCE kept each state to its own sphere, but conflict loomed. When Rome conquered southern Italy (265 BCE) only a narrow strait separated it from Sicily, then a wealthy and grain-rich prize. Carthage, meanwhile, had failed to conquer eastern Sicily, despite centuries of trying, though their forces remained in western Sicily. When, in 264 BCE, Carthage gained a foothold in the eastern Sicilian city of Messana (Messina), Rome decided to intervene.

The competition between Rome and Carthage was primarily a matter of security, although economic motives and personal ambitions played a part. Certainly, there was wealth aplenty in Sicily, for in antiquity it was not an impoverished backwater but, rather, one of the breadbaskets of the Mediterranean. Rome was unwilling to risk having a dynamic and powerful state like Carthage controlling the Straits of Messina, between Sicily and the Italian mainland, where it could block the commerce of the Greek cities of southern Italy, which were Rome's allies. Besides, ambitious Roman generals and large parts of the Roman people were tempted by the prospect of loot and glory in Sicily. For its part, Carthage could not tolerate Rome's presence in Sicily. If it seems surprising that two longtime treaty-partners like Rome and Carthage turned on each other, it should not. Before this point, Roman and Carthaginian interests had not clashed; now they did, and as Lord Palmerston observed, "nations have no eternal allies or perpetual enemies, only perpetual interests."[2] Besides, now that the two great cities of the Western Mediterranean were, for the first time, in regular close contact, both could see its own most dangerous characteristics in the other.

Indeed, this was not a conflict of polar opposites; rather, the two states were, in many ways, mirror images. Rome and Carthage shared an ethos of aggressive armed expansion. Each state was a mixed regime, an oligarchy that now dominated, now struggled with its masses. Each was controlled by a group of wealthy planters who, in spite of an agrarian ethos, owed a large part of their fortune to commerce. The Carthaginian elite was more mercantile and maritime in its outlook than its Roman counterpart, but it was also more agrarian than is often thought. Carthaginian ships traveled as far as West Africa and Ireland while, at home in North Africa, Carthage pioneered the organization of large-scale, single-crop plantations worked by slaves. While some Carthaginian elites itched for overseas expansion, others were content with the great wealth they possessed at home. Moreover, Carthage was a more sophisticated and cosmopolitan place than Rome was at the time, and Rome's near-total destruction of Carthage's cultural heritage remains one of civilization's great losses.

Rome was different. Although Italy is a sea-girded peninsula, Rome tended to look inward, maintaining the conservative mentality of a continental power. As a result, Rome possessed only a small navy, incapable of contesting Carthaginian trading dominance in the Mediterranean. Still, much of Rome's landowning elite profited from overseas trade, and there was a growing realization within Rome that its future greatness rested upon successful expansion outside Italy.

Each state had access to a substantial treasury and a large population of potential soldiers. One big difference was that Rome used citizen-soldiers while Carthage did not. If that made Rome more conservative about sending armies abroad, it also made Carthage less invested in the outcome of its foreign expeditions. After an expedition was launched, Carthage typically gave its commanders a free hand but not much support from home. In the First Punic War in particular, Carthage made liberal use of mercenaries, whose loyalty could not be taken for granted. Switching approaches in the Second Punic War, Carthage relied more on allies. But these forces were more diverse and polyglot than Rome's allies, comprising as they did North Africans, Iberians, and Northern Italian Celts, as well as a smaller number of Celts from north of the Alps. A Carthaginian commander, therefore, had to be as much a diplomat as a soldier if he hoped to hold his multiethnic force together.

Another big difference was in the treatment of allies. Both countries depended on allies, which, for the most part, both managed well. Still, this became a competitive advantage for Rome, as many of its allies were geographically closer to the center of power, and were linked by an extensive road network. Moreover, though both Carthage and Rome punished revolts brutally, Rome did a better job of wielding the carrot as well as the stick. By granting such privileges as the right to do business in Rome and to intermarry with Romans, Rome tied much of the population of Italy to itself. But the greatest privilege of all, and the most forward-looking Roman policy, was liberal grants of Roman citizenship, a boon it offered to a large part of the conquered elite. By 225 BCE, the Roman citizenry comprised one million free people, including 300,000 adult males subject to military service. Rome also had access to about 450,000 allied troops, for a total of 750,000 soldiers. This was a huge number by ancient standards. While similar statistics for Carthage do not survive, it is clear that its reliable manpower pool was much smaller.

Rome's core allies, the most loyal and dependable, were in central Italy. They represented a huge, reliable pool of soldiers. Moreover, Rome's exceptionally good alliance management kept almost all of these cities loyal, even at the nadir of Roman fortunes and prestige. Hannibal understood this and made an extraordinary effort to win new allies, but he could only do so by granting them so many concessions that the alliances proved hollow. Only Rome seemed to have the "secret sauce" that made the core of its allies love it, fear it, and serve it.

Commitment by the home government was more of a factor for Rome than Carthage. One reason was geography, as most of the Punic Wars were fought far from Carthaginian territory. The First Punic War was waged mostly in Sicily, with an episode in North Africa, and the Second Punic War mostly in Spain, Italy, and Sicily, until the final phase in North Africa. At its closest, Sicily is 105 miles from Carthaginian territory, while it is just less than 2 miles from Italy.

Another reason was domestic politics. Although Rome watched its generals warily, Carthage was even more distrustful. The Carthaginian government punished defeated generals with crucifixion. It is difficult to speak with certainty about Carthaginian domestic politics since we depend almost entirely on foreign and largely hostile Greco-Roman sources. If those sources are right, we can detect a conflict of interest between, on the one hand, a landowning nobility whose focus was on domestic agriculture and trade and, on the other, a military elite that looked to war and empire abroad and often turned to the people rather than the Council of Elders for political support. Although a similar dichotomy can be found in Rome, it was possibly more pronounced in Carthage. It might explain both why the Carthaginian government came down so hard on its generals and why it was so stingy with reinforcements and supplies.

What the Carthaginians lacked in quantity they made up for in quality. They were gifted with brilliant generalship, innovative plans, and a remarkable ability to do more with less. The Romans had no field commanders who could match the tactical élan of Hamilcar Barca or his son Hannibal. But élan works best in short, sharp bursts. The Carthaginian way of war succeeded in a quick campaign; it was not suited for a war of attrition against a politically cohesive republic equipped with enormous manpower resources, a firm alliance system, and sage leadership. In the Second Punic War in particular, the contrast between Hannibal's small but lethal professional and polyglot army encamped in enemy territory with little support from Carthage and Rome's massive allied forces working near their home base and with all the time and patience in the world could not have been greater. It took all of Hannibal's energy and brilliance just to survive a war of attrition, while Rome became progressively stronger. The time frame also gave the adaptable Romans the chance to study Hannibal's tactics and to master them. Eventually, a Roman version of Hannibal emerged in Publius Cornelius Scipio (236–183 BCE). After nearly being killed in early confrontations with Hannibal, the Roman Scipio studied his bold and brilliant tactics, and when he had mastered them he trained the Romans to turn them back on the enemy. In the final result he was rewarded with the cognomen or nickname of Africanus, "the African," a reference to the site of his final victory over Carthage in North Africa, but in some ways his success in Spain was even more crucial.

We might compare Carthage to Germany or Japan in World War II. Each had tactically brilliant militaries and each won stunning, splendid, and quick victories. Yet each state then ran up against resource-rich, politically cohesive, and well-led republics—the United States and the Soviet Union—that had little trouble absorbing early defeats and rebounding with devastating force, in some cases copying or even bettering the enemy's tactical innovations. Like the two greatest Axis powers, Carthage faced the frustration of how to turn its tactical genius into success in a war against a republic of massive strength.

For all their similarities, neither Romans nor Carthaginians understood the other fully. Since they tended to be organization men themselves, the Romans could not imagine the emergence of a genius like Hannibal. The Romans had already forced the great Greek general Pyrrhus, king of Epirus (319–272 BCE), to give up his invasion of Italy (280–275 BCE) by making the cost too high, and it did not occur to them that Hannibal could do worse—if he could even reach Italy. (Incidentally, Rome had help against Pyrrhus from its then-ally Carthage.) The issue was not only Hannibal's superiority to Pyrrhus as a general, but the power of the state behind each man. Carthage, like Rome, was a republic, not a monarchy, and an economic giant, and, even if it proved to be relatively stingy in its support of Hannibal, it could, when the need was dire, marshal resources and willpower to a degree that far outstripped the capacity of a small kingdom like Epirus.

As for Carthage, like many a clever and dynamic society, it tended to underestimate the opposition. It was easy for them to caricature the Romans as dull and unimaginative when, in fact, they were pragmatic and ruthless. Beneath a veneer of conservatism, Rome embraced change. Again and again it proved willing to ditch cherished modes of behavior in order to survive. Carthage, at times, evinced a similar propensity, but it lacked the staying power or the resources of the Romans.

It would be easy to write victor's history and tote up Rome's advantages and the reasons that it had to win in the end. It would also be wrong. Rome barely squeezed out victory in the First Punic War. It might have lost the Second Punic War had Carthage adjusted its strategy after its initial battlefield successes or if no Roman military genius had arisen to pay back Carthage in its own coin. For centuries after the Punic Wars, even when Carthaginian power was only a distant memory, the Romans frightened their children with the phrase *Hannibal ad portas!—Hannibal is coming to the gates!* Given the immense and nearly fatal damage that Hannibal did to Rome, the fear is understandable.

The First Punic War (264–241 BCE)

When Rome and Carthage began fighting over Sicily, it soon became clear that Rome dominated on land and Carthage on sea. It was a classic case of an elephant versus a whale, but with a twist—the elephant learned to swim and the whale learned to walk on land.

Over the space of a generation, Rome turned itself into a competitive sea power. It took the help of its Greek allies in southern Italy and an enormous sacrifice in blood and treasure by the Roman people. Meanwhile, Carthage became a brilliant land power that excelled on seaborne attacks on southern Italy led by a military star, Hamilcar Barca. His arrival in Sicily in 247 BCE rejuvenated the Carthaginian war effort.

In the early years of the war, the Romans drove the Carthaginians out of eastern Sicily, but they were not able to dislodge them from the western part of the island. There were indecisive battles on land (near Messina and Agrigentum) and on sea (at Mylae, Ecnomus, and Drepana). Looking for new solutions, in 256 BCE Rome invaded North Africa under the general Marcus Atilius Regulus. After initial Roman victories, the Carthaginians regrouped, defeated the Roman army, and captured Regulus.

The Romans quickly realized that, Sicily being an island, they could not prevail unless they could defeat Carthage at sea. At great expense, Rome built a series of large fleets. Still, Carthaginian rowers and helms-men were well trained and capable of dazzling maneuvers that the ill-trained Roman seamen could not hope to match. As the Romans could not compete with Carthage in a standard set-piece naval battle, they developed the *corvus*, literally "raven," a grapnel or, more precisely, a hooked metal gangplank that allowed them to send marines onto the enemy's ships. The result was to turn sea battles into land battles, a realm where Roman soldiers held the advantage. Unfortunately, the heavy corvus put Roman ships at greater risk of sinking in storms. Eventually, Roman sailors mastered maneuver warfare and so the navy was able to dispense with the corvus.

Hamilcar did not fight any set battles but relied, rather, on unconventional land tactics and seaborne raids. By such methods, he kept the Romans on the defensive in western Sicily and inflicted major casualties. Meanwhile, he raided both eastern Sicily and the coast of Italy as far north as Cumae, only about 150 miles from Rome. Worse, from Rome's perspective, he proved stubbornly impervious to all attempts to defeat and dislodge him.

Hamilcar's successes only underscored the need for Rome to expand its war aims: in addition to driving Carthage out of Sicily, they wanted to prevent it from being able to project its power into Italy. Hence the need to destroy Carthage's fleet—physically by crushing it in battle, financially by imposing a crippling indemnity, and geographically by forcing Carthage to leave Sicily and all the other islands of the central Mediterranean. But how was Rome to achieve these goals against Hamilcar Barca?

The answer lies in a debate between the two theorists Admiral Alfred Thayer Mahan (1840–1914) and Sir Julian Corbett (1854–1922) about the efficacy of sea power. Mahan argued that command of the sea, won via decisive battle, won wars. Corbett disagreed; he argued that sea power was limited in what it could accomplish, that control of the sea lanes mattered more than battle, and that wars were decided on land. In general, ancient history tends to favor Corbett. Sea power was of great importance, but it rarely won wars. The First Punic War was an exception.

Polybius argues convincingly that the war was won at sea. His Romans learned a hard lesson: they thought they could win the war by their army alone, but that turned out to be untrue because they could not beat Hamilcar Barca. Polybius wrote:

> For the last five years [247–242 BCE] indeed they had entirely abandoned the sea, partly because of the disasters they had sustained there, and partly because they felt confident of deciding the war by means of their land forces; but they now determined for the third time to make trial of their fortune in naval warfare. They saw that their operations were not succeeding according to their calculations, mainly owing to the obstinate gallantry of the Carthaginian general [Hamilcar Barca]. They therefore adopted this resolution from a conviction that by this means alone, if their design were but well directed, would they be able to bring the war to a successful conclusion.[3]

And so, although its treasury was exhausted by the long war, the Romans built one more fleet. Notably, it was financed by a small group of wealthy private citizens. The Carthaginian state was out of money as well, but no private financiers stepped forward there. Rome's new fleet surprised the Carthaginians. The Roman elite assigned a higher priority to winning the competition than did their opposite number in Carthage, and that made all the difference.

The commander of Rome's new fleet, Gaius Lutatius Catulus, understood that only by victory at sea could the whole war be decided (Polybius, *Histories* 1.59.11). The Romans won a great naval victory at the Aegates Islands off western Sicily in 241 BCE. Though the Carthaginians retained the will to fight, they had to admit that "they could not any longer send supplies to their forces in Sicily because the enemy commanded the sea."[4] Even Hamilcar Barca admitted it, although he was undefeated. And so, Carthage made peace. Rome, in an attempt to limit Carthage's future power, imposed a harsh peace treaty, the Treaty of Lutatius. In addition to paying a huge indemnity, Carthage had to evacuate Sicily, where it had held colonies for centuries. Rome then annexed Sicily, which became the first Roman province.

Carthage also had to surrender the islands that lay between Sicily and Italy, that is, the Aeolian and Lipari Islands—which were essential for ancient navigation between North Africa and Italy. As ancient warships were light and vulnerable, they needed to hug the coast when they traveled and to make frequent stops; otherwise they had to travel with heavy supply ships that would slow them down, and risk the dangers of the open sea. Without being able to land in these islands, it would be difficult for Carthage to invade Italy. As punitive as this was, Rome soon made things worse.

Unable to pay its mercenaries, Carthage now faced a revolt that found it fighting for its life in North Africa, the so-called Truceless War (241–37 BCE). Rome took advantage of Carthage's discomfit by annexing the islands of Corsica and Sardinia, treacherously claiming that they lay "between Sicily and Italy" and so were covered by the peace treaty. They certainly were possible way stations on the naval route to Italy from Carthage—now denied the enemy by Rome. Rome also upped the indemnity. By adding insult to injury, Rome stoked Carthaginian bitterness. Sardinia's loss was especially painful, as it was a major Phoenician colony with a strong Carthaginian presence. In some sense it was a foolish move, but it represented the Roman propensity for taking audacious moves when it felt its security threatened. Even if such actions made a future war with Carthage more likely, Rome preferred investing in its long-term safety by cutting the naval route from North Africa to Sicily and Italy.

Carthage also lost its naval edge—permanently, as it turned out. Rome now became the leading naval power of the Mediterranean. Although Carthage eventually built a new fleet, it could not compete with the Roman navy, either in numbers or seamanship.

The Second Punic War (218–201 BCE)

The First Punic War, like World War I, sowed the seeds for renewed conflict about a generation later. Twenty-one years separated the two world wars of the twentieth century, and twenty-three lay between the First and Second Punic Wars. Rome had reaped huge advantages from its victory in the First Punic War, but the vigorous Carthaginians fought back. Under Hamilcar Barca's leadership, they built a new empire in southern Spain, an area rich in silver and mercenaries. What Hamilcar Barca founded in Spain was continued by his son, Hannibal.

The Punic Wars were born of fear, greed, and self-interest, but honor quickly kicked in. Neither Hamilcar Barca nor Hannibal would stand for submitting to men who had never defeated them in a land battle. Nor could they forgive the treachery and insult of Rome's seizure of Corsica and Sardinia and at the very time when Carthage was fighting for its life against a mercenary revolt. The story goes that when Hannibal was still a boy, his father made him swear an oath of eternal hatred for Rome. Whether the tale is true or not, Hannibal showed that he had no trust for Rome or belief in the possibility of peaceful coexistence.

Hannibal is rightly remembered as one of history's greatest leaders. As Polybius wrote, Hannibal "was by his very nature truly a marvelous man, with a personality suited by its original constitution to carry out anything that lies within human affairs."[5] He was bright, shrewd, hardy, resilient, and honorable, but, said critics, also dishonest and greedy. He was also audacious, ambitious, and commanding in stature. His reputation alone was a force multiplier, and time and again he proved deserving of the excitement that he set off. As a young man, he studied war with a Greek tutor and with his father. He grew up to be a master commander, with sufficient boldness to invade a great empire with a small but professional army. Moreover, he was adept at propaganda and diplomacy, and he had the unquestioned loyalty of his men, who never once mutinied despite spending fifteen years in difficult conditions in enemy territory.

The stage for war was set in the 220s BCE when Rome tried to contain Carthaginian expansion in Spain. The first step was to make a treaty with Carthage in the mid-220s establishing the River Ebro in northeastern Spain as the boundary of Carthaginian territory. Nervous nonetheless about the enemy's dynamism, Rome also engaged in a series of alliances, most notably with the city of Saguntum—a Greek trading city that lay *south* of the Ebro. Rather than make a formal alliance, Rome accepted Saguntum as a friend, which, in effect, made Rome the city's patron. As Saguntum had incited several Spanish tribes to resist Carthage, Rome's new relationship with the city was viewed by the Carthaginians as an indirect attack on themselves. It is likely that Rome saw things the same way. Hannibal, though, refused to be threatened, and laid siege to Saguntum. Nor would he back off when Rome threatened Carthage with war. Rather, with the support of Carthage's home government, he not only accepted war—he brought it to Italy.

Frightened by Carthage's rebound, Rome tried to use surrogates to contain Carthage's Spanish empire, but it failed to reckon with Hannibal's brilliance. When war came, Hannibal chose not to sit on the defensive, but lacking a navy, he was forced to take a perilous path of an overland assault, through hostile territory and over the Alps (in late autumn, as it turned out).

It was one of history's most audacious and shocking strategic moves. The Romans paid a heavy price for underestimating Hannibal, a strategic blunder that rivaled Hannibal's brilliant march. At the start of the Second Punic War, Rome never dreamt that Hannibal could bring the war to Italy, so his decent from the Alps with an army at his back, in November 218, was a profound shock among the Roman people. Worse was to come because the Romans had, as of yet, no inkling of Hannibal's tactical genius or his ability to exploit Roman mistakes in the field.

Fortunately for the Romans, Hannibal's 900-mile-long trek from his capital of New Carthage to Italy was carried out with a mix of panache and error. Hannibal knew the road would be hard, but he had underestimated the difficulties and should surely have set out earlier in the year, so as to cross the Alps before the snow. As a result of his late march, Hannibal lost most of his army on his miserable overland march. He left Spain with 50,000 infantry and 9,000 cavalry; he reached Italy with only 20,000 infantry and 6,000 cavalry. Some of the losses came in combat; some died of exposure, but most probably deserted. Apparently, all of Hannibal's thirty-seven elephants survived.

Despite his depleted force, Hannibal's appearance in Northern Italy shocked Rome. The Senate was planning an invasion of North Africa but immediately canceled it and ordered the assembled legions north to defend their homeland. This first, and several subsequent attempts, to stop Hannibal did not go well. In fact, Hannibal set off an even greater series of tremors within the Roman system by smashing several Roman armies over the next few years, culminating in the horrific carnage at Cannae.

Soon after crossing the Alps, Hannibal supplemented his meager manpower with allies from the Celtic peoples of the Po Valley. He had previously sent ambassadors to them while still in Spain to gain their support. But now they were balking, having expected something more impressive than Hannibal's small, bedraggled, and exhausted force. But after a well-timed massacre of the Taurini people (in the vicinity of modern Turin), Hannibal cowed the opposition and, a bit more surprisingly, won their support.

Hannibal was a superb tactician, a brilliant and inspiring leader of men. Moreover, he was cunning, unpredictable, and hard-nosed. His specialty was combined infantry-cavalry attack, which he used to tremendous effect on the battlefield. The Romans, by comparison, were unimaginative and unsurprising. They had little taste for cavalry, which they relied largely on their allies to supply. The Romans, first and foremost, were infantrymen, and they usually deployed their men in a simple, straightforward attack. They won because of their toughness, their manpower, and their wise use of reserves. In the long term, Rome's manpower would wear Hannibal down, but, in the short term, it was not enough to outdo Hannibal on the battlefield.

Hannibal went on to defeat the Romans three times in 218 and 217: at a cavalry skirmish near the Ticinus River, a set battle in the valley of the Trebia River in which he killed or captured about two-thirds of the Roman army (i.e., about 28,000 men) while suffering few losses; and a massacre of another Roman army at Lake Trasimene in central Italy in which the Carthaginians killed 15,000 Roman soldiers and captured another 10,000–15,000, while incurring only meager losses.

At the initiative of their emergency leader or dictator (then only a six-month, temporary position) Fabius Maximus, the Romans now switched to a defensive strategy—hence the origin of the term "Fabian strategy." Their goal was now to harass the enemy and to deny him food and resources without risking another set battle. They scored a measure of success, but Hannibal still outfoxed and humiliated them on several occasions. Never comfortable on the defensive, the Romans went back on the attack in 216 BCE. The result was the greatest defeat in the history of the republic; not until the Later Roman Empire and the battle of Adrianople (378 CE) would Rome suffer a comparable battlefield loss.

The Battle of Cannae took place on August 2, 216 BCE, in Apulia in southern Italy. Hannibal had about 50,000 men, the Romans 86,000, enough of a disparity for the Romans to believe they could win with a simple steamroller tactic. Hannibal, by contrast, orchestrated a sophisticated pincer movement. His cavalry defeated the enemy on his flanks, as his infantry executed a planned retreat. Once the Romans had marched into the trap, the Carthaginian cavalry returned and cut off the enemy's rear while Hannibal's infantry surrounded the Romans on three sides and butchered them. By the time the battle was over, the Romans had suffered 48,000 deaths and 20,000 men had been captured. Hannibal had about 6,000–8,000 men killed, most of them from his Celtic allies—his least reliable troops. The Romans lost about 75 percent of their army while the Carthaginians lost only about 10–15 percent of theirs. It was one of the most stunning battlefield victories in history.

Hannibal's victories since entering Italy left the Romans fearful "for themselves and for their native soil."[6] Hannibal's cavalry commander, one Maharbal, urged him now to seize the moment. He called for an immediate attack on Rome, quipping that in five days they could be dining on the Capitol—the citadel that represented the heart of Rome. Maharbal said that he and his horsemen would take the lead, with the army following. Hannibal turned him down. Maharbal is supposed to have responded in frustration: "You know how to be the victor, Hannibal," he said, "but not how to use your victory."[7]

Hannibal might have defended himself by saying that his army was exhausted, even in victory. Because Rome was 235 miles from Cannae and so a matter of weeks and not five days away, it was bound to be an exhausting march. By the time he arrived there, moreover, the Romans would have organized their defenses. As Rome was safe behind thick and well-maintained walls, which were almost seven miles long and outfitted with an up-to-date defensive system of towers and trenches, it would require an exceptional effort to take the city by siege. It would also certainly require an infusion of manpower from Carthage, which was unlikely to arrive. Besides, Hannibal was notoriously bad at sieges, and had not brought a siege train into Italy.

And yet many Romans maintained that Hannibal's failure to march on Rome was a major blunder. Years later, Hannibal conceded the point. Maharbal might have told his chief that there was no need to take Rome by force. The mere sight of the Carthaginians on the heels of Cannae—and the cavalry could in fact have reached Rome quickly—would strike terror into Roman hearts. It might have convinced one or more of the central Italian allies to defect. It might have convinced the Carthaginian government to send reinforcements. It might even have caused traitors to open the gates of Rome.

Neither Rome nor Carthage could have competed with the other without allied support. Carthage depended in particular on the superb cavalry of Numidia (roughly, modern Algeria), which played a major role in the victory at Cannae. Hannibal obtained infantry and cavalry from his allies and subjects in Spain as well as from the Celts of northern Italy. By causing most of Rome's allies of southern Italy and some in Sicily to defect, he denied the enemy men and bases, but Carthage reaped few manpower rewards, since these new allies demanded the right not to provide troops. Carthage achieved even less with its alliance in 215 BCE with King Philip V of Macedon. In theory, Macedon could have provided men, money, and ships to the Carthaginians, but fear of Rome held them back, especially after the Romans responded by allying with Philip's enemies in Greece.

The Carthaginians' biggest blunder, however, was their underestimation of Roman resolve. They thought that Rome was a normal state of the era, that is, one that would sue for peace after having suffered major losses on the battlefield. They did not understand that the Romans were playing a different game; the Romans considered their conflict with Carthage no *Kabinettskrieg* but a struggle for survival. Nor did they understand the cohesiveness of both the Roman polity and the Roman alliance system in central Italy. Perhaps Carthage was thinking in terms of its own allies, who were far less dependable. Hence, they were surprised when Romans demonstrated the will and the wherewithal to forgo surrender and to fight until victory, no matter the setback. After Cannae they refused to even discuss Hannibal's offer of peace terms. They even sent a Roman prisoner, used as a go-between, back to Hannibal, bound and tied, as a sign of their determination. To the Carthaginian government, the wars were more on the order of *Kabinettskrieg*. They were never willing to go to the mat to win in the way the Romans were.

Although it is difficult to speak with confidence about the Carthaginian political system, it appears that there was a disjunction between leading generals and the Council of Elders that did not exist in Rome. Rome experienced tension between the Senate and great field commanders such as Fabius Maximus and Scipio Africanus, but it was not comparable to the hostility between the Elders and Hannibal. From the point of view of the Carthaginian oligarchy, Hannibal—like Pompey or Caesar two centuries later in Rome—was a dominant figure who threatened to overshadow the political system.

Carthage was now Rome's superior in land battle. Unfortunately, Hannibal's victories were hollow. Rome reacted to its terrible losses with equanimity. It was a tribute to the leadership provided by the Senate and the fortitude of the people.

Rome's position after Cannae might be compared to Britain's position after Dunkirk and the Battle of Britain. Rome and Britain each endured bitter and bloody defeats and suffered humiliation at the hands of a triumphant enemy. Yet each country knew that its position remained strong. The Royal Navy protected the British Isles and represented a successful deterrence to any German invasion. To no one's surprise, the Germans never came close to launching Operation Sea Lion, the naval invasion of England. The Royal Air Force successfully limited the damage that the Luftwaffe could do to British cities and airfields, even if it could not stop the enemy entirely. Britain could still undertake limited offensive operations overseas, sometimes with success, as in the destruction of the French fleet or the attack on the Italian fleet in Taranto, both in 1940. Meanwhile, the United States stood in the wings, officially neutral but acting as Britain's ally, supplying arms, confronting

German submarines, and readying its military manpower and industry for eventual entry into the war.

Rome likewise knew that in spite of the damage wrought by Hannibal, its main strengths remained untouched. The Romans counted on Hannibal's dislike of sieges. Siegecraft was to Hannibal in the Second Punic War what conventional naval operations were to the Germans in World War II.

No less important, Rome's central Italian alliance proved strong enough to survive battlefield losses, for which it provided plenty of replacements. Although Hannibal spent fifteen long years in Italy, he never made a serious crack in the core of Rome's alliance in central Italy.

Mahan has argued that Roman command of the sea and control of interior lines won the Second Punic War:

> To overthrow Rome it was necessary to attack her in Italy at the heart of her power, and shatter the strongly linked confederacy of which she was the head. This was the objective. To reach it, the Carthaginians needed a solid base of operations and a secure line of communications. The former was established in Spain by the genius of the great Barca family; the latter was never achieved. There were two lines possible, the one direct by sea, the other circuitous through Gaul. The first was blocked by the Roman sea power, the second imperiled and finally intercepted through occupation of northern Spain by the Roman army. This occupation was made possible through control of the sea, which the Carthaginians never endangered. With respect to Hannibal and his base, therefore, Rome occupied two central positions, Rome itself and northern Spain, joined by an easy interior line of communications, the sea; by which mutual support was continually given.[8]

Chester Starr argued that Mahan's argument was, in fact, completely wrong. That goes too far, but certainly Mahan's argument was an exaggeration. Rome's control of the sea made Hannibal's position more difficult, but it did not prevent him from winning. Three other things did: a lack of support from the Carthaginian government, an unwise strategy, and Roman fortitude and strategic wisdom.

After Cannae, Hannibal asked for major reinforcements in men, money, and grain from the Carthaginian state. What he received was meager. Instead, Carthage sent its resources to new fronts in Sicily and Sardinia. In the end, these efforts frittered away the state's strengths without reaping any rewards, since Rome held on to both islands. It was a coup for Carthage to win the support of the great Sicilian city-state of Syracuse in 215 BCE, but Rome retook Syracuse in 212 BCE after a long siege and killed its most famous defender, the great mathematician and scientist Archimedes. If Carthage had sent Hannibal more money and manpower and if Hannibal had concentrated on prying away Rome's key allies by picking off states in central Italy, one by one, he might have been able to crack the heart of the Roman confederacy. By proving to Rome's oldest and most faithful friends that Rome could no longer protect it, Hannibal might have demonstrated that there was a new hegemon in the land. He might have laid the foundation for a *pax Carthagenensis*.

In fact, one could argue that what cost Carthage the war was not too little attention to sea power but too much. It was arguably Carthage's mistaken attempt of focusing on getting back its naval bases in Sardinia and Sicily that cost it the war. Meanwhile, although Carthage did build enough warships to compete with Rome at sea, it lacked admirals bold enough to risk a battle.

Then there was Rome's ability to keep its eyes on the prize. Slowly but methodically, Rome reconquered the Italian and Sicilian states that had joined Hannibal and inflicted brutal punishment in the form of plunder, enslavement, and confiscation of land. The great southern Italian city of Capua left the Roman alliance for Hannibal after Cannae, but Rome retook it in 211 BCE. The Romans then killed, imprisoned, or enslaved the inhabitants and annexed most of Capua's territory.

In spite of Hannibal's presence in Italy for a long fifteen years, and the defection of most of southern and northern Italy, Rome still was able to muster sufficient force to send expeditionary forces strong enough to eventually conquer Carthaginian Spain. The leader of this effort was Scipio Africanus. Audacious, charismatic, and adaptive, Scipio learned Hannibal's tactics and brought them to Rome. At the age of only twenty-six he captured New Carthage (Cartagena), the Carthaginian capital of Spain. He then won two great set battles against Carthaginian armies (Baecula, 209 BCE; Ilipa, 206 BCE) and drove Carthage from Spain. Unfortunately for Rome, Hannibal's brother Hasdrubal escaped and brought a major army of reinforcements to Italy—finally. Increased by Gallic recruits, Hasdrubal's army had about 30,000 men when the Romans caught it in 207 BCE, and forced a battle at the Metaurus River (in the hills of northeastern Italy). The Romans crushed Hasdrubal before he could reach his brother, thereby ending any possibility of Carthaginian victory in Italy.

Scipio's next move was diplomatic, and it was a coup—he won over the Numidian prince Massinissa to the side of Rome. Carthage fought back, and it was a difficult struggle but, in the end, Numidia defected to Rome. Numidia had played a crucial role in supplying Carthage with cavalry, so this move was a game-changer. Hannibal had never pried the enemy's key allies in central Italy away from Rome but, by winning over Numidia, Scipio deprived Carthage of its key ally. It underlines the difference in the two sides' alliances and their importance in deciding the war.

Scipio invaded North Africa in 204 BCE, thereby compelling Hannibal to leave Italy the next year and sail to the defense of his homeland. Scipio fought a set battle against Hannibal (Zama 202 BCE), where he outdid the master and destroyed Hannibal's army. It was Massinissa's Numidian cavalry that tipped the balance and brought Scipio his victory. Carthage now surrendered and agreed to be a small state reined in to its North African homeland, weighted down once again by a huge indemnity.

Rome, meanwhile, had become a military giant. Before Hannibal's invasion it typically put six to eight legions (roughly 30,000 men) in the field; during the Second Punic War it fielded up to twenty-eight legions (roughly 120,000 men) plus allied forces. It had added two million acres of public land to its control, confiscated from rebellious allies. It had acquired a new empire in Spain, a new ally in Numidia, and it was poised to take revenge on Macedon. By guiding the state to victory, the Roman Senate gained a new ability to direct Roman policy, with the aid of impressive new leaders like Scipio Africanus. With Carthage reduced to second-rate status, no civilized power challenged Rome's domination of the central and western Mediterranean, although primitive tribes in Spain and Gaul still posed a challenge. Rome was now ready to turn eastward, where in only a dozen years it would defeat the two greatest powers of the Hellenistic Greek world—Macedon and Syria.

The Third Punic War, 149–146 BCE

The final conflict between Rome and Carthage was less a duel than a massacre. Carthage had done nothing more offensive than recover as a wealthy and vibrant city-state. Rome considered this intolerable because it feared an enemy revival, so it decided to eliminate Carthage as a political entity. It gave the Carthaginians an ultimatum: either abandon their city and disperse or fight to the death. The Carthaginians chose the latter, and the Romans sacked and destroyed the former queen of North Africa. The wars between Rome and Carthage came to their tragic end.

Five years after the end of the Second Punic War, Hannibal was elected to the position of *suffete* or chief magistrate of Carthage. During his year-long term (196 BCE), he reformed the Carthaginian government and did away with the problem of massive corruption. As a result, Carthage was quickly able to repay the tribute that Rome had imposed, and without raising taxes. In short order, Carthage was prosperous again and an economic powerhouse.

A nervous Rome forced Hannibal into exile a year later, in 195 BCE. The old warrior made his way to the kingdom of Antiochus III in Anatolia, another enemy of Rome. There Hannibal served as an advisor in Antiochus's failed war with Rome (192–188 BCE). Forced into exile again, he left for Bithynia (in northwestern Turkey). Trapped by the Romans there in 183 BCE, Hannibal took poison rather than surrender and face humiliation. He left behind an accusation that the Romans lacked the decency to let an old man die in peace.

Meanwhile, the men who ran Carthage made it a model ally of Rome. They denounced Hannibal and helped Rome in its various wars. Through it all, Carthage prospered. The city was a major port, and remained the commercial center of North Africa. The city grew rich again on its agricultural produce and manufactured goods. It was proof, if any were needed, that even without an overseas empire, Carthage was a virtual gold mine.

Unfortunately for Carthage, King Massinissa of Numidia stirred the pot. The Romans continued to use Numidia as a client state to pin Carthage down. By the treaty ending the Second Punic War, Massinissa was permitted to expand his territory, but Carthage could not wage even defensive war without Roman permission. The result was that Massinissa continuously expanded his territory at Carthaginian expense. Carthage appealed to Rome to arbitrate, and Roman boundary commissioners visited North Africa to investigate from time to time, but Rome did little to help Carthage. Over time, Massinissa reduced Carthaginian territory to a shadow of its former size.

Finally, in 154 BCE, a Roman boundary commission headed by Marcus Porcius Cato visited the city of Carthage. Cato was known for his patriotism, his ambition, his imperialism, and his eye for agricultural and commercial wealth. The riches, dynamism, and military might of the city could not help but impress. Cato declared himself horrified. When he got back to Rome, Cato immediately called for a declaration of war, ending all his speeches with the pronouncement, *Delenda est Carthago—Carthage must be Destroyed!*

On the one hand, Cato and his supporters might have imagined a new military threat emerging from Carthage. Such a worry was surely overblown, but it did not help the cause of peace when in 151 BCE Carthage dismissed its pro-Roman government and, the next year, went to war with Massinissa, whose attacks had pushed it over the edge. Not only did Carthage lose the war, it was now guilty of having violated its peace treaty with Rome.

On the other hand, Rome coveted Carthage's wealth. Carthage competed with Rome over commercial markets. Leading senators, including Cato himself, had invested in trade and shipping. For fifty years Carthage had bought off Rome annually by paying the enormous indemnity imposed at the end of the Second Punic War, but, in 152 BCE, Carthage finished making those payments.

If Sicily had been a rich prize ripe for the picking in 264 BCE, now a little over a century later, Carthage was perhaps even richer. And it could hardly take another twenty-three years to defeat it, as it had taken Rome to conquer Sicily in the First Punic War. Between fear and greed, the temptation for war was overwhelming. In 149 BCE, Rome declared war.

Carthage sent ambassadors to Rome to sue for peace. The Romans demanded that Carthage abandon and destroy the city and move inland at least ten miles from the coast. In righteous anger, Carthage prepared for a siege.

The siege lasted three years. Well-defended as it was, Carthage could not be taken easily. In the second year, Scipio Aemilianus (185–129 BCE), the adopted grandson of Scipio Africanus, emerged as the hero of the army, and was appointed commander. In April 146 BCE, Rome broke through the Carthaginian defenses. After eight days of savage street fighting, Carthage finally fell, for the first time in its long history. Rome subjected the survivors to enslavement or forced migration. Large parts of the city were burned and the territory was declared uninhabitable. The rest of the territory of Carthage (roughly equivalent to today's Tunisia) was declared the Roman province of Africa Proconsularis. The new provincial capital was the city of Utica (near modern Bizerte, Tunisia), a seaport north of Carthage and its frequent rival. Utica had rebelled against Carthage during the Truceless War. In 150 BCE, and on the eve of the Third Punic War, Utica had defected to Rome.

Carthaginian territory, with all its agricultural wealth, now belonged to Rome. Carthaginian traders no longer competed with Roman merchants. Carthaginian arms no longer disturbed the sleep of nervous Roman strategists.

Rome destroyed Carthage both as a city and an independent state. Not since the capture and destruction of their nearby rival, the Etruscan city of Veii, in 396 BCE, had the Romans inflicted such an annihilation on an enemy. It was one of the most thorough defeats in history.

Since the Romans were willing to let the Carthaginians survive if they would abandon their city, and since the Punic language and Punic culture did in fact outlive the destruction of Carthage—although in attenuated form—we might absolve the Romans of the charge of genocide. But they were certainly guilty of what might be called "civitaticide," the destruction of a state, if not of a people.

During the course of their long conflict, Rome and Carthage each adapted to changing conditions, but Rome did it better. Carthage made a series of brilliant but empty strategic choices. Rome's strategy was more conservative, less dazzling, more solid, and ultimately successful. As often in history, the tortoise beats the hare.

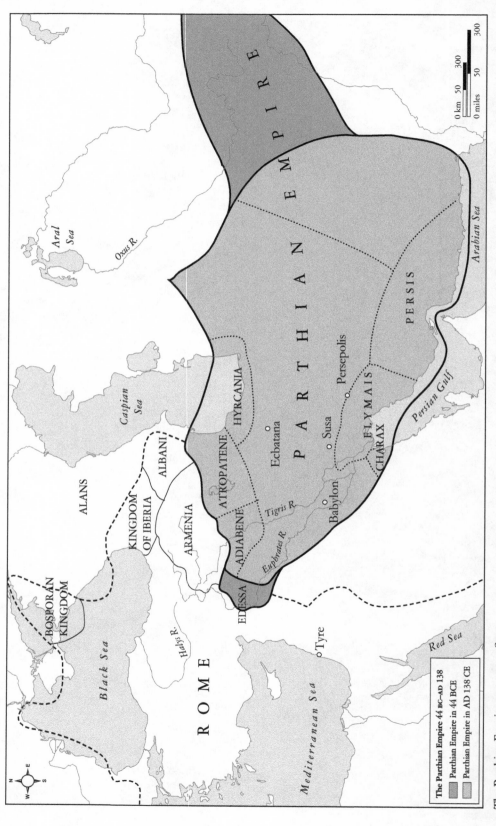

The Parthian Empire, 44 BC–138 CE.

CHAPTER 3

Rome's Greatest Foe

Rome versus Parthia and Sassanid Persia

Kenneth W. Harl

The Rivals: Rome, Parthia, and Persia

For seven hundred years, imperial Rome clashed first with Arsacid Parthia, and then Sassanid Persia, for hegemony in the Near East (today misnamed the Middle East). The two powers represented related, but fundamentally different civilizations. Rome, as republic and empire, was a Mediterranean power and was based on the civic traditions of the Classical world. Even under the autocracy of later Christian emperors, appeals persisted to the republican notions of the rule of law for and by citizens. Both Parthia and Sassanid Persia were Near Eastern monarchies, and so heir to the royal ideology and institutions stretching back to the first Mesopotamian Empire of Sargon of Akkad. Throughout the rivalry, imperial Rome enjoyed significant advantages in political organization, military power, and wealth over both Parthia and Persia.

Rome entered the Near East as an imperial republic dominated by an abundance of ambitious aristocrats who as elected magistrates commanded legions, or as members of the Senate determined strategy and operations. Throughout the rivalry, Rome fielded a superior army that could win battles and capture cities. Rome also had the political institutions to turn conquered lands into tax-paying provinces. The Roman Republic drew its strength from citizens willing to serve and sacrifice (as was characteristic of a city-state), but it enjoyed the military power of great bureaucratic monarchy. By the early first century BCE, the legions were citizens who volunteered for military service in expectation of plunder, rather than the draftees who had defeated Carthage. Legionaries saw their prime loyalty to their commander, hailed as *imperator*, who delivered victory and rewards. Hence, after 88 BCE, they turned their swords against fellow citizens as willingly as foreign foes so that the republic was rocked by successive civil wars. In 31–27 BCE Augustus ended civil war and instituted a monarchy, the Principate, which was a military dictatorship cloaked in republican symbols. Augustus transformed the army into a full-time professional one, tied to the ruling Julio-Claudian family, and composed of two arms, the legions and the auxiliary units (*auxilia*).[1] The legionaries—heavy infantry—were citizens who fought in close order formations. They opened the attack with volleys of heavy javelins (*pila*), and closed with the sword (*gladius*) for shock action. The legions employed a number of formations, depending on terrain and foe, so that they adopted a phalanx when countering Iranian cavalry. The auxiliaries, provincials who obtained Roman citizenship upon discharge, were also professionals under Roman officers who used Latin as the language of command. The auxiliaries provided light infantry, missile units of archers and slingers, and cavalry. The imperial army, even after the reforms of the early fourth century, remained primarily an infantry army, so that campaigns in the Near East required meticulous logistics. The Roman imperial army was unmatched in its chain of command, discipline, engineering, logistics, and, above all, its professionalism. Legionaries and auxiliaries served in units with distinctive banners and histories, each sanctified by its own religious rites. Officers and men forged intense bonds of comradeship, comparable to those of British regiments of the nineteenth century. Emperors promoted and rewarded, and so inspired loyalty to both the imperial family and Rome. Soldiers thus fought out of a mixture of motives—to their units, to the emperor, and to the majesty of the Roman people—down to the reign of Diocletian (284–305).

This professional army of the Principate defeated Arsacid Parthia, and drove back the armies of the first two Sassanid shahs, Ardashir I (r. 227–240) and Shapur I (r. 240–270). Yet, victory came with a high cost. The Roman monarchy was transformed into the bureaucratic autocracy of the Dominate. The first Christian emperor, Constantine I (r. 306–337), promoted a new religious ideology in the rivalry against Persia, whose shah championed a rival state monotheism. He also initiated the reorganization of the imperial army into privileged field armies, whose prime mission was the protection of the emperor, and frontier forces (*limitanei*) who steadily lost the professional advantages of the earlier imperial army.[2] Furthermore, Germans, Iranians, and Armenians from beyond the frontier were recruited, and many attained high rank—an advancement impossible in the Principate. More cavalry units were raised, especially lancers (*cataphracti*), to counter Iranian heavy cavalry, but the Roman army remained an infantry army. From the mid-fourth century, tribal regiments, commanded by native dynasts who doubled as Roman officers, were hired as federates (*foederati*). Imperial field armies declined in morale and discipline, and the defeats suffered in the late fourth century compelled the Eastern Roman emperors from Marcian (r. 450–457) on to recreate a professional field army, whereas the Western Roman Empire, which depended ever more on federates, collapsed and fragmented into Germanic kingdoms in 406–476.

The Arsacid kings of Parthia and the Sassanid shahs of Persia fielded cavalry armies comprising heavy cavalry (*cataphracti* or lancers) and horse archers (often recruited as allies or vassals from among the nomadic tribes of the Central Eurasian steppes). The Sassanid army included infantry, a siege train, and even war elephants. Sassanid armies could take walled cities—well documented by Ammianus Marcellinus's eyewitness account of the capture of Amida by Shah Shapur II in 359.[3] Yet, Parthian and Sassanid armies represented coalition forces, and they depended on foraging and ravaging for supplies so that campaigns, and strategic aims, were restricted because of rudimentary logistics. This was so even during the impressive conquests of Khusrau II (r. 590–628), who threatened to topple the Eastern Roman Empire.

War and diplomacy rested on each power's ability to exact revenues to sustain armies. Imperial Rome had by far greater revenues. The Roman historian Tacitus noted this disparity, commenting on how imperial revenues were collected in Parthia by means of compulsion, in Rome by imperial organization.[4]

At the start of the rivalry, Rome dominated the Mediterranean world, and steadily shifted from plunder and tribute to regular taxation by the opening of the first century C.E. Imperial Rome promoted cities, regional and international trade, and payment of taxes in coin.[5] By 100 CE, Roman emperors collected impressive revenues in coin to pay their professional army, reckoned at 375,000 men, that defended an empire of 60 million residents, perhaps one-fifth of the globe's population. Only contemporary Han China matched imperial Rome in numbers of cities, population, and wealth. Of the other two great imperial orders in Eurasia, the Kushan Empire ranked third, and Parthia a distant fourth. Between the first century BCE and the second century CE, Rome enjoyed an expanding economy and stable currency based on gold and silver coins. Frontier and civil wars after 235, and natural calamities, ended the prosperity of Roman peace and compelled emperors to debase the currency. But Roman emperors from Aurelian (r. 270–275) to Diocletian (r. 284–305) restored the frontiers and prosperity, and created a fiduciary currency that paid for imperial recovery in the fourth century.[6] In 395–476, Germanic tribes overran the western half of the Roman Empire, and so emperors henceforth resident at Constantinople (New Rome) ruled only the Eastern Roman (or Byzantine) Empire. They operated with, at most, two-thirds of previous imperial revenues. The emperor Justinian (r. 527–565) took as his priority the reconquest of the Western provinces, but his desultory wars and expensive diplomacy with Persia drained imperial revenues. Above all, the empire's population was ravaged by a great plague in 542, the first in a cycle of pandemics that led to a demographic collapse in the later sixth and seventh centuries.[7] Therefore, emperors after Justinian were at a significant disadvantage in revenues and manpower when the rivalry with Persia escalated to major wars in 572–590 and 602–628.

In contrast, the Arsacid kings of Parthia lacked the cities and trade that generated the currency to support a royal bureaucracy and standing army. Instead, vassal rulers and nomadic tribes on the Central Eurasian steppes rendered tribute and answered summons to serve with retainers of cavalry in war. The fiscal arrangements between Arsacid kings and the wealthy cities of Babylonia (today lower Iraq) and southwestern Iran are undocumented. These cities, along with taxes collected on the stretch of the Silk Road from Margiane (Merv) to Ecbatana (Hamadan), provided the bulk of the hard cash of the Arsacid treasury. For 250 years, the middle period of the rivalry (113–363), these wealthy cities of Babylonia were exposed to Roman attack, so that later Arsacid kings and early Sassanid shahs were at a strategic disadvantage, because they could not afford to lose these cities.

The Persian shahs have been credited with ruling a far more centralized state, but this view has been seriously called into question. The number of cities in the Sassanid Empire did not significantly increase between the third and seventh centuries. To be sure, fiscal institutions are not well documented (in contrast to the plethora of Roman records), but the shahs most likely succeeded to an imperial confederacy similar to that of the Parthians. The Sassanid shahs of the third and fourth century, however, exploited the decline of Kushan power to gain access to the wealth of the fabled caravan cities of Transoxiana and the Indus Valley. Rome thus faced a rival in Sassanid Persia that was twice the strength of Arsacid Parthia. In the early fifth century, Sassanid shahs, just like their Roman contemporaries, suffered major losses of territory and revenues when Hephthalites ("White Huns") overran these eastern lands. Persia, too, was ravaged by the cycle of pandemics after 542. Hence, both rivals, Rome and Persia, were considerably weaker when they escalated the rivalry after 572. Given the revenues and manpower available, both powers should have sought diplomatic solutions rather than waged wars to overthrow the other power. In short, both powers were fighting beyond their means in the last sixty years of the rivalry.[8]

Ideology defined and limited the rivalry against Rome. The Arsacid kings postured as heirs of the Achaemenid Great Kings of Persia (who had ruled the Near East before Alexander the Great) and the Macedonian Seleucid kings who had succeeded to the Asian domains of Alexander the Great. In the mid-third century BCE, Arsacid princes ruled over Iranian-speaking nomads, Parni, who had settled in the Tajend Valley in Khurasan. Arsaces I (246–211 BCE), founder of the royal house, seized Parthia from the Seleucid Empire, and used the region's name to design his diverse followers as Parthians. Mithridates I (171–138 BCE) decisively defeated the Seleucid king Demetrius II in 140 BCE and expanded his power from the Euphrates to the lower Oxus River. Mithridates II (123–88 BCE) received submissions from kings of Armenia, Sophene, Mesopotamia, Gordyene, and Adiabene—the strategic regions Rome would contest. He also imposed his suzerainty over the kings of Characene, Elymais, and Persis, thereby gaining control over the trade in the Persian Gulf to India. In the wake of such successes, the Arsacid kings assumed new official images. Mithridates I assumed the ancient title King of Kings, but he also styled himself as a benefactor to the Greek cities of Babylonia. Mithridates II exchanged the traditional nomadic dress for the high crown, tiara, jewels, and full beard of a Near Eastern monarch.[9] He founded on the eastern bank of the Tigris River a new capital, Ctesiphon, which was opposite the Greek city Seleucia ad Tigrim. The Arsacid kings, while posturing as Near Eastern kings, remained children of the Eurasian steppes, ruling over a loose federation of vassal kings and hereditary governors. They depended upon allied nomadic tribes of the steppes to furnish horse archers. They also followed the lateral succession principle of the steppes, so that Arsacid kings entrusted lesser kingdoms in Iran to their male kinsmen or sought for them new kingdoms. Hence, Arsacid kings frequently warred with rebellious relatives or vassals, to the strategic benefit of Rome. The strategic rivalry with Rome over Armenia and Mesopotamia stemmed, in large part, from the need of Arsacid kings to provide a kingdom in Armenia for brothers, sons, or cousins who otherwise might challenge royal authority.

The Sassanid shahs also ruled a confederation of vassal kings and cities, rather than a bureaucratic empire.[10] The Sassanid shahs, however, enjoyed significant advantages over their Parthian predecessors. They ruled a greater empire, subjecting the caravan cities of Transoxiana (Classical Bactria and

Sogdiana) and the Kushan princes of northern India. They also wrested from Rome control of eastern Mesopotamia and most of Armenia in the later fourth century; in the fifth and sixth centuries they extended their sway over the eastern and southern shores of the Arabian Peninsula.[11] Foremost, the shahs pursued their strategic rivalry with the most articulate ideology of all three powers. The first two shahs, Ardashir I (r. 227–240) and Shapur I (r. 240–270), sponsored Kartir, the religious thinker who likely reformed the Iranian cults into the orthodox monotheism of Zoroastrianism, which was universal in message, but culturally Iranian.[12] The shah presided over the great fire altars, and royal art represented the shah as receiving his legitimacy directly from Ahura-Mazda. From the start, shahs presented their wars against Rome as reflecting the cosmic clash between light and darkness. In his monumental inscription and on his victory reliefs at Naqsh-e Rustem, Shapur I stressed the submission of Roman emperors and the booty and glory won in three prestige campaigns rather than wars of conquest. Hence, shahs led their diverse armies under the potent symbols of a state monotheism that anticipated the appeals to jihad made by Abbasid Caliphs in their prestige campaigns against Constantinople in the eighth and ninth centuries.[13] Roman armies gained this advantage far later. In the brief war of 421–422, the imperial army fought against Persia under the cross for the first time.[14] Over the course of the fifth and sixth centuries, the veneration of military saints and icons proliferated, giving Christian Roman soldiers new protectors and appeals. Yet, neither Christian New Rome nor Zoroastrian Persia used its religious ideology as a policy to elevate their historic rivalry for control of strategic regions into a policy of conquest until 602. In 602, Shah Khusrau II, due to a remarkable turn of events, aimed to destroy the Eastern Roman Empire, and so end the rivalry in a decisive Sassanid victory.

Rome and her Iranian foes, Parthia and Persia, despite their differences in institutions and wealth, based their strategic aims in the Near East on the same conditions of geography and terrain. Furthermore, the rival empires shared the same broad security concerns, even though they were propelled by different ideologies and possessed very different military capabilities. Throughout this long-standing strategic rivalry, two regions were crucial to each imperial power's position in the Near East: Armenia (present-day eastern Turkey), and Mesopotamia (present-day al-Jazirah, or the borderlands divided among Turkey, Syria, and Iraq and largely inhabited by Kurds).[15] These two regions were the nexus of strategic routes between the two imperial powers.

Armenia is a high plateau of grasslands, bounded to the north by the Caucasus and to the south by the Anti-Taurus Mountains. The average elevation of the Armenian plateau is 3,000 feet above sea level, and the mountain chains rise to over 5,000 feet. Logistics proved daunting to any army accustomed to campaigning in the Mediterranean world. Roman soldiers must have found the terrain harsh and unfamiliar, and the horizon seemingly endless. Even in antiquity, timber was scarce, and today the manure of animals is the prime fuel. The growing season for grains was short, but the grasslands sustained flocks and herds. In the Mediterranean world, armies could march at the beginning of May when the winter grain was "milk ripe," and well-provisioned forces could commence a march in April, such as that of Cyrus the Younger and the Ten Thousand in 401 BCE.[16] On the Armenian plateau, few armies conducted major operations prior to July. Snows blocked passes in May and even in early June; roads quickly turned into seas of mud that are virtually impassible for infantry and carriages. Fodder posed another restriction. The Armenian plateau is best crossed in July and August, when horses and mules can graze on the vast plains of grasses. In September, conditions would have begun to deteriorate, and armies had to prepare winter quarters. Winter conditions were brutally cold. Tactius writes a chilling description of what the legionaries of Cn. Domitius Corbulo endured in their camp near Elegia during the winter of 57–58.[17] Elegia was in the vicinity of Erzurum (Classical Theodosiopolis), which is the coldest city in Turkey today.

Once Rome crossed the Aegean Sea, and acquired provinces in Western Asia Minor, it was inevitably drawn east beyond the Euphrates into Armenia to control two strategic routes. These west-east routes linked Asia Minor with Iran, with extensions that led north across the Caucasus. The first route was the Roman highway in northern Asia Minor, guarded by the legionary fortress at Satala (Sadak). It ran west to east from the Lycus Valley (Kelkit Çayı) across the plateau to the Armenian capital of Artaxata (Artashat), which lay just to the east of the Araxes (Aras) River.[18] From Artaxata, routes led via Media Atropatene (centered around Lake Urmiah) to the cities of northern Iran. This route became a section of the Silk Road.

The second, southern, highway running due east from the legionary base of Melitene (Malatya) crossed the Euphrates to Tomisa, in the Armenian kingdom of Sophene. Near present-day Elazığ (medieval Kharput),[19] the road branched into a southeastern route (leading to Mesopotamia) and a northeastern route into Armenia. This northeastern route followed the Arsanias River (Murat Nehri) to the western shore of Lake Van (Classical Thopitis), just north of the Bitlis Pass. From thence, a northeastern route followed the course of the Arsanias across high valleys and plateaus via Manzikert (the site of the decisive defeat of the Byzantine army in 1071) to meet the west-east highway near modern Ağrı. Another route went east, along the western and northern shores of Lake Van, to the cities of the eastern and southeastern shores of Lake Van—the heartland of Urartu—and then east to Iran via Hoşap, a strategic fortress during the Ottoman-Safavid Wars.

The Armenian plateau was also strategic to the rival imperial powers because of the north-south routes leading across the Caucasus mountains to the Pontic-Caspian steppes of southern Russia. The Dariel Pass, often called the Caucasian Gates by Classical authors, was a priority for Rome, because it offered to nomadic invaders easy entrance into northeastern Asia Minor.[20] The historian and imperial legate L. Flavius Arrianus Xenophon penned a tactical manual for countering Iranian-speaking nomadic invaders, the Alans, who, upon crossing the Dariel Pass, invaded Roman Asia Minor in 135.[21] The eastern Derbent Pass, often associated with the legendary "Gates of Alexander the Great," was far more important to the Iranian imperial power. Sassanid Shahs in the fifth and sixth centuries constructed fortifications south of this pass to prevent nomadic invaders from settling in the grasslands of Albania (modern Azerbaijan).

The second strategic region was called by the Romans Mesopotamia, defined by the Anti-Taurus on its northern frontier, the great bend of the Euphrates River along its western and southern boundaries, and the upper Tigris in the east. The strategic pass between Mesopotamia and Armenia is at Bitlis. Rome had to guard two strategic west-east routes across the Upper Euphrates into Mesopotamia. The first route was the highway that ran from Melitene (Malatya) across the Euphrates to Tomisa, in Sophene, and then branched southeast from Elazığ via the Ergani pass to the cities of the upper Tigris Valley, notably Amida (Diyabakır) and Tigranocerta. Roman legions stationed in eastern Asia Minor at Melitene (Malatya) and Samosata defended the crossings over the Euphrates at the western termini of this route. Between the two bases lay the rugged terrain of Commagene that restricted communications and movement.[22] Hence, down to 72, Rome entrusted Commagene to client kings. The second, southern route crossed the Euphrates at Zeugma (Birecek), and led to Edessa (Urfa) and from thence directly to the middle Tigris River, the western frontier of the Parthian Empire. Roman legions based in Syria marched over this route to reach Mesopotamia.

These grasslands of Mesopotamia are well watered in the spring by the Euphrates and Tigris, and their tributaries, and the winter rains and snow (an ecology that has been turned desiccate by the Ataturk Dam). The mountain ranges protect these lands from the most severe of the Eurasian winter winds and weather. The land is fertile, and near Edessa (Urfa) is where men first domesticated wheat and barley. In high summer the land is arid so that control of water sources is strategic. In contrast to Armenia, Mesopotamia supported caravan cities. Hence, Tigranes II, "the Great," King of Armenia (r. 95–56 BCE), who aspired to rule as successor to the Seleucid kings, built Tigranocerta (medieval Arzan) as his new Hellenic capital on the Nicephorus River (Yanarsu Çayı), a tributary of the Tigris, so that he could dominate this region.[23]

Simply put, Rome and her Iranian rivals preferred to control Armenia through a client king, but each imperial power could annex and administer Mesopotamia. Initially Rome preferred to entrust power to Arab dynasts who ruled the Aramaic-speaking caravan cities and doubled as tribal leaders commanding ethnic regiments. But in 198–200, Septimius Severus (r. 193–211) organized the province of Mesopotamia based on the fortresses of Edessa (Urfa), Carrhae (Harran), Rhesanea (Ra's al'-Ayn), Singara (Singar), and Nisibis (Nusaybin). Amida (present-day Diyabakır) on the upper Tigris was added in the early fourth century. In 299, Caesar Galerius compelled Shah Narses (r. 293–302) to cede five strategic provinces with their fortresses, including Tigranocerta, on the northeastern banks of the upper Tigris.[24] Rome directly ruled Mesopotamia from 198 to 363, when the emperor Jovian (r. 363–364) relinquished to Shah Shapur II (r. 309–379) the eastern half, including Nisibis, Singara, and the lesser fortresses north of the Upper Tigris.[25]

For Rome and her Iranian rivals, the two regions protected vital regions of their empires. For Rome, Armenia and Mesopotamia were the nexus of routes from the north and east, and so offered entrance into Asia Minor by nomadic horse archers from north of the Caucasus (such as the Alans who invaded in 135) or Parthian and Persian armies marching across Armenia. The cities of western Asia Minor were among the wealthiest of the Mediterranean world. In addition, the crossing over the Euphrates at Zeugma led to the cities of northern Syria, and so to the coastal road between Antioch and Alexandria. The prize was Egypt. Hence, when Shah Khusrau II (r. 590–628) shifted his operations from eastern Asia Minor to northern Syria in 613, he methodically reduced the Roman fortresses and seized the highways so that his armies overran the Levant and Egypt in 614–618. South of the great bend of the Euphrates, Rome only needed to secure the desert frontier by aggressive patrols against Arab raiders. Rome and her Iranian rivals never fought a strategic war over this frontier. The Byzantine *Chronicon Pascale* reports that Trajan Decius (r. 249–251) proposed increasing the lion population along this desert frontier as the most cost-effective check against Arab raiders.[26] Hence, the Roman army in the Levant and Egypt has been dubbed an army of occupation, especially after the Second Jewish War (132–135).[27] Two legions were stationed in Syria Palestina (formerly Judaea, Samaria, and Galilee), and another legion was based at Bostra in Arabia Petraea. Detachments of this legion and auxiliaries secured the caravan route over 1,500 miles south deep into Arabia. Two legions stationed at Nicopolis, near Alexandria, kept order in that unruly city and maintained the ports and trade routes along the shores of the Red Sea. Alexandria and Egypt were vital to the imperial budget, and the province always required a strong garrison lest usurpers in Alexandria carve out an independent Roman-style regime, as did L. Domitius Domitianus (294–297).[28]

For the Arsacid and Sassanid kings, Armenia and Mesopotamia were just as strategic. Armenia was vital to the defense of the approaches from the northwest via the Derbent Pass and Caspian Gates. The nomadic tribes north of the Caucasus were drawn to the grasslands and winter pastures of the delta of the Cyrus River (present-day Kura) flowing into the Caspian Sea. These lands of Classical Albania (Azerbaijan) were ideal for steppe nomads down to the time of Tamerlane (1370–1405). To the south, the main river of eastern Armenia, the Araxes (present-day Aras) flows to join the Cyrus, and its tributaries offered routes into Media Atropatene, the northern frontier lands of Iran. Mesopotamia, as defined by the Romans, was valuable to possess and tax, but it was also strategic to the defense of the cities of Babylonia, notably Ctesiphon and Seleucia ad Tigrim, the twin capitals of the Parthian Empire. The legionaries of Marcus Aurelius sacked Seleucia ad Tigrim in 165. This sack, along with changes of the river course, led to the abandonment of the city. In May 363, the emperor Julian found only melancholy ruins. The Sassanid shah Ardashir I built a successor city Veh Ardashir, the Coche in the account of Ammianus Marcellinus. Neither Arsacid nor Sassanid monarchs could afford to lose these capitals. By the treaty of 363, Shapur II secured the fortresses of eastern Mesopotamia that acted as a strategic shield against further Roman attack against Ctesiphon.

In Armenia, the Parthian kings enjoyed a significant advantage over Rome. Armenian lords, dubbed *naxarars* in the Middle Ages, were unruly, proud warriors driven by blood feud and a keen sense of honor. In martial ethos and customs they shared far more with their counterparts in Iran rather than the aristocrats of the Mediterranean world.[29] But the Sassanid shahs lost this advantage when Ardashir overthrew the Arsacid family ruling over Iran. A cadet branch of the Arsacids continued to rule in Armenia. These later Arsacid kings looked to Rome to resist their family foes, the Sassanids. In the early fourth century, Tiridates III embraced Christianity so that henceforth Armenians were linked by a common faith to Christian Rome.[30]

Given the limited sources, it is far more difficult to ascertain two important questions, namely, how the rival powers communicated with and learned about each other, and how each power assessed how it was faring in the rivalry. Surviving literary sources, public inscriptions, and official art are overwhelming from the Roman side. Little other than their coins remains to reveal how Arsacid kings devised and assessed policy vis-à-vis Rome. The Sassanid shahs from Ardashir I (227–240) to Shapur II (309–379) speak directly about the conflict in their reliefs at Bishapur and Naqsh-e Rustem and the trilingual inscription of Shapur I (240–270). Furthermore, the deeds of shahs were put to writing (preserved in the epic *Shahnameh*), from which later Arabic writers, foremost al-Tabri, drew to compose universal or Iranian national histories in the early Abbasid period.

In the first century BCE, when Romans and Parthians met, each laid claim to the Hellenistic world, and so they employed Greek as the language of communication in well-established diplomatic protocols.[31] Throughout the rivalry, envoys were routinely exchanged; violations of treaties had to be justified. From the fourth century on, diplomatic exchanges between Christian emperors and Sassanid shahs increased in frequency and in similarity of protocols as a result of long contact.[32] The Senate and magistrates of the republic, and the emperors and senatorial legates of the Principate, had a wealth of information about their Parthian rivals. From the second century BCE to the second century C.E, itineraries, navigational handbooks (*peripli*), and geographic treatises have survived, giving distances, routes, resources, and terrain. The map of the world known to the geographer Ptolemy shows the extent of Roman knowledge of relative positions of the strategic lands contested with Parthia by the mid-second century C.E.[33] Greeks and Romans, besides a tradition of mapmaking, wrote and read histories that invariably dealt with war and politics. Classical historians included extensive discussions of geography and ethnography. The Roman ruling classes, by possessing a strong sense of history, reasoned by cause and effect and displayed a curiosity for new information that proved an advantage in their dealings with Iranian foes.[34] Therefore, those determining policy at Rome had the analytical skills and sufficient information to pursue long-term strategic aims in the Near East. Arsacid kings and Sassanid shahs had access at least to some of the same information. The emperor Augustus ordered translated the work of Isidore of Charax, an itinerary of caravan routes across the Parthian Empire. Plutarch notes how the court of Orodes II enjoyed Greek literature.[35] Parthian and Sassanid ruling classes, however, lacked a tradition of writing history, and so they perceived the rivalry very much through the eyes of their monarchs, in contrast to their Roman counterparts.[36]

The rival powers also gained new or current information about each other from exiles, merchants, and pilgrims who crossed the frontiers.

Christian Roman emperors had a significant advantage in reports from Aramaic- and Greek-speaking monks and missionaries.[37] To be sure, this information had to be translated, and judged. This point raises the question of whether Rome, Parthia, or Persia pursued the rivalry with the diplomats and generals of a modern nation-state who framed long-term planning and assessed the course of a strategic rivalry. In brief, the answer is no, but then none of the powers needed such professional experts.[38] Roman generals and officers were aristocrats trained from birth to command armies, administer law, and speak to the gods. They learned politics and war by emulation. Generals in the field routinely wrote dispatches to Rome; many penned *commentarii*, or memoirs of their campaigns. Only those of Julius Caesar have survived, but *commentarii* circulated among the ruling classes because the works not only stressed generalship, but also contained a wealth of information on foes and frontiers.[39] Tacitus indicates that Cn. Domitius Corbulo, the imperial commander in the war of 54–66, likely read *commentarii* on the campaigns of L. Licinius Lucullus and Cn. Pompeius Magnus in Armenia and Mesopotamia. Julian, when assigned the command of Gaul in 357, read the *commentarii* of Julius Caesar for background and instruction in command. Iranian monarchs and nobles, reared to excel in warfare, riding, and hunting, shared the same martial outlook as their Roman opponents, as well as an education by emulation, even if they did not pen campaign memoirs.

Given the limits of communications in the ancient world, converting this information into effective policy was daunting. Commanders of the Roman Republic were given wide powers to pursue operations in the field, and to conclude wars. The final settlement rested with the Roman Senate, which sent a legation of experienced, senior members to conclude a war. Lucullus, the proconsul commanding the war against King Mithridates VI Eupator, twice in 72 and 69 BCE, had to determine strategy because it was impossible to consult with the Senate at Rome. A fast ship from ports in Asia Minor to Rome during optimal sailing conditions between May and September took three to five weeks.[40] Dispatches from Rome to these same ports would take just as long, but then mounted couriers had to deliver directives over routes in hostile territory to a commander on the move. Communication by sea during the winter was suspended. Lucullus, Pompey, Mark Antony, and Corbulo, campaigning east of the Euphrates, simply outran the lines of communication of a Mediterranean power.[41] Hence, with Trajan, the emperor marched east in every major offensive waged against the Parthian or Persian foe. This solved the problem of communications, but it simultaneously increased the costs and political risks. Parthian and Persian monarchs faced the same limitations. They depended upon mounted couriers, who would have covered between 500 and 750 miles from the frontier to Ctesiphon in five to ten days.[42] Iranian monarchs, too, usually took the field in wars against Rome. Therefore, major wars from the time of Trajan invariably risked the legitimacy and imperial power of both rivals who saw as paramount the strategic rivalry over the Near East.

Each power must have calculated and assessed its success in the rivalry, even though the precise methods are not reported beyond references of meetings of the Roman Senate, the council of the emperor, or advisors of Iranian monarchs. There is information on how Rome and Sassanid Persia officially represented successes to a wider public. Roman citizens had to be persuaded that success justified the costs of the rivalry. Rome's dissemination of success in war and diplomacy by letters, visual arts, coins, and monumental public inscriptions is without precedent. To be sure, these were official images rather than accurate news, but they were premised on the fact that Senate or emperor had to assess the course of the rivalry accurately, however they intended to publicize it. In contrast, the Sassanid shahs erected inscriptions and reliefs announcing success in the rivalry amid the royal tombs of the early Achaemenid kings. These messages were aimed for a far more limited audience of members of court, Roman envoys, or vassal kings. As designate of Ahura-Mazda, the shah did not have to inform a wider public of success in the rivalry with Rome.[43]

Therefore, the rivals were aware of the competition. Each power had a sense of its own unique greatness. Rome was a republic, then a Principate (rather than under a despot-), and finally a Christian empire. Arsacids reigned as Great Kings of Kings, and Sassanid shahs as the Kings of the Aryans and Non-Aryans. Yet, often each power had to accept long and uneasy periods of coexistence, notably in 20 BCE–113 CE and 379/382–502. Hence, the strategic rivalry undermined the very self-image of unique greatness of each power.

The First Rivalry: Rome and Parthia, 69 BCE–66 CE

On October 6, 69 BCE, the Roman proconsul L. Licinius Lucullus decisively defeated King Tigranes II, "the Great," of Armenia (ca. 95–56 BCE) before his political capital Tigranocerta, on a tributary of the upper Tigris in Mesopotamia.[44] Lucullus had crossed the Euphrates in pursuit of King Mithridates VI Eupator of Pontus (121–63 BCE), who had fled to the court of his son-in-law Tigranes II. Mithridates had challenged Rome for mastery of Greece and Asia Minor. He has the singular distinction of fighting against

Rome in three wars named after him, and Cicero hailed the Pontic monarch as the greatest king since Alexander the Great.[45] By this victory, Lucullus made Rome arbiter of the Near East. He also brought the Roman Republic into direct contact with a new rival power, Arsacid Parthia.

The Senate and people of Rome had taken little note of rising Arsacid power, for the Republic was concerned with the lands around the Mediterranean Sea. In 92 BCE, L. Cornelius Sulla, propraetor of Cilicia, received a Parthian envoy Orobazus, sent by King Mithridates II, who was concerned over Roman actions in eastern Asia Minor.[46] The meeting proved inconclusive, but Sulla treated Orobazus as the representative of a subservient ally. Sulla acted with the pride and confidence of a great *nobilis* and as the magistrate of a Republic that dealt from a position of superiority with other powers, and insisted on decisive victory in war. L. Licinius Lucullus and Cn. Pompeius Magnus (Pompey the Great) likewise treated the Parthian King Phraates III as a useful subordinate. They saw as the greater threat King Mithridates VI of Pontus, an ally turned deadly foe, and his son-in-law Tigranes II of Armenia. Mithridates and Tigranes each resented his role as a subordinate client king of Rome and Parthia, respectively. Mithridates VI exploited Roman civil wars to wrest briefly Greece and Asia Minor from the republic in 89–85 BCE. In 88–70 BCE, Tigranes renounced his Arsacid allegiance, overran Mesopotamia and Babylonia, and invaded Syria, so that he proclaimed himself King of Kings. The Arsacid kings were pushed back east of the Zagros Mountains, along the modern Iraq-Iran border, so that they lost their capital cities of Ctesiphon and Seleucia ad Tigrim. Lucullus, at the Battle of Tigranocerta, ended Tigranes's dreams of recreating the classic empire of the Fertile Crescent.

Lucullus invaded Mesopotamia to secure the person of Mithridates VI Eupator, and so end the republic's third war against the king. To this end, in 68 BCE, Lucullus negotiated an alliance with Parthian king Phraates III against Tigranes. In return for a Parthian invasion of Armenia, Lucullus promised to Phraates the return of hereditary lands lost to Tigranes since 88 BCE. In 66 BCE, Pompey succeeded to Lucullus's command, and offered the same deal to Phraates, who invaded the Araxes Valley, and besieged the historic Armenian capital of Artaxata. But Phraates failed to take Artaxata and withdrew. In the next year, 65 BCE, Tigranes surrendered unconditionally to Pompey, who restored the Armenian crown to Tigranes. Kings of Armenia were to rule henceforth as dutiful Roman allies. Pompey imposed Roman suzerainty over the Armenian king of Sophene, and the Aramaic-speaking dynast Abgar II of Osrhoene (68–52 BCE), thereby securing the eastern side of the crossings over the Upper Euphrates. In turn, Pompey conceded a

Parthian overlordship over the rest of Mesopotamia, as well as Gordyene and Abiadene (north and east of the Upper Tigris). Phraates III and his heirs felt cheated, for they had only secured Mesopotamia east of the Khabur River.

The borders between the two new imperial powers in the Near East were far from fixed. Strategically each power had reason to revise the frontiers. But Roman ambitions were long limited by popular agitation over political and economic reforms at home that plunged the republic into a new round of civil wars in 49–31 BCE. Frontier and civil wars elevated powerful commanders (*imperatores*) as dictators either for or against popular reform. At the same time, the Arsacid monarchy was rocked by civil wars among rival kings.

L. Licinius Crassus, proconsul of Syria (54–53 BCE), aimed to match the glory Julius Caesar was winning in Gaul, and so he provoked Rome's first war with Parthia. King Orodes II (57–37 BCE) was distracted by a civil war against his brother Mithridates. The king entrusted command of his western army to the Suren, the hereditary marcher lord of the eastern frontier in Drangiana and Arachosia. In the spring of 53 BCE, Crassus crossed the Euphrates at Zeugma with seven legions and 3,000 or 4,000 cavalry. He marched east to Edessa (modern Urfa), capital of King Abgar of Oshroene, and then pressed south to Carrhae (present-day Harran). The ultimate strategic aims of Crassus are uncertain, but he threatened either to overrun Mesopotamia between the Khabur and Tigris or to strike southeast along the Euphrates against Ctesiphon. In early June 53 BCE, Crassus accepted battle on unfavorable terrain east of Carrhae against a significantly smaller Parthian cavalry army of *cataphracti* and horse archers.[47] The Suren outfought Crassus. The Roman cavalry was driven off the field, and the legions had to endure thirst and a continuous barrage of arrows unleashed by Parthian horse archers. At nightfall, the Romans fell back in disorder to Carrhae. The next day Crassus botched the retreat to the Euphrates, and so he negotiated a surrender. Crassus was seized and beheaded; 10,000 Romans, along with the legionary standards, were taken prisoner. Roman losses were reported at 20,000 dead. Perhaps three-quarters of the Roman army was slain or captured. Rome's first battle against a Parthian army ended in a *clades,* an ignominious defeat that demanded revenge.

Strategically, the victory at Carrhae allowed King Orodes II to extend Arsacid dominion not only over Armenia and Mesopotamia, but the entire Near East. Twice, in 52–51 BCE and in 40–38 BCE, a Parthian army commanded by Orodes's son Pacorus crossed the Euphrates to conquer Rome's provinces and dependencies in Asia Minor, the Levant, and Egypt. Each invasion ended in failure. In 36 BCE, the triumvir M. Antonius (Mark Antony), master of the Roman East, retaliated with an invasion of Media Atropatene.

King Phraates IV (r. 37–2 BCE), in control of Mesopotamia, denied Mark Antony the crossings over the upper Euphrates. Instead, Mark Antony had to march north from Syria along the west bank of the Euphrates, and then enter Armenia from the west-east axial road in northern Asia Minor. The Roman army, numbered by Plutarch at 100,000 men, comprised perhaps twice the number of legionaries in Crassus's army, as well as strong cavalry formations. King Artavasdes II (r. 55–34 BCE) of Armenia was compelled to renounce his Parthian allegiance, and to furnish cavalry and supplies. Mark Antony reached Artaxata late in the summer, and then descended the Artaxes Valley into Media Atropatene. The expedition ended in an abortive siege of Phraata in late autumn.[48] Logistical difficulties compelled Mark Antony to withdraw, and he sustained heavy losses on the retreat, harassed by Parthian cavalry, which avoided decisive action. In 34 BCE, Antony returned to Armenia, and arrested Artavasdes, whom Antony accused of treachery. The Armenian nobles promptly proclaimed as their king Artavasdes's son Artaxias II (r. 34–20 BCE), who allied with Parthia.

Antony's invasion of Parthia proved a fiasco for his political position at Rome, but, more important, it revealed the limitations of Roman military power. Mark Antony had marched a large army over the most difficult of terrain of eastern Asia Minor, Armenia, and northwestern Iran, perhaps over 1,500 miles, in a single campaigning season. The campaign proved too ambitious.

The fighting in the two decades after Carrhae ended in a stalemate. The Arsacid kings lacked the means to conquer the Roman East. Instead, the Parthian western invasions had proved to be costly grand raids that provoked a Roman counter-invasion. In turn, Rome lacked the means to invade Iran and overthrow the Arsacid monarchy. Each power learned to respect the military of the other. The Romans appreciated the tactical and strategic mobility of the Parthian cavalry. They also learned from Crassus's failure to secure water sources and reliable local allies who could furnish cavalry and accurate information. Later Roman commanders deployed more cavalry, light infantry, and archers familiar with the arid conditions of the Near East. They adapted the tactical advantages of legionary infantry to counter Parthian cavalry.[49] The Arsacid kings learned to avoid direct battle with well-led legionaries, and to employ harassing tactics to achieve a strategic stalemate. They also realized that the lack of disciplined infantry and siege trains prevented their capture of walled cities.

In 31 BCE, Octavian, the adopted son of Julius Caesar, ended nearly three decades of civil war, and secured Rome's eastern provinces. In 27 BCE, Octavian, hailed as the first emperor Augustus (r. 27 BCE–14 CE), secured his supreme position as *princeps*, a dynast ruling in the guise of a Republican magistrate. Augustus fell heir to an unresolved eastern frontier, and loud demands by the political classes at Rome to conquer Parthia. Augustus understood the limits of Roman power, and he preferred to direct imperial expansion into northwestern and central Europe. In 20 BCE, Augustus adroitly exploited a succession crisis in Armenia to restore Rome's position in the Near East. The Armenian nobility overthrew the unpopular Artaxias II and requested a new king from Rome. Augustus obliged and sent Tigranes III (r. 20–10 BCE), accompanied by Tiberius and a Roman army that crowned the new Armenian king in Artaxata. The action risked a general war with King Phraates IV of Parthia, who claimed suzerainty over Armenia. Therefore, Augustus mobilized the legions in Syria under his able general M. Vipsanius Agrippa, and so threatened to attack Ctesiphon and Seleucia ad Tigrim. Phraates IV was persuaded to accept a diplomatic settlement.[50]

Phraates acknowledged Rome's right to crown the king of Armenia as well as Roman suzerainty over Sophene, the lesser Armenian kingdom astride strategic routes east of the upper Euphrates. The kings of Osrhoene, ruling over Edessa and Carrhae, retained a precarious independence between the two powers. Eastern Mesopotamia, with its axial west-east highways, was designated Parthian. Phraates, however, had to return Roman standards and prisoners captured at Carrhae, and to send four sons to Rome as hostages.[51] Augustus diplomatically restored Rome's boundaries to those fixed by Pompey in 63 BCE. He represented the settlement in official iconography as equivalent to a triumph; the returned standards were eventually received into the Temple of Mars Ultor at Rome. Augustus had asserted Rome's dominance over Parthia without an expensive war. Future security of the Roman East rested in the four legions stationed in Syria, as well as the armies of client kings in eastern Asia Minor, Sophene, and Armenia.[52] It was a cost-effective solution. Augustus avoided the expense of administering and defending remote provinces along the upper Euphrates. The legions in Syria thus took as their mission the defense of the coastal highway between Antioch and Alexandria. Furthermore, Augustus and his heirs had a supply of Parthian pretenders, reared at Rome, to produce as rivals to any ambitious Arsacid king who wished to revise the settlement. Phraates had little choice but to accept. He feared for his throne, and he could not risk challenges from rival kinsmen and vassal princes, as he had in the wake of the invasion of Mark Antony.

Augustus resolved the rivalry to the satisfaction of Rome, but his settlement depended on a weak Arsacid king. It also rested on a loyal king of Armenia. Rome wanted a dutiful, compliant king in Armenia, but such a king could not maintain the loyalty of regional warlords—the *naxarars* of the Middle Ages—who raided and fought over honor and blood feud. Clashes among Armenian nobles led to raids into Roman and Parthian territory so that the fighting threatened to embroil the two great powers in a greater conflict. The Armenians themselves posed little direct threat to either power. The national levy of Armenia might have numbered 80,000, but few kings could field armies larger than 5,000 cavalry.[53] Instead, Rome faced a problem of controlling the Armenians, comparable to that faced by the British in dealing with the Pathans on the Northwest Frontier of India in the nineteenth and early twentieth centuries. No Afghan ruler in Kabul acceptable to the British ever commanded the loyalty of the tribes.[54]

The settlement between Rome and Parthia held to 53 CE, when new conditions undermined it. First, an effective king, Vologaeses I (r. 51–78) secured the Arsacid throne. He had to provide kingdoms for his younger brothers, Pacorus and Tiridates, lest they challenge him. Second, another succession crisis in Armenia led many Armenian nobles, weary of philo-Roman kings, to invite Tiridates, brother of Vologaeses, to rule over them. Finally, this change of dynasty in Armenia was unacceptable to the new Roman emperor Nero (r. 54–68).[55] Even so, Nero and Vologaeses avoided a major war with each other. Instead, they waged an indirect war, better named the War of the Armenian Succession (54–66) rather than a Parthian War.

Nero aimed to place a friendly king on the throne of Armenia, and so to secure the strategic routes, rather than to conquer Armenia. From the start, Nero was willing to accept Tiridates if the Arsacid prince requested his crown from Rome. Vologaeses supported his brother Tiridates for the same reason. As king of Armenia, Tiridates would secure the strategic route by which Mark Antony had invaded Media Atropatane in 36 BCE. Vologaeses had no intention of committing the Arsacid state to a great war with Rome. He respected Roman arms and mistrusted the loyalties of Armenian nobles. Three times, they had submitted to Rome when an imperial prince— Tiberius, Gaius Caesar, and Germanicus—had marched Roman legions to Artaxata to put a king on the Armenian throne.[56]

Cn. Domitius Corbulo, the imperial legate of Cappadocia, was granted the command of operations in Armenia and Mesopotamia. Corbulo, who commanded four legions and auxiliary and allied forces totaling 75,000 men, campaigned in accordance with strategy and operations set by Nero.[57] C. Ummidius Durmius Quadratus, legate of Syria, retained two legions to guard the crossing at Zeugma. After diplomacy had failed, Corbulo invaded Armenia in a stunning two-year campaign. In the summer of 58, Corbulo marched across the Armenian plateau and captured Artaxata, where he wintered. In the next year, Corbulo ordered the destruction of Artaxata, and marched southwest. He crossed into Mesopotamia via the Bitlis Pass and received the surrender of Tigranocerta and the cities of Mesopotamia. Tiridates, discredited and deserted by his Armenian adherents, took refuge with Vologaeses. In 60, Nero promoted Corbulo to legate of Syria, and sent Tigranes VI, a scion of the Artaxid house, from Rome to reign from Tigranocerta under the protection of a Roman garrison. Tigranes, however, could not rule the Armenian plateau from Tigranocerta. He also provoked a border incident so that Vologaeses could intervene to restore his brother Tiridates. In 61–64, the fighting shifted from Armenia to Mesopotamia. In 62, L. Junius Caesennius Paetus, the new legate of Cappadocia, failed to relieve Tigranocerta, and was compelled to negotiate a humiliating truce with Vologaeses. Nero, however, dismissed Paetus, and instructed Corbulo to cross the Euphrates in force to compel Vologaeses and Tirdiates to negotiate. In 64, Corbulo threatened to overrun Mesopotamia, and so Vologaeses agreed to accept Nero's original offer. Tiridates was restored to the Armenian throne, but he had to journey to Rome to accept his crown directly from Nero.

The fighting in 54–64 resulted in an adjustment of Augustus's settlement in 20 BCE. Henceforth, an Arsacid prince ruled in Armenia, but Tiridates was mindful of the majesty of Rome, for he was awed by the city when he visited in 66. Vologaeses, too, was respectful of Rome; Corbulo's campaigns could not fail to impress. Hence, Vologaeses made no move to exploit the First Jewish Revolt (67–73) or the Roman civil war of 69–70. Foremost, Rome learned that the army in Syria was inadequate to the task of maintaining Roman hegemony in Armenia. The emperor Vespasian (r. 69–79) increased the number of legions (from four to six) and auxiliaries in the East.[58] New legionary camps were constructed in eastern Asia Minor at Satala, Melitene, and Samosata, which provided bases for Roman preemptive strikes into Armenia or Mesopotamia. Roads, bridges, depots, and auxiliary forts were constructed along the Upper Euphrates to facilitate the movement of soldiers, supplies, and communications.[59] The Flavian emperors Vespasian, Titus (r. 79–81), and Domitian (r. 81–96) poured money into creating this eastern *limes*, or frontier, on the Euphrates, and the investment proved its value in later Roman wars against Parthia.

The fighting in 54–64 revealed serious weaknesses in Roman command and communications. Cn. Domitius Corbulo clashed with his colleague Ummidius Quadratus, in 54–60, and then with Caesennius Paetius in 60–62. These proud senatorial legates of Cappadocia and Syria viewed each other as rivals for imperial favor, and so they reluctantly cooperated. Nero had to deal with delays in communication with Rome (especially from the commander east of the Euphrates), as well as contradictory reports from his legates. To Nero's credit, he selected Corbulo in 54 and again in 62 to command the offensives in Armenia and Mesopotamia. But future emperors preferred not to risk delays in communication and the problems of divided command, so they marched east to direct personally the operations against Parthia. Inevitably, the strategic rivalry between Rome and Parthia was bound to escalate, and in so doing not only increased each power's costs and aims, but transformed each power as well.

Rome and Parthia at War, 113–218

The diplomatic settlement of 66 CE held for nearly fifty years, for two reasons. First, the settlement was a sensible compromise accommodating the strategic interests of each power. Second, Parthia and Rome were also distracted by other priorities during these years. The Arsacid kings were pressed on their northeastern frontier in Areia along the lower Oxus River and to the southeast in Drangiana (present-day Sistan and the Helmand Valley). They faced a new, powerful foe, the kings of the Kushans, descendants of Tocharian-speaking nomads, who forged a great empire in Transoxiana and northern India and taxed the lucrative trade along the Silk Road. Meanwhile, Roman legions conducted major conquests in northern Europe, in Britain, Germania, and Dacia. In 113, another Armenian crisis erupted, when, King Osroes I (r. 109–129) crowned his nephew Parthamasiris as king of Armenia in violation of the settlement of 66. In part, Oroses might have acted to gain direct control of passes over the Caucasus through which the nomadic Alans had invaded Parthian domains in 72.[60] But this time the opportunism of an Arsacid king resulted in a major war. In 113, the emperor Trajan (r. 98–117) marched east in the first Parthian war in nearly 175 years.

Oroses was stunned by the speed and scale of Trajan's response, and so he urged his nephew Parthamasiris to submit and seek his crown from Trajan. At the legionary fortress of Satala, in 114, Trajan deposed Parthamasiris. With veteran legionaries and auxiliaries from the Rhine and Danube frontiers, Trajan easily overran Armenia. He appointed L. Catilius Severus, legate of Cappadocia, to organize the new province. In 115, Trajan shifted operations south, and overran the lands between the Khabur and the Upper Tigris, and annexed a second province, Mesopotamia, thereby securing the Ergani and Bitlis passes. In 116, Trajan deployed the logistics and strategy perfected in the Dacian Wars. Two Roman columns, marching down the Tigris and Euphrates, converged to storm and sack first Seleucia ad Tigrim, and then Cteisphon. Osores fled east over the Zagros Mountains, and Trajan proclaimed Parthamapastes (r. 116–117) as the Arsacid king.

From the start, Trajan pursued a strategy of overthrow, aiming to annex as provinces Armenia and Mesopotamia and to impose a compliant king on the Parthian throne ruling over lower Iraq (designated as Assyria in Classical sources) and Iran.[61] It is plausibly argued that Trajan seized upon Oroses's action to wage a war that he had already intended, because Trajan had taken a number of measures on the eastern frontier that can be interpreted as preparatory to a major war with Parthia. The Roman historian Cassius Dio, however, considered the war unnecessary.[62] Trajan could have easily restored the settlement of 66 c.e. Certainly this was what Osores and Parthamasiris expected. Instead, Trajan, weary of dealing with client rulers after his experience with Decebalus of Dacia, resolved to end the strategic rivalry decisively, by war. Trajan was rightly confident. He was bold in his strategy, meticulous in his logistics, and inspirational to his veteran officers and men. Osores and the Parthians were no match for Trajan and his legions.

It is doubtful that the Arsacid monarchy would have survived if Trajan's victory had stood, and the history of the Classical world might have taken a very different turn. On August 9, 117, Trajan's death was announced at Selinus, on the southeastern Anatolian littoral. His adopted son Hadrian (r. 117–138) was proclaimed emperor. Within a year, Hadrian withdrew all Roman forces to the west bank of the Euphrates, entrusting Armenia and Osrhoene to Arsacid client kings. Hadrian, in effect, restored the settlement of 66 c.e.[63] He is often hailed for his foresight in recognizing the limits of Roman power; his decision is considered to mark a shift in imperial policy away from expansion to one of consolidation and defense.[64]

Hadrian, however, acted not out of foresight but rather expediency. He was unpopular with Trajan's generals and the Senate, who questioned his legitimacy. He also faced Jewish insurgents in Cyprus and Cyrenaica, and defiant Parthian allies in Hatra and Adiabene, who had already forced Trajan to halt offensive operations in 117. Hadrian, to his credit, realized that he lacked the genius to suppress the rebellions and to defend the new conquests. Yet, his withdrawal proved unpopular. Subsequent events would prove that Trajan was correct, and Hadrian was wrong, on the imperial boundary in the Near East. Roman security on the Euphrates and in Armenia required the control of the highways across Mesopotamia to the Upper Tigris.

Furthermore, Hadrian never concluded a definitive diplomatic settlement with Osroes, but rather perpetuated civil war in the Parthian Empire. In 118, Hadrian withdrew support from Parthamaspates, who was quickly defeated by Osores. Hadrian compensated Parthamaspates (r. 118–123) with the kingdom of Osrhoene—an action viewed as hostile by Osores. Hadrian recognized Vologaeses III (r. 105–147), another rival to Osores, as the new Arsacid king of Armenia. The Parthian Empire was rent by civil war to 147. Hadrian had set a dangerous precedent in allowing Vologaeses III to unite the crowns of Armenia and Parthia (even though Vologaeses never controlled the entire Parthian realm).[65] Therefore, in 144 the emperor Antoninus Pius (r. 138–161) transferred the Armenian crown from Vologaeses to C. Julius Sohaemus (r. 144–161). Sohaemus, an Arsacid by descent, was a Roman senator in his manners and speech who alienated the Armenian nobility.

In the fifty years after Hadrian's withdrawal, the Parthian kings must have resented Roman arrogance and interference. In 161, Vologaeses IV (r. 147–191) sought to undo Hadrian's arrangements. He hoped to benefit from perceived Roman weakness with the accession of two new, untested emperors, Marcus Aurelius and Lucius Verus. The Parthian army expelled the philo-Roman king Sohaemus of Armenia. M. Sedatius Severianus, legate of Cappadocia, intervened, but he and the IX Hispania (based at Satala) were encircled and destroyed near Elegia. The new emperors had no choice but wage a new Parthian War (161–166).[66]

Rome entered the war at a strategic disadvantage. Roman commanders could not conduct offensive operations in Armenia until 163. Three legions and experienced officers had to be transferred from the Rhine or Danube frontiers.[67] The concentration of men and materiel required nearly three years. Imperial leadership was uninspired. Marcus Aurelius remained at Rome, while his junior colleague departed to command from Antioch in the winter of 161–162. Lucius Verus proved a disappointment, indulging in the pleasures of Antioch rather than commanding in the field.[68] Instead, experienced senior officers, notably M. Statius Priscus and C. Avidius Cassius, coordinated operations and gained the credit for victory.

Meanwhile, in 163, the Parthian army overran Osrhoene and imposed in Edessa a client king Vaël (r. 163–165). Vologaeses thus restored the Euphrates as Parthia's western boundary, and he threatened to invade Syria. In response, Statius Priscus, legate of Cappadocia, overran Armenia in a two-year campaign (163–164).[69] In 163, Artaxata was retaken and King Sohaemus (r. 163–186) was restored.[70] Meanwhile, other Roman forces were concentrated in Syria. In 165, two Roman columns struck across the Euphrates. The northern column, crossing a Zeugma, perhaps under P. Martius Verus, retook Edessa and restored philo-Roman king Mannus VIII.[71] The Parthian army retreated to Nisibis, suffered a major defeat, and fled across the Tigris. The southern column under C. Avidius Cassius marched down the Euphrates, descended on Babylonia, and took Seleucia ad Tigrim and Ctesiphon.[72] The royal palace at Ctesiphon was burned; Seleucia, even though opened by the Greek-speaking residents, was sacked. Although Avidius Cassius timed his operation to avoid the heat of summer, he feared the plague as well as shortages of supplies, so he withdrew to Syria.[73] In 166, Avidius Cassius marched across Mesopotamia, now completely in Roman hands, crossed the Upper Tigris, and ravaged Adiabene and Media Atropatene.

The war had proved a disaster for Vologaeses IV, who was compelled to accept the terms dictated by Rome. Yet, Marcus Aurelius annexed no territory. He was content that Osrhoene and Armenia were once again ruled by dutiful friends of Rome, who protected the eastern *limes*. So the frontier stood until 198.[74] This war had proved exceedingly expensive, and the returning soldiers of Avidius Cassius brought back a plague that ravaged the Roman world.[75] Marcus Aurelius needed to avoid the expense of maintaining forces in new provinces east of the Euphrates. Germans and Sarmatians on the Danube were already threatening the northern frontier, and thus legions had to be redeployed to Europe.

Twice, in fifty years, Roman legions had sacked the Arsacid capital Ctesiphon; Seleucia ad Tigrim never recovered from its second sack. Vologaeses IV and his successors learned not to challenge Rome over Armenia or Osrhoene. For Rome, the fighting revealed the value of controlling the highways across Mesopotamia from the Euphrates to the Tigris. Roman control denied Parthian armies the Bitlis Pass, and so the southern route into Armenia. The fortress cities of Mesopotamia acted as a shield against Parthian attacks and bases for future strikes against Ctesiphon. These strategic considerations were behind the decision of Septimius Severus (r. 193–211) to wage a new Parthian War in 197–199.

Septimius Severus was the candidate of the legions of the Danube in the civil war (193–197) following the assassination of Commodus, son of Marcus Aurelius. Cassius Dio censures Septimius Severus for waging a Parthian War for glory. The historian also criticizes the emperor's organization of a new province, Mesopotamia, as a costly commitment because the populations were linked by blood and customs to Parthia, so that new wars were bound to come.[76]

In fairness, Septimius Severus, who had served in Syria as a legionary legate, understood conditions in the Near East. In 194–195, he conducted a punitive expedition into Mesopotamia, alleging that Parthian vassals in Adiabene and Hatra had supported his rival Pescennius Niger, the candidate of the Eastern army in the civil war. Septimius Severus then suspended operations, and marched his legions west to defeat Clodius Albinus (r. 195–197), who had been declared emperor by the legions of Britain. In 197, Septimius

Severus returned to the East; he conducted an offensive down the Euphrates and sacked Ctesiphon in January 198. The issue was not Armenia. King Vologaeses V (r. 191–208) is not reported to have contested Roman hegemony in Armenia. Instead, Septimius Severus marched east with the intention of annexing Mesopotamia. In so doing, he knew that he would clash with Vologaeses, whose vassals had traditionally ruled over eastern Mesopotamia.

Therefore, Septimius Severus raised three new legions, I–III Parthicae, from colonies on the Danube frontier, and many new auxiliary units. Septimius Severus increased the imperial army from perhaps 375,000 to 450,000 men. With these additional forces, he fielded two columns in his offensive against Parthia. Two of the three new legions, I Parthica and III Parthia, were stationed at Singara and Rhesaena, respectively, in the new province. Septimius Severus committed the money and additional manpower to construct legionary bases and highways, and to fortify cities.[77] The military expenditures on this eastern policy proved costly, and Septimius Severus was forced to debase the silver currency. In return, he recreated the Mesopotamian province intended by Trajan. This province gave Rome a strategic advantage in future wars with the Parthians, and later the Sassanids, down to 363.

Victory over Parthia also gained Septimius Severus legitimacy as the worthy heir of Marcus Aurelius, because Severus had retroactively adopted himself into the Antonine family. His elder son Caracalla (r. 198–217), officially renamed M. Aurelius Antoninus, waged the last Parthian War (214–217). Caracalla had seized and imprisoned the Armenian royal family, and then marched east in 214, even though the Parthians had not challenged Roman control over Armenia. Caracalla acted out of impulse rather than strategic reasons. Classical sources agree that Caracalla was unbalanced, and longed for an eastern war to emulate Alexander the Great.[78] He conducted this campaign in a leisurely fashion, visiting en route celebrated sanctuaries and cities of the Greek world. He directed a single, limited offensive across the Tigris into Media Atropatene in 216, and withdrew to winter at Carrhae. On April 8, 217, the emperor was ignominiously murdered near Carrhae on the orders of his Praetorian Prefect Macrinus, who was declared the new emperor. Inconclusive fighting near Nisibis ended in a negotiated settlement between Macrinus and Artabanus V that confirmed the status quo ante bellum.[79]

Whatever his reasons, Caracalla threatened to overthrow the Arsacid monarchy. He pressured Vologaeses VI (r. 208–228) into offering his daughter in marriage in 215.[80] Perhaps Caracalla was imitating his hero Alexander the Great, who had married the daughters of the Persian king Darius III, reasoning that such an unprecedented marriage would have given Caracalla a claim to the Parthian throne. Vologaeses, at war with his brother Artabanus V (r. 216–224), lost credibility and most of his empire. Artabanus repudiated the marriage alliance, and was fortunate that Caracalla was assassinated the next year, because Caracalla might have sacked Ctesiphon. Yet, Caracalla ultimately toppled the Parthian Empire. The threat of a fourth Roman invasion during yet another Arsacid civil war emboldened Ardashir, the client king of Persis, to rebel against his Parthian masters. In 224, Ardashir defeated and slew Artabanus V at the Battle of Hormozgan. In 227, he entered Ctesiphon and was crowned King of Kings of a new Persian Empire.

Rome emerged the uncontested victor of its wars with Parthia, sacking the Arsacid capital Ctesiphon three times in ninety years. In 166, Marcus Aurelius assured uncontested Roman hegemony in Armenia, while Septimius Severus turned Mesopotamia into a bastion of Roman power in the Near East. Yet, victory came at a high price for Rome. Emperors had to concentrate ever more military forces against Parthia. To pay for the rising military costs, emperors were driven to debase the silver currency. The unintended consequences of these wars proved the most significant. In repeatedly humbling the Parthian foe, Rome had assured the demise of her rival, but in Parthia's place arose Sassanid Persia. Rome had not won the strategic rivalry, but instead had substituted for a weak opponent a far more powerful rival.

New Rivals at War: Rome and Sassanid Persia

In 224–227, Rome had, in effect, won the strategic rivalry over Parthia, because the Arsacid monarchy was so weakened that it was overthrown by Ardashir I (r. 227–240) who established a new Sassanid or Neo-Persian Empire.[81] Initial reactions at Rome are not recorded, but the court of Severus Alexander (r. 222–235) likely viewed this as merely a change of dynasty. If the Classical sources are to be believed, Ardashir soon made demands that should have disabused Severus Alexander and his mother Julia Mamaea of this perception. The new shah offered peace if Rome withdrew from Asia. In 229, Ardashir invaded Mesopotamia, and besieged the fortress of Hatra. Ardashir's attack represented a significant shift in the rivalry. Sassanid shahs, in contrast to Arsacid kings, initiated major wars with the avowed purpose of reclaiming the western lands of the Achaemenid Empire and with a zeal bred from the conviction that the shah ruled as the agent of Ahura-Mazda on earth.[82]

To Severus Alexander in 229, little seemed to have changed on the eastern frontier. The same factors that had pitted Rome against Parthia were still in place, so that the Persians in official imperial iconography were often treated as latter-day Parthians. Yet, Rome soon discovered that she faced a far more deadly rival. The shahs had a more effective army and greater resources, and so the means of waging war on a far grander scale to reverse Rome's domination in the Near East. In contrast, Rome waged war in 229–299, using the strategy devised by Trajan against the Parthians, and the professional army created by Augustus, to defend the frontiers established by Septimius Severus. Despite humiliating defeats during these seventy years of constant fighting, Rome emerged triumphant. Roman success rested on two new advantages, as well as the aims of the first two Sassanid shahs.

First, the Roman fortresses of Mesopotamia proved their value. Since they controlled water sources and the nexus of strategic routes, the Sassanid army either had to take the fortresses by lengthy siege or run risks of bypassing them as in 253. The fortifications limited the extent of Sassanid success.[83] Furthermore, loyal Arab sheiks, who commanded tribal armies and doubled as Aramaic princes or, later, senators in the cities, provided invaluable reconnaissance on Persian movements across the al-Jazirah.[84]

Second, the Arsacid kings of Armenia despised the Sassanid shah as their inveterate foe, so they henceforth allied with Rome. This shifted the strategic balance to Rome's favor, but at the same time it committed Rome to defending her position in Armenia. Invariably, eastern campaigns involved a Roman column operating to shield Armenia from Sassanid attack across the Upper Tigris, and then via the Bitlis Pass. The other route from the east, through Media Atropatene and via Hoşap, was the responsibility of the Armenian kings at Vagharshapat.

Finally, Rome was fortunate that the Sassanid shahs pursued limited aims for two reasons. First, shahs from Ardashir I (r. 224–240) to Shapur II (r. 309–379), based on their actions and boasts (in inscriptions and on bas relief monuments), warred to uphold their image as shah of the Iranians and non-Iranians and vice regent of Ahura-Mazda.[85] They boasted of humiliating Roman emperors, whereas, in contrast, Roman emperors celebrated the conquest of territory.[86] Hence, Sassanid shahs in the third century waged prestige campaigns that anticipated those of the Abbasid caliphs who, in the name of jihad, attacked Christian Constantinople.[87] At no point in the third century did the shahs obtain any significant additions of territory. At most, Shah Shapur I claimed hegemony over Armenia after 244, but the Arsacid kings refused to accept this claim. Therefore, shahs of the third century did not, as Classical sources would suggest, aim to conquer the Roman Empire.[88]

Second, the Sassanid army was primarily a coalition cavalry army composed of vassals and allies, even though it possessed a siege train and commissariat.[89] Ammianus Marcellinus was impressed by the abandoned ram used by the Persians to breach the walls of Antioch in 253, which was still to be seen in his day.[90] Even so, the lack of disciplined infantry was another weakness. Iranian cavalry, especially the allies from Central Asia, were reluctant to dismount and to attack a fortified city. They would have preferred to take plunder and captives.[91] Hence, the language of the list of Roman cities taken by Shapur during his second and third campaigns in 253 and 260 suggests that his army instead ravaged the hinterlands of most cities and pillaged sanctuaries outside the fortified cities

Therefore, during the first half of the rivalry in 229–299, fighting on the arid plains and grasslands of Mesopotamia was one of strategic maneuver and control of water sources. The Romans were long in no position to force the shah to fight for his capital city until the expedition of Odenathus in 262.[92] Roman emperor and Persian shah were each reluctant to risk his field army in a decisive battle. Shapur, on his monumental inscription, claims a battle at Mizik in which Gordian III suffered a serious defeat, but the details are vague.[93] Severus Alexander in 232 and Philip I in 244 each ended his expedition by a negotiated settlement. Each withdrew in good order and relinquished no territory.[94] The first expedition of Valerian in 254–256 was also inconclusive because Shah Shapur had retreated from Syria with plunder and captives. In 260, Valerian, after he suffered a defeat in the field, was treacherously seized during negotiations.

In 230, Severus Alexander readied to march east in the first imperial expedition in over a decade. He recruited additional legionaries and auxiliaries and ordered stockpiling of supplies and road repairs across the eastern provinces.[95] In the spring of 231, two years after the initial Persian attack, Severus Alexander, his mother Julia Mamaea, and the court set out. They reached Antioch by the autumn.[96] Severus Alexander brought significant reinforcements from the West, possibly 30,000 men, and he had in the East an army that since 198 numbered nine legions and totaled at least another 100,000 men.[97]

In 232, the Roman army crossed the Euphrates in three columns. A northern column, based on Melitene, operated against Adiabene to shield Armenia from Sassanid invasion via the Bitlis Pass. The emperor commanded the central column, crossing at Zeugma, which secured the fortresses of Mesopotamia. A southern column moved down the Euphrates, threatening Ctesiphon.[98] The historian Herodian reports that the supporting columns suffered grievous losses from privations and desultory fighting, but Ardashir also must have suffered heavy losses.[99] Both sides were ready to negotiate out of the war at the end of the campaigning season. They concluded an armistice rather than a definitive settlement.[100] From the surviving sources, it is difficult to surmise how Severus Alexander defined victory when he crossed the Euphrates. What is clear is that he did not achieve his strategic aims, and he bore the responsibility for the failure. For the first time, an emperor returned to Rome without celebrating a major eastern victory. Instead, he had negotiated with the shah on terms of equality. In so doing, Severus Alexander, long perceived as weak, lost face with the ruling classes and the army.[101]

In fairness, Severus Alexander had faced mutiny among the legions of Mesopotamia, and he had to redeploy forces to counter an invasion of the Upper Rhineland by the Germanic Alamanni.[102] Even so, the costly expedition was a political fiasco, especially in comparison to previous Roman victories over the Parthians, and the high expectations at the outset of the war. Severus Alexander had marched east, hailed by the cities across the East with traditional sobriquets of "conqueror" and "favored of the gods."[103] In 235, Severus Alexander again negotiated with invaders, the Alammani. Herodian censured the emperor, noting that officers and men concluded that "in their opinion Alexander showed no honorable intention to pursue the war and preferred a life of ease, when he should have marched out to punish the Germans for their previous insolence."[104] On March 18, 235, the soldiers mutinied and murdered the emperor and his mother at Mogantiacum (Mainz). They declared as emperor Maximinus (r. 235–238), a tough Thracian soldier who had risen to equestrian rank. The end of the Severan dynasty also ended political stability for the next fifty years. The Roman Empire was wracked by civil wars that compromised the defense of both the northern and eastern frontiers.

In 238 civil war erupted in the Roman Empire. Ardashir annually invaded and ravaged Mesopotamia. After each campaign the Persian army retired east of the Tigris.[105] By 241, Shapur I, the son and successor of Ardashir, had captured the Roman fortresses of Hatra, Nisibis, and Carrhae. The cities were sacked and abandoned.[106] It was not until 242 that a new emperor, the youthful Gordian III (r. 238–244), could take the field. The emperor's father-in-law and Praetorian Prefect C. Furius Sabinius Aquila Timesitheus commanded, and his death in 243 would put the expedition in jeopardy.[107] The Roman army reached Antioch late in 242, and opened an offensive early in the spring of 243. Timesitheus reoccupied the fortresses of Mesopotamia, and was credited with a victory near Rhesaena (modern Ras al-Ayn).[108] Then, most likely in the autumn, Timesitheus initiated an offensive down the Euphrates with Ctesiphon as the objective. The prefect, however, died of illness.[109] Philip the Arab succeeded as Praetorian Prefect, and engineered the murder of the young emperor by staging a riot among the soldiers over food shortages in the winter camp near Circesium on the middle Euphrates, on

February 25, 244.[110] The army then acclaimed Philip emperor (r. 244–249). Gordian, however, had already been discredited, because the offensive against Ctesiphon had been checked by a strategic victory won by Shapur at Mizik (Greek Misiche).[111] Philip chose to negotiate, promising 10,000 pounds of gold, which Shapur claimed as tribute on his monumental trilingual inscription at Naqsh-e Rustem.[112] The subsidy cost Philip politically. He was driven to debase the silver currency and raise taxes.[113] The higher taxes drove provincials in Syria and Cappadocia to rebel.[114]

Philip did not cede any of the fortresses in Mesopotamia, but he apparently agreed to remain neutral in Shapur's war with King Tiridates II of Armenia.[115] In 244–252, Shapur campaigned in Armenia, while short-lived Roman emperors battled rivals and Goths in the Balkans. In 253, Shapur exploited a Roman civil war. Shapur did not invade Mesopotamia, but instead advanced up the Euphrates, and invaded Syria. He defeated a Roman army, reckoned at 60,000, at Barbalissos, and his army then ravaged northern Syria. Antioch, third city of the Roman Empire, was betrayed and sacked.[116] The population was deported and settled at Gundeshapur in southwestern Iran. By his victory, Shapur not only won prestige in the eyes of his nobles and vassal kings, but he also destroyed the capacity of the Roman army in the East to wage offensive operations. In 254–256, the new Roman emperor Valerian (r. 253–260) arrived with an expeditionary force drawn from the Rhine and Danube legions. Valerian, however, had to rebuild Antioch and to restore fortresses and the imperial army of Syria.[117] Valerian was in no position to wage offensive operations, and in 256 he had to return to Rome. Shapur thereupon resumed seasonal campaigns against the fortresses of Mesopotamia so that in 258 Valerian mounted a second eastern expedition. A war of strategic maneuver for control of highways and water sources ensued.[118] In the late summer of 260, Valerian chose to parley with Shapur after he suffered a defeat in his effort to raise the Persian sieges of Edessa and Carrhae. Shapur seized Valerian, his senior field officers, and at least part of the army.[119] Roman resistance collapsed, and Shapur crossed the Euphrates to ravage the hinterlands of the cities of Cappadocia and Cilicia in eastern Asia Minor.

Two senior staff officers, Callistus and M. Fulvius Macrianus, rallied the demoralized eastern legions at Samosata and counterattacked, thereby compelling Shapur to withdraw.[120] L. Septimius Odenathus, merchant prince of Palmyra who styled himself senator and commander (*dux*), organized local forces along the Syrian frontier, ostensibly in the name of Gallienus (r. 253–268), the son and colleague of Valerian.[121] The eastern legions, however, acclaimed the two youthful sons of Macrianus, Macrianus Junior and Quietus, as emperors, and so condemned the empire to yet another civil war while Shapur retired with booty and captives into Persia. The Macrianii, father and son, marched west against Gallienus, but they were defeated and slain in Illyricum in the spring of 261. Odenathus stormed Emesa and eliminated the other young usurper, Quietus.

With his third campaign against Rome, Shapur ceased to report on his activities, and with good cause, because the war turned against him after 261. Odenathus reorganized the defenses of Syria to the benefit of his native caravan city Palmyra. In 262, Odenathus launched an invasion into Babylonia.[122] For the first time in sixty-five years, a Roman army, albeit led by Odenathus and filled with allied and auxiliary units of Syrians and Arabs, penetrated to Ctesiphon. It is uncertain whether Odenathus captured Ctesiphon, but the invasion dissuaded Shapur from waging further campaigns against Rome. Between 262 and 266/267, Odenathus secured Rome's frontiers in the Near East. Neither Shapur nor his immediate successors moved to exploit Roman disunity after the debacle of Valerian's capture.[123] The Rhine legions declared their commander Postumus (r. 260–269) as emperor, and he and his successors ruled an independent Gallo-Roman Empire to 274. Odenathus, although he professed loyalty to Gallienus at Rome, effectively ruled the Roman East. His widow Zenobia advanced their son Vaballathus (r. 270–272) as emperor of the East, but she lacked the loyalty of the eastern legions and the elites of the Greek cities. Aurelian, acclaimed emperor by the legions of the Danube, restored imperial unity and fiscal stability by his currency reforms. Aurelian initiated the restoration of the imperial army and its defenses on the eastern frontier over the next three decades.[124]

The fighting in 238–262 had ended in no settlement, so a formal state of war likely existed until the peace of 299.[125] In 283, the emperor Carus led an expedition against Cteisphon that might have invaded down the Tigris rather than the Euphrates.[126] Carus claimed a victory over Shah Bahram II (r. 276–293), but the Roman army apparently failed to take the Persian capital and withdrew after Carus was killed by lightning in late summer 283.[127] Carus's untimely death cut short a well-planned campaign, but the Praetorian Prefect Flavius Aper, father-in-law to Carus's younger son Numerian, withdrew in good order in 284.[128] Carus's death also resulted in another succession crisis that ended in a civil war in 284–285, which put Diocletian (r. 284–305) on the throne.

Diocletian, a veteran Balkan officer, ended fifty years of civil wars. He ruled as an autocrat, served by imperial officials and soldiers, rather than as a magistrate of the republic. His reforms of the court, bureaucracy, and army marked the new style of Roman government known as the Dominate. In 285, he also opted for collective rule, known as the Tetrarchy. Diocletian reigned with the superior influence (*auctoritas*) as Augustus (or senior emperor) in the East. He appointed as Augustus in the West his comrade Maximianus (r. 285–305), who resided at Mediolanum (Milan). In 293, the two Augusti adopted as their successors the junior emperors, or caesars: Galerius in the East, and Constantius I Chlorus in the West. Each emperor assumed responsibility for a major frontier. Diocletian, resident at Nicomedia (Izmit, Turkey), defended the lower Danube frontier, while his Caesar Galerius took up residence at Antioch and supervised imperial defenses in the Near East. This collective rule by a Tetrarchy failed in a new round of civil wars in 306–324, but Diocletian had ensured imperial recovery in the fourth century by his military and fiscal reforms.

Narses (r. 293–302), third and least favored son of Shapur I, needed to prove his legitimacy and bravery to the Persian nobility. In 296 or 297, Narses invaded Armenia, expelling the philo-Roman king Tiridates III (r. 287–330). Narses alleged that Diocletian had violated the treaty whereby Philip had promised Shapur a free hand in Armenia. Narses then invaded Mesopotamia and defeated Galerius, with forces drawn from the Euphrates frontier, in a battle between Carrhae and Callinicum.[129] Narses timed his attack well, because the other Tetrarchs were engaged on other frontiers.[130] The extent of the Roman defeat is uncertain, but the next year (either 297 or 298), Galerius, given crack legions from the Danube by Diocletian, restored Tiridates to the Armenian throne. Armenian lords, out of hatred for the Persians, furnished supplies and information. In two battles, at unknown locations in eastern Armenia, Galerius defeated Narses and captured the shah's tent, including his wife and harem.[131] Galerius, with Armenia secured, advanced down the Euphrates against Ctesiphon the following year. At this point, Narses had no choice but to submit to Roman demands, with his field army shattered and his capital threatened.

In 299 (or 300), Narses agreed to an unfavorable treaty that ended over forty-five years of hostilities with Rome. Tiridates III was confirmed as king, and Armenia was henceforth designated Roman. Five strategic provinces east of the northern Tigris were surrendered by Narses: Ingilene, Sophanene, Arzanene, Corduene, and Zabdaicene (the last present-day Hakkari, Turkey). These provinces controlled routes between northern Mesopotamia and Armenia, and gave Roman armies easy access into Adiabene and Media Atropatene.[132] This victory over Persia was celebrated on the triumphal arch of Galerius at Thessalonica, and Roman reliefs depicted, for the first time, a Persian shah as a suppliant.[133]

Strategically, Rome won the wars of the third century, but at a high cost that changed its institutions. Furthermore, Shapur I had won the prestige war, because his reliefs, monumental inscriptions, and building programs exalted for posterity his victories over three Roman emperors. Valerian died an ignominious death as a Persian captive. The deportees of Antioch and the soldiers taken prisoner ended their lives as subjects of the shah. Rome's victory was perhaps too complete, because Shapur II (r. 309–379) was determined to reverse this humiliation, and to regain the lost provinces.

War and Peace: Christian Emperors and Sassanid Shahs

In 299, Diocletian and Galerius imposed a treaty on Shah Narses that marked a great Roman victory over the Sassanids. Although the defeats suffered at the hands of Shapur I had been avenged, Rome had not destroyed the capacity of Sassanid Persia to renew the strategic rivalry. In 363, nearly sixty-five years later, the emperor Jovian (r. 363–364) concluded a new treaty ceding the Mesopotamian fortresses to Shah Shapur II (r. 309–379). Rome was on the defensive in the Near East for the next 265 years. This change in fortune resulted from the personal failure of the emperor Julian commanding an expedition against Ctesiphon, but Julian's defeat also rested in the decline of the professional Roman army.

Rome entered the final phases of the rivalry with Persia with a considerably different army in its professionalism and chain of command. The Eastern army had to be rebuilt and reorganized after successive defeats in 253–260 and a veritable civil war in 270–273. In the course of this fighting, at least seven, perhaps ten, more legions had been raised.[134] Diocletian reformed civil and military organization. He subdivided provinces, tripling the number from 45 to 120, to facilitate tax collection and defense. He also increased the number of legions by fourteen or seventeen, to a total of fifty-one or fifty-two legions.[135] The size of each new legion is unknown; it is surmised that each numbered 2,000 to 3,000 combatants, or the equivalent of a strong legionary *vexillatio* deployed in expeditions in the Principate. The legionary cavalry had already been detached and reorganized into independent units either by Gallienus (r. 253–268) or Aurelian (r. 270–275). The number of mounted units was steadily increased over the fourth century, especially in the three area commands under the dukes of Armenia, Mesopotamia, and Osrhoene deployed against Persia. Yet, the imperial army comprised primarily infantry into the sixth century. Diocletian also restored and extended the fortifications on the frontiers. His most celebrated fortification is the Strata Diocletiana, defining the frontier along the Syrian desert, but his repairs of the fortress cities and roads of Mesopotamia were far more important. In numbers, the imperial army under Diocletian did not increase significantly; it totaled between 450,000 and 475,000 men, or approximately the same size of the army in the late Severan Age.[136]

What changed over the course of the fourth century was the quality of the army. Successive reforms in recruitment, weapons and tactics, and the chain of command reduced its effectiveness. Many Germanic barbarians from beyond the frontiers were admitted, and the best were promoted to the highest levels of command. Weapons and tactics were simplified. The chain of command was reorganized into separate civil and military administrations. Foremost, Constantine (r. 306–337) created field armies, and so divided the imperial army into the privileged Palatine units (or *comitatenesis*), and the frontier units designated *limitanei*.[137] Constantine stationed the favored units 100–150 miles behind the frontier, not so much as a strategic reserve, but rather as a strike force ready to march during the civil wars of 306–324.[138] He reduced the Praetorian Prefect to a civil official, and in his place created new field commanders of the cavalry and infantry, *magister equitum* and *magister peditum*. The rank of *magister militum* was used to designate commands of the great regional field armies in Gaul, Italy, Illyricum, and the East by the mid-fourth century. Lesser field armies were commanded by a *comes*; the units on the frontier by a *dux*. In addition, with Constantine, the Roman army fought under Christian symbols, even though many of the soldiers remained pagans. These dramatic changes lowered morale and professionalism, and so affected the performance of Julian's army during the Persian expedition in 362–363.

Diocletian, however, conducted currency, fiscal, and administrative reforms that could pay for the increased costs of defense.[139] His successors, Constantius I and Galerius, extended the logic of his provincial organization by creating the diocesis (an intermediate level of provincial administration) and imposing ever more strict divisions between military and civil offices. This Tetrarchic administration gave the Roman Empire an overall stability, even during the civil wars waged by the regional emperors in 306–324. These wars were longer than those of the third century, but they were less disruptive. Each rival emperor aspiring to the position of Diocletian could govern and tax his dioceses effectively. Maximinus II Daia, as Caesar and then Augustus (309–313), maintained security in the East. So did Licinius, who was created Augustus for the West by Galerius in 308, and reinvented himself as Augustus in the East in 313–324. Shah Narses and his immediate successors were thus in no position to exploit the Roman civil wars to revise the treaty of 299.

In 324, he ended civil war and reunited the Roman Empire. In 330, he founded a Christian capital at New Rome, or Constantinople, and so shifted the locus of imperial power to the Bosporus, closer to Ctesiphon. King Tirdiates III of Armenia (r. ca. 287–330) either anticipated or followed Constantine by embracing the new faith. A Christian Armenian king of the Arsacid family, linked by faith to the Roman emperor, posed a threat to Persian interests. Such a king could, with the backing of a strong episcopacy, bring to heel the unruly *naxarars* and impose his authority over the Armenian plateau.

In 309, Shapur II (r. 309–373) succeeded to the Sassanid throne. As a minor, he was long in no position to challenge Rome. Shapur, mindful of his legacy and the need to impress his nobles, was determined to renew the strategic rivalry.[140] Pagan authors blame an avaricious, Christian Constantine for the resumption of war due to a trivial slight regarding pearls intended as gifts to the emperor.[141] Instead, the issue was Armenia. In 330–335, Armenia lapsed into civil war after the death of Tiridates III. Shapur and Constantine intervened in support of opposing Armenian factions. Constantine alienated many Armenians by declaring his nephew Hannibalianus king of Armenia in preference to the Arsacid Khosrov III (r. 330–339). To the relief of Armenian *naxarars*, Hannibalianus never left Constantinople, because he was slain in the riots after Constantine's death.

Shapur escalated the rivalry by ordering his general Narses to invade Mesopotamia. In 336, Constantius II, the eldest son of Constantine, arrived with forces from the West and expelled the Persians from eastern Mesopotamia. He then fortified Amida on the Upper Tigris to protect the eastern approaches to the Ergani pass.[142] On May 22, 337, the situation dramatically changed with the death of the emperor Constantine. Rioting in Constantinople led to the execution of a number of male members of the imperial family. In September 337, the three surviving sons of Constantine were declared joint Augusti: Constantine II (age twenty-one), Constantius II (age twenty), and Constans (age fourteen). The military and financial resources of the Roman Empire were divided among the three young brothers. Responsibility for the war against Persia fell to Constantius II, but he received little assistance from his brothers. Shah Shapur II, a cunning diplomat and strategist, had the advantage. He concentrated his resources on the destruction of Roman fortresses in Mesopotamia, and the recovery of the provinces lost under the treaty of 299. To this end, he repeatedly invaded Mesopotamia, besieging Nisibis on three occasions between 337 and 350.

Shapur failed to take any significant fortresses until the spring of 359, when he conducted a major offensive that climaxed in the siege and capture of Amida.[143]

Constantius II lacked the money and forces to win decisively in Mesopotamia or to launch an offensive against Ctesiphon. His jealous brothers refused to release forces from the Rhine and Danube frontiers. Twice, he faced revolts by the Western army, which proclaimed as rival emperors first Magnentius (350–353) and then his own cousin Julian (360–363). Western soldiers resented transfers to service in the East and objected to laws banning pagan sacrifices. Constantius died en route to oppose Julian, the candidate of the Western army, on May 22, 361. The new emperor Julian, who declared his adherence to the old gods of Rome, inherited the war with Shapur in Mesopotamia.

Julian II, the Apostate, with a united Roman Empire, had the means to end the Persian War. He followed the traditional Roman strategy of invading Babylonia to threaten Ctesiphon. Shapur II would then have to fight a decisive battle or negotiate. Julian also needed a clear victory to uphold the legitimacy of the ancestral gods of Rome. He immediately restored the worship of the gods and withdrew imperial support for Christianity. For the Roman world, the Persian campaign of 362–363 represented a test in divine power. On June 26, 363, Julian died from a mortal wound on his retreat from Ctesiphon. His expedition, conducted in accordance with traditional Roman strategy, had gone awry. Julian's defeat and death proved a turning point for not only strategic rivalry over the Near East, but also the religious allegiances of the Mediterranean world.

When he departed Constantinople in the spring of 362, Julian did not plan to engage in a war of maneuver in Mesopotamia, but rather to march against Ctesiphon in a classic offensive that would compel Shapur to fight or negotiate.[144] He departed Antioch on March 5, 363, crossed the Euphrates five or six days later, and concentrated his army at Carrhae. Procopius and Sebastianus, with a column of perhaps 30,000 men, marched east to defend Mesopotamia against the expected attack of Shapur across the Upper Tigris. Procopius was ordered to cooperate with King Arsaces II (r. 350–368) of Armenia in defending the Bitlis Pass. Julian achieved strategic surprise, marching, within eight weeks, a force of 65,000 men, supplied by a flotilla of 1,250 vessels, rapidly down the Euphrates.[145] By the third week of May, he reached the twin cities of Veh-Ardashir and Ctesiphon. Most fortresses along the Euphrates had been quickly taken or had surrendered. Julian's army encountered few difficulties until it reached the Nahrmalcha Canal that linked the Euphrates to the Tigris River, and so acted as the first line of defense for Ctesiphon. The Persians had flooded the fields, and so the Romans had to traverse inundated fields infested with insects in the scorching heat and humidity of high summer.[146] Nevertheless, the Romans drove the garrison into the city, and fought their way across the Tigris to secure the east bank. But Julian's army found the walls and size of Ctesiphon, perhaps 200,000 inhabitants, daunting. The Roman army only blockaded rather than besieged Ctesiphon, and Persian cavalry and supplies were able to enter the city. On June 15, 363, Julian held a council of war. His senior officers rejected a direct assault of the city and urged withdrawal. Julian was unable to press a lengthy siege (in contrast to both Trajan and Septimius Severus) or to storm Ctesiphon and thus ordered that the flotilla be burned so as to release 20,000 men for siege service. Julian realized his error, but he countermanded the order too late. The burning of the ships panicked the army and destroyed the means to use the Nahrmalcha Canal to supply the army. On the next day, Julian had no choice but to withdraw along the east bank of the Tigris. Persian cavalry laid waste the countryside and harassed the Romans on the march. On June 26, Julian was mortally wounded in a skirmish outside Maranga (near present-day Samarra).

Ammianus Marcellinus, who participated on the campaign, considered the expedition doomed from the start, but he was a pagan historian writing with the advantage of retrospect under Christian emperors. Julian, impatient to demonstrate the favor of the gods, departed Antioch in haste. He committed a strategic error by invading too early in the season. His army marched into the heat of summer rather than through it, as was the case with previous Roman armies. Julian achieved strategic surprise, but he could neither take Ctesiphon nor compel Shapur to commit to decisive battle, while the Roman army languished in the flooded fields of Babylonia. Julian failed as a commander, but he commanded a Roman army divided in its loyalties and lacking in the discipline of the legions of Trajan.[147] The officers and men of the Western army included many pagans who had served with Julian in Gaul. They clashed with the veterans of the Eastern army, which included Christians, who had served under Constantius II.[148] Finally, Shapur II outfought Julian, avoiding decisive battle and awaiting an opportunity to strike. Shapur got lucky, because the death of Julian demoralized the Roman army. The senior officers elected as emperor a Nicene Christian, Jovian, who agreed to territorial concessions beyond Shapur's expectations so that the Roman army could withdraw under safe conduct.[149] Shapur had probably expected that Julian, if he had not fallen in a skirmish, would have steadied his soldiers and withdrawn in good order. The war would have ended in a draw. Julian would not have achieved the decisive victory he wanted, but then again he would have retained Roman positions in Mesopotamia. Instead, for the first time, a Roman emperor was slain on campaign against the Iranian rival.

Under the treaty of 363, Shapur II obtained the first significant territorial gains at Rome's expense. Jovian surrendered Mesopotamia east of the Khabur, including the fortresses of Nisibis and Singara, and the five strategic provinces gained in 299. Shapur took over a superb highway system and fortress cities, which he could use to threaten Roman Syria, and Antioch. His own capital cities were no longer in danger from Roman attack. With the control of the Bitlis Pass, Sassanid armies could invade Armenia from two directions. In 379 or 382, Shah Ardashir III (r. 379–383) negotiated a most favorable partition of Armenia.[150] Most of Armenia passed under direct Persian rule. The shah also gained control of the Dariel and Derbent passes, vital to the security of northwestern Iran. In contrast, Rome made only tactical gains along the east bank of the upper Euphrates and the fortress of Theodosiopolis (present-day Erzurum), which was massively fortified to guard the northern route into Asia Minor. Theodosius I (r. 379–395), by agreeing to this unfavorable partition, acknowledged the superior position of Persia in the Near East. In fairness, Theodosius had little choice, because the eastern Roman field army had been annihilated by the Goths at Adrianople in 378, and he could not risk a war with Ardashir II.[151] Thereafter, Rome was pressed to defend Asia Minor and Syria against Sassanid attack. Rome was also committed to expensive diplomacy and wars by proxy to check Persian ambitions to acquire ports on the eastern shores of the Black Sea. The hitherto remote Georgian kingdoms of Iberia (Classical Colchis) and Abasgia assumed strategic importance for the defense of Asia Minor. These two Georgian kingdoms, linked to Constantinople by the Orthodox faith and the sea, at least preferred Rome to Persia.

Sassanid Zenith and Collapse: Byzantium and Persia, 395–628

In the fifth century, emperor and shah put aside their strategic rivalry because each had to cope with new threats posed by Huns and Hephthalites, dreaded horse archers from the Eurasian steppes.[152] The migrations of these two nomadic peoples across the Eurasian steppes from east to west set in motion other migrations and wars that transformed imperial orders in India, the Near East, and the Mediterranean world for the next 250 years. The Huns, descendants of tribes within the Northern Xiongnu Confederation, subjected the Pontic-Caspian steppes in 370–375.[153] The Huns drove the Goths into the Roman provinces of the Balkans, and so initiated the rapid collapse of the Western Roman Empire after 395. In the early fifth century, the Huns, who held sway over the nomadic tribes on the steppes between the Volga and Dneister rivers, overran central Europe and compromised imperial boundaries along the Danube. Under Attila (r. 433–452), the Huns ravaged imperial provinces in the Balkans, and so damaged the fiscal and military capacity of the Eastern Roman emperors at Constantinople. Attila also threatened to conquer the Western Roman Empire, but he was checked twice, in 451 and 452. Although his death led to the fragmenting of the Hun Empire, Attila assured that the Germanic tribes, rather than the Huns, would partition the Western Roman Empire in 452–476.[154] Therefore, Roman emperors in Constantinople, a massively fortified capital on the Bosporus, faced Sassanid Persia with fewer resources and with far more dangerous foes to the north and west.

In 395–396, the Huns first invaded the Near East via the Dariel and Derbent passes, and ravaged the northwestern provinces of the Sassanid Empire. At the same time, the shah faced an even more deadly foe, the Hephthalites or "White Huns," who ended Sassanid hegemony over Transoxiana and northern India circa 425–435. The shahs appreciated their new warlike rivals; twice shahs hired Hephthalites. Shah Peroz (r. 459–484) employed Hephthalites to oust his brother and usurper Hormizd III (r. 457–459), but Peroz soon had to battle his former allies. In 476, Shah Peroz was captured by the Hephthalites; he was released on promise of a ransom.[155]

In 484 Peroz was slain in battle against the Hephthalites, who then ravaged eastern Iran. Shah Kavad I (r. 488–531), who had spent time as a hostage among the Hephthalites, enrolled them as allies to crush rebels who backed Zamasp (r. 496–498). In 557 Shah Khusrau I (r. 531–579) entered into alliance with Ishtemi, the yabgu and vassal of Kaghan Muqan of the Gök Turks (r. 559–572), who had overthrown their masters the Juan-Juan and rapidly expanded across the Eurasian steppes.[156] In 557–565 Sassanid and Turkish armies defeated and partitioned the Hephthalite Empire, but Khusrau had merely substituted one nomadic foe with a more powerful one.

Between 379 and 502, the Constantinople emperors and Sassanid shahs avoided major conflicts with each other. On several occasions, they entered into cordial diplomatic relations based on mutual recognition of each other as equals. The emperor Arcadius (r. 395–408) concluded an alliance with Shah Yazdegard I (r. 399–420) and named the shah as guardian of his youthful heir Theodosius II (r. 408–450).[157] Shah Kavad (r. 484–531) approached the emperor Justin I (r. 518–527) to act as guardian of his heir Khusrau I (r. 531–579), but the emperor refused and gave the shah a pretext for war.[158] In each case, the emperor and the shah wished to strengthen his weak position at court by an alliance. Twice, Roman emperors assisted legitimate shahs. Zeno (r. 474–491) sent money to assist in the ransom of Shah Peroz from the Hephthalites,[159] scoring a diplomatic success and securing peace on his eastern frontier at little cost, leaving him free to face the Ostrogothic threat in the Balkans. In 590, Maurice Tiberius (r. 582–602) lent an army to Khusrau II (r. 591–628) so that the shah could oust the usurper Vahram Chobin.

These instances of cooperation seem promising at first glance. Frequent exchange of envoys led to a common diplomatic etiquette and cultural exchange between the courts.[160] But this diplomacy failed to promote a deeper understanding, or new ways of dealing with the strategic rivalry. Shahs Peroz and Khusrau II never forgot that they had lost face in turning to Rome in their hours of need. Peroz's successors Kavad and Khusrau I were spurred on to reckon with both Rome and the Hephthalites. Kavad renewed war with Rome; Khursau I entered into a fateful alliance with the Gök Turks to destroy the Hephthalites. In 602, Khusrau II seized on the pretext of avenging his ally Maurice Tiberius, who had been overthrown by mutinous soldiers, to recover territorial concessions made in 590. Therefore, the long peace of the fifth century was not a resolution of the rivalry for the Near East. It was an armistice forced on both powers because each faced greater threats elsewhere, and with reduced resources. The peace did spare Rome a major Persian war. It is doubtful that the Eastern Roman Empire could have survived the onslaught of Huns and Germans and a major Persian War in the fifth century.

The settlements of 363 and 379/382 ended the fighting but not the hostility. Rome resented her territorial losses and obviously defensive position in the Near East. The shahs would press their advantageous position whenever an opportunity arose. In the fifth century, the same borderlands emerged as cockpits for local or regional clashes that could escalate into new wars between Rome and Persia.

First, by the acquisition of the Armenian plateau, later shahs acquired three costly commitments. The shah engaged in an expensive diplomacy to court allies in the Caucasus to guard the Dariel and Derbent passes against nomadic invaders on the Pontic-Caspian steppes: Huns in the fifth century and Turks in the sixth and seventh centuries. Fortifications were constructed south of the Derbent Pass, and Persian military colonies were founded in Albania (Azerbaijan) and Armenia. The cost of defense strained Sassanid finances. Shahs in the fifth and sixth centuries postured, whenever they demanded subsidies of gold from Rome, that they needed the money to pay for the common defense against the nomadic foe.[161] Instead, emperors in Constantinople courted the Turkish tribes on the southwestern Russian steppes as convenient allies against Persia. Persian shahs were also drawn into the complicated dynastic wars and politics within the two Georgian kingdoms of Lazica (Classical Colchis) and Iberia. Persian control of Armenia depended on securing these Georgian lands.[162] Furthermore, the shah desired ports on the eastern shores of the Black Sea. But Iberia and Lazica were remote; they were beyond the capacity of the Sassanids to wage a war of conquest or to impose Zoroastrianism. Instead, the Georgian courts embraced Orthodox Christianity, and were in easy communication by sea with Constantinople. Finally, Sassanid shahs faced the insoluble question of how to maintain control over Armenia.

The shah, unlike Parthian kings, was hated by the Christian Armenians, who looked to Constantinople for aid. Shah Yazdegerd I ruled as a distant overlord and vested real power in the *naxarars* of Armenia. Vahram V (r. 399–420) and Yazdegerd II (r. 420–457) persecuted Christians and constructed fire altars in a concerted effort to convert the Armenians to Zoroastrianism. In 421–422, the virgin empress Aelia Pulcheria, who dominated the court at Constantinople, ordered a Roman army under the sign of the cross to invade Persian Mesopotamia. The fighting quickly ended in a treaty, and Shah Yazdegerd II promised to halt the persecution of Christians. In 428, Yazdegerd abolished the Arsacid monarchy and imposed Persian governors, but thereafter he faced repeated Armenian uprisings. The emperors Theodosius II and Marcian (r. 450–457), who faced Attila and the Vandals, could lend little assistance to the Armenians. In 450, Marcian rejected an appeal by the Armenian rebels under Prince Vardan Mamikonian. On June 2, 451, Vardan and reportedly 60,000 Armenians fell as martyrs against the superior Sassanid army at Avarir.[163] Yet, Shah Peroz had to abandon a policy of enforced conversion to Zoroastrianism because he had to deal with the Hephthalites. The Armenians hailed Vardan Mamikonian as a national hero. Sassanid repression had turned the Armenians into recalcitrant subjects. It also had propelled the development of an Armenian national church. But Rome reaped little advantage. The Armenians never forgot Marcian's refusal to assist. They steadily distanced themselves from the imperial church, inclining to a modified Monophysite theology. At the Council of Dvin in 553, the Armenian bishops (save those in Armenian lands under direct Roman rule) rejected the canons of the Council of Chalcedon (451), and so asserted their religious and national independence from Rome. Armenia remained strategic as ever, but the Armenians preferred neither Rome nor Persia as their overlord.

A second cockpit emerged in the later fourth century: the desert frontiers along the rim of the Fertile Crescent. Emperor and shah had long concluded alliances with Arab sheiks, styled *phylarchs* in Byzantine sources, who policed the frontiers and protected caravans. In the fourth century, Rome and Persia promoted and incited their rival Arab allies to attack each other, but they also agreed to keep the conflicts localized.[164] The Ghassanids, who united the desert tribes from the upper Euphrates to the Red Sea, championed Monophysite Christianity and allied with Constantinople. The Lakhmids, allies of the shah, favored Nestorian Christianity. They ruled an even more effective state from Hira, uniting the desert tribes south of the lower Euphrates and along the southern shores of the Persian Gulf. After 502, the fighting between the rival Arab dynasties escalated, but these clashes were sideshows to the main conflict between Rome and Persia over Mesopotamia and Armenia. It was an unforeseen consequence that proved significant. In these border wars, the future armies of Islam were trained, and, at Hira, the Arabs mastered the statecraft necessary to govern an empire.

In 502, war erupted between Rome and Persia over Lazica when a local clash escalated into a major conflict. The ensuing Persian War (502–507) was the first of five wars that raged until 628. For half this time, Rome and Persia were again at war. The fighting climaxed in the destructive war of 602–628. In 502, Shah Kavad (r. 488–531) declared war in response to objections over interference by Anastasius I (r. 491–512) in Iberia, which was regarded as a Persian vassal. It is remarkable that Kavad initiated the war, because he confronted the Hephthalites on his northeastern frontier, whereas, for Anastasius, the Huns had long passed. The Romans were taken by surprise. The Persians captured Theodosiopolis, Martryopolis, and Amida. By 505, Anastasius's generals had driven back the Persians and had stabilized the frontier; in 507, the war concluded in a seven-year truce that lasted for nearly twenty years. Anastasius ordered the construction of the fortress at Daras, the new base for the field army of the *dux* of Mesopotamia who could threaten Nisibis, which guarded the highway into Persian Mesopotamia. Kavad and later shahs objected repeatedly, claiming that the construction of Daras violated earlier conventions prohibiting the construction of new fortresses. Even more significant was the issue of money. Anastasius bought back Amida at the price of 500 (or 550) pounds of gold, paid in seven installments. Kavad claimed that this money represented arrears in tribute owed by Rome for the Persian defense of the Dariel and Derbent passes. Anastasius rejected any claim to annual payments, which could be construed as tribute to the shah. The imperial court countered with a claim that Nisibis was due to be returned to Rome after 120 years of Persian occupation under the treaty of 363 or in the year 483/484.[165] The shah and the emperor each manufactured grievances to justify war over strategic objectives that had remained the same since the first century BCE: the fortresses of Mesopotamia and Armenia.

In 526, Kavad again declared war, seizing upon the refusal of Justin I to act as his son Khusrau's guardian as an affront to his majesty. Once again, the Roman army in Mesopotamia was taken by surprise. The ailing Justin did not expect war, and his adopted son and successor Justinian (r. 527–565) inherited another costly defensive war in Mesopotamia and Lazica. The situation dramatically changed in June 530. Belisarius, recently appointed commander of Roman forces in Mesopotamia, won a crushing victory over Kavad's generals near Daras, displaying for the first time on the battlefield a tactical genius that would serve Justinian well for the next thirty years. Commanding 25,000 men, he outmaneuvered and destroyed a Persian-Arab field army of 40,000. Inconclusive fighting and the sudden death of Shah Kavad opened the way for a general peace between Justinian and the new shah, Khusrau I (r. 531–579). Both monarchs were ready to negotiate their way out of an expensive border war that would not alter the strategic balance in the Near East. Justinian wanted to secure his eastern frontier so that he could deploy Belisarius and the field army to reconquer the Western provinces. Khusrau faced Hephthalites and the repercussions of his father's suppression of the Mazdakites.[166]

Under the Eternal Peace in 532, Justinian agreed to pay Khusrau I 11,000 pounds of gold—the highest payment ever made by Rome to any foreign power. Justinian played to the vanity and avarice of the young shah, and at the same time insisted that the payment was neither a subsidy nor tribute. In addition, Justinian ordered the *dux* of Mesopotamia to transfer his headquarters from Daras to Constantia (present-day Viranşehir) so that the imperial army did not pose an immediate threat to Nisibis.[167] In return, Khusrau withdrew his forces from Lazica, and agreed to respect Roman frontiers. It was a calculated risk. Justinian needed a secure eastern frontier if he were to pursue his campaigns in North Africa and Italy. Victory in the West would restore Roman prestige and double resources in any future conflict over the Near East. Khusrau gained prestige and money and abided by the peace as long as it was advantageous. Procopius reports that Khusrau sent an embassy to Justinian requesting his share of the spoils taken from the Vandals in 532–533.[168] In 539, Khusrau received an appeal from the Gothic king Wittigis, besieged in Ravenna. The following year, Khusrau, anxious over Justinian's success in Italy, invaded Syria, and sacked Antioch.

Khusrau pursued war and diplomacy as a means to gain glory in the eyes of his nobles and to extort money from Justinian. In aims he differed little from his ancestor Shapur I. In 540 Khusrau deported the 60,000 captives from Antioch who built in Babylonia a new city Veh Antiok Khusrau to celebrate his victory.[169] This Persian War (540–545) war ended in a five-year truce at the price of 2,000 pounds of gold (although fighting continued in Lazica). Khusrau, however, is reported to have extorted an equivalent amount of gold and silver from ransoms collected from Roman cities of Mesopotamia in 544.[170] Justinian renewed the truce in 551 at the price of 2,600 pounds. The historians Procopius and Agathias deplored Justinian's policy of appeasement, a temporary expedient at best, and commented on the avaricious opportunism of Khusrau.[171] Diplomacy and treaties did little to allay suspicions or to promote cooperation between the two great powers.

In 561/562, Justinian and Khusrau agreed to a general Fifty Years Peace that reaffirmed the borders in Lazica, Armenia, and Mesopotamia as they had stood in 502. Justinian agreed to annual payments of 30,000 solidi, but he paid the first seven years in a lump sum (210,000 solidi), and promised in year eight (569/570) a payment of three years (90,000 solidi).[172] In 572, the payments were to become annual. Justinian, at eighty years of age, mortgaged the political capital of his empire to obtain peace on the eastern frontier—his successors would have to render tribute to the shah. The Fifty Years Peace epitomized the emperor's priority, namely the reconquest of the West at any cost. Justinian thus compromised imperial aims in the Near East, and almost assured future Persian Wars. Justinian's conquests collapsed almost immediately after his death so that on every frontier the empire was put on the defensive. Avars, Turkic-speaking nomads, pushed the Lombards into Italy and the Slavs into the Balkans. The Avar kaghans created a version of the Hun Empire in central Europe and on the steppes of southwestern Russia. With the strategic advantage, Khusrau fought limited wars in Mesopotamia and Lazica to win prestige, captives, and gold. He never risked the safety of the Sassanid state. Roman gold paid for his diplomacy and wars against the Hephthalites, but Khusrau compromised his empire by his alliance with the Gök Turks against the Hephthalites in 557.

In 572, the emperor Justin II (r. 565–578) and his wife the empress Sophia refused to pay to Khursau an annual tribute under the terms of the Fifty Years Peace. Byzantine sources, hostile to the emperor, blame Justin's willful pride and then delight in describing his mental collapse and illness the next year. Yet, Justin and Sophia had little choice but to refuse, preferring war over abject humiliation. Khusrau had the pretext to declare war again. This new Persian War (572–590) differed little from the previous three wars.

It was waged on the familiar battlefields of Mesopotamia by three successive emperors—Justin II, Tiberius II (r. 578–582), and Maurice Tiberius (r. 582–602)—and two successive shahs, Khursau I and Hormizd IV (r. 579–590). The belligerents repeatedly agreed to truces, but fighting resumed because neither power was willing to compromise in the interests of peace. Yet, each belligerent lacked the capacity to defeat the other. The situation dramatically changed in 590.[173]

In 590, Khusaru II (r. 590–628) succeeded his father Hormizd IV, and inherited the war with Rome. Khusrau owed the throne to his maternal uncles Vistahm and Vinduyih, who had deposed and blinded Hormizd IV and planned to rule through the young shah. Vahram Chobin, the popular Arsacid *spahbed* (commander) on the Oxus frontier, overthrew Khusrau. Khusrau, a suppliant at the court of Constantinople, requested an army from the emperor Maurice Tiberius, making his famous appeal that Rome and Persia were the divinely ordained two eyes of the world and so should support each other. Maurice Tiberius agreed, because he feared far more the usurper Vahram Chobin, celebrated for his victory over the Turks in 588. In the summer of 591, Khusrau, at the head of a Roman army, crossed into Mesopotamia, rallied supporters at Nisibis, and crossed the Upper Tigris. Khusrau and his Roman allies decisively defeated Vahram Chobin at Blarathon (modern Ganzak) in Media Atropatene. Vahram Chobin fled east to take refuge with the Gök Turks.[174] Khusrau occupied Ctesiphon and was proclaimed shah, but he spent the next ten years of his reign putting down rebellions and battling the Gök Turks.

In return for imperial aid, Khusrau II returned captured Roman fortresses, notably Daras, Amida, and Martyropolis (modern Silvan). Maurice regained the strategic fortresses and lands north of the Upper Tigris that guarded the Bitlis Pass, as well as hegemony over Armenia. Khusrau retained Mesopotamia east of the Khabur, but he renounced all the lands and fortresses acquired by the partition of 379/382, as well as claims to tribute or subsidies from Rome.[175] With a single stroke, Maurice Tiberius had ended a costly border war and regained the territorial position Rome had enjoyed in 63 B.C.E, when Pompey had settled the Third Mithridatic War. It was a stunning diplomatic success. With peace on the eastern frontier, Maurice Tiberius transferred field armies to the Balkans, scored victories over the Avars, and re-established imperial frontiers on the lower Danube.

Khusrau abided by the agreement of 590 because he had little choice. In 591, he ordered that all fortresses and border lands be turned over to Rome before he crossed back into the Persian Empire. The extent of Maurice's success made a new war with Khusrau II likely once the shah had consolidated his position in Persia. To be sure, Khusrau felt beholden to his benefactor Maurice Tiberius, but he must also have resented the fact that a Persian shah in a crisis, for a second time, acknowledged that Persia had needed Rome.

On November 27, 602, the centurion Phocas (r. 602–610), at the head of the mutinous imperial army, entered Constantinople and was crowned emperor. The legitimate emperor Maurice Tiberius, along with his six sons, had been seized and beheaded at Chalcedon while in flight to the east. Maurice Tiberius was a tireless and conscientious ruler, but he had inherited a fiscal crisis and an army battered by decades of fighting and had erred in issuing an order that his army refused to obey. The soldiers had been ordered to winter north of the Danube, in Avar territory, rather than in comfortable billets in provincial cities. The soldiers, resentful of arrears in pay and harsh campaigning, mutinied for a fourth time, but this time they deposed the imperial family and so ended the dynasty of Justinian.[176]

Narses, *dux* of Mesopotamia and commander of the Roman army that put Khusaru II on the throne, remained loyal to the memory of Maurice Tiberius and revolted at Edessa. He appealed to Shah Khusrau II to overthrow the tyrant Phocas. Khusrau seized on the pretext of avenging of his benefactor and championed a pretender impersonating Theodosius, the eldest son of Maurice Tiberius. Initially, Khusrau aimed to regain the territories surrendered in 590, but he quickly discovered that Roman resistance was uncoordinated because Phocas, unpopular with the ruling classes, faced revolts and mutinies. Khusrau thus refused to negotiate with Phocas.[177] In 603, Khusrau invaded Mesopotamia, and captured Daras in 604 after a nine-month siege. With the fall of Daras, Khusrau steadily reduced the Roman fortresses of Mesopotamia in 605–610, while Persian armies campaigned across Armenia, winning over *naxarars*. In 609 (or 610), Theodosiopolis surrendered, so the Persians could invade northern Asia Minor via the Lycus Valley (Kelkit Çayı). In 610, Khusrau extended the Sassanid frontier to the upper Euphrates; Persian armies were free to cross and ravage Asia Minor.

Meanwhile, Heraclius (r. 610–641), son of the elder exarch of Carthage, overthrew Phocas. Heraclius, on several occasions, attempted to negotiate, but Khusrau refused. Between 611 and 616, Persian expeditions commanded by either Shabin or Shahrbaraz (Khusrau's two leading generals) crossed the Euphrates near Melitene and raided across Asia Minor, reaching as far as Chalecdon on the Asian side of the Bosporus. The Persians sacked cities and ravaged the countryside with the intention of committing sufficient damage in Asia Minor to cripple the Roman capacity to wage war. In 613, Shapur shifted his main effort against Syria. In so doing, he transformed centuries of Sassanid posturing as the heirs of the Achaemenid kings into a policy of conquest. The cities of Syria fell rapidly in 613. In May 614, the Persian army under Shahrbaraz burst into Jerusalem, sacked the city, and carried off 35,000 captives and the True Cross. In 618–619, Shahrbaraz conquered Egypt. Khusrau planned to annex Syria and Egypt—his generals appointed officials, issued coinage at Alexandria, and came to terms with Monophysite bishops who resented the Orthodox emperor.[178]

Between 612 and 622, Heraclius was on the defensive against the Persians in Asia Minor, and against Avar and Slavic invaders in the Balkans. The Persian occupation of Egypt plunged Constantinople into a fiscal crisis. Khusrau's rejection of offers to negotiate forced Heraclius to fight first for survival and then for the overthrow of Persia. He drilled a new field army, cut imperial expenditures, and borrowed the wealth of the Orthodox Church, In 624, he took the offensive. In no small measure, Heraclius inspired his army because he personally led expeditions, in contravention of imperial practice since the late fourth century. He chose not to reconquer Syria and Egypt, but instead shifted the fighting to Armenia, and so control of the strategic routes into northwestern Iran. Between 624 and 628 he waged a war of maneuver over vast distances. Details are lacking, but his success speaks well of the discipline and logistics of the imperial army. Heraclius also recruited numerous allies among Armenians, Georgians, and the Turkmen tribes north of the Caucasus.

In the spring of 624, Heraclius rejoined the imperial army at Caesarea (Kayseri) and marched northeast to Theodosiopolis and across the Armenian plateau, capturing the capitals Vagharshapat and Dvin. He pressed down the Araxes (Aras) River and invaded Media Atropatene. Near Ganzak (Takht-i-Suleiman) he put to flight a superior Persian army, reckoned at 40,000 and commanded by Khusrau II himself. Then, Heraclius ravaged northern Iran, destroyed Zoroastrian fire altars, and withdrew to winter in Iberia and Albania (present-day Azerbaijan) where he entered into alliance with the Western Turks. The campaign was stunning. Heraclius, in effect, combined the strategic march across Armenia conducted by Corbulo in 58 with the invasion of Media led by Mark Antony in 36 BCE In the winter of 624–625, Khusrau ordered three armies to move against Heraclius, but the emperor outmaneuvered and defeated each one. In the spring 625, Heraclius rapidly marched southwest, circled north of Lake Van, and crossed the Bitlis Pass. Heraclius then retired along the Upper Tigris and crossed the Euphrates at Samosata into Asia Minor. A Persian army commanded by Shahrbaraz pursued but failed to bring Heraclius to decisive battle. Heraclius wintered at Trapezus (Trabzon), and sent embassies to the *kaghan* of the Western Turks.

In 626, Heraclius negotiated an alliance with the *yabgu* Zeibel of the Western Turks, whose 40,000 horse archers crossed the Derbent Pass to descend on northwestern Iran. Khusrau ordered Shabin with the main army, perhaps 50,000 men, to bring Heraclius to battle in northeastern Asia Minor. In the Lycus valley, Shabin suffered a crushing defeat, and fell in the rout. Meanwhile, Shahrbaraz led an expeditionary army of 30,000 men across Asia Minor to Chalcedon, where he pitched camp and contacted the *kaghan* of Avars, who had blockaded Constantinople. Between July 29 and August 7, 626, Avars and Slavs, reckoned at 80,000, failed to storm the Theodosian Walls. The defenders were inspired by Patriarch Sergius, and the procession of the icon of Mary Theotokos (Hodegetria) around the city walls. On August 7, the imperial navy intercepted and sank Shahrbaraz's improvised transports conveying Persian reinforcements to the European side of the Bosporus. The next day, the Kaghan raised the siege. Shahrbaraz, after wintering at Chalcedon, withdrew in the spring of 627.[179] Thereafter, he assumed a neutral position in northern Syria, and, with aims for the Persian throne, corresponded with Heraclius for a possible alliance.

The Persian offensives in 626 ended in catastrophic defeat; Shah Khusrau had lost his best generals and field armies in a final effort to destroy the Roman Empire and thus alienated the leading territorial lords of his empire. In the spring of 627, Heraclius moved his army from Trapezus to Phasis, descended the Cyrus (Kura) River, and joined his Turkish allies under the *yagbu* Khan Tong. Together, they ravaged Iberia and besieged Tiflis (Tbilisi). In September, Heraclius, perhaps commanding a veteran field army of 30,000 men, conducted a daring winter invasion of Media Atropatene. Heraclius marched to the west of Lake Urmiah, crossed the Greater Zab River, and late in the season smashed the hastily assembled Persian field army under Rhahzadh (Iranian Roch Vehan) on the plains just northeast of Nineveh. The victory ended the war. Heraclius pressed south, capturing the Persian palace at Dastagard, and penetrating to the Nahrawan Canal northeast of Ctesiphon in January 628. Heraclius lacked the manpower and siege train to capture the Persian capital, but the mere threat of a Roman army before Ctesiphon lost Khusrau his throne. Khusrau was deposed on February 25, 628, and his son Kavad II was proclaimed shah by the nobility and army in Ctesiphon. Kavad immediately concluded a peace.[180]

Heraclius regained all imperial territories lost during the war, foremost Syria and Egypt, which escaped the worst of the fighting. Imperial boundaries returned to those of 590, and so once again Rome was master of the Near East. Kavad was required to return all prisoners and the True Cross, as well as pay an indemnity. Heraclius was received in triumph in Jerusalem and

Constantinople, hailed as the greatest conqueror of the Iranian foe. He marked the submission of the shah by assuming as the imperial title (in Greek) *basileus*, previously used to designate the shah. In so doing, Heraclius indicated that the shah was no longer a monarch on par with the Roman emperor. Yet, Heraclius had won a pyrrhic victory, because the two powers had fought a ruinous war of sixteen years that exhausted both powers. The true victors were the Arabs. In 634–641, the armies of the Rashidun Caliphs overthrew the Persian Empire and overran Armenia, Mesopotamia, Syria, and Egypt. The historic strategic rivalry ended in the defeat of both powers. Sassanid Persia fell, and the Eastern Roman Empire survived as a lesser Byzantine Empire. In their place a new world empire, the Caliphate, had emerged.

The Caliphate was destined to fragment between the eighth and tenth centuries. In time, a similar strategic rivalry for the Near East emerged among Islamic powers. After the destruction of the Abbasid Caliphate by Hulagu and the Mongols in 1258, new Islamic powers arose. From the sixteenth century on, Ottoman sultans at Constantinople and Safavid shahs of Iran (representing, respectively, the positions of Rome-Byzantium and Parthia-Persia) clashed over the same borderlands. Ironically, the same strategic aims and competing ideologies drove this rivalry between the Sunni Ottoman Empire and Shi'ite Iran. The rivalry also produced results similar to those of the Roman-Iranian conflict. The Western powers ended the rivalry and created a new order of unstable nation states in the Middle East after World War I.

Conclusions and Lessons

Rome's clash, first with Parthia and then with Sassanid Persia, for domination of the Near East, offers insight to similar conflicts between two great powers. The geopolitical factors of this region have not changed, although the deposits of petroleum and natural gas have increased the significance of the Middle East. These same geopolitical factors will dictate any future conflict between the current Western power, the United States, and Iran. The United States has fallen heir to not only the position of Great Britain, but also that of imperial Rome. US success in the Middle East will depend directly on assessing the power and aims of Iran and the US ability to appreciate and respond to these Iranian aims.

Today many of the same borderlands are at stake. The civil war in Syria (should the opposition forces overthrow Bashar Hafez al-Assad and partition Syria or create a jihadist Sunni state) and the success of the policies of the regime of the AKP in Turkey (should it return the Turkish Republic to an

Islamic, Middle Eastern nation) threaten instability that could escalate into a major conflict. These two developments could result in the secession of the Kurds in southeastern Turkey, and their union with Iraqi and Syrian Kurds into a new nation-state of Kurdistan. This new state would embrace Classical Armenia and Mesopotamia over which Rome and her Iranian foes had fought. This state, besides its strategic position in the Middle East, would control significant energy resources.

Several more general lessons can be drawn. Rome, a power based in the Mediterranean world, was strained to maintain her position in the Near East. Rome defeated Parthia (even if diplomacy rather than Roman arms avenged Carrhae), but the result was the creation of a far more formidable rival. Sassanid Persia forced Rome to reorganize its army and bureaucracy to defend the vital provinces of the eastern Mediterranean. This unseen consequence of victory over Persia in the third century was to transform Rome into a significantly weaker power in the fourth century. The defeat of Julian in 363 put Rome and the imperial army on the defensive. The court of Constantinople thus could not lend significant aid to prevent the collapse of the Western Roman Empire in the fifth century. New Rome, or Constantinople, eventually triumphed, but at a high price, for the final war (602–628) led to the collapse of the entire political order in the Near East of the previous seven hundred years.

Throughout the rivalry, Rome ultimately resolved issues by war, as she had always done in previous strategic rivalries, notably in the struggle with the Samnites for the domination of Italy, or the clash with Carthage and then the Macedonian kings over the Mediterranean world. Even under Christian emperors, Rome held to a patriotic notion of victory, best captured in the pages of Livy narrating the Second Punic War (218–201 BCE). Rome never negotiated except in the wake of victory; victory was the destruction of the foe's ability to wage war; and Rome never waged an unjust war. Yet, even the Republic had to modify its view of Parthia in the wake of the defeat at Carrhae in 53 BCE. Augustus realized that expansion based on victory and unconditional surrender was impossible against Parthia, so he came to a cost-effective solution in 20 BCE. He recognized Arsacid Parthia as a significant, if lesser, power. This arrangement sufficed to secure Rome's interests in the Near East until it was repudiated by Vologaeses I. The limited fighting in 54–66 established a compromise, a new version of the Augustan settlement.

When Oroses I challenged this arrangement, Trajan responded with a strategy of overthrow and a return to traditional Roman policies of decisive victory. Trajan aimed for the annexation of Armenia and Mesopotamia, and the imposition of a pro-Roman king over a rump Parthian Empire in lower Iraq and east of the Zagros. But the Parthians rallied, and rebellions in the new conquests, along with the untimely death of Trajan, led Hadrian to declare victory and withdraw. Subsequent wars, in 161–166 and 197–199, proved that Trajan was correct, and Hadrian wrong, about the precise eastern boundary. With bases in Mesopotamia, Rome assured the security of her eastern provinces and held the Parthian capitals hostage. Hence, these two Roman invasions of Babylonia destroyed the fiscal basis and legitimacy of the Arsacid kings. Whatever the motives of Caracalla in provoking an unnecessary war, he threatened to conduct another devastating invasion, and this sufficed to undermine the Arsacid monarchy.

The ensuing rivalry between Rome and Persia represented a significant escalation over the previous one. Between 229 and 363, each power had to expand its military and fiscal institutions and the powers of its monarchy in order to compete. The shifting fortunes of war ended in Sassanid victory. The treaties of 363 and 379 (or 382) forced Rome to admit that it had lost, and was henceforth on the defensive. Rome also conceded parity to Persia. But the ensuing peaceful coexistence during the long fifth century (379–502) resulted, in large part, from each power recognizing greater new threats posed by the nomadic invaders, the Huns and the Hephthalites. The long fifth century witnessed frequent exchanges of envoys and several diplomatic solutions, but it produced no fundamental changes in the ways of resolving conflicts. It demonstrated a mutual respect, grudgingly admitted by rival powers as a result of strategic stalemate, but it never led to a change of doing business internationally. When the balance shifted in favor of one power, war was resumed. But each power understood the rules. War was honorable, victory desirable (for it conferred legitimacy and profit), and peace (even for Christian emperors) was the gift of victory. There were no appeals to appeasement or other policies promoting peace as the norm, and war as an aberration. The much vaunted pax Romana rested on victorious legions. Above all, neither rival ever really appreciated the aims and interests of the other for all the diplomatic and cultural exchange in the fifth century.

FACTORS BEYOND THE CONTROL OF THE EMPIRES

Though war remained the inevitable means to resolve a rivalry, the war need not have escalated in the seventh century to such a level that both powers were ruined and so weakened that they fell before Arab tribal armies. This outcome resulted from several factors beyond the control of either empire.

First, the threat of the northern barbarians reduced the power of each rival empire. Germanic tribes and Huns in central and eastern Europe threatened

Rome and precipitated the collapse of the Western Empire. Huns and Hephthalites, and then Turks, disrupted the northeastern frontiers of Sassanid Empire.

Second, the wars and plague of Justinian weakened East Rome, militarily and fiscally, and so the renewal of war with Persia from 540 taxed Roman resources. The impact of the plague on the Sassanid Empire is still to be studied, but both rivals had been significantly weakened by the outbreak of the final war in 602.

Third, the escalating ideologies of the rival monarchies from the third century on contributed to repeated outbreaks of wars. The Roman outlook can be traced in detail by how these wars were presented to the Roman public since the late second century. State Zoroastrianism and Christianity (even though most residents did not adhere to either orthodox faith) committed both shah and emperor to ideological aims and positions that led to war. They also hindered shah and emperor from appreciating the other's position and so developing a means of assessing the best policy and its costs in the strategic rivalry. The ruinous war of 602–628 was the result of this ideological clash and the acceptance of war as the means to resolve a conflict decisively in favor of the victor. The surprise was that Heraclius, not Khusrau, turned out to be the victor in this war, even if Heraclius won a pyrrhic victory.

Fourth, timing proved crucial in the collapse of the Persian and Roman empires in the seventh century. Muhammad and Heraclius turned out to be contemporaries, and so the Arabic attacks were timed when the two powers were most vulnerable. Heraclius personally was spent, and plunged into a deep depression after 636. He had won his victory by loans from the church. He faced ravaged imperial heartlands in Asia Minor and the Balkans, and an indifferent or hostile population in Syria and Egypt where he needed to resolve divisions within the imperial church. Given time, he and his successors might have restored imperial power, especially in light of the initial reception of the Ecthesis to unite Christendom in 638. But it was not to be. Timing, put down to divine favor (or disfavor) by the ancients or just bad luck by the moderns, proved decisive. The Arab success was as fortuitous as it was unexpected, and decisive.

France and England, Medieval Period.

CHAPTER 4

A Medieval Enterprise

England versus France I

Kelly DeVries

B Y ALL HISTORICAL LOGIC, England, a kingdom that occupies much of a large island off the northwest coast of Europe, and divided from it by—since at least the eighteenth century—what has rather egotistically been called the English Channel, should not have had the influence it did during any period of history, let alone the Middle Ages. By the beginning of the fifteenth century, it had an estimated population of only one-third that of France, which put it considerably smaller than the Holy Roman Empire, Iberia, or the ever-shrinking Byzantine Empire, and on a par with several Low Countries, principalities, and Italian cities. It was certainly larger than Ireland, Scotland, Scandinavia, or the Baltic Lands, but those in the Middle Ages were considered to be mere fringe—or frontier—lands, which is probably where England should also have been, again if historical logic is applied.

Medieval England's unlikely prominence came about because of its strategic decisions, in particular those concerning France from 1066 to 1453. These were based on three criteria. The first was politics, or, what is now a rather outdated term, *feudalism*, that is, obligation to one's lord.[1] The second was economics, in medieval England's case principally the wool trade. The third was geopolitics, the desire to achieve a European identity rather than an identity as a fringe or frontier state. This latter strategy for medieval England was an important goal, although it would have been impossible had not political and economic strategies also been pursued.

Medieval France, in contrast, seems to have regarded England for much of the Middle Ages as a strategic irritant, but little more. France's more important strategic priorities were with the Holy Roman Empire, Italy, various Low Countries states, and the papacy. Before the Hundred Years War, the French put forth very little strategic effort toward England, with most focused on forcing English royalty and nobility to abandon their lands within France (almost always to the personal profit of the French king). Outside the county of Flanders, French economic connections with England were few, with even less military interest, except in procuring those lands previously mentioned. This changed considerably during the Hundred Years War, but not entirely. Initially Edward III's (r. 1327–1377) claim to the French throne was ignored, but when he proved successful at the battles of Sluys (1340), Crécy (1346), Poitiers (1356—led by Edward's son, the Black Prince), and the siege of Calais (1346–1347), France began to focus more strategic interest on England. Although that interest declined following Edward III's death, it intensified following Henry V's (r. 1413–1422) lopsided victory at the battle of Agincourt (1415) and his conquest of Normandy and Maine (1417–1422). Even then, the French civil war, fought from 1405 to 1435 between the Burgundians and Armagnacs, was linked to and in many ways determined by the conflict with England. After that ended, England once more slipped as a strategic priority, virtually disappearing from French concern following the losses of Normandy in 1450 and Guyenne in 1453. Calais hung on, until 1558, but only barely, and only because the French saw a need in having it as the port for English wool trade.

Historical Context

In 1930, W. C. Sellar and R. J. Yeatman wrote a witty book about English History, 1066 *and All That*. Its chronological range was from Roman times to World War I,[2] even though its title focused on the single date in the history of the British Isles that not only everyone could remember no matter what their class or education, but also could identify as one when things changed—when, in popular perception, the "good" English Anglo-Saxons lost to those "bad" French Normans. That the Anglo-Saxons were themselves continental conquerors of earlier English Celts and that the Normans were pretty far from being Frenchmen, having only settled in Normandy from Scandinavia for little more than a century and retaining much of their "Viking" culture—or that the English and French had stood side by side as allies in the Great War that had just been fought—mattered little to 1930s

English perception. England was changed by William the Conqueror's victory at the battle of Hastings, fought October 14, 1066, an all-day slog.[3] England had, from then on, been forced to deal with France.

In fact, despite the number of errors in such a national historical image—that the invasion of William the Conqueror forced the English to deal with France substantially for the first time—it was accurate. In the millennium before 1066, France and England had traveled in completely different orbits. Julius Caesar in 55 and 54 BCE and Claudius in 43 CE had launched their invasions from France, but these included very few, if any, Gauls and were seen then, and ever since, as nothing other than Roman invasions. Nor, as far as the relatively extensive records reveal, did few Gauls serve on Hadrian's Wall or anywhere else in Britannia during Rome's tenure there. The Empire was perhaps concerned that too much contact between similar Celtic peoples tempted rebellion—which in fact it did when Carausius united Britannia and Northern Gaul, naming himself emperor of at least this piece of the Roman Empire in the decade 286–296, and when Constantine III did the same in the early years of the fifth century.[4] Rome never got Britannia or northern Gaul back after the latter usurpation—and eventually Constantine III removed all of his troops to the continent, with most other Romans following then or shortly afterward.

The Romans may have been gone from Britannia, but they were quickly replaced by the Angles, Saxons, and Jutes, whose conquests began in the latter half of the fifth century, and then by the Vikings, whose raids and conquests were frequent between 793 and 1016. It was these people, the Celtic-Anglo-Saxon-Jutish-Scandinavians, who fought the Normans in 1066.[5]

In between the Romans and the Normans, contact between England and France was not entirely unknown, but it was of little significance. Economic ties were minimal and dynastic marriages few. Of greater importance to England were connections with Scandinavia, the southern Low Countries (especially Flanders), the Holy Roman Empire, and the city of Rome. Genealogy explains the first, proximity the second, perception of power the third, and religion the fourth. Of those, France only brought proximity, and, even then, as Brittany and Normandy, the closest of the French lands, were not populated and had little to trade, the Low Countries offered more at an equal or shorter distance. At the same time, England, with no political unity among its numerous kingdoms, and little economic prosperity, did not offer much to entice the kingdom of France into a relationship.[6]

The year 1066 changed "all that." The conquest of England by Duke William of Normandy (r. 1066–1087) not only placed strategic focus on France, it created an unusual obligatory arrangement in which the sovereign of one medieval state owed fealty to the sovereign of another. The king of England, as duke of Normandy and count of Maine (a French principality obtained by William in 1063), was obligated to the king of France. Rather than fealty, however, William displayed open defiance of the French king, Philip I, while Philip, facing a proven warlord in William, rarely asked for it. In fact, for most of their reigns the two monarchs avoided conflict, choosing to support others in conflicts against their counterpart rather than direct war against the other. The one time they did face off, at the battle of Dol in 1076, William suffered his first defeat, but Philip could not follow his victory with any substantial gains, and the "cold war" status quo quickly resumed.[7]

Nevertheless, William remained acutely aware of the obligatory status his conquest had given to being both duke of Normandy and king of England, and at his death, in 1087, he divided his inheritance, with his eldest son, Robert, attaining the duchy of Normandy, and his second son, William II Rufus (r. 1087–1100), attaining the kingdom of England. It is suggested that such an inheritance was because of Robert's alliance with the king of France, but it might also indicate that to the Conqueror, Normandy was most important, thus going to his eldest son, and England next, to his second son. The inheritance preferences became moot, though, with the unification of both England and Normandy again by William's third son, Henry I (r. 1100–1135), following the death of William II Rufus in 1100 in a hunting accident and Henry's conquest of Normandy in 1103–1106.[8] France remained apart from England during this time, as foe or friend (King Philip I failed to come to Robert of Normandy's aid during Henry's conquest of his duchy, despite their alliance), while England was in too much turmoil to pursue any relationship with, or contention against, France.

This turmoil continued with Henry's death in 1135 without an heir, which threw England into civil war between Matilda, his daughter, then Empress of the Holy Roman Empire, and Stephen (r. 1135–1154), his nephew. Stephen is generally acknowledged as the victor, but when he died, in 1154, the throne was once more empty.[9] This ultimately led to the reign of Matilda's son, Henry II (1154–1189), whose marriage with Eleanor of Aquitaine two years before Henry became king significantly increased their French land-holdings. Beyond Normandy, Maine, Blois, and Anjou (the latter two brought by Henry), their sons would inherit Gascony, La Marche, Limoges, Perigord, Auvergne, Poitou, Brittany, and Touraine. However, with this they would gain an increased fealty obligation to the French king (who, though, at that time held far less land in France than the English king). Louis VII (r. 1137–1180), despite being replaced as the husband of Eleanor of Aquitaine by the English king (with these lands lost as a result) chose to leave Henry largely alone; but his son, Philip II Augustus (r. 1180–1223), who assumed the throne at his father's death in 1180, did not. The result was almost constant conflict between Philip and Henry over English-held lands in France, with much fighting—although no major battles—and little to show for it on either side.[10]

The two sons who followed Henry II to the English throne in 1189, Richard I *the Lionheart* (r. 1189–1199) and, in 1199, John *Lackland* (r. 1199–1216), proved militarily inadequate to hold on to most of their French lands against Philip Augustus. Initially, it looked as if this would not be the case. Richard had been rebelling on and off against his father since 1186, with the support in each instance of Philip. The two, close in age, were known to be friends, which carried into Richard's reign when, following the fall of Jerusalem to Saladin in 1187, they joined in the Third Crusade. With great ceremony, Richard and Philip met together with their numerous troops at Vézelay to begin their Crusade in the summer of 1190. Celebration was shared and oaths of allegiance given, with Philip and Richard sharing equal status on the dais.

But by the time the French and English army met again, in Sicily, bickering between the two armies had begun. Done initially by the soldiers, it quickly grew to include their royal leaders. Both allied again to capture Acre, in the summer of 1191. But that was to be the end of their cooperation. Before the month was out, Philip, ill and fatigued by crusading, retreated to France, his army following in the next few months. Richard remained in the Holy Land for another year, but was unable to recapture Jerusalem against such a formidable general as Saladin. He returned to Europe in September 1192. In the meantime, Philip had taken advantage of the English king's distance by attacking Normandy. These attacks continued after Richard was captured in Austria on his return journey to England and held in captivity until February 4, 1194. Richard would be slain in 1199 at the siege of Châlus in Aquitaine—killed by a crossbow-shooting cook.[11]

Richard was replaced by his brother, John. Without altering his goals following Richard's death, Philip continued to fight for the acquisition of English lands in France. While Henry II had fought to a draw with Philip, and Richard had been able to regain at least some of the lands captured during his Crusade and imprisonment absences, John did nothing but lose to Philip, resulting in large losses of land. Between 1202 and 1204, John lost all of his northern French lands. Then, in 1214, John attempted to recoup those losses by joining the Holy Roman Emperor, the dukes of Lorraine and Brabant, the count of Flanders, and other rebellious French counts in an alliance against the French king. The result was the battle of Bouvines, which was so complete a French victory that Otto lost his emperorship and the counts of Flanders and Boulogne were captured and imprisoned for more than a decade. John lost Touraine, Anjou, and all other French lands of his inheritance, save Gascony. The next year he was forced to sign the Magna Carta, acknowledging to his barons his ineptitude as a ruler and military leader. He died in 1216; he had proven so inept as a political and military leader that there will never be a King John II in England.[12]

While John was incompetent, his son, Henry III (r. 1216–1272), was simply weak. Henry's fifty-six-year reign, the longest of any English monarch until Victoria, was fraught with both military and political rebellions. The battles he won; the politics he lost. By his death, in 1272, the Magna Carta–initiated Parliament had increased significantly in power, with a House of Commons set to join the House of Lords in 1295. Perhaps because so much was going on in England, very little was accomplished (or even attempted) in France: an invasion of Brittany in 1230 brought no results; a rebellion in Poitou in 1241 lost Poitou; and the successful defense of Gascony in 1252 against rebels, supported by King Alfonso X of Castile, bankrupted England. Finally, in 1259, in the midst of a strong baronial rebellion in England, and worried about protecting Gascony, Henry signed the Treaty of Paris with Saint Louis IX of France in which he removed his claim on English lands in France in order to hang on to Gascony.[13]

Henry's son, Edward I, was entirely unlike his father. He was an experienced warrior, who, before taking the throne, fought against English rebels and had gone on Crusade. Initially, it seemed that Edward would simply follow his father's subservience to the French king. In 1286, he did fealty to King Philip IV the Fair, recently crowned as king of France; but eight years later, Philip declared Gascony forfeit to France when Edward refused to repeat that act in Paris. As a result, Edward allied with the rebellious Flemish Count Gui de Dampierre, sending a small army and supplies to the Low Countries. This achieved nothing in the end, however. By 1297, Edward's army had not moved from Flanders. He then reneged on his alliance with the Flemings for a French promise that Gascony would not be threatened and the marriage of his eldest son, Edward II (r. 1307–1327), to Isabella, Philip's daughter.[14]

Edward II's disastrous marriage to Isabella (which officially began in 1308) proved only less disastrous than his military command. Although he defeated several rebellions by dissatisfied nobles, Edward's loss at Bannockburn to Scottish king Robert Bruce in 1314 was one of the worst recorded by any English king. His son, Edward III (r. 1327–1377), usurped his father's throne in 1327.[15] Then, in 1328, following the deaths of Philip IV's three sons and one grandson—which Philip could not have anticipated when he agreed to Isabella and Edward II's marriage—made Edward III, as Philip's grandson, the closest heir to the French throne. So he claimed it. Yet, the French nobles, basing their decision on Salic Frankish Law, that only a direct patrilineal line denoted eligibility to the throne, chose Philip VI of Valois, Philip IV's nephew, as the new French king.

It would not be until 1337, however, that what became known as the Hundred Years War began. The earliest combat resulted in stalemate—the English campaigns of 1337 and 1339 gained nothing, and in 1340, the English won the battle of Sluys, but lost the siege of Tournai. From then on, things went mostly for the English: the battle of Crécy (1346); the siege of Calais (1346–1347); the battle of Les Espagnols sur Mer/Winchelsea (1350); the Black Prince's raid of Languedoc (1355); the battle of Poitiers, with the capture of King Jean II (1356); the battle of Auray (1364); and victory in the Breton civil war by the English-supported House of Montfort (1341–1364). The Treaty of Brétigny, signed between Edward III and Jean II in 1360, validated English land acquisitions since 1339, with Edward agreeing to renounce his claims to the French royal title.[16]

However, after this treaty, English fortunes in the war began to decline. Despite victory at the battle of Nájera in 1367 (with England and France supporting opposite sides in the Castilian civil war), English support failed to put their candidate on the throne, while other campaigns in France either yielded meager results (1370) or were turned back (1372). The Black Prince's premature death in 1375, followed by that of Edward III in 1377, made Richard II (r. 1377–1399) king. Less interested in pursuing war against France, he instead stood by while the Bishop of Norwich, Henry of Despenser, led an embarrassing "Crusade" into the Low Countries in 1383 (which attacked the allied Flemings instead of the enemy French) and then joined English forces to those of the French and other European nobles for the disastrous Nicopolis Crusade against the Ottoman Turks in 1396. During Richard's reign, Charles V (r. 1364–1380) and Charles VI (r. 1380–1422) recaptured much of the land the French had lost before Brétigny. Ultimately, in 1399, Richard II was overthrown by his cousin, Henry IV (r. 1399–1413), who, as a consequence, spent much of his reign putting down rebellions in England.[17]

Henry V's attack of France in 1415, resulting in victories at Harfleur and Agincourt, signaled a more intense English effort to regain lost lands and to reclaim the French crown. He followed this with a conquest of Normandy, Maine, and the Île-de-France, and an alliance with John the Fearless, the duke of Burgundy, then involved in a civil war over control of the frequently mentally unstable Charles VI. (After John's assassination in 1419, his son,

Philip the Good, continued the Anglo-Burgundian alliance.) The resulting Treaty of Troyes in 1420 married Charles VI's daughter, Catherine, to Henry and disowned the dauphin, Charles, making Henry heir to a much older French king. Unfortunately, Henry predeceased Charles by a few months in 1422, leaving Henry VI (r. 1422–1461, 1470-1471), less than two months old and in London, as king of England and France. This inheritance was disputed by the Armagnacs, in support of the disowned dauphin. Still, the English continued to dominate military affairs, eventually winning all the land to the Loire River and besieging the city of Orléans.

This domination began to change in 1429, however, when the siege of Orléans was raised by the French army, with the anomalous presence of Joan of Arc, who followed this up with further victories and the crowning of the dauphin as Charles VII, before being captured outside Compiègne in 1430 and burned for heresy in 1431.[18] Following the crowning of Charles VII, the alliance between Burgundy and England began to break, with the Treaty of Arras splitting the relationship permanently in 1435. The English fought on for several years, but steadily saw their French lands decrease, ultimately losing Normandy in 1449–1450 and Gascony in 1450–1453. For the English, only Calais remained under their control.[19]

Strategic Concerns That Determined English Royal Policy toward France

There were three strategic concerns that determined English royal policy toward France during the Middle Ages: politics, economics, and geopolitics.

POLITICS

Political concerns started when William, the duke of Normandy, launched ships against Anglo-Saxon England. The course of history sometimes turns on the luckiest of events (or unluckiest, depending on the results). William the Conqueror might not have earned that cognomen and the kingship of England had the winds not prevented his sailing across the English Channel when he had planned. Háráldr Hárðárði (anglicized to Harald Hardrada), the king of Norway, and another claimant to the throne, was already on his way to England with an army when William was set to sail. But bad weather on the Channel delayed the Norman fleet until the Norwegians had time to land first in northern England. The Norwegians and not the Normans were the first enemy faced by Harold Godwinson, king of England, having force-marched his army from the southern coast of England, where they were awaiting William's invasion. The Norwegians were easily defeated at the battle of Stamford Bridge on September 25.[20] William landed three days later, precisely where Harold Godwinson expected him to; but at the time, Harold was nearly 200 miles away to the north. He quickly journeyed south to meet the Normans, essentially duplicating the march his troops had made to face the Norwegians. But at Hastings he lost. It is difficult not to wonder whether the Normans would have been defeated had they been the first army encountered rather than the Norwegians. Certainly, had that occurred, the strategic concerns with France during the next four centuries would have been different.

Fealty Issues

As duke of Normandy, William was obligated by fealty to do homage to King Philip I of France. During the Middle Ages there was no uniformity in the obligatory fealty of a lord and vassal at any level of medieval society. In France, legally—although laws regarding the relationship between a king and baron were more traditional than written—a vassal with the status of the duke of Normandy or, later, the count of Anjou or duke of Aquitaine, was required to recognize his lord as king and to provide him military leadership and troops during times of war. When a strong king was on the throne, this simple fealty worked; with a weak king, the more powerful and wealthier nobles often complicated the relationship.

For example, in 1101 the powerful and wealthy Robert II, count of Flanders, agreed to help Henry I, king of England and duke of Normandy, against Philip I, the weak king of France, but Robert's legal lord. (He was Henry's, too, as duke of Normandy, but no homage had been done.) To accommodate this fealty, should Philip attack Henry without summoning Robert, the count of Flanders personally led an army of 1,000 heavy cavalry to Henry's aid. However, should Robert be summoned to assist Philip, he answered the demand for fealty, but only with a force of 20 cavalry, the other 980 assisting Henry against Philip.[21] Philip, knowing full well the strategic weight of this Anglo-Flemish agreement, chose not to invoke it by leaving Henry and Robert alone, which was, no doubt, precisely what they wanted by agreeing to such an arrangement.

The English kings always made their fealty to the French king complicated. William the Conqueror recognized his fealty as duke of Normandy and did homage to the French king as duke before his conquest of England;

he did not recognize the need for fealty as English king.[22] Henry I met with Louis VI once, in 1109, although they stayed on the opposite sides of a bridge spanning the River Epte, and Henry did not do homage as king of England or lord of any of his other lands.[23] Stephen did not do homage to either Louis VI or Louis VII, but did allow his sons, as counts of Boulogne, to do so.[24] Henry II, in August 1149, made an agreement with Louis VII, in which he promised him homage as duke of Normandy. But he was not yet married to Eleanor of Aquitaine, which occurred in May 1152; neither had he gained the English throne, which happened in December 1154. Henry again did homage to Louis, in 1183, but only specifically to acknowledge the king of France as his lord over the newly acquired county of Vexin.[25] Richard the Lionheart never did homage to Philip Augustus; despite their being together so often throughout his reign, Richard and Philip always met on equal ground. John did homage twice to Philip, in 1193, when he was not yet king, and in 1200 when he was. Neither occasion helped, though, as Philip clearly neglected keeping his end of this fealty by taking most of John's French lands between 1200 and 1214.[26]

The Treaty of Paris in 1259 and Its Implications

Henry III, no doubt trying to preserve what few French lands were left him by his father, tried a new strategy with the Treaty of Paris in 1259. Accepting that he had neither the military acumen or forces available to regain what had been lost, Henry renounced English royal claim to Maine, Anjou, Poitou, and Normandy. In turn, Louis IX allowed Henry to retain the title of duke of Aquitaine, although he only controlled the Gascon portion of the Aquitaine lands his grandmother had brought to the throne at her marriage. Henry was also forced to perform homage for these meager concessions.

There is little way not to see the Treaty of Paris as a victory for Louis and defeat for Henry. At a time when his English throne was beset by baronial rebellions, Henry III must have thought his securing peace with France would enable him to fight the rebellions and then return, stronger, to reconsider the concessions he made at Paris. If so, his plan failed: he eventually put down the rebellions, but he never managed to reassert English claims in France.

The Treaty carried repercussions for the next three English kings as well. Henry's son, Edward I, not lacking in confidence as a ruler, nevertheless did homage to Philip IV in 1286, but with the provision that it was only for the "terms of peace made between our ancestors."[27] This was still another decade before marriage could be arranged between Edward's son, Edward II, and Philip's daughter, Isabella, and another two decades before it could be consummated; yet, there is no doubt that without this homage that would not have happened.

It was that marriage, and the child it produced in Edward III, that set in motion what marked the end of the peace brought by the Treaty of Paris and the beginning of more than a century of war between England and France. Edward III became king of England in 1327 and the next year he saw Charles IV, his cousin and last patrilineal male heir of Philip IV, die. Edward was the closest male heir, but he had no patrilineal descent, as his inheritance claim to the French crown was through his mother, even though the daughter of Philip IV. As such, this violated the Salian Frankish law, which seems to have been "dusted off" and applied to this situation. There had been no need to apply the Salic law before, and there is some controversy as to whether it should have been applied at all. But the only complainant against such, Edward III, was in Westminster and not in Paris. The kingship went to a cousin, Philip VI, the count of Valois, who was a nephew of Philip IV through his younger brother, Charles of Valois, and thus patrilineal.[28]

Of course, Edward did not recognize Philip as king of France. Throughout his reign, in communication between the two, he always referred to him as Philip of Valois. So there was never any question as to Edward doing homage, even for Gascony and Ponthieu. The Hundred Years War followed eleven years later.

From then until 1356, four major conflicts were won by the English, the final—at Poitiers—netting the French king, Jean II (r. 1350–1364), among the prisoners. This imprisonment presented a problem for Edward III, however. As he had done with his father, Edward had not recognized Jean as the French king. But now, if he was interested in acquiring a ransom for Jean, he would have to decide whether he was count of Valois or king of France—a significant difference in price. The latter would require Edward to recognize Jean as king instead of himself. In the resulting Treaty of Brétigny, a ransom of 3 million *écus* was negotiated, with the added recognition of Edward's ownership of Gascony, Ponthieu, and all the lands he had conquered in the first twenty-three years of the war. In return, Edward recognized, as stated in the first line of the treaty, that *Jehan {était} par la grace de Dieu, Roy de France*—Jean [was], by the grace of God, king of France.[29]

Land Ownership

What Edward III's agreement to the Treaty of Brétigny shows, it seems decisively, is that fealty was not the greatest strategic concern England had with

France during the Middle Ages. Rather, there is no doubt that it was the ownership of lands in France that held the highest strategic priority.

This was more important than the economic produce gained from these lands. English kings who successfully retained their French lands—Henry I, Henry II, and Edward III—also had fewer problems with their lords. All other English kings faced several rebellions. Most of these failed, but putting them down cost money—funds that could have been allocated to other political and strategic concerns. Noble rebellions depicted English kings as weak, an appearance that French kings, if stronger, exploited.

No French king did this better than Philip Augustus. Philip's initial alliance with Richard the Lionheart's rebellion against his father, Henry II, gained few lands, but built a trust between himself and the soon-to-be English king that he willingly broke during Richard's longer participation in the Third Crusade, followed by Richard's imprisonment the next year. The result was French attacks on all English lands in France. Released in 1194, Richard attempted to defend these lands, with some able generalship, but his death five years later thrust a much less able general with much more noble dissatisfaction, John, against Philip, resulting in all but Gascony falling to the French king.[30] From an English perspective, Philip's actions were the very definition of treachery. But, historically, successful strategy has often been treacherous. The acquisition of these English lands in France increased Philip's personal holdings, and solidified the loyalty of his nobles, who saw by this Philip's incredible strength as a ruler. At the very moment John was signing over much of his power to disgruntled nobles with the Magna Carta, Philip had secured the largest and strongest realm in medieval French history.

The Role of Gascony

Of all their lands in France, Gascony remained most central to English strategic plans and decision-making. Brought to the kingdom in 1152 by Eleanor of Aquitaine's marriage to Henry II, it remained in English hands until 1453. During that time, Gascony is mentioned as an object of concern in every treaty between England and France, and concessions were frequently made to protect its ownership. It was also a favorite for two royals, Richard the Lionheart and Edward the Black Prince, who spent more time there— especially at the capital city, Bordeaux—than they did in England.

Even before he became king, Richard took a special interest in Gascony. His mother certainly encouraged this, but so too did the difficult relationship he had with his father—in concert with his mother and brothers, Henry and Geoffrey, he had revolted without success against his father in 1173–1174.

Henry forgave his sons, but it remained a difficult situation. As long as Henry II stayed in London, Richard stayed in Gascony. As such, Richard was on hand to crush a number of local revolts that might have otherwise developed into larger threats to English control of the region.[31]

Edward, the son of Edward III, was known even in his time as the Black Prince, although the reason is not recorded. Already Prince of Wales at sixteen when he accompanied his father on his 1346 attack of northern France, he was made a knight when the army decamped in Normandy, but did not "earn his spurs," literally in the words of one chronicler, until he commanded the center of the front line at Crécy.

Over the next few years, the Black Prince began to situate himself more and more in Gascony. By 1350, he had begun minting coins in Bordeaux, and by 1355 he had begun operating *chevauchées* (raids) from Gascony into neighboring French-held lands. The first, through Aquitaine and Languedoc, destroyed much of those lands, as the English pillaged produce, livestock, and goods—whatever they could take with them, burning what they could not. The damage caused by these raids, coupled with the Black Death of 1348–1349, devastated military recruitment. It would be a long time before either the French or English could put the same number of men into the field as they had at Crécy. The raids also brought Jean II and the French army south, where he was defeated and captured at Poitiers in 1356.

It was also from Gascony that the Black Prince, in support of Pedro of Castile, invaded Spain and fought the battle of Nájera against the French, who fought for Enrique of Trastámara.[32] (The battle was ostensibly to decide the inheritance of Castile, but is justifiably seen as an extension of the ongoing Hundred Years War.) It ended as an English victory, although little was accomplished. Perhaps the greatest casualty was that the Black Prince came down with a malady that led to a decline in his effectiveness as a military leader—including possibly his commanding the massacre of noncombatants following the siege of Limoges in 1370. A year later, he returned to England, wasting away until his death in 1375.[33]

As the English held Gascony for more than three centuries, could one suggest that the French were less interested in conquering and retaining it than other English lands in France? Evidence against this is the almost constant French attacks into Gascony by the king and neighboring barons throughout most of those years. Some of these attacks won lands, castles, and sometimes even small towns, but almost always the English and Gascons answered with counterattacks and raids of their own. The borders of Gascony were some of the most warred-over marches in medieval Europe. Still, except for when Richard the Lionheart and Edward the Black Prince based themselves in and operated out of the region, the French gained more than they lost in these conflicts. Therefore, Gascony constantly shrank, so that by the waning years of the Hundred Years War the English-controlled land was small, although it always included Bordeaux, the most important city in the region. Finally, in 1453, following the battle of Castillon and the capture of Bordeaux, it would be lost to the English for good.[34]

Scotland and Wales

Another border that saw warfare throughout most of the Middle Ages was that of England and Scotland. Scotland remained a constant strategic concern to England. Generally, however, the English regarded Scotland with little priority and respected the kingdom's sovereignty, although with a military presence in several northern counties and even a few Scottish fortifications. The English also tried to manipulate Scottish political decisions by buying off several Scottish noblemen with English lands, titles, and sinecures.

Even this small amount of military and political interference was often seen as a threat by some Scots. When this occurred, for example with William Wallace at the end of the thirteenth century or Robert Bruce at the beginning of the fourteenth century, or when Scottish raids threatened security or economics, the English military force in Scotland and on the borders increased. Large armies were marched into Scotland, often with the king in the lead. The battles of Bannockburn (1314) and Otterburn (1388) are justly celebrated for being commanding Scottish victories against these armies, but such victories were rare, with English victories at Falkirk (1298), Neville's Cross (1346), Homildon Hill (1402), and Flodden (1513) far outweighing their defeats in determining long-term results.[35]

Scotland always sought allies in these conflicts to compensate for their comparatively smaller population and considerably smaller wealth. Only France gave any assistance, although it was not until 1295 that France formed an official "common enemy" alliance with Scotland. Later called the "Auld Alliance," it lasted until 1560.[36] For most of this time it was lopsided, with the Scots providing troops and "distractions" during the Hundred Years War and the French supplying only economic assistance and military technology.

In the fourteenth century, Scottish assistance to France was largely harassment of the English along the border. It was effective, too. Although claiming the French throne in 1328, Edward III judged that the Scots posed too much of a threat to England for him to immediately go to France. Even after soundly defeating the Scots at the battle of Halidon Hill in 1333, it took Edward another four years to make it to the continent, suggesting that he was still not confident enough to leave his border open to yet another potential Scottish attack.

Despite the Auld Alliance, the French had assisted the Scots very little during Edward's campaigns against them. However, in 1346 when the French asked for Scottish assistance, it was delivered. Victory at the battle of Crécy gave Edward III the impetus to besiege Calais, while defeat meant that Philip VI could not effectively relieve it. He needed something to distract the English or Calais would be lost, and the Scottish king, David II Bruce, provided this by taking an army into England.

David II, probably expected to face only token resistance, as Edward had taken much of the English army—more than 30,000 men—to Calais. Instead, he ran into a formidable army led by wealthy northern-English barons.[37] The resulting battle of Neville's Cross was a disaster for the Scots. David was wounded, captured, and for the next eleven years imprisoned in London.[38] In the end, France's Scottish gambit did not distract Edward's attention, and Calais soon fell.

More Scottish invasions of England followed during the next sixty years. Always these were at the urging and financial assistance of the French. They achieved limited results, however: the 1385 invasion raided the Northumberland countryside, but little was pillaged or destroyed—and Richard II sacked Edinburgh in retaliation; the invasion of 1388 ended in a Scottish victory at Otterburn, but James, the Earl of Douglas and a most capable Scottish general, was killed in the process. The defeat was demoralizing for the English, but little else resulted from it; and in 1402, before a threatened Scottish invasion could take place, the English invaded Scotland and defeated a Scottish army at the battle of Homildon Hill.[39]

This was the last military conflict between Scotland and England for more than a century. By Henry V's reign, the Scottish threat to northern England had virtually disappeared. Scottish soldiers shifted their fight against the English to France. Chroniclers especially note their presence at the battles of Baugé (1421), Verneuil (1424), and the Herrings (1429), as well as with Joan of Arc at Orléans and in the Loire River campaign. They would continue to serve in France until the Hundred Years War ended.[40]

Throughout the Middle Ages, Wales had been every bit as troublesome to England as had Scotland. The difference was that southern Wales especially had a number of easily exploitable natural resources (i.e., tin and slate). So there was a more active strategic interest among English kings to conquer it. By the beginning of the thirteenth century, England had completed subjugating the south, and, by the end of that century, after Edward I had bankrupted the royal treasury to construct fourteen castles and reconstruct three more, northern Wales too came under control.[41]

From then until the end of the Hundred Years War, only one notable Welsh rebellion had to be put down, that of Owain Glyn Dŵr. Owain's rebellion developed during the reign of Henry IV, who set out to put it down with strong military force. The French wished to take advantage of this, which Owain readily welcomed. French voyages and raids along the Welsh coast in late 1403 and early 1404 prompted him to send letters and diplomats to King Charles VI on May 10, 1404, suggesting an alliance between the two. In response, later that year an army of 1,000 men-at-arms and 500 crossbowmen were sent on forty ships from Brittany to assist the Welsh rebels, but they were driven back from Wales by a storm. In 1405 a second expedition, of 800 men-at-arms, 600 crossbowmen, and 200 lighter troops on thirty-two ships, landed successfully in southwestern Wales. They raided the countryside all the way to the borders of England, but then they stopped, not moving for more than a year before returning home without causing further destruction. The reasons for this inactivity are unknown—Owain himself wrote to the French crown to plead for action a number of times during the year, but his letters went unanswered. The short-lived Franco-Welsh alliance had ended by the beginning of 1407. Over, too, was Owain's rebellion. Although he would not die until 1415, the rebellion had dwindled into insignificance long before then.[42]

ECONOMICS

In 1973, an archaeologist, Robin Birley, found a cache of 752 letters written by Roman officials and their spouses living on Hadrian's Wall in the first and second centuries CE. Called the *Vindolanda Tablets* from the Roman fortress where they were discovered, these handwritten sources have revealed the previously unknown lives of lower-level Roman military and political officials residing a long distance from the imperial capital. It was not an easy existence—one of the letters has an early second-century woman writing her Roman relatives to simply "send more socks"—but a necessary one for a man (and his family) who was hoping to move on to a much better (and, in the case of Britannia, warmer) position.[43] These letters exemplify a larger and more significant question about the geographical extent of any powerful state throughout history: Why hold on to the farthest, most isolated frontiers?

Britannia was the farthest, most isolated of Roman lands, and Hadrian's Wall was the farthest frontier of that farthest, most isolated land. Yet, there is no confusion about why Britannia remained part of the Roman Empire for more than 350 years: its natural resources. Gold, iron, copper, silver, tin, and lead ores were all abundant, and all relatively close to the surface. For Roman metallurgy, these were essential materials and were more easily mined in Britannia than elsewhere in the Empire. This more than made up for the costs of transporting it to areas at or closer to Rome for processing.[44]

However, already by the end of the fourth century, the abundance of Britannia's natural resources was in sharp decline. Most easily accessible mines had run out of their metal ores and had been abandoned. It is not difficult to tie this decline to the eventual abandonment of Britannia in the next century. Romans never had much economic foresight, with most needs in Britannia provided from elsewhere in the Empire, rather than building an economy there. Thus, grain and other foodstuffs were barely subsistence, while British pottery and other "industrial" goods were some of the lowest quality in the Empire. When the Romans left, they basically left behind no economy to speak of.

Wool Production and Trade

This is how it remained throughout the six centuries between the Romans leaving and the Normans arriving: subsistence farming and cottage industry. Essentially nothing was made or produced that had value beyond the kingdom William conquered. *The Domesday Book*, William's census of all peoples and goods in his newly conquered lands, is a spectacular document. It reveals that the kingdom was on the whole quite poor. It could do for its needs, but was highly unlikely to make any ruler or his barons rich.[45] The sheep trade changed that.

Sheep could be produced anywhere in Europe. All they need is grasslands to thrive. And all sheep will grow coats of wool that can be harvested at least once a year, and that harvesting can take place from the year after the sheep is born until its death. Because the costs of production are minimal, but the production large and consistent, wool can be a profitable item of trade. The only significant problem is that a sheep will only grow the thickness of wool it needs to stay warm, so sheep raised in more temperate climates produce only thin, short wool. English sheep—for the same reason that the Roman woman on Hadrian's Wall asked for more socks from her relatives back home—grew long, thick coats, which made their wool excellent for medieval cloth.

By whom, why, and when it was discerned that wool would become England's primary commodity to be produced and traded is not known, nor can it be narrowed to a specific region where or time when the decision was made. But, as it coincided with the wool-based economic prosperity of the Low Countries and northern Italian towns, there is likely a connection. It was during the twelfth and thirteenth centuries that these towns grew the most, and it was during those same centuries that English wool production began to develop and flourish. By the end of the twelfth century, it was substantial, with Richard I's ransom paid for by wool subsidies. And, by 1297, half of all English wealth was underpinned by wool production.[46] Wool sales to cloth-making merchants throughout Europe, but especially in the southern Low Countries and northern Italian towns, were also well established.

By this time, too, a certain number of landholders, churches, monasteries, and nobles with lands and foresight enough to produce major flocks began to control English wool production and trade: 5,500 sheep are reported on one Derbyshire estate. Selective breeding also benefited production. Sheep cost the same to feed and maintain, so the goal became breeding for the highest quality wool.[47]

English wool-producing nobles, churches, and monasteries became wealthy, as did the English kings, who recognized early that taxing wool exports could fill their treasuries. The continuation and security of the wool trade became England's major economic strategy from the mid-twelfth through the end of the fifteenth centuries.

Role of the Southern Low Countries

The English wool trade could only thrive if there was a consumer. Although there were other markets for English wool, the most consistently profitable ones were in the larger towns of the Low Countries. Southern Low Countries' cloth-makers excelled in producing large quantities of thick, warm, and full cloth that English wool was perfect for. English wool also had a natural color that allowed dying with the most lustrous, deep, and bright colors, also specialties of Low Countries' cloth-makers.

Low Countries' cloth-makers were divided into several different guilds, representing each of the various cloth-making processes—weaving, fulling (cleaning the wool to eliminate oil, dirt, and other impurities, thereby making it thicker), dying, tailoring—and sometimes specialties including tapestries and lace. The guilds were well organized and powerful, able to quell competition and set prices. But they also instituted a training program for education and established quality standards. This ensured that Low Countries' cloth-makers were the rival of any in Europe, which in turn ensured that English wool producers always had a market for their wool.[48]

In the southern Low Countries, the guilds controlled urban leadership—although sometimes they vied for power among themselves (competition between the fullers and weavers in late medieval Ghent was especially fierce[49]), so there was relatively little difficulty for the English merchants in dealing with urban authorities. However, as there was no single political authority over the various Low Countries states, English wool traders were often forced to deal not only with local but also regional governors and, increasingly in the fourteenth and fifteenth century, royal overlords: France for Flanders, Namur, and Artois; the Holy Roman Empire for Brabant and Hainaut; Holland for Liège, Limburg, and Gelderland.

This necessitated a level of diplomacy above even the most astute wool traders. But, as this was also the time when English kings wanted a larger share of the wealth generated from this trade, they stepped in eagerly. Soon, English alliances, treaties, and agreements generally took into consideration the wool trade and cloth-making industry. When other political considerations forced strategic decisions that might potentially hurt the wool trade, separate agreements and alliances were often sought. For example, in 1340, Edward III allied with numerous states so as to both launch the Hundred Years War against France and replace the wool markets that would be closed to England during the fighting.[50] England also frequently supported rebellions, especially those of Flanders against France, to ensure access to their wool markets: 1212–1214; 1294–1297; 1302–1305; 1323–1328; 1337–1345; and 1379–1385.[51] Similarly, the alliance with Burgundy during the Hundred Years War, 1418–1435, protected the Low Countries' wool markets,[52] but once those rebellions eventually failed—as they always did—and especially after the Treaty of Arras in 1435, when Philip the Good broke the Anglo-Burgundian alliance, England was forced to rely on the mutual economic benefit of the wool trade and cloth industry to both sides rather than on military force or diplomatic acuity.

Placement of the Wool Staple

As English kings began to discover how profitable the wool trade was, they realized that controlling taxation of this trade could benefit their treasuries. Collecting export taxes was not difficult, especially once, starting in 1275, Edward I imposed the "Great and Ancient Custom," a small tax placed on any sack of wool shipped through English ports. The merchants accepted this in return for the royal promise of greater protection against piracy. In times of even greater threats to their ships, during the Hundred Years War, the merchants even agreed to increase this "Custom."[53]

Import duties on the wool still had to be paid, however. By establishing the Wool Staple, which designated port towns through which wool could only be sold to foreign buyers, English kings felt they could raise revenues. The Staple allowed the English king to negotiate for consistent and lower import duties, only partly passing these savings on to the wool merchants, and thus increasing the crown's own profits and control over the trade. The first foreign Wool Staple was established in St. Omer in 1313. It went to Dordrecht in 1338, and to Bruges in 1343.[54]

Acquisition of Calais

It is only in understanding Edward III's economic strategy to protect and profit from the English wool trade that the question about why he did not march on Paris after his victory at the battle of Crécy in 1346 can be answered.[55] His strategy was to acquire a port city through which he could safely and profitably ship English wool to the continent, controlling by himself all import duties on wool. Calais's location was perfect: it was at the shortest distance across the Channel from England and proximate enough to the Low Countries' cloth-making towns to make transporting the wool easy and secure. Calais was also sufficiently isolated that only a concerted military and naval effort would enable its siege and acquisition—the time it took Edward to capture the town confirms this.[56]

Once Calais was captured in 1347, the English king removed all of its French population, replacing them with English colonists, most of whom were associated with the wool trade. The town was established primarily as a wool trading port, and by 1351, the Wool Staple had been transferred to Calais, where it remained until English occupation ended.

The Economic Role of Gascony

While the wool trade was England's most important economic strategic concern from the twelfth century through the end of the Middle Ages, exports from Gascony to England were also important: woad, dyes, and especially wine. Wine was "the beverage of choice" for the noble and wealthy classes throughout Europe, especially in England where consumption per capita was among the highest in medieval Europe.[57] Without a natural production of grapes, all wine had to be imported, with wines from Gascony of especially high quality: 9,000–12,000 tuns of wine were imported into England annually. Gascon wine was also shipped elsewhere throughout Europe—as much as 83,000 tuns in some years—with profits shared by Gascons and English.

By the time of the Hundred Years War, the wine trade was integral to England's economy. Ecological fluctuations—drought or disease—decreased the amount of trade (the severe winter of 1437–1438 dropped English tunage to 5,400), but nothing affected it so much as warfare, which threatened the grape-growing regions, ports, and sea lanes (in 1438 wine exports dropped to 4,000 tuns). Gascony was the final loss of the Hundred Years War for the English. The year before it fell, 1452–1453, 8,700 tuns of wine were imported to England; the year after, imports were negligible.[58]

GEOPOLITICS

Location

Ships were necessary to conquer the island nation of England. The Romans, Angles, Saxons, Jutes, Vikings, and Normans all had fleets. The English Channel and North Sea, which so often protected that kingdom, could also serve as a road for its enemies with strong naval capabilities and determination.

But the contrary was also true: England needed a strong navy before it could participate in European affairs. Before 1066, various English kingdoms built insignificant navies but did not unite in defensive efforts against Scandinavian incursions. Only Alfred the Great built a strong fleet, with which he successfully curtailed Viking activities against his kingdom of Wessex, but his successors did not continue with his strategic naval policies.[59]

This changed with William I's conquest. No doubt due to the means that facilitated his conquest, as well as his own needs to rule both the kingdom of England and the duchy of Normandy, he ensured that a strong fleet was constructed and maintained. Scandinavian invasions stopped and raids dwindled, while trade with northern France and the southern Low Countries proliferated. Succeeding kings followed William's naval policies, and, by the end of the Middle Ages, England could boast of the relatively unhindered ability to transport large numbers of men and goods over the seas surrounding the island and down the Atlantic coast of France to the Iberian Peninsula and into the Mediterranean. In 1497, John Cabot (Giovanni Caboto) in English ships became the first European to land on the shores of North America since the Vikings.[60]

European Identity

The core of medieval Europe, identified as such at least since the time of Charlemagne, was the Holy Roman Empire, France, the Low Countries, and Italy. It was there that could be found the greatest population, the most focused Catholic Church ties, the strongest economies, the greatest opportunity for education, and the largest amount of artistic, scientific, and technological innovation. The Iberian Peninsula and the Byzantine Empire lacked religious connections with the rest of Europe throughout most of the Middle Ages, while Scandinavia and Eastern Europe simply did not have the population or wealth to be a part of that "Europe." Had England continued along the historical path of the Anglo-Saxon period, it is likely that it would have had a similar non-European identity. But the kings of England, starting with William the Conqueror, were determined to be noticed and accepted.

William tried to do it with his conquest itself. Before undertaking his 1066 campaign, he recruited troops from Brittany, Flanders, and Boulogne. Among the latter was Eustace II, count of Boulogne, who, despite being more than fifty years old at the time of the battle of Hastings, served valiantly. William also sought the favor of the papacy and received Pope Alexander II's *vexillum* (standard) to carry with him into England.[61] Victory at Hastings brought him this increase in reputation and a military legitimacy to redefine himself as *rex anglorum* (king of the English), as well as *dux normannorum* (duke of the Normans).

This new regal status was carried into the Crusades, where English soldiers and nobles took part in large enough numbers and high enough positions to further establish their kingdom as a part of "Europe": all of the northern leaders of the First Crusade were related to those two noble veterans of Hastings, William the Conqueror and Eustace of Boulogne—Robert of Normandy (William's son), Robert of Flanders (William's brother-in-law), Stephen of Blois (William's son-in-law), Godfrey of Bouillon and Baldwin of Boulogne (Eustace's sons); on the Second Crusade, English troops were instrumental in capturing Lisbon; Richard the Lionheart took titular lead of the Third Crusade after the fall of Acre in 1191; Edward I was in Tunisia and the Holy Land from 1270 to 1272; and the future Henry IV fought on expeditions with the Teutonic Knights in Lithuania in 1390 and 1392.[62]

However, some negative efforts ironically also improved England's European identity. One of the most infamous was the assassination of Thomas Becket—archbishop of Canterbury—in 1170. When Becket opposed Henry II on issues of the relationship between church and state, he was at first exiled, in 1164. Upon his return, early in 1170, he continued to cause problems for Henry, who, as a result, made an intemperate statement that sent four of his knights galloping to Canterbury to kill Beckett as he prayed.

News of the assassination spread quickly throughout Europe. Even those who knew little about Becket were shocked by the severity and location of what soon became recognized as martyrdom. In record time, on February 21, 1173, Becket was canonized. Within fifty years, the cult of St. Thomas Becket was established, in England and elsewhere.[63] Negative reputation could also enhance a European identity.

But it was the Hundred Years War that forever changed England's image with the rest of Europe. Edward III's defaulting in 1342 on loans from the Bardi and Peruzzi banks, which he had used to fund his 1340 campaign, did not help, as it seemed to confirm that the kingdom was untrustworthy. While the English might win a battle, like that at Sluys, their setback at Tournai also seemed to confirm a pattern of defeat in military conflicts against larger, more stable states.

That changed with the 1346 campaign. Contemporary Florentine chronicler Giovanni Villani commented that Edward III's victory at Crécy brought England into Europe. Moreover, Villani was not the only Italian interested in what occurred at the battle of Crécy: ten different and unique chronicles from throughout Italy written before 1370 record details of the battle.[64]

The English would not win the Hundred Years War. But the loss hardly mattered in terms of their identity as Europeans, as they had been engaged on the Continent for so long that there was no thought within England of an identity divorced from Europe. As the Hundred Years War concluded, England was wracked by civil war from 1455 to 1485—the Wars of the Roses. This conflict tore the nobility to shreds and destroyed two royal dynasties, before ushering in a third—the Tudors. The Tudors may have been the most dysfunctional ruling family in the world's history, but they continued shaping England's European identity, strongly established by that time, into the early modern period.

Was There a Similar French Strategic Interest in England?

Victories at Crécy and Poitiers during the Hundred Years War certainly made France notice England. Before then, French kings never appeared to have the same strategic interest in England as English kings did in France. They fought with great military efforts to acquire English lands in France; Philip Augustus especially showed his generalship by defeating Henry II, Richard I, and John in campaigns, at sieges, and on the battlefield. But, even delivering these numerous defeats, he did not attack England itself. Indeed, concerted French attacks of England were few and halfhearted—for example, Louis VIII's 1215 and 1217 sieges of Dover, and the expedition of 1405–1406 in support of Owain Glyn Dŵr's rebellion. Raids were more frequent, but generally resulted in looting and pillage—for example, in 1338 at Southampton—rather than anything that could be defined as invasion.

The French also turned a blind eye to Channel piracy. Some of it was certainly state-sponsored piracy—for example, Philip VI's hiring of Genoese galleys under Aitone Doria and Carlo Grimaldi to pirate English vessels in the Channel and along the Atlantic during the 1340s and 1350s.[65] But, most piracy was a regional activity, with Norman, Breton, and Castilian vessels frequently named but, for the most part, unaligned to the French crown.[66]

The general strategy of French kings from the end of the eleventh to the end of the thirteenth centuries was simply to react to English military moves—Philip IV's diplomatic dealing with Edward I's invasion in support of Flanders in 1294–1297, for example. This changed with the Hundred Years War, when large armies were raised to stop English invasions, though that is misleading. They were, for the period, truly large armies perhaps, but even those at Crécy and Agincourt were not drawn from the entirety of France. Most English attacks and campaigns were handled by regional forces, even when those armies were royally led. In fact, during the French civil war of 1407–1435, far more of France was involved, either supporting the Burgundians or the Armagnacs, than it ever was against the English.[67]

A large number of southern and southeastern French nobles and soldiers took little to no part in fighting in the Hundred Years War. Some even continued their economic dealings with the English throughout the war, using Gascony or the Low Countries as conduits for trade. An example of these is René of Anjou, who was at times during his seventy-one years (1409–1480) duke of Anjou, count of Provence, count of Piedmont, duke of Bar, duke of Lorraine, king of Naples, and titular king of Jerusalem. Despite being tied to all of those fighting in the Hundred Years War, by fealty, family, or proximity, he stayed largely out of the fighting (except in 1431 at the battle of Bulgnéville, where he fought the Burgundians over the inheritance of the county of Lorraine). He was involved in many diplomatic affairs and intrigues, including giving final approval in 1429 to Joan of Arc's meeting with the future French king, Charles VII, his brother-in-law, and negotiating the marriage of his daughter, Margaret of Anjou, to the king of England, Henry VI (this marriage taking place in 1444). Yet, never was he required to send troops to fight alongside the French, English, or Burgundians; nor was his economy disrupted in any way by financial demands from those sides. By the end of the Hundred Years War, his lands were among the most prosperous in France, and he was among the wealthiest of lords.[68]

Strategic Lessons from the Medieval Anglo-French Rivalry

The history of medieval England and France from 1066 to 1453 teaches several lessons on dealing with long-term strategic rivalries.

The first of these concerns political strategies. This long-term strategic rivalry began in 1066 when England was "founded" with an obligation to France. William the Conqueror (and thus the new king of England) had been duke of Normandy, and as such had a fealty to the French king. It was a rare occurrence, unique at that level of political status during the Middle Ages. Thus, it is highly unlikely that modern states would ever find themselves in the same relationship; however, obligatory fealties have been defined in many ways and have taken many different forms during history. Despite its rarity, this medieval case shows that obligatory fealty is often a complicated relationship: the historical memory, if not the reality, of William's, and later Henry II's or Richard I's, obligations to the French crown was strong. Even though the fealty itself entered stasis at times, when England had stronger royal and military leadership than France, it was revived once that leadership advantage was removed.

This meant that in the strategic rivalry of medieval England and France, all diplomatic and treaty negotiations were conducted with the obligatory relationship clearly delineated—another lesson taught. The king of England was reminded in all negotiations with the French that he was obligated to the king of France. Even during what seemed to both parties small diplomatic negotiations, the French included the fealty owed them, whether it was due on that occasion or not. In the most lopsided of these, the Treaty of Paris of 1259, French success was garnered when they demanded, and received, homage from the English. However, the French king, Louis IX at the time, took advantage of a weak English king, Henry III. Stronger English kings were not so easily defeated in diplomatic negotiations, and repercussions from one success, if taken too far, as with the Treaty of Paris, may have set England on a future course of more bellicose engagements that could have been avoided by a more restrained diplomatic offensive.

What complicates obligatory relationships further is when one state possesses property (loosely defined) that another state claims. From 1066 to 1453, England always occupied lands that the French felt were theirs. These had all been brought to the English throne by inheritance and not conquest, but English kings certainly used military force to protect and retain them.

The two nations constantly fought over these patrimonial lands. Gascony was especially prized by English kings, who expended great military and diplomatic efforts to keep it. Once more, in a modern context it is not likely that the lands of one strategic rival would lie within the boundaries of another—although examples exist. However, one state might feel territorial about what it sees as its property or influence. If a rival also claims this property or influence, peace might be threatened.

A final political lesson from the long-term strategic rivalry of medieval England and France is that when there is a common rival held by two states who are not rivals themselves, an alliance between those states can prove beneficial. France used Scotland especially against England during the Middle Ages; the medieval Scots had such a political vehemence against the English that they required little from the French in their alliance—gladly taking funds, but not requiring French military intervention—and readily gave military assistance whenever required, either via military distractions or soldiers to fight in France.

However important political strategy might be to long-term rivals, as the rivalry between medieval France and England shows, economic strategic concerns are either on par with or superior to political strategies. Trade, then as now, was the most important of these. England's economy had a single profitable product to trade: wool. No doubt economists would suggest that relying on a single product for a country's economic prosperity is risky at any time. The risk was certainly there for medieval England; and yet, perhaps relying on the wool trade focused English strategic decisions in a way that having several trade items might not have. Because of wool, English kings formed a relationship with their consumer states and towns, principally in the Low Countries, that determined their diplomatic and military efforts. They needed these consumers; but, maybe more important, these consumers relied on them for the products. Especially during the Hundred Years War, the English could count on the economic, and therefore political, allegiance of the consumer states—sometimes to the point of rebellion against lords and governors allied with the French.

This medieval English economic strategy may have determined more military decisions than any political concern. Edward I recognized the funds that could be acquired from the taxation of wool exports—and that they would more than pay for the increased military and naval efforts to guarantee the safe transportation of the merchandise. Edward II recognized that funds could also be derived from directing wool imports to a single location, the Wool Staple, thereby negotiating for lower duties—with, of course, the royal treasury receiving a portion of the money saved by the merchants. Finally,

Edward III recognized that he could take advantage of his victory at Crécy to acquire his own continental port, Calais, where he could permanently place the Staple—thereby gaining all import and export duties for the treasury.

Other long-term strategic rivalries exist because both need the single product that a third state supplies. In that case, diplomatic and military decisions need to be made by a state to ensure a continued supply of the product from that third state, either provided at the same or a higher level than their strategic rival.

A final lesson learned from the long-term strategic rivalry between England and France during the Middle Ages is that geopolitics matters, especially to the state that has a geopolitical disadvantage. England's location made it difficult to be included in the European identity. Before 1066, little of Europe cared much about England. William's conquest initially did nothing to change that. But he and his successors strove to be part of the European identity. They built strong fleets of cargo and warships. They called themselves *rex*. They went on Crusade. They even assassinated archbishops (although, in fact, this was not done more than once). Above all, they developed an image by warring with France. With victories against large armies in battles and conquests of important towns in sieges during the Hundred Years War, England entered Europe. The war they would eventually lose, but the identity they retained.

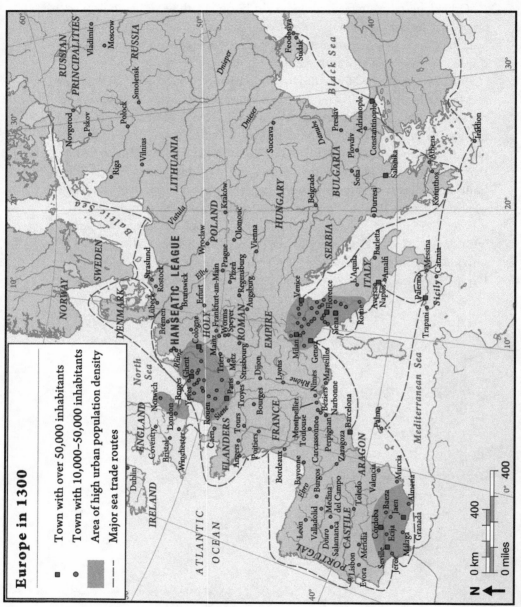

Europe in 1300

- ■ Town with over 50,000 inhabitants
- ● Town with 10,000–50,000 inhabitants
- Area of high urban population density
- – – – Major sea trade routes

ENGLAND — Dublin, Coventry, Norwich, Bristol, Winchester, London, Caen, Rouen, Bruges, Ghent, Ypres

IRELAND

North Sea

ATLANTIC OCEAN

NORWAY · **SWEDEN** · **DENMARK**

Baltic Sea

HANSEATIC LEAGUE — Stralsund, Rostock, Lübeck, Bremen, Cologne

FLANDERS

FRANCE — Paris, Troyes, Tours, Angers, Poitiers, Bourges, Dijon, Lyons, Bordeaux, Bayonne, Carcassonne, Perpignan, Narbonne, Béziers, Marseilles, Nîmes, Montpellier, Toulouse

HOLY ROMAN EMPIRE — Mainz, Trier, Metz, Strasbourg, Worms, Speyer, Frankfurt-am-Main, Erfurt, Brunswick, Augsburg, Regensburg, Vienna

POLAND — Wrocław, Kraków, Olomouc, Prague, Plzeň

LITHUANIA — Riga, Vilnius, Polock

RUSSIAN PRINCIPALITIES — Novgorod, Pskov, Smolensk, Vladimir, Moscow

RUSSIA

HUNGARY — Belgrade

SERBIA · **BULGARIA** — Sofia, Plovdiv, Preslav

PORTUGAL — Lisbon, Évora, Mérida

CASTILE — León, Valladolid, Burgos, Medina del Campo, Salamanca, Toledo, Córdoba, Écija, Jaén, Baeza, Seville, Jerez, Granada, Málaga, Almería, Murcia

ARAGON — Zaragoza, Barcelona, Valencia, Palma

Douro · **Ebro**

ITALY — Milan, Venice, Genoa, Florence, Siena, Rome, Naples, Amalfi, Salerno, Barletta, L'Aquila

Rhine · **Rhône** · **Elbe** · **Vistula** · **Danube** · **Dnieper** · **Dniester**

Black Sea — Constantinople, Adrianople, Durrësi, Salonika, Athens, Korinthos, Feodosiya, Sudak

Mediterranean Sea

SICILY — Palermo, Messina, Catania, Trapani

Iraklion

Suceava

N

0 km   400   400
0 miles   400

Europe in 1300.

CHAPTER 5

To Dominate the Mediterranean
Genoa and Venice
Christine Shaw

THE STRATEGIC RIVALRY BETWEEN the maritime republics of Genoa and Venice played a significant role in shaping the politics and economies of the eastern Mediterranean for more than two centuries in the later Middle Ages. Cooperation between them was possible, but competition, mostly of the commercial variety, easily generated hostility and suspicion and gave rise to four major wars. One of these wars turned into arguably the greatest crisis the Venetian republic ever faced in its long history. Only rarely were the two nations directly contending for the same territory, although their commercial rivalry extended to wherever the merchants of both republics were active, from Flanders to Egypt. It became a strategic rivalry only in the eastern Mediterranean, where it was principally restricted to the lands of the Byzantine Empire, or what had been Byzantine lands, and to the Crusader states of the Holy Land. In these comparatively weak states, princes would grant preferential trading privileges in exchange for military—essentially naval—support. The Venetians and Genoese, with the strongest fleets in the Mediterranean, readily entered into such arrangements, always with an eye to outdoing what privileges their rivals might enjoy.

The Context of the Rivalry

In many ways, Venice and Genoa were evenly matched. Venice was probably the more populous; it was one of the largest cities in medieval Europe.

Estimates of population for medieval cities are always hazardous, but those for Venice (based on military enrollments) are better founded than most: around 80,000 in 1200, double that for the city and lagoon by 1300, but dropping dramatically—perhaps by more than half—during the Black Death of 1347–1349.[1] More speculative estimates of Genoa's population are of around 50,000 in the mid-thirteenth century, perhaps increasing to more than 70,000 before the Black Death, then falling to 40,000 after,[2] but the Genoese could also call on the manpower of their subject territories in Liguria. There was never any suggestion that Genoa was at a disadvantage against Venice because of having a smaller population. In any case, many of the "Genoese" and "Venetians" active in the eastern Mediterranean, benefiting from the trading privileges and fighting their battles, were not natives of the cities. Rather, they were either descendants of those who had settled in the east or were from other ethnic groups who had been accepted as members of their trading communities and shared in their local privileges (but who would not be considered citizens of either Genoa or Venice).

Both were turned toward the sea; Venice had no territory on the Italian mainland beyond the lagoon until the fourteenth century; Genoa was struggling for control over Liguria. Their frontiers were far apart; they were never territorial rivals in Italy. Moreover, they had little trade with each other. Venice aimed to exploit her position at the head of the Adriatic, seeking to dominate the entirety of that sea; Genoa aspired to dominate the Tyrrhenian, but always had to contend with powerful rivals, notably the Pisans and the Catalans and Aragonese. These were territorial as well as commercial rivals of the Genoese, contending for control of the major islands of the Tyrrhenian, Corsica and Sardinia. Venice was not a party to that contest.

Both cities derived their wealth in large part from long-distance trade, because they aimed to become a hub for trade between Mediterranean lands (including Muslim lands) and western Europe. Each strove to gain commercial privileges that would give them a decisive advantage over their rivals, ideally excluding them from specific markets altogether. They did not often achieve that ideal, and then not for very long. It was not in the interests of even the weakest Byzantine emperors or other princes to give exclusive privileges to merchants from any one state.

Nor was it necessarily in their interests to abide by grants of privileges once made. Byzantine emperors and the princes of Crusader states often tried to evade implementing them in full, and there would have to be follow-up agreements, confirming or modifying the original terms. Yet the fundamental superiority of the terms granted to Italian merchants over those that applied to other merchants, including the emperors' own subjects (known generically as "Greeks"), persisted. Such commercial advantages, particularly those enjoyed over local merchants, bred resentment and hostility, increasing the unpopularity of Venetian and Genoese traders. One potent cause of resentment was that they became involved in internal trade within the Byzantine Empire. Greek merchants were discouraged from traveling far afield—the imperial authorities did not want them engaging in political intrigue or picking up heterodox religious ideas—but they were active in local and regional trade, and had to pay the standard 10 percent excise on their merchandise, while the privileged Italian competitors paid lower rates or were exempted.

Venetian and Genoese merchants also played a pivotal role in the crucial Egyptian trade, especially with Alexandria, bringing slaves and forest products from the Black Sea, buying spices that had come to Egypt via the Indian Ocean route, and other goods such as linen and cotton. Neither the Venetians nor the Genoese had any scruples about supplying war materials—wood, iron, and pitch—to Muslim Egypt. Despite this, they were never able to extract such advantageous terms from the sultans of Egypt as they did from Byzantine emperors. It was only from the late twelfth century that Venetians and Genoese (and Pisan) merchants were permitted to have their own separate compounds; before then, they all had to use one in common. The Italian merchants also had to pay taxes and were not permitted to penetrate the internal Egyptian market. As a result, Genoese and Venetians could not vie with each other for superior privileges, let alone try to exclude each other.

In their relations with the sultan, they lacked the leverage that enabled them to drive such hard bargains with the Byzantine emperors and the princes of Crusader states—the sultan had no need of their fleets; the emperors and Crusader princes did. The Crusader states of the Holy Land had no naval forces of their own; and the Byzantine emperors became increasingly unable or unwilling to maintain a sufficiently large fleet to contain the piracy endemic in their seas, let alone to adequately support their armies in war. The Venetians and Genoese made up these deficits, but they generally expected payment for the ships and crews they provided, as well as enhanced trading privileges. Crusading princes and Byzantine emperors wanted naval support, and the trading concessions they granted became political instruments, not the means to secure economic benefits to their states. Indeed, they were aware that the advantageous terms granted to the Venetians and Genoese might be detrimental to their own interests—certainly to the detriment of their own revenues from taxes on trade.

The Genoese and Venetian fleets were the key to their power, and the underpinning of their influence in the eastern Mediterranean. There was no question of either being able to deny the seas to the other. The nearest any medieval naval power could get to controlling the seas was to protect its own merchant shipping and territory and to raid those of its rivals. Still, to secure their positions, both cities kept ships and galleys well armed, and seamen were expected to be combatants. In dangerous times or waters, these vessels also carried complements of soldiers. Larger merchant ships were less maneuverable than the galleys, but could be effective in battle, serving as platforms to deploy missile weapons. The Genoese tended to make more use of the round ships, suitable for carrying bulk goods as well as larger amounts of valuable cargo, while the Venetians continued to use merchant galleys to a greater extent. One major difference between the fleets of the two cities was that Venice built and maintained state-owned galleys to protect merchant convoys and patrol the Adriatic, while Genoa usually relied on hiring private vessels or privately financed fleets to fight its wars. Still, it was easy enough to convert merchant galleys from trade to war, or, in the case of the Genoese, piracy. The Venetian government did not permit Venetians to become pirates; the Genoese government could not stop its citizens from turning to piracy.

The Venetian government was also much more active than the Genoese in directing overseas trade. While much Venetian trade was in the hands of merchants and their agents acting as individuals, traveling where and when they judged best, the distinctive feature of Venetian overseas trading was the system of convoys of galleys provided by the state, protected by escorts. Details of their organization, from their routes to their sailing dates, down to the responsibility of the shipmasters to ensure all the cargo paid due freight charges, and the wages of the oarsmen and armed guards, were decided by the government. The system matured in the early fourteenth century into the *mude*, with voyages of convoys of state-owned galleys leased to private shipmasters organized on a regular basis on major routes.[3] Genoese governments attempted to institute a similar system of organized convoys, but it never became an established practice. When Genoese merchant ships came together in convoys, it tended to be on private initiative.[4]

Similarly, when Venice or Genoa acquired or established colonies or settled trading posts in the Eastern Mediterranean, they governed them differently. Venetian colonies were directly controlled from Venice—so far as inevitable delays in communication over long distances permitted. Genoese colonies were largely self-governing, with only a few officials sent out from Genoa. Some of the most important were acquired and governed by individual families or private consortia (*maone*), over which the Genoese government had little or no control.[5]

In fact, the nature and the strength of their respective governments constituted the major asymmetry between Genoa and Venice. Directly ruled by Byzantium until the ninth century, after they became independent, the Venetians maintained a tradition of highly organized, authoritative government, and prized political stability. Genoa had been held by Byzantium from 538 to around 643, but this period left no discernible trace in Genoese traditions of politics and government. The communal government formed around 1100 never developed an institutional structure, or an ethos of authority, let alone an aura of majesty, to match that of the Venetian government. As a result of irreconcilable factional squabbling, Genoa, against some stiff competition, became a byword in the Middle Ages for political instability—it has been calculated that there were nearly sixty revolts, coups, and other changes of regime between the mid-thirteenth and mid-fifteenth centuries.[6] If the Genoese recognized that some institutions were necessary to protect and regulate common interests, and to represent the city to the outside world, the concept of public good overriding private interest, if not exactly alien to them, was rarely to the fore in their conduct of public affairs. Nevertheless, their pragmatic attitude toward government meant that the communal government could keep going despite political instability. Consequently, when there was a revolt or a change of regime when Genoa was at war with Venice, this did not necessarily mean that the Genoese would struggle to hold their own.

Their rivalry gave rise to four major wars in the thirteenth and fourteenth centuries. Principally naval conflicts, these wars were largely fought in the eastern Mediterranean. They rarely spread to the western Mediterranean—Venetian war fleets rarely entered the Tyrrhenian Sea—and never to Atlantic waters (except perhaps for clashes between their merchant ships if they encountered each other at sea). Neither side could claim clear victory in these wars, or even made decisive long-term gains as a result of them. Such wars punctuated and expressed the strategic rivalry between Genoa and Venice, rather than determining its course.

The Course of the Rivalry

The Venetians, who had maintained close contacts with the Byzantine Empire, preceded the Genoese in exploiting the commercial opportunities in the eastern Mediterranean. In 1082, Emperor Alexius I granted them favorable commercial privileges with total exemptions from customs and harbor taxes, as well as an area of Constantinople, handily situated on the inlet of the Bosphorus (known as the Golden Horn), where they could settle and conduct their business. Previously, foreign merchants had been forbidden to stay in Constantinople for more than three months at a time, and had all been obliged to trade through government warehouses. This was the first time that the emperor had renounced surveillance over any group of alien merchants. These privileges were a reward for aid from the Venetian fleet against the Normans, who, having established a kingdom in Sicily and Naples, were seizing Byzantine territory in the Balkans, aiming to hold both coasts of the Adriatic.

By the end of the eleventh century, Genoese merchants were active in the eastern Mediterranean as well, but Genoa did not become a power in the region until the Crusades. When the First Crusade was launched at the end of the century, Genoese vessels transported the Crusaders and joined in the conquest of the Holy Land. Distinguishing public from private initiative in Genoese participation in the early years of the Crusades is problematic. The communal government was only coming into being at that time, as a series of temporary sworn associations for fixed periods of a few years. Men from the same landholding families who had been prominent in the court of the bishop when he governed Genoa were among the leaders of the early commune and financed and organized the Genoese crusading expeditions. A handful of these families dominated Genoese trade in the Levant until the mid-twelfth century. Only one family, however, the Embriaci, had members migrate to the Holy Land, renting lands and urban quarters that had been granted to the Genoese commune there.[7] Though all the grants of trading privileges and quarters in the Crusader states were in return for Genoese naval assistance, not all of them went to the commune. In fact, the first grant of property in Antioch in 1098 was made to the Genoese who were there, in return for a promise to help defend the city.[8] Baldwin I rewarded Genoese help in the conquest of the Crusader kingdom of Jerusalem by an important grant, which was nominally to the cathedral church of San Lorenzo in Genoa, because that, rather than the nascent commune, still embodied the Genoese state in his eyes. By this concession, the Genoese got one-third of Arsuf, of Caesarea, and of Acre, and of the income from its port, exemption from the tax on commerce, and the promise of one-third of whatever else Baldwin conquered, provided fifty or more Genoese helped in that conquest.[9]

A Venetian fleet helped another Crusader prince, Godfrey de Bouillon, extend his control over the coast, taking Haifa in 1100, and receiving extensive trading privileges. In 1110, another Venetian fleet helped to conquer

Sidon, earning the Venetians a street and market at Acre.[10] Preoccupied with fighting the Normans in the Adriatic and the king of Hungary in Dalmatia, the Venetians did not make another major effort in the Crusades until 1123, when a fleet under the personal command of the doge came to defend Jaffa against attacks from an Egyptian fleet. Having pursued and heavily defeated the Egyptians off Ascalon, they helped to capture the port of Tyre. Before they joined the attack on Tyre, they secured a grant exempting them from all customs duties in the kingdom of Jerusalem and promising them one-third of Tyre, which they were given when the city fell in 1124.[11]

Now the Venetians had better privileges in the Holy Land than did the Genoese or the Pisans, who had also been earning grants of privileges by participating in the Crusades. It is doubtful that these grants were fully implemented. They were much too generous. Had they been properly observed, the Crusader princes would have lost control over their ports to the Italian republics. Consequently, the princes tried to go back on them. When the Crusader states came under pressure from the forces of Saladin in the late twelfth century, however, the princes were impelled to honor, if not to increase, the concessions to the Italian states and their merchants.

Of most interest to the Italians were the coastal cities, with their harbors and their connections to caravan routes along which the precious goods from Asia were brought. Only in such cities were the urban quarters they were granted really used.[12] Intentionally or not, merchants from the different states tended to concentrate their activities in different cities, the Genoese in Antioch and Acre, the Venetians at Tyre, the Pisans in Jerusalem. This may well have helped to prevent commercial rivalry turning to hostility there in the twelfth century, as it did in Byzantium.[13]

Both the Genoese and the Pisans began to challenge Venetian commercial predominance in the Byzantine lands during the twelfth century. The Venetians helped to open the doors for them, by making themselves unpopular with the Greeks through their overbearing attitude, and by crossing the emperors' interests through their ambitions to control the Dalmatian coast of the Adriatic and the harbors on the Aegean. As a result, the emperors were ready to turn to other Italians to counterbalance them. Playing Italian merchant powers against one another was a ploy that emperors would use repeatedly. It would play a significant role in generating and intensifying the rivalries between the various merchant powers.

The Pisans benefited from this policy before the Genoese did, being granted commercial privileges in 1111, which were renewed in 1136.[14] Despite the Pisans still having to pay dues of 4 percent on their merchandise from which the Venetians were exempted, the Venetians were still annoyed by this concession to their rivals, even more when Emperor John II refused to confirm their privileges. In reply, the fleet returning from its triumph against the Egyptians and at Tyre in 1123–1124 spent more than a year in the Ionian Sea, pillaging the Aegean islands and the Greek coast, until the emperor was ready to confirm their privileges in 1126.[15] Renewed cooperation against a Norman assault on the Ionian islands and the coast of Greece earned the Venetians further confirmation of their privileges in 1147, and an extension of their quarter in Constantinople the following year. A clause in the 1148 agreement by which Emperor Manuel I promised to punish anyone protesting about Venetian privileges indicated the resentment these aroused among his subjects.[16] But Venice would not support Manuel in his efforts to take the war against the Normans to Italy, or in his opposition to the Western emperor Frederick Barbarossa, preferring to remain neutral.

As part of his policy to find new allies, Manuel sent an envoy to Genoa to negotiate an agreement—just when the regime in Genoa was instituting a policy of seeking for trading privileges, in Byzantium and elsewhere.[17] Preliminary terms were agreed, with the Genoese being offered the same concessionary rate as the Pisans, 4 percent, and their own quarter in Constantinople, in return for undertakings not to occupy, or help invaders of, imperial territories (except in Syria, still regarded by the Byzantine emperors as rightfully theirs).[18] Angered by the Genoese making a commercial agreement at the same time with his Norman enemies, Manuel refused to proceed to ratification.[19] Not until 1160 were the Genoese allotted a quarter in Constantinople. Eventually, the Genoese quarter (transferred to the other side of the Golden Horn, Pera) would become one of their most important settlements overseas, but it did not get off to a good start. In 1162 the Pisans in Constantinople, backed by the Venetians there and some Greeks, sacked the Genoese quarter and it was abandoned. This was an early episode of a war between Genoa and Pisa, largely fought around Sardinia, that would last until 1175.[20]

Initially, Manuel, offended by the Genoese having made an agreement with Frederick Barbarossa (an important one to Genoa, acknowledging its independent status within the sphere of the Western Holy Roman Empire), would not let them back into Constantinople. At length, goaded by the Venetians' arrogance, he invited the Genoese to negotiate. This time they asked for, and were granted, privileges equivalent to those of the Venetians rather than the Pisans.[21] That was intolerable to the Venetians. Within months of the Genoese returning to their quarter, the Venetians sacked and burned it.[22] In reprisal, in March 1171, Manuel had the Venetians in Constantinople rounded up and imprisoned, and their property confiscated.[23] The Venetians were not slow to react, and a Venetian fleet, under the command of the doge, spent the autumn and winter of 1171–1172 raiding in the Aegean, having seized the island of Chios as a base. During the course of the campaign, many Venetians fell to disease. When this pestilence was brought to Venice by the returning fleet, rioting broke out and the doge was murdered.

In the absence of the Venetians from Constantinople, the Genoese there prospered, only to be caught up with the Pisans in the coup that brought the anti-Latin Emperor Andronicus to the throne in 1182. Genoese ships having defended the defeated regency government was added to a list of grievances Andronicus used to justify slaughtering all the "Latins" the Byzantines could find, or selling them into slavery; few escaped. Finding themselves unable to do without some western merchants and their ships, Andronicus and his successor turned to the Venetians, who began to return to Byzantium in the mid-1180s. Their privileges were confirmed, in return for another promise of naval help against the Normans, in 1187.[24] The Genoese struggled to reach a new agreement with the emperor, but finally did so in 1192, a year after the Pisans had.

Some of the Genoese and Pisan survivors of the 1182 massacres took to piracy, swelling the numbers of pirates who were making Byzantine waters increasingly hazardous for shipping in the late twelfth century. With their own navy too weak to police the seas alone, the emperors increasingly turned to hiring Italian captains and vessels to do this for them.[25] In 1197 or 1198, Pisan vessels supported the Byzantine fleet that captured a particularly troublesome Genoese pirate, Gafforio, whose ships had defeated a Byzantine fleet (under the command of a former Calabrian pirate) sent to deal with him earlier. (A former merchant who had taken to piracy after he felt unjustly treated by the Byzantine admiral, and who had commanded a Genoese ship in the Third Crusade, Gafforio was an example of how easily men could switch from one role to another.) Genoese in Constantinople thought to be Gafforio's accomplices were imprisoned, and the Genoese lost their commercial privileges and their compound, which they did not recover until late 1201.[26]

The Pisans, rather than the Genoese, were the main competitors of the Venetians in the Byzantine market in the 1190s. At one point Alexius III, who came to the throne in 1195, disastrously encouraged Pisans to attack the Venetian quarter.[27] The catastrophic result was that the Venetians decided to participate in the deviation of the main body of the Crusaders on the Fourth Crusade, for whom the Venetians were providing transport, to place a pretender, Alexius's nephew, on the throne. This operation ended in the sack of Constantinople and the installation of a "Latin" emperor, Baldwin, Count of Flanders.

Again under the personal command of the doge, the Venetian fleet played a crucial role in both the assault on Constantinople and the installation of Alexius IV in 1203, and, after he was deposed and replaced by a leader of the Greek resistance to Latin domination, in the bitter fight for the city that ended in its conquest by the Crusaders in 1204. In the election of the Latin emperor, Venetian electors helped to ensure that the leading candidate, Count Boniface of Monferrato, an ally of Genoa, did not succeed. The Genoese made no attempt to challenge the Venetian fleet off Constantinople. Individual Genoese may have been among the thousands of Latins who left the city in 1203 to assist the Crusaders, but there was no conspicuous Genoese contingent among the forces that took it in 1204.[28] Those Crusaders and others who disapproved of the deviation to Constantinople were inclined to blame the Venetians, perhaps because they so obviously became the main beneficiaries. In fact, it was probably not a Venetian plan. That the Venetians ended up becoming the dominant political as well as economic power in the Latin empire was not the outcome of a deliberate strategy.

Naturally, under the new dispensation all their trading privileges were confirmed, with the significant difference that they could now feel assured that they would be implemented in full. Another difference was that in the document drawn up by the Crusaders, as in effect the constitution of the Latin empire, it was stipulated that no one from a state at war with Venice should be admitted into the territory of the empire. Only a quarter of that territory was reserved for the Latin emperor; the rest was to be divided evenly between Venice and the Crusader barons. The Venetians, therefore, had been given a claim to three-eighths of the territory of the Byzantine Empire, including one-third of Constantinople.[29]

The lands the Crusaders allotted among themselves had to be conquered, and in reality much of the territory of the empire came under rival Greek rulers, who set up as "emperors" at Nicaea, inland in Anatolia over the straits from Constantinople, and at Trebizond on the southern shore of the Black Sea. The Venetian colony at Constantinople fitted out their own fleet of war galleys, which defended the city from attack by the Greek empire of Nicaea. Much of the burden of defense of the Latin empire was, therefore, borne by Venice. To defend the empire was to defend their own trade and merchants and colonies, but the burden was a heavy one.[30] Within the territory allotted to it—the lands on both sides of the Bosphorus, extending along the northern and western shores of the Aegean and then across to the Gulf of Corinth to encompass all of the Peloponnese—Venice concentrated on taking coastal towns, harbors, and islands that could provide anchorages along the sea route from the Adriatic to Constantinople. Much of their territory was taken and held by individuals, some of them Venetians who behaved like the other Crusaders, grabbing lands, which they were then regarded as holding in fief from the emperor or from Venice. In the Peloponnese, Venice succeeded only in securing the harbors of Coron and Modon, which became known as the "two eyes" of the republic; all vessels returning to Venice from the eastern Mediterranean were supposed to put in there to share information about pirates and trading convoys.[31] In the Aegean, their main base was the large island of Negroponte (Euboea), but they shared the island with three Crusaders from Verona who had taken it from the Byzantines. Venetian "Romania" (as the lands of the Byzantine Empire were known— not to be confused with the modern-day country of that name) was in effect divided into two spheres of influence, between Venice and the Venetians of Romania. The Venetians in Venice were less keen on the new colonies, with the attendant burdens and troubles, than were the Venetians in the eastern Mediterranean, who were eager to exploit the opportunities and potential wealth they offered. It was the Venetians of Romania who were closely associated with the government of Constantinople, rather than the Venetians in Venice. As doubts about the solidity of the Latin empire grew from around 1220, however, the government in Venice began to establish a stronger hold over the Venetians in Romania, including the colony at Constantinople.[32]

One island that had not been allotted to Venice in the division of the empire, Crete, became pivotal to the supervision and protection of Venetian interests in the region. The doge negotiated its purchase from Boniface of Monferrato in 1204, promising a substantial amount of money and help in acquiring territory in Macedonia, which he preferred to an island he lacked the means to conquer himself.[33] Negotiations had been in train with the Genoese, too, but they were not in a position to promise him such help. Genoa sent a fleet and money to back an attempt to conquer Crete by the Genoese count of Malta, Enrico de Castro (his father-in-law had been granted Malta in fief for helping the Normans). He was successful at first, yet the Venetians were bent on securing the island, so strategically placed at the entrance to the Aegean, and the Genoese had more pressing concerns, being engaged in a war with Pisa. Even after he gave up by 1212, another Genoese, Alamanno Costa, held out until 1217, waging a guerrilla war with the assistance of the native Cretans (who would rebel repeatedly against Venetian rule for more than a century).[34]

As well as trying to hinder the Venetians from taking possession of the lands they had acquired, the initial Genoese response to the establishment of the Latin empire in Constantinople was to forbid their citizens to trade in Romania.[35] This was no great sacrifice; their trade in Byzantine lands had already been dwindling before 1204. Even after the pope, planning another Crusade, incited Venice and Genoa to agree to a peace treaty in 1218, by which the Venetians consented to the Genoese having the same trading rights they had had under Alexius III, and this treaty was periodically renewed, Genoese merchants in the eastern Mediterranean concentrated on the Holy Land, rather than challenging the Venetians in their stronghold in Constantinople.[36]

In the Holy Land, however, relations between the Genoese, the Venetians, and the Pisans became more fractious in the shrunken Crusader states. Military and naval help during the Third Crusade, particularly during the defense of Tyre and the siege of Acre when the city was recovered from Saladin's forces in 1191, earned the Genoese enhanced privileges, including extensive concessions at Tyre.[37] Preoccupied elsewhere, the Venetians had not participated in the campaigns of the Third Crusade, and the Genoese were perhaps gaining the upper hand. Acre, still the center for Genoese operations in what was left of the Crusader states, and more important than ever since the loss of Jerusalem, was the flashpoint. In the first half of the thirteenth century, it was the Genoese and Pisans who fought one another in Acre, in 1222 (when the Genoese quarter was burned down) and in 1249. The major conflict came in 1256. For some years, the Venetians and Genoese had been engaged in a dispute over the property of a monastery that lay between their respective areas of the city. Losing patience, the Genoese seized the disputed property and, with the Pisans, devastated the Venetian quarter. They had the support of Philip de Montfort, lord of Tyre, who expelled the Venetians from that city. A more general civil war began, with the Genoese in one coalition, and the Venetians and Pisans as members of the opposing one. In 1257, a war fleet was sent from Venice with the merchant convoy, which burned the Genoese ships in the harbor of Acre. Reinforced from Venice and Crete, this fleet inflicted a heavy defeat on a Genoese fleet off Acre in June 1258. Forced to abandon their settlement in Acre, the Genoese moved to Tyre.[38]

Soon, however, they turned the tables on the Venetians, sending envoys to the Greek emperor of Nicaea, Michael Paleologus, and making an agreement with him, the Treaty of Nymphaeum, in 1261. It was explicitly stated that Michael was to join the war with Venice and could not make a truce or peace with them without Genoese consent. The Genoese were also to receive his protection throughout the empire, to which none of their enemies (with the exception of the Pisans, with whom Michael was on good terms) were allowed admittance. At his request, they were to supply up to fifty galleys, for which he would pay, to be used against the emperor's enemies (except Genoese allies). Should he take Constantinople—obtaining help to accomplish this was, for Michael, the real purpose of the treaty—the Genoese were to have all their former area there, with the addition of the Venetian fortress and church, if they made a substantial contribution to the conquest. They were also to be completely exempt from customs dues and tolls, on land and sea, for all imports and exports.[39]

In the event, Michael retook Constantinople before the Genoese fleet arrived. Despite this, and because Michael still wanted Genoese support in consolidating his position, he largely honored their agreement, at least at first. The Venetian fleet, which was normally at Constantinople, had been away from the city. On its return, it opted not to counterattack and try to retake the city, but instead embarked what Venetians it could, together with the Latin emperor, and returned to Venice. Michael intended to follow up the success at Constantinople with an offensive on the Aegean and the Balkans against the Latin powers, including Venice, that had established themselves there. While building up his own fleet, he still wanted Genoese naval support. What he got from Genoa was disappointing: the Genoese were more interested in raiding Venetian merchant shipping than attacking Venetian colonies. Genoese fleets in the 1260s either evaded the Venetians or when forced into engagements, at Settepozzi off Negroponte in 1263 and off Trapani in Sicily in 1266, were beaten. On the other hand, the Genoese were probably more successful than the Venetians in getting their own merchant shipping past the enemy and in attacking Venetian merchantmen. Venetian convoys, if reduced in number, generally did get through, escorted by war galleys, although the convoy sent to Acre in 1264 fell victim to the Genoese fleet when the admiral tricked the escort into leaving the convoy to try to hunt them down.[40] Under pressure from Louis IX of France, who wanted Genoese transport for a Crusade, Genoa agreed to a truce with Venice (and with Pisa, after hostilities in the Tyrrhenian) in 1270, each promising to suspend all naval operations against their rival for five years.[41]

Michael had already made a truce with the Venetians in 1268, allowing them back into Constantinople and other Byzantine cities, and recognizing their possessions of Crete, Negroponte, and in the Morea area of the Peloponnese.[42] The problem was that they still desired the restoration of the Latin empire and the predominance they had enjoyed in it, an ambition they would cherish for decades. With some misgivings, they came to accept that the best prospect for realizing this goal was an alliance with Charles d'Anjou, the brother of Louis IX, who had been brought into Italy by the pope to take the kingdom of Naples and Sicily from the heirs of the Western emperor, Frederick II. Having accomplished that, he began planning the conquest of the Eastern empire, taking over the Morea as a first step. In 1281, Venice made an alliance with him, the Treaty of Orvieto, for the recovery of the Latin empire, in which the Venetians were to enjoy the privileges they had had before 1261. Invited to participate in this enterprise, the Genoese understandably refused and sent a galley to warn Michael.[43] The Sicilian Vespers of 1282, the revolt against the Angevins in Sicily, put an end to that scheme.

By then, the Genoese were only beginning to enjoy the full benefits of the position they had been promised by the Treaty of Nymphaeum twenty years before. During that time, their relations with Michael had been troubled. Apart from his dissatisfaction with the performance of the Genoese fleet—he did not feel that he had gotten his money's worth—he was angered by the supposed involvement of the chief official of the Genoese in Constantinople in a plot to restore the Latin empire in 1263. As a result, he sent all the Genoese out of the city to Heraklea on the northern coast of the Sea of Marmora. They were not allowed back to Constantinople until 1267, after Michael had tried and failed to come to an understanding with the Venetians; they were given the quarter of Galata (Pera) on the far side of the Golden Horn.

Complicating the situation was Genoa's involvement in the confrontation of Guelfs and Ghibellines in Italy. Originally used to designate supporters of the pope (Guelfs), or the Hohenstaufen emperor (Ghibellines), these terms also became used to designate local factions throughout Italy. At a local level, especially, but also to an increasing extent at the level of regional politics, the original association of the factions with pope or emperor no longer held true, although they could often still carry that significance. With the advent of Charles d'Anjou as the papal champion in Italy, "Guelf" came to equate to "Angevin" in Italian politics. For much of Charles d'Anjou's reign, the Ghibellines were dominant in Genoa, and Michael sought their support against Charles. In 1273, Charles sent an army to attack Genoa. These troops and his Lombard allies were beaten off, but the Genoese were not anxious to renew the war, and Michael was unable to get their commitment to further operations. A peace between Genoa and Charles d'Anjou in 1276 was followed by the emperor's conclusion of a renewed truce with Venice the following year. When the threat from Charles revived, however, and especially after he made the Treaty of Orvieto with Venice, Michael turned again to the Genoese for support.[44]

Under Michael's successor, Andronicus II, who came to the throne in 1282, Genoese commercial dominance in Constantinople was secured. The populous colony they built up at Pera was surrounded by its own fortifications, which the Genoese looked to strengthen and extend whenever they could. In time, Pera became virtually another city next to Constantinople. A major reason for its growth was the extension of Genoese commerce into the Black Sea. This was a very important development, not only for their merchants, but for Genoese relations with Venice, as the Black Sea became the new focal point of their rivalry.

Byzantine emperors had excluded foreigners from trade in the Black Sea, which was a vital source of supplies for Constantinople, notably for grain from Russian lands, as well as a source of goods carried along the Asian caravan routes. Under the Latin emperors, the Venetians had engaged in limited trade there, being present at Soldaia (Sougdéa) in the Crimea as early as 1206.[45] The Genoese gained their privileges to trade in the Black Sea just during the period when the consolidation of the Mongol khanates in central Asia was bringing political unity to its northern shores. After their devastating conquests ended in the first half of the thirteenth century, Mongol control of the trade routes increased the flow of goods along them. Taking full advantage of this opportunity, the Genoese established what would eventually become one of their most important colonies, at Caffa in the Crimea.[46] When the Venetians were allowed back into the Black Sea from 1268, Soldaia became their main base. Attempts to undermine the Genoese position by diplomatic intrigue with the Mongols were fruitless, and soon abandoned, and Caffa quickly began to outstrip Soldaia.[47] Another important outlet for the caravan traffic, for the route through Persia, was Trebizond, which remained under a separate Greek emperor, though the Genoese established themselves there in 1285. Individual Venetian merchants first appeared in Trebizond in the late thirteenth century, but Venice did not negotiate commercial privileges for their merchants and their own quarter there until 1319.[48]

The Black Sea and the outlets of the caravan routes on its shores became even more important with the fall of the last Christian ports in Syria and Palestine in 1291. Genoese, Venetians, and Pisans were among the defenders of Acre, but none of their states sent any help. Commentators and chroniclers placed much of the blame for the loss of the Holy Land on the Italian merchants and their states. Earlier praise for their skills as seamen and their contributions to the Crusades had already changed to accusations of being dangerous enemies to the Crusader kingdoms. Venetians, in particular, because of the Fourth Crusade and their treaties with Egypt, were accused of putting mercantile interests first, but all them came in for criticism for the conflicts between their communities in Acre. The maritime republics' naval strength and an economic blockade of Egypt were considered crucial for the recovery of the Holy Land. But rather than institute a blockade in Egypt, they ignored the ecclesiastical council's strictures throughout the thirteenth century that banned trade with Egypt. As they provided the Saracens with arms, iron, timber, or slaves, they earned the stigma of being "bad Christians."[49]

Religion did not often enter into Italian international merchants' calculations. They had no qualms about trading with Muslim states or, for that matter, with the schismatic Greeks, which could expose them to ecclesiastical censure and sanctions. The pope had excommunicated the Genoese government and placed Genoa under interdict for concluding the Treaty of Nymphaeum in 1261 with a schismatic Greek emperor against the Latin empire and Venice. Even stronger ecclesiastical sanctions were repeatedly threatened by the popes in the decades after the Crusader states fell. Governments of the western European merchants that traded with Egypt reacted in various ways to these decrees. At first, Venice permitted trade in some products but not others, only suspending convoys to Alexandria completely from 1323, after a papal envoy came to Venice and excommunicated many leading men. The Genoese continued trading, above all in slaves brought from the Black Sea, although the government did issue prohibitions on selling war materials to Egypt. From about 1330, the papacy was ready to sell licenses to trade with the Saracens, and in 1345 papal permission was given for the unrestricted resumption of trade with the Mamluk lands.[50]

Imposition of the prohibitions had enhanced the importance of the port of Laiazzo in Cilicia, ruled by a Christian Armenian king, and an outlet for the caravan route from Persia. It was at Laiazzo that the second Genoese-Venetian war began. After a skirmish off Coron in 1293, during which some Venetian galleys were plundered, the Venetians claimed the Genoese had broken the truce. The next year, they sent a strong escort of war galleys with the convoy sent to Laiazzo, which attacked Genoese possessions in Cyprus and Genoese ships at Laiazzo. Hearing of this, the Genoese at Pera armed a fleet, which headed for Laiazzo. Catching the Venetian convoy unawares, the Genoese captured nearly all the Venetian vessels and much of their cargo. In 1295, Genoa made a massive effort, sending out a huge fleet of 165 galleys, but this returned home without encountering the Venetians. The war became a damaging conflict the following year, with each side attacking the other's colonies, as well as raiding their shipping. The Genoese (perhaps from Pera) attacked Crete, devastating Candia—the Venetian governmental and commercial centre—trying without success to link up with the Cretan rebels. The Venetians, in turn, burned Pera and Caffa, and attacked the valuable alum workings at Phocea in Anatolia, held by the Genoese Zaccaria family.[51]

The last major engagement of the war came in September 1298, when a large Genoese fleet of eighty-seven galleys entered the Adriatic and forced the Venetians to come to battle off the Dalmatian coast at Curzola. Their fleets were roughly equal in strength, and this was the largest battle Venice and

Genoa fought against each other. After hard fighting, the tide turned toward the Genoese, who captured many galleys and prisoners. One Venetian survivor of the battle sailed with a few ships to Genoese waters and got symbolic revenge by a raid on Genoa.[52] Exhausted by the struggle, both sides agreed in May 1299 not to seek reparations and signed a negotiated settlement. Andronicus II, who had become involved in the war when he arrested the major Venetian merchants and the main Venetian official in Constantinople, was not included in the peace treaty. Having run down his own fleet, and without Genoese support, Andronicus could do little to stop Venetian raids and conquests in the Aegean. In the peace he finally concluded with the Venetians in 1302, he had to agree to pay heavy reparations and to cede several Aegean islands the Venetians had taken.[53]

Although the Genoese naval victories over the Venetians at Laiazzo and Curzola did not gain them any lasting advantages, they did achieve a more decisive victory against the Pisans, in the battle of Meloria in 1284. Never again were the Pisans able to equip a war fleet that could match the forces the Genoese could muster. Pisa's power was already in decline for other reasons, from the unsuitability of their harbor for the larger vessels coming into use in the thirteenth century to the threat of the rising power of Florence in Tuscany. The Pisans, however, did not consider themselves beaten after Meloria, so the war dragged on for another four years. Pisan merchants remained active in international markets throughout the Mediterranean and beyond, but Pisa was no longer a player in the politics of the eastern Mediterranean.[54]

The last decade of the thirteenth century and the first three decades of the fourteenth century were a turbulent period in Genoese internal politics, with civil wars between the Guelf and Ghibelline factions. These had repercussions in the eastern Mediterranean when the Genoese in Pera—which had been rebuilt and enlarged—sided with the Ghibellines. When Genoa was under a Guelf regime, Genoese Guelfs were excluded from the Black Sea. Some Ghibelline exiles from Genoa took to piracy, harming the prestige and reputation of the Genoese. Ghibelline attempts to come to an understanding with Venice in the late 1320s were sabotaged by Genoese pirates attacking Venetian vessels.[55] Andronicus II helped the Perans when a fleet was sent from Genoa to bring them to heel in 1323 or 1324. The fleet penetrated into the Black Sea but fell afoul of the Turks at Sinope, whose aid they had tried to enlist.[56]

Andronicus had several reasons for dissatisfaction with the Genoese. For one, the Genoese had left him to fight the Venetians alone in 1299, though their trading privileges were based on Genoa supporting him in war. Then, in 1306, he received only scant support against Catalan mercenaries who began ravaging Anatolia when he was unable to pay them. Furthermore, when he tried to recruit Genoese ships coming from Trebizond, only pirates signed on and were rewarded with the grant of Rhodes and other Aegean islands. As a final insult, Genoese colonists at Pera abused their privileges and involved themselves in imperial palace intrigues.[57] When Andronicus's son, whom the Genoese of Pera had supported against his father, succeeded to the throne as Andronicus III, he adopted a policy of trying to recover some of the territory and authority that had been lost to the emperor. Under this policy, the major Genoese losses were the island of Chios, taken by a Byzantine fleet in 1329, and Phocea, seized in 1336.[58]

Relations between Venice and the emperor, on the other hand, had begun to improve, as the Venetians finally relinquished their dream of restoring the Latin empire of Constantinople. This greatly benefited their trade in the Black Sea, where they gained ground against the Genoese. Having made a commercial treaty with the emperor of Trebizond in 1319, with the grant of their own quarter, they began to send regular convoys there.[59] A truce with the emperor at Constantinople in 1324 lifted restrictions on their commerce in grain, an important source of supply for Venice.[60] Their trading voyages were further extended to the port of Tana, at the mouth of the River Don, which was a Tatar outpost of the Mongol Empire, whose khan granted them a quarter there in 1332.[61]

Naturally, the Genoese did not welcome these developments. Torn by their internecine quarrels, however, they were not at first in a position to react. A Venetian fleet of perhaps forty galleys, sent into the Black Sea in 1328 to exact reparations for damage that Genoese Ghibellines had inflicted on Venetians at Laiazzo, disrupted Genoese trade but went unchallenged.[62] Since the Venetians had first returned to the Black Sea after their 1268 treaty with the Emperor Michael, the Genoese had been concerned that they should not go to Tana, which was nearer than Caffa to the outlet of the caravan routes.[63] Though they had a trading post in Tana before the Venetians, they did not want it to rival Caffa, where they had much greater independent authority.

In the end, neither Genoa nor Venice was allowed to establish any extraterritorial settlement at Tana. And for a brief period, both rivals came together to defend themselves against the khan when, in reprisal for the murder of a Tatar, he expelled them from Tana in 1343. Caffa came under siege, but it was well fortified, and the Tatars retired in early 1344, only to try again in 1346. The Genoese and Venetian governments signed an alliance against the Tatars in 1344,[64] while in the Black Sea the Venetians were invited to base themselves at Caffa. Soon, however, they preferred to make a unilateral agreement with the khan in 1347 and return to Tana, much to Genoese annoyance.[65]

One hazard faced by both Venetian and Genoese shipping in the Black Sea was the establishment of the Turks on the southern shore at Sinope. By the 1330s, all of Anatolia had been conquered by the Turks, and Turkish pirates in the Aegean became a growing concern. Control from Venice over their Aegean fiefs increased, as they turned to Venice for protection from pirates.[66] On the other hand, increasing demands for men and money to combat the Turkish threat fueled discontent in the Venetian colonies.[67] When Simone Vignoso, commanding a privately financed Genoese fleet on the way to defend Caffa in 1346, learned of a plan to occupy Chios for use as a crusading base, he forestalled the Crusaders and took Chios and Phocea.[68] To the Venetians, who had contemplated offering to buy Chios from the emperor, this was a setback.[69]

Like the Venetians, the new emperor, John VI, felt that the Genoese needed to be curbed. After John VI seized power in 1347, the Genoese of Pera recognized the danger and intrigued with the deposed regent and her son. When John began to build a new fleet, to enforce a customs regime, the Peran Genoese blockaded Constantinople and destroyed the new vessels before they could put to sea in 1349.[70] No wonder that the emperor was one of the Byzantines who were convinced that the Genoese were aiming to dominate the seas, denying them to Byzantine ships.[71] Venice was also concerned about the apparent Genoese determination to dominate the Bosphorus and the Black Sea, where the Genoese from Caffa had attacked Venetian shipping after the Venetians had returned to Tana. In 1350, the doge insisted that the freedom of the seas must be preserved.[72] With its population cruelly reduced by the Black Death, Venice found it difficult to arm and man a war fleet. Nevertheless, they managed to send out thirty-five galleys (about half the size of the fleets raised in the late thirteenth century). This fleet surprised some Genoese merchant galleys near Negroponte, capturing ten, a success marred for the Venetians by the crews being more intent on plunder than pursuit of the four galleys that escaped. These four joined other Genoese vessels in the area to raid the port of Negroponte.[73]

Looking for allies, Venice found them in the emperor and King Peter IV of Aragón (whose Catalan subjects were by this time the main rivals of the Genoese in the Tyrrhenian). With the aid of these allies, the Venetians hoped to conquer the Genoese colonies, destroy the Genoese fleets, and blockade Genoa itself.[74] By a heroic effort, the Genoese, whose population also had been severely depleted by the Black Death, managed to send a fleet of sixty galleys to the east. In February 1352, in a savagely fought battle in the

Bosphorus, the Genoese managed to withstand the allied fleet. The surviving Catalans and Venetians withdrew, leaving the emperor little option but to make peace with the Genoese. Pera was given to the Genoese outright, and Greek vessels could only go to Tana with Genoese permission. Fighting shifted to the Aegean, with the Genoese and Venetians trying to capture each other's ships, and to the Tyrrhenian, where a Catalan and Venetian fleet defeated the Genoese off Sardinia in 1353. A fresh Genoese fleet managed to evade them, and to raid in the Adriatic and Aegean. Under orders to avoid battle, the Venetian admiral was wintering his fleet at Porto Longo near Modon in late 1354, when it was surprised and captured by a smaller Genoese fleet.[75]

The Genoese could not exploit this victory, however. Their defeat off Sardinia the year before had sparked renewed factional conflict in Genoa, and they had sought protection and fresh funds by submission to the overlordship of the Visconti lords of Milan. As the Visconti wanted peace with Venice, the terms of the Treaty of Milan agreed in June 1355 left neither Genoa nor Venice with any gains. An agreement not to send a fleet to Tana for the next three years was the most substantial clause.[76]

Ridding themselves of their Visconti overlords the following year, the Genoese still struggled to find political stability within their city. That did not prevent the Genoese in the east from extending their economic and political power—making their primacy over the Venetians in the Black Sea more marked—and consolidating their hold over the islands of the northern and eastern Aegean. These acquisitions were not the result of a strategy coordinated from Genoa, but were due to the initiative of the colonists at Caffa in the Black Sea, and private initiatives in the Aegean.

From Caffa, the Genoese gradually extended their control over the Crimean coast, including in 1365 Soldaia, which had been taken from the Venetians by the Tatars in 1343. Reluctant agreement to Genoese domination of the coast was wrested from the weakened khans.[77] During the war, the Genoese had seized Licostomo, on an island where the Danube met the Black Sea, and from there they built up commercial relations with the lands of King Louis of Hungary, an enemy of Venice. Later in the century, the Genoese of Caffa built up their existing trade with Poland and Moldavia, from a base at Moncastro (Bialgorod), at the mouth of the River Dniester.[78]

In the Aegean, Chios was firmly under the control of the association of shareholders in the *maona* established to compensate those who had financed the fleet that had retaken the island in 1346. Famagusta in Cyprus also came under Genoese control. Cyprus under the Lusignan dynasty, and in particular the port of Famagusta, after the fall of the Crusader states in Syria and Palestine, had been an important node in the network of trade routes for Christian merchants in the eastern Mediterranean. Both Genoese and Venetians had commercial privileges there. Although the kings of Cyprus avoided overtly favoring either, their relations with the Venetians tended to be better than with the Genoese. Fighting between the Venetians and the Genoese during the celebrations for the coronation of Peter II in 1372 developed into an anti-Genoese riot. Genoese merchants were killed and their goods plundered. In retaliation, a largely privately financed fleet was sent from Genoa in 1373. They captured Famagusta along with the king, who was forced to promise huge reparations to the Genoese, giving Famagusta to them as surety. No help had been given to the king by the Venetians. The Genoese had won a prize—Famagusta—of diminishing value, as Cyprus's significance as a commercial center was on the wane. This was a result of the growing insecurity of the overland caravan routes from Asia, which made the route via the Red Sea and Egypt more important. (King Peter I's attempt to reassert the centrality of Cyprus by launching an attack on Alexandria in 1365 had annoyed the Venetians and the Genoese, who collaborated in negotiating the return of western merchants to Egypt.) While the Venetians still had interests in the island, their merchant convoys took to avoiding Cyprus, going directly to Syria, Palestine, and Egypt.[79]

Nevertheless, these developments in Cyprus made more significant the competition between the Venetians and Genoese for Tenedos, near the mouth of the Dardanelles (each had been given a claim to the island by rival claimants to the imperial throne). The Venetians, who had been seeking possession of Tenedos for decades, sent a war fleet of ten galleys to Constantinople in 1376 to demand it be ceded to them, then occupied and fortified it.[80] In 1377, Genoa sent ten galleys to fight for the island.[81] Due to the continuing effects of the plague, both sides were still fielding much smaller fleets than in the late thirteenth century. After the king of Hungary had captured Dalmatia, depriving Venice of rich recruiting grounds for oarsmen, Genoa agreed an alliance, and provided him with some vessels, at his expense. This made it possible for the Genoese to take the war into the Adriatic again. Another useful alliance was made with Francesco Carrara, the lord of Padua, who threatened Venice from the land. Moreover, by making a treaty with the king of Aragón, the Genoese managed to deprive Venice of one potential ally, but the Venetians found another in Bernabo Visconti, lord of Milan (and enemy of Francesco Carrara). Milan also helped broker a military alliance between Venice and Peter II of Cyprus.[82]

The Cypriot alliance stipulated that Venice should help Peter recover Famagusta from the Genoese, but the attempt, backed by a Venetian fleet, in 1378 failed.[83] Fourteen Venetian galleys sent into the Tyrrhenian had better luck, defeating the Genoese fleet sent to intercept them. Undeterred, Genoa sent another fleet into the Adriatic, which wintered near Venice. The Venetians hoped to draw it away by dispatching some galleys in the spring of 1379 to attack Genoese merchant shipping, but in May the Genoese defeated the Venetian Adriatic fleet off Pola (Istria). Then, after being reinforced, the Genoese galleys blockaded and attacked Venice from the sea, while the king of Hungary and Carrara blocked the land routes to Venice. In August, the Genoese and Paduan forces took Chioggia, a Venetian settlement on the lagoon; the Venetians blockaded Chioggia in turn. Almost simultaneously, Milanese-backed forces threatened the city of Genoa, and the Venetians encouraged the Greeks and the Turks to attack Pera. Both of these assaults were beaten off, and the Genoese stubbornly held out in Chioggia until June 1380. Once Chioggia was recaptured, the Venetians claimed victory. As both sides were exhausted, Venice did not push for harsh terms in the Peace of Turin in 1381.[84]

That was the last major war between Venice and Genoa. It had been costly for both. Neither had gained definitive, lasting supremacy over the other during their long rivalry. Genoese and Venetians continued to be hostile to each other, but neither wanted another war. For instance, when a Genoese fleet was worsted in an encounter with the Venetian fleet off Modon in 1403, the Genoese decided it would be pointless to start another war, and persisted in negotiating peace with Venice. A final settlement was not reached until 1410, after an occupying French army had been driven out of Genoa.[85] Political changes in the eastern Mediterranean and the Black Sea, and associated changes to the patterns and conditions of trade, meant that both sides were forced to adjust their strategic policies and priorities. It was no longer a question of who could dominate international trade in the eastern Mediterranean and the Black Sea; in the fifteenth century it became a question of whether, and under what conditions, they could continue to operate in those markets at all.

The crucial variable keys were the declining importance of the Black Sea trade due to the disruption of the Asian caravan routes from Asia, and the rise of the Ottoman Turks. Despite the increasingly difficult trading conditions in the Black Sea, both the Venetians and the Genoese considered their trade there too valuable to abandon. Both were ready to come to terms with the Turks if they could to protect it. They did not, however, identify the Turks as a common enemy, or unite in trying to oppose or contain them, as a shared strategic interest. The Venetians had more reason than the Genoese to fight the Turks, as from the mid-fourteenth century the Ottomans had moved deep into the Balkans, increasing the pressure on what little was left of the Byzantine Empire. Venice reacted by adopting a policy of acquiring territory inland in the Balkans, wanting to block Ottoman expansion to the Adriatic, and reasserted control over Dalmatia from 1409, defeating the king of Hungary in the subsequent war. In a parallel development, the Venetians also began to expand their dominions in the Italian mainland, in a bid to keep the overland routes to their important markets over the Alps out of the hands of hostile lords.

When Constantinople fell to the Ottomans in 1453, individual Venetians and Genoese were among its last defenders. As the threat to the city grew in the early 1450s, Venice and Genoa alike recognized the danger to their interests. The Venetians organized a fleet, but the captain's primary instructions were to mediate; only if that failed, was it to be used to defend Constantinople. In the event, the city fell while the fleet was on its way. A treaty was then negotiated with the sultan Mehmed in 1454, permitting the re-establishment of the Venetian settlement there.[86] The Genoese in Pera submitted to the Turks and stayed on. Other Genoese colonies and trading posts in the Black Sea were taken over by the Turks, one by one, as were the Venetian trading posts. Genoese and Venetians alike struggled to continue trading there.

The number of Genoese colonies in the east fell precipitously, with only their hold on Chios remaining until 1566. On the other hand, Venetian trade with the Muslim East, particularly with Egypt, flourished, despite Venice fighting a series of wars with the Turks, in an eventually unsuccessful attempt to hold on to its position in the Aegean. In order to keep their colonies and harbors there, the Venetians were ready to pay tribute to the Turks. Had the Turks been content to accept this and to leave Venice in undisturbed possession of the colonies, Venice might well not have become engaged in that new strategic rivalry with the Turks. For their part, the Genoese turned their attention to developing their interests in the western Mediterranean and the Atlantic, exploiting the new opportunities opening up there far more vigorously than did the Venetians.

The Character of the Rivalry

The strategic rivalry between Venice and Genoa was a commercial rivalry between two, in many ways, similar, evenly matched maritime republics. Its character as a commercial rivalry meant that the theaters within which it was played out were beyond the control of the contending powers. They could, for example, do nothing to change the routes along which the goods from Asia traveled, nor could they influence the political and military fortunes of the Mongols, the Tatars, or the Turks in central Asia and the Near East. They played a small part in the political fortunes of the Crusader states and in the Byzantine Empire, but not a decisive one. Their rivalry was fueled, therefore, by competing in markets where access had to be negotiated and was regulated by agreements with other political powers, who granted or withheld favorable terms as their own interests and concerns suggested.

Comparing the commercial privileges each managed to negotiate was about the only way they could assess their relative performance. There was no way to measure the volume of their rival's trade; assessing their own trade and wealth was problematic enough.

For the Venetians and the Genoese, commercial rivalry was not a proxy or an instrument by which to pursue other strategic aims. In their republics, promoting and protecting trade was one of the state's primary purposes, where merchants formed a substantial part of their political elites. During their contest, both had other strategic rivalries, different in character. Until the end of the thirteenth century, the Pisans represented a greater threat to Genoa than to the Venetians. Not only was Pisa much closer to Genoa, but it was a territorial rival—for Corsica and Sardinia— as well as a commercial one. In the fourteenth century, the Catalans succeeded the Pisans as the main rivals of the Genoese in their home waters in the Tyrrhenian Sea. For the Venetians, the Normans of southern Italy, the kings of Hungary, and most formidably, the Turks—challenging them for dominance over the eastern Adriatic or western Aegean shores—served as rivals. These were primarily territorial rivalries, not commercial. They impinged on the rivalry between the Genoese and the Venetians mostly when they were at war, by occasionally distracting the resources and attention of one or the other, or by offering the opportunity to ally against the mutual enemy.

It is difficult to discern a conscious, deliberate development of a long-term strategy on either side of the Genoa-Venice rivalry, because it was not a matter of debate or controversy. There was no pro-Venetian party in Genoa, or pro-Genoese party in Venice. Neither attempted to interfere in the politics of the other state. Though Genoese and Venetians did align themselves to different sides in the Crusader states, and in Constantinople, this interference was often the work of the local Venetian and Genoese communities, not under the direction of their governments in Italy. In fact, most of the incidents in which they confronted one another in the eastern Mediterranean, including those that led to war, were not orchestrated by the home governments. Difficulties of communication, the months it took to travel from Venice or Genoa to Acre, or Constantinople, let alone the Crimea, made such central direction difficult, to say the least.

Such logistical difficulties did not prevent the Venetian government from attempting to maintain close control of Venetian colonies and trading posts and fleets. Any Venetian official or commander who took too consequential an initiative, except in an emergency, without authorization or instructions from the government in Venice risked censure, if not punishment (from fines to execution). This was particularly true if the initiative failed. Genoese governments, on the other hand, were rarely in a position to exercise comparable control. The Genoese had to rely more on private initiatives to advance and protect their economic interests; diplomatic and military backing from the state might not be forthcoming. Private initiative and finance could enable the Genoese to wage wars during internal political turmoil in Genoa. Stronger government and closer state control did not necessarily give the Venetians the advantage. The Genoese colonies' freedom of initiative and command of resources enabled them to respond quickly to threats or opportunities. In the crucial arena of the Black Sea, strategy was essentially devised by the colonists of Pera and Caffa, not in Genoa.

Neither the Venetians nor the Genoese won any lasting political friends in the eastern Mediterranean. Local people and princes alike saw them as greedy, arrogant, and untrustworthy. It was all too obvious that they were concerned with competing for profits, not hearts and minds. Neither Venice nor Genoa was interested in forming lasting alliances that were not associated with commercial treaties, although they sometimes looked for military alliances when they were at war with one another. Their naval power could be used to secure the observance of their commercial privileges when these were being undermined or rescinded. Such power could also obtain and protect access to markets. It could not, however, create markets, or prevent them from changing. Using force to try to ensure the observance of privileges could also be counterproductive, in that it made their merchants even more unwelcome and unpopular, and exposed them to reprisals. It also increased the likelihood that the host government would, if possible, turn to their rivals to counterbalance or replace them. Because of the nature of naval warfare in the Mediterranean in the later Middle Ages, when the Venetians and Genoese were at war with each other, victory in battle could not ensure victory in the war. The four wars between Venice and Genoa vented tensions between them, rather than deciding disputes.

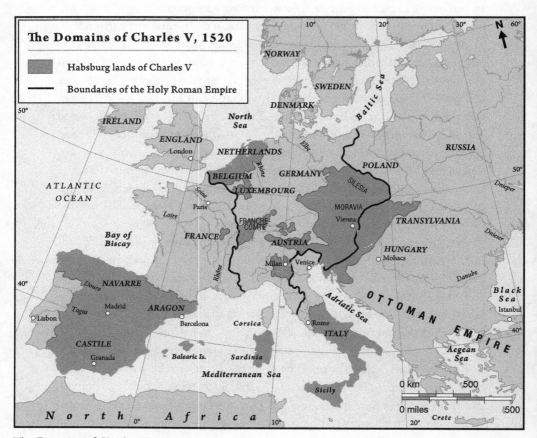

The Domains of Charles V, 1520.

CHAPTER 6

Incest, Blind Faith, and Conquest
The Spanish Hapsburgs and Their Enemies
Geoffrey Parker

"E MPIRE WAS A REMARKABLY durable form of state," Jane Burbank and
Frederick Cooper remind us in their impressive study, *Empires in World
History*. "By comparison, the nation-state appears as a blip on the historical
horizon, a state form that emerged recently from under imperial skies and
whose hold on the world's political imagination may well prove partial or
transitory." Moreover, "[e]mpires were not all alike; they created, adopted,
and transmitted various repertoires of rule."

> An imperial repertoire was neither a bag of tricks dipped into at ran-
> dom nor a preset formula for rule. Faced with challenges day by day,
> empires improvised; they also had their habits. What leaders could
> imagine and what they could carry off were shaped by past prac-
> tices and constrained by context—both by other empires with their
> overlapping goals and by people in places empire-builders coveted.
> Imperial leaders, at any time or place, could imagine only so many
> ways to run a state.[1]

The empire ruled by the Spanish Hapsburgs between 1516 and 1700
was no exception. No previous dynasty had ever controlled such extensive
territories around the world, and no European had ruled so many subjects
or commanded such extensive resources. The absence of precedents helps to
explain the apparently haphazard nature of decision-making by the Spanish
Hapsburgs: they had no choice but to improvise and experiment, to learn
by trial and (sometimes) error. Nevertheless, their "repertoire" for expansion

consisted of just two strategies: although they acquired some territories by conquest, all the major gains came through a tenacious policy of "matrimonial imperialism"—or, more accurately, of incest: intermarriage over several generations among a few dynasties in order to achieve and consolidate expansion. In the words of a humanist slogan that first became popular in the fifteenth century, *Bella gerant alii; tu, felix Austria, nube* (Others make war; you, happy Hapsburgs, marry).[2]

Although successful in the short term, the combination of conquest and incest produced three long-term disadvantages. First, each new territory (however acquired) brought not only prestige, resources, and opportunities, but also its own enduring strategic rivalries and political agendas. Second, some of the territories acquired through incest lay far from the center of government and therefore proved difficult to defend, leading to prolonged wars that exacted a high economic and human toll from the empire as a whole. Finally, incest dramatically reduced the dynastic gene pool: Crown Prince Don Carlos (d. 1568) and King Charles II (d. 1700), each of whom had only six great-great-grandparents instead of sixteen, boasted much the same "inbreeding coefficient" as the incestuous offspring of siblings, or of a parent and child. The erratic behavior of the former induced his father to place him in prison until he died; the latter—ignorant, incoherent, and impotent—was the last of the dynasty.

The Accidental Empire

Dynastic accident brought four separate inheritances together in the person of Charles of Austria (d. 1558). From his paternal grandfather, Maximilian, he received the ancestral Hapsburg lands in central Europe; from his paternal grandmother, Mary, he inherited numerous duchies, counties, and lordships in the Low Countries and the Franche-Comté of Burgundy. From his maternal grandmother, Isabella, Charles received Castile and its outposts in North Africa, the Caribbean, and Central America; from his maternal grandfather, Ferdinand, he inherited Aragón, Naples, Sicily, and Sardinia. Charles himself added several more provinces in the Low Countries, some by treaty and others by conquest; he annexed the duchy of Lombardy in Italy when its native dynasty died out; and he led the army that acquired Tunisia in North Africa.

Following the death of Maximilian in 1519, Charles bribed the leading German princes to choose him as "king of the Romans" (emperor-elect), and the pope later crowned him Holy Roman Emperor, which made him suzerain over most of Germany and northern Italy. Meanwhile, in the Americas,

Charles's Spanish subjects expanded from their bases in the Caribbean to destroy and colonize first the Aztec Empire in Mexico (eight times the size of Castile) and then the Inca Empire in Peru. In 1535, just after the acquisition of Tunis and Peru, the city of Messina in Sicily welcomed Charles with the felicitous phrase coined by the Roman poet Virgil for the possessions of the Emperor Augustus, fifteen centuries before: A SOLIS ORTU AD OCCASUM ("From the rising to the setting of the sun")—or, as the spin-doctors of his son and heir, Philip II (d. 1598), would put it, "An empire on which the sun never set."[3]

In 1555–1556 Philip inherited most, but not all, of these territories when his father abdicated. Charles had already invested his brother Ferdinand with the ancestral Hapsburg lands in Austria, and shortly before his death, he ensured that Ferdinand would succeed him as Holy Roman Emperor. Conversely, in 1554, Charles arranged Philip's marriage to his cousin Mary Tudor, queen of England and Ireland; and although Philip lost his position as king consort of England when Mary died four years later, his subjects colonized the Philippine archipelago (which they named in his honor), while the American territories over which he ruled expanded until they stretched from the Rio Grande in the north to the Bio-Bio in the south. They later included Brazil, because thanks to several generations of intermarriage with the House of Avis, which ruled Portugal and its colonies in Africa, Asia, and America, in 1580 Philip inherited them all.

Of course, Philip still faced challenges—the Portuguese settlers on the Azores defied him, supported by Queen Elizabeth of England (Mary's half-sister); while many of his former subjects in the Netherlands formally abjured their obedience and formed an independent state, the "United Provinces" (better known in English as the Dutch Republic)—but in 1582 and 1583, ambitious amphibious expeditions imposed Philip's rule on the Azores, 1,000 miles west of Lisbon; and in 1584 and 1585 the king's troops regained the southern Netherlands, culminating in the blockade and capture of Antwerp, the largest city in northern Europe, 1,000 miles northeast of Lisbon. In July 1588, after three years of preparation, an armada of 130 ships sailed majestically from the Iberian Peninsula and up the English Channel to rendezvous with 28,000 of the veteran troops who had reconquered the southern Netherlands and now stood poised to conquer England. In Madrid, a foreign ambassador observed with admiration,

> At the moment, the Catholic King [Philip] is safe: France cannot threaten him, and the Turks can do little; neither can the king of Scots, who is offended at Queen Elizabeth on account of the death of

his mother [Mary Stuart]. . . . At the same time, Spain can be confident that the Swiss cantons will not move against him; nor will they allow others to do so, since they are now his allies.

Nothing, he predicted, could now stop Philip.[4]

The ambassador erred. The following month, the Royal Navy prevented the Armada from joining the troops waiting in the Netherlands, forcing it to return to Spain through the stormy waters of the North Atlantic, where almost half of the vessels and the men aboard perished. The next decade saw the further attempts and failures by Philip's forces to invade England, as well as his efforts to place his daughter on the French throne, while a series of harvest failures and a plague epidemic killed one-tenth of Spain's population. Meanwhile, the Dutch Republic regained several cities from Philip's forces, and Anglo-Dutch amphibious expeditions captured and sacked several port-cities in Spain and America.

Shortly after Philip's death, one of his leading diplomats confided pessimistically to a colleague, Don Baltasar de Zúñiga, "Truly, sir, I believe we are gradually becoming the target at which the whole world wants to shoot its arrows; and you know that no empire, however great, has been able to sustain many wars in different areas for long. . . . Although I may be mistaken I doubt whether we can sustain an empire as scattered as ours." The "empire on which the sun never set" thus became in the seventeenth century the target on which the sun never set. By the time he became principal foreign policy adviser to Philip III (d. 1621), Zúñiga shared this fatalistic outlook. In 1619, he lamented to a colleague that "[w]hen matters reach a certain stage, every decision taken will be for the worst, not through lack of good advice, but because the situation is so desperate that it is not capable of remedy; and whatever policy is selected discredits whoever chose it." For another decade, the Spanish Hapsburgs held their own, leading the count-duke of Olivares, Zúñiga's nephew and chief minister of Philip IV (d. 1665), to crow "God is Spanish and favors our nation these days"; but the rest of the century saw a succession of losses both at home (thanks to plague and famine) and abroad (thanks to British, French, and Dutch aggression).[5] When the death of Charles II in 1700 extinguished the dynasty, it no longer ruled Portugal or its empire (save only the North African enclave of Ceuta), the Franche-Comté of Burgundy, the northern parts of Catalonia, or the southern provinces of the Netherlands; and after a bitter and prolonged war of succession, in 1713, a member of the Bourbon dynasty acquired Spain, its overseas empire, and southern Italy, leaving only parts of the Netherlands and northern Italy in Hapsburg hands.

For these failures, contemporaries and historians alike have advanced two distinct explanations:

- *A problematic inheritance.* The Spanish empire became too big to govern or to defend: structural factors—competing strategic agendas, distance, and information overload—therefore explain the failure to preserve it intact.
- *Problematic monarchs.* The Spanish Hapsburgs possessed sufficient resources, but used them inefficiently in the pursuit of impossible goals. Monarchs with superior political skills could have succeeded where Charles V and his descendants failed—or, in modern parlance, the fatal flaw lay with agents rather than structures.

Each explanation merits detailed examination.

The Poisoned Chalice: Sub-Imperialism

Each component of an empire—especially an accidental empire—brought with it a poisoned chalice: its past. Each boasted its own institutions and identity; its own economic, defensive, and strategic agendas; and often its own extensive "privileges," permanently guaranteed by the sovereign. Even at the best of times, the priorities of the local elite in Barcelona, Lima, Lisbon, Mexico, Manila, Naples, Palermo, Milan, and Brussels often differed from those of the imperial government in Madrid, leading to a sort of "sub-imperialism," in which Spain's proconsuls followed the maxim, *Obedezco pero no cumplo* (I obey but do nothing).[6] For example, when, in 1625, Philip IV ordered all his dominions to participate in an imperial defense plan, known as the "Union of Arms," the viceroy of Peru flatly refused, informing his master,

> Although I recognize that America has no Cortes, Representative Assemblies, Estates or Parliaments, so that the authority of His Majesty is free and absolute, I still believe that what matters to his royal service is not just the imposition of taxes but that his subjects should accept and pay them with obedience and enthusiasm. And to achieve this it would be good that some should hope for, and others be certain of, a reward.

When Philip flatly refused to offer bribes in return for compliance, the viceroy and his successors declined to put the union into effect for more than a decade on the grounds that "[if I] insist on it, the misfortunes that normally arise from new taxes and impositions may result."[7]

When conditions deteriorated—whether through increased government demands or decreased resources—resistance became more robust: regional elites invoked constitutional guarantees (often termed "fundamental laws," "charters," and "constitutions"), while the central government sought to override them. In 1639, Olivares reached the end of his patience with the insistence of the Catalan elite that he must respect their "constitutions" and exclaimed, "By now I am nearly at my wits' end; but I say, and I shall still be saying on my deathbed, that if the Constitutions do not allow this, then the Devil take the Constitutions." Within six months his intransigence provoked the revolt of the Catalans. It would last nineteen years.[8]

Sub-imperial agendas became even more disruptive whenever they included an "enduring strategic rivalry" with a neighbor, because this increased the likelihood of a war that might engulf the entire empire. Thus the Spanish outposts in North Africa and the Hapsburg lands in central Europe provoked the hostility of the Ottoman Empire, which also sought to extend its control in those same areas. Desiderius Erasmus, Charles V's most articulate subject, predicted a lethal contest "for the greatest of prizes: to see whether Charles will be the monarch of the whole world, or the Turk. For the world can no longer bear two suns in the sky."[9] Sultan Suleiman the Magnificent (d. 1566), who ruled over 20 million subjects and 1 million square miles of territory, led his troops up the Danube five times, on each occasion gaining lands either from the Hapsburgs or from their allies, and giant Ottoman galley fleets continued to invade the central and western Mediterranean until the two sides signed a truce in 1578.

The kings of France, for their part, coveted several Hapsburg possessions that had once been ruled from Paris: Navarre, Catalonia, Milan, Naples, Burgundy, and the southern Netherlands. Charles's election as Holy Roman Emperor in 1519 meant that his territories now surrounded France to the east as well as to the north and south, creating an unprecedented strategic threat. King Francis I of France "maintains no friendship whatever with the emperor," an ambassador observed in 1520. "They adapt themselves to circumstance, but hate each other very cordially."[10] Francis declared war on Charles the following year, mobilizing the resources of a state that, although not much larger than Spain, far exceeded it in population (twenty million French subjects compared with only six million Spaniards). The kings of France repeatedly strove to break what they saw as "Hapsburg encirclement" until 1713, when, with the Treaty of Utrect (ending the War of Spanish Succession), they finally managed to dismember the empire of their rivals.

Charles and his successors faced two other enduring strategic rivalries, each one ideological as well as political: the Protestants and the papacy. Emperor Maximilian had failed to silence Martin Luther, a professor at the University of Wittenberg in Saxony who wrote pamphlets and speeches to mobilize public support for his claims that the papacy was corrupt and required urgent reform. Although on his first visit to Germany Charles outlawed Luther and his followers, when Suleiman advanced into Hungary in 1526, and again when he laid siege to Vienna in 1529, in desperation Charles offered religious toleration to the German Lutherans (soon known as Protestants) in return for their military assistance against the Turks. Although this saved Vienna, Protestant ideas now spread both within Charles's territories (above all Germany and the Netherlands) and beyond (above all, Scandinavia, England, and Scotland). Protestants everywhere feared that the emperor would revoke his grudging toleration and that Spanish Hapsburgs intended to extirpate them if an opportunity presented itself, and therefore constantly sought to undermine Hapsburg projects and power.

The popes also felt threatened by Charles and his successors because their territories encircled Rome: Sardinia and Spain to the west, Naples and Sicily to the south, Milan and Germany to the north. Rome's commerce by sea and land, including the supply of grain on which the capital depended, therefore lay at the Hapsburgs' mercy. Two popes joined France and declared war on the Hapsburgs, provoking the sack of Rome in 1527 and a bombardment in 1557: both led to an ignominious peace. Although no pontiff ever engaged in open hostilities after this, papal support for the "crusades" of the Spanish Hapsburgs against both Muslims and Protestants, and for the acquisition of new territories, remained muted. As Philip once complained about Pope Gregory XIII's reluctance to fund his efforts to recover the Low Countries for the Catholic Church, "I believe that if the Netherlands belonged to someone else, he would have performed miracles to prevent them being lost by the church; but because they are my states, I believe he is prepared to see this happen because they will be lost by me." Gregory's efforts to prevent the union of Spain and Portugal outraged the king even more:

No one knows better than Your Holiness the love and respect that I have for you; and the setbacks that have afflicted my dominions during your pontificate are also well-known—most of them because I have taken upon my shoulders the defence of the church and extirpation of heresy. And yet the more these setbacks have increased, the more Your Holiness seems to ignore them—something that simply amazes me.[11]

These were shrewd points, elegantly phrased, but they overlooked the fact that the extent of Philip's dominions posed a permanent political threat to papal authority that no pope could ignore.

The annexation of Portugal and its empire in 1580–1583 added one more "enduring strategic rivalry." Portuguese success in monopolizing the trade in certain key commodities (notably spices and horses) throughout the Indian Ocean and Indonesia had earned the enmity of many indigenous rulers, and Philip II had to contend not only with their frequent attempts to expel his new subjects but also with many ambitious proposals for countermeasures. Thus in 1584, an official in Macao asserted that "[w]ith fewer than 5000 Spaniards Your Majesty could conquer these lands [China] and become lord of them, or at least of the maritime areas, which are the most important in any part of the world"; while the bishop of Malacca advocated pooling the resources of Spain and Portugal in order first to conquer southeast Asia, and then to annex southern China, so that "His Majesty will be the greatest lord that ever was in the world." In the 1590s, a Portuguese priest long resident in America and Africa forwarded to the king an ambitious global strategy, arguing that the fortification of six widely separated strongpoints—Johore, St. Helena, Goeree, Sierra Leone, Bahia, and Santa Catalina—would guarantee Iberian commercial supremacy around the globe.[12] Given the distances involved, such projects were totally unrealistic, but Philip still had to read and evaluate them.

Distance: "Public Enemy Number 1"

Fernand Braudel was the first historian to devote sustained attention to the role of distance in the failure of the Spanish Hapsburgs to preserve their empire. The second section of his masterpiece, *The Mediterranean and the Mediterranean World in the Age of Philip II*, first published in 1949, examined the economic constraints upon early modern empires. It began:

> Understanding the importance of distance in the sixteenth century— understanding the obstacles, the difficulties and the delays that it caused—leads one to view the administrative problems faced by sixteenth-century empires in a new light. Above all, the enormous Spanish empire: the empire of Philip II involved (for its time) a massive infrastructure of land and sea transport, and required not only the ceaseless movement of troops but also dispatch of hundreds

of orders and reports every day—links that were silent but vital. . . .
A good half of the actions of Philip II can only be explained by the
need to maintain these links, to safeguard his communications, and
to effect in each remote corner of his empire the essential transfer
of silver.[13]

In his final paper of advice to his son, the king himself blamed many of
the problems he had faced on "the distance that separates one state from
another," and in the course of his reign he repeatedly complained about delays
in the transmission of important information. So did his ministers—indeed,
one of them joked that "if we have to wait for death, let us hope that it comes
from Spain, for then it would never arrive."[14]

Nevertheless, as Braudel recognized, the same was true of all empires:
"Although much criticized, the Spanish empire was equal or indeed superior to other leading states for transport, transfer and communications."
Throughout the sixteenth century, he added, "over equal distances Spanish
communications were on the whole a match for anyone's." Contemporaries
agreed. In the awed phrase of an observer at the Court of Spain in 1566,
writing to his master in the Netherlands, "As Your Lordship knows, nothing
happens there that is not immediately known here." Five years later, when
the ambassador of the Venetian Republic (which prided itself on the speed
and efficiency of its communications network) hurried to the royal palace to
inform Philip II of the great victory of Lepanto, he found that the king had
already received the news from one of his own couriers. The same ambassador
later complained ruefully that the information at Philip's disposal "was such
that there is nothing he does not know."[15]

This superiority reflects another common denominator of empires, per-
ceptively described by Lauren Benton:

Although empires did lay claim to vast stretches of territory, the
nature of such claims was tempered by control that was exercised
mainly over narrow bands, or corridors, and over enclaves and irregular zones around them. Maritime empires represented this pattern
most clearly, with their networks of sea lanes connecting dispersed
settlements or trading posts. But territorial expansion in Europe
also occurred through the creation and protection of corridors and
enclaves.[16]

Just after he became king of Spain in 1516, Charles V signed a contract with the Taxis company (which had already created such a "corridor"

between Spain and the Netherlands through France, with 106 relay stations, each one provided with at least two horses) that established guaranteed times for various services to link him with his representatives in Germany, Italy, Spain, and the Netherlands.[17] Every week, scores of messages passed safely through these corridors. From 1560, an "ordinary" courier left Madrid for Brussels (and vice versa) on the first day of each month (and later on the 15th also), with additional "extraordinary" messengers dispatched as necessary. Seven years later, the duke of Alba established a new "corridor" from Milan to Brussels during his march to the Netherlands along what would later be called the "Spanish Road," providing an alternative chain of postal relay stations that could be used whenever civil war rendered passage through France unsafe. In 1572, he began to send two copies of all his letters to the king: one carried by couriers who rode through France, and the other by colleagues who traveled down the Spanish Road to Genoa and thence by sea to Barcelona.[18]

Hapsburg Spain maintained the largest diplomatic network in the world, with permanent embassies in Bern, Genoa, London, Paris, Rome, Turin, Venice, and Vienna (also in Lisbon until 1580), as well as temporary missions elsewhere when occasion required; and whereas the ambassadors and ministers of most other European states normally sent one dispatch each month to their principals, the kings of Spain expected at least one dispatch each week—and sometimes more. In 1557, Philip II ordered his field commander to "send me news by sending three or four messengers here, flying at top speed" every day, and "to this end, to keep post horses ready night and day." Six years later, he informed his envoy at the General Council of the Catholic Church at Trent that "there should be nothing, great or small, that is done or even contemplated in the council without you knowing all about it." In 1580, during the invasion of Portugal, the king informed his field commander that "I want you to let me know every day what is going on"; while eight years later, during the Armada campaign, the king instructed his agents that "now is the time to advise me of everything minute by minute."[19]

His ministers obliged. Some couriers managed to convey messages overland from Brussels to the king in eleven, ten, and, in one case, only nine days (an average speed of almost a hundred miles on horseback each day); while a galley carrying letters from Philip's fleet in Messina reached Barcelona—almost a thousand miles away—in only eight days, having "flown rather than sailed." A ship carrying information on Parma's preparations for the invasion of England in 1588 arrived in Lisbon in only five days. As historian Giovanni Ugolini once observed, a letter could travel faster than anything else in the early modern world.[20]

Information Overload

The Spanish Hapsburgs never seem to have recognized that their striking success in improving information transfer created new obstacles to effective government. In the words of an eminent contemporary strategic analyst,

> There is only so much that any human can absorb, digest and act upon in a given period of time. The greater the stress, the more individuals will ignore or misrepresent data, mistake and misconstrue information, and the greater will be the prospects for confusion, disorientation and surprise.

In short, "More information from more sources, made available more quickly than ever before, equals system overload." In the sixteenth as in the twenty-first century, "[p]rocessing and transmission technologies far outstrip our ability to assimilate, sort and distribute information."[21]

The Spanish Hapsburgs reacted to the information overload they had created in two distinct ways. Charles V, and initially Philip II, always briefed their principal lieutenants in person or else entrusted detailed instructions to a trusted messenger capable of explaining their intentions in detail. Moreover, they delegated the final decision on critical operational issues to those tasked with implementing them. Thus, while campaigning against France in 1557, Philip II wrote to his field commander, "These matters cannot be decided here in a timely fashion, and because opportunities and events change by the hour . . . you can put into effect whatever you see to be most appropriate and necessary for the success of this venture." A decade later, although he bombarded the duke of Alba with extremely detailed instructions on the policies to follow in the Netherlands, he added the vital concession, "I delegate all these matters to you, as the person who will be handling the enterprise and will have a better understanding of the obstacles or advantages that may prevail."[22] After the successful conquest of Portugal, by contrast, Philip's success in securing information about "everything minute by minute" led to the dangerous illusion that this empowered—entitled—him to micromanage both policy and operations. When finalizing the invasion and conquest of England in 1587–1588, the king drafted the crucial documents that explained his grand strategy in consultation with a few civilian advisors in Madrid, and then sent them by a regular courier to those who would execute it with orders to "waste no time in complaints and questions," but instead to "believe me, *as one who has complete information on the present state of affairs in all areas.*"[23] This was ridiculous. Even if the king had possessed "complete information on the present state of affairs in all areas," it would have been of little use—by the time his instructions reached their destination, "the present state of affairs" would have changed.

The Spanish Hapsburgs' second reaction to the information overload they had created was to focus on minor problems (*menudencias*, or "trivia," in the phrase of his ministers), instead of wrestling with the crucial decisions on which the fate of the monarchy depended. In 1584, Cardinal Granvelle (Philip II's senior advisor) complained bitterly,

> I see in all matters these delays, so pernicious and in so many ways prejudicial to our own affairs, including the most important ones, which become lost to view with so much delay. And the reason is that His Majesty wants to do and see everything, without trusting anyone else, busying himself with so many petty details that he has no time left to resolve what matters most.

Five years later, Don Juan de Silva, who served Philip as page, soldier, ambassador, and counselor, delivered a more comprehensive indictment of his master's administrative style. "The detailed attention that His Majesty devotes to the most trifling things is a subject for regret," Silva confided to a colleague,

> Although His Majesty's brain must be the largest in the world, like that of any other human being, it is not capable of organizing the multitude of his affairs without making some division between those that he should deal with himself and those that he cannot avoid delegating to others. His Majesty does not make this distinction. . . . Instead he leaves nothing entirely alone and takes from everyone the material that should be delegated (concerning individuals and details), and so does not concentrate on the general and the important because he finds them too tiring.[24]

The king himself recognized this problem. In 1566, with war in the Mediterranean, a rebellion narrowly averted in Mexico, and trouble brewing in the Netherlands, a royal secretary apologized for troubling his master with trivia: "When I see Your Majesty with many tasks, I am sometimes afraid to worry you with matters that could be postponed without detriment." The king replied, "I gave up on the tasks: although there are plenty of them these days, sometimes a man can relax by doing other things."[25] Everyone who has wielded executive power can sympathize with this admission—in a time of crisis, solving minor problems can provide short-term satisfaction, even relaxation, which may make the major problems seem less daunting—but Granvelle, Silva, and the rest felt that Philip did not "relax" by "doing other things" just "sometimes." They complained that he did so constantly, so that "relaxation" became escapism, and that although his "brain must be the biggest in the world," it was still too small to micromanage an empire on which the sun never set. The ministers who served Philip's successors often made similar complaints: their masters spent their time hunting, whoring, or going to the theater, instead of laboring to solve the crucial problems that faced the empire.

A Blizzard of Problems

This was especially problematic in wartime—and the Spanish Empire only enjoyed complete peace for ten years under Charles V, for six months under Philip II, and for three years under Philip III; while Philip IV (1621–1665) spent every day of his long reign at war. Each monarch often fought on more than one front simultaneously, and at sea as well as on land. War always places rulers under intense stress. Not only do hostilities require resources that may prove difficult to find, they also divert attention from other problems—just as those other problems sometimes divert attention from winning the war. Robert McNamara, secretary of defense of the United States during the 1960s, eloquently voiced this timeless dilemma in his memoirs:

> One reason the Kennedy and Johnson administrations failed to take an orderly, rational approach to the basic questions underlying Vietnam was the staggering variety and complexity of other issues we faced. Simply put, we faced a blizzard of problems: there were only twenty-four hours in the day and we often did not have time to think straight. This predicament is not unique to the administration in which I served or to the United States. It has existed in all times and in most countries ... and it ought to be recognized and planned for when organizing a government.[26]

The Spanish Hapsburgs faced exactly the same "predicament" as McNamara and others who have led a global empire at war: what they needed was "time to think straight" about what would be the best policy—and they usually failed to find it. One day, Philip II complained that although "I would like to deal with" some matters of critical importance, "there are so many other things that prevent me. What I most regret is that I am slowed down by having so many things to do," yet "if I tried to do all of them, I would get nothing done."[27]

There was much truth in this. As the French ambassador in Madrid noted in 1567, the king of Spain "has so many regions to worry about that he cannot deal with all of them"; and the previous year, on hearing of the outbreak of rioting in the Netherlands, a nobleman informed Philip to his face that "delays and procrastination had created all these problems and would create many more." He also predicted that if he continued to procrastinate, "His Majesty will face other pressing matters" that would prevent him from dealing firmly with the Netherlands. Sixty years later, the British ambassador in Madrid made a similar point: "It is no wonder that many of their designs fail in the execution, for though this great vessel [the Spanish Monarchy] contains much water, yet it has so many leaks it is always dry." In trying to do too much, the crown achieved nothing—something Paul Kennedy would later call "imperial overstretch."[28]

In 1573, with the empire at war simultaneously in the Netherlands and the Mediterranean, the duke of Alba highlighted another problem: "The Royal Treasury must be in a desperate state, and for that reason I am going almost out of my mind as I see matters proceed in such a way that if some new problem, however small, were to arise, His Majesty's resources are so exhausted that he might not have the strength to resist." Once again, there was much truth in this. In the words of a recent article, "as head of the first modern super-power," the Spanish Hapsburgs "managed a budget on a scale that had not been seen since the height of the Roman Empire. No state before had faced such extraordinary fluctuations and imbalances, both in revenue and expenditure."[29] In 1557, in 1560, and again in 1575, Philip II issued a decree (sometimes called a "Decree of Bankruptcy") that suspended all interest payments from the Castilian Treasury and confiscated the capital of all outstanding loans from his bankers. He then entered negotiations with his creditors to reschedule his debts and reduce the interest payable—but this did not change the underlying fiscal problem: his wars cost double his revenues.

In the 1590s, a decade of adverse weather and plague, Philip therefore received increasingly strident pleas to scale back his commitments. Some came from taxpayers, via their representatives in the Cortes (Congress) of Castile. In 1593, one deputy pleaded that "before anything else, You Majesty should order a reduction in war expenditure, both in the Netherlands and elsewhere"; another stated that "although the wars with the Dutch, England and France are holy and just, we must beg Your Majesty that they cease"; while a third urged "Your Majesty to abandon all these wars, making the best terms that you can."[30] Some ministers made a similar case. Mateo Vázquez, a priest who had served as the king's private secretary for twenty years, begged his master to cease spending the resources of Castile so prodigally on foreign wars. "If God had intended Your Majesty to heal all the cripples who come to you to be cured, He would have given you the power to do so; and if He had wished to oblige Your Majesty to remedy all the troubles of the world, he would have given you the money and the resources to do so." If the king persevered with the same expensive policies, Vázquez continued relentlessly, "Everything may collapse at once for lack of money." Philip addressed this passionate complaint with remarkable equanimity—although he totally rejected it. "I know you are moved by the great zeal you have for my service to say what you did," he gently chided his minister.

> But you must also understand that these are not matters that can be abandoned by a person who is as conscientious about his responsibilities as you know me to be, because they depress me and matter to me more than to anyone. Taken together, they involve far more problems than people think. . . . Moreover, these issues involve religion, which must take precedence over everything.[31]

Philip thus did not dispute the material evidence of impending disaster—but his faith-based political vision led him to ignore it.

The king could not ignore the worsening fiscal situation, however. In 1596, the marquis de Poza, president of the council of finance, sent an alarming message to Philip's most trusted advisor, Don Cristóbal de Moura:

> His Majesty must see that it is impossible to carry on as we are, because although we have already spent all His Majesty's revenues until the year 1599, his expenses continue and even increase, so that even if his revenues were unencumbered, we could not carry on. To do this, one only needs to know what I know: that His Majesty must either reduce his expenditure voluntarily until things improve, or else find a way to achieve the impossible.

A few days later Poza added despairingly, "Even if we escape from this obstacle, we will inevitably encounter another one tomorrow because each day is more impossible than the last." Moura agreed—"here we are drowning tied back-to-back" he lamented—and on November 13, 1596, "since loans are now so hard to find, and the total that we now owe" to bankers exceeded fourteen million ducats, Philip signed a fourth Decree of Bankruptcy. Castile had become the world's first serial defaulter on sovereign debt, and Philip had become, in the phrase of a recent book, "the borrower from hell."[32]

Snatching Defeat from the Jaws of Victory

Amid the "blizzard of problems" that confronted the Spanish empire, Moura also perceived a central paradox: success often bred failure—or, in Moura's own words, "however much more we acquire, the more we have to defend and the more our enemies want to take from us."[33] Experience had demonstrated that the victories of the Spanish Hapsburgs often led the vanquished to seek their revenge by forging alliances with other enemies of the dynasty. This happened for the first time after the battle of Pavia in 1525, when Charles V's troops not only routed the French field army but captured King Francis, who spent more than a year in prison until he gave his word "as a knight" that he would honor a raft of humiliating territorial concessions demanded by the emperor. As soon as he regained his freedom, however, Francis concluded an anti-Hapsburg League with representatives from several Italian states, and even sought an alliance with the Ottoman sultan. This news depressed Charles profoundly: "He is full of dumps and solitary musing," reported an English envoy, "sometimes alone three or four hours together. There is no mirth or comfort with him." The emperor had hoped that Pavia and a favorable peace would allow him to travel to Germany to extirpate the followers of Martin Luther and then to Hungary to lead the forces of Christendom against the Turks. Instead, it alarmed and unified his neighbors. "If it had not been for the conclusion of this new league," wrote the doge of Venice, "one could well assume that His Imperial Majesty would not only have laid down the law to Italy, but would have made himself the monarch of the world."[34]

This pattern persisted. The emperor's immense resources sufficed to defeat or humiliate individual enemies—the pope in 1527, with the sack of Rome; the sultan in 1532, when (assisted again by the German Lutherans) Charles led an army to Hungary that forced the sultan to withdraw; and again in 1535 when he captured Tunis; France again in 1544, when Charles advanced within fifty miles of Paris and forced Francis I to make another humiliating peace; the German Protestants in 1547, whose army he routed at Mühlberg. On each occasion, the vanquished formed an anti-Hapsburg alliance that, sooner or later, either attacked Charles or provided support to his domestic opponents, forcing him to embark on yet another campaign. Eventually, after the French king launched an attack in 1552, carefully coordinated with the

Turks, the German Protestants, and some Italian princes, forcing him to flee across the Alps virtually alone, Charles suffered a psychological and physical collapse. Defeated, humiliated, and plagued by hemorrhoids and catarrh, the emperor became sad and pensive, "and often he cries violently, and sheds many tears, just as if he were a child."[35] He abdicated shortly afterward.

His son also faced hostile coalitions that could snatch defeat from the jaws of victory. The Ottoman sultan sent not only his fleet to attack Spanish enclaves in the Mediterranean but freedom fighters to assist the rebellion by Philip II's Spanish subjects of Arab descent in 1568–1571 (the war of Granada). He also offered assistance to the Dutch rebels after 1572, while the rulers of France and England sent them troops, treasure, and political advisors (the French king's brother and the English queen's Favorite both briefly became head of state of the Dutch Republic). In 1585, Queen Elizabeth signed a formal treaty of alliance with the Dutch, expanded in 1596 into a triple alliance when Henry of Bourbon, king of France, also joined. Philip's enemies now sought to coordinate their attacks on his empire.

This development, together with a devastating famine in much of Castile, led even the royal confessor, Fray Diego de Yepes, to question his master's faith-based policies:

> God has entrusted the conservation of the Catholic faith and the expansion of the Christian religion to Your Majesty, and since they both depend on the sound government, justice and prosperity of these kingdoms of Spain, I hope you will be pleased to arrange matters so that on the Day of Judgment (which is not far off), you can appear in the presence of God confident that you have done everything possible.

When nothing improved, Yepes sent an equally stark warning to Moura that fighting wars and increasing taxes at a time of dearth "will bring down our world."

> Your Lordship can see where this leads. The poor cry out, but His Majesty does not hear them, nor does he want to hear me. I simply do not know what to do. May God in His mercy protect Your Lordship, whom the world blames for all this (along with me). . . . I beg Your Lordship to look into this carefully, and advise His Majesty, because I have had no luck in writing or speaking to him.[36]

This spiritual blackmail appears to have worked. The king, convinced that he must make peace at almost any price, empowered his nephew Albert, governor-general of the Netherlands, to undertake indirect peace negotiations with England. At first, he tied his nephew's hands—"you will conduct your-self in this matter in such a way that you do not close the door to peace, but do not open it either"—but later he conceded broad powers, similar to those he had conferred on his lieutenants in the first half of his reign: "Since you know about everything, you will be able to derive the best possible advantage; and since I have delegated everything to you, I have nothing more to say except that I await news of what happens."[37] Philip also accepted a papal offer to mediate a peace with France and approved the marriage of his daughter Isabella with Albert; shortly afterward, the king signed an act that ceded limited sovereignty in the Netherlands to Isabella and Albert, and to their offspring. Prince Philip would inherit the rest. The Spanish Hapsburgs had at last decided to trade land for peace.

The partition of the empire did not last because Albert died childless in 1621, and so Philip IV inherited all his grandfather's possessions. He immediately dissipated any potential advantage by renewing the war against the Dutch Republic, even though he was already fighting enemies of the dynasty in Germany. Shortly afterward, he provoked a war with England and also sent an army to enforce the rights of a relative to the Italian states of Monferrat and Mantua, provoking the French to intervene in support of a rival claimant. Although Spain managed to extricate itself from the wars with France and Britain, war with the former resumed in 1635, and within a decade, French troops controlled all of Spain north of the Ebro, thanks to the revolt of the Catalans who in 1641 placed themselves under French sovereignty. Portugal, too, rebelled, and (with military and naval assistance from France, Great Britain, and the Dutch Republic) in 1668 forced Spain to recognize its independence.

What had Philip IV gained by fighting so many wars? In material terms, nothing: he acquired no new territory and instead lost the vast Portuguese empire, Jamaica, important parts of the Netherlands, and northern Catalonia. Yet even this negative outcome entailed immense sacrifices. Repeatedly, imperial overstretch forced the central government to postpone or to abandon measures aimed at domestic recovery and retrenchment even as it sustained great human and material losses. Between 1640 and 1659, thousands of ordinary Catalans died violently and thousands more fled into exile. By the time Barcelona surrendered in 1652, its population halved by famine and plague, it had run up a debt of more than 20 million ducats; the diocese of Tortosa, which changed hands in 1640 and again in 1648, saw its revenues drop from more than 30,000 ducats annually in the 1630s to virtually nothing. Castilian communities close to the Portuguese border also saw their populations fall dramatically because the troops of both sides exacted so much money, food, and other local resources. As Henry Kamen has observed, "No other single event in Castilian history of the early modern period, excepting only epidemics, did more to destroy the country" than the twenty-eight-year war with Portugal.[38]

Domino Theories and Blind Faith

Few "Grand Strategies" are entirely rational. For example, no political leader wants to admit defeat and thereby lose "reputation," and the greater the resources invested in a struggle, the harder it is to walk away. The Spanish Empire was no exception: as Philip II observed in 1575, "I have no doubt that, if the cost of the war [in the Netherlands] continues at its present level, we will not be able to sustain it; *but it would be a great shame if, having spent so much, we lost any chance that spending a little more might recover everything.*"[39] Again, like other political leaders, the Spanish Hapsburgs always seemed more disposed to take risks in order to avoid losses than to make gains. It was relatively easy for Philip II to withdraw his forces from the imperial fief of Finale Liguria in 1573, unjustly occupied two years earlier, even though (as his sister María astutely reminded him) "[t]his accursed reputation makes us take leave of our senses—and sometimes reality," because Finale had never belonged to him.[40] It was a different story when a component part of the empire was concerned—not least because the central government feared that weakness in one dominion might encourage resistance in others. As Philip II's ministers reminded him in 1566, failure to crush dissent in the Netherlands would not only "place at risk the reputation of Spain" throughout Europe, but "if the troubles in the Netherlands continue, Milan and Naples will follow." A decade later, the king's advisors again argued that resuming the war in the Netherlands was the only way to uphold "the honor and reputation of Your Majesty, which is your greatest asset" when dealing with political rivals, while concessions to the Dutch rebels would endanger "the obedience of other vassals who, it is greatly to be feared, would take it as an inspiration for their own rebellion, at least in the dominions we have conquered, like Naples and Milan."[41]

Likewise, in 1608, some of Philip III's ministers opposed peace talks with the Dutch after thirty-six years of unsuccessful war because "it will appear good neither to God nor to the World if Your Majesty goes about begging for peace with his rebels. . . . If we lose our credit [*reputación*] only God by a miracle would be able to remedy the damage."[42] The ministers of Philip IV constructed an elaborate "domino theory" to justify the fighting. In 1624, they warned that "once the Netherlands are lost, America and other kingdoms of Your Majesty will also immediately be lost with no hope of recovering them." Four years later, a Spanish official in Brussels repeated the point: "If we lose the Netherlands, we will not be able to defend America, Spain or Italy." A few years later, a veteran diplomat extended the argument yet further: "We cannot defend the Netherlands if we lose Germany."[43]

This was not the only reason that the Spanish Hapsburgs continued to fight wars they could not win, however. As early as 1574, an English observer in the Netherlands discerned two motives for Philip II's refusal to negotiate with his enemies: "The pride of the Spanish government and the cause of religion"—a combination that the Hapsburgs called "religion and reputation."[44]

The religious faith of the Spanish Hapsburgs led them to react to setbacks in unusual ways. The Holocaust survivor Primo Levi, an acute observer of human nature, observed that "few are the men who draw moral strength from failure"—but Philip II, III, and IV were among them.[45] Whenever making decisions that involved complex moral judgments, all three monarchs sought the advice of special committees of theologians (*juntas de teólogos*), while on lesser issues they deluged their confessors with demands whether "in conscience" they could authorize the policy suggested by their ministers. The unswerving piety of each monarch repeatedly led them to interpret failure or even outright defeat as a sign that God was testing them: thus in the spring of 1578, when drought gripped Castile, Philip II reasoned that "[o]ur Lord must be very angry with us, because He is withholding the rain that we need so much"; and after a beloved nephew died a few months later, he observed philosophically, "It is certainly a tragedy, but God (who is responsible) must know better."[46] Although an unexpected defeat, such as the failure of the Armada, might temporarily depress his spirits, Philip soon managed to see a silver lining. Thus shortly after telling one minister in the autumn of 1588 that "I hope that God has not permitted so much evil, because everything has been done for His service," and that "I hope to die and go to God before this happens," he stated that "I shall never fail to stand up for the cause of God and the well-being of these kingdoms," and started to plan a new invasion of England.[47]

Blind faith also led the Spanish Hapsburgs to avoid formulating fallback strategies. Thus in September 1571, when the duke of Alba refused for logistical reasons to obey the king's orders to invade England and overthrow Elizabeth Tudor, Philip's first response was spiritual blackmail:

Although your influence with Us is so great, and although I hold in the highest esteem your person and prudence in all things, and especially in the matter in which you are engaged and occupied, and although the arguments you put to Us are so convincing, I am so keen to achieve the consummation of this enterprise, I am so attached to it in my heart, and I am so convinced that God our Savior must embrace it as His own cause, that I cannot be dissuaded, nor can I accept or believe the contrary. This leads me to understand matters differently [from you] and makes me play down the difficulties and problems that spring up; so that all the things that could either divert or stop me from carrying through this business seem less threatening to me.

Then the king argued that, in any case, logistics were irrelevant:

With a matter as important as this one, it does not seem right to engage in detailed consideration of the problems that would arise if we made mistakes and failed, without counterbalancing it with the benefits and advantages that success would bring—and it cannot be doubted that in terms of religion and politics, as well as of reputation and of all the other goals that I can and must try to achieve, those [benefits and advantages] would be so great and obvious that not only do they make me support and favor the cause, but they oblige and almost compel me to do so.

In short, "although it cannot be denied that we will encounter some obstacles and difficulties, they are outweighed by many other divine and human considerations that oblige us to take these risks and more." Philip subjected the commanders of the Armada to similar spiritual blackmail. When, in September 1587, the marquis of Santa Cruz pointed out the folly of sailing against England in mid-winter, and inquired about a fallback strategy, Philip replied serenely, "We are fully aware of the risk that is incurred by sending a major fleet in winter through the Channel without a safe harbor, but . . . *since it is all for His cause, God will send good weather.*"[48]

Since they continued to follow what they perceived to be a path of righteousness, the Spanish Hapsburgs always expected such miracles to bridge any gap between ends and means. Thus in 1574, as bad news poured in, Philip II lamented to his private secretary and chaplain Mateo Vázquez, "Unless God performs a miracle, which our sins do not merit, it is no longer possible to maintain ourselves for [more than a few] months, let alone years." News of further reverses, instead of leading him to reconsider his unsuccessful policies, reinforced his expectation of direct divine intervention: "May God help us with a miracle. I tell you that we need one so much that it seems to me that He *must* choose to give us a miracle, because without one I see everything in the worst situation imaginable."[49]

Admittedly the strategic vision of his grandson sometimes took a secular turn. In 1629, on hearing that Louis XIII of France had invaded Italy, Philip IV scribbled on a memorandum from Olivares that "[m]y intention is to get my revenge on France for its recent behavior," and to that end "I shall be there in person. *Fame, after all, cannot be gained without taking personal part in some great enterprise.* This one will enhance my reputation, and I gather it should not be too difficult."[50] Yet that same year the king informed another senior minister that "I seek salvation, and want to placate God by obeying His laws and by making sure that others obey them, without exception" because then, "even if misfortunes rain upon us, you need have no fear that they will harm us." Therefore, the king explained, "I desire the fear of God and executing his commands and doing Justice to be my guiding principle." He still felt the same three decades later. Upon hearing in 1656 that Britain had joined France, Portugal, and the Catalans in making war on him, Philip confided to Sor María de Ágreda, his principal spiritual confidante, that although "[t]he distress is greater than any that this Monarchy has ever seen, particularly since we lack the means to withstand even one part of such a great storm," he intended to keep on fighting because "I have firm faith that, unless our sins make us unworthy, Our Lord will deliver us from this great storm without allowing these kingdoms, so loyal to the Catholic Church, to be brought down by heretics."[51]

Agency and Structure

Many minor miracles had indeed occurred, reinforcing the Messianic vision of the Spanish Hapsburgs (apart from the providential marriages, births, and deaths that created the empire of Charles V and extended it under Philip II). In 1571, a battle fleet led by Philip's brother, don John of Austria, defeated the Ottoman fleet at Lepanto; for thirty-six hours in August 1588, the Spanish Armada ("the largest fleet that has ever been in these seas since the creation of the world") lay at anchor off Calais, only a few miles from the army assembled for the conquest of England and within sight of the designated landing zone; and in 1634 a joint Spanish-Imperial army routed their enemies at the battle of Nördlingen, recovering most of Germany for the Catholic cause.[52] As late as 1653, Pietro Bassadonna, Venetian ambassador in Spain, recalled with astonishment how, just six years before, rebellion had reigned in Naples, Sicily, and Andalusia; a devastating plague epidemic raged throughout the Spanish Mediterranean; while "the king's revenues were alienated; his credit was exhausted; his allies were either declared enemies or neutral or undecided." In short, the Spanish monarchy had then resembled "the great Colossus [of Rhodes] which had been for so many years the wonder of the world until brought down by an earthquake in just a few minutes." And yet, despite numerous earthquakes, Bassadonna noted, the Spanish Colossus remained almost intact.[53]

As long as civil wars crippled France—1562–1598, 1621–1629, 1647–1653—the Spanish Hapsburgs could hold their own, but once the French stopped slaughtering each other, the superior resources available to their monarchs tilted the strategic balance of power in their favor. Louis XIV, Philip II's grandson, therefore made major gains at the expense of Spain at the Peace of the Pyrenees (1659), of Breda (1668), of Nijmegen (1678), and of Rijswik (1697)—and at the Peace of Utrecht (1713) his grandson gained universal recognition as ruler of Spain, its American dominions, and the Philippines.

Even if the Spanish Hapsburgs had done somewhat better in each round of peace negotiations, they were congenitally incapable of preserving their inheritance intact. The repeated intermarriages that created and expanded their accidental empire inevitably reduced the genetic pool of its rulers, producing heirs with serious defects: not just poor health, physical deformities, and weakness, but also reduced fertility. The degree of inbreeding is stunning. Many of Charles V's ancestors had intermarried—Mary of Burgundy had only six great-grandparents instead of eight, while her son Philip married his third cousin Joanna, daughter of Ferdinand and Isabella, themselves the product of numerous intermarriages among the various branches of the House of Trastámara—creating an "inbreeding coefficient" for Charles of 0.037. The marriages of both Charles and his son Philip to their double-cousins dramatically increased the coefficient of Philip's son Don Carlos to 0.211. The marriage of Philip IV (who boasted only eight great-great-grandparents instead of the normal sixteen) to his niece made him the great-uncle as well as the father of his children, while their mother was also their cousin. This produced an "inbreeding coefficient" for their only child, Charles II, of 0.254—even higher than that of the offspring of siblings (0.25)—and although he lived to be thirty-nine, Charles was physically deformed, mentally challenged, and sterile.[54]

Endogamy also produced another serious problem for the Spanish Hapsburgs: insanity. Queen Joanna, grandmother of both Philip II and his first wife, María Manuela, lived in confinement at Tordesillas until her death in 1555, her behavior so idiosyncratic that her own progeny feared she might be either a witch or a heretic. Joanna's grandmother Isabella of Portugal had also been locked up, ending her days as a demented prisoner. Don Carlos and

Charles II thus not only boasted a dangerously small gene pool, but one that contained at least two cases of serious mental instability.

The Spanish Hapsburgs continued their strategy of matrimonial imperialism despite explicit warnings of the dangers involved. For example, the death of both his only son, Don Carlos, and his second wife in 1568 meant that Philip could not avoid remarrying, and he arranged to wed his niece Anne of Austria. To his surprise, Pope Pius V refused to grant the necessary dispensation. In a holograph letter, the pontiff stated that "although some of our predecessors have granted dispensations in similar cases" of consanguinity, they had erred: according to Pius, no pope had the power to override the biblical prohibition on marriages between uncle and niece. Moreover, the pope added, "we have already seen the unfortunate consequences of these marriages of the first degree"—an unsubtle reference to the mental instability of Don Carlos.[55] Philip refused to listen. Instead he blackmailed the pope, threatening to forsake the Holy League against the Ottoman sultan desired by Pius unless he got a dispensation. In November 1570, with the pope's reluctant blessing, he therefore married his twenty-one-year-old niece, producing seven children with an "inbreeding coefficient" of 0.22. Only one survived into his teens.

The material cost of the Spanish Hapsburgs' policy of conquest, blind faith, and incest was immense. The central government ran up a sovereign debt far beyond Spain's capacity to service: 85 million ducats by 1598, over 112 million by 1623, almost 182 million by 1667, and almost 223 million by 1687. Public sector borrowing on this scale—ten times total revenues, if not more—drained capital and raw materials from Spain, undercut local manufactures, and encouraged a "rentier" mentality among those sectors of the population with the potential to be entrepreneurs, while the need to create and increase taxes to repay lenders led to onerous fiscal expedients (especially duties on sales and on manufactures) with high social and economic costs. Worst of all, most tax revenues were remitted abroad, to fund armies and navies fighting to achieve international goals that mattered to the dynasty but not to most Spaniards. The government of Philip IV exported at least 150 million ducats to fund his foreign wars.

Admittedly, some of Spain's misery stemmed from an unparalleled combination of extreme weather and plague in the 1590s and again in the mid-seventeenth century, but the central government intensified these natural disasters with their disastrous policy choices. Philip IV argued that war, not peace, had become the norm in international relations: "With as many kingdoms and lordships as have been linked to this crown it is impossible to be without war in some area, either to defend what we have acquired or to divert our enemies."[56] Technically, the king was correct—he spent every day of his forty-four-year reign at war: against the Dutch (1621–1648), against the French (1635–1659), against Britain (1625–1630 and 1654–1659) and in the Iberian peninsula (1640–1668), as well as in Germany and in Italy—but he could certainly have avoided (or more swiftly ended) some conflicts, and thereby reduced the fiscal pressure that crushed his subjects and provoked so many of them to rebel. In the Netherlands, he could have renewed the Twelve Years Truce with the Dutch Republic when it expired in 1621; and he might have exploited the simultaneous Hapsburg victories in Germany and the Netherlands in 1625 to negotiate an advantageous settlement. The king himself later admitted that he should have avoided war in Italy in 1628: "I have heard it said that the wars in Italy over Casale in Monferrat could have been avoided," he later wrote ruefully, and "if I have made a mistake in some way and given Our Lord cause for displeasure, it was in this."[57] Above all, Philip IV fumbled every opportunity to make peace with France. In 1637, after just two years of war, Louis XIII sent a secret agent to open informal peace talks, but Olivares insisted on a public overture: "Let those who broke the peace, sue for peace," he pompously chided the French envoy. Two years later, the count-duke warned his master that "we need to think about bending in order to avoid breaking" and sent a special envoy of his own to Paris to start talks—but his willingness to negotiate ended as soon as a major peasant rebellion in Normandy seemed to weaken his rival.[58]

Shortly after his fall in 1643, Olivares realized the foolishness of a faith-based foreign policy, confessing to a former colleague: "This is the world, and so it has always been, even though we thought we could perform miracles and turn the world into something it can never be"—but for twenty-two years he had acted on the assumption that "God is Spanish and favors our nation." In 1650, an English statesman in Madrid marveled at the capacity of Spain's leaders for such self-deception. They were, he wrote, "a wretched, miserable, proud, senseless people and as far from the wise men I expected as can be imagined; and if some miracle do not preserve them, this crown must be speedily destroyed." A generation later, one of Charles II's ministers made the same point: "I fear deeply for Italy; I am very worried about Catalonia; and I never forget about America, where the French already have too many colonies. We cannot govern by miracles forever."[59] As Burbank and Cooper observed, "Imperial leaders, at any time or place [can] imagine only so many ways to run a state," and when the miracles ceased, and Charles II died childless in 1700, the Spanish Hapsburgs' "bag of tricks" was empty.

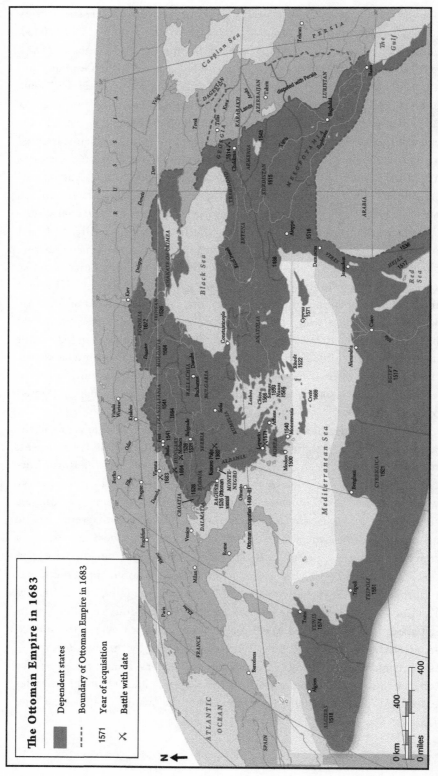

The Ottoman Empire in 1683.

CHAPTER 7	Islam's Final Push
	The Ottomans versus the Hapsburgs
	Andrew Wheatcroft

A T ITS OUTSET, THE clash between the Hapsburg and the Ottoman
empires appeared as a classic fundamental clash of faiths—Islam versus
Christianity. For contemporaries it was self-evidently a seamless extension of
the medieval wars of religion in western Asia, a confrontation between two
distinct systems of behavior and belief. Such a conveniently simple explanation obscured all other possibilities.

The synecdoche—*the clash of faiths*—explained everything in terms of
good and evil.[1] It therefore hindered even the direct discussion of the contest
in any other terms. What actually happened (as far as we know) illuminates
a different range of possibilities, as well as other narratives.[2] Moreover, the
enduring *strategic rivalry* between the Ottoman Turks and the Hapsburgs was
a conflict that ebbed and flowed over time, and in its later stages, dramatically changed its shape. At the very least, we can now see how the contest
between the Ottomans and the Hapsburgs evolved into a political constant in
European statecraft. In fact, their unremitting conflict, from the first invasion
to the last treaty of peace, continued for over two hundred years. Arguably, it
still has an impact on the present.

Like most clans or families, the origins of both the Ottomans and
the Hapsburgs take us along a similar path between evidence and myth.
The Ottomans were, literally, the sons of Osman, *Osmanli*, while the
Hapsburgs took their name from their point of origin—a small castle
known as the *Habichtsburg*, the Hawk's Fort, close to the town of Brugg,
in the area of today's Switzerland known as the Aargau. The Ottomans

were, at their start, an invisible and unimportant element in one of the great migrations of the Turkic peoples from central into western Asia. They survived among the great mass of the Seljuk Turks because of their strong group identity and fighting skills. The Hapsburgs, on the other hand, gradually extended their territory, but for many decades the full extent of their limited possessions could be seen from the tower of the *Habichtsburg*. They emerged from the mass of minor nobility when Rudolf of Hapsburg was elected King of the Romans in 1273, as a compromise candidate. Nine years later, he awarded the border duchies of Austria and Styria to his sons, and these eventually became the basis of the Hapsburg family patrimony.

Like the Hapsburgs, the Ottomans formed their base on the fringes of greater states. Their march to greatness began when Osman seized the town of Bursa from Byzantine Constantinople. His son Orhan made Bursa into the most significant city in northwestern Anatolia, and around 1350, the Byzantine emperor paid the Genoese to carry around 10,000 Ottomans, men and horses, across the straits into Europe, to fight as his shock troops in a civil war.

From the beginning, the Ottomans constructed a military state, first in Bursa and then in conquered Thrace and the wider Balkan area. By contrast, the Hapsburgs existed in the shadow of much more powerful families, building their connections by marriage, alliances, and as officeholders within the Holy Roman Empire. A century after the first Hapsburg imperial figure (Rudolf), a second, Albert, briefly occupied the same high office, and then a third, Frederick, in the 1450s, held the title, but little power. It was his son Maximilian who, by marrying the daughter of the rich and powerful Charles (Duke of Burgundy), built a solid basis for Hapsburg power.

The Ottomans and the Hapsburgs were, therefore, both self-made families, with the Ottomans following the more normal path of growth by conquest. The Hapsburgs, by contrast, had a more complex task. They were nobodies—minor counts—who slowly rose to become the elected leaders of the Holy Roman Empire. They accomplished this by building alliances and connections, similar to the techniques for rising in any large international bureaucracy today.

In 1453, the Ottoman sultan Mehmed II besieged and captured the last bastion of the Byzantine Empire, the city of Constantinople. By conquest, he assumed all of the rights and status of the Roman emperors in the east. A year before, on March 19, 1452, the Hapsburg Frederick was crowned in Rome as Frederick III, Holy Roman Emperor, by Pope Nicolas V. In that coincidence lay the deep roots of their incipient contest.

The arena for this rivalry is roughly contained in space to the territory between Belgrade and Vienna; in time the rivalry marks its start to the first two decades of the sixteenth century. By then, the Ottoman and Hapsburg empires were already engaged in a savage war for the richest prize in Europe: the Mediterranean. It was not until 1521 that an Ottoman sultan planned a new front in southeastern Europe. It was opportunistic—attacking the enemy at their most vulnerable point—but it also reflected a particular view of how the Ottoman state should develop. The Ottomans were rooted in the east, in western Asia and the Levant, with aspirations to become a great power in the Indian Ocean. With their capital since 1453 at Constantinople, their natural competitors were the Safavid rulers of Iran, Shia Muslims, with whom they shared a long border. The Hapsburgs' interests, by the first decade of the sixteenth century, centered on Germany and Europe west of the Alps. Their richest and most productive territories were the Low Countries, where two major ports—Antwerp and Amsterdam—had access to the North Sea, and the world beyond. The most recent addition to the Hapsburg domain was Spain, with its political center in Madrid. Vienna, the Hapsburgs' official capital, was far away on the distant eastern periphery.

As so often happens, the Hapsburgs' natural antagonist was their nearest neighbor.[3] France fulfilled this role perfectly, and their rivalry lasted, intermittently, well into the nineteenth century. Given the Ottoman preoccupation with their natural rivals in Iran, the opening of a second front between the Hapsburgs and the Ottomans was not inevitable. In fact, it was a result of a deliberate choice by one powerful faction within the Ottoman political system.

The united Hapsburg Empire of Charles V eventually began to come apart. On his abdication (1556), he left his Spanish domains to his son Philip II, and accepted that his brother Ferdinand would succeed him as Holy Roman Emperor. Philip II had hoped to take the imperial title himself, but talk after 1572 of a unitary Hapsburg Empire is misleading. Maximilian repeatedly rejected his cousin's entreaties to help him suppress rebels in the Netherlands, and until the 1620s, there was little cooperation or collaboration between the two branches of the family.[4]

The First Phase of the Strategic Rivalry

Everything changed in the 1520s, when a three-way contest between King Francis I of France, the Ottoman Sultan Suleiman, and Charles of Hapsburg got underway. In June 1519, Charles, supported by the limitless funds of the

Fugger family, was elected the Holy Roman Emperor. By doing so, he had trumped Francis, who had also put himself forward as the next Holy Roman Emperor.[5] The election results fueled a personal antagonism between Francis and Charles, while simultaneously engendering a political challenge between Charles and Suleiman. Proving that diplomatic necessity often makes strange bedfellows, the Catholic Francis and the Muslim Suleiman made common cause. And what was that cause? Simply put, their alliance (formalized in 1535) was built upon a common interest in wrecking or at least limiting Hapsburg power.

Suleiman and Charles inherited their huge domains, the product of good luck and able empire building.[6] Both men were driven to match or exceed their forebears: they craved the luster of conquest. Suleiman, who personally led thirteen major campaigns, eventually commissioned a series of illustrated histories of his victories to preserve them for posterity. Charles also ordered many of his feats commemorated in paintings, engravings, and other forms of art—undoubtedly, the most impressive of which were twelve large tapestries after the drawings by Jan Cornelisz Vermeyen (his war artist) to record his capture of Tunis in 1535.

Theirs was a highly personalized contest, between two individuals each highly conscious of the other's ambitions. Both men evolved an iconography that celebrated and fortified their imperial claims.[7] When Charles entered Bologna prior to his coronation as Holy Roman Emperor in 1530, his pages carried a series of helmets, the "helmets of Caesar"—one surmounted by an imperial eagle, another encircled with a crown. As reported to Suleiman, these were the emblems of ancient power. During his 1532 march toward Vienna, Suleiman on ceremonial occasions was portrayed wearing an extraordinary *helmet crown* made in Venice. This was a golden helmet in the Roman style, but crowned by a lavishly jeweled tiara, grander and larger than that worn by the pope in 1530. As heir by right of conquest to the Byzantine emperors, Suleiman was demonstrating that he outranked both the "spurious" Holy Roman Emperor and the pope of Rome.[8]

The Hapsburg ambassador to the Ottoman court became a "speechless corpse" (according to a Venetian report), when, on the march to Vienna, he saw the collection of jewels and gold in the sultan's campaign tent. Pride of place went to the helmet crown, described as Suleiman's *imperial crown*, prominently displayed and surrounded by weapons of war. Outside of these ostentatious displays, the Ottomans made it difficult for westerners to form any perception of their mysterious inner world. Ambassadors and envoys to the Ottoman court (the Sublime Porte) were under especially strict control. Rarely did any of their number speak Turkish, a language completely incomprehensible to them. Throughout the Ottoman ascendency, unfamiliarity with the language remained the central reason behind the isolation of most western emissaries. They remained reliant on their Ottoman-controlled translators, who were the means by which the Ottoman government planted ideas or hid information from these distinguished and well-guarded guests. In fact, these translators were the Ottomans' main medium for controlling the flow of knowledge to the outside world. Just to make sure that the right information was being sent back to the envoy's government, all the reports were examined by the Grand Vizier's department before they were approved for dispatch. In the west, the Ottomans had no such problems gathering accurate information, and often used their own citizens living in Vienna—mostly Greeks and Jews—to spy for them. One Grand Vizier asked for—and received—a complete set of drawings of Vienna's walls and bastions.

After his imperial coronation in 1530, Charles had begun to talk of himself as "Caesar," to which the Ottoman court responded by acknowledging him only by his lesser title as King of Spain. The Venetian ambassador to the French court told Francis I, "Sultan Suleyman . . . detests the emperor and his title of *Caesar*."[9]

What was their strategic competition about? Religion played an important part—evident in the writings on both sides of the frontier.[10] However, it was never about conversion: Christians paid a range of taxes that were not borne by Muslims, charges that varied with the local practices of the different parts of the Ottoman Empire. In aggregate, Christians were more heavily taxed than Muslims, but they were also excused from duties and services that burdened the Muslim population.[11] Nor was it about ethnic cleansing: Ottoman officials in Buda and those in Royal Hungary loathed the chaos and cruelty of border raiding and tried to control it. Nevertheless, the rhetoric used by both communities (Muslim and Christian) alluded to a limitless antagonism between these visceral as well as political enemies. For a wide European popular audience, Muslims were the "Erbfeind" (the Hereditary Enemy)—implacable enemies of all Christians. This worldview spread through propaganda in printed images and texts, drama, opera, sermons, fine art, and sculpture.[12] In the Islamic world, the visual element of antagonism was less dominant, but the ideological gulf was just as profound. The theory was of an unbridgeable chasm between their faiths, and an unremitting and enduring enmity. Still, the realities of war and politics often demanded accommodation with this enemy, but no Muslim ruler could ever make a conclusive "peace" with a Christian state. It was fundamental to the Muslim mission that the world would never be in a state of complete peace until the rule of Islam was universal. In the

Ottoman state, Islam, Judaism, and Christianity were all recognized and practiced, unlike in Catholic and Protestant states in the west that officially persecuted those who did not follow the official state faith. But there remained a huge gulf between Muslims—by birth or conversion—and all non-Muslims. Only Muslims were full members of society.

However, after periods of full-scale war between the Ottomans and the Hapsburgs there were truces and armistices. Some were ineffective and others short-lived, but many resulted in long periods of relative peace. The Truce of Zsitvatorok in 1606, terminating the Long War (1593–1606), lasted until the late 1650s, as it was extended many times.

Unusual, for a state built upon the warlike tendency of its populations, the foundation of Ottoman power was not maintained by the Ottoman warrior caste. Rather, the foundation of Ottoman power rested on a loyal, professional military corps—the new troops, the *janissaries*—forcibly recruited from among Christian villages in the Balkans. Far from home, they had no clan or family loyalties and depended upon the sultan for every scrap of food, clothing, and work. Upon their intake, they were brought to Constantinople, where they were trained to serve where they could perform best. Some became the new troops; others became officials, governors, or administrators. Women, too, entered the system, to work in the royal palaces, or to become the mothers of future sultans. The west dismissed these women merely as sexual playthings, but this assumption ignored the women of great capacity and hidden power who emerged from this system.[13]

Among the Hapsburgs, the process of military recruitment was not as formalized or structured as in the Ottoman system, but was based instead on patronage and recommendation. Hapsburg armies fighting the Ottomans were formed for the occasion from many different sources: there were local levies, mercenaries, allies, contingents from the Holy Roman Empire, and often, foreign adventurers. It was often referred to collectively by the old term *crusade*, and as such was, in fact, based on a network of mutual connection similar to that which had brought the Hapsburgs to prominence. More flexible and individualistic than the Ottoman structure, it was less able to supply reliably qualified men. The dynastic dimension was very different. The Ottoman dynasty was competitive and unstable, while the Hapsburgs were driven by a strong sense of collective, dynastic identity. The Hapsburg system also found official public roles for women members of the dynasty. Able Hapsburg women occupied key positions, such as Charles V's aunt, Archduchess Margaret of Austria, who ruled the Low Countries continuously from 1519 to her death in 1530. The marriage market, in which the Hapsburgs became so expert, not only provided the mothers of future Hapsburg rulers, but sound and loyal advisors like Philip II's second wife, Elisabeth of Valois. Perhaps the most successful Hapsburg monarch was Maria Theresa, daughter of Emperor Charles VI, who reinvigorated the entire state between 1740 and 1780.

In summary, though the processes employed were entirely different, the two dynasties both attended to the common problems inherent in creating an empire. The problem of powerful and growing local interests restricted the development of centralized power in both the Ottoman and Hapsburg polities. The process was common, but the time scale was quite different. The centralization of power in the Ottoman lands predated the Hapsburg equivalent: it took place in the fifteenth and sixteenth centuries. The same degree of centralized power only emerged in the eighteenth century within the Hapsburg domains.

Were Ottoman and Hapsburg objectives similar or dissimilar? For the Ottomans, the key objectives were their status as the dominant power, and the sultan's unique standing in the world. The long series of wars with the Hapsburgs was conducted as much to deny the same status to any possible Hapsburg rival. It was not about acquiring territory per se, nor was it about building an Ottoman colony. On the other hand, the Hapsburg objective was to resist, survive, and extend their domain. The course of the conflict was mostly driven by Ottoman military actions, which were always resisted. The Hapsburgs, for domestic political reasons, could not remain passive. Rather, they had to respond aggressively to any provocation. In reality, this rarely meant much more than marching on Buda or attacking an Ottoman fortress. But the Hapsburg goals were transformed when they took the offensive during the period 1684–1686, when the Hapsburg-led Holy League committed itself to regaining the whole of Hungary, and not to cease fighting until they had done so.

While parallelism should not be exaggerated, Suleiman I and Charles V shared common views of world monarchy, if from opposed perspectives. Both men aimed at becoming the supreme world monarch. In 1515, when Charles had visited the city of Bruges, he was hailed as the future ruler who might take back Jerusalem from Muslim hands; in 1519, as he was elected emperor, his Chancellor Mercuriano Gattinara restated the claim—that Charles would accomplish what previous crusaders had failed to do. When he was crowned emperor by Pope Clement VII in 1530, the coming crusade was the central focus of the celebrations. After Charles led the campaign to seize the city of Tunis in 1535, he was acclaimed as "the Destroyer of the Turks."

In Constantinople, equivalent claims were made. Suleiman I's childhood friend and later Grand Vizier, the key figure in Ottoman government, was Ibrahim Pasha. Ibrahim, known as the *Frenk*, or foreigner, because of his preoccupation with the west, presented his master in the same terms as Gattinara. Suleiman was the universal ruler (*sahib-kiran*), who like Alexander the Great would bring the world together under a single ruler.[14] In fact, Charles's courtiers frequently applied the Alexander analogy to their master.

The Hapsburgs were more adept at developing their family mythology and their unique commitment to the faith over the centuries than any of their European rivals. This extended to their claimed absolute dedication in the struggle against Islam, the enemy of the Christian faith. Yet the Hapsburgs came late to enthusiastic support of war between Islam and Christianity— much later, in fact, then the neighboring states to the east of Vienna.[15] The Polish Commonwealth, for example, had a better claim to be the Bulwark of Christendom than the Austrian Hapsburgs. While the Poles fought, Charles V's grandfather and his predecessor as Holy Roman Emperor, Emperor Maximilian, built his family's position through alliances and advantageous marriages for his children and grandchildren. *Bella gerant alii, tu felix Austria nube* ("Let others wage war: thou, happy Austria, marry") was a traditional couplet. The Ottomans, by contrast, waged war. It was the epicenter of their political and social system. [16]

Making War

The long strategic rivalry between the Ottomans and the Hapsburgs that developed after 1521 took a simple form: every year the Ottomans threatened the eastern Hapsburg lands, sent armies into Hungary, and regularly loosed marauders—thousands of Tartar horsemen and other freebooters—to ravage the Hapsburg border year after year. The defenses of the Austrian domains on the Hungarian frontier were feeble, and little in the way of a permanent defense force existed, except those organized by some of the cities, like Graz, and the retinues of noble families along the frontier.

The human capital of each empire was vast. Charles V, it has been esti- mated, had 25 million subjects in his territories, while Suleiman had per- haps half that number.[17] The Hapsburg domain, however, was a hodgepodge of different territories across the world, crown rights, and other sources of revenue, some highly productive and others of negligible utility. However, even the richest and best-organized territories, like the Low Countries, did not generate enough surpluses to accommodate the costs of Charles's wars of conquest. Only the silver from the Potosí mines in Peru, shipped out by the Spanish treasure fleet, produced sufficient sudden infusions of specie to support the Hapsburg campaigns against Suleiman I, and this extraordinary income was intermittent and erratic. By contrast, Ottoman tax revenue was stable and regular. For the most part, therefore, Austrian Hapsburg wars had to be financed on credit, or from sudden windfalls.

After 1545, silver and gold from the Americas became more regular, with shipments from the mines at Potosí in modern Bolivia and from Mexico. They were also vulnerable to attack by privateers, like the 1573 raids by the Englishman Sir Francis Drake. Extraordinary income might underpin the Spanish state, but the costs of war eventually forced Spain into a major bankruptcy in 1575. The Austrian Hapsburgs detached themselves from the Mediterranean campaigns. The defense of Malta in 1565 and the sea battle at Lepanto (1570) were conducted without any involvement of Vienna; the Holy Roman Empire did not even belong to the Holy League that underwrote the Battle of Lepanto.

Eventually both Vienna and Madrid withdrew from the Ottoman wars. In 1580, a truce was concluded between the Spanish Hapsburgs and the Ottomans. This resulted from the Ottoman reconquest of Tunis in 1574, and Spain's inheritance of the Portuguese throne in 1580. Following Charles V's capture of Tunis in 1535, it had become a symbol of Hapsburg determination to dominate the Mediterranean. Now, with Tunis lost and no prospect of its recovery, Spain's grand strategy shifted decisively and increasingly worldwide, with the new Portuguese acquisition. Throughout the 1580s, both Vienna and Madrid were at peace with the Ottomans. However, when in 1595 Emperor Rudolf II went to war following an Ottoman attack in 1593 on Austrian fortresses in Royal Hungary, Madrid did not support his campaign, and maintained its truce in the Mediterranean.

While lack of money constrained the Hapsburgs, the Ottoman Empire retained its capacity to wage more or less continuous war. It was organized primarily to produce taxes for wars and the manpower to fight them. The process was managed by an administration better organized and more professional than that in any part of the Hapsburg lands. In the sixteenth century, the ability of the sultans to raise armies depended on a highly organized system of fiefs (*timars*), other liabilities for military service, and their ability to financially support a permanent full-time professional military (*janissaries*)—all of which was effectively managed by a centralized palace administration. The Ottomans relied on the revenues flowing steadily year after year from Egypt, which underpinned military expeditions into Europe, campaigns against the Safavids, and their Mediterranean campaigns. However, other provinces were also expected to produce either money, services, or material in kind, including disputed Hungary. Even in the early eighteenth century, the Ottomans remained capable of financing wars through taxing the state's internal resources. Over time, however, the budget came under increasing pressure due to the increasing costs of manpower and war materiel. Most of these additional costs were a result of increasing numbers of janissary infantry and artillerymen whose salaries had to be met from the military budget. In 1527 there were only 18,000 janissaries and artillerymen, but by 1670 their number had increased to 70,000. In part, this additional cost was covered by the reduction of payments to the cavalry regiments.[18]

The administration of all of this military effort was centralized in the capital, Constantinople, with a reasonably reliable structure of government operating in the provinces. A large corps of professional officials governed the empire; even at the highest level, they were slaves of the sultan, subject to a draconian, almost military, code of discipline. They were well trained to administer the sultan's lands on a uniform basis wherever they were sent. Their goal was to design state functions so as to provide the sultan with an optimum structure for the support of war, though revenue was often diverted to luxurious living. Nonetheless, war remained an act of "merit," aimed at extending the domain of Islam, a clarity of purpose the Hapsburgs did not achieve until the nineteenth century.

The fragility of the Austrian Hapsburg state before 1700 was structural. In 1519, Charles V had inherited a ragbag of territories, of which the best ruled and organized were the Low Countries. His brother Ferdinand added three kingdoms—Hungary, Bohemia, and Croatia—to the Hapsburg domain, each with a different legal structure and administration. In each area, the common feature was that central taxation was fiercely resisted by local assemblies. Bringing the territories into some kind of harmony and administrative coherence was never wholly achieved before the nineteenth century. In 1683–1686 the Hapsburgs began the process of extending their control over all of Hungary. Although this carried major problems and high costs, it began the process of constructing a unifom (and uniformly managed and taxed) national state. At the same time, the efficiency and revenue production of the Ottoman system was in decline.

However, by the end of the sixteenth century the strain of paying for Hapsburg garrisons, fortresses, and recurring warfare was pushing Vienna to its financial limits. The Hapsburgs began searching for a suitable form of peace—it was always Vienna that sought truce extensions—and after 1606 they had no wish to reopen hostilities. However, the reputation and legacy of Sultan Suleiman the Lawgiver, or Suleiman the Magnificent, as he was known in the west, was wholly tied up with the conquest of Hungary, and that noble objective could not be abandoned by his successors. In addition to this material objective, the emperor and the sultan were also staking their reputation and status. Though the Hapsburgs had few solid political or economic interests in Hungary, their need to maintain their prestige dictated that they would fight.

Invading Hungary

The Ottoman advance in the west began almost seven years before the Hapsburgs inherited the crowns of Hungary, Bohemia, and Croatia. However, after taking Belgrade in 1521, a second stage, the assault on Hungary and putting pressure on the Hapsburg hereditary lands, was always envisaged by Suleiman.[19] The advance was twice postponed because of commitments elsewhere, but in the autumn of 1525 all was in readiness for action the following spring.

When Suleiman led the Ottoman army into Hungary in 1526, it was as a *gazi*, a Muslim warrior, fulfilling his duty to extend the boundaries of Islam. He also had the prudent motive of gratifying the Janissaries' insistence on a new land war so as to gain plunder. The objective was the Hungarian capital, Buda. Near the town of Mohács, about 180 miles from Belgrade, the smaller Hungarian army foolishly attacked the Ottomans. Janissary musketry and artillery fire inflicted huge casualties on the Hungarians, and their leader, King Louis, while making a hasty retreat, drowned in a stream, leaving no heir. Or rather, he had left a brother-in-law, Archduke Ferdinand of Hapsburg, who ruled the eastern Hapsburg lands on his brother Charles V's behalf. By the terms of the marriage settlement, Ferdinand would be Louis's successor if the Hungarian and Bohemian king died without an heir. The Hapsburgs had a legal right to defend Hungary, as a matter of principle, and this was something on which the Hapsburgs were always immovable. As the Turks continued their march to Buda, where they ransacked the royal castle, a rival contender, the governor of Transylvania, John Zápolya, claimed the Hungarian throne. As he promised to become an Ottoman vassal, the sultan backed his claim, even as his army returned to Constantinople.

Once back in Constantinople, Suleiman confronted a renewed rebellion in Anatolia, and in 1528, he faced new Safavid pressure, which culminated in three full-scale campaigns and the Ottoman capture of Baghdad in 1534. However, in 1529 he found time to mount a large expedition to besiege Vienna. This move into entirely unknown territory began in the summer, too late for a 900-mile march through unfriendly terrain. Such a late start predestined failure, and the siege ended prematurely when the first snows fell early. The forced retreat back to Constantinople during the first months of a Balkan winter cost the Sultan's army dearly. Suleiman did not make the same mistake in 1532, when he again advanced on Vienna. This time the army set out in early spring, but was delayed when the sultan insisted on besieging a small Hapsburg fortress on the frontier of Austria (Güns) with a garrison of only 700 men. It was a costly delay.

The 1532 invasion was no secret, and the Hapsburgs were given ample time to recruit an army comparable in size and professional skill to that of the Ottomans. The attack in 1529 had, however, alarmed them, and they were not sure the city could survive a second siege. But this time Charles V, supported by his brother Ferdinand, believed he had the capacity to meet the Ottomans in the field. News soon reached him of the Ottomans' advance, with Suleiman taking personal command. Writing to his wife, Empress Isabella, the emperor said that he too was "resolved to sally forth against him in my own person, with everything I can find to resist him." The Imperial Diet, on learning that the Turks had begun their advance, agreed to raise an army of 50,000 to join the emperor at Regensburg on the Danube on August 15. The emperor himself contributed a contingent of 38,000 men, including first-rate Spanish and Italian infantry, while Ferdinand was to raise almost 50,000, plus a war fleet to sail down the Danube. Not all the contingents materialized, but in theory, Europe would face the Ottomans with a huge force of about 130,000 men.

Yet the figures were not quite what they seemed. Thirty thousand of the Turkish force were marauders (*akinji*), highly effective in terrorizing the civilian population, but of little value against trained cavalry and infantry. On the other hand, the high-quality troops supplied by the Diet were funded for the war season of 1532, but only to defend the territory of the Holy Roman Empire. This included the Austrian duchies and Vienna, but excluded any action farther east. They were absolutely prohibited from crossing into Hungary in support of some ambitious Hapsburg war of conquest. In the end, this great effort was in vain, because the grand vizier, Ibrahim Pasha, in direct command of the expedition, decided to abandon the advance on Vienna, because, after the siege of Güns, too little time was left in the campaigning season to guarantee success.

Suleiman and his Grand Vizier Ibrahim had learned from the campaigns of 1521, 1526, and 1529. For one thing, they better understood just how daunting the 900 miles separating Vienna from Constantinople were, for once past Belgrade, there was no secure base or source of supply. Time and again, time and distance proved more dangerous enemies than the forces that the Hapsburgs might muster. Each Ottoman army launched against Vienna revealed new difficulties of operating so far from home. As the Ottomans had no permanent presence in Hungary, on which to build a logistical base, the difficulties of waging war in this northern environment were quite different and far greater than anything the Ottomans had encountered in western Asia or along the Mediterranean littoral.

In Ottoman terms, there were two simultaneous enduring strategic rivalries, west and east. Although the sultan and his fellow "westerners" saw the Hungarian front as a prime Ottoman concern, there was still a strong constituency within Constantinople that saw an equal (or greater challenge) coming from the Safavids in the east. Equally, the "easterners" made a strong case for not letting the growing instability in Anatolia, the Levant, and the Arabian Peninsula fester too much longer without military intervention. In 1538, Suleiman's inclination turned again and again to matters in the west. He sent an army to Moldavia and established Ottoman authority from the Black Sea inland to the frontiers of Hungary. This also allowed his reliable Tartar allies in the Crimea to join his armies operating up to the Austrian frontier. In 1540, John Zápolya died, after agreeing that Ferdinand should succeed him in Transylvania. However, shortly before his death, his young wife had borne a son, John Sigismund, who by rights should have succeeded his father. Ferdinand, sensing an opportunity to take all of Hungary, sent his army to besiege Buda.

In the following spring, ostensibly in support of Zápolya's heir, the full Ottoman army marched on Buda, brushing aside Ferdinand's force still besieging the city. This time, however, the Ottomans came to stay. The bulk of the Hungraian kingdom was now under direct or indirect Ottoman control. However, Suleiman recognized that the continued Hapsburg occupation of the Hungarian border adjacent to the Austrian provinces and Moravia, as well as Royal Hungary, was non-negotiable. He demanded a formal recognition of Ottoman sovereignty over Hungary, to be legitimated by tribute. He declared the son of John Zápolya, John Sigismund, as ruler of the new Principality of Transylvania through a Regent. This arrangement on the western front survived the abdication of Charles V, in 1556, with his brother elected emperor in his place. But when Ferdinand died in 1564, his son, Emperor Maximilian II, refused to pay the tribute agreed with Ferdinand, and the last act of Suleiman's life was a punitive expedition toward Vienna, with the sultan dying at the siege of Szigetvár in southern Hungary. After Suleiman's death in 1566, his immediate successors had no appetite at all for adventure in the north. Neither Selim II nor his son Murad III ever took command of an army in the field, while Murad's son Mehmed III only went on campaign at the insistence of his janissaries and strong pressure from the grand vizier, Koça Sinan Pasha.[20] The Austrian Hapsburgs, now led by Emperor Maximilian II, aspired to a more stable relationship with the Ottomans. This failed, but eventually a truce was negotiated in 1568, which lasted until 1593, when it was Maximilian's son, Emperor Rudolf II, who responded to a fresh Ottoman attack

The Battleground

Waging war at the eastern extremity of Europe in the sixteenth century bore little resemblance to wars waged by the Ottomans in any other region. The main reason was the nature of the battleground—the Carpathian mountain chain surrounded Hungary to the north, the Balkan ranges to the south, and the eastern Alps of Austria and the Karawanke in Slovenia to the west. From these mountain ranges, many rivers flowed down into the Danube and its tributaries. The city of Vienna, built on the banks of the great river, lay at the foot of the range of hills known as the Vienna Woods, the last of the high ground that ran north from the North Italian alpine ranges. Like the areas farther down river, the land east of Vienna was frequently inundated. Downstream in Hungary, numerous large rivers debouched into the Danube as it flowed east, with tributaries like the Morava, Raba, Váh, and Hron turning the land on both banks of the great river into a morass of impassable wetlands throughout the spring and early summer. East of Buda, the river Tisza flowed down from Ukraine, then ran parallel to the Danube, before it joined the main river at Novi Sad, above Belgrade. On the southern bend at Belgrade, the Sava and the Drava deposited a huge volume of water from the Italian and Dinaric Alps into the Danube.

The overflow from the Danube river system fed into the floodplain of the Pannonian basin, which had once been an ancient ocean floor. The skein of great rivers, their tributaries, and the streams that drained into them created fens and marshland in the saturated ground of western Hungary. In the hot summers, this turned into fertile farmland, but much of the country was still hard to traverse. On the edge of this Slough of Despond were two or three large cities—Vienna at the entry to the endless plain, Buda and Pest, before the Danube bend, and Belgrade on the southern arm of the Danube, plus many small towns on the higher ground, especially toward the frontier with Austria.

Because of climate and topography, there was only a limited number of possible routes for reaching Hapsburg lands with a full siege train. Taking any of them required thorough planning and preparation, which typically began in the autumn of the previous year. Then the army would gather at Constantinople, where the Anatolian contingents would unite with the army in Europe. In the subsequent spring, outside the capital's triple Byzantine walls, a tent city would accommodate the rapidly growing number of men. Not all the army would meet at Constantinople. The contingents from the Balkans, the allies and vassal states, and the Tartar cavalry horde would rendezvous with the main force at Edirne, Sofia, or Belgrade. Normally, Ottoman logistics and planning were far superior to those of any western army, allowing the Ottomans to maintain large armies in hostile territory for prolonged periods. Still, traversing the distance from Constantinople to Buda, the objective for the 1541 campaigning season, remained a daunting task. As only portions of the heavy siege equipment, powder, and ammunition could be produced locally, the Ottomans constructed a powder mill near Buda, and later two more, at Temeşvar and Eger.[21] The first cannon factory was set up in 1566, and a second in 1592, with a first arsenal in Belgrade in 1663. The larger pieces continued to be made at the huge cannon works (Tophane) in Constantinople. These new production facilities, closer to Vienna, greatly enhanced the Ottomans' capacity to conduct war upon Hapsburg domains.

On this unstable Hapsburg frontier, Suleiman did not trust mere words in a treaty of peace. There had to be a permanent Ottoman military presence and, therefore, central Hungary became an Ottoman province (*vilayet*) ruled from Buda. Initially, the garrison was limited to 2,500 men in Buda and 800 in Pest, but within a few years the garrison grew to 10,000. The cost of the troops and a series of new fortresses—effectively keeping the Ottoman province on a war footing—were hugely expensive. However, this provided a base from which Hapsburg fortresses beyond Buda could be captured and many towns Ottomanized.

The Hapsburgs, under threat in the Holy Roman Empire from Protestants, signed a truce that conceded all of Suleiman's main demands. The Truce of Edirne (1547) acknowledged the Hapsburg presence in western Hungary with an annual tribute of 30,000 gulden; Transylvania also paid 15,000. Suleiman's sovereign rights were recognized over the rest of Hungary. The agreement described Charles V as "king of Spain," not emperor, and Suleiman accepted this as adequate recognition of his own unique, and solitary, imperial status.

Suleiman's two personal campaigns in Hungary in the 1540s and the creation of an Ottoman province so close to Vienna—about eighty miles—stimulated a major change in Hapsburg attitudes. While Charles V was preoccupied with other challenges to his authority—in the Mediterranean,

Germany, and Italy—Ferdinand now saw the true danger of the Ottoman advance to his own patrimony. He had seen the ease with which the Ottomans' artillery fire could subdue the Hapsburg defenses: between 1521 and 1566, only thirteen fortresses were able to hold out for more than thirteen days.[22] He also had very full reports of the effect of janissary musketry, and of the lax and ill-coordinated conduct of operations against the Turks.

As a result, from the mid-1550s, serious reform and modernization were undertaken throughout the Hapsburg domains. In Vienna the formerly haphazard management of all military matters was handed over to a new Imperial War Council (*Hofkriegsrat*). Moreover, long-term modernization of the defenses was started, with the inspirational model of the defense of Eger in mind. In 1552, the key fortress of Eger in northern Hungary, manned by 2,300 defenders, had mounted a ferocious defense against an Ottoman army of about 40,000. After holding off five major Ottoman assaults, and enduring thirty-nine days of constant bombardment, the citizens watched the enemy retreat.

The idea was that these new and modernized fortresses would become—Eger-like—hubs of resistance to an advancing Ottoman army. This new Hapsburg defense line would run for 600 miles from the Adriatic to northern Hungary, with some 130 large and small forts, watchtowers, and *palanka*—low earth and timber constructions that could absorb heavy gunfire. In the most crucial sections in the north, there was defense in depth—forts only three or so miles apart. Some towns were given proper defenses for the first time. The intention was to create a barrier through which an enemy could not penetrate. To undertake this construction, the War Council commissioned the leading Italian military architects. Of course the cost of rebuilding the Hapsburg fortresses in Royal Hungary from the 1560s to the 1590s placed a tremendous strain on Hapsburg finance, greater, in fact, than the Ottoman reconstruction that had engendered it. By now, both sides of the confrontation realized that the costs were becoming ruinous and there was a decreasing appetite for full-scale military engagements that would greatly add to the financial stress.[23]

War in Hungary and on the border was cruel. Many of the horror stories of these wars are true: the massacres and atrocities, the endless lines of newly enslaved Hungarians in Sarajevo on their road of tears to Constantinople. However, it worked both ways. The Hapsburg armies also flayed men alive, impaled prisoners, and enslaved villagers. Savagery was a weapon of war and was used by both sides. Yet paradoxically, so were courtesy and a degree of humanity. When Suleiman took Belgrade in 1521, he did so upon terms that (unusually) spared the lives of the defenders. At the end, after a siege of some seventy-two days, when the survivors and their families, from a garrison of 700, opened the gates of the citadel at noon on August 29, the sultan wished to see the men whose courage and perseverance he had learned to respect. As was customary, the reprieved kissed the Padishah's hand and he gave them kaftans (robes) as a present and exchanged a few words with them. At the siege of Güns in 1532, he was once again chivalrous to a brave foe.[24] After Suleiman's death in 1566, his immediate successors had no appetite at all for adventure in the north.

The Long War (1593–1606)

The Long War, which began in 1593 and ended in 1606, marked a second phase in the enduring strategic rivalry between the Ottomans and the Hapsburgs. The first phase, beginning with Suleiman I and Charles V in 1520, had ended with the departure or death of the original protagonists. Charles V abdicated in 1556 and died in 1558, Ferdinand I died in 1564, and Suleiman I in 1566. Although the issues that had preoccupied them—world monarchy and its consequences—were occasionally revived as slogans, other tropes replaced them.

By the 1590s, although the line of Hapsburg fortresses was still incomplete, it was serving its purpose: the Ottoman armies could not penetrate the defensive cordon. However, Mehmed III did reluctantly go to war, laying siege to Eger, northeast of Buda, famous to both sides for its epic resistance to the Ottomans in 1552. However, this time the city submitted. The sultan took the surrender of the city's 7,000 defenders on October 12, 1596, and on October 25 defeated a Hapsburg relieving force at Mezőkeresztes. The twin victories were insignificant because the war dragged on inconclusively for another ten years. Once again, the Ottomans faced a coalition of Christian rulers—this time, Transylvania, Moldavia, Wallachia, all former Ottoman vassal states—an alliance promoted and partly financed by Pope Clement VIII. This intervention by the pope was significant, because it brought more men into the field against the Ottomans and provided funds collected throughout Europe to fight the war.

The long conflict forced the Ottomans into a multifront quagmire in which victory was elusive. As the length and extent of the fighting against an alliance of Christian nations—the Austrian border fortresses to the west, and Moldavia, Wallachia, and Transylvania in the east—became apparent, the exhausted Ottomans finally agreed to a truce in November 1606. The Truce of Zsitvatorok reflected the general war weariness of both sides, and held for nearly half a century.

Renewing the Struggle

From 1618 to 1648, the Hapsburgs, because of their involvement in the Thirty Years War, turned their backs on Hungary, while from 1623 until 1639 the Ottoman armies were occupied fighting local rebellions in Anatolia and the Levant, as well as the perennial war with the Safavids. On the Hungarian front there were no large-scale Ottoman invasions; however, Constantinople encouraged its Transylvanian vassal Bethlen Gabor, and his successor, György Rákóczi I, to occupy Upper Hungary.[25] The vacuum in the rest of the Ottoman border zone increased the amount of raiding by local landowners throughout Royal Hungary. The Ottoman officials in Buda, or the Ottoman garrison commanders of the border forts, responded by sending out their own raiders into Hapsburg territory.

The objectives were always the same: plunder, food, cattle, and especially prisoners, and, in addition, for the landowners who had fled into Hapsburg Hungary, collecting the rents from their former estates, now under Ottoman rule. This "little war" grew steadily because it cost the Ottoman state very little, and was extremely profitable for the raiders. There was a ready market for the prisoners, who might be ransomed by their families; if not, some were sold locally as slaves, while those who might fetch a higher price were taken to Belgrade for the long journey to Constantinople. The nature of the raiding was very harsh, for while it was the Turks who had previously been renowned for their "cruelty," now the marauders from the Hapsburg side adopted the same tactics.

The years of truce made raiding the only realistic military option along the border, but much had changed by the time war on a grand scale was renewed on the frontier. The Hapsburg commanders of the 1660s were more skillful than any comparable Ottoman general. They were battle-hardened from fighting the Dutch, the Swedes, and the French, as well as innumerable mercenaries, in the Thirty Years War. Officers like Raimundo Montecuccoli devised an organizational structure that allowed even relatively inexperienced soldiers to perform quite complex maneuvers on the battlefield.

Moreover, the Hapsburgs had built effective chains of command and control that did not really exist in the Ottoman ranks, which later proved to be a crucial weakness. Even a competent Ottoman commander could do very little to maneuver his men once contact was made. He would tell them to attack and they would attack. He could set objectives—besiege a town or fight to the death—and they would usually follow orders. A good western general, on the other hand, could devise a battle plan in terms of moving regiments or even companies around the battlefield. To accomplish this, the Hapsburgs instituted elaborate signals and battlefield communications systems within their forces. Much remained obscured by the fog of war, sometimes literally due to the all-pervasive smoke that covered the battlefield in the still early age of gunpowder. Despite this, Hapsburg commanders developed a large relative advantage in tactical execution. For the Ottomans, warfare still primarily depended on the professional skill of the individual janissary and the determination of their fighting units (*ortas*), not on the art of command.

There were no Ottoman equivalents of the Dutch pioneer military theorist, Maurice of Nassau, or inspirational commanders like Gustavus Adolphus. In the west, these men had been part of the development of kind of philosophy of war, while in the east, war remained an unchanging craft tradition. Because of this, the Turks had perfected a highly effective but very limited tactical repertoire. The sultan's professional infantry—the janissaries—still possessed a better logistical system, more experience in siegecraft, longer range and deadlier muskets than most European armies. Furthermore, with the right conditions, on the right day, they could outmatch any western foot soldiers. In the wrong circumstances, however, or under a commander they did not trust, they could easily deteriorate into a rabble. However, a defeated Ottoman army could quickly recover its spirit and sense of conviction and counterattack, with devastating consequences for an overconfident enemy.

Commanders like Raimundo Montecuccoli (a true "military intellectual") who had fought through the Thirty Years War, found the Turks a much faster and deadlier enemy than any that he had experienced on the battlefields of western Europe. Montecuccoli quickly learned new priorities. Against an enemy who used sabres, lances, and arrows, armor was essential; in western Europe it was being worn less and less. The cuirassier, out of fashion in the west, was the essential heavy cavalryman (still in armor) in the east. Against an elusive and highly trained Ottoman enemy, the ponderous western phalanxes of pikemen were of little value: commanders like Montecuccoli used more and more musketeers. As a result of such constant adaptations, the war in the east quickly became an extraordinary experimental zone in the art of war, which produced some of Europe's greatest commanders. There the west learned the value of hussars (light cavalry) and of mounted infantry (dragoons)—armed with muskets and pistols. They also learned at great cost the need for effective firepower to negate the mobility and offensive power of the janissaries.

The Ottomans learned as well, developing considerable skill with fire-arms, and more and more of them were trained in musketry and sharpshooting. But they failed to keep up with the west in the use of massed field artillery, or in the elaborate choreography of infantry drill and maneuver. The Turks honed their traditional skills to ever-higher standards: they trained the foot soldiers to use massed volley fire at the same time that this new technique was being developed in the west—but failed to develop the new skills required for maneuvering on the battlefield.[26] By the late seventeenth and the early eighteenth centuries, the janissary esprit de corps, their ideology of unit loyalty—the mess group eating from a single cooking pot—remained a huge advantage, but it was waning.

Seventeenth-century contemporaries invariably overestimated the size of Ottoman armies. It was assumed that the Turks mustered enormous forces, as many as 200,000 men. This was a fantasy, possibly born of fear. Turkish armies were terrifying to behold, and were certainly larger than those of western states. The impression of an army so large that it filled the entire horizon was partly deliberate, made possible by hordes of feudal levies and irregulars that swelled the Ottoman ranks. They vastly outnumbered the key components—the professional infantry and cavalry—which were a relatively small element of the sultan's array. Typically, though, only a small part of the Turkish army was of much value in battle, except to instill fear into those who saw (and heard) it for the first time. In quality, the best of the Ottomans were as least as good as the best of the western troops, but they now lacked the western troops' capacity to maneuver as a single organism.

Did the Ottoman military skills stagnate? None of the conventional explanations is really convincing. Was it because the Turks refused to alter a style of war sanctified by the successes of Mehmed II and Suleiman I? Was there some kind of intransigent resistance to change? Both of these causes played a part, as the Ottomans sincerely believed that their way was better, more honorable, and more courageous than the alternatives. Moreover, against their enemies in western Asia, the old ways were still effective. They had, unfortunately never experienced the new kind of war that Hapsburg commanders had endured during The Thirty Years War. So, their encounters with these new western armies and highly trained commanders came as a shock to the Ottomans, leaving them little time to adapt before they were overcome. Nevertheless, the Hapsburgs knew right up until the 1790s that on the battlefield they faced a dangerous, mobile, versatile, and implacable foe. This was their true "terror of the Turk."

The strategic rivalry between the Ottomans and the Hapsburgs resumed in earnest during the late 1650s, with army-level intervention instead of the endless raiding across the Austrian frontier. Beyond Hungary, during the Thirty Years War and in the decade that followed the Peace of Westphalia in 1648, Ottoman territory was considerably increased by full-scale campaigns. They added a huge area of Ukraine and land around the Black Sea, while a long war with Venice for control of Crete finally concluded in Ottoman success in 1672. Meanwhile, the frontier in Hungary had settled into a kind of static instability, which neither party seemed in a position to alter.

The unvoiced issue was Transylvania, which was becoming an open wound. Both the Ottoman and the Hapsburg states claimed that Transylvania was theirs, with each appointing a trusted client as their vassal prince. In reality, the clients were increasingly dedicated to pursuing their own game, to the fury of their respective suzerains. The over-mighty subject was an equal menace to both the Ottomans and the Hapsburgs.

However, neither party could cede the dominant role in Transylvania to the other. The Ottomans eventually opted for full-scale war, which had the double benefit of taking a hard line with the Transylvanians, and also renewing pressure on the Hapsburgs. Going to war, led by a sultan or the grand vizier, also had the effect of galvanizing the entire Ottoman system. War was the natural course of action for any sultan or a grand vizier of drive and energy. However, such men had, of late, been in short supply. The last successful and competent military sultan—Murad IV—had recaptured Baghdad in 1638 and then died at the age of twenty-nine two years later. Two decades of feeble government followed until 1656, when an Albanian vizier, Köprülü Mehmed Pasha, already in his eighties, was appointed grand vizier by Sultan Mehmed IV. Given power, Köprülü became a tireless autocrat, fully supported by the sultan. Mehmed Pasha deliberately sought renewal of the ancient feud with the Hapsburgs as a means to revive the old *gazi* spirit, conquest being the standard Ottoman formula for energizing the social and political structure. War with Poland or Russia may not always have been victorious, but it had produced a steady increase in the Ottoman lands on the northern frontier. The Ottomans might not win all the battles, but war-ending truces invariably gave them a little more territory.

Mehmed Pasha immediately launched a series of well-targeted offensives against a supine Hapsburg enemy. His first move brought Transylvania to heel. In 1658, he sent his son Fazil Ahmet Pasha at the head of an army of 45,000 men to besiege the Transylvanian citadel of Oradea, bombarding it for forty-nine days. In the same year, the implacable grand vizier dispatched an army of Tartar raiders to ravage Royal Hungary. It was the first full-scale Ottoman assault since the Long War had ended half a century before. The primary aim was to show what defying the sultan's army would mean. He used the devastating power of Ottoman cannon, bombarding Oradea day and night as an object lesson. The city surrendered, and its defenders were allowed to depart. Oradea and the surrounding area were put under an Ottoman governor and became part of the sultan's domain.

The Köprülü family (they produced six grand viziers between 1656 and 1701) made a demonstration of Ottoman might that had not been seen since the days of Suleiman I. The intention at Oradea was not to destroy a city, but to remind the government in Vienna of their adversary's awesome might. However, the campaign in Transylvania was Mehmed Pasha's last act, as he died in 1661. His son Fazil Ahmet Köprülü succeeded him and as grand vizier continued to the letter his father's plan for dominating the Hapsburg frontier.

The second phase was another example of the relentless and unforgiving Ottoman power. Fazil Ahmet intended to settle accounts with the Croat Zrinyi family, and especially with Miklos Zrinyi, the ban of Croatia. His new fortress, Novi Zrin, provocatively located on the Ottoman side of the heavily debated frontier, undermined the Ottoman control of the southern frontier. Its only purpose was to challenge the Ottoman castle of Kaniza, one of the key points in the frontier system.

The Zrinyis were the most powerful noble family on the southern border, hereditary enemies of the Ottomans, and equally disliked by the Hapsburgs. It was a Zrinyi who had held the castle of Szigetvár in 1566, against Sultan Suleiman. Many Ottomans implicitly believed the story that it was this resistance that brought about the great sultan's death. They, consequently, despised the Zrinyis. His new stronghold completed, Zrinyi went to war on his own account.

Early in the following year (1663), he laid siege to Kaniza, and then devastated the Ottoman province almost up to Buda, before returning with his raiders to his protective fortress in the southwest. In 1664, he set fire to and seriously damaged Sultan Suleiman's great bridge and causeway built across the river Drava and the marshes at Osijek; it was the Ottoman army's vital supply route through the southern marshes, essential for any attack on Vienna. In the eyes of the Hapsburg government in Vienna, though, he was not a hero, but a disobedient subject contemptuously breaching the peace.

Fazil Ahmet judged the mood of the Hapsburg government shrewdly. The Emperor Leopold I was desperate to maintain peace, pressing for the maintenance of the status quo every time he mooted renewal of the truce. Unfortunately for his plans, the borderers, mostly Hungarians and Croats, dissatisfied with the Hapsburgs, regarded conciliation with the Ottomans as a kind of betrayal. As a result, the Köprülü viziers rightly saw their bel-licose policy of maintaining pressure on the Hapsburgs as highly successful. Renewing the full-scale frontier war after a gap of more than half a century eroded many of the Hapsburg gains made during the Long War. The new threat to Vienna, implicit in the Ottoman campaign of 1664, caused great anxiety to the Hapsburgs, now under severe French pressure against their western territories, especially the Low Countries. However, the Ottomans seriously underestimated the greater effectiveness of the Hapsburg field army on the eastern frontier, now under the skilled commander Montecuccoli.

In July 1664, the grand vizier, with 70,000 men at his back, hit back at the Zrinyi clan, relieving his own beleaguered outpost at Kaniza, before moving on to lay siege to Novy Zrin. It held out for almost a month before the Turks overwhelmed its defences. Most of the garrison were put to the sword and the fortress blown up. Zrinyi escaped, only to be gored to death by a wild boar a few months later. Fazil Ahmet, after considering besieging the southern Hapsburg capital of Graz, which he might well have taken, instead headed northwest along the line of hills toward Vienna.

His plans were overturned by a small Hapsburg force led by Raimundo Montecuccoli, now the emperor's senior commander. Catching the much larger Ottoman army halfway across a river, he administered a stunning defeat at the Battle of St. Gotthard. It was a classic Montecuccoli victory: a small army, vastly outnumbered, but designed to take advantage of new tac-tics that proved highly effective on the eastern front: firepower, not pike-men; mobility and tactical control; field artillery working in unison with the dragoons. Then, as the janissaries floundered in the rising river waters, he unleashed his curassiers, whose heavy broadswords smashed down on the heads and shoulders of the demoralized enemy.

Despite this victory, Emperor Leopold I, more concerned with the press-ing war against the French, agreed a twenty years truce (the Peace of Vasvár, 1664), ceding all his interests in Transylvania to the Ottomans. Monteccucoli was promoted to the presidency of the Imperial War Council, and was given personal responsibility for improving the Austrian artillery. He died, aged sixty-one, in 1680, leaving his protégé, Charles of Lorraine, to carry Montecuccoli's insight into the 1690s, and to victory over the Ottomans.

Despite the shock of St. Gotthard, almost all of Mehmed Köprülü's objec-tives had been met by his son, Fazil Ahmet, leaving the Ottoman armies free once again to campaign in Poland and Moldavia. The unexpected defeat at St. Gotthard was put down to chance and made very little long-term impression on the Ottomans, and the Köprülü learned nothing from it. The celebrated traveler Evliya Çelebi was at the battle, and described how "[t]he soldiers of the One God launched their assults upon the infidels, shouting their battle cries, falling upon them as a wolf attacks a flock of sheep." Yet the sheep had remorselessly destroyed the best soldiers in the Ottoman ranks, an unparalleled event in the long Ottoman-Hapsburg rivalry.

Fazil Ahmet died in 1676 and was immediately succeeded by his adopted brother Kara Mustafa, the third of the six Köprülü grand viziers who held office between 1656 and 1703.[27] He, like his half-brother, had only contempt for the infidel. The rivalry was heightened by a new religious zeal affecting both Ottomans and Hapsburgs at the time. Kara Mustafa was also committed to the Köprülü tradition of expansive war as the most effective social cement for the Ottoman state. From St. Gotthard until 1681, the focus for Kara Mustafa's expansion shifted to Poland on the northern frontier and, with his Tartar allies, to a move into the Ukraine. However, when Russia entered the fray, the Ottomans and the Tarters concluded a twenty-year armistice, lasting until 1701. This was signed so as to give the Ottoman armies time to prepare for renewed war with the Hapsburgs when the Vasvár truce ended in 1684. When Emperor Leopold's entreaties for its extension were not answered, the Hapsburgs began readying for war.

The siege of Vienna in the summer of 1683 was the zenith of Ottoman power projection. There were good reasons that a *gazi* war had been a consistent policy of the Ottoman state since 1656, in the hands of a succession of Köprülü grand viziers. It did not matter whether the chosen enemy was the Catholic Poles, the Orthodox Russians, or the Catholic Hapsburg Empire. All were infidels. However, while the rhetoric might be sincerely Islamic, the intention was rooted in political necessity. The Ottoman Empire required the adrenaline of war, and the exact target was optional. This time the target was once again the Hapsburg Empire, which the Köprülü considered effete.[28] Vienna, in his mind, seemed ripe for the taking. It was also a rich city, and the lucrative plunder would satisfy a restless army. Moreover, the impact of capturing Vienna would strike fear and a new respect for Ottoman powers among the increasingly arrogant European powers. As a final incentive, Kara Mustafa's spies had informed him in detail about the state of Vienna's decrepit defenses.

The Ottomans, operating at the limits of their strategic reach, planned the invasion of 1683 with meticulous care. The army arrived before Vienna a little late, but the investment began immediately. Afterward, the siege's progress was slow, but steady. The most significant Ottoman weakness was Kara Mustafa himself, with his arrogant overconfidence, his contempt for his men, and his ineptitude. Still, it looked as if the city was theirs. Even the Viennese expected the worst and began preparing the city for defense in the event the walls were breached or taken by storm—the inhabitants preferring death to submission. Every building within the city was prepared for a last desperate stand, with great iron chains crisscrossing the thoroughfares to prevent the Ottomans from surging through the streets. The last stand would be in the Cathedral of St. Stephen.

What saved Vienna, apart from an extraordinarily dogged defense, was a relief army, consisting of forces contributed by the states of Germany and commanded by John Sobieski, king of Poland. Emperor Leopold, who had left the city with his family one week before the Turks arrived, had worked tirelessly to secure this expeditionary force. In all, 40,000 well-armed and well-led men had answered his call to save Vienna. Some of the most useful came from the Elector of Saxony: 7,000 musketeers, 2,000 horsemen, and the best light field artillery in Europe.[29]

On the evening of Wednesday, September 8, as on every evening, a small party of soldiers went up to the roof of St. Stephen's Cathedral to launch signal rockets. If the relief had arrived, an advance party would fire signal rockets in reply, to tell the besieged that salvation was at hand. The soldiers fired their rockets from the roof, and turned to go back down the narrow staircase to the cathedral below. As they started their decent, the last man called them back. From the hills—the Vienna Woods—they saw five rockets rise into the air, then fall back to earth. It was the agreed signal. Help was at hand. Or was it?

There was no sign on the following day. It was only on September 10 that there was any sign of movement on the hills. Then, at dawn the following morning, September 11, 1683, Vienna awoke to see the banners of the relief army strung out all along the crests of the Vienna Woods. But would they be in time to save the city? If the Ottoman engineers set off the gunpowder packed beneath the city walls, there would be huge gaps through which the Turks would surge, irresistibly. The relief force might defeat the huge Ottoman army in front of the city, but they might also enter Vienna only to find a dead calm, the streets full of slaughtered men, women, and children.

However, the miracle happened. Vienna was saved.

Many different versions of Vienna's salvation and the Ottoman rout appeared all over Europe. But the result was clear. The Turk was vanquished and driven back into Hungary. Within days, the idea of liberating Hungary from the Turks was circulating, and King John Sobieski was in favor of an immediate pursuit into the Balkans.

Reconquest

The year 1664—St. Gotthard—was chronlogically the midpoint in the Ottoman-Hapsburg encounter. It was the first time that a Hapsburg army defeated an Ottoman force in battle. It was also the first point where the Hapsburg army had the skills and the leadership to overcome their hithto unconquerable adversary. However, the Hapsburgs, with all of their other concerns in Europe, never had the power or funds to finish the job. In 1683, however, they were joined by the full might of the Holy Roman Empire, the Republic of Venice, Poland, and many other European contingents, including Russia, which joined this "Holy League" in 1686. The hidden force that drove this coalition was Pope Innocent XI, who personally bankrolled the alliance and ordered the bishops in the Holy Roman Empire and the rich monastic orders to support the long struggle financially.[30] Leopold I and his successors also succeeded in having the liberation of Hungary designated an "imperial war"—fought against a common enemy of the entire Holy Roman Empire.[31] Alomst unbelievably, given the chatoic conditon of European state relations, the coalition was sustained for the nearly sixteen years it took to reverse almost a century and a half of Ottoman occupation.

The idea of the Christians united against them terrified the Ottomans, who rightly began regarding the papacy, with its power to unify the western nations against them, as their most dangerous enemy. Still, there was little they could do against the breaking storm. In February 1684, Sultan Mehmed IV received a report from Belgrade that the European states were uniting to assail the Ottoman Empire on every side. In the spring, the Russians would strike the Tartar in the Crimea, while the Poles advanced along the River Dniester and then pushed south into Ottoman-dominated Wallachia. Venice planned to attack Bosnia, while simultaneously regaining Crete, and ravaging the Aegean. All Europe was engaged in this great encircling action: Sweden, France, Spain, England, the United Provinces of the Netherlands, Genoa, and the papacy.[32]

Although the vastness of this combined attack was exaggerated, in its essence the threat was very real. On March 5, 1684, the king of Poland, Emperor Leopold, and the doge of Venice signed an agreement to wage war on the Ottomans and not to make peace unless all three parties agreed. Even after any future peace was signed, they were to remain committed to a permanent mutual defensive alliance against any future Ottoman attack. Immediately after this alliance was signed, all the Christian nations were invited to join in this assault on the common enemy—and not merely Christian nations. Emperor Leopold even commissioned a Catholic archbishop, Sebastian Knab, already in Persia, to see if the Safavid shah could be drawn into an alliance against the common Ottoman enemy. There was expressed enthusiasm, but it came to nothing. The first major success came at Buda, stormed September 2, 1686—almost two years after Vienna was saved.

The Ottomans did not give up after the fall of Buda. Armies were regularly sent north from Belgrade; yet none of them could match the skill of the Holy League generals and their veteran troops. Annihilating defeat followed annihilating defeat: in the west, people could recite the list of the allies' six miraculous victories, like a litany of conquest.[33] Still, the Ottomans would not concede until war weariness finally compelled them to seek what was technically an armistice to run for twenty-five years and prolonged thereafter if the signatories agreed.

The allies chose to regard the peace meetings as preparation for a perpetual peace, and this was indeed its essential character. The agreement, signed at Karlowitz on the Danube in 1699, was based on the land that the Ottomans retained after sixteen years of war. This included Belgrade, which they had recaptured in 1688, the enormous Banat of Temesvar in Hungary, and the adjacent territories of Moldavia and Wallachia. Transylvania was still nominally independent but was ruled by Austrian governors.

This, in the eyes of the Holy League, was the conclusion to the Turkish wars, yet that was not how the Ottomans saw the situation. The eternal peace of Karlowitz lasted only twelve years, and in 1711 an Ottoman army fought and defeated Russia, a powerful member of the Holy League, recovering the key port of Azov that had been lost in 1697. Then, in 1717, the Ottomans declared war on Venice, another Holy League member, and recovered the Morea in Greece. They then turned on the Hapsburgs. After being routed by Prince Eugene of Savoy, they signed the Peace of Passarowitz (1718), which stripped the Ottomans of such Hungarian land that was left to them at Karlowitz.

The Final Act

The Ottomans were driven back across the Danube, confirmed by a treaty in 1699, and victory in a renewed war in 1718. Prince Eugene was able to reclaim Belgrade, but Hapsburg dreams of reconquering Constantinople and building trade with the East proved impractical. The last set of Ottoman-Hapsburg wars in 1737–1739 and 1787–1791 had, therefore, a different character from earlier conflicts. In the eighteenth century, leading Ottomans became concerned about their technical backwardness, but often had a misplaced understanding of the causes. When Claude Alexandre de Bonneval, who had fought in the French and Austrian armies, was dismissed from imperial service, he "turned Turk." His new masters carefully listened to his advice, but then ignored it, as they believed their infantry techniques and battle tactics were at so advanced a state that no improvement was possible.

Still, the Ottomans were successful in this later phase of war. This is somewhat due to some improvement in their armies, particularly the artillery, but the crucial reason lay in logistics. Before 1718, the Ottomans waged war at the limits of their logistic potential, on the frontier with Austria, and against the heavily fortified zone of Royal Hungary. Although the Ottomans twice besieged Vienna, and in 1683 they nearly took the city, they were always at the limits of their operational range. After 1718, the fighting moved 300 miles south and much closer to their sources of supply and support, while correspondingly lengthening Hapsburg supply lines.

Despite having the upper hand, the Hapsburgs remained fearful. At times they would see the Ottomans as a feeble enemy, beaten time after time, and offering no real obstacle to the grandiose plans of further conquest that still surfaced from time to time.[34] At other times, they considered the Turks as a most deadly menace, always ready to overrun Hungary and even penetrate into the provinces of Austria. No one seriously expected another siege of Vienna, but a new Tatar terror seemed entirely possible. As a result, Vienna spent vast sums of money building one of the most elaborately defended frontiers in Europe throughout the southern part of Hungary and along the frontier through Croatia. The War Council saw matters in simplistic terms: unless there were defense in depth, a garrisoned frontier, and plentiful reserves, there was no guarantee that 1683 might not be repeated. Already, by 1699, fifty miles (80 km) upstream on the Danube, the Hapsburgs were building a fortress much more substantial than the citadel of Belgrade. The key to their new defensive system was the old fort of Petrovaradin, captured by the allied army in 1687 and then the base for Prince Eugene's great victories. Work began on the vast new fortress complex in 1692, and it was only finally completed in 1760. This fortress, nicknamed "Gibraltar on the Danube," strongly suggests that the Hapsburgs still anticipated a major threat from the Ottomans in the south, against common sense and all the evidence.

It was not just Petrovaradin blocking one route north, there was also a line of new fortresses along the river Sava and at the Tverda citadel at Osijek, built between 1712 and 1721. Brod was completed by the 1770s, and Karlstadt, close to the Adriatic coast, just afterward.[35] These massive fortifications along the southern frontier cost a fortune, hemorrhaging money from the military budget. But behind this grandiose program lay a paradox. By mid-century, all Austria's principal enemies were in the west: yet there was no money left to build fortifications where they might have been valuable against the predatory French or Frederick II and his Prussian armies. Michael Hochedlinger points to an unanswerable question: "Through the second half of the eighteenth century Prussia remained Austria's main enemy. Following the loss of Silesia it became increasingly important to protect Bohemia." But relatively little was done, except strengthening Olmütz in Moravia. Yet at the same time the fortress building in the south continued with heightened urgency: "It was considered necessary to strengthen the bigger fortresses on the frontier with the Ottoman empire."[36]

So, why was it "necessary" to create these elaborate defenses against Austria's least pressing danger? The reason is that while the threat may not have been real, it was certainly there in people's minds. Like the Maginot Line between the two world wars of the twentieth century, Petrovaradin provided a sense of reassurance, of protection against a nightmare. After the siege of Vienna, Austrians feared the Turks more, if that were possible, than they had before. The folk memory recalled that the Austrian provinces had been ravaged by Tatars almost as far as Steyr—some estimates say that as many as 100,000 had been killed or taken into slavery over the years. One of the maps made at the time graphically showed villages in flames: the landscape was covered with these little symbols. The whole fabric of social life had been destroyed, with most of the parish and land records burned in the wholesale Tatar pillage. Three generations later, the memories of that time were still vivid and personal. Further south, in Styria and in the borderland with Croatia, the Turks were still very close.

However, Austrian attitudes had also changed in an opposite direction. Until the reconquest of Hungary, between 1686 and 1699, the Turks were feared, as they had been for two centuries. By the early eighteenth century, they were increasingly considered bizarre and exotic, still threatening and cruel, yet less often objects of terror. By the 1780s, they had become objects of mockery, in their eccentric dress, outlandish habits, and lubriciously imagined moral defects. Yet, they were still dangerous, like the wild beasts that Prince Eugene had collected in the zoo at his Belvedere palace, still able to inflict a savage wound. Both Turkish elements were present in Mozart's *Flight from the Seraglio*, first performed in Vienna in 1782.[37]

There would be one final encounter, a major war along the Sava River. It was not a popular war, as Austrians rightly saw the hand of Russia behind the new conflict. Since 1712, Russia had been determined to gain territory from the Ottomans, and to assert the rights of Russian protection for Orthodox

Christians anywhere in the Ottoman Empire. The Hapsburgs, useful allies, were dragged into war by Russia. Emperor Joseph II, because of a personal guarantee to Empress Catherine, committed himself wholeheartedly to this last Austrian war against the Ottomans. He even took command at the front in person, the first Hapsburg emperor to do so since Charles V had led his army against the Ottomans at Tunis in 1535. It was the largest Austrian army ever sent into battle: more than 200,000 men, and cripplingly expensive. It was, however, poorly led by the inexperienced Joseph and, as a result, it achieved virtually none of its objectives. Moreover, when Joseph was nearly captured in an Ottoman sally, he returned to Vienna and died before a peace treaty could be signed.

His brother Leopold II finally put an end to wars with the Ottoman Empire. He was content to sign the Treaty of Sistova on August 4, 1791, allowing the continuing Ottoman possession of Belgrade. Three weeks later, at the castle of Pillnitz near Dresden, Prussia and the Hapsburgs signed a united declaration against Revolutionary France. Leopold also committed himself to a formal declaration against any future claim on the territory of the Ottoman Empire. This imperial fiat definitively and finally ended the enduring strategic rivalry.

Aftermath

The end to the long state of hostility in 1791 opened the path to a new political relationship with the Ottomans. After the Napoleonic Wars ended in 1815, the Hapsburgs moved quickly to accept the Ottomans as international partners, even sending Austrian marines into the Levant to strengthen Ottoman sovereignty. Emperor Franz Joseph I also refused to enter the Crimean War in the 1850s, as a Russian accomplice against the Ottomans, causing a severe rupture in Austro-Russian relations. Finally, in 1878 Austria-Hungary accepted a mandate from the Council of Berlin to govern the Ottoman province of Bosnia and Herzogovina, but the territory remained under continuing Ottoman sovereignty. [38] In World War I, Austria and the Ottomans remained loyal allies.

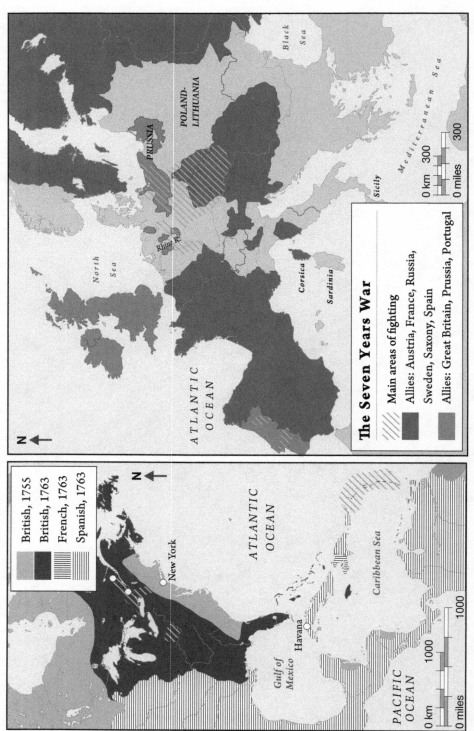

The Seven Years War

	Main areas of fighting
	Allies: Austria, France, Russia, Sweden, Saxony, Spain
	Allies: Great Britain, Prussia, Portugal

POLAND-LITHUANIA

PRUSSIA

North Sea

Rhine R.

ATLANTIC OCEAN

Black Sea

Mediterranean Sea

Sicily

Corsica

Sardinia

0 km   300
0 miles   300

N

	British, 1755
	British, 1763
	French, 1763
	Spanish, 1763

New York

ATLANTIC OCEAN

Gulf of Mexico

Havana

Caribbean Sea

PACIFIC OCEAN

0 km   1000
0 miles   1000

N

The Seven Years War.

CHAPTER 8

A Contest for Trade and Empire
England versus France II
Matt J. Schumann

F OR CENTURIES AFTER THE Norman Conquest, England and France fought intermittent contests for feudal precedence and dynastic honor. As a result of the Reformation in the sixteenth century, Anglo-French antagonisms also incorporated a religious component. Both issues figured alongside nascent ethnonationalism as the two states resuscitated their rivalry from the late seventeenth century onward, especially in the spheres of commerce and state finance. Their competition extended beyond Europe, from attacks on vital territories and institutions to allies, colonies, markets, and spheres of influence around the globe.

During the eighteenth century, competition for trade and colonies merged with ambitious political experiments. French absolutism peaked and secured a frontier on the Rhine, while a new balance between Crown and Parliament united Britain as never before. Mercantile competition abroad extended from the Baltic to the Levant, all the way to the coasts of China; the frontiers of trade, influence, and settled colonies at least abutted, if they did not overlap, in North America and the Caribbean, West Africa, and India. Finally, in the abstract, political economists on both sides of the English Channel seem to have held at least three assumptions more or less in common, that would bring their states into a series of expensive and disastrous wars:

- that "peaceful" trade was an element of international competition;
- that war was a natural outgrowth of the contest for foreign markets;
- that a gain for one state *ipso facto* represented a loss for the other.

Peace, in other words, was often merely conceived as a breathing space between armed conflicts. Even in times of notional peace, it was still the normal course of Anglo-French relations to see manipulations of third parties and foreign markets in favor of one state or the other, as well as proxy wars and closing colonial frontiers in far regions of the globe.

Background

The Anglo-French rivalry from about 1658 to 1783 was colored by its predecessors, dating back several centuries. Popular memory of older dynastic struggles and religious wars shaped the origins of what became a global competition for trade and empire. It was therefore not merely a "rational" contest for colonies and foreign markets, influenced by the thinking of the Enlightenment. Memory and myth-making on both sides also made it into a quasi-nationalist struggle, with propaganda and voluntary societies inspiring popular clamors for a larger historical reckoning.

Dynastic issues formed a key feature of Anglo-French relations for centuries after the Norman Conquest. Whereas William I (r. 1066–1087) overhauled England's succession after his invasion from the French province of Normandy, England's King Henry II (r. 1154–1189) through inheritance (Anjou) and marriage to Eleanor (Aquitaine) claimed large parts of France. The medieval rivalry peaked with the Hundred Years War (1327–1453), but dynastic meddling continued into the early modern period. As kings in the Stuart line (after 1603) tried to claim more power at home, they received sympathy and some political support from fellow absolutists in France. After 1688, however, Parliament's ascendancy and the effective political balance under the early Hanoverians inspired French as well as British ideas on constitutional monarchy, financial innovation, and popular sovereignty.

In addition to their history of dynastic rivalry, by the end of the sixteenth century, England and France also emerged on opposite sides of the Protestant Reformation. As the inheritors of religious reform under Henry VIII and his daughter Elizabeth, the people and especially the Parliament of England supported the Protestant cause across western Europe. Henri of Navarre received English support for championing the Huguenot (French Protestant) cause during the French Wars of Religion (1562–1598); but as he grasped, in the end, that the kingship of France depended on his being Catholic, he converted in 1593.[1] Through the Edict of Nantes (1598), Henry tried to settle religious differences in his own kingdom as well as mollify his disappointed Protestant allies, but religion remained a major issue after his death in 1610.

English popular sentiment, meanwhile—fired not least by the Gunpowder Plot in 1605—was violently anti-Catholic. Notwithstanding the duke of Buckingham's intrigues, the mass of English opinion favored Huguenot rebels in the 1620s; and as the Popish Plot[2] unfolded in 1679–1681, English ire turned toward France as well as Rome. Louis XIV had his own suspicions of Protestant plotting and instituted a policy of intimidation known as *dragonnades*, peaking in 1685 with the Edict of Fontainebleau.[3] Each state's intolerance toward religious minorities inflamed opinion in the other, making an enduring strategic rivalry that much easier for governments to perpetuate and sell to their respective subjects.

Neither dynastic nor religious motives, however, predicted a rivalry between France and England that would be either enduring or strategic. Rather, during a time of relative weakness when both powers struggled through domestic turmoil—the Wars of Religion (1562–1598) and later the Wars of the Fronde (1648–1653) in France, and the Civil War and Lord Protectorate in England (1642–1660)—they played a relatively passive witness to the period's major conflict: the Eighty Years War (1568–1648). The long struggle for Dutch independence pitted their mercantile fleets and dominance of the international carrying trade[4] against the resources of Spain's vast American empire. Political economists in London and Paris soon saw the quest for power and dynastic glory operating in parallel with resource extraction from overseas empires (Spanish) and trade ascendancy in Europe (Dutch). From the latter half of the seventeenth century, Bourbon heirs to Henri IV sought to extend the dynasty's influence, not only eastward to frontiers on the Rhine and in the Netherlands, but also southward—toward family ties and expanded trade with Spain and its American empire. English leaders, meanwhile, saw in the Dutch not only a long-time ally on religious grounds, but also a sometime competitor for European trade, as well as a model to follow for overseas commerce and government finance.

Spain and the Netherlands held dominant international positions for much of the seventeenth century, informing relative peace between France and England. As the latter two countries built their own American empires, however, and as their trade and influence expanded in Europe, their relationship also changed. The expansion of French territory, commerce, military force, and diplomatic prestige all posed threats in the English mind—threats echoed across the Atlantic by French claims on the Mississippi watershed, notionally pinning England's colonies against the Atlantic coast.[5] Nor was the threat merely in the distant abstract: popular myth in England by the 1670s held that Absolutist, Catholic France backed similar ambitions for Charles II and his brother, the future James II, against Parliament and

English Protestantism. Englishmen also believed that French fiscal, military, and territorial expansion threatened "universal monarchy" on the Continent of Europe, and that France's vast economic growth limited England's ability to compete in the international marketplace.[6]

The tipping point was the birth in June 1688 of James Francis Edward Stuart, son of James II and Mary of Modena. Baptized as a Catholic, the boy leapfrogged Mary and Anne—his older, Protestant half-sisters—in the line of succession, seeming to promise for England a return to Catholic monarchy and the prospect of a long-term, French-backed absolutist state. James tried to play down this notion behind a rubric of religious tolerance, but this was ultimately the context for the Glorious Revolution and John Locke's *Two Treatises on Government* (1691): a free people, discontent with their sovereign, sought to replace him with the nearest convenient alternative—Dutch *Stadthouter* William of Orange, husband of James's daughter Mary, crowned in England as William III.[7] It may therefore appear that the Anglo-French rivalry was built on dynastic and religious grounds, as England entered the Nine Years War (1688–1697) against France.[8] But as Dutch investment and rising English sea power elevated the latter to the status of a great power, commercial and imperial ambition in London began to shape the emerging rivalry and European foreign relations as a whole.

From Revolution to Rastatt (1688–1714)

Louis XIV opened the strategic game in 1688, hoping to secure "natural frontiers" on the Rhine against the Dutch-financed League of Augsburg, led by the Hapsburg emperor Leopold I.[9] If Louis were merely concerned with territory, his claim to Louisiana through La Salle's expeditions[10] might have been sufficient by the 1680s; but because dynastic and territorial concerns in Europe took precedence for him, he favored his army over France's navy and colonies. His first campaigns in 1688–1689, therefore, faced east into Germany—giving William the time he needed to secure most of his British domains. Only when the Rhine campaigns were nearing completion did Louis XIV return his attention to Britain, where three engagements in July 1690 shaped the future course of what became the Anglo-French rivalry. From the battles of Fleurus (July 1), Beachy Head (July 10), and the Boyne (July 12), Britain under William III gradually emerged as France's chief antagonist.

The Battle of Fleurus signaled a shift in French operations from the Rhine to the Low Countries. Louis was primarily concerned about dynastic glory for his son, Louis the Grand Dauphin, fighting against the Austrians on the Rhine, but the victory at Fleurus began to shift the main theater of operations to the Spanish (later Austrian) Netherlands, and the capture of Mons, Huy, Namur, and Charleroi by 1693 not only added territory to France's frontiers but also luster to Louis's crown. The Netherlands campaigns compelled William III as *Stadthouter* to return from Britain and defend his Dutch territories, losing battles at Steenkirk (1692) and Landen (1693). His military presence in the Netherlands campaigns enhanced his prestige, however, and his involvement of British troops—and especially British money, following Dutch-backed financial reforms—both increased his diplomatic influence and whetted the British appetite for deeper involvement on the continent.

The British part in the Anglo-Dutch union emerges more clearly, however, from naval operations in 1690, in the Irish Sea and especially the Channel. William's invasion in 1688 was "permitted" in a sense by a weak English fleet and James II's attempt to appear "English" by refusing French help. After a brief exile in France from December 1688 to March 1689, James sought to continue the struggle in Ireland, this time supported by French troops and money. By June 1690, William staged his own Irish campaign with 300 ships and 36,000 troops. His victory at the Boyne, outside Dublin, was not in itself sufficient to win the larger war in Ireland, but it caused James to return to France—this time for good. In England, the public increasingly began to identify James as a French puppet, and to contrast his drive for religious uniformity and dynastic glory with their values—which they shared in common with William's Dutch values of commercial dominance and political liberty.

The next major action in July 1690, at Beachy Head, acted to highlight this difference. Admiral Anne Hilarion Comte de Tourville defeated an Anglo-Dutch[11] fleet and briefly seized command of the Channel, though he was unable to exploit this success. The panic he caused in England, however, prompted not just a lot of pamphlet writing, but also a vast expansion of the Royal Navy. The Bank of England (proposed 1691, est. 1694) was one of many joint-stock ventures that emerged to serve the navy's growing funding needs, and at least a few Dutch investors transferred assets to London.[12] A revitalized Royal Navy exacted its first revenge at Barfleur-La Hogue in 1692, disabling Louis's next, and ultimately last, attempt to restore James II. Though Tourville won another battle off Lagos (Portugal) in 1693, the abortive English raids on Brest and St. Malo in 1694 offer the best insights into the emerging Anglo-French rivalry: (1) that the Royal Navy was no longer merely a defense force for the British Isles, but was emerging instead as the primary means for projecting English power; and (2) that the naval balance between France and England as a whole was undergoing what proved to be a dramatic, long-term shift in favor of the latter.

The shift, however, came on the French side as well as the English. Before his death in 1683, Jean-Baptiste Colbert led a fiscal and economic transformation in France, with high tariffs and regulated industry, making it one of the richest countries in Europe. Subsequent military expansion and reforms under Michel le Tellier and his son the Marquis de Louvois enabled France to field over 400,000 troops by the early 1690s. William and Leopold formed the League of Augsburg—titled the Grand Alliance as Spain and Britain joined at the end of the 1680s—in order to contain this power, and they gained enormously from turns of fate far away from the battlefield. Louvois's unexpected death in 1691 and a major crop failure in 1693 harmed Louis's finances, forcing him to choose by 1695 between army and naval priorities. Unable to keep up the arms race with England, France maintained a respectable fleet but largely abandoned the *guerre d'escadre* philosophy of fleet-to-fleet combat. Seeking to save money from his naval budget, Louis turned instead to *guerre de course*, or commerce raiding, based largely on privateers.

Two other actions in 1690 merit at least a passing mention for their legacy in the Anglo-French rivalry: the French-Canadian raid on Schenectady, New York, and the English colonial raid on New France's capital city, Québec. Both were part of a much larger conflict known in English colonial memory as King William's War. As the first major confrontation between English and French colonists and their respective Amerindian allies, it set a new standard of violence between North American rivals from previous colonial wars. Whereas the Dutch were quick to seize New Sweden in 1655, and the English took New Netherlands (New York) in a single campaign in 1664, the Anglo-French contest around Hudson Bay, in the Hudson-Champlain corridor, and in the waterways around Nova Scotia occurred on a scale as yet unknown in North America. Moreover, Native allies on both sides brought their distinctive way of war into the Anglo-French contest, and the long-term costs during the eighteenth century included a proliferation of expensive strategic outposts and thousands of civilians killed or taken captive.[13]

Back in Europe, French successes on land appeared to force the pace of peace. The French-imposed treaties at Turin and Vigevano in 1696 ended fighting in Italy, and more concessions seemed to be forthcoming as Barcelona (Spain) and Ath (Netherlands) fell to French arms in 1697. French generals on the Rhine also brought glory to Louis's cause, but the picture looked much bleaker at Versailles. Financial exhaustion had set in, and as far as Louis was concerned, these last conquests were no longer additions to French security. Rather, they became bargaining counters for the restoration of peace. The Grand Alliance may have continued the war beyond 1697, but the English and Dutch commercial publics had also grown tired of financing their allies and joined France in forcing Europe to peace. The resulting Treaty of Ryswick appeared as a draw between France and the allies, but the onset of peace obscured the larger reality of an emerging Anglo-French rivalry.

That reality became clear only five years later, as Louis XIV entered the last contest of his reign: the War of the Spanish Succession (1702–1714). The king and his new Spanish allies—under his grandson, Philip V—sought once again to extend Bourbon hegemony on the Continent. Though Philip managed to keep his throne against the Hapsburg claimant, the future Charles VI of Austria, the real war was against Britain and it was ultimately a losing effort. British and Dutch finances again sustained a larger, mostly Austrian war effort on the Continent, but it was British troops under John Churchill, first duke of Marlborough, that most frustrated French ambitions by land. Meanwhile, British operations by sea extended much farther around the European continent and across the Atlantic Ocean, exposing French and Spanish vulnerabilities on a vast geographical scale.

From the start, English colonies joined the mother country in pursuing an extremely aggressive war. As Britain's bulwark in the American South, Charles Town met a Franco-Spanish besieging force in 1706 with well-prepared militia and its own small flotilla. As a center for commerce and diplomacy in the backcountry, however—including a notorious Amerindian slave trade[14]—the city also projected power and reaped vengeance through its Native alliances. Failed sieges of St. Augustine (1702) and Pensacola (1707) mar an otherwise brilliant military record. Carolina-Amerindian raids annihilated the Spanish missionary presence north of the main Florida settlements, and destroyed the Spanish-allied Apalachee and Timucua nations; Chickasaw raids supported from South Carolina even displaced the French-allied Tunica tribes on the Mississippi River. England's northern colonies suffered more from French and Indian raids coming out of Canada, but they also planned ambitious operations against the main settlements of New France and staged three amphibious operations (1705, 1707, 1710) against Port Royal in Nova Scotia.

Meanwhile, the Royal Navy extended its sphere of operations far beyond its range in the 1690s. English forces led operations around the Iberian Peninsula, taking Gibraltar in 1704 and Barcelona in 1705. British ships also featured in Prince Eugene of Savoy's 1707 campaign against Toulon (southern France), and in the capture of Minorca in 1708.[15] By 1710, the Royal Navy led the blockade of Syracuse (Sicily), and nine warships and two bomb ketches crossed the Atlantic for the Quebec expedition of 1711.[16] The French navy, by contrast, managed some successful commerce raiding in 1707, but its hopes for supporting a Jacobite[17] rising in 1708 were dashed by storms, and by a Royal Navy that profited from Europe's largest intelligence network.

Led by Marlborough and supported not least by a Tory-Whig coalition under Sidney Godolphin, first earl of Godolphin, the British army also began to make its reputation on the Continent of Europe.[18] Starting at Liège in 1702, then Bonn in 1703 and racing to the Danube in 1704, Marlborough showed himself to be a different kind of leader than previous English commanders on the Continent. He took English troops deep into Germany, conducted personal diplomacy with coalition partners, and displayed both skill and boldness in a series of victories against the vaunted French army. At Blenheim (1704), Ramillies (1706), Oudenarde (1708), and Malplaquet (1709), Marlborough stymied French commanders and eventually caused a crisis of confidence at Versailles. His recall at the end of 1711 stunned both sides, and left Prince Eugene to lose at Denain in 1712.

Marlborough's recall was the product of Tory ascendancy after a landslide election victory in 1710. Benefiting from a domestic freedom-of-speech scandal, but focused mostly on the war's cost to British taxpayers, Robert Harley's Tory government quickly removed roadblocks to peace and negotiated the 1713 Treaty of Utrecht with France and Spain. The British withdrawal from the war forced their Austrian allies to come to peace at Rastatt in 1714. Austria gained the Netherlands (most of present-day Belgium), the Milanese, Naples, and Sardinia,[19] but the House of Bourbon also profited handsomely—Philip V kept his Spanish throne and a few rights in Italy, focused on the Duchy of Parma. Britain, however, gained Gibraltar, Minorca, and several North American lands, as well as trade concessions in writing for the Spanish Main and the interior of North America.[20]

In sum, although dynastic and religious issues were clearly at play, the Anglo-French rivalry ultimately hinged on land claims and state finances. Nationalized industry and trade enabled Louis XIV to seek dynastic glory with an oversized military—and to keep Europe in awe—through most of his long reign. Though allied with the Stuart kings, Louis's dominance in European affairs put the English people on edge, sparking the Glorious Revolution. With substantial Dutch help, Britain soon emerged as a major financier for France's enemies, and set France on the defensive in the colonies, at sea, on land, and at the negotiating table.

"Peacetime" and Pretenders (1714–1748)

The Treaty of Utrecht and its corollaries were mostly a compromise peace, including the revocation of Hapsburg claims to the Spanish throne, and British and French promises to adjust some of their outstanding colonial issues by committee rather than open combat. Nonetheless, Britain emerged as a clear winner, not least as a result of dominance at sea. Emerging trade and influence in the Baltic and the Mediterranean entailed their share of naval expenses for Britain, informing at least a temporary policy of peace. At the same time, France needed space after Louis XIV's death for fiscal reform and economic renewal. Both sides also faced dynastic and religious challenges, yet differing norms of peacetime trade and colonization around the globe showcased as well as any military campaign that Britain and France—even in their period of formal alliance (1716–1731)—remained strategic rivals.

Dynastic issues came immediately to the fore after Utrecht, with the deaths of Queen Anne in 1714 and Louis XIV in 1715. In Britain, new elections accompanied the accession of the Hanoverian King George I, and the Whigs won a large victory in part because of the Tories' financial mismanagement. The Whigs' anti-Catholic and antimonarchist sentiments, joined with a drive for greater continental engagement, sparked a Jacobite rising in 1715. Meanwhile, the death of Louis XIV—with a five-year-old Louis XV as heir—left France until 1723 under a regency council headed by Philippe II, duc d'Orleans. In both countries, therefore, dynastic insecurity seemed to put the rivalry on hold and prompted a formal reconciliation from 1716 to the mid-1720s.

Financial considerations also played a role, as both sides sought to enlarge public ownership of government debt. In France, the liberalization of Louis XIV's tax regime combined with John Law's involvement in the *Banque Royale*—a French lending institution backed by the Crown—and the emerging *Compagnie des Indes*, with interests ranging from Louisiana to the Indian Ocean.[21] The hope was to use financial markets as a source of revenue for the French government, much as the South Sea Company did for British debt, with a scheme based in part on insider trading. Both schemes collapsed in 1720, sinking public credit on both sides of the Channel and sending economic shock waves across Europe.

Financial speculation occurred in part as British and French governments sought to recover from wartime debts, yet a pacific partnership in Europe did little to obscure their continuing rivalry overseas. About 2 percent of all French expenditures after 1716 went to the fort of Louisbourg on Île Royale, guarding French claims to the Newfoundland fisheries—a vital nursery for seamen—and approaches to the St. Lawrence waterway.[22] In peninsular Nova Scotia, Francophone Acadiens, who were supposed to be under British rule, sought to negotiate their own "neutrality" between the two empires.[23] At the same time (1722–1725), colonists from New England faced a war with French-backed Wabanakis, Mi'kmaw, and Maliseets as they sought to expand into Maine and New Brunswick.[24] Far to the south, the Yamasee War of 1715–1717 cemented Carolina-Cherokee relations and opened British claims to Georgia. By 1718, Britain's Parliament affirmed colonial claims as far west as the Mississippi under the name *Carolana*, just at a time when Orleans's regency consolidated the *Compagnie des Indes* and sought to build in Louisiana a rival to Virginia's tobacco trade.

Britain's recovery came primarily in the forms of retrenchment, financial innovation, and a bit of gunboat diplomacy. As Britain remained mostly free of European wars during Robert Walpole's ministry (1721–1742), it was able to focus instead on economic growth.[25] Walpole was the acknowledged inventor of the sinking fund, an additional security for the repayment of public debt, and therefore a tool for lowering the long-term interest on British government borrowing. The union of Walpole's financial and naval interests neatly fell on the two major beneficiaries from the South Sea Bubble: the Bank of England, which gained near-monopoly status in servicing Britain's public debt, and the British East India Company, representing a new area of British imperial growth. In his foreign policy, Walpole was unafraid to use the navy as a diplomatic tool, but was rather more wary about committing it to war.

France's equivalent to Walpole was Cardinal Andre-Hercule de Fleury, former tutor to Louis XV, who came to political power in his own right in 1726. Like Walpole, he was a noted pacifist, though far more skilled in international relations.[26] Seeing foreign affairs as an extension of domestic robustness, Fleury, like Walpole, worked first on the colonies and the domestic economy. An early supporter of the *Compagnie des Indes*, he took Louisiana back under government control after the costly Natchez War of 1729–1731, and transferred the company interest to India. He also presided over the construction of Niagara (1727) and Crown Point (1735)—closing the frontiers between New France and New York—and later Louisiana campaigns against the Chickasaw (a close ally of British South Carolina) in 1736 and 1739. Back in Europe, he continued his predecessors' practice of encouraging French manufactures, especially of high-quality goods, and rebuilt France's trade with the Baltic and the eastern Mediterranean, not least at the expense of his British competitor.

By the 1730s, the contrast between Fleury's energy and Walpole's steady hand led many Britons to question the latter's overall strategy. A resurgent Spain forced the pace of European diplomacy at the time, with its ambitions in Italy and violent *guarda costas* trying to keep a check on British smuggling. Walpole's early gunboat diplomacy succeeded most notably when he sent twenty-eight warships to Lisbon in 1735 to defuse a diplomatic crisis between Portugal and Spain. It also had failures, however, such as an observation fleet in the Caribbean in 1726 that triggered the war it was intended to prevent (against Spain). Although the navy successfully relieved Gibraltar from a Spanish siege in 1727, the overall trend of Walpole's diplomacy tended against British overuse of the military as an instrument of international influence. At the same time, an emerging opposition party[27] began to envision a different model of gunboat diplomacy, seeing the navy no longer as a deterrent but rather as an aggressive force that could be employed to pry open foreign markets, redress international grievances, and restore Britain's diplomatic standing in Europe and around the world.

France also had a role to play in perceptions of British decline: Fleury sought indeed to wean his state from its British ties, starting with clever mediation between Britain and Spain at the Congress of Soissons (1728–1729): his foot-dragging in the peace negotiation, and impassiveness as Britain and Prussia had a war scare in 1730, signaled a new direction in French foreign policy. Walpole's withdrawal from the dying alliance—the 1731 Treaty of Vienna—appeared for a moment to isolate France, but in fact it laid grounds for the First Family Compact in 1733. This was to be the first of three Franco-Spanish treaties through the rest of the eighteenth century, largely securing the union of interests between the two Bourbon crowns. The Anglo-Austrian alliance was not nearly so perfect, and it soon took second place behind an Austro-Russo-Prussian union in 1732, targeting the Polish crown. In effect, Fleury left the British tie for a Spanish one. While he sacrificed the ambition of Louis XV's father-in-law, Stanislaus Leszczynski, to regain the crown of Poland, his clever diplomacy and Bourbon arms gained the Crown of Naples for Spain and reversionary rights for Lorraine to France, all while keeping Britain in near-helpless isolation.[28]

By partaking in the *flota*—Spain's official trade with its American colonies—France was also destined to oppose British privileges under the *Assiento*—trade concessions granted by Spain through the Treaty of Utrecht. The arrangements were imperfect, however, leaving the British short on their expected profits from trade with Spanish America. While French vessels in the *flota* were licensed at some cost, peacetime trade enabled them to cross the ocean without fear, and thus bring home the fruits of the Spanish trade. France also profited from a growing commerce in West Indian sugar—especially from Martinique and Guadeloupe—though the scale of operations soon prompted French colonization on the fringes of legality, on the islands of St. Lucia and Dominica.[29]

France thus lurked in the background as Anglo-Spanish tensions flared at the end of the 1730s. Spain had already supported a Jacobite rising in 1719, and joined France as the major power implicated in Jacobite intrigues throughout the détente period. St. Augustine also began to shelter escaped slaves from Georgia and the Carolinas, and supported the Stono Rebellion from September 1739.[30] Spanish *guarda costas* also continued to confound British commerce in the Caribbean, so that Walpole's hopes for compromise ultimately foundered.[31] By October, the Whig opposition pushed him to declare war. The Anglo-Spanish war began where the two protagonists had left off in 1729, but on an expanded scale. It was also a war fought with one eye constantly on France, whose entry was anticipated on both sides.[32]

As Europe and the colonial world returned to open conflict—the War of Jenkins's Ear from 1739 and the War of the Austrian Succession from 1740—the apparent restrictions on war over the previous quarter-century seemed to disappear. Admiral Edward Vernon's expedition to Portobello, Panama, in 1739 proved immensely popular in Britain, inspiring among other things the naming of Portobello Road in London and Mount Vernon, Virginia, and the popular song, "Rule Britannia." The abortive Cartagena expedition (1740–1741) featured Anglo-American recruits—their first service outside North America—and a squadron under Admiral George Anson sailing in 1740 was the first of the early modern period to threaten Spain's virtual monopoly on the Pacific Ocean; in 1743 it became the first in 150 years to capture the Manila Galleon.[33] In Europe, meanwhile, King Frederick II of Prussia launched a surprise attack on Austria, seizing the rich province of Silesia late in 1740. Allies seeking to exploit his success—Bavaria, Saxony, and France above all—looked forward to dismembering the remaining Hapsburg domains.[34] British diplomatic support removed some of Austria's enemies by 1742, however, and Anglo-Dutch money supported the recovery of Austrian military fortunes. Britain's King George II himself took the field the following year, leading the victorious allies—including British troops—in the battle of Dettingen.

Proper Anglo-French hostilities soon began in earnest, spreading to North America and the Caribbean in 1744, and to the Indian Ocean by 1745. Britain was notable, alongside the Dutch, for financial contributions to the allied cause in Europe, and for naval exploits that included the capture of Louisbourg in 1745–1746 and victories at Cape Finisterre (1747, 1748) that effectively ended French trade with the West Indies for the duration of the war. The French effort against Britain, by contrast, peaked with the Jacobite campaign of 1745–1746—a near-run affair that caught Hanover loyalists at a weak moment militarily, but ultimately ended with butchery at Culloden Moor and the effective end of the Jacobite threat. The rising itself inspired a second famous song from the period, "God Save the King," and French aid, though minimal in the event,[35] was sufficient to prompt the formation of anti-Gallican (anti-French) social clubs across the British Isles.[36]

In sum, Fleury understood correctly that Britain was best contained by a policy of nonconfrontation, and Walpole played into his hands from the late 1720s to the early 1740s. Mediation in the Anglo-Spanish war of 1727–1729 served French ends, as did British neutrality in the War of the Polish Succession; but when the two came to blows, as they did after Fleury's death in 1743, British sea power and financial might stymied the Cardinal's successors. European conquests and a surprise victory in India offset British gains in the Atlantic world, but French support for the Jacobites added proto-nationalist pique to what was otherwise a simpler rivalry for land and trade. British leaders meanwhile returned to the combination that had won for them before: deploying small forces and funding allies in Europe, sweeping enemies from the sea and attacking their colonies. It is notable that this strategy failed in the case of Spain—Anglo-Spanish differences were adjusted by treaty in 1750–1752—but succeeded quite well against France. For the most part, the détente period of the Anglo-French rivalry redounded to the credit of the latter; but avoiding confrontation was no easy task, and when conflict came, the fortunes of war favored the British.

British High Tide (1746–1762)

The high point of British hostility toward France occurred in the middle decades of the eighteenth century. Following the peace of Aix la Chapelle in 1748, both empires looked to their needs for defense, though British assertiveness also included attempts to build on paper one of the largest coalitions in European diplomatic history. French responses were uneven, weak, and often confused, and the major attempt to press their land claims—in the Appalachian backcountry—formed the proximate cause of the Seven Years War (1754–1763). Defeat on an unprecedented scale forced a revolutionary reassessment of French strategic priorities. At long last, about seventy-five years after the English public took on the strategic rivalry with France by accepting William III as king, ministers at Versailles led by the duc de Choiseul realized that the dynastic glory of their traditional archrival, Austria, paled in the international arena next to the finance and sea power of their new great adversary, Britain.

After the fall of Robert Walpole in 1742, many of his old allies joined with members of the opposition to form new governments. The result by 1746 was a "broad bottom" coalition led by Thomas Pelham-Holles, first duke of Newcastle.[37] The latter had been in the top tier of Walpole's government since 1724—in essence, Walpole's apprentice—yet major differences between the two men emerged by the late 1730s: the old minister held tightly to a peace and trade agenda, while the younger began to see international relations in terms of strategic rivalry. A compulsive flatterer, Newcastle's obsequiousness often made him appear to foreign diplomats as a champion of peace; but beyond wanting to please people of all parties in domestic politics, his deep suspicions of France—evident as early as the 1720s—made him much easier to manipulate than Walpole had been, in favor of more belligerent policies.

On the other side of the Channel, a cohort of French intellectuals began to glimpse from Fleury's policies the kernel of a new economic policy: *laissez-faire*. The idea may come from the Dutch notion of "free ships, free goods,"[38] but it was reborn in the 1730s, with thinkers such as Richard Cantillon, René de Voyer (marquis d'Argenson; minister of foreign affairs, 1744–1747), Francis Quesnay, his pupil Vincent de Gournay, and their protégé, Etienne de Silhouette. None of them had Fleury's grip on power, but the so-called Gournay Circle slowly gained influence in the late 1740s, especially through the king's mistress, Jeanne Poisson Marquise de Pompadour. Forerunners of the physiocrats in the 1760s, they broadly understood that state power relied on trade, and saw that peace benefited France more than Britain. "Trade" for these thinkers also meant a more assertive colonial policy—assertive, that is, until that policy gave Britain a *casus belli*.

Caution about Britain was evident in the approach toward India, where Governor-General Joseph François Dupleix had enjoyed a modicum of success in the late 1740s. He took the British base at Madras in 1746, and though it was exchanged for Louisbourg at Aix la Chapelle in 1748, the French East India Company still held a strong position. Dupleix used Company forces in 1749 to help a local ally's bid for power, and the extent of his success provoked new hostilities with the British East India Company.[39] French Company officials were concerned by Robert Clive's victory at Arcot in 1751, and began to worry that a wider war with Britain might result. French support for Dupleix dwindled after 1752, he was recalled in 1754, and the two East India Companies signed a treaty in 1755.

"Peace" as such was equally fragile in North America. There, British initiatives clearly came first—some of them apparently designed to upset regional power balances. By 1748, a trading post at Pickawillany (near present-day Dayton, Ohio) threatened to advance British claims over much of present-day Ohio and Indiana through their Miami and Wyandot allies. Meanwhile, British ministers literally advertised their ambitions on Nova Scotia, using the *London Gazette* to call for discharged soldiers willing to settle at Chebucto—soon renamed Halifax in honor of the president of the Board of Trade.[40] French governors-general in both Canada and Louisiana responded, by pursuing fort-building projects. They ranged from Fort Beauséjour in Maritime Canada[41] to expansions on Fort Toulouse in Alabama[42] and peaked with a string of outposts in the Ohio Country from Presqu'Île on Lake Erie to Fort Duquesne (present-day Pittsburgh).[43] These last forts were built soon after French-allied Ottawas and Chippewas destroyed Pickawillany in June 1752, and Fort Duquesne completed the chain early in 1754, built on the foundations of an unfinished Virginia blockhouse.

Allied to these formal French measures were what might be called the commercial intrigues of Canada's *intendant* (roughly, chief financial officer) François Bigot, the court financiers Jean Paris Montmartel and Joseph Paris Duverney, and Canada merchants from France's western littoral.[44] The Canada trade had previously dealt mostly in imports of fur and cod, but state investments in defense now opened an opportunity to speculate on the *export* of arms to North America. With the approval of the Gournay circle, French political and commercial interests were thus united in looking to contain British colonial expansion, though they apparently had few contingency plans if their projects actually led to open war.

British opposition to France is evident from Newcastle's foreign policy, almost from the moment peace was signed in 1748. He considered almost immediately an opportunity to steal away Prussia, France's strongest ally in Central Europe, and his diplomacy in the Northern Crisis of 1749–1750 forced France to pay peacetime subsidies to retain its standing in Sweden and Denmark. Newcastle also advanced the Imperial Election Plan in 1750—a project using British and Dutch funds to tie German Electors more closely to Austria—and by 1754–1755 he was close to uniting all of these with Russian interests in Eastern Europe. Such a result would contain France's allies, Sweden and Prussia, while freeing Austrian and Dutch troops to defend their (or rather, British) interests on France's frontiers. British envoys also worked behind the scenes for the 1752 Treaty of Aranjuez, securing peace in southern Europe and removing Spain and Sardinia from the French orbit. In short, aggressive British diplomacy on paper all but isolated France by 1754–1755, just as French moves in the colonial world piqued British imperial sensitivities.

Through the early 1750s, the "peace" party in Britain subsisted mainly on economic arguments. Henry Pelham—as first lord of the Treasury, chancellor of the Exchequer, and Newcastle's brother—opposed the latter's ideas on peacetime subsidies to Britain's allies and hoped to mediate disputes (Sweden vs. Russia in 1749–1750, Prussia vs. Hanover in 1752–1753) rather than go to war. His death in March 1754 removed a major block on Newcastle's natural suspicions of France. Though Newcastle—now first lord of the Treasury in his own right—still supported peace for financial reasons, he was more willing to let military and imperialist interests shape the British response to reports of French aggression. By 1753, the British diplomatic record is littered with protests about French actions in India, the Caribbean, and North America, and with secret missives to British envoys to tarnish France's image in the courts of Europe. Though Newcastle may have wanted to escalate hostilities short of open war, cabinet intrigues in 1754–1755 forced his hand:[45] French "games" that he tried to contain with diplomacy and small regional deployments soon ballooned into larger military commitments, then naval deployments, and ultimately the first global war.[46]

In 1755, the Royal Navy took two warships and 800 troops, detained about 300 French merchant ships and 6,000 sailors, and opened one of the century's most effective blockades. Though initially plagued by shipboard sickness, the navy profited from major victualing reforms. There were a few failures, such as a squadron under Admiral John Byng that failed to relieve Minorca in 1756, and French supply ships for Canada and the Caribbean that escaped the blockade in 1756 and 1757. Thereafter, there were few interruptions to Britain's voyage to global naval dominance. In 1757, amphibious operations on the French coast met indifferent success, but their lessons benefited later operations, including Gorée and St. Louis (West Africa, 1758), Guadeloupe (West Indies, 1759), and Belle Isle off the coast of France in 1761. The navy also acted decisively at Louisbourg in 1758 and Québec in 1759—the latter being notable not just for the iconic battle of the Plains of Abraham, but also for bringing advanced British surveying techniques to the St. Lawrence River. The Royal Navy also beat off an invasion scare in 1759, destroying French combat power at Lagos and Quiberon Bay, and the campaign of 1761–1762 saw the captures of Dominica, Martinique, and, once Spain entered the war, Havana and Manila. Quick and regular resupply to East India Company forces also proved decisive after 1757, with Robert Clive and Eyre Coote combining by 1761 to establish British supremacy (vis-à-vis France, at least) in both Bengal and the Carnatic. In sum, the Royal Navy was not just big (peaking around 85,000 sailors on more than 300 ships of all types), but it struck early—setting the French at an initial disadvantage—struck hard, and, often while its enemies were off-balance, learned quickly from mistakes and improved its efficiency at working with the army for amphibious operations.[47]

British operations in North America also overcame a slow start, but again exuded an unusual level of daring and confidence by the middle stages of the war.[48] French raids at Oswego and Fort Bull in 1756 continued the momentum of French advance in the North American interior dating back to 1752, but a last victory at Fort William Henry[49] shocked and enraged British colonial opinion in 1757. Taking command in North America after the defeat and death of Edward Braddock in 1755, John Campbell, fourth earl of Loudoun, proved ineffective at field command, but his reforms to the British army in the colonies—and their colonial auxiliaries—proved decisive by 1758. Following John Bradstreet's victory at Fort Frontenac—intercepting French supplies for the Ohio Country—Loudoun's emphasis on wagons and road building greatly aided John Forbes's campaign to Fort Duquesne. British troops were misemployed at Carillon in 1758, but succeeded in a long siege of Louisbourg, which set up the Niagara and Quebec expeditions of 1759. By 1760, all that remained was for British forces—some 23,000 European regulars and at least 25,000 Anglo-Americans—to take Montréal in a three-pronged operation up the Richelieu River from Lake Champlain, up the St. Lawrence from Québec, and down the St. Lawrence from Niagara. Although fraught with risk throughout, and unprecedented in its geographical scale, the British victory in North America was as convincing and impressive as the exploits of the Royal Navy, with some unforeseen results.

Following the rhetoric of William Pitt the Elder—Newcastle's partner in leading the British war effort after June 1757—historians have often argued that British victory in the Seven Years War depended on soaking up French resources in Europe. In fact, French efforts had their share of setbacks, for example retreating across most of Germany in 1757 after the defeat against the Prussians at Rossbach. Worse, their Austrian ally suffered an equally disastrous defeat at Leuthen a month later. In theory, France, Austria, and their Russian allies—even smaller allies such as Saxony and Bavaria—could replace their losses in far greater numbers than could Hanover, Prussia, and a small collection of allies in north-central Germany, but losses at sea and in Canada in particular damaged the French economy to a point where replacing losses became exceedingly difficult. It is unclear whether British leaders recognized North America as a linchpin for all of France's war efforts, but their victories, beyond mere conquests, also throttled the credit on investments in the Canada trade. These same investments supported the overall structure of French wartime finance, so their loss meant severe damage to France's ability to keep their own and their allies' armies in the field. One statistical example is the proportion of the Austrian war budget covered by French finances— 34 percent in 1758, but less than 10 percent by 1760. A fair part of the German war, it seems, was won in America.

The high tide of British antagonism and military efficacy against France coincided with peak naval performance and overwhelming commitment to colonial theaters. This was all made possible by the maturation of the financial revolution, which began with the formation of the Bank of England in 1694. As a result of the bank's lending against a well-developed sinking fund and other confidence-building measures, interest rates on British government loans remained around 3–4 percent for the duration of the war. By comparison, the French government by 1761 attempted to float a loan on an English bank at 11.5 percent interest. British patriotism was equally vital, with a lively pamphlet and ballad culture joining with Pitt's rousing speeches and the prominent place of anti-Gallican social clubs. Overwhelming British success in the Seven Years War reflected the endeavors of the entire society—not just its sharp military edge.

French Revenge (1759–1783)

Catastrophic defeat in the Seven Years War prompted major reforms in the French regime—even before the opening of peace negotiations. Gournay and his circle were mostly correct in their assessment that a strong economy was the foundation of imperial power and prestige, and that colonial holdings could support a stronger presence in Europe. Free trade and broad public access to banking and stock markets were also important for giving the larger population some sense of ownership in the war effort—something Adam Smith would remark on in his *Nature and Causes of the Wealth of Nations* (London, 1776). The major French error, though, lay in awakening the British giant far too early. When war erupted in 1754–1756, France was still in a state of unpreparedness in both Europe and the colonial world, and was utterly surprised by the scale of the British response.

France was relatively lucky that Newcastle's diplomatic schemes collapsed in 1756, leaving them allies with whom to try to win in Europe. France's army, navy, and finances were, however, nowhere near being able to support their allies' demands.[50] After several fiascos in the field and cabinet shuffles at Versailles, Madame Pompadour's last foreign minister, the

Marquis de Choiseul, finally came upon a scheme worthy of his predecessor Fleury. His *Memoire raisonné*, printed in 1761 in both French and English, gave a slanted view of the early peace negotiations with Britain. He used a careful selection of Pitt's letters to portray the wartime ministry as callous and overly ambitious, and tarnished Britain's image in the courts of Europe and on the London street. Over the medium to long term, Choiseul's scurrilous memoir combined with a change of monarchs and British war-weariness to bring the conflict to an end.[51] Yet while pundits in London sung praises of "splendid isolation" after 1763, Britain's surge from Europe out into the Atlantic world gained envy and hostility from their competitors much more than admiration.

The *Memoire raisonné* was also a first signal in French foreign policy that something fundamental had shifted—at least at Versailles. The Franco-Austrian alliance of 1756 was a major aberration from French foreign policy norms, as was the Russian tie concluded in 1757. These powers were regarded as France's traditional enemies, and the general populace of France still needed convincing that Britain was the main enemy. Diplomatic documents that "proved" British bullying in the Atlantic world played into that agenda. So too did the Affaire du Canada in 1761 and the Kourou and Malouines expeditions of 1763–1764. These were disasters of epic proportions, involving bankruptcy of the French Marine and fifty high-level prosecutions in the former case, and tens of thousands of colonists' deaths in the latter, off the coasts of South America. But they turned the attention of the French public toward the Atlantic, where France only had one major adversary: Britain.

British methods of trying to pay down their war debt feature prominently in the background to the American War of Independence. The Stamp Act, Sugar Act, Townshend Acts, and many more sought to integrate the British colonies more closely into the tax structures and political life of the United Kingdom, but communications by sea were still too slow to make this a practical possibility. Choiseul opened channels for smuggling French arms into the colonies. His revanchist agenda failed in 1770, as British colonists still refused to rebel on a large scale after the Boston Massacre, and later in the year they more or less supported the British government's position in the Falklands crisis with Spain. Avenues of French support remained open, however, at the time of the Gaspée Affair in 1772, the Boston Tea Party in 1773, and the Coercive Acts in 1774.[52] As colonists passed the Suffolk Resolves—a resolution to oppose British legislation by force—and began forming the First Continental Congress, France remained in a position to support them.

This was not merely true of Franco-American relations, but also of French relations and reforms in Europe. Choiseul expanded the French navy and encouraged the same for his ally, Charles III of Spain. By retaining good relations with Austria, he secured peace on France's landward borders and enabled himself and his successors in the Ministry of Foreign Affairs to focus on the Atlantic world. France may have been helpless to prevent the first partition of Poland (1772), but it was well positioned to continue tarnishing Britain's reputation in Europe, and to prevent Lord North's diplomats from regaining a diplomatic foothold. As the American War of Independence approached, isolation would be anything but pleasant for a Britain that lay at the mercy of France's traditional gifts: a concern with dynastic honor that resonated among many European monarchs, and subtle, rational diplomacy that portrayed a humbled France as a better ally than an overbearing, arrogant, perfidious Albion.

By the late 1770s, Anglo-American nationalism was possibly one of the most dynamic political forces in the Atlantic world, but its French and Spanish complements followed close behind, ironically inspired by the British model. French finance was, if not in brilliant shape, at least substantially reformed from the shambles that declared bankruptcy in 1759. And notwithstanding George Washington's brilliance as a general, keeping the Continental Army intact and ultimately enlarging it during hard campaigns along the eastern seaboard, the largest land campaign of the American War of Independence was the Spanish reconquest of Florida in 1779–1782. By 1781, Britain was engaged in a global war against the Americans, French, Spanish, and Dutch, isolated in Europe and even threatened in India by the emerging state of Mysore. Changing fortunes by 1782–1783 helped to bring the war to a close, but there was little denying the scale of the defeat: in 1783 alone, the London street played host to at least six editions of the bitterly satirical *Advice to the Officers of the British Army*. In sum, when France and its Spanish ally recognized Britain as their major nemesis and fully engaged in the strategic rivalry, the same British state that had overmatched France and achieved overwhelming victory in the Seven Years War was humbled in its turn.

Summation

In the decades before 1688, England made a revolutionary transition not just from a Dutch rivalry to a French one, but also from a political identity based on its religion and monarchy to one that—while still incorporating these elements—focused much more on the navy and international commerce. Built up initially by Dutch investments and financial know-how, England turned itself into a worthy rival for a France whose internal wealth had grown considerably under Cardinal Richelieu, Cardinal Mazarin, Colbert, and Louvois. Despite having only one-third of the population, far fewer resources, and less-well-developed internal communications than France, Britain greatly benefited from much more sophisticated financial systems, supporting a huge fleet and large subsidies for Continental allies. By 1748, British superiority was clear enough to prompt a major shift in French strategic thinking, marked by the rise of the Gournay circle and ambitious projects in several colonial theaters. The pace of these reforms was too slow to be effective, yet fast enough to pique British ire and lead to a catastrophic French defeat in the Seven Years War. After 1763, political turmoil in London made peace a vital interest for the British, while Choiseul turned France away from its former dynastic concerns on the Continent to concentrate more fully on its major financial and strategic rival.

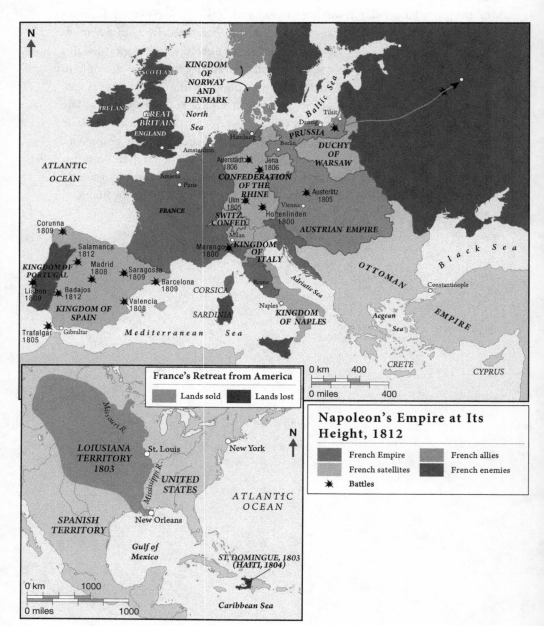

N

KINGDOM
OF
NORWAY
AND
DENMARK

SCOTLAND

IRELAND

GREAT
BRITAIN
ENGLAND

North
Sea

Baltic Sea

Tilsit

Danzig

PRUSSIA

DUCHY
OF
WARSAW

ATLANTIC
OCEAN

Hamburg

Amsterdam

Berlin

Auerstädt
1806

Jena
1806

Amiens

Paris

CONFEDERATION
OF THE
RHINE

FRANCE

Ulm
1805

Austerlitz
1805

Vienna

SWITZ.
CONFED.

Hohenlinden
1800

AUSTRIAN EMPIRE

Corunna
1809

Salamanca
1812

Madrid
1808

Marengo
1800

KINGDOM
OF
ITALY

Milan

Black Sea

OTTOMAN

Constantinople

KINGDOM OF
PORTUGAL

Saragossa
1809

Barcelona
1809

Rome

Adriatic Sea

EMPIRE

Lisbon
1809

Badajos
1812

CORSICA

Valencia
1808

KINGDOM OF
SPAIN

Naples

Aegean
Sea

SARDINIA

KINGDOM
OF NAPLES

Trafalgar
1805

Gibraltar

Mediterranean   Sea

CRETE

CYPRUS

0 km   400

0 miles   400

France's Retreat from America

Lands sold	Lands lost

N

Missouri R.

LOIUSIANA
TERRITORY
1803

St. Louis

New York

Napoleon's Empire at Its Height, 1812

French Empire	French allies
French satellites	French enemies
✴ Battles	

Mississippi R.

UNITED
STATES

ATLANTIC
OCEAN

SPANISH
TERRITORY

New Orleans

Gulf of
Mexico

ST. DOMINGUE, 1803
(HAITI, 1804)

0 km   1000

0 miles   1000

Caribbean Sea

Napoleon's Empire at Its Height.

CHAPTER 9

Napoleon's Quest

Great Britain versus France III

Michael V. Leggiere

T HE RIVALRY BETWEEN FRANCE and Great Britain during the French
Wars (1792–1815) often has been characterized as the dichotomy of the
elephant versus the whale, or the tiger versus the shark. As it stood, the shark
could not defeat the tiger on land, and the tiger could not defeat the shark in
the water: neither could defeat the other without the extensive assistance of
allies. Britain owed its position as a European Great Power to its maritime
economic strategy, while France emerged as the dominant, predatory military power of Europe. That France achieved this status is the result of many
factors released by its post-revolutionary dynamism, which are beyond the
scope of this study. However, strategy ranks as one of the crucial elements in
France's hegemonic success, as well as in Britain's multifaceted efforts to defeat its great rival during this short period.

Starting in the mid-seventeenth century, maritime economic competition gradually eclipsed issues of religion, political systems, and universal
monarchy in the Anglo-French rivalry. In their place arose an exponentially increasing competition for markets, colonies, and resources in North
America, the Caribbean, and India. As a mercantilist power, Britain's maritime security remained irrevocably intertwined with its national security,
as revenue from international trade and commerce determined the state's
power both at home and abroad. Thus, Britain's strength depended on its
merchants' ability to trade across the world's oceans. A large part of this
trade was with Continental markets, making Europe a key component
of Britain's maritime economic strategy, because successful British trade

depended on a European balance of power. Any challenge to European stability threatened British maritime security and thus Britain's power. London responded to such threats by intervening directly. Specifically, the British considered three areas of Europe vital as interdependent maritime strategic interests: (1) the Low Countries, (2) the Mediterranean, and (3) the Baltic. These three strategic spheres enabled Britain to maintain its Great Power status and influence in Europe.[1]

The British could not pursue both a maritime economic strategy and unilaterally check French ambitions on the Continent. To counter French power in Europe, protect British interests on the Continent, and maintain a European balance of power, the British looked for surrogates or coalitions of surrogates to fight France. This gave London a free hand to pursue a maritime strategy based on building a global colonial empire without depleting undo resources in grinding land campaigns. From 1793 to 1807, Britain competed with France within the framework of this maritime economic strategy. As such, it pursued a dual policy of (1) committing its own forces to strangle French maritime trade and harass the French in secondary theaters to drain French military strength, and (2) funding allied states to oppose France.

For much of the eighteenth century, France also pursued a maritime economic policy aimed at competing with Britain, while simultaneously pursuing a Continental strategy to likewise maintain its Great Power status and influence in Europe. Yet French interests and commitments as a Continental Power consumed resources on such a vast scale that it limited France's capacity to pursue a maritime strategy competitive with Britain's global reach. Due to its Continental policy, France exerted greater influence in Europe, but Britain dominated the seas and thus international trade. By the mid-eighteenth century, the decline of traditional European powers, such as Portugal, Spain, the Dutch Republic, and the Holy Roman Empire resulted in the dominance of both Britain and France in their respective spheres. Though both could exert some influence in the other's sphere, neither could dominate the other: Britain could not replace France as the main power on the European Continent, and France could not surpass Britain's maritime economic supremacy. Regardless, the competition increased as the British remained active in Continental affairs while the French pursued a dual maritime and Continental strategy. Although one could not be sacrificed for the other, success depended on allocating finite resources prudently.

Between 1783 and 1792, London's advantages in taxation, administration, and finance benefited Britain in its rivalry with the French, whose feudal foundations could not support the needs of the modern state. Throughout their rivalry, British financial systems proved far superior, more rational, and less fragile, thus providing for a more stable government. Although the American Revolutionary War had financially exhausted both states, France's systemic financial weakness led to the government's bankruptcy three years after the Peace of Paris, while Britain's finance rapidly recovered.

An absolutist political system provided the French one dubious advantage that the British government did not enjoy. Beyond the intrigues of the Bourbon court, French policymakers did not have to manage Parliament, popular opinion, and public diplomacy. Conversely, the British government perpetually faced the loss of agency due to the inability to secure formal and informal domestic support. Parliamentary opposition that combined with public outcry always had the potential to uproot any sitting British ministry. Although the French king was answerable only to God, he bore all responsibility for the success and failure of the state. While this spared the Bourbons from having to answer to parliamentary opposition parties or public opinion, it placed all responsibility for the state's welfare squarely on the king's shoulders.

In terms of economic power and resources, the rivals remained on par despite the drastic reduction of France's colonial empire as a result of the losses sustained from the Seven Years War. While the British pursued the Industrial Revolution, agriculture continued to reign in France, whose population of 24 million trebled Britain's 8 million, and whose territorial extent of 675,000 square kilometers doubled Britain's 314,000 square kilometers. The rivals had comparable economic power and resources, but growth trends in trade and industry favored the British. In geography, Britain's insular position provided London crucial advantages. Unlike France, Britain did not have to make the difficult choice between pursuing either a maritime or a Continental strategy, as its insular position provided the British greater security from direct attack. This, in turn, translated into far greater freedom of action in foreign affairs. Moreover, Britain's insular position enabled it to isolate its foreign policy from its domestic problems.[2]

To balance London's greater freedom of action, the French employed a more efficient foreign ministry apparatus that survived the French Revolution (1789–1799) and enabled Napoleon (1799–1814) to harness the resources of Spain and South Germany early in his rule. Again unlike France, which the great Vauban ringed with more than 100 fortifications for defense, water spared the British from the financial drain of fortress construction and maintenance. Britain's geographic advantage also enabled the British to focus their resources on the service branch most crucial to both their national security and their maritime strategy: the Royal Navy. While the French managed to narrow the margin of British naval superiority during the 1770s and 1780s, the British army remained quite inferior in size. Interestingly, the cost of pursuing a dual maritime and Continental strategy did not force the French to sacrifice their navy in favor of an army. By the time of the French Wars (1792–1815), the French possessed newer, larger, and better ships than the British. Moreover, France could count on help overcoming Britain's pronounced numerical superiority by the fact that the Royal Navy had global commitments. With a bit of luck and skill, therefore, the French could plan to achieve local superiority at a time and place of their choosing. Napoleonic France did, for some time, pursue a vigorous naval armaments program that would have narrowed the margin considerably. Yet, French seamanship and naval tactics continued to lag those of the British, and the gap only widened after the Royal Navy blockaded France's coasts.

William Pitt the Younger took office as British prime minister in December 1783, undertaking the unenviable task of rebuilding Britain's economic, military, and diplomatic fortunes following its defeat in the American Revolutionary War. Pitt guided Britain through its postwar economic revival by re-establishing strong commercial ties with the Americans and by concluding an advantageous trade agreement with France. The 1786 Eden Treaty brought the British closer to achieving their goal of establishing free trade between the two rivals. From the viewpoint of national security, the treaty also signaled France's inability to simultaneously continue its maritime rivalry with the British while maintaining its position as a Continental power. Unable to recover from the financial morass created by the American Revolutionary War, France made commercial concessions— despite objections from its merchant and manufacturing lobbies—to its main rival in hope of slowing the financial race that the British were clearly winning. Britain's capacity to outspend France contributed to the collapse of the French state, similar to the fate of the Soviet Union during the Cold War with the United States.

War of the First Coalition (1792–1797)

In the last years of the 1780s, the British appeared well on their way to forming a British-led European alliance system directed at France, while the French writhed in the chaos of a revolution that left their dual maritime and Continental strategy in shambles. Essentially, the French withdrew from the international stage during the early years of the Revolution. Fortunately for Paris, the British did not use the opportunity to do more than continue to erode France's standing on the Continent from afar, as Britain, too, resorted to isolationism. With Parliament and popular opinion decidedly opposed to intervention on the Continent, caution and neutrality became the guiding principles of British foreign policy, just as revolutionary France returned to the international stage in response to Austrian saber-rattling. Dynastic ties between the monarchs of France and Austria made the safety of the French royal family in the midst of an increasingly volatile revolution a matter of Austrian prestige and honor. The radicalization of the French Revolution inflamed the growing crisis and led to, on April 20, 1792, a French declaration of war on Austria, which Prussia immediately sided with, thus igniting the War of the First Coalition (1792–1797).

For Britain, the security of the Netherlands became its primary foreign policy concern when war erupted. Austro-Prussian retreats in October 1792 resulted in French advances on all fronts, including an invasion of Belgium in November. After a resounding French victory, Austrian forces evacuated Belgium, leaving nothing between the French army and the Dutch border. On November 16, 1792, Paris declared the Scheldt River open to navigation for the first time in more than 200 years and asserted the right of French armies to pursue the Austrians into neutral territory. These claims violated Dutch sovereignty and annulled prior international treaties. A decree of November 19 declaring France's intention to support revolutionaries abroad caused even greater concern in London by posing a direct threat to the British crown and government. Concurrently, French ground forces received orders to pursue the Austrians into Dutch territory, and a French warship sailed for the Scheldt. Consequently, French aggression in the Low Countries brought the British into the War of the First Coalition against Revolutionary France in 1793, rather than any ideological motive related to the fate of the French monarchy. Nevertheless, the Tory party that controlled the British government harbored no love for French republicanism. Thus, regime change became a major British objective in the French Wars.

France declared war against Britain and the Netherlands on February 1, 1793, and soon afterward against Spain. In the course of 1793, the Holy Roman Empire, Sardinia, Portugal, Naples, and Tuscany declared war against France. Successful combined operations by the British, Austrians, Prussians, and Dutch drove the French from Belgium in 1793 and opened the road to Paris, but an offensive never materialized due to the lack of cooperation between the Allies. Meanwhile, the Royal Navy attacked French colonies in the West Indies. As with previous conflicts, France found itself in the highly disadvantageous position of having to wage war on the high seas against its superior archrival while French armies contended with a formidable alliance on the European Continent.

Looking at the situation from the British perspective, London again could allocate almost all of the state's resources to its maritime economic strategy while sending only a token expeditionary force to join its allies fighting the French in Europe. Indeed this was fortunate, for, at the time, the British lacked the manpower to both garrison their global empire and commit a large army to the Continent. For the defense of the Low Countries, the British landed token ground forces to augment the larger Austro-Prussian-Dutch armies. In the Mediterranean theater, London resorted to strong-arm diplomacy to force the Italian and Barbary States not only to end their trade with the French, particularly the export of wheat, but to also provide troops for the First Coalition. The Royal Navy played its part by blockading France's Atlantic and Mediterranean coasts so as to comprehensively strangle French and neutral trade to hasten the war's end.

Although the British garnered mixed results from their diplomatic offensive in the Mediterranean, the Royal Navy crippled France in the first two years of the war. After French royalists opposed to the republican government in Paris gained control of the city of Toulon, which served as home port for the French Mediterranean Fleet, an Anglo-Spanish fleet landed a small multinational occupation force on August 28, 1793. The loss of this port and its twenty-nine ships of the line crippled France's ability to project naval power in the Mediterranean. French ground forces recaptured the port on December 18, 1793, but not before the British sank fourteen French ships of the line and sailed off with the other fifteen.

A little more than six months later, the first and largest fleet action of the naval conflict between Britain and the French Republic took place on June 1, 1794. Known as the Glorious First of June, the battle was a tactical victory for the British that cost the French Atlantic Fleet seven ships of the line. Coupled with the loss of the Toulon Fleet the year before, the Glorious First of June devastated France's ability to continue its maritime economic rivalry with the British. By default, the British were now free to conduct a campaign of blockade for the remainder of the war. Although single French ships and small squadrons pursued an active war against the British, any attempt to challenge the British control of the seas was impossible.

Like previous Anglo-French conflicts extending back to the seventeenth century, Britain's maritime triumph should have led to France's defeat. However, France avoided this fate by temporarily abandoning its dual policy and concentrating on Continental hegemony. France's bloody transformation from a constitutional monarchy to a republic had unleashed nationalistic impulses that allowed the French to turn the tide against the Coalition's land forces. By the end of 1795, French armies controlled the Low Countries and forced the British to withdraw their forces from the Continent; only Austria remained Britain's ally. Despite these setbacks, the British continued their traditional wartime policy of pursuing a maritime strategy while financing an ally to restore the balance of power on the Continent. After the British recalled their Mediterranean fleet in 1796, they only supported the Austrians by granting Vienna a considerable subsidy. While the Austrians fought the French in the Rhineland and northern Italy, the British helped themselves to the Dutch colonies at Ceylon and the Cape of Good Hope, but made minimal progress against France's colonies. Although not broken, the Austrians had had enough of an inconclusive and grinding war and opted to negotiate with the French. A separate peace was concluded in 1797 that ended the War of the First Coalition.

Despite having no allies, Britain remained at war with France. Fortunately for the British, the French could not exploit an Irish insurrection against British rule in December 1796, nor could they take advantage of a mutiny by the Channel Fleet in April and May 1797. Nevertheless, the War of the First Coalition ended with France not only shattering Europe's balance of power, but with the French in possession of the Low Countries, whose ports they would control, and periodically threaten Britain from, for the next twenty years. As noted, the British considered three areas of Europe vital to their strategic interests: the Low Countries, the Mediterranean, and the Baltic. Of the three, the Low Countries served as Britain's major maritime interest. In them, maritime security and national security were interchangeable, as the Dutch ports of Antwerp and Flushing offered the best positions from which a hostile power could launch an invasion of England. At Antwerp, the prevailing winds and currents provided easier access to the English Channel than did the French ports of Boulogne, Cherbourg, and Brest. Thus, a hostile power that controlled Antwerp posed a direct threat to Britain's control of the Channel as well as its North Atlantic trading routes; in short, much of Britain's maritime capability could be challenged from Antwerp. Control of Antwerp and Flushing also provided an enemy direct access to Essex, Kent, and the Thames estuary. Aside from the immediate problem of getting the French out of the Low Countries so as to end the threat to British maritime security, London needed long-term security against any hostile power gaining control of the Low Countries. Consequently, the issue of what political entity would replace France in the Low Countries loomed large in British diplomacy for the duration of the French Wars.

Although strategically less significant than the Low Countries, the British considered the Mediterranean vital for colonial defense. However,

Spain allied with France and declared war on Britain and Portugal in October 1796, rendering the British position in the Mediterranean untenable. The combined Franco-Spanish fleet of thirty-eight ships of the line outnumbered the British Mediterranean fleet of fifteen ships of the line, forcing the British to evacuate their positions in first Corsica and then Elba. Thus, the British temporarily withdrew their fleet from the theater for operations around Gibraltar and Iberia. In the aftermath, the British watched the French conquer northern Italy and subjugate the rest of the Italian peninsula in 1797. They returned to the Mediterranean in 1798 too late to prevent the French from invading Egypt, at that time a fiefdom of the Ottoman Empire. Unbeknownst to London, the French planned to attack Britain's maritime supremacy by building a canal across the Isthmus of Suez that would alter world trade routes, rather than launch a direct invasion of British-held India. Regardless, the Egyptian operation marked France's return as Britain's maritime economic rival. Although the British defeated a larger and more modern French fleet at the Battle of the Nile on August 1, 1798, the French remained in the Levant until 1801. This forced the British to divert resources from the main military responsibility of the Mediterranean theater: blockading the French port of Toulon. Moreover, maintaining the blockade of France's Mediterranean coast as well as French-controlled ports in Italy required friendly harbors to resupply and repair the warships on duty. To this end, the British took and retained control of Malta. Malta itself posed the problem of being unable to feed itself. Therefore, to feed Malta, the British secured Sicily, which eventually brought the shark face to face with the tiger in southern Italy.[3]

War of the Second Coalition (1798–1802)

Hatred of Revolutionary France, along with the desire to pursue traditional foreign policy objectives, led to the formation of the Second Coalition in 1798, consisting of Britain, Austria, Russia, the Ottoman Empire, and Naples. The war began with a powerful Austro-Russian surge that swept the French from Italy, while an Anglo-Russian expedition landed in Holland in late August 1799. However, as Russian forces approached the French border via Switzerland, a French army defeated them in the mountains of Zurich in late September 1799. As a result, after initial successes, the Anglo-Russian invasion of Holland stalled. Faced with early winter gales that made provisioning by sea difficult, the Allies agreed to an armistice with the French, which saw all troops re-embarked by November 19, 1799. Earlier that month, General

Napoleon Bonaparte overthrew the French government. Before year's end, he outmaneuvered his fellow conspirators to make himself dictator of France under the title of first consul.

As for the War of the Second Coalition, Russia not only withdrew from the alliance but, by virtue of a rapprochement with Napoleon, Tsar Paul I formed the Second League of Armed Neutrality with Denmark, Prussia, and Sweden in 1800. Like the First League of Armed Neutrality during the American Revolutionary War, the Baltic states sought to protect neutral shipping against the Royal Navy's wartime policy of unlimited search for French contraband and military supplies. One of Britain's three vital maritime strategic spheres, an open and friendly Baltic was essential to provide vital naval stores.[4] The situation further turned against the British when Napoleon led an army across the Alps in the spring of 1800. By mid-June he had defeated the Austrians—Britain's only remaining ally—in northern Italy. Another Austrian defeat six months later in the German theater prompted the Austrians to again forsake their British allies and make peace with Bonaparte in 1801. Seeking to likewise withdraw from the Second Coalition, the Kingdom of Naples signed the March 28, 1801, Treaty of Florence with France under Russian mediation. Naples agreed to the presence of French garrisons in their ports on the Adriatic Sea to help enforce the treaty's stipulation that all Neapolitan harbors would be closed to British shipping. Napoleon's relative leniency toward the defenseless kingdom stemmed from his need to assuage the concerns of Tsar Paul and his allies in the Second League of Armed Neutrality over further French expansion in Italy. To appease the tsar, First Consul Bonaparte allowed King Ferdinand IV to remain on the Neapolitan throne, albeit as a vassal of Napoleonic France. This turn of events jeopardized Britain's entire Mediterranean policy, which required a friendly Sicily to feed the British fueling station at Malta.

Forced to consider a war against both France and Russia, the British did the only thing they could. Rather than attempt to curry Russian goodwill, London believed that only a show of force would restore its position in the Baltic. Consequently, the Royal Navy attacked and destroyed part of the Danish fleet at Copenhagen on April 2, 1801. As a result, Denmark withdrew from the League, but the wheels for its demise already were turning. The assassination of Tsar Paul in March 1801 and the accession of the anti-French Alexander I led to a change of Russian policy and the League's collapse.

Britain's failure to defeat France after a nine-year struggle resulted in war weariness that, when combined with a row over Catholic Emancipation that saw the hawkish Pitt ousted in favor of a more conciliatory Addington administration, led to the March 1802 Anglo-French Treaty of Amiens.

After attaining peace with Britain in 1802, Napoleon attempted to revive France's colonial empire in the Western Hemisphere. A bloody uprising on the French colony of Santo Domingo, combined with deteriorating relations with Britain, soon convinced Napoleon to abandon neocolonialism; France's sale of the Louisiana Territory to the United States in 1803 reflected this policy change. For the Anglo-French rivalry, the Louisiana Purchase suggests that Napoleon realized that France still could not pursue its traditional dual maritime and Continental strategy. Although Napoleonic France appeared to relinquish its maritime strategy, the damage done to British national security by Revolutionary France guaranteed the survival of the intense Anglo-French rivalry as long as Paris controlled the Low Countries and Italy. As Napoleon considered the Rhine, Alps, and Pyrenees to be the territorial gains of the Revolution that the French nation bequeathed to him for safekeeping, nothing short of total defeat would force him to yield them. In fact, much like the Soviet Union after World War II, he would defend these "natural frontiers" by further expanding his borders.

War of the Third Coalition (1803–1806)

Lasting only fourteen months, the Treaty of Amiens did not satisfy British concerns over the Low Countries, nor did Napoleon budge on the issue of granting a commercial agreement to restore friendly trading relations between the two states. Britain's refusal to evacuate Malta per the treaty, combined with continued French expansionism, brought on renewed war in May 1803. Fresh from dropping France's maritime strategy, Bonaparte concentrated all the resources of a much stronger France against a Britain that momentarily lacked Continental allies. To defeat the British, Napoleon planned to invade England and so undertook extensive preparations to build seaworthy transports for his army. To counter this threat, the British constructed formidable coastal defenses and placed the country on a war footing. As British workers labored on fortifications, London sought allies.

With his navy ill-prepared to challenge the British for control of the English Channel and his plan to build landing barges progressing slowly, Napoleon repeatedly postponed the invasion of Britain. As he waited, he made the fateful decisions to crown himself emperor of the French in 1804 and king of Italy in 1805. Such precipitate actions challenged the tenuous equilibrium established in Europe following the War of the Second Coalition. Thanks to Bonaparte's hubris, Russia and Austria responded favorably to British alliance overtures and Albion's generous funding offers to form the

Third Coalition in 1805. Although Prussia remained neutral, the objectives of the alliance, which included a French withdrawal from the Low Countries, appeared to meet Britain's strategic needs.

To the shock of the British, Napoleon captured Vienna and crushed the Austro-Russian armies in less than four months. Austria again signed a separate peace and the Russians limped home. For all practical purposes, the Third Coalition was over; Prussia's forfeiture of neutrality to join the Coalition came too late. Moreover, a British expedition that sailed to the Low Countries in the autumn of 1805 did not disembark after its commander learned of French victories in central Europe. On the other side of the ledger, however, even while Napoleon was conducting one of the most decisive campaigns in military history, Admiral Horatio Nelson ended any chance of the French challenging British naval superiority by destroying a Franco-Spanish fleet off the coast of Spain at Trafalgar on October 21, 1805. Realizing that Trafalgar severely limited his ability to challenge the British in a fleet action and thus considerably eroded his chances of gaining control of the English Channel, Napoleon sought to exploit his victory on land.

Acknowledging that British gold had financed the three previous coalition wars, Napoleon targeted the heart of Britain's power: its maritime economy. Lacking the resources either to invade Britain or decisively defeat the Royal Navy at sea and unable to compete with Britain's maritime policy in a conventional manner, Napoleon developed an alternate maritime economic strategy: the Continental System. As a result of the Industrial Revolution, Britain emerged as Europe's manufacturing and industrial center. To ruin its economy by causing inflation and debt, Napoleon implemented an embargo against British trade with the European nations under his control. Without the European market to buy its manufactured goods and for the re-export of colonial goods, he expected Britain to experience a severe depression, hurting the nation's economy and its ability to maintain its global colonial empire. Knowing that public opinion could unseat a British Cabinet, he hoped a depression would usher in a new government that would be willing to accept French dominance of the Continent. Moreover, Napoleon believed his new System would not only cause the British grave problems, but would open the door to a tremendous expansion of French trade, which would rush in to fill the void. His hope was that France would soon replace Britain as the economic engine of Europe.

Striking at Britain by closing the French-controlled ports of Europe to British trade dated back to the third Revolutionary government of France, the National Convention (1792–1795). During the War of the First Coalition, the French forced their conquered "sister republics" to close their ports to the British. At that time, because of holes in the System, the Republic's economic attack produced only marginal success. Napoleon returned to the idea in 1806 with renewed determination; the changes France made to the map of Europe considerably strengthened his ability to wage economic warfare against the British. France now controlled the Low Countries and the Hanseatic cities of North Germany, so by extension Europe's North Sea Coast, most of Italy, the Dalmatian coast of the Balkans, and was allied with Spain and many of the German states. To make his Continental blockade more effective and to gain an ally against Great Britain, Napoleon presented the Prussians with the February 1806 Treaty of Paris as punishment for their forfeiture of neutrality during the War of the Third Coalition. The treaty forced the Prussians to close all North German ports to British shipping. As a reward for joining France's war against Britain, Napoleon ordered the Prussians to immediately occupy Hanover, a possession of the British crown. He also hinted that he would support Berlin's long-standing goal of creating a Prussian-dominated confederation in North Germany. Facing a war with either the shark or the tiger, Berlin chose to face the former.

On April 1, 1806, Berlin inaugurated Napoleon's Continental System by issuing a decree that closed the ports of Prussia and Hanover to British shipping. London responded with the Order in Council of April 8, 1806, that declared a blockade of all ports between the Ems and the Elbe rivers in Germany. A declaration of war was issued to Prussia on April 20, 1806, accompanied by the seizure of over 400 Prussian merchantmen found in British waters, as well as the blockade of Prussia's Baltic coast. However, to minimize strife with third parties, the May 16, 1806, Orders in Council opened all ports in northwest Germany and Holland to neutral shipping as long as the vessels did not come from, or were not sailing to, a French-controlled port and as long as the ship did not carry French goods, contraband, or military supplies. Five days later, London declared that the Royal Navy would not stop any neutral ships in the Baltic. On September 25, the British went as far as to open the German coast between the Ems and the Elbe. Clearly, the two Leagues of Armed Neutrality, as well as problems with the Americans, taught the British restraint in dealing with neutrals.

After Napoleon forced the Austrians in January 1806 to accept his decision to dissolve the Holy Roman Empire, he created the Confederation of the Rhine in July of that same year. With Prussia and Austria excluded, sixteen German states joined in a military and political union under protection of the French emperor. All member states received full sovereignty over domestic affairs, but a national parliament would formulate foreign policy. In return for Napoleon's "protection," member states would pay a "blood tax" by supplying forces for his armies, initially 63,000 men annually. Napoleon succeeded in making the "Third Germany" a French satellite to better harness its military resources. This did not sit well with the Prussians, who felt betrayed over the issue of a Prussian-led North German confederation.

In his glory, Napoleon began making further changes to the map of Europe. Signaling his intention to never relinquish French control of the Low Countries, he made Holland a kingdom with his younger brother, Louis, its king. In addition, the British suffered another reverse in the Mediterranean theater. In January, British ground forces evacuated the Kingdom of Naples ahead of a French invasion, taking the Neapolitan Bourbons with them to Sicily aboard British warships. Later in the year, Napoleon appointed his older brother, Joseph, to be the new king of Naples.

In Britain, the "Ministry of All the Talents" came to power in early 1806. Willing to grant greater concessions to France than any previous British administration, it favored a negotiated peace with Napoleon that would have left France possessing far more territory than it had at the height of Louis XIV's power. Reversing London's policy of sponsoring plots, typically by French royalists to assassinate Napoleon, the Cabinet initiated a dialogue with France by warning him of an impending attack. Needing to stabilize Joseph's Neapolitan regime in the face of a British counteroffensive in Calabria that resulted in a redcoat victory over the French at Maida on July 4, 1806, Napoleon secretly discussed the return of Hanover to George III, as long as London dropped its support of the Neapolitan Bourbons. Although British forces withdrew to Sicily before the end of July, they continued to support a violent insurgency in Calabria against French rule. All this diplomatic posturing came to naught, as Napoleon harbored no sincere interest in peace and only sought to cause dissension between London and St. Petersburg, which was conducting its own concurrent talks with the French emperor. Napoleon's plan partially backfired when the Prussians learned of his offer to return Hanover, Berlin's only compensation for going to war with Britain. Discovering the limits of Napoleon's friendship, the Prussians opted for war against France in August 1806.

War of the Fourth Coalition (1806–1807)

The Fourth Coalition formed after London dropped its grievances with the Prussians, and Tsar Alexander I agreed to send an army to central Europe. Although somewhat apprehensive about facing the vaunted Prussian army,

Napoleon made short work of it at the twin battles of Jena-Auerstedt on October 14, 1806. With the conquest of Prussia, Napoleon strengthened his attack on British trade in the Baltic, as French forces ensured the closure of Prussia's coast. The European-wide implementation of the Continental System began on November 21, 1806, when Napoleon issued the Berlin Decree. Although he lacked a navy, the French emperor placed the British Isles in a state of blockade, prohibiting all commerce and communication with them. More in line with his capabilities, Napoleon declared that no British goods could enter Europe, that any British subject caught on the Continent could be imprisoned and their property or merchandise seized, and that all ships in French-controlled ports registered to British owners would be seized. No ships from Britain or its colonies could enter the ports of French-controlled Europe. London only moderately escalated this paper contest with the January 7, 1807, Orders in Council that prohibited any ship from carrying commerce between two ports closed to British shipping. Any ship conducting trade between two such ports would be warned to discontinue the voyage and seized if the notice went unheeded. In response, Napoleon's Warsaw Decree of January 25, 1807, ordered the confiscation of all British goods found in the Hanseatic cities of North Germany, thus prompting the British to reclose the German coast between the Ems and the Elbe.

After Napoleon defeated the Russian army in June 1807, Tsar Alexander I signed the Treaty of Tilsit to end the War of the Fourth Coalition. Of the many developments that emerged from this agreement, Alexander's willingness to participate in Napoleon's Continental System by closing his ports to British shipping was a landmark in the Anglo-French rivalry. With the addition of Prussia and Denmark, Tilsit completed the closure of the Baltic to British trade with the exception of Sweden. Maintaining a favorable balance of naval strength in the Baltic had always figured prominently in Britain's maritime strategy, and in an instant it was gone. With Russia's naval assets now aligned with France and rumors that Napoleon planned to seize Denmark's large fleet, the British launched a second preemptive assault on the Danish fleet at Copenhagen starting on August 16, 1807. Although the Royal Navy retained control of the Baltic Sea, its ports remained closed to British shipping. London's Orders in Council of November 11, 1807, forbade French trade with Britain, its allies, or neutrals, and instructed the Royal Navy to blockade French-controlled ports. Napoleon retaliated with the Milan Decree of 1807, which declared that all neutral shipping using British ports or paying British tariffs would be regarded as British and seized.

Napoleon took further action to bolster his alternate maritime economic strategy. Of the entire European mainland, only Portugal's ports remained open to British shipping. Despite threats and ultimatums from Paris, the Portuguese government refused to join the Continental System. Nor would it break its alliance with Britain, which dated back to 1793. A warning from Napoleon to close Portugal's ports to British shipping or face a war with France convinced the Portuguese to comply, yet they refused to seize and burn British goods found on Portuguese soil. A Portuguese declaration of war against Britain amounted to little more than a farce. Following Tilsit, Napoleon reassessed the overall situation in the Iberian Peninsula. Aside from the goal of closing Portugal's ports to the British, Napoleon viewed Spain as a dubious ally, too corrupt and too inefficient to administer his Continental System. Thus, the French emperor decided to deal with Portugal overtly and Spain covertly. To align Spanish affairs with his needs, Napoleon moved French troops into Spain under the cover of an invasion of Portugal. According to the October 27, 1807, Franco-Spanish Treaty of Fontainebleau, two Spanish armies would assist a French army with the invasion of Portugal; should London dispatch British forces to save Portugal, a second French army would deploy from bases in the Pyrenees.

On November 30, 1807, French forces entered Lisbon just as the Portuguese administration sailed for Brazil with a British escort and most of the state's coin. The French established rule over Portugal, occupying its ports and fortresses and dismantling its armed forces. With the conquest of Portugal, Napoleon moved against Spain. Under the pretext of establishing a line of communication between France and Portugal, the French undertook a massive escalation of forces in Spain. More than 130,000 French troops crossed the Pyrenees between November 1807 and March 1808. Spanish officials learned that 120,000 French troops would occupy Portugal. However, instead of marching to Lisbon, the army appeared at Madrid on March 24, 1808, while other French forces took control of Spain's major fortresses. Disagreement between King Carl IV and Crown Prince Ferdinand over the right to rule brought about an invitation from Napoleon for all concerned parties to meet with him at Bayonne in April 1808. There, the French emperor arrested the king and crown prince, forcing them to forfeit the crown of Spain. Shortly after, the people of Madrid rose up on May 2, 1808, to protest the French presence in Spain. French authorities savagely suppressed the revolt but could not prevent it from spreading to the provinces. Napoleon compounded the problem by making his brother, Joseph, the new king of Spain. With every

Spanish province arming against the French, a reluctant Joseph accepted the crown on June 15, 1808.

The establishment of the Continental System in Portugal presented a tremendous setback for the British. After Sweden—Britain's only remaining European ally and trade partner—refused to comply with French demands to close its ports, the Russians invaded in February 1808 and forcibly implemented Napoleon's blockade. Like the Russians, much of the Continent initially rallied behind France in this latest showdown with "Perfidious Albion." Governments across Europe noted that while London paid the Austrians, Prussians, and Russians to fight in the Third and Fourth Coalition Wars, Britain dispatched most of the redcoats stationed on the home isles on expeditions that reflected national self-interest, such as garrisoning the recently taken city of Buenos Aires and recapturing the Cape of Good Hope. In the Mediterranean, some 6,000 British troops sailed from Sicily to take Alexandria. This appeared to be a repeat of the colonial campaigns that the British waged in the West and East Indies while their allies fought the French in Europe during the Wars of the First and Second Coalition. Although little actual colonial expansion occurred after 1803 due to the high cost of campaigning in the disease-ridden West Indies, such unilateral actions never pleased Britain's coalition partners, particularly Tsar Alexander. Consequently, just as Napoleon had to devise an alternate maritime economic strategy to compete with Britain, London likewise needed to comprehensively reassess its strategy, despite the success it had produced in previous conflicts such as the Seven Years War. As it stood, Britain's traditional strategy failed in the French Wars to protect either the Low Countries or the Baltic, and British freedom of action in the Mediterranean was considerably restricted due to the exacting costs of blockading the French Empire and the threat now posed by the Russians.

War in Iberia and a New British Strategy

British leaders explored an array of policy options and kept most on the table, but little doubt existed that British maritime security had reached is nadir and that Britain needed to plot a new course to survive the threat posed by Napoleonic France.[5] London recognized that it needed the other Great Powers as allies to defeat Napoleon; thus the timely and costly efforts of coalition building continued. After the fall of the Talents Ministry in March 1807 brought the Tories back to power under the Portland administration, London re-evaluated Britain's strategy. Napoleon's interest in Iberia upped the stakes because of the threat that he could exploit Spain's colonies in South America, whose markets some British officials hoped to break open so Britain could replace the commerce lost in the Mediterranean. As it stood, London decided to establish a strong military presence at either Buenos Aires or Mexico to secure the Portuguese in Brazil, prevent the French from exploiting Spain's colonies, and initiate trade with the major ports of South America. Plans were made to send 8,000 troops from Ireland to Venezuela in the hope of instigating a revolt against Spanish colonial rule. However, before these plans could be put into effect, the May 2, 1808, uprising in Spain altered the dynamic and provided an opportunity for the British to truly implement a new strategy. Rather than allocate its own forces to strangle French maritime trade and merely harass the enemy in tertiary theaters, London decided to commit a field army to the Iberian Peninsula. Although itself a secondary theater throughout much of the latter Napoleonic era, Iberia served as a stage where the British directly challenged the French. The British finally had skin in the game.[6]

In Spain, the revolt of the common people against the unholy French invader escalated into a general insurgency. Revolutionary Juntas (assemblies) sprang up throughout the state and mobilized Spanish forces, both conventional and guerrilla. In July 1808, French units deployed to Spain's larger cities, where they met indescribable resistance. On July 21, 1808, French forces were forced to surrender to the Spanish at Bailén, less than 200 miles south of Madrid. Although Napoleon was not present, the defeat of his forces shocked all of Europe and shattered the image of French invincibility. In the aftermath, all French armies withdrew to Madrid and then to France by the end of July. Meanwhile, a small British expeditionary force of 13,500 men landed in Portugal the first week of August 1808. After defeating the French on August 21, 1808, the British concluded the Convention of Cintra on August 30, in which they agreed to sail the 26,000-man French army back to France.

News of Bailén and Cintra prompted Napoleon to go to Spain personally. Before departing for Iberia, he held an international congress at the German city of Erfurt in October 1808. Aside from showing the other rulers of Europe his splendor, Napoleon wanted to affirm his partnership with Tsar Alexander. In particular, he sought the Russian leader's assurance that St. Petersburg would defend French interests in central Europe during his absence. Suspecting that Vienna would move against him while he campaigned in Iberia, Napoleon hoped the threat of Russian intervention would keep Austria in check. Much had changed in just one year, however, and the friendship born at Tilsit was already in retreat. Not only did Alexander evasively respond to Napoleon's requests, but he secretly assured the Austrians that he would not interfere if they attacked while Napoleon fought in Spain.

Napoleon assumed command of all French forces in Spain on November 5, 1808, and proceeded to smash four Spanish armies. By December 4, 1808, French forces again controlled Madrid. After restoring his brother as king and reorganizing the Spanish government, Napoleon turned his attention to the British expeditionary force in Portugal, which had secretly moved into Spain to attack Napoleon's flank and rear. Learning of this advance, Napoleon changed his plans from invading Portugal to chasing the British, who made a dash to the Spanish coastal city of Coruña. After one week of pursuit, Napoleon turned over command to one of his marshals and returned to France, incorrectly assuming that the war in Iberia was over. At Coruña, the Royal Navy evacuated 27,000 redcoats in mid-January 1809 as French forces closed in. The abysmal condition of the army that returned to Britain caused Parliament to seriously debate the feasibility of maintaining forces in Iberia. Regardless, the British remained committed to their new strategy, and a larger British army returned to Portugal before the French could capitalize on its absence. To augment the redcoats in Iberia, Parliament also decided to finance the mobilization and training of the Portuguese army under British direction.

The presence of a British army in Portugal did little to remove the French from the Low Countries, the Baltic coast, or Italy. Nevertheless, the Peninsula War, as it is known, served as a sponge that considerably drained French resources. In addition to supporting the guerrilla war in Spain, the British presence in Portugal forced the French to allocate an army of more than 300,000 men to Iberia. Two subsequent French invasions of Portugal were turned back by the British-led Anglo-Portuguese army in 1809 and 1810–1811, respectively. The British exploited these victories with offensives into Spain that the French likewise parried. Even after Napoleon drew down this force for the buildup prior to the 1812 invasion of Russia, 200,000 imperial soldiers remained in Spain. Although the British managed to take Madrid in August 1812 as a result of the drawdown, sufficient French forces remained in Spain to chase the redcoats back to Portugal before year's end. After receiving considerable reinforcements in the winter of 1812–1813, the Anglo-Portuguese army invaded Spain in May 1813. Again, the British benefited from the further drawdown of French forces as Napoleon summoned veteran units from Spain to replace the tens of thousands of soldiers lost in Russia. On July 21, 1813, the British defeated the French in the last great battle of the Peninsula War. In its aftermath, all French armies retreated across the Pyrenees, and, except for isolated French garrisons, the Peninsula was liberated. The British invaded France in October 1813, reaching the French city of Toulouse by the time of Napoleon's abdication in April 1814. Estimates of French losses in both Spain and Portugal from 1807 to 1814 exceed 250,000 men, with some authorities placing them as high as 400,000.

To the conquered peoples of the French Empire, the struggle in Spain appeared to be a war of liberation. Hawks in the Austrian government agitated for another confrontation with France. After being mauled militarily and diplomatically by Napoleon in the Wars of the First, Second, and Third Coalitions, the Austrians hoped to take advantage of French reverses in Spain and of Napoleon's increasing military commitment in Iberia. As Napoleon feared, war commenced between France and Austria in April 1809, when the Austrian army invaded the French ally of Bavaria. This Franco-Austrian conflict became part of the wider War of the Fifth Coalition after Britain allied with Austria. Russia remained neutral, which in itself should be viewed as a victory for Austria, considering Alexander's alliance with Napoleon. Like the previous coalitions, London financed Austria, its only ally, but continued to pursue its new strategy of direct intervention by invading Holland on July 30. More than 39,000 redcoats—an army larger than that serving in the Iberian Peninsula at that time—landed at Walcheren Island in the Scheldt Estuary; by this time, however, the Austrians had already lost the war.

Little fighting characterized the Walcheren Campaign, but more than 4,000 British troops died from sickness before the remainder returned home in December 1809. As for the Franco-Austrian conflict, Napoleon rebounded after suffering the first defeat of his career at Aspern-Essling on May 22, 1809. During the July 5–6 Battle of Wagram, he inflicted 41,000 casualties on the Austrian army. On July 12, the Austrians requested and received an armistice. The Franco-Austrian Treaty of Schönbrunn ended the War of the Fifth Coalition on October 14, 1809. Its stipulations stripped Austria of its coastline along the Adriatic Sea, thus land-locking the empire and making it a de facto partner in Napoleon's Continental System.

War of the Fifth Coalition (1809)

Although another victorious war for Napoleon, Britain's new strategy notably impacted the conflict. Much of the crack French army that had fought the Third and Fourth Coalition Wars was stationed in Iberia when the Fifth Coalition War commenced. For the first time during his reign, Napoleon had to deal with manpower problems. To raise an army to confront the Austrians, he not only called up new recruits, but also was forced to depend on foreign troops supplied mainly by his German vassals. This permanently changed Napoleon's force structure and force capabilities. Never would he have the same army qualitatively as the one that had marched to war in 1805. After exhausting that highly trained force, he became increasingly dependent on German, Italian, and Polish manpower that had not received training on par with the original *Grande Armée*. A marked change in Napoleon's tactics coincided with this qualitative decline. Instead of continuing the progression of his tactical innovations for battlefield problem-solving, he had to depend increasingly on the weight of massed batteries, huge formations, and unimaginative frontal assaults.

Although he smashed another coalition, Napoleon could not end the war that continued to rage in Spain and Portugal. Rather than cross the Pyrenees again, he left the war in Iberia to his marshals and his brother, Joseph. Despite the situation in Iberia, Napoleon's control of central Europe appeared incontestable after 1809. Allied with Russia and tightly controlling Prussia, Napoleon also hoped he had permanently settled his differences with Austria by marrying into the Hapsburg family. Yet, one year later, everything began unraveling as Russia ended its French alliance. The events between 1808 and 1811 that culminated in Napoleon's 1812 invasion of Russia are beyond the scope of this study. Those that proved particularly egregious to Napoleon included Alexander's cool demeanor at the Congress of Erfurt followed by his less than enthusiastic support of French interests during the War of the Fifth Coalition. Conversely, the lack of French diplomatic pressure on the Ottoman Empire to end its war with Russia, as well as Napoleon's ambiguity over his intentions regarding eastern Europe and the eastern Mediterranean, embittered Alexander. As a result of the crippling effects of the Continental System, Alexander issued a decree on December 31, 1810, to tax luxury goods and wines, some of France's largest exports. Moreover, the decree opened Russian ports to neutral ships carrying British exports. British goods soon flooded the markets of eastern and central Europe. Napoleon had few choices other than to force Alexander's continued participation in the Continental System. Thus, in 1811, both emperors started preparing for war.

The first quarter of 1812 initiated diplomatic realignments against France; Britain assumed one of the leading roles. Before 1808, the British mainly contributed to the successive coalition wars against France by funding in the form of loans, subsidies, and credits to allies such as Austria and Russia, whose armies would shoulder the main burden of fighting the French. Total domination of the seas then allowed the British to conduct limited military operations against secondary targets such as the Netherlands and Naples, either unilaterally or in conjunction with the Russians. However, London's 1808 decision to commit the British army to the Iberian Peninsula marked a monumental policy change for the maritime economic power. Yet this was not enough. Although the British distracted Napoleon and tied down vital imperial resources in Iberia and the Mediterranean, they realized that Napoleon's hegemony over the Continent could only be broken in central Europe. For this reason, the British could not turn their backs on Austria, Prussia, and Russia, even after all three were counted among Napoleon's allies following the failed Franco-Austrian War of 1809. The British understood that when the time came for Europe to rise against France, Britain would be expected to support it with both arms and money.

War of the Sixth Coalition (1812–1814)

Napoleon commenced the invasion of Russia on June 22, 1812. The following month, the British signed peace treaties with the Swedes and the Russians. A new British ambassador to Russia sailed from Britain in late July. Aid came in the form of a British convoy carrying 50,000 muskets and a half ton of "Peruvian" or "Jesuit's" Bark that contained natural quinine for medicinal purposes being dispatched to Russia in August. In addition, British warships operating in the eastern Baltic contributed to the successful defense of Riga by the Russians later in the year. Resolved not only to liberate Russia, but to carry the war into central Europe, Alexander became the catalyst for the formation of the Sixth Coalition. Yet Russian financial problems became so acute in late 1812 that a special finance committee informed the tsar that he would have to make peace with Napoleon unless he received massive British financial assistance. By the end of 1812, this committee sought a way for Britain to fund Russia before it went bankrupt.

After failing to destroy the Russian army at Borodino on September 7, 1812, the French reached a deserted Moscow one week later. Not only did the tsar refuse to negotiate, but the Russians burned the city. Having to choose between remaining at Moscow—1,200 miles from Paris—for the winter or withdrawing, Napoleon chose the latter. On October 19, a much smaller Grande Armée commenced the retreat. On November 3, the first snows fell; by the end of the month, Napoleon commanded no more than 40,000 walking dead. Of the 655,000 men who crossed the Russian frontier in 1812, Napoleon lost approximately 570,000 soldiers, with as many as 370,000 dead. Russian casualties have been estimated to be as high as 450,000, with two-thirds dead.

On March 3, 1813, the British formed the Sixth Coalition with Russia and Sweden against France. The Anglo-Swedish portion of the alliance obligated London to provide the Swedes with £1,000,000 by October 1813. In mid-March, Prussia joined the coalition by signing a bilateral alliance with Russia and declaring war on Napoleon. London restored official diplomatic relations with the Prussians after they formally declared the end of the Continental System in North Germany on March 20. The British bolstered the alliance by dispatching a convoy to the Baltic carrying fifty-four cannon as well 23,000 stand of arms to be shared by the Russians and Prussians.[7] Despite its commitments to Iberia, North America, and now Sweden, London offered a subsidy of £2,000,000 to be shared by the Russians and Prussians, with the former taking £1,333,334, or two-thirds, and the latter £666,666.[8] Negotiations ensued until the Prussian and Russian foreign ministers officially signed the subsidy treaties on June 14 and 15, 1813, respectively. In addition, the Russians received £500,000 for the support of their Baltic Fleet.[9] On August 11, the British government accepted an Allied proposal to issue £2,500,000 of paper money to cover the cost of military expenditure, with London accepting responsibility for the full amount of the capital and interest.[10] Signed on October 3, 1813, an Anglo-Austrian subsidy treaty granted the Austrians a subvention in the amount of £1,000,000.[11] All four subsidy treaties obligated the signatories not to make a separate peace with Napoleon. Although no British ground forces would be committed to central Europe, the British ambassadors to all four recipients of British aid would accompany the Allied armies, with the authority to withhold subsidy payments if any coalition partner failed to give its all for the general cause of liberating Germany from French control.

By early November 1813, this formidable coalition had driven Napoleon and his legions across the Rhine River and back into France. However, after reaching the Rhine, the members could not agree on their next and ultimate objective: Should they continue the war to overthrow Napoleon, or should they negotiate a peace with the French emperor? Politics eclipsed both military operations and military cooperation. In the midst of the military planning for the invasion, the allies offered Napoleon a conditional peace by which he would have remained ruler of a France that included the natural frontiers of the Rhine, Alps, and Pyrenees. Although these terms would have left France with territory that generations of Frenchmen had died in vain attempting to secure, Napoleon rejected the offer.

Into this fray arrived British Foreign Minister Robert Stewart, Lord Castlereagh, on a mission aimed at establishing allied priorities and firming up the alliance. Moreover, London sought the continuation of the alliance after the peace in order to provide collective security against future French aggression. Allied unity, which had started to crumble during January and February 1814, was restored in March thanks in part to Castlereagh's efforts and Napoleon's intransigence. His refusal to agree to terms at the Châtillon peace conference eliminated any doubt that only Napoleon's complete overthrow would bring peace to Europe. Therefore, on March 9, 1814, Castlereagh, along with the representatives of Russia, Austria, and Prussia, signed the Treaty of Chaumont, which called for Napoleon to renounce all conquests in exchange for an armistice. In effect, this would have reduced France to its 1791 pre-Revolution or "traditional" borders rather than the natural frontiers. The following day Napoleon rejected the offer, ending his last chance to negotiate a peace. As a result, the allies pledged to unconditionally defeat Napoleon. The treaty also stipulated that the Big Four (Britain, Russia, Prussia, and Austria) would work in concert for the next twenty years to prevent France from threatening the European balance of power.

After the Coalition's armies marched on Paris, Napoleon could not recover. On March 31, 1814, the ceremonial entry of the allied sovereigns into Paris occurred. Three days later, a provisional French government deposed Napoleon, but he refused to relinquish power. Finally, after some of his marshals mutinied, he agreed to abdicate in favor of his son on April 6, signing the formal act of abdication at Fontainebleau on April 11. Regardless, the British demanded the restoration of the Bourbons under King Louis XVIII; Napoleon was exiled to the tiny Mediterranean island of Elba. Although Napoleon escaped from Elba in late February 1815 and landed in France on March 1, London enacted the Treaty of Chaumont and the signatories formed the Seventh Coalition. In the aftermath of his defeat at Waterloo on June 18, 1815, by British and Prussian armies, Napoleon sought asylum in Britain. Instead, the British exiled him to the South Atlantic island of St. Helena, where he died in 1821.

Strategies for Supremacy

By adopting the new strategy of direct intervention, the British overturned the resource imbalance that had favored France since the Republic unleashed its hordes on an unsuspecting Europe in 1794. This returned France to the disadvantageous position it was in during many earlier conflicts: facing a two-front war. However, instead of fighting the British on the seas and in the colonies, the French now faced their rival in Iberia. The opening and maintaining of this second front against France transformed what appeared to be unlimited French resources to finite assets by forcing Napoleon to fight on a second front. For the first time in his reign, he had to contend with resource management; the challenges posed by this can be clearly seen in 1809, 1812, and 1813. In 1809, he relied on mainly German troops from his vassal states. Of the 600,000 men he led to Russia in 1812, only 250,000 were native Frenchmen. Of the 90,000 who returned, more than half were Prussians and Austrians who would actually fight against him in 1813. For the Sixth Coalition War that commenced in 1813, Napoleon could field only 200,000 men by the end of April. As one historian notes, the Grande Armée of 1813 provided Napoleon with an effective fighting force, "but one that suffered from the internal germs of weakness." Consequently, the Grande Armée of 1813 lacked many of the tactical attributes of previous French armies, which in turn placed strategic and operational limitations on Napoleon.[12]

The new British policy of direct intervention required London to pursue its maritime economic strategy while unilaterally challenging the French on the Continent. From the end of the Fifth Coalition in October 1809 to the French invasion of Russia in June 1812, the British, along with their Spanish and Portuguese allies, faced the might of imperial France alone. While doing this, the British confronted the Continental-wide embargo against British trade in French-controlled Europe that included a de facto state of war with Russia and Prussia. Napoleon's Continental System had a significant effect on British trade, causing British exports to fall 25–55 percent between 1806 and 1811 compared to pre-1806 levels; unemployment rose, government bonds fell by 40 percent, and the pound sterling fell in value. Britain was in crisis in 1810–1811 when bankruptcies occurred to an extraordinary extent among merchants, unemployment rose sharply, and British currency considerably depreciated. British industry stagnated, helping spur the Luddite protest movement against unemployment.[13] Yet the embargo encouraged British merchants to aggressively seek new markets, especially in Spain's South American colonies, and to increase trade with Brazil.[14] Although fighting for Spain's liberation from French rule, the British exploited these previously protected markets to replace those lost in Europe. In addition, the British smuggled extensively with Continental Europe. Napoleon's exclusively land-based customs officials could not stop British smugglers, especially as they operated with the connivance of Napoleon's chosen rulers of Spain, Westphalia, Holland, and other German states. Moreover, the British were able to counter the Continental System by threatening to sink any ship that chose to comply with French regulations and did not come to a British port. This double threat created a difficult situation for neutral nations like the United States. Together with the issues of the impressment of foreign seamen, and British support for Indian raids in the American West, tensions led to a declaration of war by the United States on Britain in 1812. This conflict indirectly aided Napoleon by further stretching British resources at a critical moment in Britain's struggle against France.

Napoleon at first benefited from the effects of the Continental System, and much of Europe initially rallied behind France. Like the modern European Economic Community (EEC), Napoleon unified Europe's states to protect their economies against cheaper British goods. Like the EEC, the Continental System aimed to enhance Europe's economy and provide it more leverage in trading. Early on, Belgium, Switzerland, and the industrialized regions of northern and eastern France benefited significantly from increased profits due to the lack of competition from British goods, especially textiles, which were produced at a much cheaper cost in Britain. Although the Continental System stimulated the French economy, the economic crisis that struck Britain in 1810–1811 spread to France, Holland, the Hanseatic Cities of North Germany, Prussia, Switzerland, and New York, demonstrating that a global economy existed in the Age of Sail. The British blockade that prevented European merchantmen from sailing severely handicapped internal European trading, which needed sea-shipping to operate at full capacity. Although Napoleon sought to replace Britain with France as the manufacturing giant of Europe, French goods lacked the same quality as British wares and they cost more. Consequently, the French economy suffered a recession as French credit declined and banks failed; French trade decreased by 33 percent from 1806 to 1813. Although the System initially stimulated manufacturing in some parts of France, it damaged regions dependent on overseas commerce. Southern France suffered from the reduction of trade, especially the port cities of Marseille, Bordeaux, and La Rochelle.

In general, the price of basic commodities and food increased throughout Continental Europe. Not only did neutrals resent the trade restrictions, but soon French allies and satellites could not bear the weight of the System, as it wrecked their economies. Illicit smuggling developed on a monumental scale. Napoleon's own brother, King Louis of Holland, allowed British goods to enter his ports. This led to his forced abdication and the annexation of Holland as well as the North German seacoast to France. Ultimately, Napoleon could not control the amount of British goods entering the Continent and so attempted to regulate the illegal trade. From 1806 to 1814, he sold 20,000 licenses to British merchants that allowed them to sell their goods on the Continent at a 50 percent duty.[15] Rebuilding France's colonial empire to a large extent on Spanish possessions had figured in Napoleon's seizure of Spain in 1808. Prior to the regime change in Madrid, French privateers operated against British trade from the ports of Spain's colonies. However, like Spain itself, the colonies refused to recognize the government of Joseph Bonaparte. After 1808, British warships used those same Spanish ports for operations against the remains of the French colonial empire, which soon fell into the hands of the British.[16]

The escalation of the Anglo-French Rivalry during the 1792–1815 period was caused by French expansion between 1793 and 1797 that produced French control of the Low Countries and northern Italy. For reasons of national security, the British refused to accept French control of Low Countries, as well as the French presence in North Italy, which threatened British economic interests in the Mediterranean. With the rise of Napoleon Bonaparte and his overthrow of the French government in 1799, the French further tightened their control of the Low Countries and further expanded their holdings in Italy. A change in the British administration led to the short-lived Anglo-French Treaty of Amiens in 1802, but neither side honored its stipulations. Napoleon's attempt to restore France's colonial empire in the Western Hemisphere caused the resumption of the Anglo-French war. With the resumption of war, London continued its policy of financing states at war with France. The rivalry further escalated after Napoleon conquered Germany and extended his power to the shores of the Baltic Sea and closed Europe to British trade. After the French invaded Iberia, the British were forced to commit a field army to Portugal. The rivalry reached its climax in 1813 and 1814, when London contributed millions in subsidies and materiel to the Sixth Coalition fighting Napoleon in central Europe, while an Anglo-Portuguese-Spanish army drove the French from Spain. The role of the military dimension of the Anglo-French rivalry during the 1792 to 1815 period was secondary. Except for 1815, British forces fought the French in secondary and tertiary theaters. Britain's greatest contribution militarily was to tie down French resources in Iberia and later liberate Iberia. The British expended much gold and materiel in supporting the Spanish insurgency in Iberia and training, arming, and equipping the Portuguese army after 1807.

The greatest asymmetry between Britain and France remained the former's maritime strength and control of the seas. Despite Napoleon's ambitious shipbuilding projects, the use of allied fleets such as the Spanish, Dutch, and Neapolitan, and the attempt to wreck Britain's economy, this advantage did not change during the French Wars. Although years of blockading Europe and supplying British forces and Spanish guerrillas in Iberia stretched the Royal Navy extremely thin, its dominance meant the difference between victory and defeat. Another asymmetry that impacted Napoleon's strategy was Britain's advanced industrial status. Mainly an agrarian state, France could not generate enough industry to fill the void created by the absence of British manufactured goods. This contributed to the collapse of France's economy, as well as the economies of those states under French control or allied to Napoleon.

Of the seven coalitions that formed during the French Wars, only Britain fought in each conflict. Indeed, Britain and France had competed for colonial mastery for more than a century prior, with Britain gaining a clear advantage due to its insular position. France could never allocate its full resources to the competition with Great Britain without undermining its position as a Continental Power, which in turn would severely jeopardize its national security. Finally solving this conundrum in the mid-1790s, France completely shattered the equilibrium of Europe and with it the stability required by the British maritime economy to sustain Britain's power both at home and abroad. In 1793, the British sent ground forces to defend the Low Countries, Britain's major maritime interest in Europe. By 1795, the French controlled both Belgium and Holland. Thus, early in the French Wars, the British perceived this episode of their rivalry with France as potentially one of life or death. The situation only escalated after young Napoleon Bonaparte conquered Italy in 1797 as a distracted Britain handed the French a free hand in the Mediterranean. Ten years later, a Franco-Russian alliance closed the ports of the Baltic to the British. Control of these three strategic spheres had enabled Britain to maintain its Great Power status and influence in Europe. This made France the primary enemy of Great Britain throughout the French Wars. Although Britain's leadership remained cognizant of other threats, such as Russia's growing maritime interests, French control of the Low Countries, the Mediterranean, and the Baltic posed a national security crisis for Britain. Nowhere is this better illustrated than London's monumental change in strategy in 1808. Before then, the British pursued their traditional strategy of committing their own forces to strangle French maritime trade, harass the French in secondary theaters, and fund allies to bear the direct brunt of fighting France on the Continent. Aside from modest colonial gains, this strategy failed. France defeated successive coalitions and made tremendous territorial gains on the Continent, while the British expended significant amounts of financial assistance to losing war efforts.

By 1808, London had drawn many lessons from its devastating failures to defeat France through containment, proxy wars, and even attempts to assassinate Napoleon. As a start, policymakers concluded that a British naval victory such as Trafalgar would not compel Napoleon to negotiate peace. Events on land, whether military, political, or economic, had to intercede to reach war termination.[17] Thus, Britain's leaders concluded that a new strategy was needed—one that featured the commitment of a British army to the Continent. This policy change reflected the priority Britain placed on defeating France. London's tough policy toward neutral shipping, two preemptive strikes against the Danish fleet, and war with the United States demonstrated how this priority moved ahead of other national interests. Due to Britain's control of the seas, the relative position changes in priorities, as reflected by Britain's willingness to accept war with every state on the European continent except Portugal, still corresponded to London's maritime economic strategy. Although British policymakers found the pursuit of a maritime economic strategy to be incongruous with unilaterally challenging French might on the Continent, after 1808 London was able to do both. Markets lost in Europe were replaced by new markets in the Western Hemisphere. Despite the tremendous strain of a Continental blockade, the Royal Navy maintained global dominance. British ground forces fought in Iberia for seven years, draining France of vital resources and providing a ray of hope for all Europeans oppressed by French imperialism. Finally, the de-escalation of rivalries with Russia and Sweden during the twilight of Napoleon's reign and the massive amounts of aid the British provided the Sixth Coalition are indicative of the priority London placed on defeating France.[18]

British policymakers rarely misperceived French intentions. The 1802 Peace of Amiens could be considered a notable exception, but neither side left the negotiating table with sincere intentions of complying with its stipulations. Napoleon's refusal to grant an accompanying commercial treaty made a permanent peace impossible. He knew this, and so did the British. Although this meant that the economic struggle would continue, the British based their hopes of victory on the strength of the Royal Navy and the pound sterling. In this they were justified. However, they miscalculated the strength of their Continental partners during the majority of the French Wars. National self-interest and the pursuit of traditional foreign policy objectives often plagued the anti-French coalitions and led to their demise. Before 1808, the British shared the blame for this because of their unwillingness to commit an army to the Continent, as well as their colonial expansion.

By 1805, Napoleon perceived Britain as France's implacable enemy because of London's ability to finance anti-French coalitions and its refusal to accept French control of the Low Countries. Yet the British naval victory at Trafalgar that same year shattered his dream of invading the British home isles. Inheriting a French fleet that had been ravished by the Royal Navy since the beginning of the French Wars, Napoleon desperately sought control of foreign naval assets to offset the balance. Despite controlling numerous foreign fleets during various periods of his reign, Napoleon could do little to counter the asymmetric nature of warfare with the British. Although his ambitious naval construction program would have yielded newer and better ships, their officers and crews would have been no match for the seasoned veterans of the Royal Navy. Even with the resources of the entire European continent at his disposal, Napoleon could not challenge the British conventionally. Along with London's refusal to recognize French hegemony, this meant that the British would continue to finance enemy coalitions as long as the Eastern Powers of Russia, Austria, and Prussia provided the manpower. Although he managed to defang Prussia, the immense populations of Austria and especially Russia meant that Napoleon would have to fight a seemingly endless series of wars. Assessment remained relatively easy, as Napoleon knew that only British gold allowed his enemies to continue the wars against him. Three years into the System, Austria took up arms against him in the Fifth Coalition War. After six years, London exclusively financed the Sixth Coalition while maintaining the war in Iberia and fighting in North America.

To defeat Britain, Napoleon developed an alternate strategy: economic warfare. Brilliant yet unrealistic, Napoleon grossly misjudged the capabilities of his empire to sustain a prolonged embargo against British trade. Ruining not only France's economy, the System wrecked the economies of satellites and allies as well. Napoleon's pursuit of defeating Britain, above all else, led him down the path of his two greatest disasters: the Peninsula War and the invasion of Russia. Interestingly, he never viewed the British field army in Iberia as a primary objective, although the empire was focused on destroying the British through the Continental System. Although London finally offered a conventional target, Napoleon placed greater hope in the unconventional economic war to crush "the little island of shopkeepers."

In his duel with the Royal Navy, Napoleon carefully balanced his strengths and weaknesses. After Trafalgar, he did not risk large-scale naval engagements, recognizing that a French naval victory, however large, would not allow him to invade Britain. By refusing fleet engagements, Napoleon forced the British to carefully balance resource-intensive deployments, despite the fact that Britain possessed approximately half of the world's total warship tonnage by the late Napoleonic period. Napoleon's massive post-Trafalgar shipbuilding program resulted in French fleet concentrations in the Scheldt Estuary and at Toulon, with smaller squadrons at numerous locations. Individual French ships and small squadrons periodically escaped to operate against the British. Napoleon accepted that the French would lose some of these encounters, but the disruption it caused the British made the losses acceptable. Should French warships escape, the British pursued them before they could inflict damage on isolated naval assets and vulnerable maritime commerce. As the number of French warships grew, the British concentrated increased naval strength in blockade squadrons. The wide range of British global commitments left few warships in reserve, as Royal Navy blockade squadrons accounted for over half of Britain's ships of the line in the years 1811–1813.[19]

Both France and Britain found that their conventional strategies failed them in the age that ushered in modern, total war. For the British, the danger posed by France seemed to threaten their very way of life. Conversely, Napoleon labored to convince the rulers and peoples of Europe's other states that Britain sought to economically enslave the Continent. He underestimated the effectiveness of both the British army in Iberia and the Spanish insurgency that the Royal Navy supported. He misjudged the ability of his subordinates, including his brother, to heal his "bleeding ulcer" in Iberia. In the end, he staked the well-being of his empire and then its survival on defeating the British. During the on-again off-again negotiations that he pursued with the Eastern Powers in 1813 and 1814, he refused to even allow any of London's demands to be discussed. Britain likewise changed its policy and adopted the new strategy of direct intervention on the Continent; its economy weathered the recession caused by the Continental System to such an extent that by 1813 London could allocate unprecedented resources to North America, Iberia, and central Europe. Its navy triumphed over the French in every fleet action during the French Wars, maintained a tight Continental blockade for seven years, and broke open new markets in the Western Hemisphere. The British assessed where they stood in terms of economic strength and control of the seas. Britain's ultimate victory over Napoleon in 1815 assured British naval and colonial dominance for the next one hundred years, when another empire challenged Britain for its place in the sun.

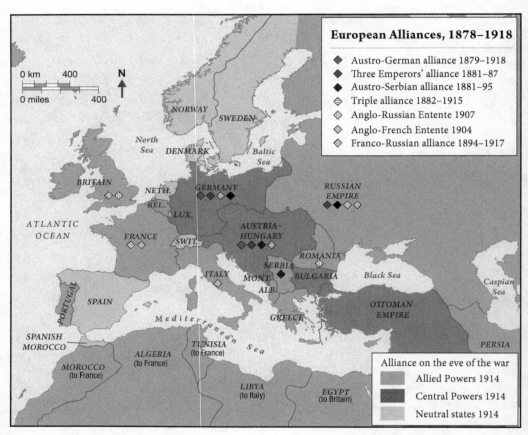

European Alliances, 1878–1918

◆ Austro-German alliance 1879–1918
◆ Three Emperors' alliance 1881–87
◆ Austro-Serbian alliance 1881–95
◈ Triple alliance 1882–1915
◐ Anglo-Russian Entente 1907
◈ Anglo-French Entente 1904
◇ Franco-Russian alliance 1894–1917

Alliance on the eve of the war

Allied Powers 1914
Central Powers 1914
Neutral states 1914

European Alliances, 1878–1918.

CHAPTER 10

A New Europe with New Rivalries
The Franco-German Rivalry
Geoffrey Wawro

T HE FRANCO-GERMAN RIVALRY CONTAINED many asymmetries: of
political structure, population, economic might, resources, and defensible frontiers. Until Bismarck, a mythic sense of inferiority afflicted the
Germans vis-à-vis the French. They felt themselves victims of the major
asymmetry in their relationship: the French had been united behind defensible borders—the Rhine, the Alps, the Pyrenees, and the Atlantic—since
the Middle Ages. The Germans, on the other hand, occupied the defenseless north German plain, where no natural frontiers existed, and which had
historically been divided into petty kingdoms with distinct dynastic and
cultural identities. Under both republics and monarchies, the French had
enjoyed a strong state tradition since Charlemagne. The Germans, in contrast, were split into three dozen states by the Congress of Vienna and, led
by an inefficient German "diet of princes" in Frankfurt, had a weak state
tradition. Indeed, Otto von Bismarck's determination to unify Germany
stemmed in large part from his experience as Prussian ambassador to the
Frankfurt diet (1851–1859), where he had seethed with frustration at the
Bund's inefficiency and at Prussia's subordination to Austria. But before this
reunification, France, wielding the power of a single coherent state, had long
possessed a controlling influence in German affairs: Richelieu dictating the
borders of the Holy Roman Empire in 1648, Louis XIV annexing Alsace and
other bits of western Germany in the 1690s, and Napoleon I liquidating the
Holy Roman Empire in 1806 and creating a French-directed Confederation
of the Rhine in its place.

Bismarck (1815–1898) devoted his career to erasing the asymmetries that favored France. First, by expanding the German Customs Union (*Zollverein*) of 1834, he and his colleagues united the thirty-nine economies of the German Confederation under the leadership of Berlin. On the international scene, Bismarck, as ambassador first to the German diet, then to Russia and France, assiduously worked to prepare the ground for German unification. In Frankfurt, he made clear to the German princes (heads of state like the kings of Saxony and Bavaria and the grand duke of Baden) that ethnically German Prussia was the natural leader of a united Germany, not the largely Slavic Austrian Empire. In St. Petersburg, he pledged support for a Russian campaign to undo the sanctions of the Crimean War, which had barred Russian naval might from the Black Sea and the Straits. In Paris, he dexterously appeared to accept French leadership of Europe while covertly planning to use French neutrality to fight a war with Austria for the command of Germany. Bismarck led the French to believe that a united Germany would behave like a loyal Napoleonic satellite state, when, in fact, he planned to unite the Germans to unlock their tremendous potential so as to overshadow the French.

The French and Prussians possessed similar political systems; both were authoritarian states with some elements of democracy. Prussia had a *Landtag*, or parliament, but voting was restricted to wealthy, educated property owners. A rising socialist-influenced working class was excluded and eventually bought off with various expedients: appeals to German nationalism, a social safety net, and then, from the 1890s, the "fleet policy" that created blue-collar jobs in the service of an expansive naval and colonial "world policy." France had a *Corps Législatif* that was gerrymandered to create a Napoleonic majority and exclude the radical urban working class; but Napoleon III also had recourse to "plebiscitary democracy," in which he would canvass public opinion on major questions (like his decision to crown himself emperor of the French in 1852) and thus tap the loyal peasantry, giving his regime a fig leaf of legitimacy in the democratic age.

Both systems permitted an activist foreign policy—with little popular push-back—but ran the risk, absent real checks and balances, of embroiling the state in dangerous conflicts that cooler heads (like the Republican bloc in the French Legislative Body or the Progressive party in Prussia) would have avoided. In short, both leaders had the ability to shape events and incite the emotions of their citizens. Unfortunately for France, Bismarck operated better in this atmosphere, chiefly because he performed a thorough net assessment of German and French capabilities and never took a step forward without carefully weighing the odds.

Napoleon III (1808–1873) was altogether different. He was sixty-two in 1870 and prematurely old, suffering from gout, kidney stones, and other ailments. Moreover, he was frequently drugged with opiates and had a short attention span. Worse, Napoleon III surrounded himself with cronies, most of whom were reactionaries or opportunists, none of whom had anything like the stature, acuity, or judgment of Bismarck and Moltke. Indeed, statesmanship in the service of Napoleon III boiled down to thinking of ways to keep the dynasty going. There was little serious political or military long-term planning. The emperor did employ a reform-minded war minister, Marshal Adolphe Niel, from 1867–1869, but then failed to insist upon implementing Niel's (attempted) reforms: an empowered general staff, promotion on merit not seniority, a reserve national guard (*garde mobile*), a military railroad department, or territorial army organization.[1] All of the reforms met institutional resistance and died; the weary emperor made no effort to revive them. In 1869, the emperor chose a former republican opponent, Emile Ollivier, to be his prime minister. Ollivier's brief was to introduce a "Liberal Empire" that would gradually co-opt France's swelling republican opposition with major political, social, and economic reforms. In fact, Ollivier never gained traction with the emperor's inner circle, all of whom viewed him as mere window-dressing. Resistant to any change, the regime's old guard planned to fight a glorious war with Prussia that would "re-found the dynasty" and permit them—in the glow of victory—to crack down on republican and radical "subversives." Napoleon III seemed oblivious or indifferent to this agenda; power increasingly accrued to his healthy, ambitious, clerical wife Eugénie. The empress was a Spanish-born arch-reactionary, who craved war with Prussia, which she viewed as a hateful Protestant upstart. Informed chiefly by emotions, nostalgia, and wounded *amour-propre*, none of the French leaders performed a real net assessment of their strength versus that of Prussia.

Overall, the French viewed the rivalry with surprising complacency. Whereas the Prussians grasped what the rivalry was about—reordering power on the basis of strength and stature—the French under Napoleon III took an absurdly amateurish and unscientific view of the rivalry. Napoleon III's *camarilla* (cabal)—and the emperor himself—viewed the Prussians as rascally little boys who had no business contesting power with France. The French, guilty of nostalgic thinking, failed to add up German assets or to grasp German resolve. They focused, instead, on Prussia alone, which Voltaire had famously dismissed as "a kingdom of mere border strips," a "land of sand and starveling pines."

The French, therefore, failed to mark Prussia's transition from a poor kingdom to an industrial powerhouse that produced more coal and steel in a year than France, Russia, or Austria, and was tied to the other economies of Germany by the *Zollverein*. Just as Bismarck had carefully assessed the Austrians before 1866 and found them more flash than substance, he assessed the French before 1870, noting their small army, flat economy, and stagnant population. Certainly much of the French public grasped their vulnerability. A joke circulating in Paris during the world's fair International Exposition of 1867 held that Napoleon III would win the gold medal "because he had exposed France" by not intervening in the Austro-Prussian War. But this sense of alarm did not penetrate the imperial government or army. Even on the eve of the Franco-Prussian War, Napoleon III still fancied himself poised for a second Jena, pushing to Berlin and crushing Prussian pretensions. The vast space, resources, troops, and technocratic competence of Germany meant nothing to him.

The rivals had the same goal—to defeat the other and dominate the German space—the Prussians directly through annexations, the French indirectly through a Confederation of the Rhine that would create new French satellites and shear off Prussia's coal and industry-rich Rhine provinces. Their rivalry gathered strength, especially after the Austro-Prussian War of 1866, because Prussia's rise was interpreted in Paris as an insult to French predominance and because continued French designs on German territory were interpreted in Prussia as impertinence in an age of nationalism. But in the frivolous way of the Second Empire, where rich, connected "friends of the emperor" gave military and foreign policy advice, French power was consistently overestimated and German power underestimated, owing to ignorance and the group-thinking need to flatter the Bonapartes, especially the increasingly powerful and bigoted empress. This was a colossal strategic failure for the French, which Bismarck and Moltke shrewdly grasped and resolved to exploit. Their net assessments were stunningly accurate, informed as they were by painstaking reporting by diplomats, spies, and smart young officers like the future general staff chief Alfred von Waldersee, who served as military attaché in the Paris embassy in the 1860s and detailed the vulnerabilities of the French army and empire in his regular reports to Berlin.[2]

Long before Louis-Napoleon Bonaparte had been elected president of France in 1848 and then overthrown the republic in 1851, Paris had become accustomed to a weak, pastoral Germany. Balzac's signature German, for example, was Schmucke, a dreamer and a musician, the stereotypical "German" at mid-century. The peak of this French manipulation was the Napoleonic period (1804–1814) when Napoleon I carved Germany into French departments and satellite states, pulled Germany into the Continental System, and compelled 250,000 Germans to serve with the *Grande Armée*. The German people rose against the French in 1813–1814 with a fury that expressed all of their pent-up resentment. For their part, the French weathered the defeats of the Napoleonic period and moved through the nineteenth century with a continuing disdain for the Germans. The German Confederation created at the Congress of Vienna in 1815 divided Germany into thirty-nine states, which tempted the French—particularly under Napoleon III (1851–1870)—to resume their manipulation of the German space to France's political and economic advantage.

Although German nationalists and Prussian chauvinists alike perceived France as their primary rival before 1866, France viewed Prussia and Germany as a weak space that still could be forged into French satellites. Louis-Napoleon sought French security, like his uncle before him, by harnessing, rather than opposing, the spread of nationalism in Europe. Napoleon I, when he created the Confederation of the Rhine, had beefed up "middle-states" like Bavaria with old imperial territory and thus had earned their loyalty. Elsewhere, he created a Polish state (the Duchy of Warsaw) as well as a Kingdom of Italy. The goal was always to empower smaller states just enough to be useful (in alliance with France), but not enough to rival French power. In the 1860s, Napoleon III renewed this program, seeking opportunities to undo the settlement of 1815 and create a new ring of satellite states that would owe their growth to France.

That explained the French emperor's interest in Bismarck. In 1865, just one year before the Austro-Prussian War, Napoleon III hosted Bismarck in Biarritz. This was an important summit; Bismarck had returned from the Paris embassy to take up the job of Prussian minister-president (prime minister) in 1862. During a long walk on the beach, the two men discussed the future of Germany, and Bonaparte agreed that Prussia would have a free hand in a war with Austria. Strategically, the French emperor was guilty of terrible shortsightedness. He wanted to weaken Austria in order eventually to break it up, into German, Hungarian, Czech, South Slav, and Polish states that would ally with Paris, still viewed as the "umpire of Europe" in the 1860s.[3] But a truly strategic thinker—without the French emperor's vanity and, as he aged, indolence—would have seen nothing but danger in *any* kind of German unification. France's population was 35 million in 1865. Austria's was 33 million. Prussia's was 19 million. Focused on its Austrian "peer competitor," Paris lost sight of the real threat: the possibility that the 19 million Prussians might annex the 20 million souls of the German Confederation and become a first-tier, heavily armed, expansive Great Power—larger, richer, and more productive than France.

This fuzziness about strategic questions in Paris was another key asymmetry. Whereas Bismarck planned for wars with Austria and France to break down the barriers to unification, Napoleon III lost himself in weird reveries that referenced the past far more than the present and future. Louis-Napoleon did not grasp what the competition was really about; Bismarck did. As late as 1866, Louis-Napoleon still believed that his strategic mission was to weaken the Russian and Austrian empires and prepare their partition into nation-states. This was a Rube Goldberg conception of strategy that depended on too many unpredictable variables, chief among them the loyalty of the minions. Napoleon III had supposed that Count Camillo Cavour would be a loyal minion (and thus facilitated Italian unification, 1859–1861), yet Cavour had merely pretended to be loyal until French power had been secured and used up; he had then asserted Italian interests against France. Bismarck, too, would play the loyal minion until he had gotten all he could from France; then he would attack France. Having already experienced this blowback with Cavour, Napoleon III should have been leery of Bismarck.

Bismarck's strategic mission contained none of the French waffle; he had to defeat Austria and France, keep the other powers neutral, and rake in the population and resources of Germany to vault Prussia into the first tier of Great Powers. He would persuade or compel the German states to give up their old identities—Bavarian, Hessian, Saxon—in exchange for a German identity that might make the world tremble. Thus, France would find itself surprised and overwhelmed by the speed and intensity of Prussia's growth in the 1860s. By the time France reacted, it would be too late.

The Austro-Prussian War of 1866

War exploded at the very moment when Napoleon III was mentally finalizing the future shape of Germany. He had been seeking to weaken or dissolve the Russian and Austrian empires since the Crimean War as a part of his plan to redraw the map of Europe along lines that would favor France. Like his uncle, Napoleon III viewed nation-states, birthed and nurtured by Paris, as the best way to leverage French power. Napoleon III would preempt German unification (either as an enlarged Austrian-led Customs Union or as an aggrandized Prussia) by reforming Germany into northern and southern confederations that would align with France to secure their independence from Berlin or Vienna. The Austro-Prussian War broke out shortly after Napoleon III had met with Bismarck, and the Prussian statesman had shrewdly pretended to support a French role in Germany. In reality, Bismarck invited the war with Austria to break out of the Congress straitjacket: the assumption in Europe at the time that any changes to the borders of 1815 would need the assent of a Congress of the Great Powers. It was just such a Congress that Napoleon III was mulling, to solve the German, Italian, and Polish questions (in the French interest), when Prussia invaded Austria in June 1866.

In 1866, Bismarck had a sophisticated understanding of his primary rival. He needed to defeat the Austrians to dissolve the German Confederation—over which Austria presided—but he knew that France lurked in the background as a more potent and threatening enemy. This was an atmosphere tailor-made for Bismarck's ingenuity. To weaken both Austria and France, he entered into alliance, in February 1866, with the new Kingdom of Italy. Italy itself was in large part an 1859 creation of the French army. But France's decision to renege on its pledge to "free Italy from the Alps to the Adriatic" (they freed it only as far as Milan, stopping short of Venice) and Napoleon III's demand for the Piedmontese territories of Nice (Nizza) and Savoy (Savoia) opened a rift between the two powers, which Bismarck slid into. He agreed that the Prussians would attack the Austrians in Bohemia if the Italians would attack them in Venetia. By making an ally of France's protégé, Bismarck not only opened a second front against the Austrians, he ensured that if the 1866 campaign became a long war, the Italians would not mobilize with the French against Prussia.

Bismarck also attempted to sow insurrection inside Austria. The Hungarians were the Hapsburg monarchy's most restive nationality, and Bismarck organized and paid for a Hungarian legion under Georg Klapka, which actually deployed in Upper Silesia to fight the Austrian army. Klapka's military contribution was nugatory, but his threat of civil war inside Austria undercut Austrian Emperor Franz Joseph I's resolve to fight the war to the bitter end. As Bismarck needed a short war—to prevent neutrals from interfering—this was a crucial contribution.

The war itself, the "military dimension of the rivalry," confirmed Prussian professionalism. The Austrian army retained an inefficient, politicized structure designed for peacetime and unsuited for war. The Austrian general staff wielded little real power, which was concentrated instead in the thirty-six-year-old emperor's military cabinet. Moreover, command on the all-important northern front was given to General Ludwig Benedek for political reasons. He was a popular commoner, known in the public mouth as "the second Radetzky." Unlike Radetzky, however, Benedek proved hesitant and incompetent. He mobilized slowly, deployed to Moravia, not Bohemia, and then tried to flank march into the path of the Prussians. Defeated in a sequence of frontier battles at Vsyokov, Skalice, and Jicin, he then made the ultimate error of resting at Königgrätz with his back to the Elbe, permitting his North Army to be enveloped and routed by three Prussian armies. Throughout, the emperor weakly chided Benedek from Vienna, but took no steps to remove him until it was too late.

Prussian arrangements were far more professional. The Prussian King Wilhelm I vested total authority in his efficient general staff chief Helmuth von Moltke and defended that vital chain of command against all inroads by Prussian generals who distrusted Moltke, resented his powers, and criticized his division of the Prussian army into three groups that were vulnerable—had Benedek been quicker—as they traversed the Sudeten Mountains into Bohemia. Buttressed by the king and Bismarck—who traveled with the great headquarters—Moltke rapidly defeated the Austrians, permitting the realization of all of Bismarck's aims. As the war wound down, Bismarck renounced annexations to avoid provoking a coalition of neutrals against him and to make it easier after the war to ally with the Austrians. "My two greatest difficulties were first getting the King of Prussia into Bohemia and then getting him out again," Bismarck later chuckled.[4] The king and the army had wanted to annex Bohemia and Austrian Silesia and parade through Vienna, but Bismarck wisely understood that the aim of German unification had been largely achieved by the war and that annexations of Habsburg territory would make the final steps—war with France, annexation of South Germany—much more difficult, if not impossible.

Prussia's unexpected and rapid victory provoked an angry outcry in France. Bismarck's defeat of the Austrians and annexation of the North German states took a Franco-German Europe dominated by France and turned it on its head. The defining asymmetry in the relationship—French unity versus German disunity—had been abruptly undone. The French called it the "surprise de Sadova": the surprise of a suddenly enlarged Prussia ("une Prusse colossale"), that now, with only half of Germany under its belt, possessed the population, national wealth, and armed strength to overshadow France. Finally, France recognized that it was in a strategic competition with Prussia, rather than a mentor relationship. "Grandeur is relative," privy counselor Pierre Magne cautioned the emperor. "A country's power can be diminished by the mere fact of *new* forces accumulating around it." Senator Lucien Murat warned that it was only a matter of time before the Prussians attacked France to extinguish Napoleon III's German influence.[5] Minister of state Eugène Rouher called for a preemptive war: "Smash Prussia and take the Rhine," before Prussia absorbed its conquests.[6]

As a strategist, Napoleon III had failed utterly to discern his primary rival or that rival's aims. Just before the war, the French emperor had boasted in a speech at Auxerre that he would use an Austro-Prussian conflict to wring major concessions and grants of territory from *both* German powers.[7] But he took no precautions to be ready when war exploded and Prussia seized the territory and influence he craved. While the Prussian army marauded in Austria and made annexations among the German states, the French emperor found himself with only 100,000 poorly armed troops to hand. That army was also poorly equipped, having not yet procured a new rifle and was, there-fore, using old muzzle-loaders. Moreover, more than half of the French army was abroad: 63,000 troops in Algeria, 28,000 in Mexico, 8,000 in Rome, and 2,000 in Indochina. Louis-Napoleon in 1866 had squandered his best chance to arrest or reshape the process of German unification. Vaguely aware that he was embroiled in a strategic competition with the Prussians, Napoleon III had not taken even the most elementary steps to win it.

The Austro-Prussian War had terminated so quickly that Napoleon III had been unable to intervene and shape the diplomatic settlement. A month after Königgrätz, the French emperor had desperately demanded "the bor-ders of 1814," which referred to the great square of German territory on the left bank of the Rhine annexed by France during the wars of the French Revolution and returned to the German states after Waterloo. Bismarck ignored the demand; how could he sell the imperative of German unifica-tion to the German people if he was prepared even to discuss the cession of Karlsruhe, Mannheim, Koblenz, and Luxembourg to the French? Bismarck then dictated peace to the Austrians, abolished the German Confederation, and drew new borders in Germany without consulting the Great Powers. Prussia annexed 1,300 square miles of German territory, adding 7 million subjects. It also took indirect control of Saxony, Hessia, Thuringia, Mecklenburg, Hamburg, Bremen, and Lübeck in a new "North German Confederation" in which Prussia controlled military and foreign affairs. Whereas Prussia had counted just one-third the inhabitants of France in 1820 and less than half in 1860, the Austro-Prussian War and the annexations almost evened the score: giving the North German Confederation a population of 30 million to France's 38 million and a Prussian army one-third larger than France's (many times larger in wartime) thanks to the Prussian use of universal con-scription. It also added greatly to Prussian economic muscle. France, once Continetal Europe's great economic power, slid down the ranks. Already in 1867, the coal mines of Prussia and the North German Confederation were out-producing French mines three to one.

With the annexations and amalgamations of 1866, the Prussian army grew from 70 to 105 infantry regiments, from ten corps to seventeen. Already in 1867, most of the North German armies had been seamlessly integrated with Prussian doctrine, drill, uniforms, and even officers.[8] French diplomatic intervention did ensure the continued independence of Saxony, Bavaria, Württemberg, Hessia-Darmstadt, and Baden, but all of those states—which had allied with the Austrians in 1866—were forced to pay crushing indemnities that fattened the Prussian war chest and made those nominally independent lands vulnerable to Prussian manipulation over the long haul. A minor Franco-Prussian rivalry characterized before the war by easy French dominance became, in 1866, Europe's preeminent rivalry, one that would forge diplomatic revolutions and drag Europe into war in 1914.

The Franco-Prussian War

Napoleon III spent the years 1866–1870 peevishly trying to assert French leadership of Europe and mastery of Germany, even though, or possibly because, his "authoritarian empire" had become stale and unpopular. Republican, anti-regime forces were strengthening, and Louis-Napoleon's only sure-fire source of popularity was an activist foreign policy in search of bold strokes and "national dignity." Yet even in this sphere, the emperor presided over a sequence of embarrassing flops. In 1863, he tried and failed to reconstitute an independent Poland over Austrian, Russian, and Prussian resistance. In 1866, he failed to wrest German territory from Bismarck after Königgrätz. In 1867, he failed to secure compensation for Prussia's German annexations in either Belgium or Luxembourg.[9] Finally, military reverses in Mexico forced his withdrawal there after several years of fruitless combat and the expenditure of 360 million francs ($1.3 billion today) in the failed effort to create a Central American satellite state.

In French parliamentary elections in 1869, the emperor's flagging government was repudiated, with more than 50 percent of voters expressing opposition to the regime. Out of options—even French army troops, given the vote for the first time, had voted against him—the emperor rather wildly (and cynically) began to ponder "a good war" (*une bonne guerre*) to rally the French. Prussia, he argued, had stymied his planned bold stroke in Germany and had insulted French national dignity in the process. Thus, the French emperor drew "red lines" around Prussia after the humiliation of 1866. Further, he insisted on a largely Catholic South German Confederation (Bavaria, Württemberg, and Baden) that would deny that region and its 8 million additional Germans (and 200,000 additional troops) to Bismarck and make the southern states dependent on France for their defense and independence.

South Germany was critical to France's military fortunes; if the Prussians controlled it, they would be still richer, bigger, and able to invade France on a broad front, from the Prussian Rhineland in the north to Alsace-Lorraine in the south. Geography and position had historically been an asymmetry that favored France against Voltaire's "kingdom of mere border strips." Prussia's spread southward would change that asymmetry in Berlin's favor, enabling Moltke to plan the sort of broad, concentric invasion of France that he had used so successfully against the Austrians in 1866. Thus, in 1868, Napoleon III warned the British foreign secretary that if Bismarck tried to annex South Germany, "our guns will go off of themselves."[10] For his part, Bismarck wrestled with South Germany's stubborn wish to retain its political independence and concluded that the only sure way to annex it was to provoke a French invasion of Germany that would rally all Germans to the Prussian throne.

The Franco-Prussian War arose from Napoleon III's need to humble and weaken the Prussians and Bismarck's need to provoke a French invasion of Germany that might serve to complete the process of German unification. Bismarck forged defense agreements with the South German states, assuring the involvement of their armies in the event of war. This was another feat of Bismarckian politics; in a few short years, Bismarck had reversed an asymmetry favoring the French: military strength. Enlarged by the North German Confederation plus the allied South German armies, Prussia added seven corps between 1866 and 1870 and became a million-man army. With just 400,000 troops, France found itself exceedingly vulnerable. Both sides now pushed for war—Napoleon III recklessly, to nip Prussian growth in the bud, Bismarck prudently, to cast Prussia as a victim of French arrogance and to complete national unification. Once again, the French displayed alarming strategic negligence. They knew the dangers of Prussian military organization—"the energy and speed of your movements [mean] that we're in danger of finding you in Paris one day unannounced," the French Empress Eugénie had complained to the Prussian ambassador after Königgrätz. "I will go to sleep French and wake up Prussian."[11] And yet in the interwar period, the French did nothing to improve the speed and energy of their movements to stymie the Prussian war machine.

The French government also failed to complete the key rail line (Verdun to Metz) to the eastern frontier. Moreover, the war ministry failed to make any arrangements to take the railways under government control. The French army also retained its extraterritorial and "non-divisioning" system to make the army a school of the nation, despite the fact that the Austrians—with the same system—had required two *months* to mobilize in 1866 and, as a result, had been overwhelmed by the vastly more efficient Prussians. No matter. The French, with a smug belief in their ability to improvise—*le système D, on se débrouillera toujours*—kept their battalions scattered around France and the overseas possessions, while planning to form divisions on an ad hoc basis during mobilization.[12] Nor did the French make much progress creating a Landwehr-style reserve army or *garde mobile*. In the four years between 1866 and 1870, the French army trained only 90,000 *mobiles*, less than a quarter of the 400,000 they had planned to recruit. Finally, the French general staff remained a backwater, which meant that the army had neither proper maps nor even firm war plans in 1870. Indeed the only substantive steps the French took between the wars were to revise their tactics and to procure a new breech-loading rifle—the Chassepot. They abjured the tactical offensive altogether, resolving instead to lure Prussian attacks into the "battalion fire" of the rearmed French infantry.[13]

Crises ensued, any one of which might have triggered the Franco-Prussian War. "Messaging" was critical here, and hinged on another key asymmetry: that of national goals, objectives, and stakes. Because the French regime was played out—Louis-Napoleon was old and ill, his government infiltrated by republican opponents (hence the "Liberal Empire" of 1869–1870)—the French message was strident and panicky, sure to excite the French masses on the issue of "national dignity" but also to alienate skeptical international opinion. The French message was also clouded by Napoleon III's unpopularity; the engine of Bonapartist progress had broken down, the sick old emperor no longer represented the future. Everything he now undertook seemed fraudulent.

Bismarck's messaging was easier, more credible, and shrewder. The right of Germans to unify was generally accepted in all but the most reactionary circles. Bismarck used German nationalism, which had not yet earned a bad name, to conceal his aggressive strokes against the powers that hemmed him in. This gave Prussia a distinct advantage; Germans and neutral Great Powers alike rallied to the calm, sensible Prussian "optics": that Bismarck sought nothing more than German unity. In each crisis—the Luxembourg Crisis of 1867, the *Zollparlament* crisis of 1868, and then three successive crises in 1870, which culminated in the Spanish throne crisis that sparked the war—Bismarck appeared merely to be defending German sovereignty, whereas Napoleon III appeared in every crisis the reactionary, petulant aggressor.

Those crises demonstrated how shrewdly Bismarck actively managed the strategic competition, always with an eye on international opinion. "Great crises provide the weather for Prussia's growth," he liked to say.[14] Occasional

European dust-ups (provoked by others) would divert the attention of the European powers from the threat of German unification and Prussia's creeping borders. He understood that amid such crises, Prussia could pose as the victim and defeat Great Powers like Austria and France singly. He worried, however, that all of his plans would shatter against a great coalition, or even against the intervention of one or two neutrals on the side of his intended victim. The European neutrals had given Bismarck a free hand against Austria in 1866 because the Austrians had foolishly declared war and because everyone had expected an Austrian victory or, at the very least, a long, inconclusive war. The trick, now that Prussia had demonstrated its military excellence, was to make the European powers believe that France was the more threatening power. If Bismarck could do this, the other powers would probably sit out the next war as well, providing yet more fair "weather for Prussia's growth."

And so in the Luxembourg Crisis of 1867, in which Napoleon III demanded the Dutch fortress town of Luxembourg—which had doubled as a fortress of the German Confederation—as compensation for the Prussian gains in 1866 and French "benevolence," Bismarck quietly engaged the British (who feared that a French step into Luxembourg might carry them into Belgium), and then agreed only to neutralize the place. Bismarck had won all sorts of dividends in this; he appeared the "reasonable man" to the British. He avoided a public relations disaster inside Germany by merely neutralizing but not ceding the territory to the unpopular French. Better still, he enraged and humiliated Napoleon III. ("When a hunter is ashamed of returning from the chase with an empty bag, he goes to the butcher, buys a rabbit and stuffs it into his bag, letting the ears flop out. *Voilà le Luxembourg*," Adolphe Thiers, one of the emperor's most persistent critics, hooted in the Legislative Body.)[15] This made it more likely that the French emperor would eventually declare war on Prussia, permitting the Germans to wage an internationally acceptable war of national defense against French aggression.

Bismarck managed another aspect of the strategic competition between France and Prussia just as carefully. South Germany was Catholic, and so inclined to accept French protection in the event that the Protestant Prussians tried to annex the southern states, as opposed to merely federating and cooperating economically with them. To Bismarck, leaving the political and cultural obstacles separating Germany's North and South to resolve themselves naturally might take decades. But a French invasion— even better, a *Napoleonic* invasion—would smash the obstacles down in an instant. Francophobia lingering from the Napoleonic Wars would set the war machinery of the North German Confederation in motion and put the

South German armies at Moltke's disposal. Thus, discreetly goading Louis-Napoleon would not only make it likely that the French emperor would alienate neutral powers, but that he would alienate his South German protégés as well.

The crises that eventually provoked the war—three successive crises in 1870—Bismarck engineered to cast France in the worst possible light. First, Bismarck floated the idea that the Prussian king might take the title of "German emperor," to more accurately reflect his control of the North German Confederation. The French reacted indignantly to the provocation, threatening war, which made them appear increasingly reckless to the other powers. Bismarck then supported constructing a railway from Prussia to Italy via Switzerland, which, in a public speech, he called a "strategic interest." Again, the French government and legislature reacted furiously. The final crisis, which triggered the war, was the Spanish throne crisis. Having offered a Hohenzollern candidate to Madrid, the Prussian king then withdrew him from the running when faced with French threats of war. There the matter should have rested, but Napoleon III upped the ante, demanding not only withdrawal of the Hohenzollern candidate, but a pledge by the Prussians that they would never again offer a candidate for the Spanish throne. This was regarded all over Europe and the world as unconscionable arrogance, for it reopened a war scare that had seemed settled by the Prussian king's climbdown.[16]

By July 1870, the French were well aware that they were on the verge of a major war with Prussia, yet the French foreign ministry under the duc de Gramont made no effort to pursue alliance strategies that might have given France an overpowering hand. Gramont merely assumed that the Austrians would intervene in any Franco-Prussian conflict "to erase the memories of 1866." He also assumed that the Italians would join the war to show their gratitude for French assistance in the war of 1859 (and he assumed that the Austrians would permit an Italian army to cross their territory to join the war against Prussia). Further, he was convinced that the Danes would join the war to take back Schleswig, seized by the Prussians in 1864.[17] Had Gramont breathed life into these assumptions with an active foreign policy, they might have resulted in sturdy alliances, a "revenge coalition" against Berlin. Instead, he merely took for granted that Prussia's old victims and France's old protégé would join the war spontaneously. For a nation locked in a harrowing strategic rivalry, this was gross negligence, and a real contrast with Bismarck's careful management of any off-stage actors who might have been expected to intervene.

Bismarck made it all but impossible for Austria to join the war by appealing to the monarchy's increasingly influential Hungarian political elite. Austria had become Austria-Hungary in 1867, and Budapest had received its own parliament and government in part through Bismarck's encouragement. Bismarck saw Hungary's veto power over Austrian decision-making as vital to curbing any resumption of Old Austrian—that is, anti-Prussian—policy, and his ministrations bore fruit in 1870 when the Hungarian prime minister, Gyula Andrássy, counseled against intervention in the Franco-Prussian War. Bismarck drew off the Italians by taking their side against the pope in the ongoing struggle for Rome, at a time when the French were still witlessly defending the Papal State—to Italy's chagrin—with a large garrison in the Holy City. Russia, in 1870, was the most important off-stage actor. Whereas Gramont merely assumed that the Russians would not support the creation of a great German state that might eventually menace Russia, Bismarck secretly purchased Russian benevolence by pledging to support repeal of the orders to the Russian Navy in the Black Sea that had restricted Russian movements since the Crimean War.

The military dimension of the rivalry now proceeded without outside interference, which was precisely what Bismarck had planned for. France's army had had four years to react to the lessons of the Austro-Prussian War, but presented itself in 1870 as an only superficially reformed force. Vital changes had simply not been made due to bureaucratic infighting, turf wars, political interference, and the pathetic inertia that increasingly affected the drifting Second Empire. The general staff had not been empowered. The pace of mobilization had not been improved. The army organization remained primitive, without a permanent division structure. Only infantry tactics had been reformed, but in a wooden way—defensive at all times—and without accompanying changes in artillery and cavalry equipment and tactics. Indeed, the Franco-Prussian War would be an artillery war; the Prussians had rearmed with Krupp steel breech-loaders, while the French retained their bronze muzzle-loading cannons. In every battle, the superior Prussian guns would hammer the French artillery, infantry, and cavalry and put them to rout.

Ultimately, the French were defeated almost before the first shot was fired. Napoleon III insisted on taking command of the Army of the Rhine despite his inexperience. That alienated the putative commander—Marshal Achille Bazaine—who sulked and did nothing throughout the deployment phase in July 1870, giving Moltke a head start to cross into Lorraine and Alsace and begin enveloping the French army with three widespread columns, the same operational approach he had used against the Austrians in 1866. Stunned and thrown back at Froeschwiller and Gravelotte in August 1870, the French Army of the Rhine broke into two pieces. Marshal Patrice MacMahon's piece retreated toward Paris, turning eventually north to Sedan. Bazaine's piece retreated into the fortress of Metz. Every pundit and analyst active at the time goggled in disbelief at French incompetence. With their vast reserve system, the Prussians were easily able to replace casualties and even increase their field army as the war lengthened. With their derisory *garde mobile*, the French were not. Moltke was, therefore, able to hive off a single army to maintain the siege against Bazaine, and then send three armies to encircle MacMahon and his reinforcements at Sedan. In just a month of fighting, the Prussians captured or destroyed the entire French army, including the emperor himself, who was taken prisoner at Sedan. As in 1866, the Prussian king defended Moltke's authority, enabling the general to move his vast armies efficiently across a broad theater of war and execute decisive victories.

A New Geopolitical Tide (1871–1914)

Bismarck overreached in 1871. In earlier wars and crises, he had been unimpeachably moderate. "We don't live alone in Europe," he regularly reminded King Wilhelm I and the generals, "but with three other powers who hate us." Like most Germans of his generation—molded by wicked tales of Napoleon—Bismarck had a real loathing of France. He would not show France the moderation he had shown the Austrians. He not only feared France's resurgence (for which he wanted insurance), he feared republics, and France had become one after its defeat at Sedan. Thus, Bismarck annexed Alsace-Lorraine and demanded reparations of five billion francs—sixty times the indemnity he had charged the Austrians in 1866. The addition of South Germany plus Alsace-Lorraine to an already enlarged Prussia eclipsed French power. "You have a new world, new influences at work. . . . The balance of power has been entirely destroyed," Benjamin Disraeli observed from London.[18]

The asymmetries that most defined the rivalry after 1871 were now economic and demographic. Germany, which the French had regarded before 1866 as a rather harmless space of drowsy landscapes and dreamy poets, became Europe's powerhouse. The German population surged from 41 million in 1871 to 60 million in 1890 to 70 million in 1914. German industrial production surpassed British levels in the 1890s, and Germans led the world in patents and during the "second industrial revolution" in chemicals, electrical equipment, and transport. By 1914, only the United States had a larger economy. France, in contrast, stagnated, its population stuck at 39 million for decades before 1914 and its economic output half of Germany's in 1880, a fourth of Germany's in 1900, and just a sixth of Germany's on the eve of World War I.[19]

Faced with this juggernaut, the French rather desperately looked for solutions. The French "Opportunist" republicans viewed overseas empire as the best way to match German power and population. Africans and Asians might provide the bodies and resources that were not springing in sufficient quantity from France. French Radical republicans dismissed the empire in Africa and Indochina as a distraction from the central mission of developing France and imbuing the French people with republicanism and nationalism— through school, the press, and military service—and a desire to re-conquer "the blue line of the Vosges."

The total defeat of reactionary forces in the Boulanger and Dreyfus Affairs meant that French republicans after 1900 could embark on a vast militarization of society without fear of strengthening anti-republican forces. Until then, the army had been a haven for monarchist cliques and conspiracies. The post-Dreyfus change in the French army led to a disturbing new asymmetry in the relationship: French spending on the military was so high and the French draft so extensive that France matched German military efforts, despite Germany's economic and demographic superiority. This was accomplished by conscripting .75 percent of their population in the years before 1914, compared with German conscription of .47 percent. Thus it was that in 1914, 2 million French troops faced 1.7 million Germans. That said, because the Germans drafted a smaller fraction of eligible males, they were able to train the draftees better and could endow them with more heavy artillery, leading to better results in the Great War. The Germans also had much bigger reserves contained in their larger, younger population.

Net assessment methods became more institutionalized and professional in this period. The Prussian victories in 1866 and 1870–1871 had enshrined the general staff everywhere, and every European army became better at gauging its relative strengths and weaknesses. Indeed, the arms races that preceded World War I were premised on net assessments that sought—in every power—to level the playing field. This was a quite different state of affairs from 1866 and 1870–1871, when the Prussians had plotted shrewdly in both conflicts, but the Austrians and French had lurched haphazardly and unintelligently into war, with little truly professional net assessment.[20]

The Germans, too, suffered a kind of strategic schizophrenia before 1914. Berlin's perception of its "primary enemy" shifted wildly between 1871 and 1914. The army was focused on the European Continent and the threat of the French and Russians—hence the Schlieffen Plan—but the navy, a powerful force under Wilhelm II, gratuitously alienated Great Britain with its "risk theory" aimed at British ports and its demands for an overseas empire. The consequences of Berlin's inability to fix a primary enemy/rivalry were disastrous. The Germans poured vast resources into the battle fleet (envisioning fifty battleships and thirty battlecruisers by 1920) that were never recouped in war, and made the relatively underfunded German army vulnerable to the stalemate of 1914 and the fatal war of attrition.[21]

"Messaging" had favored Prussia until 1870, when it began to favor France. Like Napoleon III, Kaiser Wilhelm II was his own worst enemy, isolating himself in an entourage of reactionary yes-men and spewing provocations like the *Daily Telegraph* Affair, the Kruger Telegram, and *Weltpolitik* ("I hold a trident in my fist") that gradually alienated all of the other powers except Austria-Hungary and Italy, which were negligible assets. In the Kruger Telegram of 1896, the kaiser offered congratulations and the suggestion of aid to the Boer president at a time when the British government was trying to take all of South Africa under its wing. *Weltpolitik* was the kaiser's determination in the two decades before World War I to build a great colonial empire—a dangerous proposition in view of the fact that all of the prime resource areas had already been taken by the British, French, Americans, Portuguese, Japanese, Dutch, Belgians, and Italians. War scares like the two Moroccan Crises in 1905 and 1911 stemmed from forceful German attempts to wrest away European colonies (France's, in these two cases) with gunboat diplomacy. In the *Daily Telegraph* Affair of 1908, the kaiser pulled off a rare feat: he insulted the British, French, Russians, and Japanese in a single interview.[22] These gaffes and provocations left Germany less alliance-worthy than ever. Only abject Austria-Hungary, nearly devoured by its own nationality problems, and Italy—hoping to secure German support in its own quest for colonies like Libya—remained as German allies. Bismarck had always said that Germany needed to be "one of three on the European chessboard," but he would never have gone to war with a trio like *this*.

The asymmetry in political structure—a balanced, democratic republic in Paris versus an irresponsible camarilla in Berlin—deeply affected the rivalry. German military and naval planners were free to provoke the world with their aggressive, unchecked procurement, planning (the Schlieffen Plan was an open secret) and saber-rattling over issues like Bosnia and Morocco. On the surface, the French *réveil national* was far less threatening; it emanated from the country's parliamentary and presidential system and lodged itself in a powerful, credible coalition. Overall, German braggadocio and freelancing facilitated the great diplomatic revolution that would eventually destroy the German Empire: the Triple Entente of France, Russia, and Britain.

The rivalry de-escalated for a time in this period. The chief factor in the de-escalation was the nature of the French Third Republic. It was democratic, and the French people, in general, gradually lost their fascination with Alsace-Lorraine and the "blue line of the Vosges." In 1870, Tsar Alexander II had opined that Berlin "had created an inexpugnable hatred between the two peoples," and indeed the Germans had, for a time, but tempers had cooled by 1914. Urban aesthetes and peasants alike rejected war for the "lost provinces." "As for me," French thinker Remy de Gourmont wrote on the eve of World War I, "I wouldn't give the little finger of my right hand for those forgotten provinces. My hand needs it to rest on as I write. Nor would I give the little finger of my left hand. I need it to flick the ash from my cigarette."[23] As for the French peasants, most would have been hard-pressed to tell you exactly where Alsace and Lorraine were. Having successfully lobbied their politicians to decrease military service from three years to two in 1905, French peasants, still the majority, were in no mood to fight a war to recover the provinces that had been thoroughly Germanized in the years since 1870. They would troop off willingly to war in 1914 not for *revanche*, but because the Germans had invaded France again.

The Dreyfus Affair, which dragged on from 1894 to 1906, ended the "golden age" of the French army that had run for twenty years after the war of 1870–1871. The army's squalid comportment in the Dreyfus Affair— framing a Jewish officer to whip up anti-Semitism and undermine the republic—replaced the "golden age" with a deep distrust of the military. When the French war minister appeared before the Assembly in 1899 and declaimed—in the usual way—that "the army belongs to no party; it belongs to France," he was met with jeers and insults, so deeply was the French military discredited by its political machinations.

Bismarck would have noted this calming of the French temper and encouraged it with deft concessions or mere forbearance. His successors under Kaiser Wilhelm II lacked his moderation. The French *réveil national*— which made Alsace-Lorraine its centerpiece again—began in 1911 after the Second Moroccan Crisis. In 1905 and again in 1911, the Germans had bid for French Morocco and had been repulsed, but had inflicted humiliating diplomatic blows on the French in both episodes: forcing the resignation of French foreign minister Théophile Delcassé in 1905 and shearing off French Congo in 1911. The second crisis led to the dismissal of Joseph Caillaux's government, which had worked for détente with the Germans, and the appointment of *"Poincaré la guerre"*: Raymond Poincaré, a revanchist Lorrainer, determined to embark on a more confrontational policy with the Germans.[24]

Just as democracies can discourage war, they can also encourage it. In America today, the US military has been sanctified by all parties, because it is politically expedient. Everyone "supports the troops" and congressional assent to any cuts in wages, benefits, or platforms is a rare thing indeed. This is a dangerous development today—it makes wars easier to contrive—and it was dangerous for France because, in the notoriously fractious National Assembly (particularly fractious after 1911), military spending and grandstanding became the only issue that all parties could agree on. The left supported military expansion because they had thoroughly purged the officer corps after the Dreyfus Affair and now had reliable republican officers in place who would "make the army the very image of the republic."[25] The French right supported military expansion because, after the Dreyfus Affair, they gave up resisting the republic and supporting the old Bourbon, Orleanist, or Bonapartist pretenders and made a strong, assertive military their cause instead. New right-wing pressure groups like the *Camelots de Roi* and the *Ligue des Patriotes* advanced the nationalist cause and expressed indifference on the old restoration questions. Thus, all parties in the French system besides the Socialists— who controlled 10–15 percent of the seats in the French chamber at any given time—needed the *réveil national* to legitimize themselves. Even the French school system became a party to the revival: black-robed teachers ("the black hussars") coaching students on the need to recover Alsace-Lorraine and the necessity of military service. All of this, in turn, explained the *union sacrée*: the otherwise unthinkable "sacred union" of all French parties under the banner of the nation to resist German pressure.

After 1911, the French army grew sharply and became a threat to the Germans. Military service was restored to three years in 1913, and the French added artillery, machine guns, and aviation. The Franco-German rivalry, which had burned for twenty years after 1871 and then cooled considerably during France's internecine Dreyfus Affair, sparked into life again after 1911. There was a lack of strategic discernment displayed by both France and Germany in this last phase of the rivalry. The French had seemingly come to terms with the loss of Alsace-Lorraine. Jules Ferry had successfully rebuked revanchists in the 1890s thus: "You'll make us believe that you prefer Alsace-Lorraine to France," and Ferry had embarked on an overseas empire to replace the losses of 1871. Now the French swerved back to an unhelpful obsession with the provinces, not for strategic reasons—the lost frontier had been sealed with a belt of new fortresses from Verdun to Belfort in the 1870s—but for opportunistic political ones.[26] French politicians wanted to intoxicate voters with fairy tales about resurgent French pride and power.

For their part, the post-Bismarck Germans were witlessly alienating every Great Power that mattered: the French in the Moroccan Crises and outrages like the Zabern Affair of 1913; the British with their Navy Race and colonial offensives; and the Russians with their tariffs on grain, military buildup, and unyielding support for Austria-Hungary in the Balkans. The figure of Kaiser Wilhelm II loomed large. Groupthink dominated his councils, where ministers and service chiefs were selected for their tractability, not their sound advice. The kaiser wanted his "place in the sun," and his generals, admirals, and ministers would have to provide it, at almost any cost.

This, then, accelerated the rivalry toward war. Neither side had a firm grip on the tiller, for both sides were milking the rivalry for domestic-political benefit; concessions were viewed on both sides as weakness and even as cause for a change of government. The Germans had used "fleet policy" and "world policy" to try to drum up popular support for an increasingly unpopular regime. The *réveil national* pointed less to the strength of the republic in France than to the weakness and tenuousness of republican institutions: the need to attire them in pomp and glory that could be found only in the army.

This period was rife with strategic miscalculations and just plain nonsense. French diplomacy was generally strong—making sure to lock in British and Russian support—but French military planning did not keep step. This was in part because of the purges undertaken after the Dreyfus Affair. Many good French officers were driven into the wilderness along with the bad ones. To make the army "politically correct," officers' eating habits (did they eat fish or meat on Fridays?) and church attendance (a bad thing in a determinedly secular republic) were cause for demotion or dismissal. Fewer bright thinkers remained to contest the tactical innovations of General Joseph Joffre (named General Staff chief in 1911) and the head of the French war college Colonel Louis Grandmaison. Joffre was stolid, not brilliant; a deputy said of his choice to lead the army, "in a democracy, every fat man is a good man." He had been chosen for his girth and amiability as well as his willingness to play the game.[27] He ostentatiously ate a beefsteak every Friday to demonstrate his anticlerical credentials.

Joffre and Grandmaison worked up Plan XVII and new tactics to win the next war. Offensive doctrine was undertaken to undercut Germany's technical and material advantages (more heavy artillery, three times as many NCOs.) Quality (of red-trousered French infantry) was sacrificed to quantity. At the French war college, General Ferdinand Foch propounded the following formula as if it were all one needed to know: "war = moral superiority of the victors, moral depression of the vanquished." No account was taken of the real lessons of the Franco-Prussian War, that casualties had been far higher than in 1866, and would be ruinous in an age of quick-firing artillery and machine guns (of which the French had only half as many as the Germans in 1914). Joffre and Grandmaison also eschewed the defensive—the flaw in 1870–1871. Rather, they would mass their armies on the eastern frontier, and attack the Germans with the bayonet, emphasizing the "moral element." When more prudent and scientific officers like General Philippe Pétain or Foch (awaking from his war college reveries) protested that the offensive doctrines would not succeed in an age of trenches, machine guns, and quick-firing artillery, they were reassigned.[28]

The Germans made an irreconcilable enemy of France in 1871, and then successively alienated the Russians and British, assuring their diplomatic and military isolation in 1914. The Schlieffen Plan was conceived in Berlin as a way out of this isolation, yet it guaranteed British intervention (because of its path through neutral Belgium) and assured a long war of attrition that Germany could not win easily or at all. France, laboring to keep the German threat under control, increased spending on the military and poured loans into Russia to modernize the Russian railways and increase the striking power of the Russian military. That strategy—a key piece of the Franco-German rivalry—paid off, as the Russian "steamroller" destroyed the Austro-Hungarian army in 1914 and diverted increasing numbers of German troops from west to east.

Whereas the French focused on Germany as their main rival down to 1914, the Germans wavered on this question. By 1914, they were alarmed by the revival of the French military, but they had competing concerns. Berlin tended to view Russia as the most threatening land power, Chancellor Theobald von Bethmann Hollweg famously instructing a relative not to plant new trees on his East Prussian estate "because the Russians would conquer it" before the trees matured. The Germans viewed the British as the most threatening naval, colonial, and economic power and the one keeping them from their "place in the sun." *Britenhass*—hatred of Britain—would be the most conspicuous German emotion in 1914. The French, on the other hand, could focus on the Germans because of the Triple Entente coalition that they had assembled to guard their flanks. The Germans were more reckless, eschewing the prudent rapprochements with the various powers that would have permitted them to focus their strength on a single rival and instead inviting an unwinnable confrontation with them all.

Both rivals expected 1914 to decide the rivalry in the manner of 1870. France's Plan XVII called for a brutal stab into the heart of Germany by the massed French army. Germany's Schlieffen Plan would envelop that French thrust from the flank, seize Paris, compel the surrender of the French and

British armies, and then turn everything against the Russians in the east. Both visions failed to materialize. Moltke the Younger reduced Schlieffen's mighty "right hook" from sixteen corps to eleven in order to attempt a double envelopment of the French from Belgium and Lorraine. Schlieffen had always demanded a ratio of 7:1 between the right and left wings of the German army in France; Moltke reduced the ratio to 3:1. Logistics also undercut the Schlieffen Plan; the further the Germans advanced from their railheads (140 kilometers in the case of the First Army), the fewer critical supplies they received. All of the armies began to run low on ammunition, as their horse-drawn supply wagons were fully taxed hauling fodder: two million pounds of hay and oats daily for the horses of a single army.[29] Granted this respite, the French and British hurled the Germans back at the Marne. Kaiser Wilhelm II called the reverse "*the* great turning point in his life," as it consigned the Germans to a war of attrition that they would not win against the better armed, better supplied, better financed Entente.[30] The French did not allow for modern firepower and were savaged in the Battle of the Frontiers and the Battle of the Marne. They lost one million men in the first month of the war, carnage that would multiply more than fivefold in the course of the conflict, leaving the nation of 38 million broken, dismayed, and unready for the rivalry with Germany that would resume after the war.

Conclusion

The figure of Bismarck loomed over this rivalry from beginning to end. He had served as a kind of magician, achieving a unity that no one had thought possible. Germany had been divided at the Congress of Vienna precisely to deny its awesome potential to a single Great Power. Bismarck overcame this division by deftly isolating his most incorrigible enemies and managing "offstage actors" like Britain and Russia that might have interfered with his plans.

Magicians are a rare breed, and Bismarck's successors proved less competent at directing the rivalry with France that might have been peacefully managed—to Germany's long-term benefit—by better, more supple leaders. Unfortunately, the entourage of Wilhelm II contained no such men. France recovered smartly from the defeat of 1870–1871, but vacillated dangerously through the period until 1914. Leaders like Ferry and Delcassé tried to make the country forget Alsace-Lorraine, which it largely did. But military affairs once again became a hot-button issue in the Third Republic. Before the Dreyfus Affair, the army (covertly) assailed the republic for its "cowardice" vis-à-vis the Germans. After the affair, and the taming of the army, the republic itself seized upon the army and its Continental aims as a way to rejuvenate and legitimize itself. Thus, Alsace-Lorraine was dragged back into the center of the frame by the *réveil national*. Both France and Germany would have had a far happier and more prosperous twentieth century had they resisted the pull—by generals, journalists, and politicians—to war, but they did not. The rivalry would bathe itself again in blood.

Like most rivalries, this one saw perceptions of relative power change radically. Underdogs until 1870, the Germans emerged after Sedan as the top dog, relegating France to the underdog role. The Germans overplayed their hand, insisting eventually on a global dominance that called every major power into the field against Berlin, while France made the most of its own downward spiral. A France that had been isolated and threatening under Napoleon III suddenly became alliance worthy. Because Germany had become so powerful and obnoxious (insisting on European and overseas domination under Wilhelm II), France emerged as a helpful makeweight to the Russians in 1892, and then to the British in 1904. The timeless lesson is clear. A power eclipsed by another is not disarmed; on the contrary, it can use military deterrents, alliances, finances, trade, and levers of the media and public opinion (soft power) to improve its relative situation and thwart the "winner." How did this strategic competition end? The French won. But in their own efforts to win the peace, they antagonized a Germany that was really only lightly wounded by the Treaty of Versailles. True, the Germans surrendered 13 percent of their pre-war territory (25,000 square miles) and 10 percent of their population (6.5 million subjects), and their army and navy were reduced to 100,000 troops and a dozen lightweight ships, but the Germans remained the most potent power in a central European space that had become a contested vacuum with the breakup of Austria-Hungary and the retreat of Soviet Russia. The advantage in "optics" would flip again, the Germans after 1919 becoming a victim of French pride and revenge—and merely trying to reclaim areas that were "rightfully theirs"—the French an overweening victor. Germany would rebound to defeat France in 1940.

CHAPTER 11

A New World in Dispute
The British Empire versus the American Empire
Kathleen M. Burk

T HROUGHOUT MOST OF RECORDED human history, empires have been
the normal way of organizing people into political units. Naturally
they have come in different shapes, sizes, structures, and powers. Looking
specifically at the British and American empires, both were, more often
than not, extended by private explorers, farmers, and businessmen rather
than by the state; both were dominated by whites; both (eventually) were
democracies; both supported private enterprise; both insisted that they were
bringing the blessings of civilization and good government to those who
had suffered by their lack; and both justified the use of force as a way of
providing those blessings. There were also distinct differences. The British
had created a seaborne empire, while for most of its existence, the American
Empire has been land based. Most important of all, the British Empire was
a colonial empire, while the United States, once it had conquered the land
from sea to shining sea and gone through its Philippine phase, was much
less a colonial empire than the semi-controller of a range of client states—
besides, once it reached its apogee in the mid-twentieth century, there was
not a lot of "empty" territory left to conquer and colonize. Economic interests in particular often brought them into conflict, but, partly because of
the similarities and in spite of the differences, the two empires often worked
together against threats from others.

Comparing the Two Empires

Looking at the period from the beginning of the War of 1812 (called the American War in Britain while it was taking place) to the outbreak of World War II, there are three overarching themes.

- First of all, where the two empires shared borders, such as the Canadian-American border, there was repeated conflict—military, diplomatic, or economic.
- Second, when there was no common enemy, such as in Latin America, there was competition.
- And third, where there was a common enemy, such as in the Far East, there was cooperation.

There was also a trajectory. In 1812, they were both expanding empires, but the British Empire was already global, while the American was continent-bound. During the nineteenth century, while the United States was manifesting its destiny westward, it was also an economic, social, and cultural colony of Great Britain; however, in the thirty years from the acceleration of its own industrial revolution to after the end of the Civil War, the United States surpassed Britain industrially.[1] By the 1920s, the United States was also financially stronger than Britain. Nevertheless, it remained militarily weaker: the United States Navy was significantly smaller than the Royal Navy, and the US Army was smaller than the British Army. It is mistaken to call the United States in the 1920s—as many historians have done and American politicians in the 1920s did—the strongest Power in the world.[2] The United States was a potential but not an actual global Power: it had the resources but not the sustained will. Its ability to project power was distinctly more limited than that of Great Britain. Only when it devoted its population and its domestic financial, economic, and natural resources to this did the United States succeed Great Britain as the predominant Global Power.

Comparing the general positions and powers of the two empires is illuminating. First, Great Britain was a small island nation with a large and growing seaborne empire, while the United States was a large, continental nation with a growing land-based empire. (This began to change in 1867 with the annexation of the Midway Islands, a movement that accelerated in 1898.) Despite being an island nation, Britain was extremely vulnerable to invasion, as had been demonstrated by the Romans, the Angles, the Saxons, the Jutes, the Danes, the Normans, and the Dutch; only with the growth in the strength and power of the Royal Navy could Britain feel safe enough to explore and conquer across the wide oceans. By contrast, fundamentally the

United States in the nineteenth century was unconquerable by an outside power, although it was perfectly capable of destroying itself. Yet during the entire period from 1812 to 1940, the British army and navy were larger than those of the United States, and overwhelmingly so in the nineteenth century. During this time, Great Britain was occupied primarily with imperial activities, problems dealt with by the Indian army, made up of Indians but officered by the British in a ratio of roughly two to one; in the mid-1860s, they totaled about 180,000. In addition, there were in 1870 roughly another 120,000 members of the armed forces.[3] The American army in 1870 was authorized at about 45,000, falling to about 27,400 in 1876.[4]

This was not because of a lack in American population numbers. While in 1801, the population of the United States was 5,486,000 and that of Great Britain was 15,902,000, in 1856 the lines crossed: now the American population was 28,212,000 and the British was 28,011,000. By 1901, the American population was nearly twice that of the British.[5] In truth, the reason that US military power was limited was that Congress did not like spending money on a standing army or navy, which might prove to be dangerous, and the money in any case could be more usefully employed elsewhere, such as leaving it "to fructify in the pocket of the taxpayer" (in the words of Prime Minister William Gladstone). As a quick comparison, in 1890, the British regulars plus the Indian army stood at roughly seven times the size of the US army. The Spanish-American War changed things for the United States, and the numbers of American soldiers shot up to over 250,000; thereafter they stabilized at around 100,000 until World War I. Nevertheless, even then, the United States could put many fewer men in the field than could the British.

There were other points of strength as well. First was natural resources, and these the United States had in abundance; what it lacked for much of the nineteenth century was a wide range of domestically manufactured goods, and for many of these it depended on imports from Britain. Conversely, except for coal and iron, Britain was considerably more dependent on imports of raw materials, such as timber for its ships before steel was used and cotton for its textile industry, than was the United States. But this hardly mattered, because where the British Empire was supreme was in its financial and commercial power, and it could purchase what it needed. During the nineteenth century, the City of London was the world's financial center, while the pound sterling was the world's primary transaction and reserve currency. Not only did the city finance, for example, the building of the Argentine railway system and the movement of the Southern US cotton crop to market, it was the home of the Bank of England, essentially the manager, if not the controller, of the gold standard. But there is another important point about this financial strength, which is that it enabled Britain to carry out a wide-ranging and influential foreign policy, including the wherewithal to subsidize allies. At the Battle of Waterloo in 1815, the Prussians helped to turn the tide, and the Prussians were subsidized by Britain; during World War I, Britain financed or guaranteed the purchases in the United States of France, Russia, Italy, Belgium, Greece, and Rumania.[6] Once the United States joined the war, it loaned but never gave. This was probably wise, because the British effort, which saw it lose 15 percent of its wealth during the war, enabled the United States to supplant Britain as the world's major financial power.

There were two more important components of British strength during this period—diplomatic and naval power. Looking at diplomacy, Britain was excellent at maneuvering countries less powerful than it was, but it was also exceptionally good at building coalitions, especially with the European Powers. The United States suffered for a good part of its history from the general lack of status of diplomats—often called cookie-pushers—and men of ability tended to look elsewhere for careers. At the same time, it feared the ability of crafty Europeans, and especially of the British, to outwit and cheat Americans. Strong distrust was never absent from Anglo-American relations.

The second component was British strength on the oceans and seas. From the time of the Battle of Trafalgar in 1805, when the Royal Navy, under the command of Admiral Horatio Nelson, essentially destroyed the French and Spanish fleets, and particularly after 1815, Great Britain was the dominant naval power. This did not necessarily mean that it physically controlled the oceans; rather, it controlled the western approaches to the United Kingdom and Ireland, and the narrow seas around Europe, the Baltic, and the Mediterranean, as well as strategic waters elsewhere:

- Gibraltar controlled the western Mediterranean;
- Malta gave it control of the central basin of the Mediterranean;
- Alexandria controlled the eastern Mediterranean, including the entrances and exits from the Black Sea and the Suez Canal;
- Simonstown kept an eye on the Indian Ocean and the route to India, the Antipodes, and the Far East;
- Control of the Channel protected the home islands, the Low Countries, and access to the Baltic Ocean, the latter hemming in Russia;
- The West Indies Squadron protected economic interests in Central and South America;

- The Atlantic Squadron based at Halifax protected Canada and, at the same time, the east coast of the United States; and the fleet in the South China Sea protected British interests in China.

The Royal Navy also patrolled the sea lanes, supported by a network of some 157 principal coaling stations around the world that it controlled or to which it had access (much envied by the Americans, although many were open to American ships after 1815), protecting the largest merchant marine in the world.[7] This had two elements: first of all, this supported British trade, the largest in the world and the lifeblood of the empire; second, it also ensured that the merchant marine continued as the "school for sailors," upon whom Britain could call in time of need.

A brief comparison with the United States Navy is illuminating. In the 1880s, the Royal Navy had 367 modern warships, while the United States had fewer than 90, only 48 of which could fire a gun and 38 of which were made of wood. In 1889, however, a near war with Germany over Samoa drew Americans' attention to the fact that the United States Navy ranked twelfth in the world, behind those of the Austro-Hungarian, Ottoman, and Chinese empires, none of which was a noted naval power. Congress now responded by appropriating the funds for the first three modern armored battleships in the United States Navy; in 1904, fourteen battleships and thirteen armored cruisers were being built simultaneously in American shipyards.[8]

The two empires' goals did not differ much. The United States wanted to extend across the continent in physical terms and to extend across Latin America and the Far East in economic terms. Great Britain wanted sometimes, although not always, to extend and maintain the empire in physical terms, although this desire very much fluctuated according to political, diplomatic, and economic pressures; more unending was the intention to extend and maintain its economic informal empire, ideally without having the bother and the expense of exerting political control.

North America

With the Treaty of Paris of 1783, Great Britain recognized the independence of the United States. However, both sides found it difficult to shake loose from each other. Many British, and indeed Europeans, doubted that a republic would have the internal strength to survive, and many expected that, sooner or later, the new country would fall apart, allowing Britain and others, such as Spain, France, and Russia, to pick up some of the pieces (this expectation was nearly fulfilled, although it would take eighty years and the Civil War for it to be tested and found to be wrong). For their part, many Americans expected to continue to enjoy the economic and especially trading privileges that they had enjoyed as part of the empire, even though they had rejected it. The British for their part were incredulous at the American expectation that commercial life could go on as before the separation.[9]

A bit of context will be useful to make it clear why the United States and Great Britain engaged in a second war less than thirty years after the end of the first. During the period from 1783 to 1812, war between Great Britain and the United States was repeatedly threatened and, from 1812 to 1815, actually took place. An extremely important grievance for the United States was the treatment of Americans and American vessels by the Royal Navy. First, the British claimed that once a Briton always a Briton, and impressed—that is, hauled off American merchant ships—any sailors whom they believed were British. And second, the British claimed the right during time of war to prevent neutral ships carrying contraband—which they themselves defined—from trading with the enemy; American ships were often the victims of the British interpretation of the rights of neutrals, which was a narrow one. These issues would be a direct cause of the War of 1812. Another important issue was the putative British support of Indians who were attacking American settlers attempting to move into and colonize the Indians' lands. And finally, it was simply not clear whose writ ran where, with the result that there was conflict over the boundary.

The American territorial objective was to conquer Canada, which the United States assumed would not be difficult. Thomas Jefferson, for example, wrote in August 1812 that "[t]he acquisition of Canada this year, as far as the neighbourhood of Quebec, will be a mere matter of marching, and will give us experience for the attack of Halifax the next, and the final expulsion of England from the American continent."[10] The United States also wanted to eliminate, if possible, the Indians' ability to block western expansion, with the assumption being that the fall of Canada would deprive them of supplies and support. As a result, American forces crossed into Canada in 1812, 1813, and 1814, and won some victories; but in only one of eight attempts did they successfully occupy British territory for more than a short time, and even that exception, in southwestern Upper Canada, was returned to Great Britain in the peace treaty.

For the British, the war was defensive, in that its primary goal was to retain Canada, and in general to end the United States' ability to threaten the British colonies in America. (Before the Revolution, Great Britain had had twenty-three American colonies; after 1783, it still had ten.) It also wanted to avenge the sufferings of the Canadians and, if possible, to redraw the Canadian-American border to make it more defensible. It is likely that it wanted to humble the Americans.

Empires always fear unstable borders, since, unlike those of long-established states, they are not fixed by consent. A threat exists on the other side. Particularly bad stretches of the border, such as those between Maine and New Brunswick, in New York along the Niagara boundary, between Minnesota and Ontario, and just west of the Great Lakes around the Pigeon River Falls, desperately required precise delimitation. Without it, conflict continued, and in 1812 erupted into war. The ferocity was fed by myriad small conflicts during the years since 1783 over parts of the border whose legality was denied by one or both sides. Most of the land battles of the War of 1812 were fought at and over that border (although the fact that a good deal of fighting took place in the southeastern part of the United States should not be forgotten).

Border conflict included attacks on each other's capitals. On April 27, 1813, Americans launched an assault against York (now Toronto), the village that served as the capital of Canada, and drove out the British soldiers. A surrender agreement was negotiated, whereby the United States commanders agreed to respect private property, allow the civil government to function, and permit doctors to treat the British wounded. Despite the agreement, during their week of occupation American soldiers, including some officers, broke into homes and robbed the Canadians, pillaged the church, and locked up the British and Canadian wounded without food, water, or medical attention for two days. At one point, the priest John Strachan rescued a woman who was about to be shot by the Americans while they were looting her house. Strachan's own pregnant wife was assaulted, robbed, and probably raped by a group of American soldiers. When the Americans withdrew, they set fire to the parliament buildings and the governor's home—the Canadian equivalent of the Capitol and the White House.[11]

The British effected a bit of retaliation a year later by invading and burning parts of Washington. On May 20, 1814, Lord George Bathurst, the secretary for war and the colonies, instructed Major-General Robert Ross, a veteran of the Peninsular War against the French, "to effect a diversion on the coasts of the United States of America in favour of the army employed in the defence of Upper and Lower Canada."[12] Sir George Prevost, the governor-general of Canada, wrote to Vice-Admiral Sir Alexander Cochrane on June 2, 1814, suggesting that he should "assist in inflicting that measure of retaliation which shall deter the enemy from a repetition of similar outrages" as had taken place in Canada. Cochrane on July 18 then issued an order to the squadrons blockading the east coast of the United States "to destroy and lay waste such towns and districts upon the coast as you may find assailable."[13] The army, however, paid no attention to the order. If a town was willing to surrender, the British neither shot nor burned, but would require a contribution of supplies or money, and then return to their ships. In the case of Washington, after the American surrender,

> General Ross . . . did not march the troops immediately into the city, but halted them upon a plane in its immediate vicinity, while a flag of truce was sent in with terms. But . . . scarcely had the party bearing the flag entered the street, than they were fired upon from the windows of one of the houses, and the horse of the General himself, who accompanied them, killed. . . . All thoughts of accommodation were instantly laid aside; the troops advanced forthwith into the town, and having first put to the sword all who were found in the house from which the shots were fired, and reduced it to ashes, they proceeded, without a moment's delay, to burn and destroy every thing in the most distant degree connected with government. In this general devastation were included the Senate-house, the President's palace, an extensive dockyard and arsenal, [and a number of military buildings, equipment, and stores.] But, unfortunately, it did not stop here; a noble library, several printing offices, and all the national archives were likewise committed to the flames, which, no doubt the property of the government, might better have been spared.[14]

Neither side won and neither side "lost" the war, in spite of the American conviction that, because they had won the Battle of New Orleans, they had won the war. Negotiations over the Treaty of Peace and Amity—that is, the Treaty of Ghent—that ended the war took place for virtually the entire year of 1814, although news of its signing did not reach the United States until early 1815, just after the Battle of New Orleans. Five of the articles pointed out the lack of agreed boundaries around islands, on land and on the Lakes, and set out arrangements for commissions to survey and decide on them, but this took nearly six decades to accomplish. The Treaty did not prevent further conflicts after 1815, but the conflicts were often, although not always, private rather than state-sponsored: men on the frontier, eager for land or furs, had little regard for what Great Britain and a distant federal government had agreed.

The result was that for the remainder of the century, there were recurrent conflicts between the two empires over the place of the boundary between the United States and Canada, a thinly populated country. Why should both countries care? For the British, who had taken it from the French by conquest, it belonged to the empire and they were willing to fight for it. The Americans viewed things differently. God had clearly not intended that the United States end at the 48 degree parallel and they were convinced that, once conquered, the Canadians would rapidly embrace the blessings that being American would bring.

As a diversionary tactic, Britain tried to construct a balance of power by encouraging Texas to remain independent, which would weaken the United States and turn its attention from the northern border.[15] Americans invaded Canada a dozen times during the nineteenth century, although no member of the United States Army itself did so after 1814. Interestingly, the 1896 Republican platform still insisted that Canada should join the United States, although it was conceded that this would be achieved by negotiation rather than invasion. Most Americans apparently refused to believe that the Canadians were not eager to become American citizens and assumed that they were only prevented from joining the United States by the might of Great Britain. The two countries nearly went to war several times over parts of the border during the century: Who can ever forget the Aroostook or Lumberjack War of 1838, or "Fifty-four forty or fight" in 1848, or the Pig War of 1859?[16]

The Webster-Ashburton Treaty of 1842 sorted out most of the border conflicts by negotiation, with the northern boundary of Maine being the most difficult, in a compromise that broadly favored the British. Although Lord Ashburton believed that Americans made "troublesome neighbours" with whom "nothing [was] more easy than to get into war . . . any morning with a very good cause," he also believed that a good Anglo-American relationship was vital for both countries. Daniel Webster, the secretary of state, shared that belief.[17]

Central to Anglo-American conflict now was control of the Oregon Territory, comprising the future states of Oregon and Washington and the province of British Columbia. President Thomas Jefferson sent out the most famous exploring expedition in American history, that of Meriwether Lewis and William Clark, with instructions to explore, discover, and map a route to the West and especially to Oregon, to enable the infant nation to expand.[18] More specifically, he instructed them to bring the Indians into the US orbit, wrest the fur trade from Britain, and lay claim to the Pacific Northwest (rather a large task, it must be said). The expedition took more than two years and covered several thousand miles. The outcome was the Oregon Trail, followed by dozens of wagon trains; the British became alarmed and moved to protect their own claims.[19] The result was a standoff, which occasionally developed into local conflict.

During the presidential election of 1844, candidates cried for war with Great Britain if it did not concede the American demands for Oregon in full, including a border set at "Fifty-four forty or fight," as trumpeted by the Senator from Ohio, William "Foghorn Bill" Allen.[20] In his inaugural address on March 4, 1845, President James K. Polk claimed all of the Oregon Territory; in April 1846, he denounced the Joint Occupation by the United States and Great Britain, asked Congress to extend American laws to Oregon, and recommended a military buildup. In late January 1846, disgusted with Polk's bombastic threats, the British Foreign Secretary, the Earl of Aberdeen, threatened war, and then began active preparations to defend Canada. Upon receipt of the British warning, the Americans drew back, since the United States was woefully unprepared for war with Great Britain: there were only 480 men on the northern frontier; even worse was the navy, with only one ship of the line, six frigates, and another twenty ships—the United States had seven steamships, while the British had 146. Thanks partly to the fact that the Royal Navy ruled the waves while the US Navy hardly had the ships to rule a lake meant that hot heads had to cool and diplomacy took over. The Americans scrambled to repair the damage. Neither country wanted war, and negotiations rapidly began, culminating in the 1846 Treaty in Regard to Western Limits Westward of the Rocky Mountains. Yet the wagons trains, and the people inside them, were to determine the outcome: Americans soon outnumbered Canadians.[21]

Latin America

In Latin America, Great Britain and the United States were strong competitors—or rather, the United States wanted American commercial expansion in Latin America, but came up against the commercial might of the British. This seemed wrong, since from the early days of the Republic, American expansion southward was taken for granted—Thomas Jefferson, for example, considered Cuba "the most interesting addition that could ever be made to our system of States."[22] The British, however, did not constitute the only threat to American expansion.

In 1823, John Quincy Adams, the US secretary of state, received the news that the Russians were trying to claim the Pacific Coast down to San Francisco Bay, and he determined to thwart them. At the same time, the newly independent Latin American republics were threatened with invasion by France, who wanted to take over Spanish power in Latin America. George Canning, the British foreign secretary, proposed to the Americans that they should jointly issue a warning to the Spanish and French governments that the United States and Great Britain would not allow this: for the first time, Britain proposed to the United States that they act together as independent powers.[23] Adams was not convinced. His response in Cabinet was that "[i]t would be more candid, as well as more dignified, to avow our principles explicitly to Russia and France, than to come in as a cock boat in the wake of the British man-of-war."[24]

The result of the Cabinet's decision to decline the suggestion of the British and to act alone was the Monroe Doctrine, which stated that any attempt by an outside power to attempt to colonize or to recolonize any part of the Western Hemisphere would be taken by the United States as "the manifestation of an unfriendly disposition toward the United States," and the United States would not allow any such attempt to succeed.[25] This was a bit bombastic, since the United States, with a miniscule navy, could have done nothing about it: only the Royal Navy could have prevented any such attempt. Fortunately for the United States, Britain was no less inclined than the United States to allow any development of significant European interests in the hemisphere.

In South America, the British increasingly controlled an "informal" empire, not an "empire of rule," in which they were not particularly interested.[26] Commercial profit was what was wanted, and with the help of local collaborators, Britain was able to enjoy power without the costs of responsibility. Behind these financial and commercial links always lurked the threat of force, of "gunboat diplomacy" provided by the Royal Navy, or of local coercion. In South America, Britain wielded overwhelming commercial power. As a French agent in Colombia wrote in 1823, "The power of England is without a rival in America; no fleets but hers to be seen; her merchandises are bought almost exclusively; her commercial agents, her clerks and brokers, are everywhere to be met with."[27] Great Britain financed, for example, the Argentinian railways, and was overwhelmingly dominant in Brazil into World War I. It was only by the turn of the century that Germany and the United States challenged Great Britain's dominance.[28]

Americans found this frustrating, some claiming that Americans had the God-given right to extend their economic reach, particularly in Central and South America: some politicians argued that British control contravened the Monroe Doctrine. As James S. Hogg, the governor of Texas, asked rhetorically in 1884,

Why is it that the seat of commerce and finance now in control of and dominating the United States and the whole world is located on the little island of England? Why does not the United States control both the finance and commerce and proclaim herself the mistress of the seas?[29]

Americans, after all, were also a commercial and maritime people, and since mid-century their interests had expanded into Central America and the Far East. But dramatically increasing this commercial expansion appeared an imperative after 1870. The Americans experienced their own industrial revolution, but the American market itself was not big enough to absorb the wheat and preserved meats produced by farmers or the huge increase in manufactures, and there was a real fear that, if these goods could not be sold, there would be depression, with rural and urban unrest and perhaps even uprisings. But wherever the United States turned, it found the British already in possession of markets. This was particularly galling in Latin America, since the United States saw the hemisphere as its own.

In 1895, the growing American desire for predominant influence in their own backyard clashed with an existing British interest, in a now-forgotten part of South America, and the Americans won. By 1895, US strength had increased hugely, as had its confidence in its conduct of foreign affairs. At the same time, Great Britain was feeling increasingly threatened by the European Powers. This combination resulted in a major adjustment in the relationship between the two empires. The locus for the change was some territory disputed between Venezuela and Great Britain. Venezuela called for American help, invoking the Monroe Doctrine, a call that the United States had in fact ignored for a number of years.[30] Secretary of State Richard Olney, however, decided to answer the call. He decided that Britain was the guilty party and Venezuela the innocent. Writing to the secretary of state for foreign affairs, the Marquis of Salisbury, who was also the prime minister, he suggested that the conflict should be decided by arbitration. He also demanded that Britain deal directly with the United States and included a somewhat intemperate paragraph:

> To-day the United States is practically sovereign on this continent, and its fiat is law upon the subjects to which it confines its interposition. Why? It is not because of the pure friendship or good will felt for it. It is not simply by reason of its high character as a civilized state, nor because wisdom and justice and equity are the invariable characteristics of the dealings of the United States. It is because, in addition to all other grounds, its infinite resources combined with its isolated position render it master of the situation and practically invulnerable as against any or all other powers.[31]

Known as the Olney Doctrine, this came close to claiming that might makes right. When it was made public, the Canadians and Latin Americans were outraged: "If Washington won its point with Salisbury, the Chilean minister to Washington observed, 'the United States will have succeeded in establishing a protectorate over all of Latin America.' "[32] Britain responded in its best Foreign Office prose, which outraged President Grover Cleveland, and he went to Congress and made a speech that, if it had been in a traditional diplomatic exchange between nations, would have been understood as a call for war. Canada began military preparations and looked to its defenses.[33]

To the disgust of the prime minister, the British Cabinet decided that it had to agree to arbitration (that, in fact, came to a conclusion that favored the British position).[34] Why did it do so?

- First of all, there were increasing threats from two imperial rivals, the French and Russian empires. There was chaos in the Ottoman Empire, where the Turks were slaughtering thousands of Armenians; the British feared that Russia would take advantage of the chaos to seize Constantinople and the Dardanelles Strait, which would allow Russia to move warships into the Mediterranean, instead of remaining bottled up in the Black Sea.
- Second, the Russians were making alarming progress in building railways southward to the northern border of India; in addition, Russia was trying to supplant the British position in Persia and Afghanistan—a contest termed the "Great Game" in central Asia. In short, India was gravely threatened.
- Third, France meanwhile was thrusting eastward in Africa, trying to cut off the British drive to control a contiguous line of territories from the Cape to Cairo; indeed, they met at the headwaters of the Nile at Fashoda and had a not unfriendly standoff (they dined together). However, the French had to withdraw because British control of the Mediterranean meant that the French troops could not be reinforced. France was also threatening the British position in the Far East, although not as much as was Russia, which was pushing through Siberia and into Manchuria through to Port Arthur. The problem here was the Dual (Franco-Russian) Alliance of 1892/1894, which meant that Britain had to consider their threats as combined.

To cope with growing imperial problems, Britain had, in 1889, adopted a "two-power standard" policy, by which the Royal Navy had to be larger than the next two threatening fleets, which were those of France and Russia.[35] In 1900, the naval threat was significantly increased by the German announcement that it intended to build a High Seas Fleet that could match the strength "of the mightiest naval Power"; this was required, Germany said, because it intended to achieve *Weltmacht*, or world power, a position that required colonies.[36] Germany had already joined the crowd of countries threatening China and the positions of the Powers already ensconced there. Britain now had to worry about three fleets and another imperial rival. A navy is considerably more expensive than an army is, and Britain's finances were increasingly stretched. Great Britain also appeared to have few friends.

How did the United States fit into this? Quite simply, the British Cabinet feared that if the United States was not accommodated in the Venezuelan matter, it would become so anti-British that if Britain went to war against one or more of the European Powers, the United States would join Britain's enemies, and the result would be a British defeat. In the larger scheme of things, Venezuela did not matter. Financial pressure had increased in Britain, not helped by expenditure on the 1899–1902 Boer War, and the Cabinet finally authorized reconfiguring British naval strength to meet what it saw as increasing threats. In 1902, Britain concluded its first-ever peacetime alliance, the Anglo-Japanese Alliance. Japan's responsibility was to patrol the China Waters, enabling Britain to move part of its fleet to the Mediterranean to meet the increased French and Russian threats. A portion of the Mediterranean fleet was moved to join the Channel fleet, in order to protect the home islands and the Low Countries from the increasing threat from Germany.

As for the Western Hemisphere, it was assumed by the Cabinet that the United States and Great Britain would never again go to war—it would be, they felt, akin to a civil war if it happened—and thus the West Indies and the Atlantic Squadrons could be moved, letting Canada take care of its own defense and leaving the Americans in control of the Caribbean. Indeed, the Americans believed that they had, in effect, taken control of their own sphere of influence by driving the British away. They had certainly taken control, but the British saw things differently: because the two countries would not go to war with each other, it was perfectly safe for Great Britain to leave the Americans in charge of protecting British as well as American interests. In short, the British had incorporated the Americans into their defense strategy. Nevertheless, at the end of the century, the British Empire still held the "five strategic keys" that "lock up the world," controlling or patrolling from the great naval bases at:

- Dover (the English Channel);
- Gibraltar (the western entrance to the Mediterranean);
- Alexandria (the eastern Mediterranean and the Suez Canal);
- Cape of Good Hope (the route to the Indian Ocean and the South Pacific); and
- Singapore (the Far East).[37]

The Far East

CHINA

The two empires were more cooperative in the Far East. Britain, of course, opened up China by means of the Opium War of 1842, while the United States opened up Japan by means of the "burning ships" (Japanese) or the "white fleet" (American) in 1856. Lin Yse-hsü, the governor of the Chinese province of Hu-Huang, was a man of integrity and high morals. In October 1838, he was instructed by the emperor to stamp out opium addiction in China. After dealing with many of the Chinese dealers by public strangling, he turned to the foreign smugglers of opium. The British were by far the most important, but every American trading house at Canton, the only port open to foreigners, also traded in opium. The biggest US trader, Russell & Company, which was also the third largest dealer in the Indian opium trade, was headed by Warren Delano, the grandfather of President Franklin Delano Roosevelt.[38] After a group of British merchants tried to prevent the strangling of a Chinese smuggler, Lin put all two hundred British merchants under house arrest in their factories, which contained their homes as well as their warehouses. Blockading the factories with thousands of soldiers, he refused to let any food supplies pass through the lines until the merchants had agreed to hand over all of the opium in their warehouses and on their ships. The British superintendent, after six weeks without new supplies of food, promised the opium merchants that the British government would compensate them for their loss of £2.6 million and persuaded them to turn the opium over to Lin. Chinese soldiers removed it from the factories, and Chinese sailors in war junks removed it from the ships and poured it into the sea. The British traders then left Canton.

Lord Palmerston, the foreign secretary, was angry at the restrictions on trade. But he and the British government had a more important reason for intervening. The millions earned from smuggling opium into China were used to buy tea to sell at home. The duty on tea leveled by the British government had, since the late 1820s, raised £3 million a year, equal to half the yearly cost of the Royal Navy. At the beginning of June 1840, a large British expeditionary force, which included steam-powered gunboats and thousands of marines, arrived in China. Lin sent out eighty war junks, but many of them were blown out of the water. The raiders imposed a blockade and then attacked and took control of strategically important sites along the China coast.[39] Meanwhile, the Americans, who had remained neutral, stayed at Canton and cleaned up: they carried the tea for British traders through the ineffectual Chinese blockade and loaded it onto British ships—all at stiff rates, about which the British could do nothing but complain. As one Briton said, "While we hold the horns, they milk the cow."[40]

The result of the First Opium War was the August 1842 Treaty of Nanking, the first of the "Unequal Treaties" imposed on the Chinese by the British. China ceded Hong Kong, an island opposite the approaches to Canton, in perpetuity; opened up five Chinese port cities to trade and foreign residence; lowered all tariffs; and paid a large indemnity to compensate the merchants for their losses and to pay for the war. The treaty was supplemented in 1843 with an agreement giving Britain Most Favored Nation status. In 1844, by the Treaty of Wanghia, the Americans gained the same, and thereafter, through what became known as "hitchhiking imperialism" or "jackal diplomacy," the United States demanded for themselves whatever the British got.[41] According to one British official, "the Americans hide behind our guns, and when the shooting has stopped, they run forward to get as much as they can." Or as one Chinese official put it, "the English barbarians' craftiness is manifold, their proud tyranny is uncontrollable. Americans do nothing but follow in their direction."[42]

The British saw the Americans as fellow believers in what was termed the "open door," that there should be equality of access to all parts of China: the strongest economic power always wants free trade, because they can wipe out the competition. For this reason, the other Powers refused to agree. Why should they open their territories to British traders and watch the decline of their own? The Americans, however, confident in their commercial prowess, also called for free trade, and the British accepted—to the extent that any business interest welcomes strong competition—rather than discouraged American entry into the China market. In any case, the Americans had to work against entrenched British interests, as the latter remained by far the dominant economic interest in China during the nineteenth century, while the United States played a minor role. During this entire period and into the twentieth century, the Americans benefited from the British willingness to allow them full access to Hong Kong for their ships, both commercial and military, and for their traders: all of the American trading houses had their headquarters on the island. Yet for the following half-century, they disagreed over Hong Kong. President Wilson's call for the self-determination of peoples became for liberal Americans an important principle, and Hong Kong was repeatedly the focus of the attention of President Franklin Roosevelt. In 1945, he nudged the British colonial secretary, Oliver Stanley, remarking that "I do not want to be unkind or rude to the British, but in 1841 [*sic*], when you acquired Hong Kong, you did not acquire it by purchase." Stanley snapped back, "Let me see, Mr President, that was about the time of the Mexican War, wasn't it?" by means of which the United States had acquired a good chunk of the Southwest.[43] History does not record Roosevelt's response.

JAPAN

The British had opened up China to foreign trade; the Americans opened up Japan. In 1853, the American Commodore Matthew Perry began the forced opening up of the country by steaming defiantly into Edo (later Tokyo) Bay with a fleet of four very large ships, two of them black-hulled coal-burning steamships—the "burning ships" to the panic-stricken Japanese—that carried sixty-one guns and a crew of nearly a thousand men. Perry carried a letter from President Millard Fillmore to the Japanese, which asked that Japan open its borders to trade with the Americans; the United States also needed to use Japan as a coaling station on the way to China. Perry left, but warned that he would return. The Japanese fortified the harbor, but this failed to prevent the arrival of the Americans the following year with a considerably larger fleet.

Perry had been instructed to "do everything to impress" the Japanese "with a just sense of the power and greatness" of the United States. Consequently, he brought with him huge quantities of champagne and vintage Kentucky bourbon "to grease the wheels of diplomacy" and a pair of Colt six-shooters and a scale model train to display US technological advancement. He employed Chinese coolies and African Americans to show the superiority of white over color, and he used uniforms and pageants as manifestations of American cultural supremacy.[44] It is probable that American power rather than American culture convinced the Japanese to deal with the Americans. This was not an easy decision for the Japanese: aware of the West's technological advances, they disagreed over whether to resist or receive, the latter providing the chance to learn about the threat. The Japanese were alarmed by the violence produced by foreigners in China, led by the British, and they decided to deal with the United States rather than with Great Britain. They also decided to make limited concessions rather than have worse forced on them.

They signed the Convention of Kanagawa in March 1854, which opened up the two small and isolated ports of Shimoda and Hakodate to trade, and agreed to provide refuge for the crews of wrecked American ships, rather than, as was usual, hunting them down and killing them. The American consul general, Townsend Harris, arrived in 1856 and was soon relegated to one of these ports by the Japanese government and, in the first instance, forced to share a run-down temple with rats, bats, and spiders.[45] They did, however, assign him a Japanese mistress.

During the next several years, Japan was increasingly forced to open its doors to foreign trade, a right that had been restricted to a small handful of Dutch traders on one island in Nagasaki harbor. After two years' negotiations, the Japanese in 1858 signed a new treaty with the Americans, the Treaty of Kanagawa, which increased trading privileges, but they delayed ratification. Then one morning Harris rushed to warn Japanese officials that a British fleet of forty ships was about to enter the bay, followed by those of France, and that if the Japanese did not ratify the treaty with the United States before the British arrived, the British would insist on more extensive privileges. Furthermore, it was more honorable and seemly to sign a treaty to which they had agreed rather than have one imposed on them. The Japanese signed, and the enraged British were forced to accept what the Americans had agreed to, with the addition of a clause of their own covering woollens.[46] There was sometimes a certain amount of tension thereafter between the American and British diplomatic representatives. The British representative got his own back by his elevation to the status of ambassador, leaving the mere American minister far down the pecking order in a country that used ritual and position as a weapon.[47]

This conflict over position in Japan swayed back and forth for several years. Ironically, by the end of the decade, the United States was, as in China, the junior partner to the British, with whom the Japanese preferred to deal— for one thing, the Japanese preferred British manufactures to American commodities. And of course, there was greater British power much closer: the Royal Navy had only to steam from China, while ships—or even just one ship—from the very small United States Navy only called in every three to four months. It was more dangerous to irritate the British.

THE PHILIPPINES

There was one colony in the Far East where the United States reigned supreme, and this was the Philippine Islands, collected, along with Puerto Rico and Cuba, as a result of Spain's defeat in the 1898 Spanish-American War.

The British positively encouraged the acquisition of the Philippines. Indeed, the full title of Kipling's poem was "The White Man's Burden: The United States and the Philippine Islands." Why might this be? A short answer was that the British Empire was increasingly under threat from Russia, France, and Germany, and the British feared that if the Americans did not take the Philippines, the Germans would. Optimists among the British political elites, as well as journalists and commentators, believed that if the Americans had their own empire, they would stop criticizing the British, and understand that the two countries had many of the same ideals and interests and should work together—they were "our American Cousins," after all, according to one writer.[48] Even Sherlock Holmes got into the act:

> It is always a joy to me to meet an American ... for I am one of those who believe that the folly of a monarch and the blundering of a Minister in fargone years will not prevent our children from being some day citizens of the same world-wide country under a flag that shall be a quartering of the Union Jack with the Stars and Stripes.[49]

This was delirium rather than destiny, a dream rather than a possibility.

When the United States was in Manila Bay preparing to invade the Philippines, the German fleet was also there, ready indeed to claim the islands if the Americans did not want them. The Americans had already decided that they did want them, along with Hawaii and Guam; furthermore, they had already mapped a number of Pacific islands and atolls. The Americans were trying to build a commercial empire exactly as the British had done in the eighteenth and nineteenth centuries—although they did not think of it that way—and they needed the Philippines to protect their trading routes to China and Japan, as well as to provide supplies. A less obvious reason to grab the islands was the intention of the Navy Department to weaken Spain by depriving it of revenues from them: the squadron was first to destroy Spanish ships, then to capture Manila, and thereafter to blockade all of the principal ports.[50]

The US Asiatic Squadron under Commodore George Dewey had been concentrated in British-held Hong Kong Harbor since the receipt of a cable dated February 25, which instructed Dewey to prepare for an attack on Manila. The British also allowed Dewey to maintain communications with Washington through the Hong Kong cable, the only trans-Pacific link. The order to attack Manila was finally approved by the president on April 24, and the squadron left Hong Kong for Manila Bay at the end of the month. In Manila Bay, the American and German admirals came into conflict. To the anger of the Americans, the Germans were provocative, cutting in front of

US ships, taking soundings of the harbor, landing supplies for the besieged Spanish, and refusing to salute the American flag, as required by naval courtesy. The Americans called the German admiral's bluff, threatening a fight if his aggressive activities continued, and the Germans backed down.[51]

The task for Dewey was to be considerably easier because of the weakness of the Spanish fleet, and this was partly because of further British aid. Late in June, a Spanish squadron left for the Philippines by way of Suez. In Alexandra, Rear Admiral Manuel de la Cámara sought permission to take on coal, water, and other supplies, but Egypt was a British protectorate and the Egyptians were induced to refuse permission; a week later, the fleet returned to Spain.[52] As a consequence, the Spanish fleet in Manila Bay was so weak that its commander, "anticipating destruction, anchored his ships in shallow water to minimise the loss of life. In a seven-hour bombardment of the sitting ducks, Dewey destroyed Spanish naval power in the Pacific."[53]

In sharp contrast to the threatening activity of the Germans, the British appeared to support the Americans. When the Americans began to bombard Manila to soften it up before landing, the British commander moved two ships nearby to observe the effects of the bombardment. In doing so, he appeared to place them deliberately between the American and German ships, thereby saving the Americans from a stab in the back (although it is highly unlikely that the Germans would have fired on the Americans in any case). Support for this myth came from the fact that only the British fired a twenty-one-gun salute when the American flag rose over the city.[54] Furthermore, the American fleet then refueled in Hong Kong, and the American president first learned of the victory by means of the British-owned trans-Pacific cable. In short, to keep the Germans out, and to grow a powerful ally, the British encouraged the United States to assume the "responsibility" of an imperial power and turn the Philippines into an American colony, which it remained until the end of World War II. At that point, the Philippines became part of the American informal empire in which, in the classic manner, the Philippines retained nominal independence, but local collaborators enabled the Americans to enjoy great political and economic influence without the costs of political responsibility. Usefully, the Philippines sit astride the route from the Indian Ocean to the South China Sea, just north of Britain's Malay possessions and southeast of Hong Kong.

The main point here is that, unlike in North America, the Far East saw Anglo-American cooperation rather than conflict. Great Britain aided the American conquest of the Philippines in a number of ways, as the United States supported the British during the Boer War of 1899–1902, while the

European Powers did not. The major threat to both was Germany. Mutual Anglo-American support helped to limit the tearing apart of China by the Russians and Germans (France was gobbling up Indo-China) and, for a while, the expansion of the Japanese Empire. They all challenged the interests of the two empires, both of which feared the closing-off of markets.

The Near and Middle East

From the nineteenth century until a few years after the end of World War II, Great Britain was the dominant Power in the Middle East, a position sometimes challenged by France, but maintained by the power of the Royal Navy, the Indian Army, and British financial power. The Americans accepted the position as a fact of international life, and increasingly benefited by it, as during the Spanish-American War. Yet after World War I, the need for oil began to drive them apart, a situation that ended with the Suez Crisis of 1956, by which the United States essentially ensured the final destruction of the British Empire.

SUEZ CANAL

A central component of British power in the region, as well as in other areas of the world, was for nearly a century their control of the Suez Canal. Built in 1869 by the French, within a decade, the British determined to control the Canal, the gateway to India, the Far East, and the Antipodes. When, in November 1875, the opportunity arose to secure a substantial block of shares in the Canal, Prime Minister Benjamin Disraeli acted quickly. For political reasons, he could not ask Parliament for the money, since it would have been blocked; he could not ask the Bank of England, because providing that amount would have deranged the markets. So he turned to the Rothschilds, then the most important merchant or investment bank in the world. The story, as told by Disraeli's principal private secretary, Montagu Corry, goes like this:

> Disraeli had arranged with him [the Secretary] that he should be in attendance ... just outside the Cabinet room and, when his chief put out his head and said "Yes," should take immediate action. On this signal being given, he went off to New Court and told Rothschild in confidence that the Prime Minister wanted £4,000,000 "tomorrow"; Rothschild ... picked up a muscatel grape, ate it, threw out the

skin, and said deliberately, "What is your security?" "The British Government." "You shall have it."[55]

This was hardly a small sum: it was equivalent to more than 8 percent of the entire UK budget.

In 1882, there was an Egyptian nationalist revolt against their overlord, the Turkish Khedive—as Egypt was part of the Ottoman Empire. There were riots in Alexandria between Europeans fearing massacre and Egyptians fearing occupation; the revolt raised fears in Britain for the security of the Canal. The British fleet shelled Alexandria, and troops landed, securing the Canal; the British then fought their way to Cairo and took control. Army and Naval Intelligence were eager to maintain their grip: they were becoming more and more convinced that the security of imperial routes required direct control of the Canal, and the addition of a naval base at Alexandria, which, when added to those at Cyprus and Malta, would considerably strengthen Britain's regional position. Economic benefits were also foreseen: Egyptian long-staple cotton for Lancashire mills, markets for British exports, and opportunities for British investments. There was also the familiar British conviction that the Egyptians were unable to run their country effectively, and thus it would be a kindness to remain and do it for them. Therefore, British advisors were placed in all government departments, and British forces were stationed in the country.[56] At the outbreak of World War I, Turkey allied with Germany; military reinforcements were sent to Egypt, and in December 1914, the British declared it a protectorate. They were to control the Canal until 1956.

PERSIA AND MESOPOTAMIA

The second important step for Great Britain in the Near and Middle East concerned Persia, or later Iran. At the outset, its importance arose because it was a vital factor in the nineteenth-century Great Game over central Asia between the Russian and British empires, with India the prize, but there was soon a second factor, and that was oil. In 1907, the two Powers divided Persia into spheres of influence, with the southwest of the country neutral territory between them. The British were soon to regret this, because an important oil field was discovered there in 1908 by an Englishman, the oil from which Britain badly needed for the Royal Navy. In fact, the Navy would, in 1913, decide to equip all of its ships to be powered by oil rather than coal.[57] The British moved, and by 1914 the area containing the oil fields, where the Persian writ did not run, was essentially a British protectorate. As a consequence, the Anglo-Persian Oil

Company (later the Anglo-Iranian Oil Company, and later still, British Petroleum), the largest shareholder of which was the British government, controlled the oil.

Next came Mesopotamia. On December 9, 1917, British troops led by General Sir Edmund Allenby, a soldier of great vigor and imagination, captured Jerusalem. At noon on December 11, the general, the thirty-fourth conqueror of Jerusalem, together with his officers and some foreign diplomats and military attachés, dismounted at the Jaffa Gate. They entered the city on foot, out of respect for the status of Jerusalem as the Holy City of Christians, Jews, and Muslims. Allenby had been told to do so by London, who wanted everyone to notice that whereas the German kaiser had entered the city on horseback, Allenby, like Jesus, had done so on foot. This was part of the campaign to defeat the Ottoman Empire, and Britain would receive Palestine, together with Mesopotamia, as part of the spoils during the Versailles Peace Conference. But what was Britain doing in that part of the world? The answer, again, was oil.

In early October 1914, an expedition was sent to secure the head of the Persian Gulf, and by the end of November the British occupied the port of Basra. For the next three years, the British fought to conquer Mesopotamia, and by the end of October 1917, the Turks were forced to surrender. During the war, the British government, and especially Prime Minister David Lloyd George, were determined to extend the empire to the Middle East; thus they were desperate that Britain and its allies essentially win the war before the United States actually sent many troops over to Europe. The American president, Woodrow Wilson, had insisted that one outcome of the war would be self-determination for all peoples—that self-evidently included those in colonies (for the Americans, the Philippines were self-evidently not a colony, since they were bestowing the benefits of religion and democracy on a backward people). The British needed the Americans as allies, and could not be seen to be defying Wilson's moral crusade. Lloyd George's plan was to present the United States with a fait accompli. If the Americans could claim to have won the war for the Europeans, Great Britain would find it difficult to win the argument to maintain their empire without making harsh sacrifices in their relationship with the United States. When the Americans actually arrived on the battlefield, they did make a difference, but not enough to claim that by their arrival they had won the war.[58] The British withstood American pressure, and received Mesopotamia, now Iraq, and Palestine and Trans-Jordan, but under the guise of their being League of Nation mandates. This fooled very few.

After the end of World War I, increasingly anxious about oil supplies, American oil companies also moved into the Middle East and by 1940 had acquired concessions in Iraq and Kuwait, and particularly in Saudi Arabia, with the establishment of the Arabian-American Oil Company (ARAMCO) in 1938, when American oilmen hit a gusher. Private enterprise made the running, but it had the support of the US government, which saw Saudi Arabia as its own sphere of influence. World War II was to demonstrate just how essential dependable supplies had become: between December 1941 and August 1945, the Allies used seven billion barrels of crude petroleum.[59] Competition between the United States and Great Britain in Saudi Arabia deepened, and in 1944 the two leaders sought to calm the rising tensions with mutual assurances about each other's stake in Middle Eastern oil: Roosevelt insisted that the United States was not casting "sheep's eyes" toward British holdings in Iran; Churchill responded that Britain would not "horn in" on US interests in Saudi Arabia.[60] The Anglo-American Petroleum Agreement of 1944 eased only very temporarily the fierce competition for oil concessions in Iran. As for Saudi Arabia, by the end of the war the United States had consolidated its control of Saudi oil.

World War I

World War I was a partial turning point. In spite of the British urging that American interests were also at stake, the United States refused to join the war until it was torpedoed into it. After all, where was the danger? The United States had moats to the east and west and extremely weak countries to the north and south. During the period of their neutrality, Americans railed against the British for the use of their power against neutral countries. In this context, the power resided in the Royal Navy and the overwhelming control of the transoceanic cables. As with the War of 1812, the Royal Navy stopped American merchant ships and hauled them into port, when their cargoes might be confiscated (and paid for), or, at the very least, held up. The United States could not object to the confiscation of armaments for Germany and their allies, since traditionally neutrals were not free to carry them to belligerents. But they did object, for example, to foodstuffs being deemed contraband.[61] A real problem was US trade with other neutrals: Would the goods continue on to the Central Powers? And second, there was the British blacklist of American firms that the British believed were trading with the enemy, especially in Latin America.[62]

However, once the United States had joined the war, it equaled and even surpassed British depredations. The United States also increased its industrial war-making capacity, a sector whose expansion had, in fact, been substantially financed by Britain from 1915 to 1917.[63] Otherwise, the United States was expected to contribute an endless supply of Iowa farm boys. But crucially, as noted earlier, Britain lost its position to the United States as supreme financial power, which had endless repercussions.

On the other hand, Britain retained its military superiority in the interwar period. True, the United States forced Britain to choose between Japan and the United States, and thus Britain did not renew the Anglo-Japanese Alliance in 1922, an alliance that had served the British well.[64] Yet the United States Navy did not succeed in supplanting the Royal Navy as the greatest in the world, in spite of support by many in the US government and public. This would unfortunately have required that money be spent on the armed forces, as well as a much deeper involvement in international affairs, a path that few Americans wished to follow. As for the British, to the dismay of the Royal Navy, the alarming postwar financial position convinced the Cabinet to accept a one-power naval standard in battleships and cruisers—that is, British and American naval parity—thereby overturning the policy of decades.[65] At the Washington Conference of 1921–1922, this was accepted for capital ships, but not for cruisers and destroyers, which led to intense competition and tension between the two navies. The result was that the following decade saw the worst level of Anglo-American hostility in the twentieth century. The US Congress, however, repeatedly refused to appropriate the funds to out-build the British, and the Royal Navy retained its status until World War II.[66] As for the two armies, the United States Army numbered 852,000 in 1919, but was down to 137,000 by 1925, where it remained until 1935; the numbers then rose to 185,000 by 1938.[67] The British Army in 1920 numbered 550,000, but was expected to fall to 280,000 during the financial year; it was down to roughly 220,000 by 1938.[68] The numbers then began to grow, and, until mid-1943, the British had more men in the field than did the Americans.

As the atmosphere darkened in the 1930s, the British had a growing fear that they might have to fight a three-front war: against Germany on the Continent, against Italy in the Mediterranean, and against Japan in the Far East, as, in fact, they did. The United States was not sure just what, if any, foreign policy it wished to maintain, given the Depression, but Britain did not have that luxury. They tried to convince the Americans that US interests in the Far East were also gravely threatened by Japan, but they were difficult to convince.[69] Britain knew that it needed American aid, particularly financial but also military, and fortunately, the Japanese came to their aid by bombing the United States into the war.

Conclusion

From 1814 to 1940, the two empires were intertwined, but the emotional element changed during this period. There was never a serious chance that they would again go to war: after all, neither could actually defeat the other, although during the nineteenth century, Great Britain could inflict a huge amount of damage on the United States, while the United States could only damage Canada—important, but not life threatening. At the turn of the century, the United States was a potential Great Power, but not an actual one: it was an extremely potent economic power, and it was *primus* in the Western Hemisphere, where the competition was weak, but it had little military power to project and few means with which to project what it had. In contrast, the British empire was a global power of the first magnitude. World War I began to change both positions, although this was not necessarily very evident during the interwar period; it was only World War II that cemented the change in the two positions.

There are two unusual points to be made about this strategic rivalry. First of all, from the late nineteenth century on, Great Britain repeatedly tried to convince the United States to act as a world power, which meant taking on the necessary responsibilities, not just enjoying the fruits of others' work (such as the American piggy-back diplomacy in China: whatever concessions Britain won, the United States insisted should be granted to it as well). Great Britain's attempts to get the United States to join World War I are well known; the United States' desire to benefit economically from Europe during the 1920s while refusing to become involved in European power struggles is also well known; but British attempts to make the Americans understand that their interests were also threatened in the Far East, and thus they should prepare, are perhaps less familiar. Of course, the British expected to benefit as well: countries are seldom altruistic. But the fact that they took it for granted that both countries shared the same interests demonstrates that they feared that if one went down, both would be in dire straits, as would have indeed been the case. This segues nicely into the second point: this is the only case in known history in which one Great Power, or empire, handed on the torch of supremacy to another without a battle between them having been fought.

CHAPTER 12

A Whale against an Elephant
Britain and Germany
Williamson Murray

The Approach of War (1904–1914)

If anyone in Britain or Germany in a leadership position from 1914 through 1945 had actually read, much less grasped, Sun Tzu's admonition to understand "the other," there is not much evidence of such an effort in the actual decision-making processes that those two nations and their leaders made throughout this period.[1] Given the close ties between the two nations—economic, cultural, and intellectual—this appears to be an extraordinary state of affairs. Yet it may represent an understatement. That understanding "the other" represented such a block to developing effective strategic approaches in the Anglo-German competition suggests how difficult it has always been to navigate the shoals of grand strategy.

On June 28, 1914, Serbian student Gravrilo Princip assassinated the Archduke Franz Ferdinand, the heir to the Austro-Hungarian throne, in Sarajevo. One might have thought that a British government, which had found itself engaged in a naval and economic competition over the past several decades with the Germans, might have concerned itself with the possibility of a major European war.[2] Instead, as the momentum for war gathered on the Continent over July 1914, the British cabinet focused on the troubles in Ireland. Not until events on the Continent had reached the tipping point did Winston Churchill, First Sea Lord of the Admiralty, note the effects of the crisis on his colleagues. On July 24, 1914, as the cabinet meeting on

Ireland was about to break, Sir Edward Grey read out the ultimatum the Austrians had presented to the Serbs:

> As the reading proceeded it seemed absolutely impossible that any State in the world could accept it, or that any acceptance, however abject, would satisfy the aggressor. The parishes of Fermanasgh and Tyrone faded back into the mists and squalls of Ireland, and a strange light began immediately, but by perceptible gradations, to fall and grow upon the map of Europe.[3]

Conventional wisdom has it that World War I was largely an accident that never needed to happen, or that Britain had no legitimate strategic interest in involving itself in what many Britons believed should have remained a Continental squabble.[4] Both views are nonsensical because they ignore the nature of the German polity and the threat its values and culture represented not only to peace, but also to the security of the Second Reich's neighbors.[5] Nearly all of the German military and political leaders were only too willing to consider war a reasonable solution to their nation's strategic and political problems; so when the crisis came in July 1914, they delightedly leaped into the dark, launching a massive invasion of Belgium and northern France.

The rivalry between Britain and Germany had grown steadily in the aftermath of the Franco-Prussian War (July 19, 1870–May 10, 1871) that had created a unified German state and a kaiser.[6] And yet, for the forty years after Otto Bismarck's triumph, the intertwining of economic and financial interests seemed strong enough to prevent a clash of arms between the two powers. However, after his accession to the throne, Kaiser Wilhelm II, in 1888, removed the steadying hand of the Second Reich's founder and great statesman. Bismarck's successors never managed to understand the reality the Iron Chancellor had grasped in the aftermath of the "War-in-Sight" crisis of 1875.[7] Simply put, Bismarck recognized that Germany, at the heart of Europe, surrounded on three sides by Great Powers, would find itself dangerously exposed to the effects of any major war among the European powers. Above all, the new Germany must put strategy and policy in control of a cautious and careful military strategy. Such an approach demanded that the Reich follow Clausewitz's dictum that "war should never be thought of as *something autonomous* but always as an *instrument of policy*...."[8]

However, that was not the case in Wilhelm II's Reich. The German military no longer read Clausewitz.[9] Instead, they turned the Prussian thinker on his head. Where Clausewitz argued that political goals and aims should drive military strategy in balance with the means at hand, the German military argued that in the modern era, "military necessity" should now drive policy as well as strategy.[10] Therein lay the disastrous strategic choices the Germans made in designing their campaign plan, if war were to break out in Europe. In the late nineteenth century, the French had heavily fortified the Franco-German frontier, particularly the Belfort Gap. In response, the chief of the German general staff, Graf Alfred von Schlieffen, redesigned the Reich's war plans to outflank those defenses by invading Belgium and Luxembourg. On the outbreak of any major European conflict, Germany would violate a nation whose neutrality the Prussian monarchy had originally guaranteed.[11]

Schlieffen dismissed the possibility that the British, who had also guaranteed Belgium's neutrality, might intervene as an irrelevancy.[12] In his calculations, Britain's small army did not represent a significant force in a future Franco-German War. Since in the event of war Schlieffen desired to overwhelm the French before France's Russian allies could retaliate in the east, "military necessity" overrode concerns about strategic consequences, short term as well as long, from a violation of Belgian neutrality. Thus, in July 1914 in response to Russian mobilization over troubles in the Balkans, the Germans launched a massive invasion of Belgium and France without provocation. The larger problem was the fact that Germany had no strategic framework within which its senior political and military leaders could debate operational choices such as the Schlieffen Plan.[13]

There were alternatives. Had the Germans remained on the defensive in the west but concentrated their offensive strength against the Russians, it is likely that the British would have stood aside, at least in its first months of the conflict. At the height of the diplomatic crisis, the kaiser suggested to Moltke the Younger, now chief of the General Staff, that Germany move against the Russians rather than the French. For Moltke, "military necessity" demanded that the German army move as quickly as possible into Belgium before the Russians could mobilize.[14] The invasion of Belgium went forward. As to Schlieffen's assumption that it was irrelevant whether the British arrived to fight on the Continent, the British army was to play an important role in the initial fighting. Without the arrival of a British Expeditionary Force (BEF) on the left wing of the French armies, the Germans would probably have won the war in the west and then pivoted east to crush the Russians.[15]

The most important factor in Britain's increasing involvement in Continental affairs had been the massive increase in the *Kriegsmarine* in the decade before the war. In terms of Germany's geographic position, no strategic move could have made less sense than building a large fleet that could threaten the Royal Navy's control of the world's oceans. Yet, that is precisely what the Germans had proceeded to do, beginning in 1900. Despite German claims that the Reich was building a High Seas Fleet, the range of the *Kriegsmarine*'s battleships could barely reach beyond the North Sea. There was only one potential opponent, Britain's Royal Navy. In reality, the Germans continued their naval buildup through to the outbreak of the war in the belief that the British would be deterred from an anti-German foreign policy. Not surprisingly, they were wrong.

Winston Churchill characterized debates in the British government about matching the German threat in the following terms: "The Admiralty had demanded six ships; the economists offered four; and we finally compromised on eight."[16] What made the German naval challenge particularly egregious was the fact that, just in geographical terms, the British Isles would block the *Kriegsmarine*'s access to the world's ocean in any conflict. The Royal Navy could easily block the English Channel, while Scotland, the Orkneys, and the Shetlands provided the naval bases to block the North Sea. It was the unheeding buildup of the German navy that spurred the British to settle their differences with the French in 1904 by forming the *Entente Cordiale*, and three years later to sign a similar agreement with the Russians. These agreements did not represent an alliance, but rather a willingness of the powers to settle their major points of disagreement. Yet in terms of a German threat, as late as August 1908, Churchill declaimed, "I think it is greatly to be deprecated that persons should try to spread the belief that war between Great Britain and Germany is inevitable. It is all nonsense."[17]

Nevertheless, in the last days of July, the British cabinet remained divided about the wisdom of intervening in a European conflict, in spite of the implications of the Entente Cordiale—an agreement that came closer to an alliance in 1912 when the British moved their major fleet units out of the Mediterranean to the North Sea, with the French moving their major fleet units from the Atlantic Coast to the Mediterranean.[18] Nevertheless, as war loomed in late July 1914, nearly two-thirds of the cabinet opposed Britain's intervention—a division that reflected the deeply fractured nature of the Liberal Party.[19] As late as August 1, the British foreign secretary, Sir Edward Grey, warned the French ambassador that should France find herself drawn into a war with Germany because of her alliance with Russia, it would be "unreasonable to say that, because France had an obligation under an alliance of which we did not even know the terms, therefore we were bound, equally with her by the obligation of that alliance, to be involved in war."[20]

But the German invasions, first of Luxembourg and then of Belgium, settled the matter.[21] To rub salt in the wound occasioned by the invasion of Belgium, the German chancellor, Theobald von Bethmann Hollweg, told the British ambassador that the 1839 Treaty of London guaranteeing Belgium's neutrality was nothing more than "a scrap of paper." The Kaiser joined with Bethmann-Hollweg in blaming the war entirely on the British, who had failed to keep their Allies in check.[22] Britain was now in the war. Had the Schlieffen Plan worked, this would not have mattered, but because the plan failed, Britain's participation with its industrial and financial resources, its access to the global economy, and the blockade that the Royal Navy was able to impose on the Reich would matter a great deal.

The Great War (1914–1918)

As if its performance during the prewar period leading up to the outbreak of war had not been sufficient to persuade the world that the Reich was a rogue power, the Germans inflicted a series of atrocities to crush the possibility of guerrilla resistance to their military operation and occupation as they advanced through Belgium and northern France. In slightly more than a month, they shot over 6,000 *French and Belgian civilians* as hostages for the supposed attacks of *franc tireurs* (supposed guerrillas) on German troops.[23] In nearly every case, these incidents involved either German friendly fire incidents or the continued resistance of French and Belgian troops after the German advance had bypassed them. By the standards set by the *Wehrmacht* in World War II, these actions represented an insignificant total.[24] But for a Europe that still possessed standards, such actions represented an appalling level of barbarism.[25]

WAR ERUPTS (1914)

With its declaration of war on Germany, the British cabinet agreed to dispatch four of the six infantry divisions then present in the United Kingdom to the Continent on August 5. It kept the other two divisions at home to resist a possible German invasion. In a series of prewar staff talks, the French and the British had already accomplished the planning and coordination for such a move.[26] As a result, the BEF would play a crucial role in three of the major battles in France in 1914. By being at Mons on the left flank of the French Fifth Army in late August, the BEF prevented General Alexander von Kluck's First Army from outflanking the French. Thereafter, Sir John French, the BEF's commander, seemed wholly committed to running away from the Germans. As a result, the BEF, when presented with an opportunity at the Battle of the Marne to break apart the tenuous connection holding the German First and Second Armies together, the French and the BEF failed to act with dispatch.[27] Nevertheless, by their mere presence between the German armies, the British forced the Germans to break off the Battle of the Marne. Then the BEF, though not its commander, redeemed itself in the ferocious battles in Flanders in October and November 1914 that helped the French and Belgians deny the Germans from seizing the Channel ports.

By the end of the fighting in Flanders in 1914, little remained of Britain's professional army.[28] Individual soldiers and junior officers had performed in outstanding fashion, but the BEF's leadership at the higher ranks had ranged from indifferent to bad. In fact, British generals had proven no more incompetent than those of other armies, all of whom had proven equally inept. The loss of nearly one million soldiers *killed in action* in the first five months of the war was the direct result of gross incompetence on the part of the senior military leaders in all the nations.[29]

Only the French commander-in-chief, General Josef Joffre, displayed a modicum of competence in his conduct of the Battle of the Marne, but that occurred after he had entirely misread the German drive through Belgium and had launched French armies eastward into Alsace and the Ardennes in a series of disastrous attacks. The criticisms that historians have leveled about the BEF's poor generalship miss the fact that poor generalship marked military leadership in all of the nations throughout the four murderous years that followed.[30] Admittedly, a larger systemic problem confronted all the armies in World War I: *their tactics and doctrinal frameworks were completely inadequate for the successful conduct of larger operations in the conflict* in which they found themselves involved.[31] To add to their problems, not only did they confront the issues of adapting their tactics and doctrine to an unexpected environment, but their opponents were adapting at the same time.[32] That said, the leadership of the opposing British and German armies hardly deserves praise for the conduct of the war on any level.

The numbing casualties that all the major powers had suffered in the opening campaigns put to rest any ideas of the possibility of a compromise peace. In November 1914, General Erich von Falkenhayn, von Moltke's replacement, suggested to Chancellor Bethmann Hollweg that the war was no longer winnable and that Germany should seek a compromise peace with the Russians. The chancellor turned the general down cold: Germany would seek victory and political aims that were already at megalomaniacal levels—among other goals, he suggested the annexation of Belgium, much of northern France, and unspecified territories in the east that would make an invasion of eastern Germany impossible.

STRATEGIC STALEMATE (1915)

At least in 1915, the chief of the general staff sought relatively limited military aims, clearly in the hope of exhausting Germany's opponents.[33]

Nevertheless, because of "military necessity," the Germans unleashed gas warfare on the Western Front in April 1915.[34] Similarly, that month the *Kriegsmarine* launched unrestricted submarine warfare as a counter-blockade of the British Isles. The Germans even went to the extent of announcing in New York papers, including the *New York Times*, that they intended to sink any ships that entered the waters off the British Isles on the same day that announcements appeared that the passenger liner *Lusitania* was about to sail. The dubious success that followed with the sinking of the Cunard liner *Lusitania* off the Irish coast on May 7, 1915, with a considerable loss of American lives (128 out of the 1,198 drowned) almost brought the United States into the war, while it also provided the British with the justification to tighten the blockade. Because of American pressure, the Germans halted unrestricted submarine warfare for a time.

On the British side, matters did not go much better. Field Marshal Lord Herbert Kitchener, appointed to head the War Office on the outbreak of war, believed the conflict would be long and drawn out. While he believed that Britain needed to commit a large army to the Continent, the fashion with which he went about establishing that army minimized much of its potential. He ignored the Territorial Army and focused mobilization on the creation of new formations. The army's High Command had not helped matters by shipping nearly all its staff officers over to France with the BEF in August 1914. Thus, it fell to superannuated and retired officers to train the mass of volunteers who had joined in the war's first months—the new model army to be referred to as the Kitchener armies after Kitchener, now the secretary of war in the cabinet. Meanwhile, the French army had to bear the burden of the fighting on the Western Front in 1915 until the British finally had mobilized sufficient forces to launch a major offensive in 1916.[35]

Not surprisingly, Winston Churchill apprehended the larger strategic issues. Late in December 1914, he sent the following message to the prime minister, Herbert Asquith:

> I think it quite possible that neither side will have the strength to penetrate the other's lines in the Western theatre. Belgium particularly, which it is vital for Germany to hold as a peace counter, has no doubt been made into a mere succession of fortified lines. I think it probable that the Germans [will] hold back several large mobile reserves of their best troops. Without attempting to take a final view, my impression is that the position of both armies is not likely to undergo any decisive change—although no doubt several hundred thousand men will be spent to satisfy the military mind on the point. . . .[36]

Churchill aimed to avoid the impasse he predicted in two ways. First, he set in motion the development of the tank by using the Admiralty's resources and technical manpower.[37] The other path led to the Dardanelles and the ill-fated assault on Gallipoli. That campaign represented an effort to attack what Churchill would call Axis's "soft underbelly" in the next war. Whatever the strategic merits of the Dardanelles campaign, its execution by British military forces was lamentable, the defeat a fatal combination of incompetence and chance.[38] The upshot of the failure was that there was no alternative but to dig the Germans out of the Western Front and hope that the Royal Navy's blockade would eventually break German morale, as well as place unacceptable pressure on the Reich's war economy. Thus in 1915, the British found themselves mobilizing their economy for a major ground war, while at the same time they were organizing and training the so-called Kitchener armies. They also found themselves having to supply the Western Front with sufficient troops to keep the French from collapsing, but the Kitchener divisions would not be ready for full-scale commitment until summer 1916.

In the first war years, German military operations won tactical victories on the battlefield that seemingly suggested that the Reich would win the war. In the spring and early summer of 1915, the Germans achieved major successes against the Russians that drove Tzar Nicholas II's forces from Poland. Nevertheless, there were no indications that the Russians were willing to quit. Moreover, the British blockade was beginning to bite. The Reich quite simply lacked access to many of the raw materials essential for the conduct of modern war, such as rubber, copper, and nitrates, and especially foodstuffs. Throughout the year, Germany's commanders in the east, Field Marshal Paul von Hindenburg and Eric von Ludendorff, pressured Falkenhayn to reinforce their front with the aim of crushing the Russians by driving into the depths of Russia. Their arguments were largely fallacious and ignored the logistical and strategic problems created by fighting deep in Russia.[39] The political pressure they exerted on German decision-making was considerable, but not yet sufficient to force the kaiser to replace Falkenhyn and change the Reich's strategic approach.

THE YEAR OF ATTRITION (1916)

In response to the claims of Hindenburg and Ludendorff that the Reich needed to follow an eastern strategy, Falkenhayn focused German military strategy in the west. He completed a major strategic assessment of Germany's position immediately before New Year's Day, 1916. It represented a mixture of acute observations with bizarre conclusions. He argued that the war had exhausted both France and Russia, but that the "enormous hold which England still has on her allies" was the only thing keeping them in the conflict. Falkenhayn particularly worried that "our enemies, thanks to their superiority in men and material are increasing their resources much more than we are. If that process continues a moment must come when the balance of numbers itself will deprive Germany of all remaining hope."[40] But at the end, his strategic proposal fell off the table with the statement that the way to strike at Germany's main opponent was not to attack the British, but rather to attack the French. He was not deluded enough to expect a decisive victory, but he did aim to draw the French into a great battle of attrition that would bleed them white. To do that, Falkenhayn proposed attacking Verdun to draw the French in, and then to hammer them to pieces with artillery.

The Germans began their attack in February 1916. Falkenhayn had badly miscalculated. However, the French imposed a casualty exchange ratio of one-to-one on the attackers, as opposed to the four-to-one ratio Falkenhayn had hoped to achieve. Verdun was just the start of German troubles in 1916. In June, the Russians launched a devastating attack on ill-prepared Austro-Hungarian positions on the Eastern Front, which Germany's allies had weakened, to launch an offensive against the Italians. For a time the Brusilov offensive threatened to collapse the ancient Hapsburg monarchy. Then in July, after a massive artillery bombardment, the British launched a great offensive on the Somme. Shortly thereafter, the Rumanians joined the war on the Allied side.

Too much of the history of the Somme Battle that began on July 1, 1916, understandably, but misleadingly, focuses on the disastrous casualties the British suffered on the first day of the battle.[41] The 57,000 casualties on that terrible day were indeed a monument to British incompetence. But subsequently British forces performed much better. Over the remainder of the battle, they inflicted nearly as many casualties on the Germans as they suffered themselves. In effect, they created another artillery battle, of *attrition*, from which the German army never fully recovered. The Germans termed the Somme a new kind of battle, a "battle of materiel," one in which they were at a distinct disadvantage.[42] The problem for the Germans lay in the fact that Falkenhayn demanded that the defending troops hold every piece of ground, no matter how tactically useless; and if lost, that they immediately regain the ground lost. Thus, throughout the battle the Germans were still packing their troops in front-line trenches, where the weight of the British artillery bombardments massacred them.

By early August 1916, Germany and its army were in serious trouble, with major difficulties in the west and with its ally Austria-Hungary on the brink of collapse. Pressured from all sides by demands for a change in military leadership, the kaiser removed Falkenhayn and replaced him with Hindenburg and Ludendorff, the latter the main driving force. Upon taking over command, the two generals discovered just how weak Germany's strategic situation was. The heavy casualties suffered at Verdun and on the Somme had exhausted the army, while the increasing Allied advantage in materiel was having a significant impact on the battlefield.

On the tactical level, Ludendorff executed a massive reordering of German tactics. In September 1916, he carried out an extensive survey of the Western Front to include extensive meetings and debriefs with front-line officers and soldiers. Arriving on the Western Front, Ludendorff demanded that the staffs and the front-line soldiers with whom he discussed the tactical situation not give "favorable report[s] made to order."[43] He recorded in his memoirs his impressions in the following terms:

> The loss of ground up to that date appeared to me of little importance in itself. We could stand that, but the question how this and the progressive falling off of our fighting power ... were to be prevented was of immense importance.... [O]n the Somme the enemy's powerful artillery, assisted by excellent aeroplane observation and fed with enormous supplies of ammunition, had kept down our own fire and destroyed our artillery. The defense of our infantry had become so flabby that the massed attacks of the enemy always succeeded.... I attached great importance to what I learned about our infantry.... Without doubt it fought too doggedly, clinging too resolutely to the mere holding of ground, with the result that the losses were heavy.[44]

What now occurred was no less than a revolution in tactics: the creation of defense-in-depth tactics that would revolutionize modern warfare.[45] *The differences between British and German lessons-learned processes, through which both came to grips with the tactical problems raised by the fighting, underline the very different cultures of their armies.* Having made a major effort to discover what the *actual problems* were on the Western Front, Ludendorff systemized a coherent response through the use of the general staff. Within two months, the general staff had come up with *The Principles of Command in the Defensive Battles in Position Warfare*, which it duly issued to troop units on December 1, 1916. Through the presence of general staff officers down to division level, Ludendorff was then able to ensure that the manual was thoroughly understood *and applied*. Here, Ludendorff stands out as one of the few senior generals in the war to display an interest in what was happening on the sharp end and what could be done to improve tactical effectiveness.

On the other side, Field Marshal Douglas Haig, commander of the BEF since 1915, and his staff displayed little interest in finding out was occurring on the sharp end with either artillery or infantry tactics.[46] In many respects, Haig has received unfair criticisms from historians for his "incompetence": what they ignore is Haig's considerable and impressive role in the buildup and administration of Britain's first massive ground force based on the conscription of the British people.[47] Moreover, far more than was true of his German counterparts, Haig was interested in technology, and in this regard was a major supporter of the development of the tank. But British tactical adaptation was slower and less effective than that of the Germans, partially because of command disinterest and partially because their means of disseminating lessons learned were less effective.[48]

Nevertheless, in the end, it was the *strategic vision* that mattered. Here, the British recognized that support for their allies, particularly the French, was essential to victory. Moreover, they made every effort to win the battle for the narrative in the United States. Their blockade of the Central Powers, which steadily tightened as the war progressed, caused considerable friction with Woodrow Wilson's administration, the policy of which seemed largely concerned with keeping the United States out of the conflict, whatever the national interests.[49] The British compromised with American demands to the extent possible, while delightedly replying to American protests about the blockade by drawing examples drawn from the Union blockade of the Confederacy during the American Civil War.[50]

Whatever the American protests, the blockade was biting deeply into the German economy both in terms of military capabilities and on the home front.[51] By 1916, it was affecting German combat and logistic capabilities.[52] Moreover, it was having a serious impact on the Reich's food situation. Not only was Germany dependent on the import of major foodstuffs before the war, but the cessation of fertilizer imports resulted in a significant decrease in agricultural output.[53] The winter of 1916–1917 became known throughout the Reich as the "Turnip Winter" because the civilian population had so little to eat.

In the fall of 1916, as Ludendorff struggled to reform German tactical capabilities, he was also pushing for strategic decisions that would guarantee the Reich's defeat. In spite of the Kaiser's decision to halt unrestricted submarine warfare in 1915, the *Kriegsmarine* had waged a relentless campaign in favor of its resumption. The figures that the German navy presented were largely bogus. Among other numerical manipulations, its advocates calculated that neutral shipping would refuse to sail to Britain, but they forgot that American shipyards possessed enormous capabilities. As Isabel Hull has pointed out, "the navy underestimated Britain. It ascribed less intelligence and will power to its foe than it assumed for Germany."[54] Not surprisingly, almost from their first moments in the *Oberste Heeresleitung* (OHL, the Army High Command), Hindenburg and Ludendorff had become enthusiastic supporters of the "military necessity" of resuming unrestricted submarine warfare. In early January 1917, Hindenburg bluntly stated that "[w]e fully expect war with America and have made all the preparations for it."[55] Having paid no attention to Chancellor Bethmann Hollweg's worries about the danger of bringing the United States into the war, Hindenburg and Ludendorff instigated his removal in 1917. In effect, Germany was now a military dictatorship.

The fact that Ludendorff worried in the fall of 1916 about the possibility that either Holland or Denmark might enter the war on the side of the Allies suggests how prepared the army was to take on the United States. In fact, Ludendorff's tactical reforms, by enabling the army to fight on for another two years, ensured that the war's price in casualties and wealth would be that much higher for Germany when the war was over. So short of troops were the Germans that Ludendorff ordered a major retreat on the Western Front in the spring of 1917 to free troops up for the defensive battles that he anticipated would occur later in 1917. In Operation ALBERICH, fittingly named after the malicious dwarf of the *Niebelungen* saga, the retreating Germans destroyed every building, cut down every fruit tree, poisoned the wells, and left the area they evacuated a virtual desert.[56]

GERMANY ON THE BRINK (1917)

With the new tactics, the German army in the west wrecked the French army's Nivelle offensive of spring 1917. Moreover, with the new tactics it fended off the massive British offensive at Passchendaele in the late summer and fall. Matters went reasonably well in the East with the steady march of Russia toward revolution and utter collapse—a revolution that the Germans enthusiastically aided and abetted. Not only did they ship Lenin across German territory in the spring of 1917 so that he could further the disintegration taking place in Russia, but they also supplied the Bolsheviks with gold to carry out their revolution.[57] All of this would come back to have a disastrous impact on Germany's fate for much of the remainder of the twentieth century.

As he presented Germany's decision to resume unrestricted warfare to the Americans, the German ambassador in Washington also passed along the German government's terms for a compromise peace. The terms indicated why no peace was possible with the Reich, other than its complete defeat. The German proposals included the following:

- a frontier in the east that would protect Germany and Poland [then a German client-state] economically and strategically against Russia;
- a provision of colonies worthy of Germany's population and status as a Great Power;
- a withdrawal of German troops from the territory they had occupied in France with "reservation concerning the strategic and economic boundaries, as well as financial compensation" (as if the French had invaded Germany!);
- the restoration of Belgium under what to all intents and purposes would have been under German control; and
- compensation for whatever injuries German industry and commerce had suffered during the war.[58]

The German ambassador understood that such proposals had no chance of acceptance by the Allies. For the Germans, it was a matter of *Weltmacht oder Niedergang* (world power or defeat).

For the Allies, 1917 was a dark year. While their army was becoming more tactically effective, especially in use of artillery, the application of its improving capabilities proved inept. The first and perhaps most important was the fact that mutinies throughout the French army, as a result of the failure of the Nivelle offensive, had severely debilitated French military capabilities. Thus, the British were going to have to launch major military operations, with their concomitant heavy casualties, in 1917. Ironically, the BEF was now in a position to impose an unacceptable level of attrition on the Germans. In a series of smaller operations in April and then June 1917, the British had destroyed the German defenses on Vimy Ridge and then at Messines and had imposed heavy losses on their opponents in taking those positions. Here British counter-battery fire proved particularly effective. Those two operations underlined that relatively limited attacks, which possessed overwhelming superiority in artillery, could severely hurt the Germans, even with their new defensive system. But Haig was set on launching a great offensive in Flanders. The result would be a bloody, indecisive battle fought over land that had once been a great swamp, drained by the French and Belgians in the Middle Ages. Now British, Canadian, and Anzac formations would flounder in the mud of Flanders with little success.[59]

Around the Battle of Flanders—its origins, conduct, and results—would swirl a political tempest and a breakdown in civil-military relations that came close to losing Britain the war. To a certain extent, British difficulties mirrored those besetting the Germans as well. In both cases, those troubles reflected the effects of the war on the two societies. The coalition government of Herbert Asquith had collapsed in November and December 1916, largely based on dissatisfaction with Asquith's lackadaisical conduct of the war.[60] His replacement was David Lloyd George, a Welsh Liberal politician of considerable talent and drive. Lloyd George had taken over the War Office after Kitchener had died in July 1916, when the ship carrying him to Russia had hit a mine off the Orkney Islands and sunk. Almost immediately, Lloyd George had found himself at odds with the strategy of attrition that Haig and the chief of the imperial general staff, General William "Wully" Robertson, were advocating. Nevertheless, he was to be constrained in his relationship with the generals in articulating a more effective strategy for Britain. On one hand, he was depending on the Conservatives to keep him in power since Asquith had taken a sizeble portion of the Liberal Party into opposition, while Robertson and Haig had close connections with both the Conservatives and the king, George V. Well before operations began in Flanders, Haig had made clear that he intended to launch a powerful blow to break through German lines and crush the German army in the field. Robertson attempted to persuade Haig to attempt the more limited approach that had worked so well in the Arras and Messines attacks, but Haig would have none of it.

As casualties ballooned into the hundreds of thousands in Flanders in late summer 1917, Lloyd George found himself appalled by the losses. Nevertheless, he refused to rein in Haig and stop an offensive that was going nowhere.[61] In retrospect, Lloyd George was looking for somewhere else other than the Western Front to achieve a decisive victory. In fact, there was no place, other than the Western Front, where the Allies could defeat the Germans. In one of the more shortsighted political moves of the war, as the British offensive in Flanders burned itself out, the prime minister hit upon the dubious expedient of preventing Haig from continuing offensive operations in the spring of 1918 by starving the BEF of replacement soldiers to make up for the losses suffered at Passchendaele.

THE YEAR OF DECISION (1918)

At the start of 1918, the Second German Reich stood at a momentous point in its history. In the east, Ludendorff and Hindenburg imposed a peace treaty, the Treaty of Brest Litovsk, on the new Bolshevik regime in Russia that sliced off Poland, the Baltic states, Finland, the Ukraine, and much of White Russia (present-day Belorussia).[62] Moreover, even after signing the peace treaty, Ludendorff pursued further goals in the east to include the Crimea region and the Caucasus. In the west, the situation seemed equally propitious for the Germans. Only a few Americans had arrived in France, while Passchendaele had exhausted the British army, starved as it was for reinforcements. The French army had recovered from its own mutinies, but it remained a brittle instrument. Nevertheless, the German army was not in much better shape; its discipline was beginning to crack. Already in January 1918, no less than 200,000 soldiers had deserted, a number that would grow to over 700,000 by October 1918.[63] Moreover, troop trains transferring soldiers from the east to the west in 1918 faced a constant problem of desertion, while a substantial number of the troops arriving on the Western Front from the east were susceptible to Bolshevik propaganda.

Ironically, it is possible that, had the Germans proposed reasonable terms for a settlement in the west, they might have achieved a peace that would have left them with most of the gains they had made from the Treaty of Brest Litovsk. But for Ludendorff, it was all or nothing. Thus, he planned a series of major offensives to knock the Western Powers out of the war before the Americans arrived. Ludendorff's offensives aimed at achieving tactical gains. When Crown Prince Rupprecht of Bavaria, one of the few sensible senior officers in the German army and commander of the first great offensive, the MICHAEL Offensive, asked what the operational objective of the upcoming offensive was, Ludendorff replied: "I object to the word operation. We will punch a hole into [their front line]. For the rest we shall see."[64]

Ludendorff was right. MICHAEL tore an enormous hole in British lines and pushed the British Fifth and Third Armies back almost to Amiens. But moving over the wasteland they had created the previous year in Operation ALBERICH, the German advance steadily slowed while their artillery units found it almost impossible to displace forward.[65] With neither strategic nor tactical goals, the Germans seized worthless territory that proved far more difficult to defend than the well-sited positions they had abandoned. Moreover, the Germans now had to defend their great bulging salients that reached deeply into Allied-held territory. That decreased the number of German troops defending each sector, as well as the reserves available for counterattacks.[66] By early July, Ludendorff had exhausted the German army's fighting strength, having gained nothing worthwhile either operationally or strategically. The Germans had lost nearly 900,000 men in these attacks. It was maneuver warfare at an unacceptable cost.[67] And there was virtually nothing left in the east on which the Germans could draw.

The Allies survived the storm. Moreover, by the summer of 1918, with the flow of reinforcements restored, Haig disposed of a stronger force than in the spring. In addition, a flood of American troops were arriving in France, 250,000 every month. While these troops were certainly not trained to the standards of the French and British, they proved exceptionally fast learners, and their opponents were on their last legs. The German collapse began on August 8. A massive British combined-arms attack, supported by large numbers of tanks, shattered German forces near Amiens. Ludendorff characterized the defeat as the "Black Day" of the war for the German army. Much worse followed, as Allied attacks drove the Germans back into Belgium and the French territory they had seized in the war's first days. The BEF carried much of that effort, the fall campaign representing its most impressive tactical and operational performance of the war.[68]

The German army found itself bludgeoned into submission; by early November it was a completely beaten force.[69] On October 1, 1918, Ludendorff admitted in a staff meeting of the Army High Command that "[t]he *OHL* and the German Army are finished; the war could no longer could be won; rather, the final defeat was probably inescapably at hand." With the arrival of American troops, the Allies were on the brink of "a *great* victory, a *breakthrough in grand style*. . . . One could *no longer* rely on the troops."[70] Confronted with defeat on the Western Front, Ludendorff desperately sought an armistice.[71] This the exhausted French and British were willing to do, although the commander of the American Expeditionary Force, General John J. Pershing, argued that only a peace treaty dictated in Berlin with Germany prostrate would achieve a lasting peace.

In every respect, the contest between Britain and Germany in World War I represented *a contest for the future of Europe*. Without the British effort, the Germans would have won the war. The most significant British advantage lay not necessarily in their own strength but in the obdurate beliefs of their opponents—*that what mattered in war was its conduct, not its strategy or political ends*. From the war's opening moments, the Germans placed "military necessity" before political concerns and thus made impossible any reasonable connection between means and ends. The German military's demand that "military necessity" override all other concerns not only ensured that Britain would enter the war at its outset, *it also guaranteed that the United States eventually would find the Second Reich's behavior intolerable and would throw its immense economic weight on the side of the Allies*.

In contrast, the British consistently placed support for their Allies high on their list of priorities. They also ensured that their actions did as little as possible to harm the interests of the major neutrals, especially the United States. At the same time, to control the narrative, they highlighted the willful German disregard for international law and neutral rights. *Whatever their weaknesses in military effectiveness, the strategic effectiveness of Britain's leaders ensured an Allied victory.*

The Treaty of Versailles and the Interwar Years (1919–1939)

The armistice granted by the Allies reflected French desiderata. It required the German army to surrender all of its artillery and most of its machine guns and retreat back across the Rhine, while granting the victorious powers bridgeheads on the river's right bank. But because military operations had not reached German territory, a substantial number of the Reich's political and military leaders almost immediately claimed that the German army had stood unbroken and undefeated in the field, only to be stabbed in the back by the communists and the Jews. Even the president of the German Republic, who had replaced the kaiser, the Social Democratic politician Friedrich Ebert, greeted the troops returning to Berlin with the pronouncement that "no enemy has subdued you."[72]

Somehow, the Germans expected that their opponents would grant them an easy peace of reconciliation, in spite of the fact that they had wrecked much of Western and Eastern Europe and had made it clear throughout the war that if they won they intended to impose a Carthaginian peace on the Allies.[73] Ever since the signing of the Treaty of Versailles, historians have criticized the peace efforts that took place in Paris in 1919 for their supposed harshness.[74] In fact, the peacemakers failed for reasons that lay beyond their control.[75] The extraordinary harsh and merciless behavior that the Germans had exhibited throughout the war hardly made a soft peace possible: the execution of over 6,000 hostages in France and Belgium in the war's opening months, the introduction of gas war, the dragooning of tens of thousands of Belgian and French males for forced labor in Germany, the launching of unrestricted submarine warfare in 1915, the imposition of ruthless rationing in parts of Belgium and northern France that brought the population of the occupied areas close to starvation,[76] the Treaty of Brest Litovsk, and the massive demolitions carried out by the German army in Operation ALBERICH, as well as during the retreat in the fall of 1918.

Moreover, such a peace, with the incorporation of German-speaking territories set adrift by the collapse of the Austro-Hungarian Empire, namely Austria and the German-speaking fringe that surrounded Czechoslovakia, would have made Germany a victorious power after all. As it was, Germany now found itself sharing a frontier with only one major European power, the badly damaged France. The fallout from the collapse of the empires meant that a group of quarrelsome, weak powers—none of which displayed much strategic sense—now bordered the Reich to the east and south. Moreover, the success of the communist regime in Russia ensured that the Germans were not the only major power fundamentally dissatisfied with the peace settlement.

The Peace of Versailles, which left Germany unified and the strongest economic power in Europe, confronted the victorious Western Powers with a conundrum. For the French, the most pressing issue in their relations with the new Weimar Republic was a desire for the Germans to pay reparations for the damage they had inflicted on France. However, there was a catch, namely that to pay that bill, the German economy would have to be the most powerful in Europe, hardly what the French viewed as in their best interest. On the other hand, the British viewed the recovery of Germany and its economy as essential to their economic stability. After all, the Reich had been Britain's largest trading partner before the war. Admittedly, Lloyd George had run an election campaign in the immediate aftermath of the war promising the British people that the coming peace treaty would squeeze the Germans until "the pips squeaked." But the economist John Maynard Keynes's devastating critique of the economic consequences of the peace treaty, published in 1919, reverberated throughout the British economic and political elite.[77]

The Anglo-French unity over what to do collapsed in 1923 when the French occupied the Ruhr, a major industrial region, after the Germans had failed to pay the reparations that were due. The economic consequences from the French move were disastrous. The collapse of the mark and the resulting massive inflation deliberately induced by the German government in response to the French move into the Ruhr further exacerbated Germany's economic difficulties. Equally important was a breakdown in Anglo-French relations that would not fully recover until the late 1930s. Here the traditional British view that aimed at keeping any one Continental power from dominating Europe pushed the British into a policy that was distinctly unfriendly toward the French.

The failure of the Ruhr occupation underlined for the French that they could not act against the Germans unless they had British support, a factor that had an important effect on events in the late 1930s. The economic recovery of Europe, especially Germany, largely through extensive American loans, helped bring about an improvement in the relations among the powers. In addition, the arrival of the master diplomat and statesman, Gustav

Stresemann, the Weimar Republic's foreign minister (1923 and 1924–1929), also had a considerable effect. But while Stresemann was willing to agree to the frontiers of the Germany's western neighbors, he was unwilling to extend such guarantees to Germany's *eastern* neighbors.

Yet one should not assume that economic and political concerns were the only factors influencing Anglo-German relations. To begin with, the German Foreign Office mounted a massive disinformation effort to persuade the British and Americans that Germany was no more responsible for starting the war than the other powers.[78] The German aim was to disprove the claim in the Treaty of Versailles that, supposedly, Germany had started the war, on which the French claims for reparations rested. This effort involved the careful selection and doctoring of the documents in the volumes on the Second Reich's prewar diplomacy that the Germans published.[79] It also included offering English and Continental scholars not only fellowships to Germany but also access to the carefully culled files of the German Foreign Office—provided, of course, they wrote their histories from the German point of view.[80]

The literature of the postwar period also reflects how differently the popular cultures of Great Britain and Germany viewed the events of the period 1914–1918. Beginning in the late 1920s, some of the most moving literature written in Britain in the twentieth century began to make its appearance in the United Kingdom. Fundamentally, literature examined the horror of the war and its terrifying impact on the young men who had served in the BEF. The message of these works was clear: the war was an unmitigated, inexcusable waste of those whom British society had sent off to the charnel houses of the Western Front.[81] The literature in Germany was quite different. Two of the great German remembrances of the war were Ernst Jünger's *Storm of Steel* and *Copse 125*.[82] Jünger was one of those few soldiers who love war. Wounded innumerable times in the conflict, and winner of the highest medal Germany could bestow on a soldier, the *Pour le Mérite*, Jünger fought on the Western Front from 1915 to the conflict's end, except when he was in the hospital or recovering from his wounds. To Jünger, war was a test that every generation should experience. His message was quite different from that which the British public was hearing, and it was one that reflected much of the other German writings on the war.[83]

The Great Depression represented a disastrous watershed in European history. The response of both the German and British leaders initially was to cut back on government expenditures, which only exacerbated the problems of recovery. The collapse of the world economy, however, hurt the Germans far more, because their economy was far weaker and far slower to recover from the war. By 1932, well over a third of the German workforce was unemployed. The Reich's economic travails destroyed the political stability of the Weimar Republic and drove the majority of the public to the political extremes. With the political center destroyed, the choice was between the communists and the Nazis.

Matters were somewhat better in the United Kingdom, but not by much. The British recovery was fragile, and its very fragility played a considerable role in the major efforts by Conservative politicians and the Treasury to hold down defense spending to minimum levels through to the late 1930s.[84] Nevertheless, it is clear that British rearmament could have begun far earlier and posed less serious risks to the nation's economic stability than was the case with the Germans, given Britain's access to financial markets.

THE RISE OF HITLER (1933)

At the end of January 1933, Adolf Hitler came to power in Germany. His political success reflected three separate events that exercised a powerful influence on the German political scene: the disastrous end to the four-year war that had bled Germany white; the great inflation of 1923; and the nightmarish impact of the Great Depression that threw half of the Reich's workers on the welfare rolls. Hitler made no secret of his goals in his turgid statement of Nazi ideology, *Mein Kampf,* and he was equally explicit in a conversation with Germany's military leaders four days after becoming the chancellor of the Third Reich. He made clear his intention to overthrow entirely the European balance of power that had largely remained the basis of Europe's strategic relations since 1648.[85] Whatever the military leaders may have thought of Hitler's long-term megalomaniacal goals, they were delighted to hear that their new leader had no intention of continuing the limitations on Germany's military but instead would provide the army, the navy, and the *Luftwaffe* (once the latter had been created in 1935) with blank checks to begin rearmament. In effect, Hitler was willing to break with the penny-pinching that had characterized the response of the world's powers to the Depression and to embark on a massive program of defense spending to finance Germany's rearmament program.

For the immediate future, Hitler had to navigate through a hostile European environment with minimal power. Nevertheless, he embarked on a risky policy of destroying the restrictions of Versailles piece by piece through diplomatic means. To do so, he presented himself as a man of peace—except to the Germans—who only wanted for the German people the same rights that Versailles had granted to other Europeans.[86] In short order, Hitler destroyed the protective screen that the peacemakers of 1919 had placed around the Reich. In 1933, Germany withdrew from the League of Nations; in 1934, it signed a nonaggression pact with the Poles; in 1935, it announced conscription and the creation of an air force; and in March 1936, Hitler ordered the *Wehrmacht* to occupy the demilitarized zone of the Rhineland. Immediately after each one of these initiatives, Hitler announced that Germany's intentions were entirely peaceful.

It was a message all too many Europeans enthusiastically embraced. In 1936, Britain's former prime minister, David Lloyd George, came away from a meeting with Hitler, impressed by the *Führer*'s peaceful intentions.[87] In his assumptions about the Germans, Lloyd George was no different from the great majority of his countrymen. Typical of British attitudes was passing of the Oxford Union's resolution, "[t]hat this House refuses in any circumstances to fight for King or Country," by 275 votes to 153.[88] Winston Churchill was the great exception: above all, he saw the Third Reich not only as a great strategic danger but as a moral one as well. In July 1934, Churchill commented in one of his many warning columns in *The Daily Mail*:

> I marvel at the complacency of the Ministers in the face of the frightful experiences through which we have so newly passed. I look with wonder upon our thoughtless crowds disporting themselves in summer sunshine, and upon this unheeding House of Commons, which seems to have no higher function than to cheer a Minister; [and all the while, across the North Sea,] a terrible process is astir. *Germany is arming.*[89]

But most in Britain regarded Churchill as a relic from an earlier age.

Germany's program of rearmament encountered major problems from its inception.[90] With minimal foreign exchange to purchase the raw materials on which arming the Reich would depend, with an economy still in desperate shape from the Depression, and with the restrictions of Versailles still influencing the Reich's industrial capabilities, Hitler's rearmament program took far longer than the *Führer* had hoped or expected.[91] Luckily for the Germans, European attention was focused on other issues beside the German danger for much of the mid-1930s. In 1935, Benito Mussolini launched the Italian military against Abyssinia (modern-day Ethiopia). British public opinion demanded a stand against Italian aggression and support for the League of Nations—but at the same time expressed a strong desire to avoid war. Thus, British policy fell between two stools.[92] Consequently, British policy failed to stop the Italians, while at the same time angering them so much that whatever chance there may have been to keep Mussolini's support for an anti-German front had disappeared.[93]

During the crisis, the British chiefs of staff weighed in with military assessments that considerably overestimated Italian capabilities and underestimated those of the Western Powers, should a shooting war break out with the Italians. However, they were far more optimistic in their own meetings. One suspects that the pessimistic analyses they provided the government reflected their hope that British politicians would finally address the major weaknesses in the British military—weaknesses that had resulted from the government's parsimony over the previous decade and a half. In November 1933, the government formed the Defense Requirements Committee, consisting of the chiefs of staff and several important civil servants. After interminable meetings that drew in the Treasury, the cabinet, the Foreign Office, and other committees, the cabinet agreed to an increase in defense spending of £71 million, to be spread over the next five years.[94] That represented at best a drop in the bucket.

The year 1936 brought an even bigger distraction from the threat posed by German rearmament. A military revolt in Spain failed to overthrow completely the Republic, but instead resulted in a civil war that pitted the radical right (the Nationalists) against the radical left (the Republicans). The Italians and the Soviets sent major forces and massive supplies to support the contending sides. Early in the revolt, the Germans provided key support to General Francisco Franco's fascists with their Ju 52 transports that flew the Spanish Foreign Legion across the Straits of Gibraltar to the Spanish mainland to participate in the fighting. But thereafter, Hitler reduced the German contribution to a small group of advisers and weapons that the Germans wanted to test.[95] As he pointed out in late 1937 during a meeting with senior advisors, continuation of the civil war in Spain, rather than a quick victory by the Spanish Nationalists, was much more to Germany's advantage.[96]

The next year, 1937, would prove to be the key year during which both defense and strategic policies for both Germany and Britain would be determined. In late spring 1937, Neville Chamberlain succeeded Stanley Baldwin as prime minister. He immediately made clear that his government would place major constraints on defense expenditures. The Royal Air Force (RAF) would receive most of the increases in defense spending, the Royal Navy less, and the army virtually nothing. In a May 1937 cabinet meeting, the prime minister warned his colleagues:

> He did not believe that we could, or ought, or in the event, would be allowed by the country, to enter a Continental war with the intention of fighting on the same line as in the last war. We ought to make up

our minds to do something different. Our contribution by land should be on a limited scale. It was wrong to assume that the next war would be fought by ourselves alone against Germany. If we had to fight we should have allies who must ... maintain large armies. He did not accept that we also must send a large army.[97]

Chamberlain's strategic approach represented a disavowal of Britain's traditional policy from the eighteenth century on, which had committed major ground forces to the Continent in support of its allies.[98] The Royal Navy and the RAF hardly received significant increases in funding. In retrospect, the only sound decision made by the government regarding defense had to do with the RAF. It ordered that Service to emphasize *fighters* rather than *bombers* in its program. But even that decision had little to do with *strategic realism*, but rested on the fact that fighters were cheaper.

The British predicated their defense policy on two basic assumptions: that whatever the militaristic policies of Nazi Germany, Hitler did not want war; and that his aim was solely to reassert Germany's position as a major European power. Thus, given that assumption, then Britain should right the "wrongs" of Versailles and by so doing ensure Europe's peace. However, that assumption rested on a fundamental misreading of Nazi aims, part wishful thinking, and part guilt, that somehow Britain had to make things right. In July 1937, Chamberlain commented to the Soviet ambassador that "if only we could sit down at a table with the Germans and run through all their complaints and claims with a pencil, this would greatly relieve all tension."[99] The next year he would note to his foreign secretary, Lord Halifax, that "dictators were men of moods—catch them in the right mood and they will give you anything you ask for."[100]

But one should not ascribe the entire blame for such attitudes to Chamberlain and his closest advisors. Rather, the British establishment wholeheartedly supported the policy of appeasement. Thus, the Baldwin government had signed the Anglo-German Naval Agreement in July 1935, which allowed the *Kriegsmarine* to build up to 35 percent of the Royal Navy's tonnage. In effect, the agreement destroyed the naval provisions of the Treaty of Versailles, undermined relations with Italy and France, and placed no real restriction on German naval construction, which was moving ahead at the maximum speed German resources would allow.

Reinforcing attitudes in London was the pernicious influence of the British ambassador in Berlin, Sir Nevile Henderson, who made every effort to place German actions in a favorable light and to minimize the aggressive nature of Nazi foreign policy. A letter Henderson wrote to Lord Halifax in the summer of 1938 underlined the tone and substance of his reporting from Berlin:

> Personally I just sit and pray for one thing, namely that Lord Runciman [the British politician sent by Chamberlain to mediate the differences between the Czechs and the Sudeten Germans] will live up to the role of [an] impartial British liberal statesman. I cannot believe that he will allow himself to be influenced by ancient history or even arguments about strategic frontiers and economics in preference to high moral principles.[101]

Fears that any significant increases in defense spending would put the British recovery from the Depression in jeopardy reinforced such attitudes. As Chamberlain noted in 1937, the maintenance of Britain's economic stability represented an essential element in the maintenance of its defensive strength.[102] Thus, through March 1939, the British made every effort to place restrictions on defense expenditures. The fundamental aim of British rearmament was not national security, but rather that military expenditures should not interfere with the normal course of British business. A comparison of the British national income devoted to defense with that of Nazi Germany's suggests the extent of these limitations. In 1935 and 1936, British defense expenditures were less than 30 percent of the Third Reich's, while in 1937 and 1938, they barely reached 30 percent. Not until 1938 did British defense spending reach 8 percent of GNP, a rate the Germans had reached in 1935.[103]

Finally, of note was the role played by the British chiefs of staff committee and the many assessments it passed along to the government, all of which played a major role in providing Chamberlain the justification he needed to support his policy of appeasement. In 1937 and 1938, these reports were almost all uniformly negative about the balance of forces between those of the United Kingdom and those of the Third Reich. Admittedly, there was some justification for the positions they took. Nazi Germany obviously represented an increasingly dangerous threat in Europe; Italy in the Mediterranean was now hostile and a threat to the sea lines of communications to India and the Far East; and Japan, who after July 1937 was embroiled in a major land war in China, represented a dangerous opponent and threat to British colonies in the Far East, as well as to the British Dominions of Australia and New Zealand.

Nevertheless, the chiefs of staff committee consistently worst-cased their reports, overestimated the military power of potential opponents, and minimized the real and latent strength of the Western Powers. Emblematic of their reports was their pessimistic report of March 1938 immediately before the Czech crisis broke. They concluded

> that no pressure that we and our possible allies can bring to bear, either by sea, on land, or in the air could prevent Germany from invading and overrunning Bohemia and from inflicting a decisive defeat on the Czechoslovakian army. We should then be faced with undertaking a war against Germany for the purpose of restoring Czechoslovakia's lost integrity and this object would only be achieved by the defeat of Germany and as the outcome of a prolonged struggle. In the world situation today it seems to us . . . Italy and Japan would seize the opportunity to further their own ends and that in consequence the problem we have to envisage is not that of a limited European war only, but of a World War. On this situation we reported as follows some four months ago: "Without overlooking the assistance we should hope to obtain from France and possibly other allies, we cannot foresee the time when our defense forces will be strong enough to safeguard our territory, trade and vital interests against Germany, Italy, and Japan simultaneously."[104]

Such assessments did not drive appeasement; rather, they allowed Chamberlain to justify his best-case analysis of German intentions to cabinet and parliamentary doubters.

Meanwhile, Hitler's all-out rearmament program was running into serious difficulties with production runs canceled or delayed because of a lack of raw materials, all resulting from major shortages in hard currency.[105] In November 1937, he summoned his senior military and diplomatic advisers to examine Germany's strategic and economic policies.[106] The *Führer* made clear in his opening remarks that Germany needed to move in the immediate future before the Reich's enemies completed their rearmament. He did not lay out a rigid program, but suggested rather that Germany would have to use military force to achieve its aims of overthrowing the existing European order. Austria and Czechoslovakia would be the first targets. As one writer has noted, "even if it were not a timetable for aggression, it was a ticket for the journey; and the first stops Prague and Vienna were clearly marked."[107]

But the meeting did not go as Hitler clearly planned. The minister of war and commander-in-chief of the Armed Forces, Field Marshal Werner von Blomberg, and the *Wehrmacht* commander, Colonel General Werner Freiherr von Fritsch, raised serious doubts as to whether the *Wehrmacht* was ready for war. They were supported by the foreign minister, Constantine von Neurath, who warned that Germany lacked serious allies. Hitler's response came the following January: he fired Blomberg and Fritsch, the latter on trumped-up charges of homosexuality, and retired or transferred a number of senior officers to new positions. However, the Fritsch firing exploded into the most serious civil-military crisis in the history of the Third Reich.[108] But Hitler, ever the gambler, doubled the bet. While he was dealing with the political fallout from the Fritsch case, he manufactured a crisis with Austria. After Hitler had bullied the Austrian chancellor Kurt Schuschnigg into surrendering, German troops marched into Austria in March 1938 to an enthusiastic reception from the great majority of the population. To a certain extent, the *Anschluss* alleviated the Reich's economic situation by providing much-needed foreign exchange and a substantial number of workers. Nevertheless, its greatest significance lay in the fact that it placed Czechoslovakia in an impossible strategic situation.

The reaction of the other European powers was minimal. As one British commentator noted, the Germans were only moving into their own backyard. That lack of reaction only confirmed to Hitler that he was on the right track. He had claimed in *Mein Kampf* that the kaiser's major mistake had been to make an enemy of Britain and believed he could keep Britain out of a future war on the Continent as his military forces built a great eastern empire on the ruins of the "season" states and the Soviet Union. In fact, the *Füher* knew little about the British, and what he thought he knew was dangerously skewed. In 1936, he appointed Joachim von Ribbentrop to be the German ambassador to London, Ribbentrop's qualifications being that he was fluent in English, was not a part of the diplomatic formal corps, and was slavishly devoted to Hitler. He made an appallingly bad impression on the British, including many appeasers, most of whom quite rightly regarded him as a jumped-up *parvenue*. There were, of course, a number of pro-appeasement supporters who were glad to fill Ribbentrop's ears with nonsense. Like Henderson, Ribbentrop provided a filter that reinforced the preconceptions of those for whom he worked. Named as Germany's foreign minister in February 1938 during Hitler's purge of his senior advisors, Ribbentrop then provided the *Führer* with consistently anti-British advice, much of it underestimating the British. By this point, Hitler appeared to have concluded that Britain was not a natural ally of Germany and that he was going to have to deal with the British eventually.

The ease with which the Germans incorporated Austria into the Reich led Hitler to turn next to the Czechs. He might not have brought the crisis to a boil in 1938, but for the fact that in May 1938 the Czechs accused the Germans of preparing a surprise attack on their nation. In fact, that was not the case. But London and Paris warned Hitler against any move the Germans might make against Czechoslovakia. The appearance that Nazi Germany had backed down to warnings from London and Paris, as well as the fact that the Czechs had mobilized and occupied the fortifications on their exposed borders, infuriated the *Führer*.[109] Hitler responded by issuing a new military directive for "Case Green," plans for a war with Czechoslovakia. The covering letter, signed by the new commander of the *Oberkommando der Wehrmacht* (OKW), General Wilhelm Keitel, made clear that preparations for such an eventuality were to be completed by October 1, 1938. The preamble now ominously read, "It is my unalterable decision to smash Czechoslovakia by military action in the near future."[110]

In early June 1938, Joseph Goebbels's propaganda machine moved into high gear against Czechoslovakia, while the *Wehrmacht* deployed forces to the German-Czech border for eventual offensive operations. Meanwhile, in the west the Germans made desperate efforts to fortify their border with France. It was not a bluff. Hitler fully intended to smash the Czech state in a swift military operation. However, the German military was not yet ready for a major conflict or in a position to take advantage of whatever weaknesses Britain and France may have had in their own strategic positions.[111] What is of particular interest in this period are the strategic analyses, or net assessments, of the British and German military. Read side by side, it is almost as if those responsible for making strategic assessments existed in separate worlds.

The German assessment processes—not surprisingly given their disinterest in strategic matters—were not nearly as sophisticated as those of the British. The best of these were a series of strategic memoranda written by the chief of the *Wehrmacht*'s general staff, General Ludwig Beck. His first strategic assessment, dated May 5, 1938, argued that Japan and Italy would not stand by the Reich, particularly in the case of Japan, involved as it was in a major war in China. Moreover, Beck warned, it was entirely possible that Rumania, Yugoslavia, and Poland would eventually intervene on the Allied side. Should war occur, the chief of the general staff believed that the Allies would be content to launch minor offensives into the Rhineland, but would place their emphasis on the war at sea and in the air.

General Beck had no doubts as to who would win such a war. Germany's military position had admittedly improved since the 1920s, but the *Wehrmacht* was simply not ready for war. The Reich possessed neither the economic nor the military base to fight a major war, much less a world war, against the Allied powers with any chance of success.[112] Not surprisingly, Beck resigned as chief of the general staff in late August 1938. The other German generals, for the most part, showed no disposition to follow Beck's lead. Erich von Manstein, supposedly the army's most competent general, noted in a letter to

Beck in August 1938, "Hitler has so far always estimated the political situation correctly."[113]

For the British, the crisis and worries over the possibility of another war created a flurry of activity. The most obvious were the three trips that Chamberlain would make to Germany in September 1938—the first to Berchtesgaden, the second to Bad Godesberg, and the third to Munich at the end of the month to surrender Czechoslovakia. Over the course of August and September, one sees an increasing annoyance in both the population and cabinet at the fact that Hitler was clearly aiming at war. In particular, the meeting at Godesberg, where the *Führer* turned down cold Chamberlain's mediation efforts, hardened British distrust of the Germans.[114] Not surprisingly, there was considerable muddle in British policymaking circles, as it became increasingly clear that Britain needed to make hard decisions as to what course to take if the Germans were to invade Czechoslovakia. In late August, Lord Halifax summed up the emerging situation for the cabinet. There were, he noted, two possible explanations for Germany's military preparations. The first was that, against the advice of the "moderate party" in Germany, Hitler had determined to use military force against the Czechs. The second possibility was that although Hitler had determined to solve the Sudeten problem in 1938, he had not yet resolved to use military force.

Halifax then added for the benefit of his colleagues that "[w]e were, in effect, concerned with the attempt of the dictator countries to attain their ends by force. But he asked himself whether it was justifiable to fight a certain war now in order to foster a possible war later."[115] As the cabinet debated German intentions and the overall strategic situation in meeting after meeting, its members failed to come to grips with perhaps the most important strategic question that German actions should have raised. What would the strategic situation be if the West surrendered Czechoslovakia, its well-armed military, its foreign exchange, and its significant armaments industry, personified by Škoda Works, and then Britain and France had to fight the Germans in 1939? No cabinet member raised that question until Oliver Stanley on September 16, and none of the military committees ever addressed that question before Chamberlain surrendered Czechoslovakia at the Munich Conference at the end of September 1938.[116]

For much of September, the military assessments, as well as those of British intelligence, worst-cased the strategic situation. Then, on September 23, the chiefs of staff produced a far more optimistic assessment. They questioned the experience level of the German general staff; failed to mention any significant air threat; and suggested that should war break out over Czechoslovakia, the French would have significant opportunities to make larger inroads into

Germany. The chiefs' conclusion was on a note totally different from their previous estimates—and completely at odds with a strategic assessment produced by their joint planning committee that same day: "until such time as we can build up our fighting potential we cannot hope for quick results. Nevertheless, the latent resources of the Empire and the doubtful morale of our opponents give us confidence as to the ultimate outcome."[117] How to explain this change in assessment of the strategic situation? Most probably, it reflected the intelligence from Germany—and not through Henderson, the British ambassador in Berlin—that indicated the *Wehrmacht*'s and the economy's weaknesses.

Such a change in the military assessment had no effect on Britain's strategic policies. Prime Minister Chamberlain, accompanied by the French premier Edouard Daladier, agreed to Hitler's demands that Czechoslovakia surrender the Sudeten districts. In that territory lay Czechoslovakia's fortifications, and so the Czechs were now defenseless. In strategic and military terms, the Munich agreement was a disaster for the Western Powers. It delivered the Czechs, their substantial military armaments, and their industries into Nazi Germany's hands, although the Germans would have to wait until they seized the remainder of the Czech state in March 1939 to gain access to most of the plunder.[118] For his part, Chamberlain returned home to receive a hero's welcome for having saved Europe from war. To the cheering crowds, he announced that he had brought "peace for our time." But almost immediately, the prime minister confronted discomfort in the ranks of his own party for the heavy emphasis he and his advisers had placed on the lack of preparedness of Britain's military.

The prime minister attempted to finesse this political difficulty by announcing an effort to increase defense spending. In fact, the government obfuscated—it did nothing to repair the army's sorry state; it provided a few small ships for the navy, along with the dredging of Dover and Rosyth harbors; and finally, it increased the number of Spitfires and Hurricanes on order, but only by extending the two-year contract to a third year. In other words, for the immediate future there would be no increase in orders for fighters.[119]

While Chamberlain continued efforts to minimize defense expenditures, reports from Germany were anything but encouraging. Ambassador Henderson had been diagnosed with cancer and had returned to London for a major operation that would keep him out of Berlin until February 1939. Thus, the British embassy in Berlin no longer represented a filter to reassure those in London who had devoured Henderson's optimistic reporting about the peaceful intentions of the Nazi regime. To add to the gloom, the German opposition supplied the British with reports that Hitler was about to seize the Netherlands in the opening move for an all-out aerial and naval attack on the British Isles. Worried by these reports, the British approached the French to see what aid they could supply. The French replied that there was nothing they could do, since by pushing for the surrender of Czechoslovakia, the British had removed approximately thirty divisions from the order of battle available to the Western Powers. In February 1939, confronted by harsh strategic realities, Chamberlain finally agreed to major increases in the British army that would allow it to support the French on the Continent.[120]

While the British were dithering, Hitler was profoundly unhappy about Chamberlain having robbed him of the opportunity to wage a short, quick war to smash the Czechs. Within three weeks of Munich and the occupation of the Sudetenland, he ordered the OKW to draw up plans to occupy the remainder of Czechoslovakia. At the same time, he confronted the fact that Germany's massive mobilization during the Czech crisis had seriously overstretched the German economy. The Reich Defense Committee went so far as to warn in early October that "in consequence of *Wehrmacht* demands (occupation of the Sudetenland) and unlimited construction on the West Wall so tense a situation on the economic sector occurred (coal, supplies for industries, harvest of potatoes and turnips, food supplies) that continuation of the tension past October 10 would have made an [economic] catastrophe inevitable."[121] As a result, Hitler confronted the unpleasant need to slice the allocation of raw materials to *Wehmacht* armament production—steel by 30 percent, copper by 20 percent, aluminum by 47 percent, rubber by 14 percent, and cement by 25–45 percent.[122] It is not hard to see why he was so eager to rip up the Munich agreement only five months after he, Chamberlain, Daladier, and Mussolini had signed it.

In mid-March 1939, the Germans occupied the remainder of Czechoslovakia on the trumped-up charges that the Czechs were mistreating their minorities. That move finally destroyed British illusions about Hitler's intentions. In the immediate aftermath, Neville Chamberlain attempted to minimize Hitler's action in destroying the Munich agreement. He suggested to the cabinet that the guarantee extended to the Czechs in October 1938 was no longer operable. "[T]he state whose frontiers we had undertaken to guarantee against unprovoked aggression had now completely broken up."[123] That evening in the House of Commons, he confirmed that while he regretted German actions, he had no intention of altering "our course."[124] However, an enormous outpouring of public outrage in Britain, exemplified by virtually the entire press, quickly changed his mind. What followed was a decision to draw a diplomatic line in the sand. As rumors swirled about impending German actions, the British reacted with haste; they extended guarantees to Poland and Rumania to make clear to Hitler that Britain would intervene should the *Wehrmacht* attack those countries. In fact, Britain and France were in a position to do little to help those countries in war. Churchill summed up Britain's strategic errors in his memoirs:

> There was some sense in fighting for Czechoslovakia in 1938 when the German army could scarcely put half a dozen trained divisions on the Western Front. . . . But this had been judged unreasonable, rash, below the level of modern intellectual thought and morality. Yet now at last the two Western Democracies declared themselves ready to stake their lives on the integrity of Poland. History, which we are told is mainly the record of crimes, follies, and miseries of mankind, may be scoured and ransacked to find a parallel to this sudden and complete reversal of five or six years' policy of easy-going placatory appeasement, and its transformation almost overnight into a readiness to accept an obviously imminent war on far worse conditions and on the greatest scale.[125]

Hitler's response was immediate and furious. Throughout the winter of 1938–1939, the Germans had been putting increasing pressure on the Poles to do a deal that would have turned their nation into a satellite nation. But the Poles had proven stubborn and had turned the Germans down cold. The British guarantee set the stage for the opening moves of the war. The chief of the *Abwehr* (German intelligence), Admiral Wilhelm Canaris, heard the *Führer* declaim that he would cook the British a stew on which they would choke.[126] On April 3, 1939, Hitler ordered the OKW to draw up plans for an invasion of Poland under the code name of *Fall Weiss* (Case White). The *Wehrmacht,* he ordered, was to consider a target date of September 1 for the initiation of military operations against Poland.[127]

For Hitler there was no alternative other than war against the Poles. He believed the Munich settlement had robbed him of the opportunity to conquer the Czechs. He was now not going to allow anyone to prevent him from having a war of conquest against the Poles. Ribbentrop continued to give the *Führer* the same flawed advice that the British would not go to war over Poland. Here, back channel messages from London reinforced such assumptions. In July, Sir Horace Wilson, senior civil servant in the British government, and Sir Joseph Ball, a senior official in the Conservative Party's bureaucracy, suggested to Helmuth Wohlthat, an official in the Reich's Four Year Plan, that the British were willing to make concessions about Poland, as well as extend major financial assistance through major loans to German industry. This effort at further appeasement blew up when someone high up in the British government leaked the British proposals to the press.[128]

The German reply to these efforts was short and to the point. The Reich had no intention of disarming or changing its policies in exchange for "peace loans."[129] The signing of the non-aggression pact with the Soviet Union further convinced German leaders that the British would fail to declare war once they confronted a German-Polish war. But at the same time, Hitler and his advisers had no clear thoughts on what they were going to do should the Western Powers respond to a German attack on Poland by declaring war. As Hitler exclaimed to Ribbentrop at news the British had declared war on September 3, "What now?"

For the British, the summer of 1939 was one of general confusion. On one hand, as the Ball-Wilson negotiations suggest, they were willing to deal with the Germans. On the other, facing an election in the first half of 1940, Chamberlain's maneuver room had narrowed. Still, for the most part the British government thought largely in diplomatic terms. Its hesitant approach to the Soviets about a military alliance underlined its unwillingness to recognize that war was inevitable.[130]

Interestingly, the chiefs of staff were far more optimistic about the overall strategic situation than they had been the previous year. What appears to have happened is that the government's willingness to untie the Treasury's purse strings resulted in a more optimistic mood among military leaders.[131] Moreover, the pessimistic reports of the previous year emanating from the German military and the opposition to Hitler had convinced British military leaders that the overall German strategic and military situation was far weaker than they had thought before the Czech crisis.[132] The irony of this change in assessments from 1938 was the fact that, while Germany the country had been in a weak position the previous year in economic as well as in military terms, the three German Services had considerably improved their combat capabilities over the course of the year. This was particularly true for the army, where Czech arms dumps had a major effect. Czech tanks would equip three of the panzer divisions that invaded France in May 1940, while Czech arms would equip the formations of *Waffen SS* divisions that supported the German army's drive into France and the Low Countries in May and June 1940.[133]

World War II (1939–1945)

With the German invasion of Poland on September 1, 1939, and the British declaration of war two days later, the second great war between Britain and

Germany broke out. The European theater of the conflict would last for the next five and a half years. The real contest between Britain and Germany, however, would be concentrated in the first twenty-two months of that terrible struggle.

After the Germans invaded Russia in June 1941 and unnecessarily declared war on the United States in December of that year, the struggle for the Germans became multifaceted and less focused on Britain. For the British, Germany always remained the main focus. It would only be with the massive and effective attacks of the Allied Bomber Command during the Battle of the Ruhr Valley in spring 1943 that German attention was refocused on the threat that Britain represented. In the end, it would be the critical period between June 1940 and June 1941 when the competition between Britain and Germany would determine the war's eventual outcome.

PRECARIOUS STRATEGIC BALANCE

One should not believe that the Allies were in a hopeless position in September 1939, or that the Germans did not have substantial weaknesses. Allied strategy focused on building up economic and military strength for an eventual military confrontation with the Germans two or three years down the road. Given Allied weaknesses as well as strengths, this made some sense. However, what the Allied political and military leaders failed to understand was how weak Germany's economic situation was, or for that matter, how deeply the blockade would wreck the Reich's economy.[134] But for the blockade to have full effect, the Allies needed to conduct major military operations that would force the Germans to make unpalatable decisions, such as supporting the Italians or launching a major offensive in the west in the fall of 1939. To understand the precarious strategic balance between the opposing sides, I will examine the war's first half-year, first from the German perspective and then from the perspective of the Allies.

For Hitler and Ribbentrop, the British declaration of war on September 3, 1939, had come as a nasty surprise. If the German economy had improved considerably over what it had been in the fall of 1938, it still confronted difficulties. Petroleum stocks were dangerously low. Germany only escaped the full consequences of its petroleum difficulties by minimal imports from Russia and Rumania and because Allied passivity allowed the *Wehrmacht* to stretch out the limited supplies available in stockpiles.[135] Equally threatening was the collapse of imports, the result of the successful Allied blockade. Imports of raw materials fell from 4,445,000 tons to 1,122,000 tons from prewar totals in the war's first months.[136] Equally serious was the sudden end of the imports of iron ore from French and other sources, with the loss of access to 9.5 million tons as a result of the blockade. This situation made the import of Swedish iron ore with high Fe (iron) contact (50 percent) of particular importance for the further functioning of the German economy.[137] In October 1939, an OKW memorandum warned that time worked more in the favor of Germany's enemies than in Germany's. The same memorandum also pointed out that "the danger in case of a prolonged war lies in the difficulty of securing from a limited food and raw-material base for a population while at the same time securing the means for the prosecution of the war."[138]

Almost immediately after the completion of the Polish campaign, the dangerous economic situation led Hitler to demand that the *Wehrmacht* launch a major campaign in the west before oil and raw material shortages placed Germany's military forces in a position where they could no longer launch such an effort.[139] In early October, the *Führer* issued a directive as to what a campaign in the west needed to achieve in strategic terms:

1. An offensive will be planned on the northern flanks of the Western Front, through Luxembourg, Belgium, and Holland. This offensive must be launched at the earliest possible moment and in the greatest possible strength.
2. The purpose of this offensive will be to defeat as much as possible of the French Army and of the forces of the allies fighting on their side, and at the same time win *as much territory as possible in Holland, Belgium, and northern France, to serve as a base for the successful prosecution of the air and sea war against England* and as a wide protective area for the economically vital Ruhr [author's italics].[140]

The emphasis on the operational objectives was clearly focused on Britain. Unfortunately for Hitler, he had formed his impression of Britain's resolve based on his dealings with Sir Neville Chamberlain, the British prime minister during the Czech crisis. As he declaimed in the spring of 1939, "I saw my enemies at Munich and they are worms."[141] Hitler appears to have believed that a major air and maritime offensive against the British would convince their leaders to make peace at any price. Hitler, who had not accounted for the rise of Winston Churchill, was, in this assessment, spectacularly wrong.

The fall offensive did not occur for three reasons:

- First, the German army was most unhappy with the performance of its troops at the tactical level. The army leaders argued for a postponement of the offensive against the west to the following spring, which led to a major blow-up with Hitler.[142]

- The second reason was bad weather, which on a number of occasions forced the Germans to postpone major military operations in the west.
- The third reason was that the Allies failed to conduct any significant military operations over the course of the fall.

The Allied failure to conduct serious military operations lay in the pusillanimity of military as well as political leaders in Britain and France. Ironically, despite his reputation, Chamberlain had argued for the Allies to make a major effort to push the Italians into the war on Germany's side if the *Wehrmacht* were to invade Poland. In late June 1939, the prime minister argued in the foreign policy committee that there were important advantages in having the Italians at Germany's side in any future conflict. In that meeting, Samuel Hoare, a leading appeaser, went so far as to argue that an early offensive against Italy would force the Germans to divert forces from Poland.[143] Such assessments sounded on the mark, but they immediately ran into opposition from the British military, as well as French military and political leaders. In July, the British joint planning committee opined that Italy might "be in a position to hit us more effectively at the outset than we can hit her. . . ."[144] Such nonsense fit in well with the worst-casing that had marked so many of the assessments of the British military throughout the 1930s. The French were no more eager to take on the Italians.[145]

Yet it would not have taken much to persuade Mussolini to pitch Italy into the conflict on Germany's side.[146] Had the Italians joined the war in September, they would likely have suffered a series of disastrous defeats that fall, which would have forced the Germans to either intervene in the Mediterranean or launch their offensive in the fall of 1939 against northern France and the Low Countries, whatever the weather conditions. Leslie Hore-Belisha, secretary of state for war, contradicted such assessments in July:

> [E]ven if Italy remained neutral, we still had to leave our forces in the Mediterranean to watch her. It would be preferable to devise means to smash Italy and thus release forces for action elsewhere. As a neutral, Italy would sustain Germany whereas an ally, she would constitute a drain on German resources.[147]

The disasters that Italian military forces would suffer in North Africa during the last half of 1940 against attenuated British forces suggest how vulnerable the Italian military would have been against the combined military forces of Britain and France a year earlier.[148]

The second possibility for Allied military action lay in the location of the Saar up against the French border. That area, while of less industrial importance than either the Ruhr or Silesia, was, nevertheless, of considerable economic importance. Not only was the region a center for heavy industry, but it produced 8 percent of Germany's coal. An offensive against the Saar would have forced the Germans to use substantial amounts of ammunition, the stocks of which the Polish campaign had dangerously drawn down, as well as increasing the Third Reich's economic difficulties. Both factors would have increased pressure on Hitler to launch the *Wehrmacht* in the fall to seek an immediate decision.

However, in spite of its promises to the Poles in August 1940, the French High Command did nothing. The French commander-in-chief, General Maurice Gamelin, reported to the Poles in mid-September that he had "already fulfilled his promise to undertake the first French offensive within fifteen days of mobilization. It is impossible for me to do more."[149] In fact, Gamelin was being economical with the truth in his communications with the Poles: no military operations occurred on German territory throughout this period, known as "the phony war." French patrols did not even reach the outlying positions of the West Wall.

The final vulnerability in the German economy lay in the import of Swedish iron ore. For six months of the year, that ore moved through the Baltic Sea when it was ice free. During the other six months, the ore freighters had to travel from the northern Norwegian port of Narvik down the coast until they finally reached the Skagerrak and could turn into the Elbe estuary. On September 19, Sir Winston Churchill, back at the Admiralty as the First Sea Lord, suggested that the ore trade was of great importance to the German war economy and that, if the political pressure failed to persuade the Norwegians to shut down the trade, he "would ... propose the remedy adapted in the last war, namely the laying of mines inside Norwegian territorial waters."[150] Churchill then waited until November 19 to propose formally that the Royal Navy mine the Norwegian *leads* (the sea corridor between Norway's offshore islands and its mainland). He immediately ran into stiff opposition from Lord Halifax and the Foreign Office. The Soviet invasion of Finland in late November then involved the mining of the Norwegian leads with the purpose of aiding the Finns. In the end, the British failed to mine the leads until early April 1940, thereby providing the Germans with the justification for their invasion of Scandinavia.[151]

An Allied strategic study in April 1940 summed up the strategic results of the failure to undertake any serious military actions against the Germans by that point in the war.

Hence, the Reich appears to have suffered relatively little wear and tear during the first six months of the war, and that mainly as a result of the Allied blockade. Meanwhile, it has profited from the interval to perfect the degree of equipment of its land and air forces, to increase the officer strength and complete the training of troops, and to add further divisions to those already in the field.[152]

The disastrous defeat of Allied ground forces was a direct result of the failure of the Allies to undertake *any* serious military action, combined with the gross incompetence of the French commander-in-chief, Gamelin.[153]

Winston Churchill became prime minister on May 10, 1940, the same day that the German panzers came west. For the next sixty days, Prime Minister Churchill would confront the most daunting set of problems that any political leader has confronted in history:[154]

- First, he had to deal with the strategic issue of how much aid to extend to a France that, from the first moments of the German invasions, was sinking slowly but steadily in the sloughs of catastrophic defeat.
- Second was the political challenge he confronted as early as the end of May, as a cabal of appeasers, led by Halifax, pushed for Britain to make peace with the Germans.
- Third was how Britain was to meet a German air and amphibious assault on the British Isles if it stood alone. This demanded the mobilization of the British people in psychological terms to stand against what appeared to be the unbeatable power of Nazi Germany. It would also demand that the Royal Navy neutralize the French fleet to prevent it from falling into the hands of the Axis.
- Fourth, and perhaps most important in the long term, was the problem of connecting with the United States and the Soviet Union to persuade them that it was in their national interest to help Britain. Only in his attempts to reach out to the Soviets in 1940 and early 1941 would Churchill fail.

In the largest sense, the bloody-mindedness of the British triumphed over the apparently more rational approach urged by the likes of Halifax and Samuel Hoare. As King George V noted in his diary shortly after the French surrender, "[p]ersonally, I feel happier now that we have no allies to be polite to and pamper."[155] After the war, Churchill would comment that in his speeches he had only given voice to the feelings of the British people. What enabled Churchill to win out over those who wanted to drop out of the war was the fact that the Germans never made a serious offer that might have tempted those who saw no reason to continue the fight. The crucial point for Churchill in June 1940 was the indication he received from President Roosevelt that the United States would back up Britain with financial and military aid. That in turn led the prime minister, late in the afternoon of July 3, to order the Royal Navy to attack the French fleet at Mers-el-Kébir, its base in North Africa. The French suffered 1,297 sailors killed in the attack, but it was a clear signal that Britain was in the war to the end.

What Churchill brought to the British war effort was a penetrating mind, a ruthless unwillingness to put up with incompetence, and a capacity to see the larger issues involved in decision-making. In early June 1940, twenty-eight-year-old physicist and RAF intelligence analyst R. V. Jones went before Churchill, a group of RAF senior officers, and the War cabinet to argue that the Germans had developed a system, based on radio beams, to improve significantly the ability of their bombers to hit targets at night and in bad weather. Jones's evidence was scanty, but he possessed an extraordinary ability to connect the dots. Everybody in the room, except for Churchill, was willing to dismiss Jones's arguments as nonsensical and not test out his theory. Churchill, however, recognized that, whatever the odds, the possession of such a capability by the Germans could have a disastrous impact on Britain's security. Thus, he ordered the RAF to fly the necessary test flights—and that night a test flight discovered the beams. Exactly one month later, the *Luftwaffe*'s commander-in-chief Hermann Göring suggested that German bombers using the beams should make nighttime attacks on British aircraft factories. By that time, British emergency measures to distort or jam the beams were already in place, and the Germans achieved no notable success in these attacks.[156]

Perhaps emblematic of the response of the British people to Churchill's call for resistance was the major increase in fighter production. In May 1940, the target for Hurricane and Spitfire production was 261 new fighters; the Supermarine and Hawker factories turned out 325. For June, the target was 292; actual output was 446. Over the next two months, the target was 611; actual production reached 972.[157] However, on the German side, there was no increase in the production of Bf 109s, in spite of the heavy losses that squadrons equipped with that aircraft had suffered beginning with the campaign in the west.[158]

While Churchill was shoring up Britain's strategic position and preparing for a massive German assault on the British Isles, the Germans went on vacation. After all, the war was over. Hitler toured the old Flanders battlefields with his cronies and visited Paris with Albert Speer as his guide. While the *Führer* was enjoying himself, his staff was congratulating themselves on the ease of the German victory in the west. The OKW's chief of staff, General Alfred Jodl, noted in his diary that "[t]he final victory over England is only a matter of time."[159] His boss, Field Marshal Wilhelm Keitel, commented that crossing the English Channel was simply a matter of a "powerful river crossing."[160] At least the German army and the *Kriegsmarine* had the sense to recognize that Operation SEA LION, code name for the invasion of the United Kingdom, needed air superiority over the Channel and southern England, or it was a no-go. In fact, SEA LION never had a chance of succeeding, even if the Germans had been able to achieve temporary air superiority over the Channel.[161] The British had thirty-five destroyers stationed at Harwich and thirty-five more at Plymouth and Portsmouth, which, moving up and down the Channel, would have made mincemeat out of any German invasion force, most of which would have been transported on Rhine River barges.

The most significance contrast between the opposing sides lay in their ability to understand their upcoming opponent. One of the leading analysts in the British Y Service, which monitored *Luftwaffe* radio transmissions, underlined the advantage the British were already enjoying in intelligence by summer 1940 in her memoirs:

> [b]y the end of the summer of 1940 the Air Ministry intelligence had an almost complete picture of the *Luftwaffe's* Order of Battle, particularly in Western Europe. . . . [E]ven in the summer of 1940, we could almost certainly confirm the height at which the [enemy] formations were approaching, and we were also able to give some indication, from what we were hearing, of their intended action.[162]

Standing in stark contrast was the performance of German intelligence, *Luftwaffe* intelligence in particular. On July 16, General Joseph "Beppo" Schmidt, chief of *Luftwaffe* intelligence, issued his organization's assessment of "the other." Virtually every one of his estimates and assumptions was wrong, from underestimating the capability of British fighters and the production capabilities of British industry to (and most important) failing to mention that not only did the Allied Fighter Command possess radar but had managed to integrate it into a systemic approach to air defense.[163] General Schmidt concluded with the upbeat comment that "the *Luftwaffe*, unlike the RAF, will be in a position in every respect to achieve a decisive effect this year."[164]

Given the correlation of forces and the limited range of the Bf 109, it is doubtful that the Germans could have won the Battle of Britain under any conditions except massive British incompetence. Additionally, the appalling ineffectiveness of the intelligence being fed to the *Luftwaffe* planners and flight crews certainly did not help matters. In retrospect, the outcome of the Battle of Britain and the following nighttime assault on British cities is not surprising: in 1940, the Germans possessed neither the air nor naval capabilities to accomplish that task.

Significantly, German attention was focusing on other possibilities even before the Battle of Britain began. In early July, General Walter von Brauchitsch, the army's commander-in-chief, and General Franz Halder, chief of the general staff, set in motion the planning for an invasion of the Soviet Union. Both apparently failed to consider Britain a long-term strategic problem.[165] At the end of July, they met with Hitler; during their conversation, the *Führer* mentioned that he believed that the only reason that the British were rejecting the possibility of peace lay in their belief that the Soviet Union and the United States would enter the war. In this case, he was right, but his solution, namely to launch a massive assault on the Soviets, made little sense. Yet, that decision delighted the army leaders. The *Luftwaffe*'s chief of staff, General Hans Jeschonneck, greeted the prospect of invading the Soviet Union with the comment, "at last, a proper war."[166] For the Germans, what they had supposed was going to be a short war with the Soviet Union turned into a nightmarish war of attrition. Much as in the Battle of Britain, German intelligence became a major factor in the catastrophes that began to swamp the *Wehrmacht*.[167]

Once it was clear that the Germans had failed in the Battle of Britain, Churchill's problem was how Britain was going to win the war against a Germany that controlled the Continent. The romance that followed between Churchill and President Roosevelt, aimed at drawing the United States into the conflict, proved more difficult at first than Churchill had anticipated, while the Soviets proved obdurately obtuse about the danger gathering on their borders in the west.[168] Beyond air defense, the British confronted the problems raised by the defense of Britain's trade lines to bring in the foodstuffs and raw materials required to fight the war.[169] But air and sea defense of the British Isles would not by themselves lead to anything other than stalemate.

Therefore, Churchill had to address the problem of what Britain could do that would strike at the Germans directly. As early as the summer of 1940, he placed Britain's emphasis at hitting back at the Germans with bombers. At the same time, he pushed the cabinet to establish the Special Operations Executive (SOE), as he suggested, to set "Europe ablaze." The resistance groups that SOE helped to create and support would prove to be of considerable help in tying down German troops. In the case of Operation OVERLORD, the invasion of France on June 6, 1944, resistance sabotage and hit-and-run attacks would make the *Wehrmacht*'s efforts to reinforce the Normandy battlefront more difficult. Nevertheless, in the end the resistance movements proved less effective than Churchill had hoped.

Initially, Churchill was optimistic about the prospects of a strategic bombing campaign against Nazi Germany. He commented in summer 1940, "There is one thing that . . . will bring [Germany] down and that is an absolutely devastating, exterminating attack by heavy bombers from this country upon the Nazi homeland."[170] A year later, Churchill was not so optimistic, especially after the Butt Report, which had studied the efforts of Bomber Command, indicated how little effect the bombing of Germany was achieving. He minuted Air Marshal Sir Charles Portal that

> . . . it is very disputable whether bombing by itself will be a decisive factor in the present war. On the contrary, all that we have learned since the war began shows that its effect, both physical and moral, are greatly exaggerated. . . . The most that we can say is that it will be a heavy and I trust a seriously increasing annoyance.[171]

To a certain extent, Churchill was being too cautious. Its impact was to prove devastating on German morale as well as on the Reich's economy. In the case of the former, while its impact on morale did not lead to Germany's collapse, it seriously affected the support the Nazi regime enjoyed among the general population.[172] Moreover, it pushed Hitler and his advisors down an unintended path, namely to invest heavily not only in bombers rather than in fighters, but in the development and deployment of the V-2 rocket, perhaps the most expensive and useless weapons system of the war.[173] Göring commented in October 1943 that all the German population "wished to hear when a hospital or a children's home in Germany is destroyed is that we have destroyed the same in England; then they are satisfied."[174] Nevertheless, whatever its effect on German morale, British bombing failed to cause the collapse of the Nazi regime, as so many of the prewar air power predictions had posited. The Nazi regime proved more than capable of controlling the German population with the ruthless means at its disposal until the end of the Third Reich in April 1945.

Equally damaging to the Reich's continued survival were the direct effects created by Bomber Command's efforts. By early 1943, what had been mere pinpricks turned into massive hammer blows. In the spring of 1943, in the Battle of the Ruhr, British bombers smashed up the major cities of the Ruhr. These attacks came perilously close to breaking the Reich's war economy, particularly by damaging the German ability to transport coal to the rest of the economy. As the foremost economic historian of the Reich, Adam Tooze, has noted,

> Reading contemporary sources, there can be no doubt that the Battle of the Ruhr marked a turning point in the history of the German

war economy, which has been grossly underestimated by post-war accounts.... Most significantly, the shortage of key components brought the rapid increase in *Luftwaffe* production to an abrupt halt. Between July 1943 and March 1944 there was no further increase in the monthly output of aircraft.... As Speer himself acknowledged, Allied bombing had negated all plans for a further increase in production. Bomber Command had stopped Speer's armaments miracle in its track.[175]

At this point of the war, the Third Reich was fighting against two enormously different kinds of opponents.[176] On the Eastern Front, the *Wehrmacht* found itself engaged in a massive battle of attrition with the Soviet Union that much resembled the terrible battles of World War I, with its slaughter of infantry by firepower, except in this case with maneuvers that covered hundreds of miles. In the west and in the North Atlantic, the Germans confronted the Anglo-American powers in a battle of attrition, but one that was quite different from what was happening in the east. In this case, attrition came in terms of *equipment* and those who *crewed the weapons systems*: fighters versus bombers, and merchant shipping and escorts versus U-boats. In both battles, the losses were terrifying. The U-boats lost over 75 percent of their crews. The Allies lost nearly 15 million tons of merchant shipping. The losses for Bomber Command were equally depressing. Half of the crews died before the end of their tours; 25 percent were wounded or captured by the Germans, while only 25 percent survived the war unscathed.[177] In the summer and fall of 1943 and well into the spring of 1944, America's Eighth Air Force was losing between 25 and 35 percent of its bomber crews *every month*.[178]

In the technological sides of the war, there was a sharp difference between how the British and the Germans conducted the war. The British folded in the best and the brightest of their civilian world into their intelligence and scientific assessment. And, while the German military and civilian leaders consistently undervalued and underutilized the civilian expertise that they might have used to bolster the Reich's war effort, the British did not. Scientists such as R. V. Jones and Solly Zuckerman provided not only brilliant intelligence analysis to the tactical and operational problems confronting the British military, but in some cases they were able to provide insights that formed the basis for crucial military operations.[179]

In early 1944, Zuckerman, serving as the chief scientific adviser to Air Marshal Arthur Tedder, General Eisenhower's deputy, suggested that the Allies conduct a major air offensive against the French transportation network as a means of preventing the *Wehrmacht* from reinforcing the battlefront in Normandy. Using Zuckerman's arguments, Eisenhower and Tedder were then able to force the most unwilling British and American bomber barons to conduct such a campaign, which proved to be a major enabler of Allied efforts in the Battle of Normandy. One cannot imagine the Germans utilizing a zoologist, which is what Zuckerman was, as an adviser to the most senior commanders in the German military—moreover, one whose advice those senior commanders consistently followed.

But it was much more than simply taking a few scientists into the analytic community that made the Allied analytic effort so effective in the war. Bletchley Park and the breaking of the Enigma codes was not just the triumph of mathematicians like Alan Turing. Integrating German-speaking historians and others into the effort played a large role in comprehending the intentions of German military commanders. Perhaps the best example was the incorporation of the Cambridge undergraduate history major Harry Hinsley into the naval intelligence effort. It was Hinsley, at the age of twenty-two, who figured out that the German weather ships off Iceland were using the same code settings as the U-boats. Similarly, the key intelligence officer in analyzing the German U-boat campaign was Rodger Winn, a forty-year-old barrister who had been crippled as a child by polio and who could not stand for long periods of time without excruciating pain.[180] Again, one cannot imagine the Germans utilizing similar individuals in the battle to understand what Sun Tzu so accurately characterized as "the other."

In the largest sense, the Germans were incapable of understanding "the other." It was not just a matter of their intelligence failures, which admittedly were immense. Above all, it was their strategic assessments, skewed as they were by nonsensical ideological preconceptions, that led the Germans in 1941 to invade the Soviet Union and then, at the end of the year, to declare war on the United States. Thus, within two years and three months of the invasion of Poland, the Germans had managed to repeat every major strategic mistake that they had made in World War I, thereby setting in motion their doom. Admittedly, through the end of 1942 there was no Western Front, but by the spring of 1943, Bomber Command, soon to be augmented by the Eighth Air Force, had recreated a Western Front with a vengeance—in this case one that played to Allied strengths, rather than weaknesses.

Conclusion

This chapter covers the nearly thirty-one years of competitive interaction between the British and the Germans. Of those years, slightly less than a third involved direct action by their military forces. In many respects, the

Germans enjoyed considerable advantages at the tactical level against their British opponents. This was true, certainly in the first stages of both wars, but particularly throughout the second. And yet, in the largest sense, the inability of the Germans to assess the strategic equations in both world wars completely negated their tactical advantages.

Contributing to their flawed strategic assessments was the general inability to understand the British, either strategically or operationally. Not surprisingly, the British proved particularly adept in their handling of allies in both wars, while the Germans proved almost completely inept. It was only in the interwar period that British leaders floundered strategically and politically in their assessment of the degree of menace that the Germans represented. Those errors of judgment are perhaps understandable, but not excusable, given the nightmarish war through which Britain had so recently passed. In the end, strategic leadership demands vision and a willingness to strip away the fog with which one's facile assumptions encompass harsh realities. The real strike against the Chamberlain government's appeasement policies in the late 1930s was the fact that it followed, rather than led, the British public in recognition of the German danger.

As suggested in the opening paragraphs, the ties between Britain and Germany should have provided these competing powers with some sense of "the other." For the most part, they did not. In World War I, only obdurately stupid behavior on the part of the Germans forced the British to commit themselves to the struggle. The interwar period saw the British pile illusory assumption on top of illusion. Only when they were looking over the brink into the catastrophe of absolute defeat, with the fall of France, did the British finally recognize the nature of the German menace. But even then, it took the extraordinary intellectual toughness and perceptions of Winston Churchill for the British to hang on in the face of the existential threat that the Third Reich represented.

This chapter should warn those who make strategy and policy in the future how extraordinarily difficult it is to understand "the other," even when that "other" is by history, culture, and economics intimately connected to their world. Where that is not the case, and a vast gulf of history, culture, and intellectual understanding exists between two powers in a long-term competition in the international arena, the problem of understanding "the other" becomes exponentially more difficult. Facile assumptions and hopes for the future inevitably will lead to disaster.

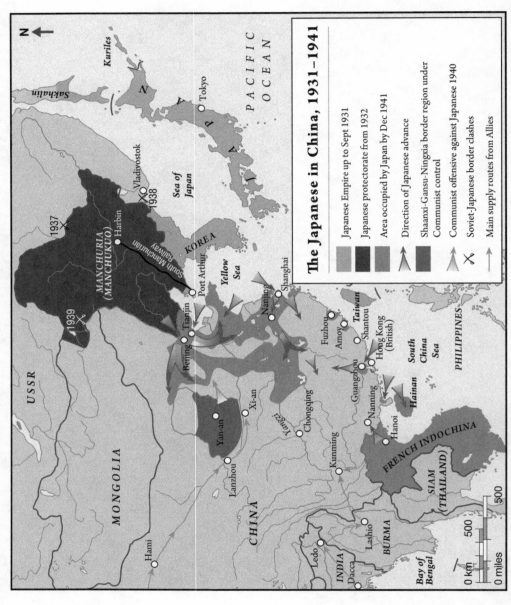

The Japanese in China, 1931–1941

- Japanese Empire up to Sept 1931
- Japanese protectorate from 1932
- Area occupied by Japan by Dec 1941
- Direction of Japanese advance
- Shaanxi-Gansu-Ningxia border region under Communist control
- Communist offensive against Japanese 1940
- Soviet-Japanese border clashes
- Main supply routes from Allies

N

USSR

MONGOLIA

MANCHURIA (MANCHUKUO)

Harbin

South Manchurian Railway

KOREA

Sakhalin

Kuriles

Vladivostok
1938

1937

1939

Sea of Japan

J A P A N

Tokyo

P A C I F I C
O C E A N

Beijing
Tianjin
Port Arthur

Yellow
Sea

Yan-an

Xi-an

Lanzhou

Hami

CHINA

Yangzi

Chongqing

Kunming

Nanjing

Shanghai

Fuzhou

Amoy
Shantou

Taiwan

Guangzhou

Nanning

Hainan

Hong Kong
(British)

South China
Sea

PHILIPPINES

Hanoi

FRENCH INDOCHINA

SIAM
(THAILAND)

BURMA

Lashio

Ledo

INDIA

Dacca

Bay of
Bengal

0 km   500
0 miles   500

The Japanese in China, 1931–1941.

CHAPTER 13

China, Russia, and Japan Compete to Create a New World Order

S. C. M. Paine

I N THE WEST, WE think of peace as the norm and war as the aberration. In the nineteenth and twentieth centuries, however, war was the norm for Asia.[1] China and Russia generally rejected the Westernizing global order and, with varying degrees of determination, sought to overturn it. Japan typically tried to adapt but, when that proved impossible, it too tried to create an alternate order. Sweeping changes in the global economy set the context for the diplomacy and wars among China, Russia, and Japan. Occasionally these changes were of such a magnitude and the effects so long lasting that they constituted framing events—they decisively influenced what followed by introducing new constraints and by opening new opportunities, and their sweeping nature ultimately forced all to alter their previous courses of action.

Two sets of framing events upended the international context of Sino-Russo-Japanese relations: first, the industrial revolution, and second, the combined effects of World War I and the Great Depression. After the Napoleonic Wars, the industrial revolution spread from England to the Continent and gradually to the rest of the world in a process that continues to the present day. Wherever it spread, it upended the regional and ultimately the global balance of power. Then mismanagement of military strategy in World War I and of economic strategy in the Great Depression destroyed the European political and economic order. The combined effects put communism and fascism on steroids both in Europe and in Asia, producing pernicious effects felt to the present.

Framing Events: The Industrial Revolution

The industrial revolution was a catastrophic event for traditional societies. Previously successful foreign policy paradigms suddenly and inexplicably, from their points of view, no longer worked. In fact, changes made far, far away had put them on a very unequal footing with industrialized countries. A new era had dawned based on steam power, the iron industry, textiles, the insurance industry, banking, and in its later stages on railways, telegraphs, and steamships. Together these changes transformed static societies into the rapidly changing world taken for granted today. The new institutions and technologies produced economic growth, something virtually unknown in traditional societies, and, over several generations of compounded growth, the differences in wealth between those who industrialized and those who did not became enormous.[2] Today, the international balance of power and per capita standards of living reflect different degrees of industrialization.

The industrial revolution gave rise to an emerging Westernized global order conducive to the promotion of trade and the creation of wealth. It was based on freedom of navigation, international law, and a growing set of international institutions to facilitate trade and communication. At its root, it was a maritime global order because its members were bound together by maritime shipping, which was far cheaper than the overland trade, which it soon eclipsed. Russia had risen to greatness, in part, as an essential link of the Silk Road, transporting Asian luxury goods to Europe. Steam navigation and the Suez Canal (opened in 1869) marginalized the overland trade and removed the economic foundation of Russian greatness.[3]

Historically, Russia and China had been great land empires. By the nineteenth century, geography and ambitious autocrats had endowed them vast territories, numerous contiguous colonies, and security paradigms that heretofore had been effective at maintaining and expanding their empires. Meanwhile, Japan, as an island separated from security threats by an oceanic moat, had generally focused inward. It traded with neighbors and had harmonious relations with China, whose cultural achievements were admired by educated Japanese. The industrial revolution, however, upset this traditional world, forcing the Chinese, Russians, and Japanese to respond or submit to the bidding of others.

China's Pre-Industrial Revolution Security Paradigm

China long failed to grasp the economic, technological, and military implications of the industrial revolution.[4] The Chinese government, rather than devising ways to profit from the growing commerce with Europe, resisted the increasingly strident Western demands for trade. China, the reigning superpower of the known world (that is, the world known to China), did not accept the dictates of others. It set the rules of the world order. For millennia, China had dominated its much smaller East and Southeast Asian neighbors culturally, technologically, militarily, and economically. Burma, Indochina, Korea, Japan, and Thailand belonged to China's Sinicized world. They emulated its governmental institutions, educational system, and society. Their governments followed the international norms of the Chinese global order, in which China played the grand puppeteer and choreographer of international relations.

The Han, the dominant ethnic group in China, considered their civilization to be the acme of human achievement and did not recognize the existence of other civilizations. China's destiny was to spread its civilization across the known world to unite "all under heaven" (*tianxia*, 天下), one of the names that the Han used to designate China. Each emperor sought to maintain and, if possible, to expand the territory his predecessors had amassed. In times of population growth, the Han migrated outward in search of arable lands. They encouraged or coerced minority peoples to adopt Han practices and, over time, many of these peoples lost their original ethnic identities to become Han. Those who refused to assimilate were driven first into the hills—areas not suitable for the settled agriculture of the Han—and eventually to the frontier. Such a strategy produced ethnic homogeneity in the core lands of the Chinese Empire.

The Han considered those not adhering to their practices to be barbarians, ignorant people living on the periphery, whom the Han would either buy off with trade or militarily crush when necessary. Historically, lethal security threats came not from the Sinicized world but overland from the nomadic tribes from the northwest and north, the Muslims, the Mongols, and the Manchus. The latter two had conquered China to form conquest dynasties, the Mongol Yuan dynasty (1271–1368) and Manchu Qing dynasty (1644–1911), the two territorially largest dynasties in Han history. Muslims, however, mostly rejected the Sinicized order.

During China's last dynasty, the Qing, the emperor garnered the acquiescence of diverse subject peoples by adopting their religious practices— Buddhism for the Mongols and Tibetans, and Daoism and Confucianism for the Han. The emperor gave generous gifts to the leaders of his subject peoples and married daughters by secondary concubines to the sons of Inner Asian leaders, in return for compliance with Han norms for foreign policy. But the Muslims of Xinjiang, Gansu, and Yunnan rejected Han and Manchu attempts to pose as representatives of their religious hierarchy and periodically rose up to secede from the empire, a problem that continues to bedevil present-day Chinese rule over Xinjiang.[5] These civil wars included bitter fighting in

- Xinjiang (1820–1828, 1847, 1862–1878);
- Gansu (1845, 1895);
- Yunnan (1846, 1855–1873); and
- the Donggan Rebellion in Gansu and Shaanxi (1862–1873).

According to Han norms, both foreign policy and military decisions were made in Beijing. Retreat, loss of arms, and battlefield defeat could all yield a death sentence for the unlucky commander. Rigidity in mission fulfillment did not allow for reassessment in the field and presumed that China, as the superior power, always had the ability to win each battle.[6] The Han dealt with neighbors separately and worked to prevent them from coordinating. If facing multiple adversaries, China would appease one—often through preferential trade arrangements—while annihilating the most dangerous threat. For example, in the eighteenth century, rather than contest Russian expansion along the northern banks of the Amur River, the Chinese chose to buy harmony with trade at the border town of Kiakhta (south of Lake Baikal), the precursor to the treaty ports that the Europeans would use. At the time, China was busy suppressing the Zunghar Empire. Chinese victory over the latter entailed genocide for the Zunghar Mongols, permanently eliminating both the threat and the ethnic group.[7] As long as the Han remained technologically and organizationally superior to their neighbors, and as long as the neighbors could not coordinate, the strategy worked. The era of rapid communication beginning with the telegraph would make enemy coordination possible, with lethal effects for China.

By the late eighteenth century, the Qing Empire had reached its maximum territorial extent. In fact, the final military campaigns of conquest had been costly and produced little further expansion. The campaigns to subdue the Tibetan Jinchuan minority in Western Sichuan (1747–1749, 1771–1776) succeeded, but at enormous cost. The Qing then practiced genocide on the Jinchuan who, like the Zunghars, have disappeared from the ethnic map. The Qing Burma Campaign (1766–1770) failed, as did the Vietnam Campaign (1788–1789).[8]

Although territorial conquests and New World crops introduced in the eighteenth century increased the available arable land, by the early nineteenth century, population had outrun agricultural productivity, yielding rural poverty and the increasing frequency and lethality of rural rebellions.[9] Endemic civil wars have been a persistent feature of Chinese history, and dynastic change often rides on a wave of horrific peasant rebellions against their urban overlords.

Such civil wars came in two variants: minority groups attempting to secede from the Chinese Empire or Han groups rebelling, with the goal of usurping central rule in Beijing. (These were in addition to the many Muslim revolts listed earlier.)

- Secession attempts by minority groups
  - Miao (1795–1806, 1855–1872); Yi (1817–1821); Li (1831, 1887); Yao (1832, 1836, 1847)
  - In Qinghai (1822)
  - In Taiwan (1787–1788, 1826, 1832–1833, 1862–1864, 1888–1889)
- Rebellions by Han groups
  - White Lotus Sect (1796–1805); Heaven-Earth Society (1853–1865)
  - Eight Trigrams (1813)
  - Small Knife Society (1853–1855)
  - Taiping (1851–1864)
  - Boxers (1899–1900)
  - Nian (1851–1868)

Civil wars of both types reached a crescendo in the third quarter of the nineteenth century, the worst possible timing, as they coincided with the spread of the industrial revolution in Europe, the consequent growth of Western trading interests in Asia, and the expansion of the Russian Empire into Central and East Asian lands belonging to the Chinese sphere of influence. For the first time in history, China faced not only the usual pairing of a landward threat with a civil war at home, but also an unprecedented additional seaward threat. To survive the rebellions, China tried to buy off the Russians with territory in the north and the maritime West with trading privileges on the coast. The West decided to help the dynasty by providing military expertise. Had it fallen, the West risked losing the many treaties setting up the treaty port system—China's interface with the global maritime order and precursor to Deng Xiaoping's special economic zones, set up more than a century later. China then used Western technology to defeat the most threatening rebellions: the Taiping, Nian, Donggan, and Xinjiang. There were many other factors that went into the Qing victory, but it was such a close call that the Qing may have required all factors to survive.[10] Not millions, but tens of millions died, and much of the country was devastated. Western aid did not save, but may have delayed, the demise of the Qing dynasty for two generations. The dynasty fell in 1911, instead of at the height of the civil wars in the 1860s.

Thereafter, China responded with a "self-strengthening" movement. Han officials rapidly understood the efficacy of Western military technology and set about learning how to use and manufacture it. In the 1860s, various Han governors set up provincial arsenals and during the next two decades established some of the heavy industry necessary to manufacture weapons. They also hired foreign military experts to form Western-drilled armies.[11] The self-strengtheners understood Western power strictly in military terms. At the end of the Xinjiang Rebellion in the 1870s, when China had a large standing army in place, it forced Russia to back off from an attempt to absorb the Ili Valley on the Russo-Xinjiang frontier. Russia, which lacked the transportation system to deploy troops in sufficient numbers, had to withdraw and rescind its 1873 declaration of Russia's newest region of Kuldja.[12] With this success, the Chinese incorrectly believed that they could resume foreign policy as usual.

Russia's Pre-Industrial Revolution Security Paradigm

Like China, Russia was a great land empire, whose leaders saw power and prestige in terms of territorial extent and so aimed at maximizing all three. Likewise, Russia's neighbors were much smaller both in territory and population. But unlike China, historically Russia was not culturally central; rather, it was a backwater of Europe that could boast superiority only in military and territorial terms. Russians tried to make a case for their own spiritual superiority, connecting the Russian spirit (*russkaia dusha*, русская душа) with a mystical quality associated with the Russian Orthodox Church and Russian culture. Their technologically superior neighbors were struck not by Russia's soul, but by its general poverty juxtaposed to the lavish living of a small aristocracy. Long historical connections with Europe meant that Russia rapidly felt the effects of the industrial revolution and began importing technology much earlier than did China. These effects would become lethal after the unification of Germany in 1871, putting a technologically superior great industrial power on Russia's border.

Like China, Russia also had a highly successful strategy for empire. Russian peasants fled their enserfers and spread out in search of new land on the frontiers. Fortune seekers also gravitated toward the frontiers. Farmers soon sought government help to defend their new lands against marauders. Nearby military commands tended to provide help. Civil officials followed. If the local Russian population and skeletal administration could take and retain territory on the cheap, the Russian government recognized their actions. If they could not, the Russian government disavowed them (a scenario that Russian President Vladimir Putin may have been trying to replay in 2014 vis-à-vis Ukraine).[13]

Under the tsars, Russia often absorbed new territories administratively as military governorships, but later civilianized them as regular provinces after the gradual emplacement of regular administrative structures. Peasants and adventurers then tried to escape these structures by moving ever further afield, beginning the process anew. The preeminent historian of the late tsarist period, Vasilii O. Kliuchevskii, famously wrote:

> The history of Russia is the history of a country in the process of colonizing itself. Her area of colonization grows in tandem with her national territory. At times shrinking and at times growing, this age-old movement continues to this very day.... Therefore, the periods in our history are the stages which our people have gone through in the occupation and development of the land acquired by them.[14]

These methods produced an empire spanning ten time zones, but they did not bring prosperity to Russia's citizens. The gap in their standard of living relative to those of western Europeans grew rapidly after the advent of the industrial revolution, closed somewhat during the Great Depression and the decimation of World War II, before again diverging.[15] After the industrial revolution, agriculture, and therefore land, was no longer the key source of wealth. Rather, manufacturing, trade, and (later) services were. An expanded empire brought expanded and costly security requirements. The emerging maritime order and the old order of land empires each required different institutional structures. Under the tsars, the Russian government protected the interests of the rural landed gentry, not of the urban commercial interests central to the development of the industrial revolution.[16]

Russian geography precluded a seamless transition to the institutional structures favored by the maritime trading nations. Out of very real security concerns, continental empires funnel resources into the military at the expense of the civil economy and of economic growth. An empire the size of Romanov Russia had many neighbors, which were often its most lethal adversaries. Protection from hostile neighbors required a large standing army, which had a palpable presence in the capital and consequent influence on political institutions. Under the tsars, education of the elite was militarized, with gentry children donning cadet uniforms. The two rules for continental empire were (1) no great powers on the borders, and (2) no two-front wars. So Russia worked assiduously to prevent the rise of any neighboring great power. This entailed the destabilization of neighbors (the three eighteenth-century partitions of Poland), the piecemeal ingestion of territories (applied to the Ottoman Empire, Persia, and China),[17] and, in the Soviet period, the funding of multiple sides in civil wars to create a failing state (the long Chinese Civil War).[18] It is no accident that so many dysfunctional states ring Russia. This traditional paradigm for continental empire entailed a negative-sum global order: Either Russia absorbed the contested territory or a neighbor kept it, but the fight to determine sovereignty damaged the contested lands, producing a negative sum.

As two expanding land empires, Romanov Russia and Qing China began to overlap in the mid-seventeenth century. The modus operandi established in the early eighteenth century at the time of the Qing suppression of the Zunghar Empire lasted nearly two centuries. As a result, Russia had the earliest European presence in Beijing, an ecclesiastical mission dating to the early eighteenth century. It took advantage of the coincidence of China's great internal rebellions with the Opium Wars to negotiate their shared frontier. Without firing a shot, it acquired territories five times the area of Japan by posing as China's mediator, supposedly to help fend off the British and French Opium War demands, while China desperately dealt with the Taiping Rebellion.[19]

Had China acquiesced to Western trading demands and taxed the trade, it could have avoided the Opium Wars, profited from the trade, and developed its economy. In the event, the West forced China to give in on trade, but at a cost of bitterness on both sides and increasingly intrusive treaties, while China ceded vast swaths of territory to Russia for no services rendered. To this day, the Chinese have failed to appreciate the gross strategic error committed by their government of fighting the wrong enemy. The commercial relations the West sought to develop were indicative of future global economic trends, a wave China should have tried to ride, instead of futilely trying to stop. The solution to the commodity of opium was not war but diplomacy, regulation, and taxation. Moreover, there was no need to cede any territory to Russia whatsoever, since, without a railway system, Russia could not deploy troops to take and hold the territory. Russia simply had one extremely clever diplomat in Beijing, who duped the Manchus.[20] The Chinese have attributed their defeat in the Opium Wars to Western actions instead of the existential problem caused by a wave of internal rebellions, whose causes were internal, overlaid by Chinese officials' long-standing lack of curiosity about Europe, which left them ignorant and soon blindsided.

Because China did not adhere to the Western belief that treaties were permanent, it had no intention of honoring the terms of coerced documents; rather, it would bide its time to overturn them when the opportunity arose. But attempts to disregard the terms led to more lost wars and more onerous treaty terms: the Treaty of Nanjing (1842), the Treaty of Tianjin (1858), the Treaty of Beijing (1860), the Yantai Convention (1876), and the Treaty of Shimonoseki (1895).[21] As it turned out, repeated defeats in war, in combination with regime-threating internal rebellions, produced permanent treaties that protected Western commercial interests and gave Russia permanent sovereignty. In Chinese history books, these became known as "the unequal treaties," and they named the period "the era of humiliation." The Han, however, never considered their own dire treatment of ethnic minorities, entailing expulsion from traditional homelands or genocide.

Russia derived little wealth from its new territories, whose resources often duplicated the rich and undeveloped natural endowment of European Russia. In any case, the new resources were mainly inaccessible until the Trans-Siberian Railway was completed in 1916, and difficult to access even then. But the goal was not wealth maximization. Rather, Russian leaders clung to the pre-industrial view of territorial extent as the key to greatness and land as the ultimate source of power.

Until the late nineteenth century, Russia faced industrial powers only in Europe, but Japan's rise introduced the prospect of a two-front, Great Power war. For Russia, the rise of Japan and Germany, in combination with the decline of China, were game changers. In World War II, Russia would play China against Japan to prevent a combined German-Japanese invasion.

Japan's Decision to Westernize in Order to Defend against the West

In the late nineteenth century, Japan observed with horror China's vivisection by Russia and its subjugation by the West, and feared it would be next.[22] When the Tokugawa *shogunate* seemed to be following the footsteps of the Qing that led to military defeat and unequal treaties, mid-level samurai rose up against Tokugawa rule. The last Tokugawa *shogun* fell to a brief civil war, the Boshin War (1868–1869), ending the *shogunate* system. The new leaders became known as the Meiji generation in honor of the ruling monarch, the Emperor Meiji (r. 1867–1912). Rather than pursue the strategy of military resistance favored by China, senior statesmen went on a series of fact-finding missions to study the West to learn more about the nature of the threat. They concluded that resistance would boomerang and instead embarked on a strategy of Westernization, not out of any affinity for Western culture, but out of the painful conclusion that Japan must adapt Western civil and military institutions in order to fend off the West.

Their grand strategy had two phases: a domestic phase, followed by a foreign policy phase. During the former, Japan carefully eschewed foreign policy crises by compromising with the Great Powers, lest war derail the domestic reform program. China took the opposite approach. Chinese resistance led to a series of regional wars that China lost—the Opium War (1839–1842), the Arrow War (1856–1860), the Sino-French War (1883–1885), the First Sino-Japanese War (1894–1895), and the foreign intervention in the Boxer Uprising (1899–1900). The constant warfare—both civil and regional—precluded domestic reforms until the last decade of imperial rule, when China belatedly tried to introduce a broad reform program along the lines of what Japan implemented, but the military modernization led to a regime-changing mutiny of the Westernized army, whose Han officers and conscripts overthrew Manchu minority rule forever.[23]

Japanese leaders, by contrast, intended to protect their national security by transforming their country into a Westernized great power. This would entail creating the domestic institutional structures to eliminate the pretext for extraterritoriality—the adherence of Western nationals to Western law while residing in Japan—and other discriminatory articles of the so-called "unequal" treaties. Japan's leaders also believed that Great Powers required empires. Geography dictated that theirs would be on the Korean Peninsula and extending into Manchuria in order to create a resource base sufficient for prosperity and national security.

The domestic reform phase lasted from 1869 to 1894. The reforms included compulsory education, universal military conscription, an army general staff, the Bank of Japan, a new criminal code, a Cabinet subordinate to a prime minister, Imperial Tokyo University, civil service examinations, a constitution, a parliament, a reorganized court system, and a code of civil procedure. Together they became know as the Meiji Reforms. Japan made these painful and highly unpopular changes in order to become not just a consumer but also a producer of the modern technology necessary to protect its national security.

The domestic phase of these institutional reforms ended in 1894 when Great Britain, the reigning superpower, renegotiated its "unequal" treaties with Japan with a new set that treated Japan like any European power because Japan had the Westernized institutions necessary to conduct diplomatic and commercial relations according to the norms of the Westernized maritime order. Meanwhile, China did not rid itself of its unequal treaties until the height of World War II and, arguably later, with the return of Hong Kong and Macau to Chinese sovereignty in the late 1990s.

Upon completion of the domestic phase of its reforms, Japan immediately began the foreign policy phase to create an empire. Japan colonized its neighbors to stabilize failing states in the belief that only with stability and economic integration could they all prosper. Japan and Russia simultaneously became interested in the same territory. In the third quarter of the nineteenth century, Russia conquered the khanates of Central Asia and in 1891 began construction of a Trans-Siberian Railway that promised to overturn the balance of power in Manchuria, when Russia alone would be able rapidly to deploy troops. Like the Qing dynasty, Korea's Yi dynasty became ever more dysfunctional with each passing nineteenth-century monarch. Similarly, Korea faced the largest peasant rebellion in its history. Before Russia could use the railway to dash Japan's plans for empire by dominating northeast Asia, Japan fought two wars of Russian containment: the First Sino-Japanese War (1894–1895) and the Russo-Japanese War (1904–1905). It won both and gained not only Korea, but also Taiwan, the Pescadores, and southern Manchuria. Initially, the West extolled Japan's transformation into a Great Power and its constructive participation in the maritime global order.

The Meiji generation developed a new security paradigm. Each major conquest began with a surprise attack—on Korea in the First Sino-Japanese War, Russian interests in Manchuria in the Russo-Japanese War, and throughout the Pacific in World War II. After winning the first two wars, Japan installed administrative institutions under the Imperial Japanese Army to maintain public order and to extract resources. It invested heavily in infrastructure, pacification, resource extraction, commercial crop development, and education. These created a literate population, a superior infrastructure, and rapid economic growth, particularly in urban areas.[24] By World War II, it had transformed Manchuria into the most economically developed part of Asia outside the Japanese home islands.[25] These factors were essential for the post–World War II economic miracles in Japan's primary colonies of Korea and Taiwan. Under Deng Xiaoping, China emulated Japan's very successful economic development strategy, but without crediting Japan.

The Meiji generation understood the dawning post–industrial revolution global order far better than did Russia's leaders, let alone China's. The latter two saw the threat posed by the industrial revolution in military terms, so their solution entailed the importation, use, and manufacture of military technology. The Meiji generation saw the interconnections between civil and military institutions. Because many senior leaders had served in both, they had connections crossing institutions. The Meiji Constitution, however, did not set up any requirements to maintain these connections. The next generation would have better formal educations, but career tracks within particular organizations, so that military leaders would lose their appreciation for the civil side of governance and civil leaders would lack military credentials and, therefore, their military counterparts often did not respect them. In the early twentieth century, although the West continued to approve of Japanese goals, it increasingly loathed their methods that relied on coercion when those undergoing colonization resisted. The more concerted the resistance, the more vicious Japan's reprisals became. By the mid-1930s, a proclivity for reprisals would make Japan's empire ungovernable by creating determined enemies wherever the Imperial Japanese Army deployed.[26]

China, Russia, and Japan all responded to the industrial revolution in different ways. In the nineteenth century, China was the least receptive and Japan the most receptive to cooperating within the developing Westernized global maritime order and to initiating comprehensive reforms that Westernized its civil and military institutions. In the process, the samurai lost their preeminence and, when they resisted in the Satsuma Rebellion of 1877, conscripts in the new Westernized army rapidly defeated them. After defeat in the Crimean War (1853–1856), Russia implemented a much more modest reform program, whose most notable feature was the emancipation of serfs in 1861. In the 1880s and 1890s, the government invested heavily in infrastructure development and after defeat in the Russo-Japanese War, followed immediately by the Revolution of 1905, set up a weak parliament and implemented agrarian reforms to relieve rural poverty. Throughout this long, slow process, the government continued to protect its agrarian-based class structure and autocratic governing institutions, empowering one clan to rule.[27] And unlike Japan, it did not eschew foreign crises while it reformed, but under its last tsar, staggered from foreign crisis to foreign crisis—the Russo-Japanese War, followed by a succession of Balkan crises that culminated in World War I, which destroyed tsarism itself.[28]

Lessons from the Industrial Revolution

- Those who ignore fundamental structural changes in the international economy do so at their peril. Time does not wait for the stubborn.

Nor does time wait for the blind. It is imperative to distinguish one's primary, secondary, and tertiary enemies.

- China correctly identified the primary enemy as Chinese seeking to overthrow the dynasty, but it did not grasp that Russia, a country after Chinese territory, was the secondary problem, while the West, separated by seas, could never pose an equivalent threat.
- Ignorance of one's enemies is dangerous. A deeper Chinese knowledge of the West would have revealed the latter's primary interest in trade, which the Chinese could have turned to their mutual benefit.
- Finally, power is as much about a country's economic base and the structure of its civil institutions as it is about military institutions and hardware. Japan was the lone developing country of the nineteenth century to grasp the importance of institutions, whose structure then either predisposes or impedes the formulation of effective strategies.

Framing Events: World War I and the Great Depression

The combined effects of World War I and the Great Depression upended the global order yet again. Between the Napoleonic Wars and World War I, there were no global wars. Most European conflicts were short. Until the Russo-Japanese War, Europeans won all their wars against non-European powers and usually at minimal costs to themselves, as was the case for their nineteenth-century conflicts with China. In World War I, relentless trench warfare destroyed a generation of young men across Europe, sent time and again over trenches into oncoming machine-gun fire with predictable results. The army leadership across Europe stuck with costly military strategies, rather than carefully coordinating offensives with allies and military services. The scale of the bloodshed made a spectacle of European governments for their colonies, which now found much more to criticize in their overlords, and for European voters and veterans, who lost faith in their governments. The war severely weakened all European states politically and economically, although the expansion of the British Empire disguised the severity of Britain's wounds. Regime change occurred not only among the Central Powers, but also much more ominously in Russia and soon in Italy.

Russia could not endure the relentless battlefield casualties. The autocracy already faced a growing revolutionary movement prior to the hostilities. After relentless defeats, support for the tsar evaporated in the armed forces. When the successor provisional government tried to continue the war, the army collapsed, opening the opportunity for a communist coup in the capital. Civil war (1917–1922) followed. The new communist government rejected not only the traditional political and economic order, but also the social order. Communism entailed the imposition of centralized political institutions under the Communist Party, the nationalization of all private property, and the physical elimination of huge classes of people who resisted these changes or simply had no place in the new scheme of things. Their elimination required vicious civil wars when those slated for death resisted and, as a consequence, an omnipresent secret police developed in countries with successful communist revolutions.

Meanwhile, in postwar Italy, fascists assumed power in the midst of a severe postwar depression and public outrage over the denial of territories promised by Italy's wartime allies. The fascists promised to restore prosperity and greatness with a new Roman Empire. They emphasized nationalism, the martial races, government economic planning, and the evils of the maritime global order. The Russian communists and the Italian fascists inspired copycat movements across the globe. Both movements constituted violent attempts to replace the maritime global order.

Alternate World Orders: The Bolshevik Revolution

Upon taking power in Russia, the communists (then known as the Bolsheviks) ceded some of the most productive parts of the empire to the Central Powers in return for peace under the Treaty of Brest Litovsk. In addition to a large indemnity, Russia lost 25 percent of its population, 33 percent of its manufacturing, and 27 percent of its agricultural lands.[29] At the time, the Bolsheviks controlled certain cities but little of the countryside. During the course of a vicious civil war, they gradually extended their territorial control over Russia. When the Entente won, it returned Russian territory, but not its colonies of Finland, Poland, and the Baltic states that desired independence.

The Bolsheviks built effective civil and military institutions with incredible speed, and the Soviet model became the road map to seize power in a shattered land that Soviet allies followed the world over: starting with the like-minded banding together to establish a Communist Party, which in tsarist Russia's case operated in exile for many years to protect the leadership from arrest. Within Russia, the party operated at two levels: the public and the covert. It had as large a public presence as the host legal system would allow and a covert presence engaged in terrorism, cadre recruitment, and propaganda to discredit the incumbent government. The plan was to destroy the host government from within, seize power, and implement a social revolution to eliminate elites of all ilk.

To win the civil war, the Bolsheviks leveraged their central position in St. Petersburg and Moscow to use the railway system that fanned out from these two hubs. They paired each military commander with a party member, connected with the secret police, who could eliminate uncooperative commanders as well as their families. Likewise, it paired party members with experts in the civil bureaucracy. This assured Communist Party control. The Bolsheviks also had a strong social program, promising land to the peasants and literacy education for recruits. Land gave peasants a reason to fight, but in a classic bait-and-switch strategy, after the civil war, the new government deployed its battle-hardened army to take back the land from the peasants. It did so out of communist principles as well as financial necessity.[30]

The government transferred wealth from the countryside in order to fund its ambitious urban investment program to develop the heavy industry central for armaments production. These plans excluded rural areas from the benefits of industrialization and modernization, even while making them pay the bill. The government needed to control agricultural production to force the wealth transfer, accomplished by low purchasing prices for agricultural commodities. Not surprisingly, many peasants resisted, slaughtered their animals, and hid their harvests. The government, desperate for food to feed the cities, then sent in the army, confiscated the crops, deported many to prison camps, and a terrible post-collectivization famine ensued in which millions died. [31] Rural living standards plummeted and only slowly recovered before stagnating, but initial industrial growth rates were impressive.

The Russian communists, like the tsars before them, saw greatness in terms of territorial extent and had the even more grandiose vision of transforming communism into the new world order, with Russians in the leadership position. They immediately developed the export version of their road map to power. They set up the Communist International, or Comintern, to train party members and funnel economic and military aid abroad. Although the public face of the Comintern was an organization independent of Russia, in reality it was an arm of Russian foreign policy. The Comintern helped others set up legal front organizations and recruit the like-minded, while also developing a covert organization to engage in proscribed activities—often propaganda, in countries restricting press freedom, and assassinations. In the 1930s, it encouraged the establishment of communist parties along its borders and throughout Europe:

- Denmark and Ukraine in 1919
- Estonia, France, Great Britain, India, Persia, and Turkey in 1920
- China, Czechoslovakia, Ireland, Italy, Mongolia, Portugal, Romania, Spain, and Sweden in 1921
- Japan in 1922
- Norway in 1923
- Syria–Lebanon in 1924
- Korea in 1925
- Vietnam, Siam, Laos, Malaya, and the Philippines in 1930

Other neighbors already had communist parties: Bulgaria (1903), the Netherlands (1909), and Austria, Belorussia, Finland, Germany, Greece, Hungary, Lithuania, and Poland (1918).

Russia was particularly active in China, where its propaganda efforts were more effective than in any other country. The Bolsheviks promised to eliminate all tsarist unequal treaties, gaining instant popularity among Chinese intellectuals, but then secretly reneged without the intellectuals' noticing.[32] Russia funded numerous parties and warlords, most particularly the Chinese Communist Party and also the incumbent Nationalist Party. Its military aid made possible the Northern Expedition (1926–1928) that swept away many of the warlords dividing China to produce a nominal unification under Nationalist rule. When the Communists tried to take over the Nationalist government during the expedition, the Nationalists turned on the Communists and, after a series of extermination campaigns (1930–1934), sent the Communists on the Long March to the north to desolate Yan'an. On the eve of the Northern Expedition, Russia denied repeated Chinese Communist petitions to leave their alliance with Nationalists. As a result, the Nationalists virtually wiped out its urban presence. In 1929, when the Manchurian warlord demanded that Russia give up its railway concessions as a good communist should, Russia deployed its army, and China lost the ensuing Railway War. Thus, despite the communist propaganda, Russia continued to follow the foreign policy of a traditional land power aimed at territorial maximization.[33]

Alternate World Orders: The Fascist Hybrid of Autarky and Empire

The Great Depression was the second of two for Japan.[34] Immediately after World War I, Japan lost its lucrative wartime exports to Europe, and Europeans returned to Asia to recover markets lost to Japan. This caused a postwar depression in Japan, which proved damaging, particularly to rural areas. The Great Depression made a bad situation far worse, with foreign markets eliminated worldwide.

Economic depression created an environment conducive to extremism. It is no coincidence that Japan began the Second Sino-Japanese War in 1931, the year after the United States fatefully introduced the Hawley Smoot tariff, raising its rates to historic highs. The other industrial powers followed suit, leaving trade-dependent Japan out in the cold and its civil leaders, who had long advocated cooperation with the West, in disgrace. This opened the door to the military's eclipse of Japan's civil leadership. Military-backed assassinations of both civil and military leaders silenced surviving moderates and produced cabinet appointments of members favoring an aggressive foreign policy. The finance minister was no longer included in key policy discussions so that the economic and financial consequences of military decisions were no longer carefully analyzed. Government decisions became measured in terms of operational, rather than strategic, success—in terms of military victory in the field of battle, rather than the long-term impact on economic growth, the actual foundation of both military power and personal prosperity. Japan's military lacked their grandparents' understanding of the civil underpinnings of effective governance and confused means with ends. Military victory was a means; prosperity and security were the ends, which the military means soon precluded. In many ways, the Chinese Nationalists followed a similar path. In China, as the Great Depression persisted and Japanese military intervention escalated, the Nationalist Party emasculated the civilian leadership, leaving the military in charge.

In 1931, Japan abandoned the maritime order in which it had long been a constructive member, with fateful consequences for all. Its leaders chose a strategy of autarky to survive in a protectionist world. This entailed an empire expanded to a size sufficient to practice autarky, beginning with the invasion of Manchuria, an area larger than Germany and France combined. When the League of Nations condemned Japan's actions, it withdrew from the organization in 1933, signaling its rejection of the maritime global order for an alternate order based on conquest, autarky, nationalism, and military dominance over politics and society. Some have called this order *fascism*. Japan did so, just as the Nationalists developed a strategy that finally seemed capable of defeating the Chinese Communists. The escalation of Japanese military operations derailed this process, even though the Communists were the primary adversaries of both the Japanese and the Nationalists.

Russia observed with great concern the rise of fascism on two fronts in Germany in the West and Japan in the East. Russia had fallen to a one-front war in World War I when allied with the world's wealthiest nations. This time it was diplomatically isolated and had yet to recover from the combined effects of World War I and the Russian Civil War. In the 1930s, it tried to set up Germany to fight the West so that Russia could play the role of a jackal state late in the war. In fact, when Russia joined with Germany in 1939 to destroy Poland and divide Eastern Europe, it allowed Germany to acquire the resource base necessary to go to war. Germany then turned on Russia, the real target of its ambitions, as Adolf Hitler had made so clear in *Mein Kampf*, a book Joseph Stalin should have read, but apparently did not. So Russian strategy was disastrous in Europe.

However, the strategy was highly effective in Asia, where the Russians brokered a truce in the Chinese civil war. China rejected Japan's plans to transform it into a colony, but did not replay the Manchus' failed strategy of conventional military resistance along the accessible coastline. Instead, the Nationalists and Communists together delivered a mixed conventional-guerrilla strategy that overextended Japan's limited manpower in a futile attempt to garrison the vastness of China. The Japanese army forgot about the rationale for the invasion, which was primarily economic, to become focused on operational wins that led to overextension ever farther inland as the Chinese traded space for time and implemented a ruinous boycott of Japanese goods. China lacked the conventional arms necessary to eject Japan, so the war stalemated. In the end, Japan's strategy of warfare impoverished both China and Japan.

In late 1936, within two weeks of the German-Japanese Anti-Comintern Pact, threatening an alliance that could visit a two-front war on Russia, Russia intervened diplomatically in the Chinese civil war. On the Russian promise of conventional military weapons, the Nationalists and Communists agreed to halt the civil war in order to combine against Japan, whose invasion of China had proceeded without interruption from Manchuria (1931–1933), Jehol (1933), and throughout North China (1933–1935). In 1937, after the Russian diplomatic intervention, the Second Sino-Japanese War escalated to encompass Central and South China, when the Nationalists abandoned their strategy of defeating the Communists before fighting the Japanese and went to war against Japan. Both the Communists and Nationalists believed that the Russians would also provide soldiers, but once they were in, Russia was out. Millions of Chinese died fighting Japan so Russians would not have to.

In 1941, when Japan decided to cut off foreign aid to the Nationalists by attacking US, British, and Dutch interests throughout the Pacific, it transformed the Nationalists from an isolated adversary into a member of a Great-Power alliance. This decision made victory impossible. By excluding the finance minister from high-level government meetings, the military ignored the mortal economic effects of its preferred strategy, which rested increasingly on wishful thinking rather than on a hardheaded assessment of capabilities and goals. Japan's leaders forgot the roots of their prosperity, which lay in trade, not warfare.

Before these irretrievable strategic mistakes, the West missed an opportunity to work with Japan in the 1920s when civil war wracked North China and when Soviet involvement became manifest. Japan's leaders correctly warned of the long-term dangers posed by the spread of communism to China, not only for Japan, but also for the world. The West, however, remained fixated on exacting retribution from Germany for past misdeeds, rather than focused on forestalling future disaster. If the West had not chosen to export its economic problems through protectionism, the speed if not the actual rise of communism and fascism might have been slowed. We will never know whether active Western diplomacy in China, in combination with US membership in the League of Nations, would have helped Japan remain engaged in the Western global order.

Key Lessons from World War I and the Great Depression

- Keep the global economy healthy so that constructive participation in the global maritime order offers economic growth, not poverty.
- Align military campaigns with allies in order to maximize the damage on those who would overturn the global order.
- Likewise, cooperate with friends and coordinate economic policies. The failure to do so by civil and military leaders alike in World War I and the Great Depression—the sins of omission—came at a huge cost, paid not only by their children who fought their war but by their grandchildren, who fought yet another world war that grew

out of the botched termination of World War I and the economic mismanagement of the Great Depression.

World War II leaders, the conscripts of World War I, did not repeat the mistakes of their grandparents, but paid careful attention to allies, joint and combined operations, war termination, enforcement of the peace, and the health of the global economy.

So World War I was not the war to end all wars. It destroyed neither the will nor the ability of Germany to rise again. Instead, it gave rise to two potent world orders hostile to the maritime global order: communism and fascism, which both promised to right the wrongs of unfettered capitalism. The Great Depression put both movements on steroids when democracies throughout the developed world failed to end the depression, leaving workers and factories idle in societies in desperate need of income and manufactures. In contrast, the communists' and fascists' breakneck military spending and comprehensive government economic planning restored their economies to growth long before the conventional strategies followed elsewhere yielded results. For the Anglophone world, World War II was fought to undo the damage.

The Long Cold War Stalemate

In the 1930s, Britain and the United States observed global events with increasing dismay. Adolf Hitler's invasion of Western Europe then made clear that fascism, not communism, posed the greatest threat. Hitler's invasion of Russia soon convinced Russia that the fascists posed a greater danger than the capitalists. German and Japanese actions created a lethal opposing alliance out of the most unlikely partners. Imperial Britain, communist Russia, and the anti-colonial United States cooperated in a way that would have been unthinkable prior to the rise of Hitler. Britain, the guarantor of the prewar world order, and the United States, which would become the guarantor of the postwar peace, spent the war years not only carefully coordinating military campaigns with Russia, but also planning the institutional structures to maintain the postwar order. Their plans ran counter to those of Russia, so it is not surprising that the unlikely alliance dissolved immediately after the common threat of fascist Germany disappeared.

Postwar, the Western allies and Russia set about building opposing global orders. The West tried to reintroduce the maritime global order through the United Nations, the Bretton Woods system, the Marshall Plan, regional alliances—most notably the North Atlantic Treaty Organization, the European Economic Community, and, at the national level, through democratic elections. Membership in these institutions and alliances was voluntary, and, over time, more and more countries found that membership was in their own interests, thereby contributing to the spread and deepening of the maritime global order.

Although the war left fascism in tatters, it invigorated communism. After World War II, Russia helped communists in Eastern Europe infiltrate the host Ministry of the Interior to arrest their way to power by incarcerating or executing members of noncommunist parties. The presence of the Red Army, which after World War II never left, provided backbone to Communist Party rule.[35] As Winston Churchill observed,

> From Stettin in the Baltic to Trieste in the Adriatic, an iron curtain has descended across the Continent. Behind that line lie all the capitals of the ancient states of Central and Eastern Europe. Warsaw, Berlin, Prague, Vienna, Budapest, Belgrade, Bucharest and Sofia . . . [where Russian influence had become decisive].[36]

In China, Japan had eviscerated the Nationalists' conventional military forces, leaving the Chinese Communists in a far stronger position than at the start of the Second Sino-Japanese War. Post–world war, the Russians transferred to the Chinese Communists immense stores of captured Japanese conventional weapons. The Nationalists then made the fatal strategic mistake of risking all their assets in the Manchurian theater, the only theater where the Communists had critical advantages, including proximity to their Great Power ally, proximity to well-developed base areas, an extensive railway system to deploy troops, and the geographic position to surround the Nationalists on three sides, leaving a narrow egress along a single railway line to the south. The Nationalists would have done better consolidating their control over China south of the Great Wall, where they, not the Communists, had all the advantages.[37] Communist victory in the long Chinese civil war transformed Asian politics and made communism far more dangerous, with the addition of China to the Communist bloc that now extended through Eastern Europe.

When the Chinese Communists won the civil war, they added a chapter to the Communist playbook on taking power—not from the cities but from the countryside. The Chinese Communists created armies from scratch through a long process of turning peasants into party members and cadres into guerrillas, whose forces over the years became more proficient at larger military operations. Their strategy to take over the host from within entailed three stages of military development that ultimately brought victory in large conventional battles. Transition to the final stage required imported conventional weapons, which presumed a Great Power ally (i.e., Russia, the only available Great Communist Power). So Russia and China armed and funded communist movements the world over. The West countered with its own aid programs, leaving all sides in the wars of independence well armed.[38]

In the post–World War II wave of decolonization, the Chinese Communists' rural model seemed highly relevant. It proved to be extraordinarily effective for establishing military, police, and party institutions while fighting a civil war to take control of a failing state. For much of the Cold War, communism seemed to be spreading more rapidly than capitalism. Nevertheless, the maritime order prevailed in the most productive areas of the world: the industrialized countries of Western Europe, North America, Australasia, and Japan. Costly wars in Korea and Vietnam proved divisive for the Western alliance and for their voting populations. The communists became more adept at imposing costs on the West. In Korea they fought largely conventionally, whereas in Vietnam they emphasized a guerrilla war that the United States found no way to counter at an acceptable cost as long as Russia and China kept their aid flowing. The West also had a learning curve. It replayed the successful communist strategy in Vietnam against Russia in Afghanistan, where the communists bogged down in an endless guerrilla war.

China's Role in the Termination of the Cold War

China played a critical role at the end of the Cold War. The Chinese Communists had required Russian military, economic, technical, and other aid in order to win the long Chinese civil war. Yet both countries remained true to their continental traditions that made them wary of Great Power neighbors. Russia had funded multiple sides throughout the Chinese civil war to delay the rise of a bordering Great Power. Russian advisers had even tried to discourage the Chinese Communists from crossing the Yangzi River in 1949 to unite the country.[39] The Korean War then served Russian interests to bog down both China and the United States, forestalling the rise of a Great Power neighbor while bloodying its primary adversary. During the Vietnam War, Russia and China clashed over differences in strategies.

Mao Zedong proved much more astute at politics and war than at economics. His insistence on the Great Leap Forward (1958), collectivizing and nationalizing all of China, produced the country's first nationwide famine, the Great Famine (1958–1962), in which 40 million died.[40] Not surprisingly, this produced critics within the party, among them those partial to Russia. The Sino-Soviet split became public in 1960, but it had been in the making since Stalin's death in 1953, when Mao began jockeying for leadership of the international communist movement much to the horror of Nikita Khrushchev. The rivalry expressed itself during two Taiwan Strait crises (1954–1955 and 1958). With the Great Famine and Khrushchev's mockery of the Great Leap Forward, Mao set about eliminating his critics, through the Cultural Revolution (1966–1976), with particular attention to the pro-Russia faction. Once China developed atomic weapons (1964) and nuclear weapons (1967), it could strike out even more independently. Border disputes nearly brought the two countries to nuclear war in 1969, when Russia sounded out the United States on a possible Russian atomic strike against China. The United States strongly opposed the suggestion.[41]

At this point, Russia had become the primary adversary not only for the Western maritime order but also for China. US president Richard Nixon seized the opportunity to initiate secret diplomacy with China in 1970, followed by his official visit in 1971. This paved the way for the US exit from the Vietnam War and Sino-American cooperation on a strategy of assisted suicide for Russia.[42] Leonid Brezhnev overextended Russia financially and territorially by failing to fix the economy, whose growth had stagnated, while still funding an expanding list of expensive adventures in the Third World and missile deployments in Europe.[43] The assisted suicide included the militarization of the Russo-Chinese frontier, which was far more expensive for Russia than for China, whose population density formed a powerful defense. Russia, whose eastern periphery had hardly any Russian population, relied on expensive mechanized forces. These expenses, in combination with Russian military expenses garrisoning Eastern Europe and defending against NATO, constituted an enormous financial burden on a not particularly productive economy.

Although the communist model proved effective for imposing and maintaining one-party rule and installing a dictator for life, it was ill-suited for creating prosperity thereafter. Communists correctly emphasized the primacy of economics but did not understand how modern economies produce wealth. So they executed the very categories of people necessary to run a modern economy. Likewise, they eliminated the very institutions and laws necessary to promote economic growth—most notably, private property and free markets. And they also eliminated the freedoms necessary to run effective markets, the principal ones being freedom of expression and freedom of movement.

The extraction of investment capital from agriculture impoverished the bulk of the population, who were originally peasants, even in Russia. The focus on heavy industry in order to build a state-of-the-art military retarded the development of light industry and the production of consumer goods, so that living standards stagnated after reaching pre war levels. Moreover, full nationalization of industry put the party in complete control over the urban economy, and central plans dictated production thereafter. Modern economies, however, turned out to be far too complicated to plan. The decentralized markets of capitalist countries proved to be far more adept at allocating resources and maximizing production and innovation. The human costs of imposing and maintaining communist rule kept on mounting, requiring extensive prison camp systems to deter critics.

Although the model produced the rapid growth of heavy industry, it set the conditions for the stagnation of agriculture and light industry. Because the growth was not balanced or self-sustaining—the gains from collectivization and nationalization occurred but once—over time economic growth rates lagged far behind those in the West. There was also the yawning gap between the tale the communists told about how they ruled and the actual historical record. This became known as the "Big Lie," which did not set the conditions for an innovative society either; rather, unorthodox thinking risked imprisonment. Communism yielded extreme political repression and long-term economic stagnation detrimental to its ultimate survival.

It took several generations before the evidence concerning divergent living standards became overwhelming even to the communist elite, who by the 1980s must have realized that their own purchasing power at home was literally inferior to that of US welfare mothers with access to Walmart. (The author's anecdote: while living in Moscow at that time, the local "super" market sold a total of about 75 different goods, comparing unfavorably with the variety offered by standard candy racks lining US supermarket checkout lanes.) The cumulative effects of communism left Russia so far behind technologically that its military equipment could no longer match that of its rivals, and trend lines indicated that its economic problems were compounding.

Russia and the Soviet Union formed an odd, inverted empire. According to communist theory, the mother country by definition was the most economically developed part of the empire that extracted primary resources from the underdeveloped and impoverished periphery. In the Soviet Empire, Eastern Europe and the Baltic States were far more prosperous and economically developed. Indeed, those parts of the empire with the deepest historical association with Western Europe and the maritime world remained the wealthiest.

The Russian government was the primary victim of the Big Lie. When Mikhail Gorbachev tried to reform Russia so as to save communism, he sequenced political reforms before economic reforms, while planning to fund the economic reforms from savings generated by terminating the Cold War. This would allow him to shift money from foreign to domestic policy. He apparently had no idea how hated Russian rule was in Eastern Europe and among Russia's many nationalities, so that when central power weakened, the colonies bolted. He also apparently did not understand that Russia was one of the most backward parts of the empire and had long lived off the labor of others. When Eastern Europe became independent and no longer had to subsidize Russia, Russian living standards collapsed. Even in Russia proper, the Communist Party of the Soviet Union lost power before the economic reforms could bear fruit.[44] China's leaders have carefully studied Gorbachev's mistakes and have focused on economic reforms that have restored China to its historical position as an economic powerhouse. It is unclear whether or not the Chinese Communist Party ever intends to engage in political reforms. Unless its leaders are content with the prospects of multiparty governance, it is unlikely that they will risk far-reaching political reforms. The latter would guarantee the end of one-party rule.

Lessons from China's Role in Terminating the Cold War

- Mistakes the magnitude of World War I and the Great Depression take generations to repair.
- Immersion in domestic politics to the exclusion of the vital interests of friends and foes (the United States in the roaring twenties and during the Great Depression) risks reaping the whirlwind.
- Not only is it important to prioritize (and correctly) one's enemies, it is equally important to treat one's friends right.
- Soviet coercion of Eastern Europe and China yielded long-term hostility among its closest neighbors—hardly a recipe for security in the modern age. Indeed, strategies entailing the oppression of allies or occupied lands boomerang in the long term, delivering the opposite of intended outcomes.

- Japanese strategy in the Second Sino-Japanese War yielded a unified viscerally anti-Japanese China in 1949.
- Soviet postwar strategy in Eastern Europe yielded their earliest possible departure from the empire and entry into NATO, while Soviet strategy in China made the latter so angry that it teamed up with the United States to destroy the Soviet Union. Russian strategy transformed friends into enemies.
- In contrast, Western treatment of West Germany and Japan turned lethal enemies into stalwart allies.

Possible New Framing Events: The Communications Revolution

The Cold War ended in 1991 with the dissolution of the Soviet Union. It was followed by two decades of unprecedented economic growth in less developed countries.[45] For a time, triumphalists proclaimed an "end to history,"[46] but turmoil in the Islamic world, a Russia suddenly on the march, and a China poised to march or perhaps to sail posed potentially serious threats to the maritime global order, on which the unprecedented global prosperity in the post–Cold War decades was based. Several unprecedented changes will affect strategy and perhaps together become framing events in the form of a communications revolution: The cell phone has brought telephone service throughout the world, while the Internet has made knowledge accessible worldwide. It is no longer possible to close off populations in the way required by past dictatorships unless one intends to live (and die) in the abject poverty of North Koreans. With instant media, foes can no longer be fought sequentially, in the way required by past continental powers. Rapid communication allows small countries to recognize threats in real time and combine forces to counter a Great Power foe.

Today, prosperity requires connections with the outside. Communist countries that intend to become prosperous, or just wealthy enough to maintain strong militaries, cannot remain walled off financially, as in the past. Much of their wealth, particularly in the case of China, is based on participation in the global maritime order through mutually beneficial trade. These connections make countries that threaten the global maritime order more vulnerable to sanctions than in the past. Moreover, the myriad international organizations that form the backbone of the global maritime order have grown stronger as more and more countries find participating in them beneficial and whose participation then strengthens these institutions. The communications revolution has put dictatorships of all kinds in a far more disadvantageous position than in the past, both at home and abroad.

With the implosion of the Soviet Union and the many revelations from its archives concerning the brutality of its rule and the poverty of its citizens, communism has been defanged. Communism became a lethal threat to the global order because so many people around the world believed its message and emulated its model. Even China has now abandoned the economic model, which, according to Marxist teachings, justifies communist political institutions and one-party rule. It is unclear how long the political superstructure can survive the demolition of its economic foundations. In any case, communism no longer has any export value. China's abandonment of communist economics has restored its historical place as the dominant economy of Asia and funded its ambitious foreign policy that gives little consideration to the interests of close neighbors, but focuses on old grievances from the Second Sino-Japanese War.

Japan long acquiesced to US foreign policy dictates, but with the sixtieth anniversary of World War II, according to conventional Japanese periodization, the World War II era has ended and a new era has begun. China's continued reliance on hatred as the motivating force for its foreign policy, however useful domestically, boomeranged internationally. Hatred creates enemies and spikes tensions in ways that are ultimately self-defeating. Already, Chinese militancy toward Japan rapidly eroded the latter's strong postwar pacifism. China responded to the 1989 Tiananmen uprising with a thorough revamping of textbooks in order to restore student loyalties to the government. Past texts had rallied student sympathies around hatred of the Nationalists and class enemies. Post-Tiananmen texts vilified Japan and the West (i.e., the maritime global order).[47] China has also lined its coast with missiles aimed at Japan and Taiwan, even though neither poses a threat. Starting in 1994, Japan introduced a succession of political reforms to strengthen the office of prime minister.[48] In 2007, for the first time since World War II, its defense minister rejoined the cabinet. The subject of constitutional revision to remove limitations on Japanese military power (Article 9) is no longer taboo but under active discussion. Twice Japan remade itself to respond to a dire threat: the Meiji reforms in response to Western intrusions, and the postwar economic miracle in response to defeat in World War II. If China continues to goad Japan, it may trigger a third rebirth antithetical to its own interests.

Final Lessons from the Competition in Creating a New World Order

Overextension is a real problem that real people face, more often than one might think. The Russian Empire imploded twice in the twentieth century because of overextension: once mid–World War I and once at the end of the Cold War. Japan succumbed to overextension in the Second Sino-Japanese War, the Nationalists in the Chinese Civil War, and arguably the Qing dynasty conquered too much to hold forever. In all cases, the results were catastrophic. Allies are often essential to avoid overextension. A growing list of enemies is disastrous. Therefore, competent foreign policy must take into careful consideration the interests of other countries. There are at least two types of overextension: military and economic. A competent foreign policy aligns ambitions with the underlying economic base. Those who think offensive weapons are the ultimate currency of power are wrong, as the fate of China's self-strengtheners and the Soviet Union demonstrates. The underlying economic base in combination with the roster of one's friends is the ultimate currency of power.

It is important to fight the right enemy. China fought the wrong enemies in the Opium Wars—Britain and France, instead of Russia, which took something valuable—a huge swath of territory that was never returned. Japan fought the wrong enemy in the Second Sino-Japanese War. The Communists were the primary enemies of both Japan and the Nationalists. By fighting each other, they predisposed a Communist victory in the Chinese civil war— a problem that still endures.

Censorship and dictatorship impeded the flow of information necessary to make the accurate assessments on which a sound foreign policy depends. Dictatorships have been best at deceiving themselves, as they succumb to their own propaganda, with dire consequences for themselves. Note, for example, the fate of both the fascists and communists whose lies eventually could not hide the reality. Communism was a nonfunctional economic and political model that Russia and China would have been better off discarding sooner rather than later. Censorship, however, allows bad paradigms to survive far longer than their natural shelf life, victimizing censors and censored alike.

As seductive as the idea of deterrence is, in practice, if the value of the undesirable activity is associated with regime survival by the undesirable party, then deterrence is unlikely to succeed. US attempts to deter Japan by embargo before World War II precipitated the very attacks they were designed to forestall. Japan viewed its problems in China as existential and therefore was not susceptible to deterrence. Likewise, Japan's attempt to deter further Western intervention in China by bombing Pearl Harbor and targets across the Pacific produced the very march on Tokyo that Japan could not parry. Isolationist America turned on a dime when the attacks made clear to voters that the global order on which their prosperity depended was at stake.

In high-stakes disagreements when deterrence is not feasible, then the very lethality of the threat can be used to strengthen the international system to put time on one's side. Threats can be used to build alliances, strengthen international institutions, and facilitate cooperation to create enduring mechanisms and precedents that both further constrain undesired actions and continue to strengthen the international order long after the crisis subsides. Thus, the threat can be used to set the conditions for its elimination. This approach replaces a negative objective (deterrence), with a positive objective (strengthening of the global order). In World War II, the Allies set precedents for cooperation that the Western Allies further developed after the war. The Western alliance in the Cold War then deepened the global order. The lethality of the threat of fascism during the global hot war, followed by the communist threat in the ensuing cold war, made this possible. In this way, the more dire the threat, the stronger the international order becomes.

In 2014, Vladimir Putin took the first steps to restore the Russian Empire with the seizure of the Crimea, beginning anew the age-old process described by the tsarist historian Kliuchevskii. Although the communists reconstructed the fallen tsarist empire, Vladimir Putin faces a more difficult task. A repeat performance may not be possible in the age of modern international law that rejects unilateral territorial changes; when real-time news shows tanks as they cross borders, allowing others to respond immediately; with a global financial system controlled by the maritime order, which can freeze, seize, or restore assets; and, most important, without a highly marketable ideology, as communism once was. Moreover, the wealth gap separating Russia from members of the maritime order has only grown, positioning Russia ever more poorly to impose its will on others. Russia's best course of action is to join the maritime order, but, like China, it prefers to forge its own path.

Historically, Russia has been incredibly savvy at the operational level, combining diplomacy, propaganda, and coercion to take contiguous territory, often on the cheap. Its methods depend on failing state, non-state, or defeated state neighbors, as well as secrecy. But Russia has been incompetent at the strategic level because its strategies have produced death on a massive scale both at home and abroad, and poverty for itself and its friends. Likewise, Chinese history has been unbelievably bloody. Ongoing civil war in some part of the country is the norm, not the exception. Times of prosperity have been brilliant, but shorter than the devastating periods of unremitting warfare.

There are unsettling parallels between China today and Japan of the 1930s. Both divide the world in terms of island chains, allude to an Asian Monroe Doctrine, and try to make neighbors follow their wishes. In both systems, the military holds great power. These similarities follow earlier parallels between the economic reforms of Deng Xiaoping and those of Meiji Japan. Will China's rise also be followed by a strategic suicide? Watching the evolution of China's maritime territorial disputes that have alienated its neighbors, one wonders whether China will repeat Japan's mistake to confuse ends with means. If the ends are security and prosperity, then a fight over small islands and even energy rights will not be worth the candle.

Today, there are no economic problems of the magnitude of the Great Depression that set Japan (and Germany) on the road to self-destruction. But the Chinese Communist Party faces an existential domestic threat to its continued rule of the magnitude of that faced by the Qing dynasty and the continuance of Manchu minority rule. The survivors of the twentieth-century Communist killing spree may wish to settle scores with their government. Certainly, there is much domestic anger at perceived corruption of party members. Should events and desires not align, one wonders whether China's leaders will suffer the same sort of amnesia that Japan's did in the 1930s and forget the international commercial connections on which their prosperity depends. They are correct that democracy poses an existential threat to one-party rule. The two systems are mutually exclusive. China's leaders must decide whether their goal is the perpetuation of one-party rule or the prosperity of China. So far, it has been possible to pursue both goals simultaneously, but a fork in the road approaches when they will have to choose.

The goals of land and maritime powers differ fundamentally.

- Land powers strive for the domination and absorption of neighbors, producing a negative-sum international environment not conducive to wealth generation. Their global order emphasizes wealth confiscation, not creation.
- Maritime powers focus on positive-sum transactions to create wealth through trade.

Japan has embraced the maritime world. Russia continues to reject it. And China remains torn.

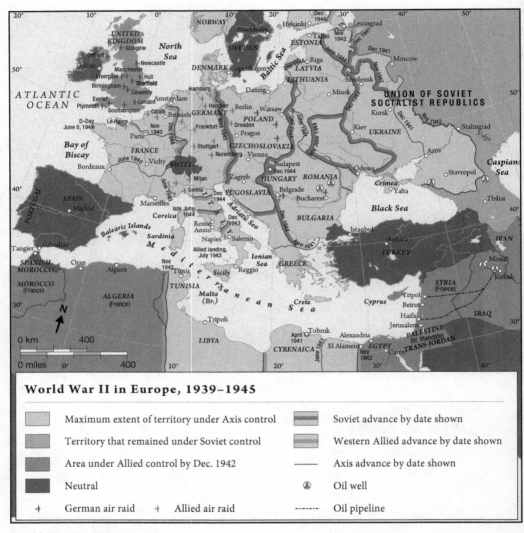

World War II in Europe, 1939–1945.

World War II in Europe, 1939–1945

Maximum extent of territory under Axis control	Soviet advance by date shown
Territory that remained under Soviet control	Western Allied advance by date shown
Area under Allied control by Dec. 1942	—— Axis advance by date shown
Neutral	⊕ Oil well
+ German air raid + Allied air raid	------- Oil pipeline

CHAPTER 14

The Bear against the Imperial Eagle
Russo-German Competition
Robert M. Citino

Introduction: Symmetries and Asymmetries

Germany and Russia's "enduring strategic rivalry" lasted almost exactly seventy-five years and embraced two world wars. Within that time frame, there were occasional periods of *rapprochement* and even strategic cooperation between the two, first as common guarantors of monarchical stability and solidarity in the late nineteenth century (1873–1879, 1881–1894), then as bitter opponents of the post-1918 Versailles settlement (1921–1933), and then, for a relatively brief but terrifying period, totalitarian partners standing against the Western alliance (1939–1941). These periods of calm were not the same as friendship, however, and the two never dropped their mutual attitude of wary suspicion. Their enmity culminated in the two world wars, and indeed, was a principal cause of both conflicts. In both world wars, Russia and Germany fielded the largest armies, fought the greatest campaigns, and spilled more blood against one another than any other combatant powers.

It is tempting to seek the roots of tension between the two in the distant past, and historians have been doing just that for decades. The standard historical narrative points to struggles for land between Teuton and Slav in the medieval or even ancient worlds. Key signposts along the way include the wars on the eastern marches of the Carolingian Empire, the German *Drang nach Osten* ("eastern impulse") or *Ostsiedlung* ("eastern settlement") of the Middle Ages, and—richest of all in terms of myth and legend—the

Teutonic Knights carving out a monastic principality in the primeval forests of East Prussia, ruling the conquered natives as overlords from their dark, forbidding castle at Marienburg (today, Poland's Malbork).[1] Their destruction in 1410 at the Battle of Grunwald, also known as the First Battle of Tannenberg, marked the culmination point of eastern settlement by the Germans.[2]

While we must use history with caution (the army that laid the Teutonic Knights low at Grunwald was an alliance of Poles and Lithuanians, for example, not Russians), we can make a case that a clash between the two powers was inevitable, at least in the modern period. Both Russia and Germany sought to dominate the domain of "strategic landpower," judging themselves not by the size of their overseas holdings but on their influence on the European mainland itself.[3] Both powers supported massive ground forces, backed by much smaller naval (and later, air) components, and both societies were heavily militarized. These very symmetries lay at the root of their strategic rivalry. As there could be only one dominant land power in Europe, one hegemon, Russia and Germany were probably destined for war at some point.

Upon closer analysis, equally dramatic asymmetries present themselves, and they, too, played a role in fostering conflict. Seen from the Russian perspective, Germany was smaller but more densely populated, much more heavily industrialized, and thus far more dynamic and potentially expansionist. Germany was a powerful spring that might break its ties at any moment, uncoiling itself and wreaking havoc on anyone unlucky enough to be in the way. After 1871, the Germans held a hegemonic position in the European littoral, from which they not only blocked Russian access to the west but were also well poised to turn and devour the lumbering eastern empire whenever they chose. In such a scenario, Russia's vast size would be a hindrance rather than an advantage, retarding military readiness and turning mobilization into a matter of months rather than days. Fear of Germany was, therefore, the latest incarnation of a long-standing Russian xenophobia, generated by Russia's sense of its own insecurity and reified over the centuries by the devastating Mongol, Swedish, and French invasions.

For all its dynamism and power, Germany, too, could look to the east and conjure a vision of its own nemesis. Germany was a relatively crowded land, constricted in a geographical and strategic sense. It occupied a dangerous spot in the middle of the North German Plain, lacked much in the way of defensible borders, and possessed only the narrowest access to the sea. Historian Michael Stürmer has described it as *der Macht in der Mitte* ("the power in the middle"), surrounded by enemies or potential enemies in the course of its historical development: France to the west, Austria to the south, Sweden to the north, and, of course, mighty Russia to the east.[4] For German policymakers, Russia was a mysterious behemoth, a land of unfathomable expanse and an apparently inexhaustible supply of men and resources. If Germany was a coiled spring, Russia was the steamroller, or perhaps better, the glacier. Russian armies might take time to get started, but once they did, they would be inexorable in the advance and impossible to stop, grinding down everything in their path.

These very differences led Russia and Germany to view each other primarily through a lens of fear, and as strategists from Thucydides on have recognized, fear is a potent engine of rivalry and armed conflict.[5] Both conjured worst-case scenarios against the other, a fact that would lead them to war twice. In World War I, the Germans destroyed the Russian Empire (before going down themselves for unrelated causes). But strategic rivalry never stops, and a few short years later, in World War II, the "Russians" (actually now the Soviet Union) returned the favor many times over, smashing the German Wehrmacht in the greatest series of military campaigns in world history, destroying Hitler's Third Reich, and planting their flag over the Reichstag building in the very heart of Berlin.

Bismarck's Failure: The Rise of Rivalry

Before 1871, good relations between Russia and Prussia were a bedrock of European diplomacy. Not only were they two of Europe's most conservative monarchies—staunch enemies of the French Revolution and Napoleon, for example—but their self-interest also ran in parallel directions, and Polish weakness and instability were a magnet to them. In the eighteenth century, both had taken part in the most hardheaded and cynical event of the era: the three partitions of Poland in 1772, 1793, and 1795.[6] Although Austria had been a partner in the First and Third Partitions, Russia and Prussia were the big winners. Prussia gained massive new territories, including "West Prussia," linking the kingdom proper with the detached province of East Prussia; "New East Prussia," the lands between the East Prussian border and the Niemen, Vistula, and Bug rivers; and "South Prussia," including the districts of Posen, Kalisch, and Warsaw; while Russia acquired new lands that together were larger than many European kingdoms, including Lithuania, Livonia, Kurland, Podolia, and Byelorussia (modern Belarus). In the end, they erased the very name of Poland, as a secret protocol declared:

In view of the necessity to abolish everything which could revive the memory of the existence of the Kingdom of Poland, now that the annulment of this body politic has been effected, the high contracting parties are agreed and undertake never to include in their titles the name or designation of the Kingdom of Poland.[7]

The name "Poland," the robber-monarchs declared, would "remain suppressed as from the present and forever."[8]

Their mutual violation of Poland acted as cement that held together the friendship between Prussia and Russia. Both powers had a vested interest in maintaining the status quo, both in the former Polish territories and in Europe at large. Over the course of the next century, they crushed Polish uprisings, imposed ruthless Germanization or Russianization laws on the restive Polish population, and stood ready to crush any talk of national liberation or the freedom of subject nations.[9]

It is easy to identify the event that destroyed this picture of cooperation and replaced it with bitter rivalry: the creation of a unified German Empire in 1870–1871. The new state was a *Kleindeutschland* ("little Germany," a largely Protestant German state, excluding the Austrian lands) that was the result of clever cabinet diplomacy by the formidable Prussian minister-president, Otto von Bismarck, meticulous military planning by Field Marshal Helmuth von Moltke (the Elder), and an upsurge of popular nationalism within the various German states. In the course of the wars of unification, the Prussians had laid Denmark, Austria, and France low.[10] In place of Prussia, traditionally the fifth of the five Great Powers, a mighty unified Germany had now arisen, and the Russians, like the rest of the European powers, had to pause and take stock of the changed strategic environment.

Just a few years earlier, they had it within their power to halt the entire process. Unfortunately, the creation of modern Germany dovetailed neatly with a period of internal consolidation in Russia. The Crimean War (1854–1856) had been a disaster, with the armies of Tsar Nicholas I displaying ineptitude in the field, losing one battle after the other, and failing even to defend Sevastopol, a powerful fortress on their own soil.[11] Defeat led to the humiliation of the Peace of Paris (1856), which demilitarized the Black Sea and prevented Russia from operating in waters it had long considered its own.

The positive side of defeat in the Crimea was that the Russians realized how much trouble they were in, how far behind Great Britain and France they had lagged, and how urgent it was to reform the state. Nicholas I died in 1855 while the war was still ongoing—perhaps, it was said, of a broken heart. The reign of the new tsar, Alexander II (1855–1881), would see thoroughgoing reform in three areas:

- the reorganization of the judicial system;
- the creation of a new model army based on universal military conscription; and
- the encouragement of local self-government through the *zemstvo* system (a form of rural self-government for the peasantry communes and landed gentry who would send their elected representatives to a provincial assembly[12]).

Most important, Alexander abolished serfdom in 1861. The abolition of serfdom was fraught with all sorts of complexities, including compensation for the landholding class, and historians continue to discuss its successes and failures. Nevertheless, it is no exaggeration to say that the reforms of Alexander II created the modern Russian state.[13]

For all these reasons, it was an inward-looking, even distracted Russia that observed the growth of German power in central Europe. The buzzword in St. Petersburg was now *recueillement* (i.e., recovery or introversion).[14] "Russia is not sulking," declared Chancellor A. M. Gorchakov, but it might have looked as if it were.[15] While Prussia was on the march, fighting three wars in seven years, Russia actually offered it benevolent neutrality. Historians often label Russia's policy an error, but that is unfair. After all, no one knew how dangerous Prussia was about to become, nor did any other power lift a finger to stop it. Britain was just as distracted as Russia, for example, thrashing out the domestic issues associated with the Reform Bill of 1867. The Austrians actually fought alongside the Prussians against Denmark in 1864, and France offered Prussia diplomatic support against Austria in 1866. Russian policy was no more or less skillful than anyone else's in this era.

Bismarck also played his diplomatic cards adroitly. Taking the occasion of a massive Polish uprising in Russia in 1863, he was quick to offer his cooperation to Alexander II.[16] Prussia, he promised, would track down escaped rebels and hand them back to the Russians, and Russian forces would have the right to cross the Prussian border in hot pursuit. He also encouraged the Russians to be as brutal as possible: "Strike the Poles in such a way that they will despair of their lives," he wrote at the time. "I have every sympathy for their plight but if we are to exist we can do nothing other than exterminate them."[17] Bismarck's words were meant to be familiar and comforting to St. Petersburg, to remind the Russians of their long-standing friendship with Prussia over the one issue on which the two could never compromise: Poland. It also reminded them of the real threat to the status quo in Europe at the time: not Bismarck and the Prussians but Napoleon III of France, the nephew of the grand ogre himself, and a figure who constantly invoked the modern spirit of nationalism and national liberation.[18]

Bismarck backed up his words, as well. He mobilized the Prussian regiments in the eastern districts, sent the fire-breathing General Gustav von Alvensleben, one of King Wilhelm I's aides-de-camp, to Petersburg to sign an agreement with Chancellor Gorchakov, and rebuffed warnings by the British ambassador to Berlin, Sir Andrew Buchanan, that Prussia's actions were offensive to Europe. "Who is Europe?" Bismarck scoffed. ("Several great nations," Sir Andrew replied.)[19] As so often in this period, Bismarck got what he wanted: Russian neutrality in Prussia's upcoming wars. Moreover, the sudden appearance of Russian troops on the Austrian border in 1866 played a material role in the Prussian victory, and a replay of the process in 1870 may have helped to prevent Austria from intervening against Prussia in its war with France.

All these wars were short and decisive victories for Prussia, however, and they ended with the old order in ruins and a new hegemon in town. Like that other Great Power on the European periphery, Great Britain, Russia had a vested interest in maintaining a balance of power, and had little inclination to see any one power dominate the European heartland. Napoleonic France had been trouble enough. Bismarck's Germany was hundreds of miles closer to Russia than France had been, and it was sitting on a featureless invasion plain ideal for modern military operations. Moreover, Prussia had just increased its power two- or threefold without fair compensation, and that is not how western Europe played the balance of power game. Barbara Jelavich describes Russia as playing "the role of a bystander" in German unification. "Russian approval" had been essential to the process, she argued, but Russia never enjoyed "control of events."[20] Nor had it sold its cooperation to Prussia at anything like fair market value. Certainly, Alexander II had taken the opportunity of Europe's distraction to abrogate the Peace of Paris and remilitarize the Black Sea in October 1870, but that seemed a paltry return for the vast increase in Prussian power.

It did not take long for that realization to set in. The old Prussia had been a reliable and conservative junior partner—and the new Germany was anything but. In terms of military power, economic production, internal dynamism, and brilliance of leadership, it had leapfrogged its former friend. The foundation of the Reich had also undermined the notion of monarchical solidarity and legitimacy. In destroying the German Confederation, Bismarck had dethroned one prince after the other, and had even seized the treasury of George V of Hanover. Historians may well argue today about the nature of the "real Bismarck"—the great unifier, the balance of power genius, the "white revolutionary."[21] The Russian tsars, their ministers, and the informed Russian intelligentsia (particularly of the pan-Slav type, those who "saw a conspiracy in every corner west of the Vistula," in Henry Kissinger's words) never trusted him from the start.[22]

Bismarck could see the danger that loomed. Germany was now a satisfied power, one that had achieved all its goals in foreign policy and had no further demands to make in the diplomatic realm. "*Wir sind satt!*" he liked to say, "We're full!" What his new creation needed above all was a period of internal consolidation, and for that, it needed peace, quiet, and the status quo. He also knew that France was in the irreconcilable camp and would not cease until it had its revenge, and he needed to make sure that it remained a camp of one and that French anger stayed an isolated phenomenon.

To achieve these ends—maintenance of the status quo and isolation of France—one of his first diplomatic moves after the victory over France was to propose the formation of a Three Emperors' League (*Dreikaiserbund*)— Germany, the Hapsburg Empire, and Russia, united in common opposition to radicalism, revolution, and restive subject nationalities.[23] Signed in October 1873, it lacked much in the way of specific clauses or mutual obligations, but that was hardly the point. On the surface, Bismarck seemed to be creating a throwback to the good old days—the Holy Alliance, the Concert of Europe, and the right of the conservative courts to serve as international anti-revolutionary gendarmes. In reality, the League served his ends, linking Germany with potential French allies and making war less likely.

Unfortunately, it was doomed from the start. The foundational problem was that the three powers were no longer conservative in any real sense. Post-1866 Austria had become Austria-Hungary, the land of the *Ausgleich* and power-sharing between the German and Magyar populations. Forcibly expelled from its dominant role in German affairs, it had shifted its center of gravity to the east and south. The only place where it could exhibit the dynamism and expansionism that were so *de rigueur* in the late nineteenth century was the Balkan Peninsula, where Ottoman Power continued to recede.

That same description applied to the other two partners. Stripped of its old role as protector of Orthodox Christianity by defeat in the Crimea, Russia had adopted a new one: active protector of the small Slavic nations, the "little brothers," against the depredation of Magyar, Teuton, and Turk. The center of gravity for this effort would be the Balkans, and Russian foreign policy began to focus there in an increasingly aggressive manner. As for Bismarck, no one could possibly have taken him seriously as a conservative, least of all he himself. As he proved throughout his career, he was ready to take whatever actions he believed were necessary at the moment, unfettered by promises or principle. It was both the beauty and the flaw of *Realpolitik*.[24]

The problem of managing allies who were at cross-purposes in a traditionally volatile corner of Europe eluded a solution, even for a diplomat as skilled as Bismarck. His frequent suggestions to partition the Balkans, placing the western half under Austria-Hungary and the eastern under Russia, were always halfhearted (and unworkable), and his tendency to say one thing to Chancellor Gorchakov and another very different thing to the Austrian foreign minister, Jules Andrassy, only exacerbated the problem—increasing suspicions and keeping tensions at a high level. But there was no easy solution, and in Bismarck's defense, keeping the two potential adversaries talking was preferable to seeing them go to war, a war that would have set Europe aflame and dragged in both Germany and France at some point.

Given its systemic problems, the quick demise of the Three Emperors' League was no surprise. The Balkans had long been a graveyard of empires and overly precious diplomatic schemes. The Great Power here, the Ottoman Empire, was in the midst of a long, slow decline that had once led Nicholas I to dub it the "sick man" of Europe. Already in the nineteenth century, the Serbs, the Greeks, and then the Romanians had risen up and won first their autonomy, and then their independence. In August 1875, it happened again, as an anti-Turkish rebellion broke out among the ethnic Serbs of Herzegovina, spread to neighboring Bosnia, and thence, by 1876, to Bulgaria. The Turks suppressed rebellion in all these *vilayets* (provinces) with their customary vigor, atrocities broadcast to the west in full living color in W. E. Gladstone's grisly pamphlet *Bulgarian Horrors and the Question of the East*.[25] Within months, tens of thousands of Christian refugees were fleeing their homes and seeking the relative safety of neighboring Serbia and Montenegro. The two principalities reacted by declaring war on the Ottoman Empire in June 1876. The war went badly (as Serbia and Montenegro probably knew it would), badly enough to precipitate the tsar's intervention, a declaration of war, and the dispatch of Russian troops to the Balkan theater in April 1877. Prince (later king) Nicholas I of tiny Montenegro once famously stated the formula of his successful foreign policy in this crisis: "We and the Russians— 100,000,000 strong!"[26]

Russia's war with Turkey was far more difficult than expected. The "sick man" still had some life left in him, as he would prove repeatedly until 1918. The initial drive south came up against tough Turkish fortifications just after crossing the Danube at Plevna, and Russian assaults on the works in July and September broke down with heavy losses. The Turks did little more in this war than defend passively, however. While they proved that entrenched infantry employing modern firearms could inflict heavy casualties on the attackers, they did nothing to wrest the initiative away from the Russians. Plevna fell in December, followed by Adrianople in January 1878, twin losses that completely unhinged the Ottoman defenses. With Russian armies driving swiftly toward Constantinople, the combatants agreed to an armistice on January 31.[27]

By this point, the other European powers had become concerned about the prospect of a decisive Russian victory, which seemed to herald the end of the Ottoman Empire as well as Russian dominance of the entire Near East. Warnings flew from the various capitals to St. Petersburg, and Great Britain sent its Mediterranean squadron fleet to the Dardanelles, its ritual sign of support for the Ottomans. Tensions simmered, then exploded in March 1878 when Turkey and Russia signed the Treaty of San Stefano. Its key clause was the establishment of a large, independent Bulgaria straddling the Balkan Peninsula, which most European statesmen presumed would be a puppet state of the power that had liberated it—Russia. Austria-Hungary, Great Britain, and France all protested angrily at what appeared to be a naked Russian power grab in the Balkans, and a general war seemed on the near horizon.

Bismarck had intentionally held back from the crisis up to this point. For public consumption, he declared Germany's utter disinterest in the Balkans. The entire region, he once proclaimed to the Reichstag, was not worth "the bones of a single Pomeranian grenadier"—not worth the life of one German soldier, in other words. He now proposed an international conference to settle the dispute, promising to act as an "honest broker" at the deliberations, an individual who had no dog in the fight but who simply wanted to see justice done. In June 1878, the Great Powers dutifully convened at the Congress of Berlin, with the representatives of the Great Powers, among them Otto von Bismarck, first chancellor of the German Empire; Gyula, Count Andrássy, Austro-Hungarian foreign minister; A. M. Gorchakov, chancellor of Russia; Benjamin Disraeli, prime minister of Britain; and William Waddington, minister of foreign affairs, for France.

The Congress resulted in an apparently reasonable compromise, splitting Greater Bulgaria into three sections: the autonomous principality of Bulgaria (north of the Balkans, including the city of Sofia), Eastern Rumelia (between the Balkan and the Rhodope mountains, placed under an Ottoman-appointed Christian governor and Great Power supervision); and Macedonia, which was returned to the Ottomans. To compensate for Russia's presumed dominance in Bulgaria, the Congress gave Austria-Hungary permission to occupy and administer (but not to annex) Bosnia and Herzegovina, while Great Britain signed a separate convention with the Ottoman Empire that ceded the island of Cyprus to British rule. [28]

Russia therefore came away from Berlin with precious little to show for its troubles. It had, in its own view, fought a good fight. It had gone beyond base national interests, stood up for the rights of small nations, launched itself into a war, and crushed its opponent after a series of difficult and bloody campaigns. It then had to stand by and watch as international rivals snatched away the fruits of its labors. Austria-Hungary, in particular, had made greater territorial gains than had Russia, and it had not fired a single shot. The same thing was true for the British. Russia had suffered over 100,000 men killed, by contrast, and had come away practically empty.

The Russians knew whom to blame for their travails at Berlin. Not Britain, whose support of the integrity of the Ottoman Empire was a pillar of foreign policy. Not Austria-Hungary, which had stolen in at the last moment to pick up the spoils from Russia's military victory. Not France, certainly, which as deranged with anger as it was toward Germany, still managed to come away from the Congress with something to show: permission to occupy and administer the North African city of Tunis.

All of them had signed the Treaty of Berlin, but to the Russians, the identity of the culprit was clear. It was the statesman who stood at the center of the talks, the one around whom everyone seemed to be revolving, the one who claimed to be an "honest broker," but now, suddenly, did not seem very honest at all. He was a genius; everyone in Europe said so. Anything that took place at this Congress in his own backyard had to be his doing.

The Russians—government and public opinion alike—blamed Bismarck. In the aftermath of the Congress, he and his new Germany became punching bags for the Russian press and for Pan-Slavs in general, with one newspaper claiming that "[t]he honest broker acted for a big commission."[29] Alexander II went so far as to write Wilhelm I an angry letter in August 1879, warning of the "fears that concern me and whose consequences could be disastrous for both countries."[30] When Bismarck read the note, he remarked that if he released it to the German public (something he had done in the past), they would think it was a declaration of war, and Wilhelm was sufficiently alarmed that he traveled to Alexandrovo, Alexander's hunting lodge in Russian Poland, to meet the tsar in person and iron things out.

At the Congress of Berlin, Bismarck's *Realpolitik* had "turned on itself," in the famous formulation of Henry Kissinger.[31] Honeyed words about conservative solidarity and the traditional friendship between Prussia and Russia apparently meant nothing in the face of national self-interest. The Congress not only killed the Three Emperors' League, it marked an end to over a century of warm relations between St. Petersburg and Berlin, and in that sense really was the end of an era. But perhaps it is fairer to say that *Realpolitik* never had a chance of succeeding at Berlin, given the context of the times. Breaking with Austria-Hungary was never a realistic option for Bismarck, since German public opinion would never have stood for it. Maintaining an alliance with Austria-Hungary, however, meant that friendship with Russia was impossible. Every now and then, the statesman faces a situation in which there is nothing to be done. For Bismarck, the Russian question was a "wicked problem" devoid of a quick fix, or any sort of fix at all.[32]

The best evidence for the intractability of Russian-German strategic rivalry comes from the decade after the Congress of Berlin. These were the years of the mature Bismarck in all his dazzling brilliance, signing treaties with all comers, juggling conventions, Dual and Triple alliances, replete with published and unpublished protocols, codicils, and appendices. The result was a complex web of European alliances with Germany at the center that has long been the subject of fascination by historians.

It began in 1879, when Germany and Austria-Hungary signed the Dual Alliance, a mutual defense pact directed against Russia:

> Should, contrary to their hope, and against the genuine desire of the two high contracting parties, one of the two empires be attacked by Russia, the high contracting parties are bound to come to each other's assistance with the whole war strength of their empires, and will accordingly conclude peace together and upon mutual consent (Article 1).[33]

It was almost exactly twenty-five years after Bismarck had written that he wanted to avoid "tying our trim and seaworthy frigate to the worm-eaten and old-fashioned Austrian man-of-war."[34] Perhaps he was legitimately frightened by Russian anger over the German machinations at the Congress of Berlin; perhaps he wanted to impel Russia into better relations by forcing it to recognize the reality of the German-Austrian link. At any rate, he had trouble selling it even to his own monarch, for whom "friendship with Russia was a sacred bequest from his parents."[35]

Bismarck had his way, of course, but as always he hedged his bets by reaching out to St. Petersburg. Alexander II's assassination by terrorists of the *Narodnaya Volya* ("People's Will") in 1881 brought his son, Alexander III, to the throne. Bismarck greeted the new tsar with a *démarche* emphasizing their mutual interest in international order and conservative values. The result was a revived and expanded Three Emperor's League, although

Bismarck styled this one as an "alliance" (*Dreikaiserbündnis*), rather than a mere "league." Despite the rhetorical flourish, it was much less than meets the eye, amounting to little more than a vague promise of mutual consultation in Balkan affairs:

> Russia, in agreement with Germany, declares her firm resolution to respect the interests arising from the new position assured to Austria-Hungary by the Treaty of Berlin. The three Courts, desirous of avoiding all discord between them, engage to take account of their respective interests in the Balkan Peninsula. They further promise one another that any new modifications in the territorial status quo of Turkey in Europe can be accomplished only in virtue of a common agreement between them (Article 2).[36]

The Alliance was a cooperative vision, in other words, but a minimalist one. As such, it was entirely suitable for two powers—Austria-Hungary and Russia—who despised one another, and a third power—Germany—attempting to stand between them and be friends with both.

But even this minimal policy was unable to withstand the reality of Balkan politics. Although the next few years passed uneventfully enough, and the Russians renewed the Three Emperors' Alliance on schedule in 1884, another Bulgarian crisis arose the next year that overturned Bismarck's carefully wrought alliance system altogether—a sign of how fragile any treaty relationship is if it crosses paths with strategic realities. The original ruler of Bulgaria, *Knyaz* (Prince) Alexander of Battenberg, was a cousin of Alexander III and an officer in the Russian army. His reign thus seemed to fulfill the promise of Russian primacy in the new state. In 1885, however, after an uprising in Eastern Rumelia, the separated principality declared union with the mother country, and the Grand National Assembly of the new enlarged Bulgaria broke with Russia and forced Alexander's abdication. Eventually, the Assembly offered the throne to another German prince, Prince Ferdinand of Saxe-Coburg and Gotha, a figure with close familial ties to the western dynasties. Now Russia's humiliation from 1878–1879 was complete, as its one legitimate gain from the war with Turkey had apparently slipped through its fingers.[37] Russia would continue to contest Ferdinand's legitimacy for years.

By now, the well-established ritual of Russian foreign policy admitted only one possible scapegoat for this development: Bismarck. The Pan-Slavs were particularly outraged. M. N. Katkov, writing in the Moscow newspaper *Vedomostei*, accused Russia of "losing its identity as an independent power" and being "pushed out of the East {Balkans} step by step":

Our allies used everything imaginable—cajolery and lures, cheating and sophistry, a charade of principles, psychological pressure, the cosmopolitan orientation of our diplomacy, the illiteracy of our politics, and the threat of [hostile] coalitions. . . . We see with great concern that, due to the Three Emperors' League [*sic*], Russia's authority was shaken; that its policies, injurious to Russia, and to which Russia contributed on its own, alienated from Russia those countries for whose independence Russia had shed so much of its own blood.[38]

In such an atmosphere, Alexander III had little choice but to allow the Three Emperors' Alliance to lapse when next it came up for renewal, in 1887.

Events had now driven Bismarck's vision of peaceful cooperation with Russia into the last ditch. Part of him despaired altogether, but that was nothing new. He was given to depression. This was, after all, a man who even at the peak of his power suffered from nightmares:

I go on dreaming what I am thinking awake, if I can sleep at all. Recently I saw the map of Germany in front of me, on it there appeared one decaying patch after another and peeling off.[39]

But another part of him was the supremely confident operator, and his reaction in extremis was to send one last proposal to Russia, perhaps his signature diplomatic move. It usually goes by the name of the "Reinsurance Treaty" in English but perhaps the German term is more evocative: *Rückversicherungsvertrag*, a treaty to "cover your back."[40]

Promising "benevolent neutrality" in the event that either party "should find itself at war with a third Great Power" but specifically excluding a German war with France or a Russian war with Austria, the Reinsurance Treaty was Bismarck at his Machiavellian best. At the very least, it violated the spirit of the Dual Alliance (since expanded into a Triple Alliance with the addition of Italy), and later attempts by historians to defend it fall into hairsplitting legalism at best. The new Kaiser, Wilhelm II, who succeeded to the throne in 1888, regarded it as dishonorable and unworthy of a Great Power, and so did many of the advisors around him. Wilhelm II was a callous and crude young man in so many ways, but even he could see that treaties so complex they required a team of lawyers to interpret were no treaties at all. His refusal to renew the Reinsurance Treaty was one of the crucial issues leading to Bismarck's forced resignation in 1890. Bismarck's successor as chancellor, Leo von Caprivi, complained that conditions in the Balkans have increased the antagonism between Russia and Austria. Germany would run the danger of someday having to decide between Austria and Russia. . . . What value are alliances if they are not founded on a community of interest between nations?[41]

It was a good question, one that Bismarck had never asked. The denouement of the story was predictable. With Russia now disillusioned and cut loose from any treaty tie with Germany, it began to search for allies. The word "search" hardly qualifies, however, implying as it does difficult issues and hard choices. There was already an obvious candidate, the one revisionist state that craved revenge on Germany. An exchange of diplomatic letters between Russia and France began in August 1891, followed by economic agreements that promised massive French loans to Russia, and then by General Staff talks that hammered together a military convention and realistic war plans—a step even Bismarck would never have dared. The Franco-Russian Treaty, ratified by the French Chamber of Deputies in January 1894, could not have been clearer in its terms, in sharp contrast to Bismarck's parsing, word-splitting, and occasional prevaricating:

> If France is attacked by Germany, or by Italy supported by Germany, Russia shall employ all her available forces to attack Germany. If Russia is attacked by Germany, or by Austria supported by Germany, France shall employ all her available forces to fight Germany. [42]

It had all happened so quickly, and it amounted to nothing less than a diplomatic revolution. France and Russia were now allies, and Germany was encircled in a strategic sense by a hostile coalition. The new dispensation did away with discussions of "benevolent neutrality" or countries "finding themselves at war" against a third party—the words that reality had imposed on Bismarck. Here was the language of strategic clarity, as Russia had come to understand it, and so was the proviso that the "available forces to be employed against Germany shall be, on the part of France, 1,300,000 men; on the part of Russia, 700,000 or 800,000 men," so that "Germany may have to fight at the same time in the East and in the West."[43] Germany would no longer have the luxury of contemplating a war against France or Russia alone. An attack on either one of them would be an attack on both, perhaps the first true expression of what the world would come to know as "collective security."

Apparently—and this is a point rarely receiving the attention it deserves—being a diplomatic genius like Bismarck was not half as important as representing a sensible, balanced, and mutually acceptable strategic position. Strategic realities tend to trump diplomatic skill, personal insight, or glibness. Even a mediocre diplomat can make history, if the position is strong. Russo-German rivalry was too much even for Bismarck to handle. Who today, outside of a few scholarly specialists, can name a single individual who concluded the Franco-Russian alliance of 1894? And yet it was they who had triumphed. It is food for thought for present and future policymakers.

From Rivalry to War

The run-up to World War I has generated a standard historical narrative. It begins with Germany's turn toward "world policy" (*Weltpolitik*) and fleet building, and goes on to include a series of treaties and diplomatic crises: the Anglo-French *Entente Cordiale* of 1904, the First Moroccan Crisis of 1905, the formation of the Triple Entente of 1907, a Second Moroccan Crisis in 1911, and the Balkan Wars of 1912–1913. All were important to the outbreak of war, but none as important as the Bosnian Crisis of 1908–1909 (also known as the First Balkan Crisis). Taking place precisely in the middle of the seventy-five-year era discussed in this chapter, it may be the single most important event in the history of Russian-German rivalry—the defining moment.

In October 1908, Austria-Hungary made a unilateral decision to annex Bosnia-Herzegovina. The move was defensive rather than aggressive. With the onset of the Young Turk revolt in the Ottoman Empire, reform, centralization, and constitution-writing were the order of the day in Istanbul. Bosnia-Herzegovina was still under the nominal suzerainty of the sultan, and with a new Ottoman Parliament expected to make a declaration affirming the empire's territorial integrity, the position of the provinces would once more come into question. Indeed, the Hapsburgs themselves had never settled on a satisfactory definition of "occupation and administration," the language used in Article 25 of the Treaty of Berlin, as opposed to outright annexation. It therefore seemed prudent to the Austrian foreign minister, Alois Lexa von Aerenthal, to settle the ownership of the provinces once and for all with a definitive annexation.

Of course, prudent or not, this was a Balkan issue of international importance, and the Austrian declaration touched off a violent reaction. Serbia, which had the best ethnic claim to Bosnia-Herzegovina, spearheaded the outrage, but the Russians, too, objected to this clear breach of the Berlin treaty. The Serbs had successfully drawn Russia into war in the past, and they did their best to do it again this time. The Serbian foreign minister, Nikola Pasic, approached the Russians to ask for their support in a war against Austria-Hungary. His Russian counterpart, Alexander Izvolsky, demanded the convening of another international congress. He had just met with Minister Aerenthal, privately at Buchlau Castle in Moravia in September.[44] While the two had discussed the Bosnian issue, Aerenthal had announced the annexation prematurely, springing it on the world before Izvolsky had even returned home and prepared public opinion. Austria-Hungary refused categorically to turn over the issue to a congress, on the grounds that the annexation had been a domestic decision and was thus not subject to international approval.

Back and forth went the war of words, with Serbia and Russia both threatening military action against Austria-Hungary. War might very likely have broken out were it not for German intervention. In March 1909, the acting state secretary in the German Foreign Ministry, Alfred von Kiderlen-Wächter, presented an ultimatum to the Russian government demanding that it cease its agitation over the issue. Germany had already advised the Austrians to seek international approval for suspending Article 25 of the Berlin Treaty:

> But before we make this proposal to Austria-Hungary, we have to know with certainty that Russia would accept the Austrian note and that it will agree, without reservations, to suspend Article 25. Please tell Mr. Izvolsky categorically that we expect a precise answer—yes or no. Any evasive, hedged, or unclear answer we would have to regard as a rejection.

In case of rejection, Kiderlen went on to warn, Germany "would then withdraw and let events take their course."[45]

But allowing events to "take their course" was impossible for Russia at the moment. It had just fought a war—against Japan—and lost it in embarrassing fashion on land and at sea. Defeat had plunged the country into revolution (the Revolution of 1905), the aftermath of which was still rippling through Russian politics and society. Its ally and principal bankroller, France, also had massive investments in the Ottoman Empire, and French investors had little stomach for another war in the Balkans that might draw in the Ottomans. Izvolsky had no choice but to back down. Russia now added its signature to the Five Power Memorandum of March 30, 1909, demanding that Serbia climb down from the precipice and accept "the *fait accompli* in Bosnia-Herzegovina."[46] Once again, Russia's humiliation was complete.

The Bosnian Crisis is the key to understanding Russian behavior in the summer of 1914. Once again, events in the Balkans—in this case, the assassination of Archduke Franz Ferdinand—had thrown Europe into crisis. Once again, Austria-Hungary appeared to be on the march. Just as it had taken Bosnia-Herzegovina in 1908, so now it seemed poised to swallow up Serbia in revenge for its alleged role in the murder of the Archduke. Once again, Germany was backing Austria-Hungary to the hilt, threatening language was emanating from Berlin, and it seemed as if Russia's allies might prefer talking the issue to death rather than act. Once again, Russia promised to come to Serbia's defense, but backing down as it had done in 1909 was not an option this time. Russia's prestige, indeed its very status as a Great Power, was on the line. This time, Russia would force the issue—declaring mobilization and setting its armies in motion toward the Austrian border. But not merely the Austrian border: Russian troops were also pouring into Poland and the Baltic littorals, heading toward the frontier with the real enemy, the foe who had blocked Russian advancement at every turn for the past forty years: Germany. In that sense, German-Russian strategic rivalry was the real and proximate cause of World War I.

The same is true of World War II—that is to say, the war arose out of the complex relationship between Germany and Russia. On the surface, both of them had a great deal in common in the post-1918 era. The tsarist and German empires were gone, the victims of popular discontent and revolution. In their place were regimes dominated by modern ideologies—communism for the Soviet Union, first democracy and then fascism for Germany. Both states had suffered grievous territorial losses as a result of the war, and worst of all, the postwar settlement had resurrected the state of Poland, a fact that neither was inclined to accept in the long term. Indeed, the chief of the German Army High Command in the early 1920s, General Hans von Seeckt, had gone so far as to say that Poland's existence was "unbearable" (*unerträglich*) for Germany.[47] Thus, while Soviet communism was hostile ideologically to both democracy and National Socialism, the interwar period would witness a fair amount of cooperation between the two states. The absurd strategic situation after 1918—in which the Western Powers attempted to maintain the peace while reducing both Germany and the Soviet Union to the status of pariah powers (while the United States sat things out altogether)—had forced them to be friends.

The Treaty of Rapallo in 1922, for example, took the Western Powers by surprise. While the two greatest land powers in the world had apparently buried their hatchet, closer inspection shows it in less dramatic colors. The two did agree to a mutual renunciation of claims resulting from the war, a sensible path, since the regimes that had incurred those debts and obligations no longer existed on either side. The victorious allies would have done well to treat Germany in a similar fashion. In addition, a limited military cooperation began, with the Germans sending personnel to a Soviet tank school at Kazan and a flying school at Lipetsk.[48] The Germans could get hands-on practice with weapons forbidden them by the Treaty of Versailles; the Soviets could acquire German technical prowess and know-how. While it features prominently in every history of the period, the relatively small number of Germans who actually attended the school should give pause to anyone trying to make too much of it. The Rapallo treaty was never a fundamental shift to true *rapprochement*, but rather a limited and temporary response to a given set of conditions. Both powers had lapsed into one of their periodic moods of introspection, and Rapallo suited the mood perfectly.

Even this limited form of cooperation ended abruptly when Adolf Hitler came to power in January 1933. Hitler had risen to power on the basis of his anti-communism, and one of his first acts upon becoming German chancellor was to toss every official of the German Communist Party into concentration camps. As the man who claimed to have saved Germany from Bolshevism, he would have had a hard time sending German military personnel to the Soviet Union. At any rate, his decision to rearm (begun immediately but not announced formally until March 1935) soon rendered the military link unnecessary.

As in 1870–1871, this momentous change that was taking place in Germany did not evince much of a reaction from Russia. Once again, it was a time of introversion in Russia—another looking inward. Vladimir Lenin's death in 1924 had thrown the Communist Party of the Soviet Union into chaos, and a succession struggle dominated the next four years. By 1928, Josef Stalin had emerged victorious, liquidating or expelling his rivals for power. That same year, he introduced the First Five-Year Plan, a grandiose vision for transforming the Soviet economy through an instant industrial revolution from above. It featured the seizure of all private property in the countryside, the forced collectivization of agriculture, and the mass murder or starvation of millions of those unfortunate enough to be labeled "kulaks," or wealthy peasants. The horrors of this current round of domestic introversion would culminate in the late 1930s with the purges, Stalin's bloody war against his domestic political enemies.[49] A handful of them were, no doubt, real and dangerous foes, but millions and millions of victims were trumped up or imagined altogether.

In terms of relations with Germany, Stalin stood for "socialism in one country." He focused almost exclusively on domestic and social policy and suspended attempts to subvert capitalist regimes abroad. Nevertheless, from Moscow's point of view, a very familiar pattern soon began to appear. In the 1920s, a beaten-down and depressed Germany had posed little threat to anyone. But now Germany had rearmed, had revived economically, and was undertaking all sorts of provocative acts. It left the League of Nations, declared rearmament, remilitarized the Rhineland, forced the Anschluss with Austria, and provoked the Sudeten crisis in 1938. Each time, the Western Powers objected, sometimes on their own and sometimes as a group through the League of Nations, and each time they failed to follow up their words with actions. The phrase "collective security" was on everyone's lips, but if the term implied going to war on behalf of someone else's interests rather than self-interest, no one seemed eager to take the first leap. Thus, Germany's recovery of the hegemonic position it had lost in 1918 once again seemed inevitable, and it appeared that the West was willing to acquiesce in it, just as it had acquiesced to the Germans during the Congress of Berlin and the Bosnian Crisis.

As always, the key to understanding the German-Soviet relationship was Poland. In January 1934, Nazi Germany and Poland signed a non-aggression pact. It was an improvement in relations compared to the Weimar Republic, which had steadfastly refused, even under its most accommodating Foreign Minister Gustav Stresemann, to sign any sort of "Eastern Locarno" recognizing Germany's borders with Poland.[50] The pact with Poland allowed Hitler to play a favorite role of his, that of peacemaker. No speechmaker of the day invoked his service as a *Frontsoldat* ("front line soldier") and pled for international reconciliation more often than Hitler did. The pact also cut a fissure in the French alliance system, in which France had enlisted the small successor nations of the interwar period in place of pre-1914 Russia, signing treaties with Poland as well as with the "Little Entente" (Romania, Czechoslovakia, and Yugoslavia). While the German pact with Poland called into question Poland's reliability as a French ally, it brought some peace of mind to Polish dictator Jozef Pilsudski. The Poles had become concerned about French support, now that France had announced the building of the Maginot Line in 1929. A Great Power patron who sheltered behind a fortified line and refused to sally forth was no patron at all. Finally, the pact matched the relationship that Poland already had with the Soviet Union. The two had signed their own nonaggression agreement in November 1932, and would renew it in May 1934, after Poland's pact with Germany.

Germany and the Soviet Union eyed each other warily, in this, the one region that both considered to be a vital state interest. Whoever controlled

Poland was ideally positioned to launch a war on the other—the reason they had partitioned it in the first place and the reason they rejected its current existence. As German power waxed in the late 1930s, and war came to seem more and more inevitable, each side became progressively more terrified of the other establishing a predominant position in Eastern Europe and Poland. The Munich Conference, which handed the Sudetenland to Hitler after a summer of war fever, without even inviting the Soviet Union, did nothing to allay Soviet anxieties. Stalin feared that the West was trying to divert German aggression to the east, luring the Reich into a war with the Soviet Union. Usually attributed to Stalin's "paranoia," his reaction can also be seen as a conditioned response from the Kremlin leadership since the formation of Germany in 1871, whether that regime was a tsarist autocracy or a communist dictatorship.

The stage was set, therefore, for the dramatic events of the summer in 1939. Munich had destroyed Czechoslovakia and saved the peace, but not for long. Hitler's seizure of Prague in March 1939 seemed to portend a strike against Poland. The subsequent Anglo-French Guarantee to Poland (as well as Romania) in April 1939 was to Hitler an intolerable example of meddling in Germany's backyard. It was, by British standards, "a continental commitment with a vengeance,"[51] and Hitler reacted by signing a formal military alliance with Fascist Italy, the so-called Pact of Steel.

With the Western Powers having thoroughly alienated both Germany and the Soviet Union, there could be only one logical solution: a *rapprochement* between the two giants. Hitler intended to invade Poland all along, and he wanted to avoid the two-front war that had sunk Germany in World War I. Stalin wanted to stay out of a European war, not least because of Japan's threatening attitude in the Far East, and he certainly had no desire to fight Germany one-on-one in Poland while the Western Powers held back, as he suspected they would (and as they actually did).

The first feelers came from Moscow. They included hasty public denials that the Soviet Union would aid Poland in the event of war, a declaration by the Soviet chargé in Berlin that no real quarrels existed between the Soviet Union and Germany, and, in May, the dismissal of Maxim Litvinov as foreign minister and his replacement by V. I. Molotov.[52] Litvinov was the man of Geneva, who stood for collective security, disarmament, and closer ties with the West. He was also Jewish, and the "Jew Litvinov" had been a regular figure of mockery and caricature in the controlled German press.[53] The Germans responded to the Soviet overtures, toning down their anti-Soviet rhetoric, agreeing to open trade talks, and publicly denouncing their non-aggression pact with Poland.

Finally, as the summer wore on and the September 1 date for the invasion of Poland approached, Hitler became personally involved in the diplomatic process. After he sent a direct message to Stalin, the Soviet Union agreed to receive German foreign minister Joachim von Ribbentrop in Moscow on August 23. Here, Ribbentrop and Molotov signed a ten-year nonaggression agreement, but that was only the public face. The Nazi-Soviet Pact also contained a "Secret Additional Protocol" dividing Eastern Europe into German and Soviet spheres of influence "in the event of a territorial and political transformation of the territories belonging to the Polish state."[54] Germany received primacy in western Poland and Lithuania, the Soviets much more: the province of Bessarabia, the eastern half of Poland (the Kresy, or "borderlands" region), Latvia, Estonia, and Finland. An early September revision of the terms would hand Lithuania to the Soviets and transfer more of central Poland to the Germans. Essentially, the Protocol re-created the borders of the old tsarist empire as they had stood around 1795, at the end of the Third Partition of Poland. Stalin had therefore won back the territories that had broken away from Russia after the Bolshevik Revolution of 1917. Here was a classic example of foreign policy "realism," an ideology of power politics with the strong taking what they wanted and the weak having to pay the price.

The Nazi-Soviet Pact exploded on the world like a bombshell. Ideological enemies who had been "pouring filth over each other" for years were suddenly embracing like old friends.[55] Late in the signing ceremony between Molotov and Ribbentrop, Stalin appeared in person in a white dinner jacket and actually proposed a toast to Hitler. "I know how much the German people love their Führer! I want to drink to his health!" he beamed. Hitler returned the favor by phone. "Give my congratulations to Mr. Stalin, leader of the Soviet people!" he told Ribbentrop.[56] All over the world, leftist intellectuals had to turn on a dime and repudiate condemnations of Germany they had written only weeks or days before. Fewer events in the twentieth century held more drama.

Ideology aside, the Pact offered obvious benefits to both sides. In the words of one analyst, not for a long time "had the possibility of territorial expansion been so real and apparently without risk for the Soviet Union, and not since 1870 had Germany been so hopeful of securing a war on one front."[57] It is easy to explain why Hitler signed it. He never intended to keep it, since his brutal, expansionist ideology demanded a near-term invasion of the Soviet Union itself. He once described Bolshevism in a 1938 speech as "the incarnation of the human destructive instinct," an *idée fixe* that was impervious to reason or change.[58] A few years later, Hitler would get his war, the one he had wanted to fight all along, only two years into the ten-year term of the Pact.

Stalin's willingness was more problematic, and appears on the surface to be a massive blunder. The pact made perfect sense for the Soviet Union, however. The West was offering Stalin a chance to fight Germany by himself, at least in the opening phase of the war, and promised him nothing in return. Hitler wanted to him to do nothing, and promised him everything. The amount of blame heaped on the Western Allies for not pursuing the negotiations with Stalin more aggressively is equally misplaced. Having backed Poland, they had nothing to offer Stalin, no matter how aggressively they might have pursued it. Despite the rage directed at Stalin at the time—and by historians ever since—for signing a treaty with Hitler, he was not blind to strategic realities. He warned Hitler's foreign minister, Ribbentrop, that Germany should not expect an easy victory in the upcoming war, since Britain would fight "stubbornly and cunningly,"[59] and in private at least, he was prone to refer to the Nazi leaders as "cheats" and "frauds."[60] Nevertheless, he did what every statesman tends to do: he took the best deal he could get at the time, no matter how many problems it might cause in the future. In the process, he won himself almost two years to reform the creaking Soviet military, and also acquired vast buffer regions: two factors that might have made the difference between victory and defeat.

The key to understanding the Pact, however, is that it restored the original historic basis for a Russian-German modus vivendi. It was the same as it had been in the great era of Prussian-Russian friendship from 1770 to 1870: the destruction of Poland. This time there were no distractions, no diversions or detours into the Balkans or anywhere else. The conflict unleashed by Adolf Hitler in 1939 soon became known as "World War II." In its opening phase, however, with the German Panzers driving into Poland on September 1, 1939, and the Soviets responding from the east two weeks later, it was nothing more or less than the Fourth Partition of Poland.

The Rivals at War: The Great Asymmetry

Although German and Russian interests often ran in parallel and symmetrical paths over the decades, we cannot say the same about their warfighting. Once the shooting began between them, powerful asymmetries were more likely to come to the fore. Germany truly was a coiled spring. Its initial blows were always its strongest ones. German planners had long recognized that they could not fight and win sustained wars of attrition—neither the state's geographical position nor limited resource base would permit it. Rather, it had to fight a high-tempo war of maneuver, seeking out and destroying as much

TABLE 14.1 Territorial Partitioning of Poland

1772	Austria, Prussia, and Russia	Maria Theresa, Frederick II the Great, Paul I
1793	Prussia and Russia	Frederick William II, Alexander I
1795	Austria, Prussia, and Russia	Francis I, Frederick William II, Alexander I
1939	Germany and USSR	Hitler, Stalin

Source: "Partitions of Poland," *Encyclopedia Britannica Online Academic Edition*, accessed September 9, 2014.

of the enemy force as possible in the opening weeks of the fighting. The Germans called it *Bewegungskrieg*, the "war of movement," and its goal was to keep Germany's wars *kurtz und vives* (short and lively), in the memorable phrase of its most successful practitioner, Frederick the Great.[61]

German *Bewegungskrieg* was a way of war that stressed maneuver on the operational level, not simply tactical maneuverability or a faster march rate, but the movement of large units like divisions, corps, and armies. Prussian commanders, and their later German descendants, sought to maneuver these formations in such a way as to strike the mass of the enemy army a sharp, annihilating blow as rapidly as possible. It might involve a surprise assault against an unprotected flank, or both of them. On several notable occasions, it even resulted in entire Prussian or German armies getting into the rear of an enemy army. The desired end-state was the *Kesselschlacht*, literally, a "cauldron battle," but more specifically a battle of encirclement, hemming in the enemy on all sides prior to destroying him in an aggressive series of "concentric (*konzentrisch*) operations." The Germans had to win early, in other words, or they would probably not win at all.

If the Germans had the ultimate "front-loaded" military machine, the Russian and Soviet armies were the opposite. They really were a steamroller—not only in their power and inexorability but in the time they took to get assembled and rolling. Like the Germans, this posture was not so much a choice that they had made at any discrete point but rather a result of systemic factors of time, space, and transport. The land was immense, the communications network—roads and railroads—primitive by the standards of western Europe. By definition, then, the Russians had to absorb the initial blow from German armies, no matter how grievously it might land. They could trade space for time, as they had against Napoleon, that is, they could retreat, abandon tens of thousands of square miles, and scorch the earth as they went, denying it to their advancing adversaries. It would always be a painful process, but Russia knew it had to survive a great deal of pain early in order to have any chance of winning in the end.

Both world wars saw the asymmetries play out more or less precisely. In World War I, the Germans quickly encircled and destroyed an entire Russian field army at the Battle of Tannenberg (the "Second Battle of Tannenberg," to German nationalists) in August 1914.[62] Their subsequent invasion of Russian Poland, however, came to grief in September at the battle of Warsaw, as rain, mud, inadequate logistics, and Russian numbers began to tell. A vicious back-and-forth struggle for Lodz in October inflicted massive casualties on both sides but ended in Russian retreat.[63] The Germans renewed the offensive in May 1915 with a well-coordinated offensive between Gorlice and Tarnów, blasted a hole in Russian defenses, and forced the Russian armies into a headlong retreat that did not end until they had evacuated the great Polish salient altogether.[64] The next year would see Russia's last great operation of the war, the Brusilov Offensive of June 1916, targeting Austro-Hungarian forces on the southern portion of the front.[65] It virtually destroyed the Habsburg Army in a single blow, taking hundreds of thousands of prisoners, before itself collapsing against a German counterblow.

In the end, the Russians went down. The loss of the key Baltic port of Riga in January 1917 led to the February Revolution that overthrew the tsar.[66] The new Provisional Government that replaced him never stabilized, and its insistence that the war must go on alienated the masses in both city and countryside. The October Revolution overthrew the Provisional Government in turn, and the new Bolshevik regime sued for peace and got it at Brest-Litovsk in March 1918.[67] Nevertheless, the Russians had stayed in the field long enough, and diverted enough precious German manpower and resources, to play a key strategic role in saving the British and French armies from defeat earlier in the war. In preventing the Germany army from winning the war quickly and forcing it into a war of attrition from the start, the Russians had prevented it from winning at all.

World War II would display the asymmetries even more vividly. The Soviet Union spent the two years after signing the Nazi-Soviet Pact supplying the German war machine with key materials of all sorts: oil, grain, cotton, manganese.[68] The terms were generous, the payment schedule leisurely. Without these resources, the Germans would have suffered serious hurt from the British naval blockade, the very strategy that had beaten them in World War I. The term "non-aggression" had given way to "friendship" now, a relationship that in Stalin's words had been "sealed in blood."[69] The powers signed a new treaty in late September 1939 that ratified the partition of Poland, declared that there was no longer any reason for the war to continue, and stated that if efforts to produce a general peace should fail, the record would show that "England and France are responsible for the continuation of the war."[70]

Their friendship ended almost as abruptly as it began, however, with the German invasion of the Soviet Union in June 1941. Historians may describe a process of disillusionment and building tensions on both sides that led to the conflict, with the Soviet advance into Finland (the Winter War of 1939–1940), the Baltic States, and Bessarabia (June 1940) stoking German fears.[71] The occupation of Bessarabia, in particular, put Soviet forces just a few days' march from the Ploesti oil fields that were so crucial to the German war effort. But in reality, none of these factors produced the German invasion. Hitler had intended to invade the Soviet Union all along, perhaps since he was a penniless street person in a Viennese homeless shelter in 1912. Stalemated now in his war with Great Britain, Hitler saw an opportunity for the grand gesture, the bold military stroke that would cement German power once and for all, and demonstrate to Britain how hopeless its wartime position was. He decided to invade the Soviet Union, in other words, because he wanted to.

His complete lack of strategic basis for the move had one beneficial impact: it surprised the Soviets, especially Stalin, who simply could not understand why Hitler would do such a thing. Stalin had reports of military preparations along the border, even German reconnaissance overflights of Soviet territory, but they seemed to make no sense. "I think Hitler is trying to provoke us," he muttered to one of his generals on the evening of June 21, 1941. "He surely hasn't decided to make war?"[72] The very next day, the German ambassador to Moscow, Friedrich Werner von der Schulenberg, handed Molotov the official declaration of war. Molotov responded with an incredulous, "What have we done to deserve this?"[73] The answer was that in this case, at least, they had done nothing at all.

Partially as a result of this surprise, never had the German "war of movement" found a more lucrative target than it did in the opening days of Operation Barbarossa. The Germans began by wrecking the gigantic Soviet air force on the ground in a series of devastating air raids. Once the Germans had established air superiority over the front, quick-moving "tank armies" (*Panzergruppen*) slashed through Soviet defenses. With the Panzers ranging wide and deep, the German armed forces (*Wehrmacht*) sealed off one immense encirclement after another: at Bialystok, Minsk, Smolensk, Bryansk, and Vyazma on the central front, and the biggest one of all at Kiev in the Ukraine. By December, the Germans had fought their way to the very gates of Moscow. They had inflicted four million casualties on the Red Army, about three million of whom were prisoners, and to many outside observers, the Soviet Union seemed finished.

But it was not. The Red Army had survived the worst military onslaught in the history of war but it was still in the field. Its manpower reserves were just beginning to be mobilized, its industries were getting into high gear, and its weaponry was far better than German intelligence had reported. In all these early battles—even when its leaders were inept and its levies poorly trained—it had taken a toll on its German adversary. The Wehrmacht was designed for fighting short campaigns in central and western Europe, lands with a relatively temperate climate and an excellent road network. The wear and tear of a logistics-intensive campaign deep inside Soviet Russia and Ukraine had wounded it deeply, and it was a shadow force that reached Moscow by December.[74] Here a massive counteroffensive by no fewer than seventeen fresh field armies, under the capable direction of General G. K. Zhukov, hit the Germans, driving them back in some confusion and inflicting massive casualties on them. There was much hard fighting yet to do, but the mauling in front of Moscow effectively ended any chance of the Germans winning the war early, and thus of winning at all.[75]

Conclusions: The Great Symmetry

For the next forty months, the two adversaries engaged in some of the hardest and bloodiest fighting in the history of warfare. Two bitter rivals, each dedicated to stamping out the other, two monstrous regimes, the wholesale killing of civilians on all sides: the Russo-German War set new standards in all these areas, turning eastern Europe into a slaughter-pen, "the Bloodlands," and we should all hope we never see anything like it again.[76] Not until April 1945 did the Soviet army blast its way into Berlin. With Soviet troops just blocks from his bunker, Hitler committed suicide, and the long strategic rivalry between Germany and Russia finally came to an end.

Even today, analyzing that rivalry is not easy. It did not arise out of economics. For much of their history, the two had a mutually beneficial economic relationship, with the Germans producing manufactured goods and the Soviets providing raw materials out of their bountiful surplus. Nor was ideology at its root. National Socialism and Marxist communism may have been bitter ideological rivals, as far apart on the spectrum as possible, but the two states found enough in common to ignore their ideologies and sign a treaty of cooperation in 1922 (Rapallo), a trade treaty in mid-August 1939, and the Molotov-Ribbentrop Pact later that month. They even became "friends," according to the official record, in late September 1939. Mutual stereotyping of national character may have played a role. Russian Pan-Slavs saw themselves as the bearers of an organic, spiritual culture, and the Germans as materialistic and soulless. Pan-Germans did the same in reverse; they were the bearers of *Kultur* in the highest sense and the Russians were uncouth brutes from the steppe. Such absurd propaganda did inform public opinion to a certain extent, but was never determinative to policymakers.[77]

With economics, ideology, and national character excluded, what factor was left? In 2012, Robert Kaplan published *The Revenge of Geography*.[78] Anyone studying the tortured relationship between Germany and Russia/USSR should read it carefully. Kaplan's point was that analysts always need to read "what the map tells us." The map, in this case, tells us a great deal. The German nation had come of age as a disunified gaggle of small states, trapped in a precarious geographical position. Even after the Germans overcame their early disadvantages by unifying and forming the dominant power in Europe, they still saw themselves in terms of their vulnerabilities. They had enemies all around, and sat on a flat North German Plain devoid of terrain protection. The same was true of Russia. Seen by neighboring powers as a threatening giant, it was far more prone to see itself in terms of its weaknesses. The Russians sat at the opposite end of the Plain, and felt just as vulnerable to the more developed peoples to the west.

Given these assumptions, control of the open geographical space between them—the Baltic States, Byelorussia, and especially Poland, medium and small-sized peoples with weak militaries and vulnerable geographies—was absolutely essential to national security. At the very least, each side needed to deny such control to the other, and each was highly jealous of any attempt by the other to steal a march in the area. They did not view Poland as a buffer zone, but rather as a threat whose very weakness might invite the other power to dominate it. For that reason, Germany and Russia were both most comfortable when they had partitioned Poland between them, their borders were contiguous, and they could keep a close watch on one another. This was the great symmetry of the Russian-German relationship: the long-term abhorrence of an independent Poland. It did not change over time. It was as immutable as geography itself.

The post-1945 world said goodbye to all that, of course. Germany was no longer a rival to anyone, but a truncated and divided pawn between the United States and the Soviet Union in the Cold War. Even today, while a reunified Germany is an economic and financial giant, it has apparently been weaned off military adventurism and expansionist policies altogether—to the world's relief.[79] Unfortunately, the situation to the east is not so clear. The fall of the Soviet Union seemed to have heralded a new era in Eastern Europe, as the subject nations won their independence. "The Russians swallowed up Eastern Europe," wrote John Lukacs in 2010. "Then it went on for forty years during which they had serious instances of digesting some of it (as Churchill had foretold); and it ended with their disgorging just about all of it."[80]

But Russia today seems to be once again on the march. The regime of Vladimir Putin fosters Russian separatism in Ukraine, using the grievances of ethnic Russians in the Crimea and the Donbas, and it is difficult to say where the process will stop. Ethnic Russians live all over the countries that broke away when the Soviet Union fell apart, not just Ukraine but Moldova, Belarus, and the Baltic states. If these lost Russians have real a sense of grievance, then Russia can exploit it. If they do not, then Russia can foment one. Some of Russia's potential victims, however, already have a "security guarantee" from the West: NATO. The tragedy of such Russian policies is that there is no better way to encourage Germany to take a more active military role, a development that could have ominous possibilities.

In 1989, looking back from a distance of fifty years, the dean of US diplomatic historians, Gerhard Weinberg, described the Nazi-Soviet Pact as a result of "terrible miscalculations made by both parties." He went on to comment:

Perhaps a new perception of the past will enable the Soviet Union to see the secret protocol as part of a mistaken and adventurous policy by Stalin—a policy that cost Russia the most horrendous losses. . . . As Europe moves into a new phase, perhaps the Soviets as well as the Germans may come to see that allowing the peoples living in between them to enjoy a real independence can contribute to the security of all countries.[81]

As tensions rise in Eastern Europe, the world would do well to heed these words. The future peace may well depend on a strong and stable Poland. The broad plain of the Vistula has historically been the arena in which Germany and Russia have played out their strategic rivalry. It is here that both powers have spied their greatest opportunities and conjured their most frightening nightmares. For centuries, both spent their blood and treasure trying to subjugate Poland, and both failed. Over and over again, Poland has survived and re-emerged as an independent state. The words of the Polish national anthem describe a bittersweet but defiant arc: "Still Poland has not perished" (*Jeszcze Polska nie zginęła*).

And let us hope it never does. A secure and free Poland keeps Germany and Russia separated, and therefore serves as Europe's best proof against a potential catastrophe: a rebirth of the strategic rivalry between the two giants. As we peer into an uncertain future, the issue of Polish liberty comes once more to the fore, as it has many times in the past.

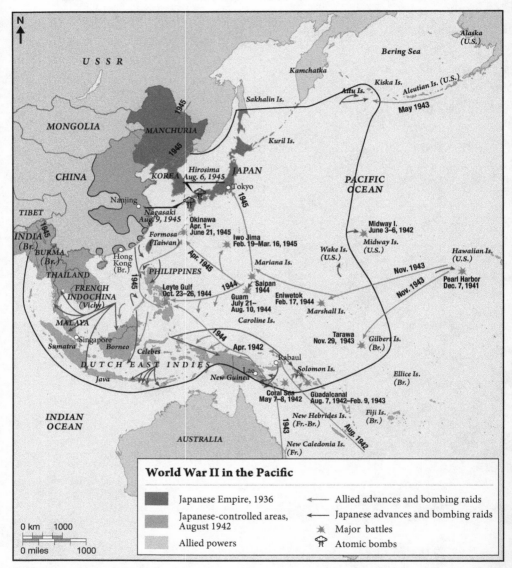

World War II in the Pacific.

CHAPTER 15

Pacific Dominance
The United States versus Japan
William M. Morgan

A S JAPAN AND THE United States warily circled each other, and the possibility of war loomed, the Japanese ambassador in Washington, though publicly courteous and conciliatory, secretly urged an attack on Hawaii. In an encrypted telegram to his prime minister, he insisted that a "strong naval armament should be at once dispatched for the purpose of occupying the islands by force."[1] Surprisingly, this incendiary message was sent not in 1941, but in 1897.

Only recently have historians become aware that forty-four years before Pearl Harbor, there was another possibility of a Japanese attack on Honolulu. In 1897, Japan was no longer the weak, semi-feudal nation that Admiral Perry encountered in 1853. The capable Imperial Navy, its core composed of modern British-built steel cruisers, quickly defeated the Chinese Navy in the 1894–1895 war. Fresh from that victory, Japan turned its attention not only to Korea and northern China but eastward to the Hawaiian Islands. Both the United States and Japan sought to control the independent Republic of Hawaii, run by a small white oligarchy that, in 1893, overthrew the Native Hawaiian queen. An 1896 census showed that Japanese sugar plantation workers, nearly all males between twenty and forty years of age, represented a quarter of the population. For these male immigrants, the Imperial Government demanded suffrage equality with white males, who numbered fewer than half the Japanese. Suffrage and equality might, however, turn Hawaii into a Japanese possession—a development the United States would not accept.[2]

Long the most influential foreign power in Hawaii, by the late 1890s, the United States deeply embraced the Mahanian (Alfred Thayer Mahan) strategic value of the archipelago. In 1887, the United States negotiated rights to develop a huge base at Pearl Harbor. Operating from that base, the United States Navy could control a vast stretch of the North Pacific, especially as coal-fired warships lacked the range to strike the American West Coast from Asian or Pacific bases and to return without re-coaling at Hawaii. Given the islands' significance to power projection and coastal defense, the United States would tolerate no Japanese meddling. In early 1897, as the immigration spat grew nasty, both nations sent flotillas to Honolulu. President McKinley accelerated his plans to annex the islands, signing an annexation treaty with Hawaii on June 16, 1897. He instructed the commander of the Pacific Squadron to occupy the islands if Japan landed troops to pressure the weak Republic into suffrage concessions. He readied more warships, including the new battleship *USS Oregon*, then the most powerful warship in the Pacific. Tough diplomacy, backed by naval deployments, caused the Japanese to slowly back off, and the United States soon absorbed Hawaii.[3]

The 1897 crisis over Hawaii was the first time the two nations considered military action against the other. The Hawaiian episode was a target of opportunity, not so important that Japan would risk war. Nevertheless, 1897 is the most appropriate beginning date for the Japanese-American rivalry. During the next four decades, the rivalry evolved from wary and conditional friendship, to quarrels, to confrontation, and finally to war.

Two Rising Powers

Though in 1897 the two powers tussled over the same objective, the episode was important for its uniqueness. Until shortly before Pearl Harbor, the two nations pursued different goals, though both were expansionist powers.

Throughout the rivalry, both were rising powers. The United States became a global power after the 1898 war with Spain. After World War I, the United States was the world's most powerful nation, though it demobilized most ground forces and possessed overseas bases only in the Caribbean, the Philippines, and Hawaii. Japan was a rising middle power, stronger in military than in economic terms. While possessing less material power overall than the United States, it was, by 1941, the most powerful country in Northeast Asia.

During the 1897–1941 rivalry, the United States remained much larger in terms of population and the economy. The US population grew faster because of much greater immigration. When the Meiji era (1868–1912) began, Japan's population was 34 million, climbed to 53 million in 1914, and reached 74 million in 1941. The United States population was 38 million in 1868, 99 million in 1914, and 140 million in 1941. In GDP, the American economy was four times bigger in 1870, and five times bigger in 1941. In per capita GDP, therefore, the gap narrowed slightly. In 1941, the American per capita GDP was three times that of Japan. This was partly because the Japanese economy weathered the Great Depression better than the American giant. Though American growth in the 1920s had exceeded Japan's, during 1929–1941 the Japanese economy grew 66 percent, with an actual decrease in GDP only in 1930. The much larger American economy grew 23 percent, most of that growth coming in 1939–1941 (but then doubling during World War II).[4]

Though the macro statistics show that Japan coped with the Great Depression better than most advanced economies, there were significant sectorial differences. The depression hammered agriculture. Japan exported mainly agricultural products such as silk, and those exports dried up. Traditional village life—still a core component of Japanese identity—seemed wrongly undervalued by modernization. And from these disgruntled villages came most of the Imperial Army's recruits.

Location and resources were the most dramatic and persistent asymmetries. The United States was ideally located, with oceans separating it from its biggest rivals, and no meaningful threat in its own hemisphere. But Japan lived in a tough neighborhood, with Russia always a threat, the Europeans lurking about, and China, though constantly in political turmoil, able to field forces strong enough to tie down the Japanese army and drain the Japanese treasury.

Unlike the United States, Japan had few resources: little iron ore, not much coal, few steel plants, no strategic minerals, and worst of all, no oil. It sought those resources first in Korea, Taiwan, and South Sakhalin, then in Manchuria and North China, next in all of China, and, in 1941, in Southeast Asia. Until shortly before Pearl Harbor, Japan imported many essentials—oil, scrap steel, aviation fuel, machine tools—from the United States. The comparatively closed international trading system complicated Japan's quest to diversify supply. As the big British, French, and Dutch colonial empires privileged imports from their home countries, especially manufactures, exports of raw materials back to their home countries took precedence over exports to outsiders. It was difficult, therefore, for Japan to buy as many resources as it wished, and even more so to sell into the colonial empires to earn money to buy resources. Only Northeast Asia was not "locked up," but even there Japan competed with Russia, as well as the European colonial powers, first in Korea, then in Manchuria, and finally across China.

Aside from material factors—population, military capability, the size of the economy and its growth, resources, and location—Japanese imperialism differed from American imperialism in its ideological and psychological underpinnings in at least five ways.

First, feelings of vulnerability infused Japanese policymaking down to 1941. The West used Japan's military vulnerability to pry open the *shogunate* and trigger its 1868 collapse. The feudal samurai class and its successor, the professional military, played an important role in Japan's swift embrace of many Western practices, partly to strengthen the country to resist military threats. Japan swiftly built up its military, but for decades, Western powers could intimidate Japan into surrendering hard-won gains. As the decades passed, Japan sought ever more strength to act—if it wished—with impunity in Northeast Asia. And as Japan grew stronger, the target area for unilateral action expanded.

Second, anger at inequality undergirded Japanese diplomatic and security policy. In the Meiji era, Japan worked unceasingly to rid itself of the hated unequal treaties that allowed extraterritoriality and tariff oversight. Even as Japan shed the treaties, it confronted the racial superiority that the Western powers assumed for themselves. American racial discrimination was the most publicized, as few Japanese immigrated to Europe and a great many went to Hawaii and the American mainland. We need not linger over the many incidents of anti-Japanese, anti-Asian sentiment, such as discrimination in housing and workplaces, unequal pay, separate schools for "orientals," restrictions on immigration, and finally the 1924 ban on Asian immigration. This sad history made it emotionally much easier for Japanese to see the United States as disrespectful and unfair and unlikely to give Japan its due.[5] At the state-to-state level, Japanese policymakers felt constrained by international rules invented by Westerners after they had completed their dirty-handed conquests.

Third, intertwined with vulnerability and inequality was an ambitious quest to build a self-sufficient and militarily invulnerable empire. Initially confined to interests in Korea and the Liaotung Peninsula in southernmost Manchuria, this imperial vision grew by leaps and bounds until, by 1941, it encompassed most of Asia.[6] Its two most familiar names were "A New Order in East Asia" and "The Greater East Asia Co-Prosperity Sphere."

Fourth, the Japanese military played a disproportionate role in national policy until 1945. Early in the Meiji era, when the idea of a prime minister and a national legislature formed by political parties first appeared, the military insisted that politicians could not be trusted to place national interest above politics and therefore should not control the armed forces. Thus both the army and the navy general staffs were placed under the emperor's authority instead of the civilian cabinet. The army and navy ministries henceforth focused on administration, budgets, and personnel. As members of the cabinet, the army and navy ministers reported to the emperor through the prime minister. The ministers did not command the powerful chiefs of staff, who controlled the actual forces. This did not mean that the ministers were not often supportive of the general staffs. It soon became the practice that the army and navy ministers must be appointed from among active duty officers, making the ministries as well devoted to service interests. This system, called the "independence of the Supreme Command," endured until Japan's surrender in August 1945. Foreign policy could not be made without integrating the views of the services. Should the army or navy ministries disagree with the cabinet, they would resign and the government would collapse. Until the services nominated an active duty officer as minister, no government could be formed. Politicians tended, therefore, to defer to military recommendations on foreign as well as domestic policy.[7]

Fifth, Japan had a flawed governmental decision-making system. Only the emperor could command both the cabinet ministries and the Supreme Command. In practice, the emperors almost never issued orders to the chiefs of staff or to the cabinet. Policy was confirmed, therefore, only at Imperial Conferences, held in the presence of the emperor, who would sit silently. He was attended by the prime minister, the army and navy chiefs of staff, the army and navy ministers, the foreign minister, often the finance minister, and the president of the Privy Council, a senior advisor to the throne. Starting in 1937, the government held Liaison Conferences to achieve policy consensus before holding Imperial Conferences. The attendees were the same as for Imperial Conferences but without the emperor and the president of the Privy Council. Before Liaison Conferences, there was much cross-agency compromise. Thus the decision-making structure did not force the emperor, the prime minister, or the cabinet to face contradictions or make tough choices; rather, differences were papered over at lower levels.

The Rivalry's Early Years

As spoils from the Sino-Japanese War of 1894–1895, Japan wanted the island of Formosa, control of the Shandong Peninsula on the mainland, the end of Chinese meddling in Korea, and key ports on the Liaotung Peninsula in South Manchuria. China agreed to these terms, plus a $135 million indemnity. But the war spoils infringed on Russian and German desires for concessions and bases. In April 1895, Russia, Germany, and France successfully pressured Japan to give the Liaotung Peninsula back to China. This was a body blow to the proud Japanese, despite a last-minute increase of the indemnity to $200 million. A huge outcry of dissatisfaction with the Triple Intervention toppled the Ito Hirobumi cabinet in 1896.[8]

After the war, a weakened China fragmented faster, enticing foreign powers to enlarge and protect their interests. France, Germany, and Britain acquired leaseholds, and, to Japan's dismay, Russia acquired the Liaotung Peninsula that the Triple Intervention had forced Japan to return to China. Germany, by manipulating an 1897 incident in which two Germans were killed, gained control of the important port of Kiaochow on the Shandong Peninsula. Britain browbeat the Chinese into ceding Weihaiwei port, also in Shandong. Within their spheres of influence, the powers operated railroads, mines, and other concessions, privileging their own commercial and financial interests.

Japan, too, adopted the spheres of influence approach. And the spheres of influence related to territory, so in some ways the commercial competition was actually territorial competition. Russia, one of the most aggressive countries, was on Japan's doorstep. The most likely area for Japan to create its own sphere of influence was precisely the region in which the Russians were deeply involved. In the early 1900s, as China disintegrated, Japan became more aggressive on the mainland. There was consensus that national security depended upon control of the Korean Peninsula. Even if Japan pushed the Russians out of Korea, the peninsula would not be safe with Russian domination of Manchuria, so Manchuria became a prime focus. Between 1895 and 1904, Japan slowly won this political and economic struggle. Japan built several key rail lines within Korea. Many Japanese settlers went there. Japan provided 60 percent of Korean imports and took 80 percent of Korean exports. Even in these early days, Japan was unique among the competing powers in seeking an absolutely reliable supply of strategic resources. Reliability implied eliminating threats to the region from which strategic resources were found, threats to the transport routes to Japan, and an enhanced level of administration and financial controls to assure that the development of the resources met Japanese needs.[9] This trend strengthened as the years passed.

After acquiring the Philippines and Guam in 1898–1899, the Americans became more engaged in Asia, though less aggressively than the Europeans. The Open Door Policy defined that engagement as peaceful commercial activity without further territorial acquisitions. The United States declined to establish an exclusive sphere of influence and insisted on trading through-out China. Why confine ourselves to one sphere, the Americans reasoned, when with our broad and competitive economy we can out-compete the Japanese and the Europeans across all of China? Secretary of State John Hay's Open Door notes of 1899 and 1900 announced that all powers agreed to his plan to renounce spheres of influence and to respect Chinese territorial and administrative integrity. In reality, the skirmishing for national advantage continued.

The Open Door Policy remained the basis of American policy in Asia to 1941. The Open Door inherently ran against Japanese expansion, which was increasingly characterized by the use of force, direct administrative control of acquired territory, and the exclusion of other powers. Given later Japanese complaints of American hypocrisy, the United States applied the Open Door only in Asia. In its own hemisphere, the United States welded Puerto Rico and Cuba into the American economic system via tax and tariff policies. It ruled out sharing the ownership or control of the Panama Canal. It intervened frequently in Central America and the Caribbean. The Greater Caribbean region became, in fact, an American lake. On the other hand, unlike Japan in Asia, the United States faced no constellation of powers com-peting for Caribbean influence. Practically and realistically, the distinct situ-ation in Asia called for a different approach by Japan and perhaps by the United States.

South of the Great Wall, Japan had less success in gaining railway conces-sions and other advantages. In that region, Japan had to cooperate with the major European powers, especially Britain, while in Manchuria and Korea, Japan had to cope with Russia. In this situation, Japan had to choose which countries to confront and which to embrace. It embraced Britain via a 1902 alliance, freeing itself to focus on Manchuria and Korea. The alliance recog-nized that Japan was "interested in a peculiar degree politically as well as commercially and industrially" in Korea. In short, Japan committed to the Open Door in China below the Great Wall in exchange for British recog-nition of Japanese special interests in Korea and Manchuria.[10] The alliance provided for military help from Britain if Japan became involved in a war with more than just one other power. That meant fighting Russia alone. But it also meant that no third country could intervene to upset the war spoils, as during the hated Triple Intervention.[11]

The Russo-Japanese War of 1904–1905 resulted from a Japanese desire for total control of Korea and for increased influence in Manchuria. An important new development was that Japan now defined Korea as essential to its national security.[12] The inclusion of ever-larger regions as essential to national security was another trend that strengthened steadily until 1941. The war with Russia was a series of Japanese victories won at great and, on the ground, unsustainable cost, hence the willingness to accept American mediation. Russia acknowledged Japan's dominance of Korea and transferred to Japan the Liaotung Peninsula leaseholds and the spur of the Chinese Eastern Railway south from Harbin. Japan now had significant interests in South Manchuria.

Yet there were still worries. The Russian threat was beaten but hardly eliminated. Japan needed to solidify its hold on Korea and expand its interests in Manchuria. Japan poured advisors and troops into Korea. Soon there were 5,000 civilian advisors scattered throughout the Korean government, making sure Japan's wishes were followed. Two army divisions kept order. In 1910, Japan annexed Korea. The powers were not overly concerned because they had no great economic interests in that country. But Manchuria was part of China. Japanese actions there might affect the treaty port system throughout all of China. Yet Manchuria was precisely where Japan now set its sights.

The army and navy sought force levels that would allow expanded operations on the mainland, but the Diet, conscious that the war savaged national finances, refused big military increases. The inter-service competition for resources accelerated, troubling cabinet stability and becoming a fixture in Japanese politics.

General Yamagata Aritomo, one of the *genro* (elders who were informal but trusted advisors to the emperor) sent Emperor Meiji a plea calling for an army strong enough to undertake on the mainland whatever policy the government decided. This was a striking example of the cart before the horse, an early manifestation of what became a characteristic of army (and, later, navy) planning: pushing for larger resources without reference to a policy goal. Logically, the government should decide the policy goal and the military should ask for the resources to attain it. Instead, military strength itself became the goal. In essence, the policy objective became unhindered unilateralism. It encouraged overly ambitious military requests, because if the policy goal was expansive but undefined, who could say how much was enough?

In this aggressive atmosphere, Japan's first national defense plan appeared. The Imperial National Defense Policy of 1907 planned a military capable of unilaterally achieving any and all ambitious policies. This meant an army of twenty-five divisions in peacetime, with a surge capacity of twenty-five additional divisions in wartime. A bigger fleet would be built on the so-called "8-8" plan: two fleets built around 8 battleships, 8 heavy cruisers, and 268 light cruisers, destroyers, and submarines. That said, the naval increase merely kept Japan at rough parity with the growing American navy and preserved the battleship ratio with Britain.[13]

With the Russians at least temporarily subdued, and the British negated by alliance, the 1907 defense plan imagined the United States as the most likely potential enemy. Why? Partly this was simple logic. With China in disarray, Britain neutralized by treaty, Russia defeated, and France and Germany focusing on European rivalries, the only major power left was the United States. Moreover, the anti-Japanese hysteria in California and elsewhere offended many Japanese, despite Roosevelt's vain attempts to mute it. Third, the Portsmouth Treaty dashed excessive popular expectations of war spoils, and many Japanese blamed Roosevelt's intervention in the negotiations.

No specific American military or even diplomatic actions in East Asia forced Japan to identify the United States as a prime threat. No large ground or naval forces were based in China, or in Asia for that matter. The Philippines had not been turned into a naval bastion. There was no large dry-dock or other necessities to support a fleet. Nor on the diplomatic front had the United States done much more than voice the Open Door mantra of "equal access to China" while American business interests tried to make money. What was the real as opposed to the imagined threat? If the policy goal is the ability to intervene anywhere, then the threat picture worsens rapidly. In this period, there was no increase in American military capacity to damage Japan itself or Japanese interests or freedom of action in Korea, Manchuria, or North China. Nor was there intent to do so. Japan simply imagined a large American military threat where none existed.

Imperial Army leaders considered diplomatic and administrative issues related to Korea and Manchuria as embedded within military policy and therefore solely within the army's purview.[14] This was a mistake on the army's part, because the situation was not static. The Russian reaction could not be anticipated, nor could the course of Chinese revolutionary nationalism. Either or both might lead to changing involvement in North Manchuria and North China, with huge diplomatic and economic consequences. More and more army officers embraced the sentiment that military judgment should prevail in Manchuria and, later, China. Officers believed themselves responsible to the emperor, not to the cabinet, to defend Japan's interests on the mainland. This way of thinking accelerated the autonomy of the two services from cabinet supervision. The services won the elimination of the requirement that the prime minister confirm, by signature, changes in administrative and personnel policies within the army and the navy. The army general staff no longer funneled national defense plans and budget estimates through the Army Ministry to the cabinet. Instead, budget requests went directly to the throne, and the cabinet was expected to approve whatever was sent. Partly because of the debts left by the Russo-Japanese War, the Diet did not fund the increase from nineteen to twenty-five peacetime divisions recommended in the 1907 Imperial National Defense Policy. Many army officers believed that the government thereby abandoned its duty to the nation. Soon Saionji Kinmochi's government fell when the army minister (a former army chief of staff) resigned because the government failed to fund two additional divisions in Korea. The army would not identify a general officer to fill the minister's position, so Saionji could not form a new cabinet. Finally the *genrō* installed General Katsura as prime minister.[15]

When civilians tried to balance military needs with diplomacy, the militarists pounced. In 1913, Abe Moritarō of the Foreign Ministry proposed pushing for economic advantage in China without angering, by reckless army actions, the ruling warlord Yuan Shikai and turning public opinion against Japan. The ultra-nationalists saw Abe's idea as abandonment of their hopes to take over Manchuria. In fact, Abe concurred with further expansion of Japanese influence in Manchuria and North China. His error was suggesting a cautious means to that end. A young rightist fanatic stabbed Abe to death, then disemboweled himself over a map of China, presumably suggesting the area of Abe's weakness. The intimidation or assassination of men who would use moderate means, even toward expansionist ends, was another trend that would increase over the years.[16]

Japan used the Western powers preoccupation with World War I as an opportunity to expand its interests. First, it began by occupying German possessions in the Pacific, which it would later retain under a League of Nations mandate.[17] Second, Japan acquired German interests in China. Declaring war on August 23, 1914, Japan seized Kiaochow and other German facilities in Shandong. Third, Japan sought greater influence in all of China. The Foreign Ministry welded proposals from the army, navy, and the cabinet into the Twenty-One Demands, presented to China in January 1915. The Demands considerably expanded Japanese interests, confirming the occupation of Shandong, extending mining and railway rights in Manchuria, and establishing a veto over any additional rights to foreign powers.[18] The so-called Group Five demands would have gutted the Open Door, placing Japanese officials in charge of administrative and financial matters across much of China.

Japan kept the Group Five demands secret, but when China leaked them to the United States, American distrust skyrocketed. Pressure from the United States and Britain and a resolute China forced Japan to drop the Group Five demands. China accepted the remainder. The United States threw a sop to

Japan by recognizing that "territorial contiguity creates special relations" between Japan and the Chinese regions of Shandong, South Manchuria, and North China (eastern Inner Mongolia).[19] Nevertheless, as in the 1895 Triple Intervention, Japan focused not on its gains but on what it had lost. The whole episode created bad feelings between Washington and Tokyo.

The 1917 Lansing-Ishii Agreement attempted to smooth the waters. The so-called agreement between Viscount Ishii Kikujiro and Secretary of State Robert Lansing settled nothing. The two sides simply restated their positions without true compromise or meeting of the minds. Once again, the United States accepted Japan's special interests in China, but did not spell out either the geographic range of "China" or exactly what "special interests" meant. The two countries did, however, reaffirm their devotion to the Open Door and the territorial and administrative integrity of China, but did not specify how they had now harmonized their previously discordant views. Japan merely repeated its devotion to principles it had recently violated.

The fourth opportunity of World War I was Japan's intervention in Siberia. The Siberian Intervention was an American brainchild to assist the Czech Legion, which had been fighting the Germans on the Eastern Front, to fight its way through the Bolsheviks along the Trans-Siberian Railway to Vladivostok and then travel by ship to Europe. Several nations sent small contingents. Wilson dispatched 7,900 Americans and asked Japan for 7,000 soldiers. The Japanese agreed to intervene militarily, but for reasons of their own: to build a buffer against the traditional Russia enemy, and to lay the base for control of Siberian resources should the Russian state disintegrate. The Imperial Army sent more than 70,000 troops as far as Lake Baikal. It was an extremely costly venture in money and lives (5,000 casualties); and Japan did not withdraw until 1922, after the Washington Conference.

The Rise and Fall of the Washington System

In the idealistic atmosphere of the Fourteen Points and the creation of the League of Nations, many people thought cooperation was better than the arms races, competition, and secret treaties that had led to the human and economic catastrophe of 1914–1918. In the new atmosphere of peace, it seemed senseless to boost peacetime military spending above wartime levels. For various reasons, Japan, Britain, and the United States desired a respite from buildups and confrontation. Though the United States did not join the League of Nations, it rejected total isolationism and put forward a new framework for international relations that emphasized arms limitation, cooperation governed by legalistic principles, and consultation. Historians now call this new framework the "Washington System" because Secretary of State Charles Evans Hughes hosted a conference in the capital that produced three important treaties. The Five Power Treaty set capital ship ratios at 10 for Britain, 10 for the United States, 6 for Japan, and 1.75 for France and Italy. The Four Power Treaty pledged Britain, Japan, the United States, and France to consult, rather than act unilaterally, in any crisis. The Nine Power Treaty bound the major powers to respect the Open Door principles of equal access to China and no seizure of Chinese territory. During the 1920s, additional treaties and conferences tackled arms limitation and forged no-war pledges. The Washington System aimed to stabilize international politics by adherence to overarching principles such as maintaining the Open Door, renouncing war, ending arms races, and abandoning imperialism.

Prime Minister Hara Takashi supported this new approach. Hara was the first prime minister to come from a political party and the first commoner to hold the office. He was despised by the ultra-nationalists and disliked by the conservatives, who thought he was too reliant on diplomacy rather than force in dealing with the often-rebellious colony of Korea. Facing severe budget shortfalls, Hara wished to avoid a costly naval race with Britain and the United States, the latter of which was already contemplating a major fleet expansion. Hara appointed Admiral Kato Tomosaburo, who had been both commander of the Combined Fleet as well as navy minister, as a key negotiator at Washington, along with Japan's ambassador Shidehara Kijuro. The two men accepted the premise that Japan was better off constraining the growth of British and American navies than by trying to out-build them. Not all Japanese agreed. In November 1921, during the naval negotiations, an ultra-nationalist assassinated Hara as he walked through Tokyo Station. He was replaced by Finance Minister Takahashi Korekiyo, who also was well aware of Japan's inability to out-build the United States, and who approved Admiral Kato's agreement to the final 10-10-6 capital-ship ratio among the great naval powers.

The Washington Conference made most admirals angry. Japanese officers complained about unequal ratios. British officers grumbled that their navy, traditionally the largest and most powerful, now merely equaled the American fleet. Some American officers argued that, by freezing the fleet, the agreement made it impossible to defend the Philippines or to defeat Japan quickly in its home waters. This point of view ignored two points: first, that such freedom of action would be unobtainable if Japan matched the American buildup; and, second, the Philippines were not a crucial American interest, and therefore huge peacetime expenditures to defend it were not justified.

Japan tried to comply with the spirit of the Washington treaties. In 1922, it abrogated its alliance with Britain, returned Shandong Peninsula to China, and withdrew troops from Siberia. The question would be whether Japan could consistently attain its goals within the System, as it might fail to protect existing interests, or Japan might develop goals that could not be attained within the established rules-based regime. Both happened.

In fact, Japanese opposition to the Washington System began at the Washington Conference itself. Admiral Kato was the leader of the "treaty faction," a group of naval officers who realized that Japan's relative naval power was best maintained by treaties that limited the growth of the other powers rather than by trying to out-build them. Kato's subordinate, Admiral Kato Kanji (the two were not related) was the navy's chief technical representative on the delegation. He demanded that as a great power, Japan should have parity with the United States and Britain. Overruled, he insisted on a 10-10-7 ratio. As Japan's navy did not patrol globally like the Anglo-American fleets, a 10-10-7 ratio would make the Imperial Navy dominant in East Asia against either power. Kato Kanji lost that battle as well. His biographer describes him simply as an expert doing his job.[20] Fair enough, but he had little understanding or appreciation for the broader political goals espoused by Kato Tomosaburo. Nor did he stick to "technical" opposition. Kato Kanji returned to Japan to lead the political charge against the Washington Treaty as the leader of the "fleet faction" of officers who wanted a stronger navy, no matter what. Kato Kanji's protestation did not take long to start weakening domestic support for cooperation within the Washington System. Later, as chief of staff of the navy, he pushed out moderates among the officer corps and installed men of his own thinking. The atmosphere among the naval officer corps became progressively more hostile to the remaining moderates, such as Yamamoto Isoroku, and, in the end, the "fleet faction" triumphed.

The Washington System worked for about ten years. It then began failing in Asia, as Japan could not obtain its desired level of benefits (growing trade and resource access on the continent) via peaceful cooperation. Three developments doomed Japan's attempt at cooperation.

First, strengthening Chinese nationalism damaged Japan's attempt to extend its mainland interests. During 1924–1927, Foreign Minister Shidehara Kijuro tried to avoid disputes with China, even as nationalism expanded the Kuomintang (KMT), whose 1926–1928 Northern Expedition under Chiang Kai-shek extended KMT control northward toward Beijing. The KMT even attacked foreign concessions on the coast. Japan began viewing the KMT as a threat to Japan's interests in Manchuria and north China. In 1927, the retired general Tanaka Giichi became both prime minister and foreign minister, and ordered the selective use of force to slow the KMT's advance. At the same time, the Kwantung Army leadership sensed that the Manchurian warlord Chang Tso-lin was abandoning his cozy relationship with Japan, so without consulting Tokyo, mid-level officers killed Chang by blowing up his railway car as he passed through southern Manchuria. Prime Minister Tanaka's inability to hold the army accountable for this rash action toppled his government. His successor, Hamaguchi Osachi, attempted to stay loosely within the Washington System. The Hamaguchi cabinet was noninterventionist, attempting to restore good relations with Chiang Kai-shek's government in Nanjing. Japanese militarists charged Hamaguchi with weakening the country, especially after the conclusion of the London Naval Conference in 1930, which precipitated a major political crisis.

Second, the Great Depression hugely complicated Japan's resource quest. The "standard" interpretation is that the Great Depression caused hardship across Japan but especially in rural areas, where the military recruited heavily and with which military leaders identified (as opposed to an excessively Western "big business," which identified with modern urban areas). In December 1931, Inukai Tsuyoshi became prime minister with Takahashi Korekiyo as finance minister. Under Takahashi, finance minister until 1936, the government intervened more often in the economy. He banned currency exchanges, stopping the outflow of gold. He boosted exports by allowing producers to fix prices and share export markets as they wished. He subsidized mining companies to bring in more gold. His strong guiding hand helped Japan weather the Great Depression better than most countries. Whereas GNP dropped in the United States, it grew in Japan, at least until the mid-1930s. That said, traditional sectors like agriculture and silk and textiles fell on hard times, while the modern conglomerates such as Mitsui and Mitsubishi profited, especially as military procurement grew dramatically. Military spending composed 43 percent of government expenditures by the mid-1930s, far higher than that of the Western powers.[21]

Third, the metastasis of the notion of an impregnable self-sufficient empire eventually doomed cooperation. Germany's World War I defeat shocked Japanese military and civilian planners. How could a country so strong and militarily capable lose? They reasoned that future conflicts, like World War I, would be long, fight-to-the-death "total wars" in which economic, technological, and demographic strength would triumph. Japan in the early 1920s lacked the resources for such a war. In the late 1920s and 1930s, however, the total war thinkers—of which Ishiwara Kanji, the arch-fomenter of the

1931 Manchurian Incident, is the best known—urged that Japan build an autonomous empire, including a self-sufficient security sphere that embraced all resources needed for a total war economy. The total war concept mandated the domination of mainland resources and, as such, ended cooperation with other powers under the Open Door principles reiterated in the Washington System. Alas, the expensive force structure and military operations needed to expand the autonomous empire consumed the newly acquired resources. In 1938, just to maintain the military's imported steel quota, the government cut 15 percent from the merchant shipbuilding industry and 25 percent from the railroads.[22] The 1941 Materials Mobilization plan gave the military 38 percent of steel production.[23] Military expansion was increasingly diverting funds from the civilian economy, which, therefore, grew more slowly than it could have and, as a result, generated less tax revenue to purchase strategic resources. It was a vicious circle. The costs of expansion consumed the benefits of expansion. The bigger the autonomous empire grew, the more resources it needed. Hence expansion could never stop. It was one long slippery slope from Korea to Manchuria to China to Indochina to Southeast Asia.

Even as Chinese nationalism, global depression, and wrongheaded expansionist thinking ruined cooperation, Japan made a final, vain attempt to stay within the Washington System. At the London Naval Conference of 1930, Japan pursued compromise and win-win solutions. But what once would have been considered foreign policy successes were now viewed, back at home, as sell-outs and surrender. After the unpopular London treaty, the ultra-nationalists would have their day.

The discord over the London treaty carried over from the Washington naval negotiations in 1921–1922. It was really a single, long, contentious period. By 1930, Admiral Kato Kanji's "fleet faction" had equaled the influence of the "treaty faction." Kato himself was chief of the naval general staff. The London treaty extended limitation from capital ships to other warship classes. Japan received its much-desired 10-7 ratio in destroyers and submarines, but there was a huge fight over the cruiser ratio. Japan wanted 10-7 in cruisers as well. Partly this resulted from different needs. Britain preferred to have a lot of light cruisers to patrol its global empire, but the United States and Japan wanted 10,000-ton heavy cruisers that were more useful in major fleet actions. In the end, because the United States pledged to defer building to its treaty limits before 1936, Japan got better than a 10-7 ratio in heavy cruisers in fact, if not in the treaty itself. Overall, Japan improved its relative position in naval strength. But Kato Kanji and the hardliners successfully portrayed the London treaty as adverse to Japan. Within the Imperial Navy, the moderates were increasingly shunted aside. By 1934 Japan decided against participating in future naval conferences and after 1936 no longer adhered to Washington System limits.

The final success at London was perversely the kiss of death to moderate civilian government. Prime Minister Hamaguchi Osachi was tough, stubborn, and not inclined to toady to ultra-nationalists, who were offended by Hamaguchi's nontraditional attempt to give women the vote. That bill failed to pass the Diet. In the midst of the depression, with government revenues slumping, Hamaguchi cut government expenditures, which upset militarists who thought military budgets should be sacrosanct. But the final straw was the London Naval Treaty. Right-wing politicians and conservatives raged that Hamaguchi sold out Japanese national security. The result, as so often in the 1930s, was assassination. In November 1930, walking through Tokyo Station not far from where Prime Minister Hara had been murdered in 1921, Hamaguchi was shot by Tomeo Sagoya, a member of an ultra-nationalist secret society. Hospitalized for several months, Hamaguchi died in early 1931.

The Manchurian Incident, 1931: Turning onto the Road to Pearl Harbor

If Kato Kanji was an example of a senior officer crossing the line into national policy formulation, Lieutenant Colonel Ishiwara Kanji is a good example of a second growing phenomenon—the inordinate influence of mid-level officers. Ishiwara came to Manchuria in 1928, after preaching a fervent expansionist message to eager young officers at the Army Staff College. Ishiwara was a "total war" believer and advocate of an invulnerable, autonomous empire.[24] As the Great Depression cut the profits of Japanese railway and other concessions in Manchuria, the Kwantung Army, filled with mid-level extremists, concluded that the profit slump was a Chinese plot. Led by Ishiwara and his colleague, Colonel Itagaki Seishiro, the army manufactured a pretext for unilateral action. Soldiers planted a bomb beneath the South Manchurian rail line, then used the explosion to launch a broad military offensive. Vainly hoping that the Tokyo civilian government would set things right, the League of Nations and the United States reacted slowly and cautiously, then ramped up criticism as Japanese troops fanned out across all of Manchuria. Rather than rein in the young hotheads, Japan established the puppet state of Manchukuo and withdrew from the League. Secretary of State Henry Simpson authored the American response. What became known as the Stimson Doctrine was in reality a toothless pledge to not recognize the legality of territory transfers made as a result of conquest—basically a rote reiteration of the Open

Door's principle of no territorial aggrandizement in China—but the Hoover administration understood that American interests in Manchuria were not worth a war.

After the Hamaguchi shooting in late 1930, there was a rash of ultra-nationalist murders of moderates. Some junior officers joined plots to cleanse the government of perverse Western thoughts by killing political and business leaders. The Cherry Blossom Society, a secret group of ultra-nationalists within the Imperial Army, had similar aims. A third group under Inoue Nissho aimed to kill twenty people but succeeded, in February and March of 1932, in murdering only Finance Minister Inoue Junnosuke and Takuma Dan, the director of the giant Mitsui *zaibatsu*. In May 1932, eleven young naval officers stormed into the prime minister's residence and murdered Prime Minister Inukai for insufficient support for military expansionism in Manchuria. They attacked the homes of Count Makino, Lord Keeper of the Privy Seal, and Prince Saionji, the last *genro*, but both men slipped away before the attacks.

The assassinations, if not the intimidation, peaked in the February 26, 1936, coup attempt by the ultra-nationalist Imperial Way faction of the military. Coup leaders, mostly majors, backed by 1,500 troops, fanned out to kill six men, including former prime minister Okada Keisuke and Admiral Suzuki Kantaro (who was the emperor's grand chamberlain). They missed Okada and Suzuki but murdered the able finance minister Takahashi Korekiyo, the current Keeper of the Privy Seal Saito Makoto, and Watanabe Jotaro, who oversaw military education. This time, the army suppressed the rebels, considering their extreme demands illegitimate.

After 1936, the government and the military largely stopped outright murder, as senior military officers supported militarism but not social revolution and overthrow of the government that they sat atop. But the radicalism of junior and mid-level officers and excessive deference to them continued. To manage the simmering lower and middle ranks, the aptly named Control Faction, of which General Tojo Hideki was a leader, dominated the army. There was little daylight between the basic goals of the ultra-nationalists, the Control Faction, and its civilian fellow travelers, and so-called moderates. All groups believed that Japan should be Great Japan. And murder was still a possibility. In August 1941, the ultra-nationalists sensed that Hiranuma Kiichiro, a cabinet minister, was quietly working with US Ambassador Joseph Grew to prevent war. A man slipped into his house and pumped six shots into him. Hiranuma somehow survived, but the threat of such violence was always on the minds of policymakers. In his biography of Yamamoto Isoroku, Agawa Hiroyuki describes how the militarists intimidated the navy minister and vice minister, barging into their offices with rants and extreme demands. To preclude an attempt on the moderate Yamamoto's life, he was transferred afloat as commander of the Combined Fleet. Even prime ministers were not immune. Eri Hotta notes that fear of assassination led Konoe to meet secretly with Ambassador Grew in the fall of 1941.[25]

Though Manchuria was part of China, most scholars date the China War to 1937. After occupying all of Manchuria in 1932, in 1933 Japan occupied Jehol province, just southwest of Manchuria. For several years, Japanese forces avoided full-scale combat south of the Great Wall. However, in July 1937, incidents around the Marco Polo Bridge near Beijing triggered a full-scale war that Japan steadily enlarged in a futile attempt to win. The Chinese fought well enough that Japan could not end the China War on its terms. American aid helped the Chinese, but recent studies note that the KMT fought more skillfully than previous historians have recognized.[26]

During these years, American policy was adrift. Though attempts to confront or punish Japan were made by some officials, such as Treasury Secretary Henry Morgenthau, these measures were small-scale or were not embraced by President Roosevelt. Domestic politics did not allow for strong policy or rearmament. As the political situations in Europe and Asia deteriorated, popular books charged that World War I had not been an idealistic crusade and that American intervention had been a mistake. The most famous book blamed secret alliances, militarism, and rampant nationalism as primary causes of the war. This was Sidney B. Fay's *The Origins of the World War*, which the American Historical Association acclaimed as the best book on European history published in 1928 and which remained a basic college text into the 1960s. University of Chicago professor Helmuth Engelbrecht attacked munitions makers in *The Merchants of Death* in 1934. Smedley Butler, a Marine general, wrote *War Is a Racket* in 1935. During 1934–1936, a Senate committee chaired by Senator Gerald Nye (R-North Dakota) investigated whether bankers and munitions makers had pushed the United States into World War I. The Nye committee hearings energized opposition to any new involvement in Europe. As a result of these tomes and other works, the American public adopted a more isolationist attitude, and Congress passed neutrality acts in 1935, 1936, 1937, and 1939. The acts banned arms trading with belligerents, declared that Americans traveled in war zones at their own risk, and barred American ships from carrying cargo or passengers to nations at war. Clearly, a tough policy against Japan would run against the public and congressional mood.

Late in the decade, the isolationist mood began to lighten. While Japan was fighting the Chinese, the United States grew increasingly alarmed at the 1938–1941 Nazi rampage. In American eyes, Japan linked itself to the hated Nazis by signing the Anti-Comintern Pact, joining the Axis Pact, and emulating Nazi expansion by enlarging the China War and moving into northern and southern Indochina. Around 1938, the United States began to think that there was no hope that Japan would return to normal behavior on its own and began applying economic embargoes. FDR successfully lobbied for inclusion, in the 1939 Neutrality Act, of provisions for arms and war materiel sales to belligerents—meaning Britain and France—on a cash-and-carry basis. By 1940–1941, the United States was quite pessimistic about a change in Japanese behavior and ramped up economic pressure. In January 1941, FDR wrote Ambassador Grew, "we must recognize that the hostilities in Europe, and Africa, and in Asia are all parts of a single world conflict. . . . We are engaged in the task of defending our way of life and our vital interests wherever they are seriously endangered."[27] In March 1941, Congress replaced the remaining neutrality legislation with the Lend-Lease Act, which allowed massive sales to American allies, after previously approving a huge naval expansion. For many years, the navy remained below the limits set in the 1922 Washington treaty. However, from the mid-1930s, Representative Carl Vinson worked with several senators to pass bills that eventually built the fleet that won World War II.

Two Conflicting Visions, Two Uncompromising Nations

The Pacific War began from two clashing visions, and the unwillingness or inability of either country to change positions. China was a major, core issue for Japan, which identified very significant interests there. In the peculiar thinking of many nationalists and militarists, loss of Japanese interests in China was an existential threat to the Greater Japan imagined by those groups. On the other hand, the United States was essentially a status quo power in the Pacific. Rather than a competition—with both nations striving for the same goal—it was a worsening political-ideological clash of ideas about Japan's ambitious vision of its future, how rapidly it would reach that ambitious objective, and whether the United States could accommodate itself to both the process of getting there and the ultimate Japanese goal of an autonomous empire. At its most basic, the rivalry was an aspiring hegemon versus a status quo power.[28]

Japan and the United States also had different visions of the political and economic meaning of the Open Door and its offspring, the Washington System. For the United States, the Open Door would supposedly produce win-win solutions. Businessmen and bankers from all countries could develop opportunities and make money for themselves and their shareholders. Personal and corporate profits were the goal. Both the United States and Japan played this game, though for the United States it was the only game played. It was purely and simply economic factors and trade, with personal and corporate profits as the main goal. That all powers, again with the exception of China, would be peaceful and content was an important political side benefit, but not the main goal of bankers and businessmen. The Open Door aimed to stabilize East Asia while delivering economic benefits to the powers.

Japan's view of the Open Door steadily diverged from the American vision, as it increasingly pursued national security goals using economic and military tools. Personal and corporate profits were not the main goal. Security autonomy was—hence the Japanese focus on access to raw materials, which in large part went into the production of military goods. Moreover, the military managed a good chunk of the industries that produced weapons and warships, and their goal was not profits, but rather the building of a powerful military. Thus, while one can say that economic factors were important to explaining the behavior of both countries, the meaning of "economic factors" differed greatly, as Japan's motivation was to build a security sphere, an invulnerable, self-sufficient Greater Japan.

When did war become a probability? The main driving force for eventual war was the failure to settle the China war, either by outright Japanese victory or by compromises and accommodations by either Japan, the United States, or both. But the timing of that failure was equally important. As Japan enlarged a China war it could not win, Americans increasingly connected Nazi aggression with that of Japanese militarists. American sensitivity to Japanese actions heightened after 1938, and American policy stiffened. The United States began to think that there was no hope that Japan would return to normal behavior on its own and began applying economic embargoes. Rather than make Japan malleable, the embargoes and freezes made the militarists even more determined to cut off and isolate the Chinese and replace imports from the United States with oil and other strategic materials from Southeast Asia. Barring compromise, war became unavoidable, particularly after Japan's occupation of northern Indochina in 1940, quickly followed by the Axis Pact in September 1940. After the move into southern Indochina in July 1941 and the subsequent oil embargo, the only compromises that would prevent war were politically impossible in either country.

What broader themes distinguished the rivalry?

1. **The two countries sought dissimilar economic goals.** Though both sought economic penetration of Northeast Asia, Japan's goal was state driven and security related: to control nearby territory as a security buffer and as a resource base to build a modern military and an industrial state. America's goal was a state-encouraged search for new markets to profit investors, entrepreneurs, and shareholders. Resource acquisition was not a significant goal.

2. **Japan sought its goals with a much higher level of intensity.** Those goals were essential to building the secure, self-sufficient, hegemonic Japan that many badly wanted. Japan's vision was so strong that it could not give it up in 1941, as the Japanese were certain that an architecture of unfair rules made by others constrained their future. Though the United States pursued its goals with less intensity, it clung to the Open Door, China-centric policy, backed by embargoes that directly challenged Japanese aspirations. That weak American pushback was unsuccessful. Over forty plus years, Japan's span of interests grew immensely. The Sino-Japanese War of 1894–1895 was fought over competing aspirations in Korea. In 1941, Japan occupied much of East Asia and Indochina and pondered the conquest of Southeast Asia. In short, America followed a "failed containment" policy.

3. **The two nations made accurate net assessments of material factors.** They understood each other's resource base, trade flows, productive capability, and existing and planned force structure. Virtually all American and most Japanese policymakers knew intellectually that Japan would lose a total war.

4. **But war came anyway. Why?** Because national goals and policy positions were defined by ideology—by ideas and beliefs and values. Japan chose to define its future as a powerful, autonomous empire, an Asian hegemon. The United States chose to overvalue its national interests in Asia and hold tightly to Open Door principles. Rather than accept the certain loss of compromising, Japan gambled on war with little chance of victory. By standing pat on its Open Door principles, the United States too avoided the certain loss a compromise would entail, confident that its obvious material superiority would bring Japanese compliance and American "victory" without a war.

5. **Japan had a particularly complex set of constitutional and legal procedures that complicated the process of getting to the right answer.** Moreover, the military, increasingly dominated by persons with extreme

views, especially beneath the very top, wielded disproportionate weight. The independence of the general staffs, and the requirement that the army and navy ministers be active duty officers gave the military great influence on the formation of cabinets and shaped the understandings and agreements on future policy that were part of cabinet formation. The military supplanted civilians in several key posts. It was not uncommon for military men to serve as prime minister, as Tojo did from 1941 to 1944.

6. **As a group, Japanese leaders increasingly tended toward stronger positions, rather than caution and moderation.** This was partly because those positions came from ultra-nationalists, whose mindset prized boldness, a pure spirit that foreswore compromise, and a belief that will and commitment could prevail over material reality. The inner circle performed no analysis that resolved policy contradictions and conflicts. Platitudes—such as "We must work hard to prepare"—glossed over serious planning flaws and wrongheaded assumptions. As Eri Hotta noted:

> The leaders' shortsighted and wishful thinking went hand in hand with ready references to Japan's high moral ideals, the superiority of the Japanese spirit, Japan's grand mission to liberate the whole of Asia from Western colonialism, and their wish for a peaceful resolution of the diplomatic and economic stalemate. None of these were conflicting aims in their mind—so long as they remained abstract. They created the illusion of ideological consistency and uniformity in Japan's leadership.[29]

A senior planner in the Naval Ministry wrote long after the war that "we had no inkling that the United States would be so angry" over the move into southern Indochina.[30] Robert J. C. Butow observed that whenever the top leadership faced contradictions or inconsistences, "the day was saved for the advocates of action by the *decisive* influence expected from Japan's allegedly superior fighting morale, military training, and general esprit de corps." The mind-over-matter factor had worked before, according to unchallenged but mistaken cultural assumptions of Japanese policymakers. In 1941, "the tendency to divide 4 by 2 and come up with 3 proved Japan's undoing." So did a refusal to back down. Asked how he and his colleagues could have taken such a gamble, Tojo replied that Japan "had been challenged and had to fight, no matter what the state of her preparedness. . . ."[31]

7. **Japanese imperialists operated in a congenial atmosphere.** Imperialism did not spring from popular demand, but there was popular approval after significant imperialist ventures. There were few vociferous opponents of imperialism, and those voices were often silenced by

assassination and intimidation. The Japanese people as a whole accepted imperialism. Certain sectors welcomed it, such as the military, a large chunk of the civilian bureaucracy, nationalist intellectuals, and traders and manufacturers with mainland interests and aspirations that imperialism would further. Those who opposed imperialist ventures usually did so because they thought Japan lacked the resources for quick victory, or questioned whether the specific goal was worth the resource expenditure. They did not embrace a radically different vision for Japan's future.

8. Prewar Asia held no vital US national interests. America aimed at a very slow alteration of power balances in Asia under the principles enshrined in the Washington System: naval limitation, equal access, and no territorial aggrandizement. A status quo power in the Pacific, the United States had little economic interest in the Philippines and Guam, and for decades, until just before Pearl Harbor, considered the Philippines indefensible. As William Braisted has shown, without big investment in dry docks and other facilities in the Philippines, a big fleet could not be based there.[32] During the 1920s and 1930s, the United States paid little attention to Dutch, British, and French colonial empires in Asia, and it had acknowledged Japan's special paramount interests in Korea and Manchuria. That left China as the focus of American interest, but even that interest was, initially, to preserve and protect rather than annex. (This is not to say that the American business interests making money in China were not ambitious or exploitative.) Only in the final years before Pearl Harbor, as the United States linked Nazi and Japanese behavior, did the United States perceive vital interests in Asia, and toughen policy toward Japan. A fair question is whether American interests were worth the blood and treasure of the Pacific War.

9. There was plenty of misinterpretation and misjudgment. On the American side, throughout the prewar period, far too many American policymakers mistakenly believed that normal economic pressures would control Japanese behavior. Such normal economic growth would naturally require Japan to free up resources being drained off by the military, which in turn would make aggression on the mainland less likely. When that aggression occurred anyway, most American policymakers turned to economic pressure via embargoes and sanctions. When those measures failed to moderate Japanese expansion, American officials had no answers. They could not imagine that Japan, supposedly a rational actor, would launch a war. Many officials thought of themselves as realists. Realism postulated that in the anarchical international system, states always behaved in ways that strengthened their power relative to other states. Power consisted of material power, especially military and economic. Knowing that Japan's military and economic strength, though sizable, could not defeat the United States in a long war, American officials reasoned that Japan would not start a war that it was certain to lose. Realism prevented them from imagining that Japan might, if pushed to the limit, go to war for non-realist ideological and emotional reasons. Hence the primary American misjudgments were assuming that Japan would behave according to an American vision of rationality and that the United States had enough leverage to change Japan's policy.

On the other hand, Japan misjudged the threat picture. It saw threats everywhere. Foreign Minister Matsuoka asserted that joining the Axis would deter the United States from "encircling" Japan by leasing bases in New Zealand and Australia, despite the fact that those two countries were five thousand miles from Tokyo, as far from Tokyo as Seattle.[33] Japan consistently misinterpreted defensive hedging as an offensive threat. When Foreign Minister Toyoda met British Ambassador Robert Craigie in August 1941, Craigie claimed that Japan was exaggerating the threat of encirclement. Toyoda replied that Britain had frozen Japanese funds and opposed the move into southern Indochina. Craigie said Britain was acting defensively. Japan's occupation of Indochina triggered the asset freeze. A look at a map, Craigie said, showed that Japanese airfields in southern Indochina were aimed at British and Dutch possessions further south. A passive Britain sought only to protect Malaya and Burma, whereas Japan had aggressively occupied several countries. Toyoda claimed that Britain was aiding Chiang Kai-shek; Craigie said the aid was slight. Toyoda said Britain was pressuring the Netherlands East Indies not to export to Japan. Craigie said Britain had not pressured the Dutch and that Britain had only reacted defensively to Japanese offensive moves. Unable to agree, they parted.[34] Threat was in the eye of the beholder. The weak US response to the Manchurian Incident and the fairly low level of aid to China in the early years of the China war were misperceived by the Japanese as strong measures.

Paths Not Taken

Was there no possible middle ground? The two most commonly mentioned "off-ramps" from the road to Pearl Harbor were (1) a fall 1941 summit between Prime Minister Konoe and President Roosevelt, and (2) the *modus vivendi* notion of late 1941. Before analyzing those possibilities for last-minute compromise, let us examine bilateral relations in 1940–1941.

By 1940, even some strong supporters of Japan's hardline position began to question the government's policy, but they made no headway. Prince

Fushimi, the chief of the naval general staff from 1932 to April 1941 and the emperor's second cousin, had long endorsed Kato Kanji's "fleet faction." He backed the occupation of northern Indochina but questioned the signing of the Tripartite Pact, which he feared would cut off steel, oil, and other key imports from the United States and lead to a protracted war. He raised those points during the Imperial Conference of September 19, 1940.

Prince Konoe, just returned as prime minister, admitted that trade relations would worsen. But he claimed that with consumption controls "we should be able to supply the military and thus withstand a rather prolonged war" with the United States.[35] The director of the Planning Board, Hoshino Naoki, accurately described Japan's dependence on imports for strategic materials but glossed over the difficulty of obtaining adequate supplies during wartime.

The president of the Privy Council, Hara Yoshimichi, asked, "I wonder if our taking a firm stand might not have a result quite contrary to the one we expect." Matsuoka replied that the United States would react reasonably: "Japan is not Spain. We are a great power with a strong navy in Far Eastern waters. The United States may adopt a stern attitude for a while, but I think she will dispassionately take her interests into consideration and arrive at a reasonable attitude."

Then Matsuoka, who never seemed to grasp the internal contradictions in his analyses, stated, "As to whether she will stiffen her attitude and bring about a critical situation [war], or will levelheadedly reconsider, I would say the odds are fifty-fifty." The Imperial Conference then approved this rash plan of joining the Axis, accepting a 50 percent chance of a crisis with the United States—hardly a prudent course given Japan's vulnerability.[36]

On July 1, 1941, the Liaison Conference considered the move into southern Indochina. The Germans had just launched an attack on Russia, and the Conference briefly discussed whether to take advantage of that fact by invading Siberia. Minister of Commerce and Industry Kobayashi Ichizo warned that Japan did not have the resources to support a war. He was ignored. The following day, an Imperial Conference blessed the southward advance and rejected any moves against Russia.[37] Able to read the Japanese diplomatic code, the United States immediately knew that Japan would invade southern Indochina and began planning a freeze of Japanese assets and an oil embargo. On July 25, when Japan informed the United States of the move south, the United States froze Japanese assets and soon cut off the oil flow.[38] The asset freeze and oil embargo made securing resources from Southeast Asia imperative if war stocks were to be maintained.[39]

Preparing for a decisive Imperial Conference on September 6, 1941, a Liaison Conference adopted "The Essentials for Carrying Out the Empire's Policies" that enshrined the policy of planning for war while continuing to negotiate. This policy continued until war began. During August 1941, various offices in the army and navy ministries and general staffs assembled drafts of "The Essentials." Neither the army nor the navy directly assessed the chances for victory. The army thought war with the United States would be chiefly a naval affair, and left it to the navy to evaluate how the war would turn out. The navy did no evaluation, probably because Navy Chief of Staff Nagano and most of the naval general staff supported war.[40] Remarkably, Prime Minister Konoe and Foreign Minister Toyoda accepted the army-navy recommendations. In the crucial summer conferences, Konoe was largely mute, not even opposing the occupation of southern Indochina. Ike suggests that they may have pinned their hopes on a successful Konoe-FDR meeting so that they would never have to carry out the war.[41]

At the Imperial Conference, the prime minister, the army and navy ministers, and the service chiefs of staff mouthed ritual professions that diplomacy was the first option and war second. Nevertheless, Japan's "minimum demands which are necessary for the self-preservation and self-defense of our Empire" increased, making a diplomatic settlement more difficult. Admittedly, US sanctions and an oil embargo forced Japan to choose between war or concessions, but it was the Japanese occupation of southern Indochina that triggered those strong American measures. But even distressed by the oil embargo, Japan did not envision significant concessions. Instead, Japan wanted the United States and Britain to freeze force levels in Asia, "cooperate in the acquisition of goods by our Empire," restore commercial ties including the oil trade, and supply resources from their Asian possessions. These demands would result in a better situation for Japan than before the embargoes. In return, Japan would not have to withdraw from Indochina but merely promise not to move farther south. It might withdraw someday from Indochina, after a "just peace was established in the Far East." It would also guarantee the neutrality of the Philippines. For the Anglo-Americans, this was a lopsided bargain: stopping military buildups and reopening the resource flow while Japan actually improved its position.[42]

Ending the China war on favorable terms was the sticking point. Japan insisted on ending the conflict in such a way as to maintain Japanese dominance and unrestricted access to resources. This was essential to building the self-sufficient empire. So the China war not only had to end, but it had to end in a certain way, as stipulated in "The Essentials." That meant that the British had to close the Burma Road. Western nations had to cut off all aid to Chiang, and accept continued Japanese military operations. No Liaison Conference participants addressed whether these conditions could possibly be accepted by FDR, even if he agreed to meet with Konoe.[43] After Munich, any concessions to aggressors would be politically unacceptable appeasement.

Navy Chief of Staff Nagano stated that there was a "very high" probability of a prolonged war with the United States. But he stressed careful preparations, without ever considering whether Japan could actually win a long war. Instead, Nagano focused on seizing "the enemy's important military areas and sources of materials quickly at the beginning of the war ... obtaining vital materials from the areas now under hostile influence." If the initial attacks were successful, "our Empire will have secured strategic areas in the Southwest Pacific, established an impregnable position, and laid the basis for a prolonged war." Ultimate success in a prolonged war was "closely related to the success or failure of the first stage in our operations." Moreover, as the embargo on oil and other resources was already eroding Japan's warmaking ability, war had to come soon—barring significant Anglo-American concessions.[44]

Japan's basic problem of self-sufficiency was still a dream. Despite substantial economic benefits from the years of conquest and control of mainland territories, the resource supply was woefully inadequate. Only Southeast Asia now held enough promise to wean Japan's economy off American imports. After the surrender of the Netherlands, Japan pressured the Netherlands East Indies to sell much more aviation-grade crude, other crude oil, and gasoline. In negotiations from September 1940 through June 1941, Japan demanded 3.15 million tons of fuel of various types, but Batavia never offered more than 1.85 million tons. Japan became convinced that only force would deliver the supplies it wanted.[45] In the mind of the top leaders, the only solution was to quickly seize the East Indies and ramp up production swiftly, before Japan's reserves were exhausted. Alas, this was a pipe dream.

The problem was that no realistic preparations or battle plan could do the trick. Nagano and others grossly overestimated Japan's capability to extract resources from conquered areas. In 1941, the Naval Ministry and the government's Planning Board made separate but similar estimates of Japan's oil supplies for waging war. Both utterly overestimated how much and how fast oil would flow from Southeast Asia. These estimates assumed that by the third year of war, oil from the conquered south would almost satisfy wartime consumption needs, but left aside consideration of whether Japan could safely bring the oil home. Director of the Planning Board Suzuki Teiichi stated that "if important areas in the South were to fall into our hands without fail in a period of three or four months, we could obtain such items as oil, bauxite, nickel, crude rubber, and tin in about six months, and we would be able to make full use of them after two years or so."[46] These estimates were fantasy.[47]

The navy and army leaders never directly and comprehensively analyzed whether Japan could win the war. When they got past the opening stages of the war, they said there were too many variables to make an accurate assessment. More prudent and realistic leaders might have declined to go to war until the variables became clearer. Essentially, Japanese leaders rolled the dice. They counted on favorable future political and diplomatic developments, such as a German defeat of Britain. They assumed a bloodied, timid America would negotiate an early peace rather than fight a long war. They hoped a devastating strike at the beginning of the conflict would lead to an early peace, as had happened at the outset of the 1894–1895 war against China and the 1904 Russo-Japanese war. They made wildly unrealistic estimates about resource consumption and supply from conquered territories. They blundered ahead, avoiding hard realities and comforting themselves by stringing out pointless negotiations.

Off-Ramp: Fall 1941 Summit between Prime Minister Konoe and President Roosevelt

Many historians have considered whether the proposed Konoe-FDR summit could have led to peace. Most believe that neither nation's domestic politics would allow a compromise, so a summit would have been fruitless, though a sizable minority think it could have worked.[48] In early August, egged on by moderate aides, Konoe decided to try to meet FDR. The idea was that a meeting on neutral ground would decrease, physically and psychologically, the ability of hard-liners to squelch any compromises. Moreover, Konoe would be responsible for compromises, allowing the militarists to save face. Konoe got approval from Army Minister Tojo and Naval Minister Oikawa, though Tojo, who assessed only a 20 percent chance of a good result, extracted Konoe's promise that if a summit failed, the prime minister would finish the war preparations.[49] On August 26, 1941, a Liaison Conference approved Konoe's message to FDR urging a broad discussion of all important issues.[50]

Konoe believed that once he sat down with FDR, they could hash out a deal, even one that involved Japanese compromise. As Eri Hotta describes it, Konoe and a few other advisors and military staffers believed that a summit might play out like this: "Konoe meets Roosevelt; Konoe conveys

Japan's conditions, pre-approved by the military; Roosevelt refuses to accept such conditions; Konoe telegraphs the U.S. reply; the army gets furious; the emperor steps in to reprimand the army for its intransigence; and a peace—which was sure to include Japan's troop withdrawal from China and Indochina—is reached. . . ."[51] This scenario was a possibility, but an unlikely one. Though Konoe had gotten Tojo and Oikawa's approval for a meeting, there is no sign that they or the military and civilian hard-liners were willing to concede anything, much less withdraw from China.

A summit was a gamble. It would probably have failed, but it was worth trying. Even if unsuccessful, as it very likely would have been, it would not have worsened the diplomatic crisis or accelerated the Pearl Harbor attack. FDR had shown initial interest in a summit, but after reflection and likely pressure from Hull, replied that there must be preliminary agreement on key issues before a meeting. No American, certainly not FDR, contemplated a meaningful concession without extracting an even greater concession from Japan, such as withdrawing from Indochina and possibly from China as well. Konoe probably knew that he must make a big concession and that he would have to sketch that concession before FDR would even consider a summit. Yet preliminary agreements—better said, preliminary compromises—were exactly what Konoe could not extract from the hardliners. Only a summit without pre-conditions could lead to a settlement, at least in his mind. Was the United States justified in failing to arrange the summit? It is almost impossible to imagine, after examination of the well-dug-in policy positions, that Japan would have withdrawn, in the short term, from Indochina, much less from China itself. A summit without Japanese concessions would have been seen as appeasement. US policymakers judged that the chances for real compromise and agreement were nil, so they did not pursue the summit proposal. They were probably right, but a summit was worth the gamble to save the blood and treasure later expended on the war.

Off-Ramp: The Modus Vivendi Notion of Late 1941

The second off-ramp on the road to war was a modus vivendi that was never presented to the Japanese. On November 6, 1941, FDR suggested that a modus vivendi would postpone war and give the American military more time to prepare. As FDR sketched on November 20, the modus vivendi would restart the oil flow and provide some rice shipments if Japan froze further deployments.[52] Though the modus vivendi may have postponed war, it did nothing to solve the policy contradictions. Proponents still hoped, however, that a broader accommodation could be reached within the modus vivendi time limits. With few people in either government prepared for real compromise, a modus vivendi would likely have merely delayed war. But that delay would have favored the United States, allowing more time to build up, and—as Sidney Pash and others have noted—made it harder for Japan to go to war in mid-1942. Why was the modus vivendi unappealing? Partly because restarting the oil flow and removing the asset freeze and other restrictions meant that American resources would continue be used against China, now a quasi-ally. Indeed, Chiang Kai-shek bitterly opposed the modus vivendi idea, as did Britain, the Netherlands, and Australia. Second, policymakers were—mistakenly—convinced that there was no need for the modus vivendi because Japan would rationally decide against a war it would lose.

$$* * * * *$$

Aside from a summit or a modus vivendi, could the United States and Japan have reached a workable compromise? What if the United States had resumed oil, steel, and other shipments, and coerced the Dutch, British, and Vichy French to break open closed colonial systems to supply Japan with much greater amounts of resources? Japan wanted those resources to maintain military freedom of action and specifically to win the China war. If the Japanese had gotten the resources from the United States and Southeast Asia, they might not have attacked. A major sticking point remains: the China war. With its imagined close relationship to China, the United States predictably objected to Japan's use of US resources to wage a vicious war on its friend. But if the resource flow was guaranteed, Japan might have ended the China war south of the Great Wall and returned, more or less, to the pre-1937 situation that the United States had tolerated. Neither nation would have been particular happy with that solution, but it might have prevented total war. The Chinese in Inner China and Manchuria and the Koreans would still have been under Japan's thumb, but it can be argued that correcting that unfortunate situation was not a critical national interest of the United States.

The US-Japan rivalry is best characterized as a strong status quo power versus an impatient aspiring hegemon. Within that overarching structure, several themes shaped the rivalry. Side effects from the Great Depression and strengthening Chinese nationalism convinced Japan that its interests could not be served under the Washington System. An aggressive, increasingly nationalist Japanese military unduly influenced foreign and security policy. The civilian policymaking structure was weak, diffuse, and structurally incapable of resolving contradictions in policy ends or ways and means. The ever-stronger quest for an autonomous empire consumed the very resources it acquired. The military capability to intervene anywhere became a policy objective, and this mindset naturally found threats everywhere. By 1941, Japan somehow felt encircled, though there was no existential threat. As Japan's goals on the mainland and Southeast Asia expanded steadily, the United States remained a status quo power, without vital interests in East Asia, and responding weakly until the late 1930s. Underlying Japanese policy was an unrealistic culturally derived belief that the indomitable Japanese spirit could triumph over any material disadvantage. A related belief, held in some quarters, was that the United States was not tough enough to fight a long war, especially if severely bloodied at the outset. As the United States linked Nazism to Japanese militarist expansion and toughened policy toward the empire, neither the United States nor Japan was willing to accept the other's key goal: autonomy approaching hegemony for Japan, and peaceable status quo application of the Open Door for the United States. In the end, Japan rashly gambled on a war that many Japanese realized might be lost.

CHAPTER 16

A New Global Paradigm
The United States versus Russia
James H. Anderson

Introduction

Strategic rivalries include momentum shifts, unexpected twists, and outright reversals of fortune, and the Cold War is no exception. Reeling from Vietnam, Watergate, the twin oil shocks, and stagflation, the United States appeared on the defensive in the 1970s. Meanwhile, Soviet imperialism reached new heights in the Third World, with Moscow backing proxy forces in Angola, Ethiopia, and Nicaragua, among other places. By the time Soviet tanks rumbled into Afghanistan in 1979, détente was already a dirty word among US leaders, and the "correlation of forces" seemed very much in Moscow's favor.

But a snapshot—even one that stretches over a decade—does not give sufficient context to a strategic rivalry, let alone determine its outcome. Armed with hindsight, the Cold War's outcome today appears obvious, but this was far from self-evident while events were unfolding. Most observers—and most participants, for that matter—expected the strategic stalemate to last much longer.

Then, in 1991, the Soviet Union collapsed—suddenly, completely, and, for the most part, peacefully. To understand this stunning reversal, it is necessary to reassess the larger context of this rivalry. My goal is to provide a thematic assessment, with an emphasis on the interplay of geopolitical and ideological factors, the development of strategy, and the role of military power, including its nuclear, conventional, and unconventional dimensions. First, however, I address what distinguished the Cold War from other strategic rivalries.

Distinguishing Features

The atomic revolution provided the Cold War rivalry with a novel risk—global destruction. Throughout history, strategic rivalries have led to the elimination of empires, states, and even entire civilizations. Yet the risk of nuclear war threatened future generations in a way that previous strategic rivalries never could, possibly to the point of humanity's extinction.

Moreover, the technological marriage of long-range missiles and atomic warheads produced the revolutionary combination of unprecedented destruction at unprecedented speed. By the 1960s, both sides had intercontinental ballistic missiles (ICBMs) capable of reaching the other in a half hour. Beginning in the late 1970s, Moscow deployed mobile SS-20 missiles in Eastern Europe capable of quickly destroying NATO targets. In the early 1980s, NATO responded by deploying Pershing II and ground-launched cruise missiles, giving it the capacity to strike Moscow in ten minutes. Not to be outdone, Moscow periodically positioned ballistic missile-laden submarines off the Atlantic coast capable of reaching Washington, DC, in similarly short order. These reduced warning times meant that neither superpower could rule out nightmarish, nuclear bolt-from-the blue scenarios.

Commonalities

Even strategic antagonists can share common psychological scars, and the Cold War is no exception. Hitler's invasion of the Soviet Union and Japan's attack on Pearl Harbor left Moscow and Washington with a primal fear of surprise attack. Such shared experiences led the superpowers to keep their strategic forces on high alert levels (at least compared to the interwar era), and to place a premium on strategic warning. For the United States, this led to extensive reconnaissance flights over the Soviet Union, with the resulting embarrassing shoot-down of Francis Gary Powers's U-2 spy plane (1960).

The Soviet Union and the United States also shared military superiority over other potential rivals. World War II left Britain and France exhausted; Italy, Japan, and Germany prostrate in defeat; and China entangled in a costly civil war from 1945 to 1949. The Soviet Union, though it suffered horrendous casualties, had found the resources to crush the *Wehrmacht*, Hitler's armed forces, and it maintained a much superior land force than its European and Asian neighbors long after World War II ended. The United States, on the other hand, suffered comparatively light casualties but demonstrated the capacity to churn out military hardware at a jaw-dropping rate (the United

States produced nearly 100,000 aircraft in 1944 alone).[1] While its land forces underwent a huge postwar drawdown, it maintained sufficient air and naval forces to intimidate or, if necessary, obliterate other nations.

The superpowers also shared a mutual interest in avoiding direct military conflict with each other, given the capacity for destruction and potential for escalation (proxy wars were another matter). The Soviets aggressively probed Western weaknesses, but they were neither reckless nor suicidal. Some US military leaders embraced bellicose rhetoric—for example, General Curtis LeMay was the inspiration for General "Jack D. Ripper" in Stanley Kubrik's movie *Dr. Strangelove*—but political leaders generally behaved cautiously when it came to nuclear matters. This common ground helped to keep the *Kalter* in the *Kalter Krieg* (the "cold" in the Cold War).

Asymmetries

Beside these common interests, asymmetries permeated the strategic rivalry from the outset. Except for Pearl Harbor, the United States exited World War II with its homeland unscathed, a maritime nation capable of generating large land and aerial forces, possessing an atomic monopoly, championing democratic capitalism, and committed to leaving its recent isolationist past behind. The Soviet Union emerged from the same contest with its homeland ravaged, an immense land power with modest naval and aerial power, determined to prevent Germany from ever again dominating *Mitteleuropa*, and animated by Marxism-Leninism-Stalinism and deeply rooted tsarist imperial traditions.

These asymmetries flowed largely from *geography*. The Soviet Union and the United States ruled over huge landmasses—the first and third largest countries in the world, respectively—that provided each with strategic depth. But the geographic similarities end there. The United States, a maritime power, exploited its lengthy coastlines and port facilities; the Soviet Union, a continental power, had far less access to ports. Located in the temperate zone, the United States also possessed the world's most fertile agricultural lands; the Soviet Union's landmass was located in much colder climes (mostly north of the US-Canadian border), which made farming, already difficult with forced collectivization, even more so.

Geography provided the United States with some clear security advantages: its oceanic moats, combined with friendly states to the North and South, obviated the need to defend its territorial borders against invaders. As such, the United States homeland was secure from physical attack, at least until the Soviets developed long-range bombers and ICBMs. In contrast, the Soviet Union had to cope with long-range, US-based delivery systems; medium-range systems based on its periphery; and more traditional security concerns along its vast European and Asiatic borders.

Interplay of Geopolitical and Ideological Factors

Ideological and geographical asymmetries combined to provide the Cold War with a blended reality, with the relative weight of each varying according to time, place, and circumstance. Ideological tensions antedated the Cold War, with President Woodrow Wilson and Bolshevik leader Vladimir Lenin articulating the principles of democratic capitalism and international communism, respectively. Between the two world wars, the ideological rivalry festered while both powers focused on domestic concerns. The one exception was when President Wilson sent US troops along with the Allied expeditions in 1918 to the far north (Archangel, Murmansk) and to the far east (Vladivostok), thus fueling the Bolsheviks' suspicions about the capitalist West. The United States, in fact, found Marxism-Leninism-Stalinism so repugnant it withheld diplomatic recognition from the Soviet Union until 1933—an early form of ideological containment. The United States later practiced a similar policy against the People's Republic of China, withholding formal diplomatic recognition until 1979. (The key turning point in US-Sino relations occurred earlier, with President Nixon's opening to China in 1972.)

The Soviet fear of foreign invasion had deep geopolitical roots. "At the bottom of the Kremlin's neurotic view of world affairs is traditional and instinctive Russian sense of insecurity," observed George Kennan, the architect of containment, in his famous Long Telegram to George C. Marshall, then secretary of state, in 1946.[2] Echoing English geographer Sir Halford Mackinder's argument made nearly a half century earlier, Kennan added: "Originally, this was insecurity of a peaceful agricultural people trying to live on vast exposed plain in neighborhood of fierce nomadic people."[3] At the Yalta Conference, February 4–11, 1945, these ancestral fears reinforced the Soviet determination to prevent a resurgent, postwar Germany.

Geopolitics trumped ideology during World War II. President Roosevelt and Prime Minister Churchill found common cause with Joseph Stalin in defeating Nazism. As long as both sides were locked in a desperate struggle for survival, ideological tensions remained muted. The Soviets even disbanded the Third Communist International in 1943. So, for most of the war, the erstwhile allies focused on geostrategic concerns: the timing of a second front, the dangers of a separate peace, and the division of postwar Europe. Unfortunately, goodwill engendered by wartime cooperation soon dissipated, hastened by Roosevelt's death in April 1945. By the time of the Potsdam Conference (1945), if not earlier, ideological differences were reasserting themselves.

The early Cold War assumed a Eurocentric focus, given unresolved questions about Germany's future. As the conflict escalated, it became clear that the Soviets were not going to allow free elections in countries they occupied. This dispute over elections marked an early inflection point in reigniting the rivalry, and it foreshadowed other early Cold War crises, including the Czechoslovakian coup d'état (1948) and the Berlin blockade (1948–1949).

Europe was not the only area the rivals found themselves contesting. They were also at loggerheads in the Middle East, with access to oil resources a key focus. In 1946, the United States pressured the Soviets to withdraw their military forces from northern Iran, pursuant to the Tripartite Treaty of Alliance (1942) signed by Great Britain and the Soviet Union.

US and Soviet maneuvering in Iran reflected an early case of Cold War containment. The Soviets wanted to maintain a military presence in Iran for geopolitical reasons—chief among them securing access to additional oil supplies and providing its border with a greater security buffer. To these ends, they established a puppet regime in the northern province of Azerbaijan. The United States had its own geopolitical interests in the region, including access to oil and protecting Iran against communist thrusts. These interests, when combined with a more idealistic desire to strengthen the credibility of the United Nations (UN), led Washington to pressure the Soviet Union by backing multiple UN Security Council (UNSC) efforts to resolve the issue. (Three of the first five UNSC Resolutions focused on the Iran crisis.) The United States scored a diplomatic victory when Stalin, sensing US resolve stiffening, agreed to withdraw his forces.[4]

The United States also dissuaded Stalin from bullying Turkey over access to and control of the Dardanelle Straits.[5] Stalin demanded changes to the Montreux Convention (1936), which recognized Turkish control over the straits, and he massed troops along the Turkish border. These moves alarmed Truman. "There is not a doubt in my mind that Russia intends an invasion of Turkey and the seizure of the Black Sea Straits to the Mediterranean," he wrote to Secretary of State James Byrnes in January 1946.[6] In April, the president dispatched the battleship USS *Missouri* to pay a visit to Istanbul, and in late August, he sent a naval task force to the Mediterranean to apply additional pressure to the Soviets.[7] By late October, the Soviets, once again sensing American resolve, withdrew their claim to the Turkish Straits. For its part, Ankara moved steadily closer to the United States. The following year, the Truman Doctrine helped solidify Turkey's status as a dependable US ally by providing Ankara with defense and economic aid.

Containment rested on the assumption that one's adversary was rational, not fanatical. Stalin's willingness to back down, at least in the case of Iran and Turkey, provided some reassurance to Truman that, with the proper mix of geopolitical incentives, he could influence Moscow's behavior.

Ideological Dimension

Cold War dynamics, however, cannot be explained in geopolitical terms alone. As the Cold War progressed into the 1950s (and beyond), ideology pushed the superpower competition into remote and forbidding locales. Small islands such as Quemoy and Matsu, off the southeastern coast of China, assumed importance far in excess of what geography alone would dictate. Likewise, conflict spread to the steep hills in Korea, dense jungles of Vietnam, and jagged mountains in Afghanistan, among other places.

The incompatibility of democratic capitalism and Soviet communism represented the taproot of Cold War hostility. The competing worldviews sidelined prospects for any negotiated resolution. The superpowers, therefore, tailored their respective narratives to internal and external audiences, using all the public diplomacy and propaganda tools at their disposal, including leaflets, pamphlets, newspapers, and television and radio broadcasts.

Stalin and his successors up to Mikhail Gorbachev viewed the conflict through the lens of class conflict. Nikita Khrushchev put it colorfully when he said, "If anyone believes that our smiles involve abandonment of the teaching of Marx, Engels, and Lenin, he deceives himself poorly. Those who wait for that must wait until a shrimp learns to whistle."[8] Much later, Gorbachev emphasized the salience of ideology:

> The flaw in Soviet foreign policy . . . consisted in the fact that all its energy came from an ideological source. A hard core of ideological constructs ultimately determined the behavior of the USSR on decisive questions of international relations. . . .[9]

All that said, communist ideology permitted some flexibility. Even Karl Marx adjusted his initial thesis when it became clear that worldwide revolution was not imminent. In 1921, at the Tenth Party Congress, Lenin abandoned "War Communism" that was bankrupting the Soviet Union and

stirring social unrest. In response, he abolished food requisition and reintro-
duced private ownership in agriculture and light industry. These changes
endured, at least until Stalin assumed power.

Later, the nuclear revolution also forced communist ideology to adapt,
especially after both sides acquired the hydrogen bomb. Acknowledging
the potential for nuclear catastrophe, Khrushchev rejected the idea that
world war was "inevitable." He, instead, embraced "peaceful coexistence"
at the Twentieth Party Congress, invoking a concept developed by Lenin.
Khrushchev's reformulation did little to assuage the ideological conflict,
however. Met with suspicion in the West, this announcement—and subsequent Soviet behavior—failed to ease tensions.

The Soviets considered the United States its number one foe throughout
the Cold War, but China also figured prominently in their calculations. Here,
too, ideology played a major role in determining the arc of Soviet-Sino relations, with its progression of alignment, alliance, and bitter estrangement.
The fallout, in turn, had significant implications for the US-Soviet rivalry.
For example, North Korea under President Kim Il-Sung invaded South
Korea with Moscow's and Peking's moral and material support. Worse, from
a long-term perspective, the Soviets helped China develop its atomic weapons. Much later, the United States exploited the Soviet-Sino schism with
President Nixon's opening to the People's Republic of China in 1972.

Ideology also played a crucial role in the Cold War's bloodless resolution,
a remarkable event that will be covered in more depth later in this chapter.
Here it suffices to note that Soviet ideological malaise, rather than conviction, proved a contributing factor. A loss of ideological confidence, born of
economic stagnation and the bitter fruits of imperialism, preceded the Soviet
Union's political disintegration.

Containment

Mindful of the ideological and geopolitical nature of the threat posed by
the Soviet Union, the United States adopted *containment* as its overarching
strategy for the Cold War. Stationed in Moscow, diplomat George Kennan
outlined his framework of containment in his famous Long Telegram and his
Foreign Affairs article (1947), written under the pseudonym "Mr. X." Kennan
described, in general terms, the rationale for countering Soviet aggression,
leaving others to craft the particulars of implementation.[10] Seeking to avoid
the pitfalls of war and appeasement, Kennan's description of containment provided the strategic rationale for a series of far-reaching initiatives, including

the Truman Doctrine (1947), the Marshall Plan (1948), and the North Atlantic Treaty Organization (NATO) (1949). These initiatives reflected the newfound determination of the United States to counter the threat of Soviet expansion economically, politically, and militarily.

The Soviet atomic bomb test (1949) spurred President Truman to undertake a comprehensive review of US strategy. Drafted in early 1950, National Security Council report NSC-68 painted the competition between superpowers in stark terms and emphasized the risks the United States faced unless it changed course. "The issues that face us are momentous, involving the fulfillment or destruction not only of this Republic but of civilization itself."[11] After rejecting options involving a continuation of the status quo, preemptive war, and disarmament, NSC-68 recommended a much more muscular version of Kennan's framework to deter communist aggression over the long haul. North Korea's invasion of South Korea seemed to validate the gravity of the threat, prompting President Truman to approve the document in September 1950.

The Soviet strategy had a dual-edged quality. The defensive element aimed to address Moscow's fears of "capitalist encirclement"; the offensive component sought to advance Soviet power, preferably without engaging the United States in direct military conflict. As Kennan noted in his Long Telegram in 1946, the Soviets, comforted with the ideological certitude of ultimate victory, did not have a fixed timetable to advance their conquests.[12] This meant that Moscow could afford to be patient in probing Western weaknesses and preparing the ideological battlefield with a steady torrent of peace initiatives, disarmament proposals, and disinformation campaigns.

Intelligence

While both sides clearly recognized the nature of the strategic competition, they often erred with respect to intelligence estimates. Most resulted from faulty extrapolations—such as the "missile gap" in the 1950s, when the United States overestimated the size and projected growth of the Soviet missile force. Deception efforts also played a role, as happened at the 1955 Moscow Aviation Day parade, when the Soviets circled a small number of bombers around the reviewing stand to create the illusion of a larger force.

Other US intelligence assessments underestimated Soviet strengths and timelines. The Soviets' testing of an atomic bomb in 1949, for instance, took place much earlier than expected. In 1957, the Sputnik satellite provided another unwelcome surprise, foreshadowing the Soviets' capacity to deliver long-range nuclear payloads. Later, post–Cold War assessments revealed the Soviet biological arsenal to be much larger than estimated.[13]

Despite all the attention devoted to intelligence failures, the United States accurately discerned the relative weaknesses of the Soviet economy in the latter stages of the Cold War and sought to play off US strengths against them. As will be explored later, the Office of Net Assessment played a key role in recognizing the competitive nature of this strategic interaction.

Multiple factors contributed to Soviet intelligence failures, starting with their highly centralized intelligence system that focused mostly on ensuring party loyalty. As a result, analytic efforts received far fewer resources. Soviet intelligence products often consisted of little more than press summaries.[14]

> Professional prudence was the principal reason for the inadequacy of Soviet intelligence analysis . . . it behove [sic] the KGB not to take any chances in suggesting a reality that might challenge the next day's resolution of the Presidium.[15]

The problem was not just the production of intelligence, but the consumption side as well. As one scholar of Soviet intelligence put it,

> The top Soviet leaders received intelligence polluted by ideology and deliberate lies. In turn, they themselves ignored data conflicting with the ideological postulates.[16]

Another intelligence-related asymmetry resulted from the nature of the two societies. US analysts were always struggling to discern clues from a society shrouded in secrecy, while Soviet analysts faced the opposite problem. They were forced to gauge intentions and gather political intelligence from a cacophony of opinions emanating from Washington, allied capitals, and a myriad of other locations

This failure to comprehend the West's open societies led the Soviets into several costly intelligence missteps. For example, Moscow believed that it could sneak missiles into Cuba, first without the United States discerning their presence, and then, even if the missiles were discovered, that the US reaction would be limited. The first part of this assessment is stunning, given thousands of Soviet personnel and hundreds of trucks and transporters that accompanied the missiles. Worse, they could not foresee that the United States would risk nuclear war to keep missiles out of the Western Hemisphere. Evidently, "no one in the KGB was asked for a formal assessment of the likely American reaction to the placement of missiles in Cuba."[17]

Later, Moscow failed to anticipate NATO's so-called dual-track decision in December 1979 in response to the Soviets' earlier SS-20 intermediate-range

ballistic missile deployment.[18] The Soviet SS-20 deployment strained relations between the United States and its NATO allies by placing NATO under
a new threat. But it also galvanized NATO to link its own intermediate-range
nuclear force modernization (Pershing II and ground-launched cruise missile deployment) with arms control efforts to reverse the Soviet deployment.
The arms control track failed mainly because Soviet leaders did not want to
relinquish their initial advantage, and they underestimated the resolve of
NATO leaders in the face of massive public protests. But the result was that
the Soviet Union was rendered less secure because of NATO's deployments,
which effectively denied Moscow a sanctuary to threaten European targets.[19]

Role of Military Power

Faculty intelligence estimates, such as the Soviet SS-20 deployment, also
suggest the broader significance of military power assessed in relation to the
capabilities of other powers and specific historical contexts. Consider, for example, the Soviet Union's possession of the world's largest land army after
World War II, most of it positioned in Eastern Europe. This force provided
Moscow with strategic depth and political leverage, thus serving both geopolitical and ideological purposes. In time, though, the deployment of these
same forces engendered resentment.

Military power, and the spending required to sustain it, also imposed
an ever-escalating strain on an increasingly wobbly economy. In the long
run, the cost of mainlining military forces that absorbed roughly 20 percent
of GDP crippled the Soviet economy beyond the point of repair. Unable
or unwilling to challenge hard-liners within the defense establishment, the
reform-minded Gorbachev maintained these spending levels until the late
1980s, though the economic damage was clearly visible to all.

In the near term, though, the Red Army's defeat of Nazi Germany provided the Soviet regime with a deep reservoir of political legitimacy. Military
power helped Moscow maintain its superpower status, even as France, China,
and the United Kingdom joined the nuclear club during the 1950s. But
the arsenals of these second-tier powers remained puny when compared to
Moscow's nuclear capabilities, which only the United States could afford to
match. Likewise, no other nation-state could match the two superpowers'
conventional capabilities.

The Cold War also placed new demands on US military power, including
the sustainment of a permanent defensive perimeter overseas. Maintaining
the forward deployed military posture required a level of continuous global

engagement that was new to American diplomats, as they worked to secure overseas bases and security alliances. The success of these efforts provided the United States with strategic depth and forward-based military forces to contain communist aggression. Moreover, the US global military posture was bought at roughly one-third the price the Soviet Union was paying, as measured in terms of a percentage of GDP.

The United States not only helped form a series of global security alliances, in direct contrast to its isolationist course after World War I, it undertook a leadership role within these alliances, particularly within NATO (established in 1949). This was a striking departure from past practices, where the United States, following President Thomas Jefferson's advice to avoid "entangling alliances," had remained aloof from formal alliances with any foreign power since the Revolutionary War.[20] These requirements resulted in the United States maintaining, for the first time in its history, what it had long despised—a large standing army during peacetime.

Over time, the costs of maintaining such large forces at home and overseas—though never as crippling as what the Soviets endured—left a deep imprint on the US economy. The military-industrial complex that Eisenhower warned America about in his Farewell Address (January 17, 1961) came into existence and continued growing. Large, and by US historical standards, *unprecedented peacetime military spending distorted the economy*: the government soaked up research dollars at the expense of the private sector, and the practice of spreading procurement dollars across a large number of congressional districts made defense spending more responsive to political interests than to strategic ones.

But US defense spending also had positive effects on the economy. Spinoff and dual-use technologies, ranging from microelectronics to aviation design, not to mention the networking capabilities that underlay the Internet, all provided significant benefits to the civilian sector. In contrast, the Soviet civilian sector gained comparably little from its military expenditures—a fact that partially explains Soviet efforts to steal Western technologies.

More broadly, US military spending had a powerful effect well beyond protected narrowly defined security interests: it underwrote the strategy of containment and US global engagement, and ushered in *Pax Americana*, a period of peace that allowed the global economy to surge forward unscathed by major interstate wars. In fact, it is hard to conceive the globalization of the world's economy without the shield of US arms.

This dominance did not occur by happenstance. American strategists understood the importance of *comparative analysis* in assessing the relative strengths and weaknesses of national power and how best to exploit asymmetries in force structure, strategy, and doctrine. Created in 1972, the Office of Net Assessment focused on making just such comparisons and interactions, giving the United States an important analytical advantage over the Soviet Union, especially during the latter stages of the Cold War.

For their part, the Soviets expended considerable efforts to determine the so-called correlation of forces. Their methodology also considered a wide range of political, military, economic, and cultural variables. In this regard, both the US and Soviet approaches avoided the perils of drawing too many conclusions from "bean counting" military hardware. But the Soviet approach differed since its practitioners viewed trends and events through the lens of ideological determinism.

In wartime, a belief in the inevitability of victory can help nation-states recover from initial battlefield disasters, as the Soviet Union did during World War II. In terms of peacetime economics, however, the same certitude promotes a stay-the-course mentality, even when overwhelming evidence indicates that changes are necessary. This helps explain why Soviet leaders were able to rationalize their economy's declining performance—and their resultant inaction—over several decades. Substantive reform efforts began only after Gorbachev and his like-minded cohorts cast aside the ideological blinders worn by their predecessors.

Military Risk and Nuclear Weapons

Nuclear weapons played an important role in the superpowers' thinking about military power and the nature of victory, both in ideological and practical terms. Military power played a decisive role in winning World War II. In the Cold War, it also played a crucial role in some contexts—including multiple Berlin crises, the Korean War, the Cuban missile crisis, and Vietnam—but a secondary or even marginal role in other situations. In all cases, Washington and Moscow wrestled with the same fundamental challenge: how to convert unprecedented military power into political influence without provoking a direct superpower clash of arms and the attendant risk of nuclear war.

This continuous risk of direct superpower conflict assumed several forms and shaped military force structure, alert levels, and doctrine. For example, the superpowers took the threat of surprise attack very seriously. Fearing a sudden "bolt from the blue," they each placed a tremendous emphasis on strategic warning. Moreover, both rivals had to guard against allies and client-states leading them down risky paths they would prefer to avoid. For instance, the United States found itself restraining South Korean strongman

Syngman Rhee's desire to attack North Korea prior to the Korean War. Moscow faced a similar challenge with Cuba's Fidel Castro, who repeatedly attempted to goad the Soviet Union into war with the United States.

Though Castro appeared unconcerned about the potential for escalation, the Soviets and their American counterparts always had to weigh the risk of war against the backdrop of nuclear weapons. These weapons shaped superpower thinking about military power, and nuclear strategy represented an important subset of containment strategy. The United States' atomic monopoly (1945–1949) presented unique challenges for the Soviet Union. Privately, the Soviets worked furiously on the development of their own atomic weapon; publicly, they assumed a posture of studied nonchalance, treating the atomic bomb as just another weapon. Later, the Chinese adopted similar rhetoric for much the same reason, with Chairman Mao disparaging the Soviet advantage in nuclear weapons.

Even after the United Kingdom, France, and China joined the nuclear club, the United States and the Soviet Union measured their arsenals almost entirely against one another, and hence retained, by a wide margin, the two largest nuclear arsenals throughout the Cold War. There was no template for the superpowers to harness the latent destructive power of nuclear weapons into meaningful political ends, though the Allied strategic bombing campaigns of World War II provided a point of departure. Thus, for much of the Cold War, policymakers and strategists on both sides found themselves working in uncharted territory, with few signposts to guide them. In fact, military strategists, who one would have thought could make major contributions in this era, refused to undertake the deep thinking required in an increasingly complex strategic environment, perhaps because the unprecedented destructive power of nuclear weapons appeared to gut the concept of military victory—hence, the rise of the "civilian defense intellectual" who, for much of the Cold War, did almost all of the original thinking on US nuclear strategy—starting with the scholars at the RAND Corporation, including Herman Kahn, Bernard Brodie, and Albert Wohlstetter.[21]

While nuclear theory was still in its infancy, President Eisenhower faced a real-world strategic quandary: how to prevent debilitating, Korean War–type conflicts from recurring. This meant finding a way to contain the Soviet Union without risking fiscal ruin. After a strategic review (Project Solarium), the Eisenhower administration placed a premium on leveraging nuclear weapons to achieve these ends. In October 1953, President Eisenhower signed National Security Directive 162/2, thus ensuring the growth of America's strategic nuclear arsenal.[22] Constrained by a lack of technical expertise, the Soviet arsenal grew more slowly, at least until the 1960s.

Somewhat unevenly, the superpowers eventually came to similar conclusions about the political utility of nuclear weapons, as leaders on both sides anticipated that the costs of a large-scale nuclear exchange would far exceed any potential policy gains. This was an inescapable conclusion after the superpowers developed the hydrogen bomb—the United States in 1951, the Soviet Union in 1953—which increased their destructive power by several orders of magnitude. Overall, though, nuclear weapons had, in practice, reduced the risk of direct conflict between the superpowers, save for the glaring exception of the Cuban missile crisis in October 1962, which provided some of the most dangerous moments of the Cold War, and highlighted the risk of superpowers backing hot-tempered leaders like Fidel Castro. As such, the crisis marked an important inflection point, inducing both rivals to greater caution, at least insofar as nuclear weapons were concerned. In its aftermath, the superpowers signed the Partial Test Ban Treaty in 1963 and established a "hotline" to enhance communication during crises.

Yet despite its seriousness, the Cuban missile crisis did not denude nuclear weapons—or nuclear threat-making, for that matter—of their political utility. For example, during the Yom Kippur War in October 1973, when an Arab coalition prepared to attack Israel, US Secretary of State Kissinger made a very public and calculated reference to the dangers of nuclear escalation so as to deter Soviet intervention in the Middle East.[23] Nor did the Cuban missile crisis curb the superpowers' appetite for building more nuclear weapons and upgrading delivery systems. On the contrary, in the mid- to late 1960s, Moscow embarked on a significant expansion of its nuclear arsenal, spurred in part by the humiliation it experienced after withdrawing its missiles from Cuba.

As the Cold War matured, the advent of increasingly accurate delivery systems and second-strike capabilities ensured a nuclear stalemate at the strategic level. The inability of either side to achieve a clear advantage eventually opened the door to strategic arms negotiations and to beginning the long process of creating alternatives to mutually assured destruction.

Still, much nuclear posturing continued along the road to, if not peace, at least strategic parity. For instance, the United States underwrote most of its security guarantees to Europe through its strategic nuclear umbrella. This required that Western European nations demonstrate their commitment to NATO by allowing Washington to deploy nuclear weapons on their soil. The hope was that such measures would enhance deterrence, but the Europeans understood that these deployments would undoubtedly attract Soviet nuclear strikes on their nations in the event of a conflict. Forward deployed nuclear weapons thus reassured US allies—and frightened them at the same time.

These fears led NATO to adopt the Harmel Report in 1967, which committed the alliance to a policy of détente while simultaneously reaffirming its security commitment to deter Soviet expansion.

Nuclear posturing had far less effect in the superpowers' battle for influence and dominance in the Third World, as such weapons meant little to Third World revolutionaries, save the special case of Fidel Castro and the Cuban missile crisis. Clearly, the Viet Cong did not feel threatened by the US nuclear weaponry any more than the Afghani *mujahedeen* feared Soviet nuclear weaponry. Their defiance in the face of nuclear supremacy was proved well founded, given the opprobrium the superpowers would receive from any use of nuclear weapons against nonnuclear adversaries.

Impact of the Nuclear Stalemate

In the late 1960s, the Soviet Union had achieved a rough equivalence with the United States insofar as nuclear capabilities were concerned. This opened the door for strategic nuclear weapons negotiations where both sides admitted that their nuclear weapon stockpiles had reached the point of diminishing returns.

By the early 1970s, the atmospherics surrounding US-Soviet détente created an additional incentive for the superpowers to negotiate. Despite these conditions, strategic arms negotiations proved tortuous and protracted for several reasons:

- Many of the problems revolved around the rivals' different capabilities: the Soviets placed great emphasis on land-based intercontinental missiles, while the United States allocated its weapons more evenly among land, sea, and bomber-based systems. These and other asymmetries bedeviled negotiators.
- At times, the negotiations themselves took on the character of a medieval theological debate, complete with high priests of nuclear theology strategy and esoteric terminology that was beyond the ken of mere mortals.
- The rough parity of strategic nuclear forces did provide, however, enough of a basis for ensuring a modest agreement pursuant to the Strategic Arms Limitations Talks (SALT). As a result, in 1972, the superpowers signed SALT I, and codified the doctrine of mutual vulnerability with the Anti-Ballistic Missile Treaty, which placed severe limits on the superpowers' defensive capabilities.

- The superpowers nevertheless continued to modernize their nuclear arsenals, which the terms of SALT I permitted, but this had more to do with bureaucratic inertia than any realistic attempt to alter the calculus of mutually assured destruction.

Broader Implications of the Strategic Defense Initiative

Though compelling for its parsimonious logic, mutually assured destruction came at a cost. By holding each other's population hostage to nuclear annihilation, the superpowers reinforced preexisting ideological and geopolitical hostility. From this angle, the underlying logic of mutual vulnerability violated civilized norms, a necessary evil in the absence of viable policy alternatives such as disarmament or strategic defense. This calculus changed after the Reagan administration took office.

Long before assuming the Oval Office, Ronald Reagan developed an interest in strategic defense, stimulated in part by visits to Lawrence Livermore Laboratory and the North American Air Defense Command.[24] Reagan's distaste for mutually assured destruction, combined with technological advances, convinced him to embark on a new strategic path, against the advice of some of his closest advisors. After deeming mutually assured destruction immoral in a nationally televised address on March 23, 1983, President Reagan challenged the scientific community "to give us the means of rendering these nuclear weapons impotent and obsolete."[25] Some critics immediately challenged the president on purely technical grounds, saying it would never work. Others deemed it provocative, believing the Soviets would conclude that the Strategic Defense Initiative (SDI) was a cover for the United States to achieve a first-strike capability.

Though clearly aspirational in the near term, SDI jarred the Soviets. So did Reagan's later refusal to consider SDI a bargaining chip at Reykjavik, Iceland, talks in October 1986.[26] After spending decades and hundreds of billions building their land-based ICBM force, Moscow found itself at the wrong end of a cost-imposition strategy. To be sure, the ensuing SDI debate included lots of talk about the potential for the Soviets to use cheap countermeasures to defeat an American missile defense system. Since Reagan's initial concept of SDI did not specify technologies in advance, these scenarios reflected far more speculation than analysis. This much was clear: the United States changed the strategic debate to favor its own technological potential at the expense of the Soviet Union.

The Reagan administration's newfound commitment to strategic defense exploited the Soviet's relative disadvantage in microelectronics and computer technology. The Soviet leadership grasped the implications of this revolution even before Reagan announced his SDI initiative. In the past, the Soviets' wide-ranging espionage efforts offset some of the US technological advantages, as Soviet agents pilfered certain weapons designs, including, most spectacularly, that of the atomic weapon. But the microelectronics-based revolution was too broad and too deep for the Soviets to steal their way to technological equivalency. Equally problematic, the Soviet's centralized economic system lacked the ability to create disruptive technologies of its own, let alone match those of the United States. In this case, as it usually does, entrepreneurship handily beat centralized planning in generating technological innovation.

Revolution of Military Affairs

Technological innovations also had a profound effect on how both sides thought about organizing and employing conventional forces. In fact, dramatic advances in conventional weaponry, particularly those that favored the United States during the latter stages of the Cold War, began shaping the strategic rivalry almost as much as nuclear weapons. When, in the 1980s, the Office of Net Assessment took careful note of Soviet marshal Nikolai Ogarkov's writings about a Military-Technical Revolution (MTR), Andrew Marshall and his staff began reformulating these ideas into a broader concept, emphasizing the integration of dramatic technological advances, doctrine, and organization to achieve decisive battlefield effects. Collectively, these ideas became known as the Revolution of Military Affairs (RMA).

The US military operationalized elements of the RMA in the Air-Land Battle Doctrine, as the US Army reoriented its focus back to Europe in the wake of the Vietnam War. By providing the United States with the capacity to attack Soviet rear-echelon forces, the Air-Land Battle Doctrine offset numerical disadvantages that NATO faced in the European theater with a marriage of superior technology and doctrine. These doctrinal and technological advancements greatly enhanced the deterrent value of conventional forces in Europe, thereby reducing the risk of political coercion. For their part, Soviet thinkers recognized that highly accurate conventional weapons could, in localized circumstances, achieve nuclear weapons–like effects without incurring the opprobrium associated with actually using nuclear weapons.

The development of the Air-Land Battle Doctrine and emerging RMA had a number of long-term effects. The Air-Land Battle Doctrine generally reflected close cooperation between the US Army and Air Force.[27] But its development also exposed a broader lack of inter-Service cooperation at the same time. These difficulties, along with inter-Service communications failures during the US intervention in Grenada (1983), thus set the stage for Congress to pass the Goldwater-Nichols Act (1986), which mandated jointness among the Services. At another level, the evolving RMA inadvertently provided added incentives for US and Soviet adversaries to embrace unconventional and asymmetric military strategies—a trend that continues in the Cold War's aftermath, as evidenced by the enduring popularity of irregular warfare in Afghanistan and Iraq, among other places.

War in the Shadows

Unconventional conflicts had far-reaching implications for the Cold War writ large. The Cold War began in Europe, but most of the bloodletting occurred in the Third World. Proxy wars involved slow, grinding conflicts, largely outside the glare of media attention. They had their own dynamics and were quite divorced from the superpower competition in conventional and nuclear arms. Decolonization, which gained momentum in the aftermath of World War II, provided the backdrop for many of these conflicts. Colonial powers struggled against the nationalistic tide, seeking to maintain their empires by intimidation or, in some cases, by outright force. The superpowers courted, cajoled, and, at times, coerced the new nationalistic leaders. Some proved willing stooges. Other leaders of newly independent states, such as Egypt's Gamal Abdel Nasser, played their own game, seeking to play superpowers off one another to advance their own political ends.

With its markedly anti-Western overtones, decolonization provided Moscow with opportunities to exploit. In January 1961, Khrushchev pledged Soviet support for "wars of national liberation," which displaced Stalin's earlier emphasis on "socialism in one country." Khrushchev's commitment to support revolutionary struggles also strained Soviet-Sino relations, as Chairman Mao had his own ambitions in the developing world. Soviet interventions included the deployment of combat troops, advisers, supplies, and various forms of economic and political support, all a further drain on the tottering economy. Soviet imperialism reached its zenith in the 1970s, with Moscow subsidizing a wide range of activities in Africa, the Middle East, the Caribbean, Central America, and Latin America.

The US defeat in Vietnam marked another turning point in the Cold War, calling into question the utility of using force to achieve policy ends. Presidents Ford and Carter became far more gun-shy about foreign military intervention abroad, except for narrowly focused operations such as the Mayaguez incident (1975) and a failed attempt to rescue US hostages in Iran (1980). An equally shaken Congress passed the War Powers Act in 1973, aiming to curtail the president's authority to use military force. Even after prosecuting a series of small-scale interventions, including the raid on Libya in 1982 and intervention in Grenada in 1983, the United States remained leery of large-scale foreign military adventures for the remainder of the Cold War.

Several factors prompted the superpowers to vie for power and influence in the Third World.[28] Prior to World War II, the United States and the Soviet Union each focused their energies inward: Stalin tightened his personal grip on power at home, and Roosevelt struggled to lift his country out of the Great Depression. After the war, however, international circumstances changed dramatically: *decolonization opened up a new battleground* for the Cold War rivalry.

The Soviet Union sought to exploit the colonial legacy of Western powers, backing anti-colonial movements and wars of national liberation. Rhetorically, Moscow also lumped together the United States with European powers, even though US colonial possessions were quite limited—most notably the Philippines, a consequence of the Spanish-American War. The United States found its own anti-colonial perspective, a byproduct of the Revolutionary War, at odds with the views of its European allies.

Moreover, the United States had mixed emotions when it came to intervening in the Third World. Its idealistic impulses tugged in opposite directions: its desire to retreat from the Old World competed with a messianic urge to remake it in its own image. These idealistic sentiments, in turn, intersected with more *realpolitik* concerns, including the need to contain Soviet expansion without driving the United States into financial ruin and risking costly stalemates like Korea. Domestic US debates over Cold War intervention abroad thus reflected a swirl of intersecting interests and values. The defeat in Vietnam effectively ruled out large-scale US military intervention abroad for the remainder of the Cold War.

Ideological competition magnified the importance of superpower territorial gains and losses abroad. Soviet leaders believed that gains in the Third World validated their political system. Much later, reformers like Gorbachev considered Soviet difficulties abroad to be symptomatic of deeper problems at home. By the 1980s, the "wars of national liberation" had long since lost their luster for the Soviet people and their leaders.

The *quest for new markets* also played a role in the superpowers' quest for influence in the Third World, but more so for the United States, given its commitment to promote international trade. Scarred by memories of the Great Depression, the United States clearly wanted to create a post–World War II international economic world order based on low tariffs and the rule of law. Radical critiques of US foreign policy, however, often exaggerated the influence that markets had on Washington decision-makers by interpreting their every move abroad through the lens of economic imperialism.

The Soviet Union was less interested in developing markets abroad. The Soviet Union's reliance on autarky in the 1930s largely insulated it from the Great Depression, and left a lasting—and mostly favorable—impression on its leaders. Until the mid- to late 1980s, Moscow's insistence on maintaining a centralized economy stifled innovation and largely limited trade to within the Soviet bloc. In the selected markets where Moscow permitted trade, shoddy workmanship made most Soviet products unattractive and uncompetitive with buyers in the outside world.

The Cold War competition for allies and client-states, as well as the value that newly independent states placed on their sovereignty, stimulated the growth of the Non-Aligned Movement (NAM), beginning with the Bandung Conference in 1955. The Non-Aligned Movement lacked the capacity to prevent superpower intervention in the Third World, but its ability to mobilize political opposition presented another cost to foreign military intervention. Most NAM countries sharply criticized US intervention in Vietnam, for example. Soviet interventions in the Third World also elicited sharp criticism from NAM leaders. Yugoslavia's Josip Broz Tito, for example, denounced the Soviet invasion of Czechoslovakia in 1968. Later, when Politburo leaders were considering military intervention in Afghanistan in 1979, Soviet foreign minister Andrei Gromyko anticipated—correctly, for the most part—that "[a]ll the non-aligned countries will be against us."[29]

Arming the Proxies

US-Soviet competition included various forms of security assistance to allies and client-states. Foreign military sales and transfers provided the superpowers an avenue for leveraging their military power in order to gain inroads into the Third World. There was no shortage of demand, with revolutionary movements and governments clamoring for superpower arms. Such arms fueled proxy wars in Angola, Mozambique, and El Salvador, among other hot spots, throughout the latter half of the 1970s and much of the next decade.

America's efforts to supply such weapons were often hampered by oversight imposed by a post–Vietnam-Watergate Congress, which moved to rapidly reassert its authority on a wide range of oversight matters. For instance, Congress passed the Arms Export Control Act (1976), making US arms transfers subject to intense oversight by Congress, as well as the Clark Amendment curtailing US military aid to insurgents in Angola. This created an asymmetry, as the Soviets leaders faced no such restrictions on whom they could help. With a much freer hand, Moscow subsidized Cuban arms purchases, which fueled Havana's intervention in Central America and Africa. At times, however, these arms transfers also proved problematic for the Soviet Union. In 1972, for instance, Egyptian president Anwar Sadat kicked out thousands of Soviet advisers, after confiscating millions of tons of war materiel the Soviets had obligingly sent him. Moreover, there was a growing perception that Soviet military equipment was inferior to what the United States had to offer. Egyptian and Syrian military commanders blamed Soviet-supplied arms for their battlefield humiliations, pointing to how much better US-supplied technology fared in Israeli hands.

Superpower efforts to arm proxies were both a cause and effect of their strategic rivalry. Their efforts reflected the intensity of the rivalry and helped to sustain it by fueling a wide range of protracted Third World contests. These battlegrounds provided an attractive outlet for competition, given the superpowers' reluctance to fight one another directly. The security risks were generally low because neither superpower exported their most advanced weapons. Security assistance—whether in the form of government or direct commercial sales—had the added appeal of providing another stimulus to the superpowers' industrial bases.

In some cases, superpower efforts to provide arms for proxy fights had a significant battlefield impact. These included Soviet support for the Viet Cong during the Vietnam War and US assistance to the *mujahedeen* in Afghanistan. The competition in the Third World also had a lopsided economic effect with its adverse impact on the Soviet Union. Moscow's economic burdens, at this time, were also growing, as the Soviets discovered what previous empires had all endured: at some point, client-states stop providing net economic gains, and, instead, become a resource drain. As a result, the Soviet Union's efforts to update its own economy were greatly hampered by the fiscal and resource drain imposed by Moscow's Eastern European clients. For a time, the Soviet Union's abundant natural resources and growing populations could compensate for these disadvantages, but stated GDP growth was masking the system's pervasive structural weaknesses.

Dispensable Allies

Throughout the Cold War, the superpowers constantly reassessed how well their interests and values aligned with those of the states and non-state actors requesting various forms of security assistance. Here, as elsewhere, ideological factors colored Soviet thinking, especially regarding the desirability and durability of alliances and partnerships. Marxism-Leninism predicted that the capitalist powers would fight one another as well as members of the socialist camp. As the Cold War progressed, however, it became clear that capitalist powers were not going to fight one another—despite intra-alliance rivalries and periodic crises. Post-Stalin Soviet leaders concluded that, far from being imminent, intra-capitalist wars were not even likely. Flexibility on this particular point did not, however, detract from the Soviet view (pre-Gorbachev) that the superpowers remained locked in a fierce ideological competition, notwithstanding periodic thaws in the relationship.

The ideological trajectory of the Soviet-Sino relationship, another key dynamic of the Cold War, also morphed over time. Stalin initially supported nationalist leader Chiang Kai-shek and the Kuomintang when they were much stronger than the Chinese Communist Party. After the Chinese Communists' victory in 1949, the Soviet Union moved to back the new People's Republic of China. The early Cold War period witnessed a genuine alliance between the communist giants. Nowhere was the intimate nature of this cooperation more apparent than in the field of nuclear weapons cooperation: Soviet scientists provided their Chinese counterparts with technical knowhow and assistance throughout much of the 1950s. But just as a common communist ideology brought these two historic rivals into a quasi-alliance, so ideological differences played a role in the split. The most contentious issues involved de-Stalinization and "peaceful coexistence" with the West—two concepts the Chinese communist party found repugnant, even though they did not affect the essence of the US-Soviet rivalry.

The ideological differences were exacerbated, as often happens in international relations, by the personnel animus between the two state's leaders, Khrushchev and Mao. The Soviet leader remarked in his memoirs: "Politics is a game, and Mao Tse-tung has played politics with Asiatic cunning, following his own rules of cajolery, treachery, savage vengeance, and deceit."[30] Against this backdrop, the Soviet Union faced an increasingly hostile China.

Their long-simmering differences first erupted in public view in October 1961, at the Twenty-Second Party Congress. In a thinly veiled attack on China, Khrushchev unleashed a fusillade against Albania's embrace of Stalinism. Zhou Enlai, the head of the Chinese delegation, stalked out of the Congress and departed Moscow early. Before long, the Soviet Union found itself fighting a two-front ideological war against democratic capitalism and Maoism. By the end of the decade, the Soviet Union and China were engaging in division-sized border skirmishes along the Ussuri and Amur Rivers in the Soviet far east.

President Nixon and Chairman Mao found common ground in their opposition to the Soviet Union—another example of how geostrategic concerns often trumped ideology during the Cold War. Both nations cast aside their ideological differences and normalized relations in 1972. The significance of this turning point is hard to overstate, especially if one imagines—notwithstanding the hazards of counterfactuals—the security challenges the United States likely would have faced if the Soviet-Sino split had never occurred.

NATO and the Warsaw Pact

If the Soviet-Sino split revealed the importance of alliances in a negative sense, NATO provided a positive example, demonstrating the importance of successful alliances in shaping the Cold War. US political and military power ensured its status as first among equals within NATO, but it was rarely capable of bending NATO to its will if the other member states were opposed to a particular action. On the other hand, the country-members of the Warsaw Pact assumed only a pretense of equality, as the Soviet Union dictated policy.

NATO's resilience is clear when one considers the long list of crises that strained the alliance—among them tensions over Suez, the disaster in Vietnam, France's withdrawal from command structures, the collapse of détente, and the Soviet deployment of SS-20s—not to mention chronic bickering among allies over defense spending. NATO muddled through all of them, retaining its cohesion against the Soviet threat.

Tensions within the new Warsaw Pact also resulted in bloodshed: Soviet troops crushed rebellions in Hungary (1956) and Czechoslovakia (1968). Each of these proved costly not only in economic terms, but in maintaining alliance unity, which the Soviets always viewed as suspect. Moscow probably realized that its heavy-handed approach to enforcing order fueled a smoldering resentment among its client-states and tarnished its image abroad, but

Soviet leaders worked within a system that could imagine no other policy solutions to perceived betrayal.

NATO and the Warsaw Pact reflected asymmetries on several levels:

- In the first place, conventional military force ratios heavily favored the Soviets throughout the Cold War; the Soviet-dominated alliance led in tanks, troops, artillery pieces, and aircraft.
- However, the West's technological prowess helped to compensate for the Warsaw Pact's numerical advantages, especially when combined with doctrinal and organizational changes, as happened with the United States Army's adoption of the Air-Land Battle Doctrine.
- Geographically, the Warsaw Pact reflected a tighter grouping than NATO (the accession of Greece and Turkey stretched the concept of a "North Atlantic" alliance). For NATO, geography mattered less than the common values and interests that knitted the alliance members together. The experience of the Warsaw Pact clearly showed that political coercion did not engender reliable, let alone enthusiastic, allies. Though NATO members routinely vented their frustrations, giving the appearance of disunity, there was never any real danger of dissolving the Alliance, despite persistent Soviet efforts to split the alliance.

Washington sought to build on NATO's success by creating other anti-communist alliances, including the Baghdad Pact and the Southeast Asian Treaty Organization (SEATO). US efforts to link the alliances via common members (Turkey was part of NATO and the Baghdad Pact; Pakistan a member of the Baghdad Pact and SEATO) reflected the "architectural ingenuity" of Secretary of State John Foster Dulles.[31]

The United States recognized that its own membership in the Baghdad Pact might prove problematic, given Arab-Israeli dynamics, so instead it became an "associate member" and sought to bolster the alliance by pledging its support to member states. No amount of external support, however, could offset regional instability, which proved to be the bane of the Baghdad Pact. Iraq pulled out after its monarchy fell in 1959, and the organization renamed itself the Central Treaty Organization (CENTO). Riven with regional rivalries, including Pakistan's efforts to enlist CENTO's support against India, the alliance also had to defend against charges that it was a cover for neo-imperial adventures—a theme that Soviet propaganda pounded home relentlessly.

Southeast Asia proved similarly ill-suited to a NATO-like security alliance. Alarmed by the French disaster at Dien Bien Phu (1954), the United States created SEATO to protect the region against further communist predations.

With a geographically dispersed membership—only the Philippines and Thailand actually resided in Southeast Asia—SEATO found itself encompassing a disparate set of national security interests. As historian Bradford Lee noted, "Each of them was more wrapped up in its own specific problems than in the general American project of extended containment."[32] Pakistan proved a problematic alliance member, just as it did in the CENTO Pact. Pakistan left SEATO in 1973, after failing again to enlist the alliance in support of its rivalry with India.

From a strategic perspective, both the SEATO and Baghdad alliances lacked the internal cohesion of the NATO alliance (critics dubbed SEATO a "zoo of paper tigers"). Writing in 1957, Henry Kissinger noted that ". . . [in] neither SEATO nor the Bagdad Pact are we associated with partners with whom we share the degree of common purpose conferred by the cultural heritage which unites us with our European allies."[33] Prophetically, he added, "In such circumstances, a system of collective security runs the danger of leading to a dilution of purpose and to an air of unreality. . . ."[34] The "air of unreality" led to the formal demise of SEATO in 1977 and CENTO in 1979.

The Role of Civilian Leaders

The Cold War's scope and complexity created extraordinary challenges for national leaders. The superpowers had to consider each other, outside actors, and long-term historical forces over which they had limited influence. Yet a select number of leaders, through their force of personality, retained the ability to shape events and trends during the Cold War. Stalin and Truman exerted the greatest influence during the early Cold War, while Gorbachev and Reagan dominated its endgame.

Joseph Stalin

Ruthless and opportunistic, Stalin viewed the world primarily from a Marxist-Leninist perspective. He also treated everything—from his own standing within the Soviet hierarchy to the Soviet Union's standing relative to Western powers—with the same zero-sum mentality. Stalin backed down on occasion, to be sure, but only when outmaneuvered or faced with an unfavorable constellation of factors, as noted earlier with early Cold War crises involving Iran and Turkey. With Stalin in charge, the prospects for any type of détente, let alone negotiated resolution of the Cold War, remained dismal.

No other Soviet leader would come close to matching his iron grip, and Nikita Khrushchev and Mikhail Gorbachev, while heads of the Communist Party, never wielded power over the Politburo to anything approaching the degree that Stalin achieved. Other Soviet leaders served as mere caretakers given their short tenures. During Reagan's first term, Soviet leaders Yuri Andropov (November 1982 to February 1984) and Konstantin Ustinovich Chernenko (February 1984 to March 1985) died within a year of one another.

Harry S. Truman

On the US side, President Truman did more than any other Western leader to shape the Cold War's early trajectory. He embraced major initiatives with relish, such as his eponymous doctrine (1947). The Truman Doctrine grew out of specific concerns that communist guerrilla forces might prevail in Greece and Turkey, especially after cash-strapped Britain informed the United States it could no longer provide the two countries with financial assistance. Ideological concerns imbued the Truman Doctrine, and it assumed a more universal cast with its pledge to "support free peoples who are resisting attempted subjugation by armed minorities or by outside pressures."

Conceptually, the Truman Doctrine fit well with the framework of containment. But like Kennan's formulation, the Truman Doctrine did not specify what type of support the United States would provide. Politically, it had the benefit of strong bipartisan support, as did the Truman administration's other major national security initiatives, including the Marshall Plan (1948) and the creation of NATO (1949).[35]

Leonid Brezhnev

The voluntary nature of these initiatives contrasted with the Soviet approach toward its client-states. The Brezhnev Doctrine reflected this view, declaring, in effect, that becoming a member of the communist bloc marked an irreversible transition (once a communist, always a communist). Initially cited to justify the Soviet invasion of Czechoslovakia (1968), this doctrine came under strain as the Soviet Empire increasingly experienced political and economic woes. The Polish crisis in 1981 effectively ended the Brezhnev Doctrine.[36] Soviet sources indicate that Brezhnev himself was strongly opposed to intervening in Poland.[37] Even KGB chairman Yuri Andropov—an ardent champion of Soviet interventions in Hungary, Czechoslovakia, and Afghanistan—realized that military intervention in Poland would be politically and diplomatically disastrous for the Soviet Union.

Reagan and Gorbachev

The sudden and bloodless end of the Cold War was atypical for strategic rivalries. A closer look at the interplay of President Reagan and President Gorbachev is, therefore, crucial to understanding why these dynamics unfolded the way that they did. Gorbachev understood that a stagnant and overcommitted Soviet Union could no longer compete with the United States and the West. True, Gorbachev had his own reasons for pursuing reform, but the Reagan administration calibrated its pressure—playing US strengths against Soviet weaknesses—to reinforce his natural inclinations.

Over time, George Kennan's initial conception that resistance to Soviet thrusts would lead to its "break-up or the gradual mellowing of Soviet power" morphed into an approach that became comfortable with an enduring stalemate.[38] In other words, successive. administrations strived to manage the competition, rather than to end it. President Reagan's approach to containment, however, marked a departure from his predecessors.[39] Echoing criticisms of containment dating to the 1950s, he believed that containment lacked imagination and condemned those living under communist regimes to hopelessness. Not content with denouncing the Soviet Union, Reagan turned Marxist-Leninist ideology against itself, asserting that communist regimes were themselves subject to the "inevitability" of decline. While retaining elements of containment, he committed the United States, in a measured yet determined fashion, to promoting changes within the Soviet system. Codified by the National Security Decision Directive 75 (NSDD-75), "US Relations with the USSR," January 17, 1983, this initiative signaled a controversial change from previous variants of containment that aimed at limiting communist expansion.[40] In practical terms, this new approach, backed by dramatic increases in the defense budget, focused on pitting US advantages against Soviet weaknesses:

- support for anti-communist guerrillas in the Third World ("Reagan Doctrine") to exploit an overextended Soviet Empire;
- an unapologetic defense of democratic capitalism;
- a greater willingness to use military force in pursuit of policy objectives;

- elements of economic warfare; and
- the sabotage of Soviet espionage efforts aimed at stealing US technology.[41]

The willingness to use military force yielded mixed results. A US peacekeeping intervention in Lebanon (1983) ended in disaster. Later the same month, however, US military intervention in Grenada (Operation URGENT FURY) proved far more successful. The effort mattered little in geostrategic terms, but it helped to discredit the Brezhnev Doctrine by forcibly ousting a Marxist-Leninist regime. Although a relatively small-scale operation, the decision to intervene represented a dramatic move at a time when the Vietnam experience still had many questioning the utility of military force.

While the United States appeared rejuvenated in the 1980s, signs of Soviet political-military strains mounted. Domestically, the Kremlin appeared on autopilot after Brezhnev's death in 1982, leading to Yuri Andropov and then Constantin Chernenko, a pair of short-time successors. Internationally, the Kremlin had precious little to show for its efforts in the Third World, particularly in its most ambitious intervention—Afghanistan—where the human and economic costs were mounting at an unsustainable rate. It would take a forceful leader to change the Soviet Union's trajectory at home and abroad—Mikhail Gorbachev.

Gorbachev's accession to general secretary (1985) marked another turning point in the Cold War. He understood, for example, that Soviet efforts to impose socialism on Afghanistan were doomed to failure. Tellingly, he implored Moscow's handpicked leader, Mohammad Najibullah, accordingly: "Give up on the leftist bent in economics. Learn to organize the support of the private sector."[42] Gorbachev's instructions, in this case, provided an early clue about his willingness to eschew ideology and embrace market-based reforms.

On the domestic front, Gorbachev's pursuit of *Glasnost* ("Openness") and *Perestroika* ("Restructuring") got underway, slowly and unevenly at first, but soon picked up speed. Acutely aware of the Soviet Union's systemic weaknesses, he sought to reform Soviet communism but failed to anticipate what these reforms would unleash (in this he was far from alone).

With the benefit of hindsight, the Soviet collapse had the trappings of inevitability. Gorbachev's effort to reform the communist system proved self-defeating. Though he understood that military spending was crushing the Soviet economy, the apparent necessity of keeping hard-liners in check made it impossible to lower defense spending levels. It was not until 1989 that Gorbachev announced significant cuts in the military forces.[43]

NSC-68's assessment of two incompatible political-economic systems proved correct after all. Ultimately, Gorbachev's attempt to implement market-based reforms to salvage communism proved self-defeating. The outcome was no more surprising than if the United States had tried to save capitalism by stamping out free enterprise and implementing a centrally directed economy. If the ultimate outcome was not in doubt, the timing and nature of the Soviet Union's dissolution was subject to the complex interplay of human agency, including Gorbachev's coming to power and the election of Ronald Reagan to the US presidency.

Reagan and Gorbachev were a study in contrasts. The former actor and governor was a more intuitive decision-maker than his younger, legally trained counterpart. Still, they developed a personal chemistry, and though their relationship did not end the Cold War, it helped to set the final trajectory. Their effectiveness was enhanced by their shared gift for reaching well beyond their natural constituencies: Reagan connected with people behind the Iron Curtain, and Gorbachev gained favor among Western elites. Unfortunately, for the Soviet Empire, it was Reagan's message that resonated among the "subject" populations. And though Gorbachev could get on *Time Magazine*'s cover as Man of the Year, and his wife became a fashion leader, he had no message that appealed to the Western masses. In the end, Western populations were, on the whole, satisfied with their lot, while those within the Soviet Empire yearned for a system that could deliver consumer goods on the scale they could readily see in the West.

The Role of Chance

While this chapter has emphasized the role of strategy, it is important to remember that chance occurrences also shape historical outcomes. The notion that the White House—or the Kremlin, for that matter—managed crises with rheostat-like precision is more myth than reality. The famed "eyeball to eyeball" moment that Secretary of State Dean Rusk recalled during the Cuban missile crisis was wildly inaccurate: the ships in question were approximately 500 nautical miles apart at the time.[44] Moreover, the Cold War saw dozens of accidents involving nuclear weapons and strategic delivery systems, and those are just the ones declassified on the US side.[45] The cool, detached logic of nuclear deterrence often did not make sufficient room for real-world messiness and unpredictability. Unpredictable and consequential wildcards played a role, too. Chernobyl (1986) provided still another mortal blow to the Soviet system. Bureaucratic stonewalling and bumbling in the aftermath of this disaster convinced Gorbachev of the need for greater transparency.

Endgame

The Cold War did not endure for more than four decades because of some basic political misunderstanding or failure to communicate. Even before the super-powers had a dedicated "hotline" (a byproduct of the Cuban missile crisis), they had plenty of direct and indirect means to communicate. The problem was that the rivals understood each other too well, knowing that the incompatibility of their political systems meant that the rivalry could not be ended by negotiation or compromise. Ending it without recourse to suicidal military conflict could only be accomplished if one or the other surrendered the ideological underpinnings of its system, and adopted in large measure that of the other.

In the end, this is what happened, and the superiority of US strategy played a significant role in the outcome. Less an iron rule of conduct than a roomy framework, the "containment strategy" allowed successive administrations to put their own stamp on specific policies while adhering to a larger national approach to what was viewed as a continuing Soviet menace. In fact, "containment" proved flexible enough to adapt on the fly to changes of policy, which sometimes took place within a single administration, as happened with President Carter's adoption of a more hawkish posture after the Soviet invasion of Afghanistan. At other times, the changes were more tonal than substantive, such as President Reagan's modulating his anti-Soviet rhetoric during his second term.

As a strategy, containment proved remarkably effective over the long haul, despite costly setbacks in Korea and Vietnam. Part of the answer is with the institutional checks and balances that, combined with a political culture of domestic restraint, provided the United States with built-in shock absorbers to cope with internal and external pressures. In contrast, the Soviet Union's ideological rigidity and geostrategic ambitions proved a lethal combination. Additionally, Moscow's imperial overreach drained the Soviet Union's resources and diminished whatever ideological appeal the Soviet Union once enjoyed.

Cold War momentum shifts made it difficult for outside observers to make predictions in mid-stream. Writing in 1987, historian Paul Kennedy made the right argument (imperial overstretch) but focused on the wrong super-power (United States) in his widely read book, *The Rise and Fall of the Great Powers*. The Soviet Union's weaknesses are clearer in retrospect, as is often the case with defeated rivals. The Soviet Union certainly gave the appearance of a formidable enemy well into the 1980s—and with good reason, given its vast territorial expanse, dominant position in Eastern Europe, far-reaching inter-ventions in the Third World, and bulging conventional and nuclear arsenals. But it was also a fragile empire that had long passed the point of imperial overstretch. It was only waiting for a catalyst to precipitate the fall.

US institutional strengths also are clearer in retrospect:

- Democratic discourse allowed stakeholders to blow off steam, while elections provided citizens with the opportunity to remove incompetent leaders in an orderly fashion. Juxtaposed next to the rigidity of the Soviet system, Western democracies appeared supple. Institutional checks and balances, combined with a political culture based on civic restraint and the rule of law, allowed the United States to self-correct its excesses.

- In contrast, the Soviet Union's ideological rigidity and geostrategic ambitions worked at cross-purposes as the Cold War matured. Domestically, the Soviet *apparatchik* system cultivated short-sighted leaders, which made the entire system less responsive, like barnacles accreting on the hull of a ship. Internationally, Moscow's imperial overreach drained the Soviet Union of resources, crimped its growth, and sullied its ideological appeal. Third World nationalism, as well as US-backed anti-communist resistance movements, further complicated Soviet efforts.

- Gorbachev's increasingly frantic efforts to reform the system proved self-defeating: instead, they served to expose the system's underlying contradictions and hasten its demise. Gorbachev said it best: "The delusion was that at the time I, like most of us, assumed this could be accomplished by improving and refining the existing system."[46]

* * * * *

The United States endured economic and financial shocks aplenty during the Cold War, as did its allies. But for every crisis there was a recovery that strength-ened the economy. Centralized planning helped the Soviets mass-produce arma-ments during World War II, but as the Cold War advanced beyond the 1950s, this system proved ill-equipped to compete with capitalist countries. The Soviets enjoyed strong economic growth rates in the early years of the Cold War, but this was in part because the devastation wrought by World War II left the country with a low baseline. The ideological rigidity of the Soviet Union limited its capacity to enact political and economic reforms, and it fell further and further behind the West. "Above all, this was because the totalitarian system possessed tremendous inertia," Gorbachev would later note.[47]

Successive US administrations demonstrated a principled pragmatism—recognizing, for example, that countering Soviet-backed expansion necessitated the need to support democratically challenged allies such as Sygmann Rhee (president of South Korea, 1948–1960) and Ferdinand Marcos (president of Phillipines, 1966–1986). But there were matters of principle beyond which the United States would not bend, even if this meant risking outright military conflict with the Soviet Union. The United States never recognized Soviet claims to the Baltic nations and remained committed to the territorial integrity of Western Europe and securing access to the Middle East. On other matters, though, the United States accommodated harsh realities on the ground, whether this involved accepting a military stalemate in Korea (1953), abandoning South Vietnam (1975), or standing back while the Soviet Union rolled tanks into Hungary (1956) and Czechoslovakia (1968).

For all its permutations among different administrations, the strategy of containment retained its overall coherence. Continuity along these lines excluded the extremes of conciliation and preemptive military action against the Soviet Union. The Soviet Union's strategy, by comparison, reflected a mix of offensive and defensive elements, as the geopolitical fear of encirclement combined with ideological thrusts aimed at destabilizing the United States and its allies. The ideological and geopolitical differences dividing the superpowers ensured a rough stalemate until Gorbachev ushered in *Glasnost* and *Perestroika*, and President Reagan embraced a more muscular form of containment designed to reinforce the effects that political changes within the Soviet system were having.

The Cold War's aftermath also provides insights into the nature of the rivalry. The ideological underpinnings of the Soviet Union were thoroughly discredited, save for communist remnants in Cuba and North Korea. However, the geopolitical impulses underlying Soviet foreign policy have since reasserted themselves with a vengeance, especially under President Vladimir Putin's neo-imperial reign. For the US side, policymakers spent over a decade after the Soviet Union's collapse grasping for a new overarching strategic concept to replace containment, only to find that airy formulations such as "enlargement" lacked coherence and utility in the face of new security challenges wrought by 9/11.

NOTES

Introduction

1. I am talking here about addressing rivalries as a theme. Political scientists had, of course, conducted many examinations of specific rivalries, particularly the US-Soviet, Israeli-Arab, and Indian-Pakistani rivalries.

2. This Introduction lays out the key findings of political scientists. These are all drawn from the following articles: J. Joseph Hewitt, "A Crisis-Density Formulation for Identifying Rivalries," *The Journal of Peace Research* 42, no. 2 (March 2005): 183–200; Zeev Maoz and Ben D. Mor, "Enduring Rivalries: The Early Years," *International Political Science Review/Revue internationale de science politique* 17, no. 2, *Crisis, Conflict and War/Crise, conflit et guerre* (April 1996): 141–160; Gary Goertz and Paul F. Diehl, "Enduring Rivalries: Theoretical Constructs and Empirical Patterns," *International Studies Quarterly* 37, no. 2 (June 1993): 147–171; Jack S. Levy, "Historical Trends in Great Power War, 1495–1975," *International Studies Quarterly* 26, no. 2 (June 1982): 278–300; Erik Gartzke and Michael W. Simon, " 'Hot Hand': A Critical Analysis of Enduring Rivalries," *The Journal of Politics* 61, no. 3 (August 1999): 777–798; William R. Thompson, "Identifying Rivals and Rivalries in World Politics," *International Studies Quarterly* 45, no. 4 (December 2001): 557–586; Daniel S. Geller, "Power Differentials and War in Rival Dyads," *International Studies Quarterly* 37, no. 2 (June 1993): 173–193; William Moul, "Power Parity, Preponderance, and War between Great Powers, 1816–1989," *The Journal of Conflict Resolution* 47, no. 4 (August 2003): 468–489; Henk W. Houweling and Jan G. Siccama, "Power Transitions and Critical Points as Predictors of Great Power War: Toward a Synthesis," *The Journal of Conflict Resolution* 35, no. 4 (December 1991): 642–658; Woosang Kim, "Power Transitions and Great Power War from Westphalia to Waterloo," *World Politics* 45, no. 1 (October 1992): 153–172; Henk Houweling and

Jan G. Siccama, "Power Transitions as a Cause of War" *The Journal of Conflict Resolution* 32, no. 1 (March 1988): 87–102; William R. Thompson, "Principal Rivalries" *The Journal of Conflict Resolution* 39, no. 2 (June 1995): 195–223; Michael Colaresi, "Shocks to the System: Great Power Rivalry and the Leadership Long Cycle," *The Journal of Conflict Resolution* 45, no. 5 (October 2001): 569–593; Michael Colaresi and William R. Thompson, "Strategic Rivalries, Protracted Conflict, and Crisis Escalation," *Journal of Peace Research* 39, no. 3 (May 2002): 263–287; Gary Goertz and Paul F. Diehl, "The Initiation and Termination of Enduring Rivalries: The Impact of Political Shocks," *American Journal of Political Science* 39, no. 1 (February 1995): 30–52; James P. Klein, Gary Goertz, and Paul F. Diehl, "The New Rivalry Dataset: Procedures and Patterns," *Journal of Peace Research* 43, no. 3 (May 2006): 331–348; Vally Koubi, "War and Economic Performance," *Journal of Peace Research* 42, no. 1 (January 2005): 67–82; Douglas Lemke and William Reed, "War and Rivalry among Great Powers," *American Journal of Political Science* 45, no. 2 (April 2001): 457–469.

3. Ibid.
4. Ibid.
5. Proto-rivalries have all the characteristics of an enduring rivalry, but have not been going on long enough to warrant the "enduring" label. The developing US-China rivalry would fall into the "proto" category.
6. Michael P. Colaresi, Karen Rasler, and William R. Thompson, *Strategic Rivalries in World Politics* (Cambridge: Cambridge University Press, 2007), 79.
7. Thucydides 1.75 and 1.76. See Robert B. Strassler, ed., *The Landmark Thucydides* (New York: Free Press, 2008), 43.
8. See http://wwi.lib.byu.edu/index.php/Agadir_Crisis:_Lloyd_George's_Mansion_House_Speech.
9. Donald Kagan, "Our Interests and Our Honor," *Commentary Magazine* (April 1997), 42-45.
10. Henry Kissinger, "Realpolitik Turns on Itself," in *Diplomacy* (New York: Simon & Schuster, 1994), 137–167. See also Robert M. Citino's Chapter 14 in this work.
11. For an explanation of why the Numidian excuse may have been more pretext than reason, see Donald Walter Baronowski, "Polybius on the Causes of the Third Punic War," *Classical Philology* 90, no. 1 (January 1995): 16–31.
12. For a recent example, see Graham Allison, "Avoiding Thucydides's Trap," editorial, *Financial Times*, August 22, 2012, http://belfercenter.ksg.harvard.edu/publication/22265/avoiding_thucydidess_trap.html.
13. Nadia Shadlow, "Peace and War: The Space Between," War on the Rocks, August 18, 2014, http://warontherocks.com/2014/08/peace-and-war-the-space-between/.
14. Winston Churchill, *The Grand Alliance* (Houghton Mifflin, 1950), 331.

15. Stephen Broadberry et al., "British Economic Growth, 1270–1870," January 10, 2011, http://www.lse.ac.uk/economicHistory/seminars/ModernAndComparative/papers2011-12/ Papers/Broadberry.pdf.

16. See the statistics available at the "Angus Maddison Project," http://www.ggdc.net/maddison/maddison-project/home.htm.

17. This was the cost of a single coalition; there were seven before the wars ended, all subsidized by Great Britain.

18. Although this appears to be a trifling number, despite the heavy demands of the war in Iberia, the British shipped 120,000 muskets to Sweden and Russia before the end of 1812. In February 1813, the first shipment of arms sailed for Russia carrying 50,000 stands of arms. Without the arms and ammunition required to confront the enemy, there might not have been a coalition for the British to create. Shipments in the spring and summer of 1813 amounted to over 100,000 muskets for the Prussians, 100,000 muskets for the Russians as well as 116 guns and 1,200 tons of ammunition and shells. In the summer of 1813, the Swedes received 40,000 muskets. In November 1813, Castlereagh reported that nearly 1,000,000 muskets had been sent to Iberia and Central Europe. During the course of 1813, the British provided the following supplies to the Russian, Prussian, and Swedish governments: 218 pieces of ordnance complete with carriages and the necessary stores for the field, rounds of ammunition, and "a suitable quantity" of gunpowder, shot, shells, and caissons; 124,119 stands of arms with 18,231,000 musket cartridges; 23,000 barrels of powder and flints; 34,443 swords, sabers, and lances; 624 drums, trumpets, bugles, and cavalry standards; 150,000 uniforms complete with great-coats, cloaks, pelisses, and overalls; 187,000 yards of cloth of various colors; 175,796 boots and shoes "with a proportionate quantity of leather"; 114,000 blankets; 58,800 linen shirts and pants; 87,190 pairs of gaiters; 69,624 pairs of stockings/socks; 90,000 "sets of accoutrements;" 63,457 knapsacks; 14,820 saddles with blankets; 22,000 forage caps; 14,000 stocks and clasps; 140,600 shoe-brushes, combs, and black-balls; 3,000 gloves and bracers; 20,000 great-coat straps, brushes, pickers, and sponges; 5,000 flannel shirts, gowns, caps, and trousers; 14,000 haversacks and canteens; 702 pounds of biscuit and flour; 691,360 pounds of beef and pork; 28,625 gallons of brandy and rum; and "marquees, tents, forage carts, and necessary camp equipment; surgical instrument cases, medicines, and all necessary hospital stores." John Sherwig, *Guineas and Gunpowder: British Foreign Aid in the Wars with France, 1793–1815* (Cambridge: Cambridge, 1969), 287; Charles Stewart, *Narrative of the War in Germany and France in 1813 and 1814* (London, 1830), 366.

19. Brian Arthur, *How Britain Won the War of 1812: The Royal Navy's Blockades of the United States, 1812–1815* (Rochester, NY: Woodbridge, 2011), 57. The British government's gross tax income in 1813 was £70,300,000, which equates to $5,038,412,390.86 in 2011 using a conversion based on the GDP Deflator. In 2011, the relative value of £1,333,334 from 1813 was equal

to \$95,560,263.82, while that of £666,666 was \$47,780,060.24 using a conversion based on the GDP Deflator.

20. In 2011, the relative value of £500,000 from 1813 was equal to \$35,835,081.02 using a conversion based on the GDP Deflator.

21. In 2011, the relative value of £2,500,000 from 1813 was equal to \$179,175,405.08 using a conversion based on the GDP Deflator.

22. In 2011, the relative value of £1,000,000 from 1813 was equal to \$71,670,162.03 using a conversion based on the GDP Deflator.

23. See James G. Lacey, *Gold, Blood, and Power: Finance and War through the Ages*, IDA Paper P-4924, final (Alexandria, VA: Institute for Defense Analyses, September 2012).

24. Paul Kennedy, *The Rise and Fall of Great Powers* (New York: Random House, 1987), 439.

25. Lacey, *Gold, Blood, and Power*, 1.

26. Garrett Mattingly, *Defeat of the Spanish Armada* (London: Jonathan Cape, 1959), 223.

27. Neil Hanson, *The Confident Hope of a Miracle: The True History of the Spanish Armada* (New York: Vintage Books, 2006), 116.

28. George Kennan, "The Long Telegram," sent to George Marshall, dated February 22, 1946, photocopy at the Truman Presidential Library, Harry S. Truman Administration File, Elsey Papers, http://www.trumanlibrary.org/whistlestop/study_collections/coldwar/documents/pdf/6-6.pdf. This was the framework for the later article Kennan wrote for *Foreign Affairs*, "The Sources of Soviet Conduct" (July 1947), http://www.foreignaffairs.com/articles/23331/x/the-sources-of-soviet-conduct.

29. Kennan, "The Long Telegram."

30. Geoffrey Parker, *The World is Not Enough: The Imperial Vision of Phillip II of Spain* (Waco, TX: Markham Press Fund, 2001), 17.

31. Eberhard Kolb, *Der Weg aus dem Krieg* (Munich: 1989), 58–64, 77–82.

32. Biblioteca del Real Monasterio de San Lorenzo de El Escorial, Spain, *Ms* I. III. 30/122v, "Raggionamento" of Philip II for his son; E. Poullet and C. Piot, eds., *Correspondance du Cardinal de Granvelle 1565–1586* [hereafter *CCG*], 12 vols. (Brussels, 1877–1896), 4:558, Granvelle to Morillon, May 11, 1573, quoting with approval Don Pedro de Toledo, viceroy of Naples 1532–1553. Fernand Braudel, *The Mediterranean and the Mediterranean World in the Age of Philip II*, 2 vols. (London, 1972—1973), 1: 372–374; and G. Parker, *The Grand Strategy of Philip II* (New Haven, CT: Yale University Press, 1998), chap 2, provide copious examples.

33. Braudel, *The Mediterranean*, 1:372; Universiteitsbibliotheek, Leiden, Manuscript Department [hereafter UB], *Hs Pap* 3/3 Alonso de Laloo to Count Hornes, August 31, 1566; Parker, *Grand Strategy*, 49, quoting Leonardo Donà; L. Firpo, ed., *Relazioni di ambasciatori veneti al Senato, tratte dalle migliori edizioni disponibili e ordinate cronologicamente*, 14 vols. (Turin, 1965–1996), 8:670, Final Relation of Donà, January 1574.

Chapter 1

1. In citing the classical texts and certain standard secondary works, I use the standard abbreviations found in Simon Hornblower, Antony Spawforth, and Esther Eidinow, eds. *The Oxford Classical Dictionary*, 4th edition revised (Oxford: Oxford University Press, 2012). All translations are my own.

2. See Hdt. 5.32, 8.3.2; Thuc. 1.95.1–5, 128.4–131.1 (with 75.2, 96.1), 134.1; Arist. *Pol.* 1306b22–1307a4; Diod. 11.44.3–6, 46.1-3; Nep. *Paus.* 2.2–3.4; Plut. *Arist.* 23.1–5, *Cim.* 6.1–6, 9.1–6; Justin 9.1.3. Note Hdt. 4.81.3 with Nymphis of Heracleia *FGrH* 432 F9.

3. For a comprehensive discussion of Sparta's situation and of the manner in which she coped with the challenges she faced, see Paul A. Rahe, *Republics Ancient and Modern: Classical Republicanism and the American Revolution* (Chapel Hill: University of North Carolina Press, 1992), 136–162. See also Donald Kagan, *The Outbreak of the Peloponnesian War* (Ithaca, NY: Cornell University Press, 1969), 9–30; *The Spartan Regime: Its Character, Origins, and Grand Strategy* (New Haven, CT: Yale University Press, 2016).

4. See Thuc. 1.95.6–7; Xen. *Hell.* 6.5.34; Isoc. 4.72, 7.30, 12.67 with Meiggs, *AE*, 23–67, and Kagan, *The Outbreak of the Peloponnesian War*, 31–43, 377–379.

5. For a comprehensive overview, see Pierre Briant, *From Cyrus to Alexander: A History of the Persian Empire*, translated by Peter T. Daniels (Winona Lake, IN: Eisenbrauns, 2002).

6. The best recent discussion of the logistical challenges faced by the Persians and of their ability to surmount them can be found in Christopher J. Tuplin, "Achaemenid Arithmetic: Numerical Problems in Persian History," in *Recherches récentes sur l'Empire achéménide*, ed. Pierre Briant (Lyon: Topoi, 1997), I 365–421 (at 366–373). Cf. T. C. Young, "480/79: A Persian Perspective," *Iranica Antiqua* 15 (1980): 213–239, who errs in adopting uncritically the minimum calorie-intake calculations of Donald W. Engels, *Alexander the Great and the Logistics of the Macedonian Army* (Berkeley: University of California Press, 1978), 1–24, 123–130.

7. The Athenians had long been itching to take on the Hellenes' leadership at sea: Hdt. 7.161, 8.2–3; Plut. *Them.* 7.3–4.

8. See Hdt. 7.144; Thuc. 1.14.3; Arist. *Ath. Pol.* 22.7; Plut. *Them.* 3.4–4.3. On the significance of a city's possession of mines of this sort, see Robin Osborne, *Classical Landscape with Figures: The Ancient City and Its Countryside* (London: G. Phillip, 1987), 75–81.

9. See John S. Morrison, John F. Coates, and N. Boris Rankov, *The Athenian Trireme: The History and Reconstruction of an Ancient Greek Warship*, 2nd edition (New York: Cambridge University Press, 2000), with Lucien Basch, "Roman Triremes and the Outriggerless Phoenician Trireme," *The Mariner's Mirror* 65, no. 3 (November 1979): 289–326, and *Le Musée imaginaire*

de la marine antique (Athens: Institut Hellénique sur la Préservation de la Tradition Nautique, 1987), 303–336, as well as Boris Rankov, "The Dimensions of the Ancient Trireme: A Reconsideration of the Evidence," in *Trireme Olympias: The Final Report*, ed. Boris Rankov (Oxford: Oxbow Books, 2012), 225–230. Cf. Alec Tilley, *Seafaring on the Ancient Mediterranean: New Thoughts on Triremes and Other Ancient Ships* (Oxford: Hedges, 2004), and see John R. Hale, "The Lost Technology of Ancient Greek Rowing," *The Scientific American* (May 1996): 82–85; and "Rowing Ancient Warships: Evidence from a Newly-Published Ship-Model," *International Journal of Nautical Archaeology* 36 (2007): 293–299. Cf. Herman T. Wallinga, "The Ancient Persian Navy and Its Predecessors," *Achaemenid History* 1 (1987): 47–78; *Ships and Sea-Power before the Great Persian War: The Ancestry of the Ancient Trireme* (Leiden: Brill, 1993), 171–185; and *Xerxes' Greek Adventure: The Naval Perspective* (Brill: Leiden, 2005), 32–46, who insists that triremes were habitually undermanned, with George Cawkwell, *The Greek Wars: The Failure of Persia* (Oxford: Oxford University Press, 2005), 117–118, 228–229, 271, who shows that this claim is unproven and argues on the grounds mentioned in my text that it is improbable in the extreme.

10. See Hdt. 7.144; Thuc. 1.14.3; Arist. *Ath. Pol.* 22.7; Plut. *Them.* 4.1–3; Polyaen. *Strat.* 1.30.5.

11. Note Hdt. 8.3; Thuc. 1.96.1; Arist. *Ath. Pol.* 23.4–5; Diod. 11.46.4–5; Nep. *Arist.* 2.2–3; Plut. *Arist.* 23, *Cim.* 6.1–3; and see Thuc. 1.96, 3.10.3–4, 6.76.3–4; Arist. *Ath. Pol.* 23.4–5; Diod. 11.44.6, 47; Nep. *Arist.* 2.3; Plut. *Arist.* 25. 1 with Meiggs, *AE*, 42–67, 459–464.

12. See Vincent Gabrielsen, *Financing the Athenian Fleet: Public Taxation and Social Relations* (Baltimore, MD: Johns Hopkins University Press, 1994).

13. See Paul A. Rahe, *The Grand Strategy of Classical Sparta: The Persian Challenge* (New Haven, CT: Yale University Press, 2015), Chapter 4. Cf. Peter Krentz, *The Battle of Marathon* (New Haven, CT: Yale University Press, 2010), and James Lacey, *The First Clash: The Miraculous Greek Victory at Marathon and Its Impact on Western Civilization* (New York: Bantam Books, 2011).

14. On hoplite warfare, see Victor Davis Hanson, *The Western Way of War: Infantry Battle in Classical Greece*, 2nd edition (Berkeley: University of California Press, 2000). Note also Victor Davis Hanson, ed., *Hoplites: The Classical Greek Battle Experience* (London: Routledge, 1991). For the way of life to which this mode of warfare gave rise, see Victor Davis Hanson, *The Other Greeks: The Family Farm and the Agrarian Roots of Western Civilization*, revised edition (Berkeley: University of California Press, 1999). Although Hanson's analysis has given rise to considerable controversy, no one to date has proposed a plausible alternative: see Donald Kagan and Gregory F. Viggiano, eds. *Men of Bronze: Hoplite Warfare in Ancient Greece* (Princeton, NJ: Princeton University Press, 2013).

15. See Thuc. 1.90.2–91.7, 93.2; Diod. 11.39.4–40.4; Nep. *Them.* 6–7; Plut. *Them.* 19.1–2.2.

16. See Ar. *Eq.* 813–816; Thuc. 1.93, 2.13.6–7; Diod. 11.41–43; Nep. *Them.* 6.1; Plut. *Them.* 19.3–5 with Johannes S. Boersma, *Athenian Building Policy from 561/0 to 405/4 B.C.* (Groningen: Wolters-Noordhof, 1970), 46–50, and Robert Garland, *The Piraeus: From the Fifth to the First Century B.C.* (Ithaca, NY: Cornell University Press, 1987), 14–22, 163–165.

17. See Thuc. 1.135.3; Aristodemus *FGrH* 104 F6.1; Pl. *Grg.* 516d; Nep. *Them.* 8.1, *Arist.* 3.3; Diod. 11.55.1–3; Plut. *Them.* 22.3; Cic. *Amic.* 12.42 with Anthony J. Podlecki, *The Life of Themistocles: A Critical Survey of the Literary and Archaeological Evidence* (Montreal: McGill-Queens University Press, 1975), 30–37, 185–194.

18. For the difference that commerce makes and the divide that separates ancient from modern international relations, see Paul A. Rahe, *Montesquieu and the Logic of Liberty: War, Religion, Commerce, Climate, Terrain, Technology, Uneasiness of Mind, the Spirit of Political Vigilance, and the Foundations of the Modern Republic* (New Haven, CT: Yale University Press, 2009), 1–60.

19. See Alfonso Moreno, *Feeding the Democracy: The Athenian Grain Supply in the Fifth and Fourth Centuries BC* (Oxford: Oxford University Press, 2007).

20. Note Moses I. Finley, "The Fifth-Century Athenian Empire: A Balance Sheet," in *Imperialism in the Ancient World*, ed. P. D. A. Garnsey and C. R. Whittaker (Cambridge: Cambridge University Press, 1978), 103–126.

21. An epitomator of Ephorus (*FGrH* 70 F191) and, after him, Diodorus (11.60.4–62.3) appear to have conflated this battle with a later struggle of a very similar character that took place in the vicinity of Cypriot Salamis in 451. For the likely date of Eurymedon, see Plut. *Cim.* 8.8–9 with *ATL*, III 160.

22. For the terms of the Peace of Callias and its timing, see Pl. *Menex.* 241d–e; Isoc. 4.120; Plut. *Cim.* 13.4–5; Ammian. Marc. 17.11.3; *Suda* s. v. *Kímōn* with Ernst Badian, "The Peace of Callias," *Journal of Hellenic Studies* 107 (1987): 1–39, reprinted in Badian, *From Plataea to Potidaea: Studies in the History and Historiography of the Pentecontaetia* (Baltimore, MD: Johns Hopkins University Press, 1993), 1–60. Cf. P. J. Stylianou, "The Untenability of Peace with Persia in the 460s B.C.," *Meletai kai Upomnemata* 2 (1988): 339–371, with Badian, *From Plataea to Potidaea*, 61–69.

23. See Antony Andrewes, "Sparta and Arcadia in the Early Fifth Century," *Phoenix* 6, no. 1 (Spring 1952): 1–5, and W. G. G. Forrest, "Themistocles and Argos," *Classical Quarterly* n. s. 10, no. 2 (November 1960): 221–241. For a partial corrective, cf. J. L. O'Neill, "The Exile of Themistocles and Democracy in the Peloponnese," *Classical Quarterly* n. s. 31, no. 2 (November 1981): 335–346.

24. See Thuc. 1.128.7, 129.2, 131–138; Nep. *Paus.* 3.5–5.5; *Them.* 8.2–10.5; Diod. 11.45; Paus. 3.14.1, 17.7; Plut. *Them.* 23–29, *Mor.* 560f. Cf. Diod. 11.54.2–55.8, where the chronology and the details seem muddled.

25. See Thuc. 1.100.2–101.2 (with 4.102.2–3); Diod. 11.70.1; Plut. *Cim.* 14.2.

26. See Thuc. 1.101.2, 128.1, 2.27.2, 3.54.5, 4.56.2. For the year in which the earthquake took place, see Paus. 4.24.5–6; Plut. *Cim.* 16.4.

27. See Plut. *Cim.* 16.4–5; Cic. *De div.* 1.112; Pliny *NH* 2.191; Ael. *VH* 6.7.2; Polyaen. 1.41.3.

28. Consider Hdt. 9.33–35, 64.2, in light of Thuc. 1.101.2; Diod. 11.63.4–64.1; Plut. *Cim.* 16.6–7; Paus. 1.29.8, 3.11.8, 4.24.5–6.

29. See Thuc. 1.102.1–2; Xen. *Hell.* 6.5.33; Diod. 11.64.2; Plut. *Cim.* 16.8–10; Paus. 1.29.8, 4.24.5–6; Justin 3.6.2.

30. See Thuc. 1.102; Ar. *Lys.* 1138–1144; Plut. *Cim.* 16.8–17.4; Diod. 11.64.2–3; Paus. 1.29.8–9, 4.26.4–7; Justin 3.6.3.

31. See Plut. *Cim.* 17.3, *Per.* 9.5–10.1; Pl. *Grg.* 516d; Nep. *Cim.* 3.1.

32. See David H. Conwell, *Connecting a City to the Sea: The History of the Athenian Long Walls* (Leiden: Brill, 2008), 37–107.

33. See Thuc. 1.105.2–3, 108.4–5, 115.1; Diod. 11.84.2–7, 85.1–2, 88.88.1–2; Plut. *Per.* 19.2–4.

34. What, we can surmise, the Athenians did during the great Peloponnesian War is an indication of what they are likely to have done in this earlier conflict: Thuc. 2.69.1, 93.4.

35. That an attempt was made by the Athenians to renew the peace can be inferred from Hdt. 7.151.1.

36. See Thuc. 1.104, 109–110; Ctesias *FGrH* 688 F14.36–39; Diod. 11.71.4–5, 74.1–75.4, 77.1–4, 13.25.2; Isoc. 8.86. For the date, the Egyptian evidence, which accords with the claims of Ctesias and Diodorus and not those of Thucydides, is dispositive: see Dan'el Kahn, "Inaros' Rebellion against Artaxerxes I and the Athenian Disaster in Egypt," *Classical Quarterly* 58, no. 2 (December 2008): 424–440. For what the Athenians suffered, however, Thucydides is far more likely than Ephorus, Diodorus's chief source, to have known what he is talking about. See Jan M. Libourel, "The Athenian Disaster in Egypt," *American Journal of Philology* 92, no. 4 (October 1971): 605–615, and Meiggs, *AE*, 92–151, 473–476. In this connection, see Hdt. 3.12.4, 15.3, 160.2 (with 7.82, 121.3), 7.7. Even those who believe Thucydides' figures inflated concede that something like one Athenian citizen in five died in the Egyptian campaign: see A. J. Holladay, "The Hellenic Disaster in Egypt," *Journal of Hellenic Studies* 109 (1989): 176–182, and Eric W. Robinson, "Thucydidean Sieges, Prosopitis, and the Hellenic Disaster in Egypt," *Classical Antiquity* 18, no. 1 (April 1999): 132–152.

37. See Mogens Herman Hansen, "Demographic Reflections on the Number of Athenian Citizens, 451–309 B.C.," *American Journal of Ancient History* 7 (1982): 172–189.

38. See Thuc. 1.107.2–108.2; Hdt. 9.35.2; Diod. 11.79.4–80.6; Plut. *Cim.* 17.4–9, *Per.* 17.1–4; Paus. 1.29.6–9; ML no. 35.

39. See A. J. Holladay, "Sparta's Role in the First Peloponnesian War," *Journal of Hellenic Studies* 97 (1977): 54–63, and "Sparta and the First Peloponnesian War," *Journal of Hellenic Studies* 105 (1985): 161–162, as well as David M. Lewis, "The Origins of the First Peloponnesian War," in *Classical Contributions: Studies in Honour of Malcolm Francis McGregor*, ed. Gordon Spencer Shrimpton and David Joseph McCargar (Locust Valley, NY: J. J. Augustin, 1981), 71–78, which is reprinted in Lewis, *Selected Papers in Greek and Near Eastern History*, ed. Peter J. Rhodes (Cambridge: Cambridge University Press, 1997), 9–21.

40. See Theopompus *FGrH* 115 F88; Andoc. 3.3–4; Nep. *Cim.* 3.3; Plut. *Cim.* 17.4–8, *Per.* 10.1–6.

41. As Meiggs, *AE*, 181–182, points out, it is hard to believe that Pleistoanax simply withdrew.

42. See Thuc. 1.35.2, 40, 44.1, 45.3, 67.2, 4, 78.4, 140.2, 144.2, 145, 7.18; Diod. 12.7; Paus. 5.23.3 with Kagan, *The Outbreak of the Peloponnesian War*, 128, and G. E. M. de Ste. Croix, *The Origins of the Peloponnesian War* (Ithaca, NY: Cornell University Press, 1972), 293–294.

43. The testimony of Ephorus *FGrH* 70 F193 ap. Schol. Ar. *Nub.* 858 and Plut. *Per.* 22.2–23.2 is confirmed by Thuc. 2.21.2, 5.16.3.

44. Given the semi-public nature of the meetings of the Spartan alliance, it is highly likely that the Athenians heard about the Spartan proposal quite soon thereafter. The reference to this event made by the Corinthians in the debate at Athens certainly presupposes that their listeners are already fully familiar with what took place. Cf. Donald Kagan, *The Outbreak of the Peloponnesian War*, 170–179, and *On the Origins of War and the Preservation of Peace* (New York: Doubleday, 1995), 77, n. 20, with A. H. M. Jones, "Two Synods of the Delian and Peloponnesian Leagues," *Proceedings of the Cambridge Philological Society* 182 (1952–1953): 43–46, and Ste. Croix, *The Origins of the Peloponnesian War*, 200–205.

45. See Paul A. Rahe, "The Peace of Nicias," in *The Making of Peace*, ed. Williamson Murray and James Lacey (Cambridge: Cambridge University Press, 2009), 31–69.

46. For an overview, see J. B. Salmon, *Wealthy Corinth: A History of the City to 338 BC* (Oxford: Clarendon Press, 1984), 1–256.

47. For details and a full citation of the evidence, see Kagan, *The Outbreak of the Peloponnesian War*, 203–228.

48. The date can be inferred from a comparison of the speech in which the Corinthians sought to dissuade the Athenians from making an alliance with Corcyra (Thuc. 1.36.4–43.4), in which there is no mention of the Megarian Decree, and Thucydides' summary of the arguments presented at Sparta after the battle of Sybota by the Megarians (1.67.4), in which the decree is not only mentioned but stressed.

49. See Kagan, *The Outbreak of the Peloponnesian War*, 254–267.

50. For an elaborate, ingenious, and ultimately unpersuasive piece of special pleading aimed at getting around the evidence strongly suggesting that, in passing the Megarian Decree, the Athenians voted to adopt a policy tantamount to an empire-wide embargo on Megarian trade, cf. Ste. Croix, *The Origins of the Peloponnesian War*, 225–289.

51. See Kagan, *The Outbreak of the Peloponnesian War*, 222–250.

52. I see no reason to join George Cawkwell, *Thucydides and the Peloponnesian War* (London: Routledge, 1997), 31–34, in supposing that Thucydides deliberately or inadvertently omitted to mention a clause within the Thirty Years Peace guaranteeing freedom of the seas and access to the Aegean ports.

53. I see no grounds for joining Ernst Badian, "Thucydides and the Outbreak of the Peloponnesian War: A Historian's Brief," in *Conflict, Antithesis and the Ancient Historian*, ed. June Allison (Columbus: Ohio State University Press, 1990), 46–91, reprinted in *From Plataea to Potidaea*, 125–162, in thinking that Thucydides deliberately failed to mention a clause within the Thirty Years Peace guaranteeing the autonomy of the members of either league.

54. See P. A. Brunt, "Spartan Policy and Strategy in the Archidamian War," *Phoenix* 19, no. 4 (Winter 1965): 255–280, and Donald Kagan, *The Archidamian War* (Ithaca, NY: Cornell University Press, 1974), 18–24. Cf., however, Thomas Kelly, "Thucydides and Spartan Strategy in the Archidamian War," *American Historical Review* 87, no. 1 (February 1982): 25–54, and Cawkwell, *Thucydides and the Peloponnesian War*, 40–43.

55. Cf. Kagan, *The Outbreak of the Peloponnesian War*, 254–272, 278–281, 321–324, 347–349, 369–372.

56. For the details, see Kagan, *The Archidamian War*, 1–123.

57. That Pericles' strategy was offensive is but rarely appreciated: for an exception to the rule, see H. T. Wade-Gery, "Thucydides," in *The Oxford Classical Dictionary*, 1472–1475 (at 1474–1475). Cf. Kagan, *The Archidamian War*, 24–123. To grasp the significance of the Epidaurus expedition, one need only compare Thuc. 2.56.4 with the passing observation at 6.31.2, and see 5.53.

58. Cf. Thuc. 3.87.3 with 2.13.6–8.

59. See Kagan, *The Archidamian War*, 43–146.

60. For an overview, see ibid., 218–259.

61. See Cawkwell, *Thucydides and the Peloponnesian War*, 64–66.

62. See Kagan, *The Archidamian War*, 260–349.

63. For the details, see Donald Kagan, *The Peace of Nicias and the Sicilian Expedition* (Ithaca, NY: Cornell University Press, 1981), 17–137.

64. See ibid., 157–353.

65. See Donald Kagan, *The Fall of the Athenian Empire* (Ithaca, NY: Cornell University Press, 1987), 1–50.

66. See Thuc. 6.27–29, 53.1–2, 60–61, 88.9–93.3, 7.18.1, 8.6.1–14.3.

67. For the details, see Kagan, *The Fall of the Athenian Empire*, 51–426.

68. On this period, see Charles D. Hamilton, *Sparta's Bitter Victories: Politics and Diplomacy in the Corinthian War* (Ithaca, NY: Cornell University Press, 1979), and *Agesilaus and the Failure of Spartan Hegemony* (Ithaca, NY: Cornell University Press, 1991), as well as Paul Cartledge, *Agesilaos and the Crisis of Sparta* (London: Duckworth, 1987).

69. See John Buckler, *The Theban Hegemony, 371–362 B.C.* (Cambridge, MA: Harvard University Press, 1980).

Chapter 2

1. Unless stated otherwise, all translations are the author's.

2. Speech in the House of Commons, March 1, 1848, http://hansard.millbanksystems.com/commons/1848/mar/01/treaty–of–adrianople–charges–against.

3. Polybius, *Histories* 1.59, trans. Evelyn S. Shuckburgh (London; New York: Macmillan, 1889; reprint, Bloomington, 1962). http://www.perseus.tufts.edu/hopper/text?doc=Perseus%3Atext%3A1999.01.0234%3Abook%3D1%3Achapter%3D59.

4. Ibid. http://www.perseus.tufts.edu/hopper/text?doc=Perseus%3Atext%3A1999.01.0234%3Abook%3D1%3Achapter%3D62.

5. Polybius, *Histories* 9.22.6.

6. Polybius, *Histories* 118.5.

7. Livy, *History of Rome*, 22.51.4.

8. A. T. Mahan, *The Influence of Sea Power Upon history 1660-1783* (Little Brown & Company, 1890), 20.

Chapter 3

1. For the evolution from a conscript army into a professional one, see Lawrence Keppie, *The Making of the Roman Army from Republic to Empire* (London, 1984), 57–171, and P. A. Brunt, "The Army and the Land in the Roman Revolution," *Journal of Roman Studies* 52 (1962): 68–86. For weapons and tactics, see A. K. Goldsworthy, *The Roman Army at War, 100 B.C.–A.D. 200* (Oxford, 1996), and Graham Webster, *The Roman Imperial Army of the First and Second Centuries A.D.* (London, 1969), 107–265. For the auxiliary units, see Ian Haynes, *Blood of the Provinces: The Roman Auxilia and the Making of the Provincial Society from Augustus to the Severans* (Oxford, 2013). Still fundamental for the Roman command structure is Alfred von Domaszewski, *Die Rangordnung des römischen Herres* (Vienna, 1907).

2. For the later Roman army, see Pat Southern and Karen R. Dixon, *The Late Roman Army* (New Haven, CT: Yale University Press, 1996). For the late Roman field armies, see D. Hoffman, *Die spätrömischen Bewegungsheer und die Notitia Dignitatum*, 2 vols. (Düsseldorf, 1969–1970). For fielding more heavy cavalry against Iranian foes, see John Eadie, "The Development of Roman Mailed Cavalry," *Journal of Roman Studies* 57 (1967): 161–173. For the

recruitment of barbarians, see Thomas S. Burns, *Rome and the Barbarians, 100 B.C.–A.D. 400* (Baltimore, MD: 2003), 248–373, and Hugh Elton, *Warfare in Roman Europe, A.D. 350–425* (Oxford, 1996), 128–155.

3. Amm. Marcel. XVIII. 8. 1–9. 1; see Noel Lenksi, "Two Sieges of Amida (A.D. 359 and 505–503) and the Experience of Combat in the Late Roman Near East," in *The Late Roman Army in the Near East from Diocletian to the Arab Conquest: Proceedings of a Colloquium Held at Potenza, Acerenza and Matera, Italy (May 2005)*, ed. A. S. Lewin and P. Pellegrini (British Archaeological Reports, International Series 1717, Oxford, 2007), 219–236, and R. C. Blockley, "Ammianus Marcellinus on the Persian Invasion of A.D. 359," *Phoenix* 42 (1988): 244–260.

4. Tac., *Ann.* II. 60. 5 (Penguin translation, 110–111). Tacitus makes the remark after discussing inscriptions reporting the revenues of the Egyptian pharaoh Ramses II, which were seen by Germanicus outside of Thebes in 19 CE. Classical authors appreciated the economics of war; see Thuc. I. 19, I. 140. 5–141. 1, and II. 13. 35, on the financial resources of the rivals Athens and Sparta.

5. See Keith Hopkins, "Taxes and Trade in the Roman Economy, 200 B.C.–A.D.400," *Journal of Roman Studies* 70 (1980): 101–125, For the imperial budget, see Kenneth W. Harl, *Coinage in the Roman Economy, 300 B.C. to A.D. 700* (Baltimore, MD: 1996), 207–249.

6. See ibid., 143–175, and Kenneth W. Harl, "From Aurelian to Diocletian: Financing Imperial Recovery by Debasements and Fiduciary Currencies," in *Money in the Pre-Industrial World: Bullion, Debasement, and Coin Substitutes*, ed. John H. Munro (London, 2012), 33–45.

7. See P. Horden, "Plague in the Age of Justinian," in *Age of Justinian*, ed. Michael Mass (Cambridge, 2005), 134–160. In 542–543, the plague carried off between one-quarter and one-third of the population; see P. Allen, "The 'Justinianic' Plague," *Byzantion* 49 (1979): 5–20, and D. Sathakopoulos, "The Justinianic Plague Revised," *Byzantine and Modern Greek Studies* 24 (2000): 256–276. For the long-term demographic impact, see Michael McCormick, *Origins of the European Economy: Communication and Commerce, A.D. 300–900* (Cambridge, 2001), 38–41, 114–116, and 753. For the impact on recruitment into Justinian's army, see J. L. Teall, "The Barbarians in Justinian's Armies," *Speculum* 40 (1965): 294–323.

8. See P. Pourshariati, *Decline and Fall of the Sasanian Empire: The Sasanian-Parthian Confederacy and the Arab Conquest* (New York, 2008), 160–280, and *contra* James Howard-Johnson, *Witnesses to World Crisis: Historians and Histories of the Middle East in the Seventh Century* (Oxford, 2010), 438–474, minimizing the impact of these wars as enabling the rapid Arabic conquests. For the Muslim view on their success, see Fred M. Donner, *The Early Islamic Conquests* (Princeton, NJ: 1981), 251–272.

9. See M. Rahim Shayegan, *Arsacids and Sasanians: Political Ideology in Post-Hellenistic and Late Antique Persia* (Cambridge, 2011), 39–49.

10. See Pourshariati, *Sasanian Empire*, 33–58. For a survey of the economy, see Christopher Brunner, "Geographical and Administrative Divisions: Settlements and Economy," in *The Cambridge History of Iran* III. 2, edited by E. Yarshater (Cambridge: Cambridge University Press, 1983), 747–777.

11. See C. E. Bosworth, "Iran and the Arabs before Islam," The *Cambridge History of Iran* III. 1, edited by E. Yarshater (Cambridge: Cambridge University Press, 1983), 604–612.

12. See J. Duchesne-Guillemin, "Zoroastrian Religion," in *Cambridge History of Iran* III. 2, 474–888, and cf. Martin Sprengling, "Karitr, Founder of Sassanian Zoroastrianism," *American Journal of Semitic Languages and Literature* 57 (1940): 197–228.

13. See Hugh Kennedy, *Armies of the Caliphs: Military and Society in the Early Islamic State* (London; New York, 2001), 105–107.

14. See G. Kenneth Holum, "Pulcheria's Crusade and the Ideology of Victory," *Greek, Roman and Byzantine Studies* 18 (1977): 153–172. For morale, a subject still requiring a major study, see Southern and Dixon, *Late Roman Army*, 168–178.

15. See C. S. Lightfoot, "Trajan's Parthian War and the Fourth-century Perspective," *Journal of Roman Studies* 80 (1990): 123–124. Roman authors designated the regions below the confluence of the Khabur and Euphrates as "Assyria" rather than Babylonia. Mesopotamia was strictly applied to the northern regions between the Euphrates and Tigris later organized as a province by Septimius Severus. Throughout I have used the conventional designation of Babylonia for lower Iraq.

16. See D. Engels, *Alexander the Great and the Logistics of the Macedonian Army* (Berkeley, 1976), 11–25 and 137–158.

17. Tac., *Ann.* XIII. 35. 5–10.

18. Circa 120, Vologaeses III moved the Armenian capital east to Vagharshapat. Tiridates III, who converted to Christianity, founded Ani as the third capital in what became the heartland of the medieval Bagatrid kingdom.

19. Kharput may be Classical Carcathiocerta; see Strabo XI. 14. 2. See D. H. French, "New Research on the Euphrates Frontier: Supplementary Notes 1 and 2," in ed. Stephen Mitchell (Oxford, 1983), 71–101, and cf. Stephen Mitchell, *Anatolia: Land, Men, and Gods in Asia Minor*, vol. I: *The Celts and the Impact of Roman Rule* (Oxford, 1993), 129–132.

20. For the Dariel Pass, or Caucasian Gates, see Strabo XI. 500. For Nero's plans to cross the Dariel Pass to campaign against the Alans, see Suet., *Nero* 19.2; Dio 68. 8. 1; Tac. *Hist.* I. 6. 2, and Plin., *NH* VI. 40. The Derbent Pass was usually identified as the Gates of Alexander (although sometimes called the Caspian Gates); see Jos. *Ant.* XVIII. 4–6. For the Sassanid

fortifications, see K. Kleiber, "Alexander's Caspian Wall: A Turning Point in Parthian and Persian Military Architecture," *Folia Orientalia* 42–43 (2006–2007): 193–195.

21. For texts and commentary of Arrian, see J. G. De Voto, *Arrianus Flavius: Teckne Taktika (Tactical Handbook) and Ektaxis kata Alanos (The Expedition against the Alans)* (Chicago, 1993). See E. L. Wheeler, "The Legion as Phalanx," *Chiron* 9 (1979): 303–318, and A. B. Bosworth, "Arrian and the Alani," *Harvard Studies in Classical Philology* 81 (1977): 217–255.

22. See David Magie, *Roman Rule in Asia Minor to the End of the Third Century after Christ* (Princeton, NJ: 1952), 573–574, and 1434–1435, n. 19. Nemrut Dağ (2,150 meters/6,880 feet above sea level) dominates the region.

23. For the site, see T. A. Sinclair, *Eastern Turkey: An Architectural and Archaeological Survey* (London, 1987), 361–365, citing the older scholarship. In 2011, I confirmed Sinclair's suggestion by a visit to the site. The ruins of the city are just northeast of Beşiri and just south of the modern railway line.

24. Pat. Patr., *FHG* IV, 189, frag. 14 = M. H. Dodgeon and S. N. C. Lieu, *The Roman Eastern Frontier and the Persian Wars, A.D. 226–363: A Documentary History* (London; New York, 1991), 133. See W. Ensslin, "Zur Östpolitik des Kaisers Diokletian," *Sitzungsberichte der Bayerischen Akademie der Wissenschaft* 1 (1942),: 1-83. For redating the treaty from 299 to 300, see T. D. Barnes, "Imperial Campaigns, A.D. 285–311," *Phoenix* 30 (1976): 174–193.

25. Amm. Marcel. 25. 7. 9–10; cf. Zos. III. 31. 1–2, and Oros. 7. 31. 1–2; see discussion by N. Lenksi, *Failure of Empire: Valens and the Roman State in the Fourth Century A.D.* (Berkeley, 2002), 161-162.

26. See *Chronicon Paschale*, 504–505 (Dindorf edition); cf. Amm. Marcel. 16. 7. 5, for lions in the Euphrates valley in 359.

27. See Benjamin Isaac, *The Limits of Empire: The Roman Empire in the East*, revised edition (Oxford, 1990), 101–150, for the imperial army as an occupation force.

28 See S. I. Oost, "The Alexandrine Seditions under Philip and Gallienus," *Classical Philology* 56 (1961): 1–20, and Ramsay MacMullen, "Nationalism in Roman Egypt," *Aegyptus* 44 (1964): 179–199, for social unrest at Alexandria. Rome could not tolerate a regime in Egypt comparable to the Gallo-Roman or Romano-British Empires. Hence, Aurelian sent the future emperor Probus to secure Egypt in 271 before the emperor marched against Palmyra; see SHA, *Vita Prob.* 9. 5, and see J. Schwartz, "Palmyrenes et l'opposition à Rome en Égypte," in *Palmyre: Bilan et Perspectives* (Strasbourg, 1976), 139–151. For the threat posed by the usurper L. Domitius Domitianus (295–297), see J. Schwartz, *Lucius Domitius Domitianus* (Brussels, 1975, Papyri Bruxelles 12), 110–176, and J. D. Thomas, "The Date of the Revolt of L. Domitius Domitianus," *Zeitschrift für Papyrologie und Epigraphik* 22 (1976):

253–279. The loss of Egypt in 617–619 was fiscally, and nearly politically, disastrous for Heraclius; see Walter E. Kaegi, Jr., *Heraclius, Emperor of Byzantium* (Cambridge, 2003), 88–92.

29. See Tac., *Ann.* II, 2–3, contrasting the Roman manners of the unpopular Arsacid king Vonones (8–12) to the traditional Parthian habits of his rival Artabanus III (10–38).

30. See Elizabeth K. Fowden, "Constantine and the Eastern Peoples," in *The Cambridge Companion to the Age of Constantine* (Cambridge, 2006), 387–389. The story of the baptism of Tiridates III by Gregory the Illuminator, before the conversion of Constantine, dates from the fifth century.

31. See E. S. Gruen, *The Hellenistic World and the Coming of Rome* (Berkeley, 1986), I:132–157.

32. See Matthew P. Canepa, *The Two Eyes of the Earth: Art and Ritual of Kingship between Rome and Sasanian Iran* (Berkeley, 2009), 122–153.

33. See Alexander Jones, "Ptolemy's Geography: Mapmaking and the Scientific Enterprise," in *Ancient Perspectives: Maps and Their Places in Mesopotamia, Egypt, Greece, and Rome*, ed. R. J. A. Talbert (Chicago, 2012), 109–128. Ptolemy's map represented the summation of knowledge gained from war, diplomacy, exploration, and trade. For Roman authors' access to geographic knowledge, see Benet Salway, "Putting the World in Order: Mapping in Roman Texts," in *Ancient Perspectives*, 193–234. The celebrated Peutinger Map was a presentation piece rather than a reference map; see Richard J. A. Talbert, *Rome's World: The Peutinger Map Reconsidered* (Cambridge, 2010), 162–172.

34. *Contra* Susan Mattern, *Rome and the Enemy: Imperial Strategy in the Principate* (Berkeley, 1999), 1–24.

35. For text, translation, and commentary, see W. H. Schoff, ed. and trans., *Isidore Characenus, Parthian Stations: An Account of the Overland Trade Route between the Levant and India in the First Century B.C.* (Philadelphia, 1914). See also Plut, *Crass.* 32, for the Suren, who was conversant in Greek, mocking the low taste of Greek works seized from Crassus and his officers in 53 BCE.

36. See Thuc. I. 22. 3–4, on the value of history, and cf. Plut, *Alex.* 44, for the value of biography as instruction.

37. See Peter Brown, "Diffusion of Manichaeism in the Roman Empire," *Journal of Roman Studies* 59 (1969): 92–103, for trade, communication, an exchange of religions across the political boundaries of the Fertile Crescent.

38. See Edward N. Luttwak, *Grand Strategy of the Roman Empire from the First Century A.D. to the Third* (Baltimore, MD: 1976) 1–39, 55–61, 130–145, and 191–194. Luttwak assumes an imperial government with modern style institutions; see critique by J. C. Mann, "Power, Force, and the Frontiers of the Empire," *Journal of Roman Studies* 69 (1979): 175–183. But it is also misleading to argue that the absence of professional experts rules out the ability of Romans to implement long-term strategic policy; *contra* Gruen,

Hellenistic World and Coming of Rome, I:203–249, arguing for the republic, or Mattern, *Rome and the Enemy*, 81–92, arguing for the Principate.

39. For Caesar's composition of his *Commentarii*, see T. D. Wiseman, "The Publication of *De Bello Gallico*," in *Julius Caesar as Artful Reporter: The War Commentaries as Political Instruments*, ed. K. Welch and A. Powell (London, 1998), 1–19, and K. Barwick, *Caesars Commentarii und das Corpus Caesarianum, Philologus* Supplement 31. 2 (Berlin, 1938). Three times, Caesar reports sending dispatches to Rome; see discussion by Kimberley Kagan, *The Eye of Command* (Ann Arbor, 2006), 110–111 and 222 n. 243. A single quote from the *Commentarii* of Trajan survives from Priscian, and so the column acts a pictorial narrative of Trajan's account; see F. Lepper and S. Frere, *Trajan's Column* (London, 1988), 226-227, and cf. 187–193 and 275–308. These works are best compared to the memoirs of British officers of the nineteenth and twentieth centuries or of German generals of World War II. These works, far more than anecdotal collections of Polyaenus, handbooks, or Homeric epics (which have survived), were read for generalship, strategy, and tactics, *contra* J. E. Lendon, *Soldiers and Ghosts: A History of Battle in Classical Antiquity* (New Haven, CT: Yale University Press, 2005), 261–289. See instead J. B. Campbell, *The Emperor and the Army, 31 B.C.–235 A.D.* (Oxford, 1984), 317–367, and, for the ethos of bravery, William V. Harris, *War and Imperialism in Republican Rome, 327–70 B.C.* (Oxford, 1979), 9–53.

40. See R. Duncan-Jones, *Structure and Scale in the Roman Economy* (Cambridge, 1996), 7–29, and cf. Lionel Casson, *Ships and Seamanship in the Ancient World* (Princeton, NJ, 1971), 281–298, for the transmission of news by ship between Rome and ports in the Eastern Mediterranean. Even during favorable sailing conditions in the early spring or the summer, directives from Rome would take four weeks to reach Euxine ports Amisus (Samsun) or Trapezus (Trabzon), the main ports of communication for Lucullus or Corbulo. It would take another four to six weeks for the directives to reach any Roman commander operating east of the Euphrates. Directives from Rome to Antioch could be delivered in under three weeks.

41. See Piers MacKesy, *The War for America 1775–1783* (Cambridge, MA: Harvard University Press, 1964), 60–78, for comparable problems of communication between Lord George Germain and British commanders in North America, as well as the shipment of supplies and reinforcements.

42. See Hdt. V. 52–53, for the Persian Royal Road. Herodotus, writing in the fifth century BCE, reports that the Achaemenid king at Susa could receive news from Sardes by mounted post covering 1,500 miles within a week. Cyrus the Younger and the 10,000 covered an equivalent distance from Sardes to Babylon in a march of four months in 401 BCE; see John W. I. Lee, *A Greek Army on the March: Soldiers and Survival in Xenophon's Anabasis* (Cambridge, 2007), 18–26.

43. See Canepa, *Two Eyes of the Earth*, 46–53, for Sassanid (and possibly Arsacid) responses to Roman official images of the rivalry.

44. For the sources, see Plut., *Luc.* 26–29; App., *Mith.* 84–85; Dio. 36. 1–3; Memnon 38. 2–4 = *FHG* IIIB, 365–366. For the campaign, see E. Eckhardt, "Die armenischen Feldzüge des Lukullus," *Klio* 9 (1909): 72–115 and 10 (1910): 192–231, and cf. A. Keaveney, *Lucullus: A Life* (London; New York, 1992), 104–110.

45. Cic., *Acad.* 2. 1. 3.

46. See A. N. Sherwin-White, *Roman Foreign Policy in the East, 168 B.C. to A.D. 1* (Norman: University of Oklahoma Press, 1984), 219–220, with review of the sources. The date is disputed as either 96 or 92 BCE The year 92 BCE is the more plausible; it is surmised that Mithridates II sent the legation because he was concerned that Sulla had restored King Ariobarzenes to the throne of Cappadocia. Tigranes II of Armenia, then a Parthian vassal, sided with Mithridates VI of Pontus against this action.

47. Plut., *Crass.* 19–33 and Dio 40. 16–30; see Sherwin-White, *Roman Foreign Policy*, 287–288, for the chronology of the campaign.

48. See ibid., 307–310, critiquing the hostile sources of Plut., *Ant.* 34–52 and Dio, 49. 23. 1–31. 4. Mark Antony invaded on the invitation of the Median king Artavasdes I, who aspired to revolt from Phraates IV. Phraata is unlocated, but it was on the strategic highway in Azerbaijan between Lake Urmiah and Hamadan (Ecbatana). It might have been near Takht-e Soleyman ("the fires of Solomon"), seat of a later Sassanid fire altar complex.

49. See Dio 40. 38–40; in 51 BCE, C. Cassius Longinus, a legate of Crassus, employed a feigned retreat to defeat a Parthian detachment near Antioch. Cassius strategically forced a Parthian withdrawal from Syria. In 38 BCE, P. Ventidius, the legate of Mark Antony, positioned his infantry on gently sloping ground at Mount Gindarus so that the Parthian cavalry charged uphill, lost cohesion, and was driven back. The Parthian prince Pacorus fell in the Parthian rout that ensued. See Dio 49. 20. 1–3; Justin 42. 4. 8–10; and Florus 2. 19. 5–6.

50. See Sherwin-White, *Roman Foreign Policy*, 322–341.

51. See Jos., *BJ* 18. 2–4. Augustus sent the sophisticated *hetaira* Thermousa, whom Phraates made his principal queen. This was tantamount to an admission of subordination to Rome. She was accorded a unique rank of honor. Their son Phraates V (Phraataces; r. 2 BCE–4 CE) struck coins featuring on the reverse the portrait of his mother, named Thea Urania Musa; see David Sellwood, *An Introduction to the Coinage of Parthia* (London, 1971), 176–178, no. 58/1–10. For portrait sculpture, see E. Strugnell, "Thea Musa, Roman Queen of Parthia," *Iranica Antiqua* 43 (2008): 275–298.

52. These were the kingdoms of Cappadocia, Commagene, Pontus, Armenia Minor; they were annexed as provinces in 17, 72, 62, and 64, respectively; see Magie, *Roman Rule in Asia Minor*, 463–467.

53. See Plut, *Ant.* 37, for King Artavasdes II of Armenia arriving with 6,000 cavalry to serve with Mark Antony in 36 BCE. The full Armenian levy was likely comparable to the 80,000 men summoned as the national levy at Harkh by the Bagatrid king Ashot III to oppose the Byzantine emperor John I Tzimisces in 976. See G. Schlumberger, *L'Épopée byzantine à la fin de dixième siècle* (Paris, 1896), 216–234.

54. See T. R. Moreman. *The Army in India and the Development of Frontier Warfare, 1849–1947* (Basingstoke, UK, 1998), 35–67, and cf. Kenneth W. Harl, "Along the Hindu Kush: Warren Hastings, the Raj, and the Northwest Frontier," *Historically Speaking* XIII, no. 4 (September 2013): 19–23.

55. See M. T. Griffin, *Nero: The End of a Dynasty* (New Haven, CT: Yale University Press, 1984), 37–41, for the role of Nero's ministers L. Annaeus Seneca and Sex. Afranius Burrus in directing policy. This perception led to the tradition of an initial five years of sound government (*quinquennium*); see Aur. Vic., *De Caess.* 5. 2–4 and *Epitome* 5. 2–3.

56. See Magie, *Roman Rule in Asia Minor*, 481–484, for Gaius Caesar putting Ariobarzanes on the Armenian throne, and 496–498, for Germanicus putting Polemo on the Armenian throne.

57. See H. M. D. Parker, *The Roman Legions* (Cambridge, 1958), 182–188. In 58, Corbulo commanded III Gallica, IV Scythica, and VI Ferrata, and a strong *vexillatio* (battle detachment) of X Fretensis, along with large numbers of auxiliaries and allied contingents. See Tac, *Ann.* XIII. 35. 6, for Corbulo as a strict republican commander and foil to the depraved Nero. See Tac., *Ann.* XIII. 34, 5, and XV. 14. 2, and 27. 1, for implied comparison of Corbulo's achievement to those of Lucullus and Pompey.

58. See Parker, *Roman Legions*, 106–115, and 145–160. The Eastern army was increased to six legions: in Cappadocia, VI Ferrata, XII Fulminata, and XVI Flavia; in Syria, III Gallica, IV Scythica; in Palestine, X Fretensis.

59. See Magie, *Roman Rule in Asia Minor*, 566–592; the annexation of the client kingdom of Commagene in 72 was part of the reorganization of the frontier. Cappadocia and Galatia were combined into a single province under a senior propraetorian legate who supervised the construction of highways and installations across central Asia Minor; see Mitchell, *Anatolia*, 118–142. For imperial military expenditures stimulating urban development and striking of civic token bronze coinage, see Kenneth W. Harl, *Civic Coins and Civic Politics of the Roman East, 180–276 A.D.* (Berkeley, 1987), 22–23.

60. Jos. *BJ*, VII. 244.

61. The chronology and movements, as argued by Lightfoot, "Trajan's Parthian War," 114–120, are to be preferred over those of Julian Bennett, *Trajan: Optimus Princeps*, 2nd ed. (Bloomington, 2001), 192–196.

62. See Dio 68. 17. 1–2, and cf. 29. 1–2, for Trajan's desire for glory and rejection of negotiation. For reorganization of the eastern *limes*, and annexation of Arabia Petraea in 106, as preparations for a Parthian War, see Bennett, *Trajan*, 177–179, and Isaac, *Limits of Empire*, 349–351.

63. SHA, *Vita Hadr.* 22 (Penguin translation, 81): "The Parthians he retained in a state of friendship, because he took away from them the king that Trajan had imposed. He allowed the Armenians to have a king, whereas under Trajan they had had a legate. He did not exact from the Mesopotamians the tribute Trajan had imposed. He kept the Albani and Hiberi on very friendly terms, because he bestowed bounties on their kings. The kings of the Bactrians [i.e. Kushan emperors] sent ambassadors to him, to request friendship."

64. See Isaac, *Limits of Empire*, 26, and Lutttwak, *Grand Strategy*, 57–61 and 73–74. Except for SHA, Latin authors criticized Hadrian for his decision to withdraw west of the Euphrates; see Bennett, *Trajan*, 203–204, with full discussion of the sources.

65. See Anthony Birley, *Hadrian: The Restless Emperor* (London, New York, 1997), 153–154, for Parthamaspates' appointment to the throne of Osrhoene. For the sources and chronology of the Parthian civil wars, see K. Schippmann, *Grundzüge der Parthenischen Geschichte* (Darmstadt, 1980), 65–67, and David Sellwood, "Parthian Coins," in *Cambridge History of Iran*, III:1, 295–297.

66. Anthony Birley, *Marcus Aurelius: A Biography* (New York, 1987), 120–121.

67. See ibid., 123–125. Three legions marched east: II Adiutrix from Aquincum, I Minervia from Bonna, and V Macedonica from Troesmis. P. Julius Geminius Marcianus, legate of X Gemina at Vindobona, was also transferred east. M. Annius Libo, consul 161 and cousin of the emperor, departed to succeed as legate of Syria.

68. SHA, *Vita Ver.* 7. 2; see Birley, *Marcus Aurelius*, 129–131, for the indolence of Lucius Verus at Antioch.

69. SHA, *Vita Marc. Aur.* 9. 1. Imperial coins of 163 style Lucius Verus Armeniacus; see *RIC* III:254–256, nos. 470–526, and 321–323, nos. 1360–1411. In 164, Marcus Aurelius assumed the title on his coinage; see *RIC* III:219–223, no. 78–133, and 281–283, nos. 861–910.

70. *RIC* III:255, nos. 509–513, and 322, nos. 1364–1376: REX ARMENIIS DATVS. Lucius Verus is depicted as investing Sohaemus with the crown of Armenia. In 164, Artaxata was leveled and a new capital was constructed, "Kaine Polis," at an unknown location; see Birley, *Marcus Aurelius*, 131.

71. See ibid., 140, and cf. Harl, *Civic Coins and Civic Politics*, 189 n. 97, for the coins styling Mannus βασιλέυς and φιλορώμαιος.

72. See SHA, *Vita Ver.*, 7.1 and 8. 1–4, for capture of the Parthian capitals. Coin hoards support a date of 165 for the sack of Seleucia; see R. N. McDowell, *Coins from Seleucia on Tigris* (Ann Arbor, 1935), 125–128.

73. See Birley, *Marcus Aurelius*, 140–141. Avidius Cassius retreated north along the Tigris late in 165 and then marched back to bases in Syria. This expedition was a model for Julian II.

74. See Tac, *Ann.* IV. 5. 1–6, who treats client kingdoms as part of the dominion of Rome; and cf. Gruen, *Hellenistic World and the Coming of Rome*, I:54–95; *contra* Luttwak, *Grand Strategy*, 20–40,who draws false distinctions between client states and provinces.

75. See J. F. Gilliam, "The Plague under Marcus Aurelius," *American Journal of Philology* 82 (1961): 225°–251. For debasement of the silver coinage, see Harl, *Coinage in the Roman Economy*, 126–128.

76. Dio 75. 3. 2; see F. Millar, *A Study of Cassius Dio* (Oxford, 1964), 138–158, for Dio's hostility to the eastern policy of Septimius Severus.

77. See Isaac, *Limits of Empire*, 255–257. The cities of Edessa and Carrhae each received colonial rank and struck civic bronze coins; see B. V. Head, *Historia Numorum: A Manual of Greek Numismatics*, 2nd ed. (London, 1911), 814–816. In 242, Gordian III restored Abgar X to the throne of Osrhoene, but Philip deposed Abgar and restored direct rule.

78. See Dio 78. 7–8, and cf. Herod. 4. 10. 1, for Caracalla's unjustified provocation of the war. For the campaign, see Magie, *Roman Rule in Asia Minor*, 684–686, and Pat Southern, *The Roman Empire from Severus to Constantine* (London, New York, 2001), 53–54, 299 n. 69. Caracalla proceeded east in a leisurely fashion so that he could visit shrines of the East; see Harl, *Civic Coins and Civic Politics*, 54–56 and 60–61, and cf. Barbara Levick, "Caracalla's Path," in *Hommages à Marcel Renard*, ed. J. Bibauw (Brussels, 1969), II:426–446.

79. See P. Salama, "L'Émpereur Macrin *Parthicus Maximus*," *Revue des Études Anciennes* 66 (1964): 140–150. For civic coins proclaiming the same victory, see Harl, *Civic Coins and Civic Politics*, 45 and 161 n. 69.

80. See Shayegan, *Arsacids and Sasanians*, 142–143, with critique of sources. There is no reason to reject the marriage proposal as a fiction invented by Herodian.

81. See Pourshariati, *Sasanian Empire*, 37–56, for critique of arguments for centralization. Many Arsacid princes were co-opted and incorporated into the Sassanid hierarchy.

82. See Duchesne-Guillemin, in *Cambridge History of Iran* III. 2:873–807, for the evolution of royal ideology. For numismatic iconography, see Andrea Gariboldi, *Sasanian Coinage and History: The Civic Numismatic Collection of Milan* (Costa Mesa, CA, 2010), 6–46, for titles and crowns depicted on coins.

83. See Kenneth W. Harl, "Roman Experience in Iraq," *Journal of History Society* VII, no. 2 (June 2007): 217–219, and cf. Isaac, *Limits of Empire*, 255–257.

84. For the co-opting of the Aramaic-speaking elites as Roman equestrians or senators, see the example at Edessa discussed by S. K. Ross, *Roman Edessa:*

Politics and Culture on the Eastern Fringes of the Roman Empire, 114–242 C.E. (London; New York, 2001), 83–117.

85. See Shayegan, *Arsacids and Sasanian*, 340–349, for the shahs adopting the Achaemenid titles and ideology. See Duchesne-Guillemin, in *Cambridge History of Iran* III. 2:866–874, for the emergence of a royal Zoroastrianism in Persis since the third century BCE.

86. Roman imperial sculpture and coins celebrated the conquest of peoples and territory. See, for example, the reliefs of subject peoples depicted on the Sebasteion; see R. R. R. Smith, "The Imperial Reliefs from the Sebasteion of Aphrodisias," *Journal of Roman Studies* 87 (1987): 88–138. For celebration of imperial victory on coins, see M. P. Charlesworth, "*Pietas* and *Victoria*: The Emperor and the Citizen," *Journal of Roman Studies* 33 (1943): 1–10, and cf. A. C. Levi, *Barbarians on Roman Imperial Coins and Sculpture*, vol. 123 of Numismatic Notes and Monographs (New York, 1952).

87. See Kennedy, *Armies of the Caliphs*, 105–107.

88. See Canepa, *Two Eyes of the Earth*, 38–52, arguing that the shahs in time adopted these territorial aims as propaganda and finally as policy as a result of contact with Rome.

89. See B. Dignas and E. Winter, *Rome and Persia in Late Antiquity: Neighbours and Rivals* (Cambridge, 2007), 63–69, for Sassanid army. See also A. D. H. Bivar, "Cavalry Equipment and Tactics on the Euphrates Frontier," *Dumbarton Oaks Papers* 26 (1976): 271–292.

90. Amm. Marcel. XX. 11. 11.

91. See M. L. Chaumont, "Conquêtes sassanides et propagande mazdéene (IIIeme siècle)," *Historia* 22 (1973): 664–709, noting that even those Persians who were strict Zoroastrian monotheists gladly plundered rich pagan shrines, including cults ultimately of Persian origin. For a comparable case of the Cossacks employed by the Polish and Hapsburg kings, see P. H. Wilson, *The Thirty Years War: Europe's Tragedy* (Cambridge, MA: Harvard University Press, 2009), 292.

92. SHA, *Trig. Tyr.* 15. 1–5 and 18. 1–3, and Zos. I. 39. 1 = Dodgeon and Lieu, *Roman Eastern Frontier*, 74–75. The long-term aim of Odenathus might have been Charax on the Persian Gulf and so access to sea-borne commerce to India; see L. de Blois, "Odenathus and the Roman-Persian War of 252–264," *Talanta* 6 (1975): 7–23.

93. *RGDS* ll. 6–9 = Dodgeon and Lieu, *Roman Eastern Frontier*, 35–36. The defeat of Gordian III is only reported by Shapur in his inscription and depicted on his victory reliefs at Bishapur. Classical sources stress the treachery of Philip; see sources in Dodgeon and Lieu, *Roman Eastern Frontier*, 35–45. For the depiction of Roman emperors on Sassanid reliefs, see B. C. MacDermont, "Roman Emperors in Sassanian Reliefs," *Journal of Roman Studies* 44 (1954): 76–80.

94. *RGDS* ll 9–10 = Dodgeon and Lieu, *Roman Eastern Frontier*, 45. Shapur claims that Philip paid tribute of 500,000 aurei, or the equivalent of 10,000 Roman pounds of gold. On his coins, Philip advertised a peace with, rather than a victory over, Persia; see *RIC* IV. 3, 76, no. 69 (PAX FVNDATA CVM PERSIS). Classical sources criticize the peace as disgraceful, but they do not elaborate on the terms; see Dodgeon and Lieu, *Roman Eastern Frontier*, 45–46, for sources. Philip, a Praetorian Prefect who had his emperor assassinated, was just as unpopular as Macrinus (r. 217–218), who had ordered the assassination of Caracalla.

95. See E. Winter, *Die Sasanidischen-römischen Friedenverträge des 3. Jahunderts n. Chr.: ein Beitrag zum Verständis der aussenpolitischen Bezeihungen zwischen den beiden Grossmächten.* (Frankfurt am Main, 1988), 45–79, for the course of the war and armistice. See H. M. D. Parker, "Legions of Diocletian and Constantine," *Journal of Roman Studies*, 23 (1933): 175–177, for Legio IV Italica, which might have been raised by Severus Alexander, but more likely by Gordian III.

96. See C. R. Whittaker, trans., *Herodian Books V–VIII* (Loeb Classical Library; Cambridge, MA: Harvard University Press, 1970), 108–109, and cf. F. Millar, *The Roman Near East, 31 B.C. to A.D. 337* (Cambridge, MA: Harvard University Press, 1993), 150.

97. Severus Alexander brought II Parthica, possibly IV Italica, the Praetorian cohorts, and legionary *vexillationes* and auxiliaries from the Danube or Rhine. In the East, the legions were XV Apollinaris and XVI Flavia in Cappadocia; I and III Parthica in Mesopotamia; IV Scythica, III Gallica, VI Ferrata, X Fretensis, and III Cyernaica in the Syrian provinces; and II Traiana in Egypt.

98. David Potter, *The Roman Empire at Bay, A.D. 180–395* (London; New York, 2004), 167, who surmises that the northern column might have planned to put a philo-Roman Arsacid prince on the throne of Adiabene; the southern column aimed to restore the king of Mesene. The objectives are admittedly speculative. The northern column operated north of the Tigris and south of the Tur Abdin, and so in the fertile lands of Gordyene (present-day Siirt).

99. See Potter, *Roman Empire at Bay*, 167 n. 119, critiquing Herodian.

100. Herod. 6.7. 1–6.; see also Winter, *Die Sasanidischen-römischen Friedenverträge*, 45–79.

101. See Pat Southern, *The Roman Empire from Severus to Constantine* (London; New York, 2001), 59–63, for the unpopularity of Severus Alexander with the army (in contrast to the popularity of Septimius Severus and Caracalla), because of his favor to the Senate and the influence of his mother Julia Mamaea.

102. See Potter, *Roman Empire at Bay*, 166–167, for mutiny of legionaries of I and III Parthica, who slew prefect Flavius Heracleo. Hence, the mint at Rome struck coins announcing FIDES MILITVM; see *BMCRE* VI, 190–191, nos. 762–763. Later literary sources speak of a usurper Uranius, but this seems

to be a confusion with Uranius Antoninus (r. 253–254); see H. R. Baldus, *Uranius Antoninus: Münzpragung und Geschichte*, 1971, 246–252, and *contra* Potter, *Empire at Bay*, 165 n. 215.

103. See Harl, *Civic Coins and Civic Politics*, 48–48, 60–61, and 173–174 n. 68.

104. Herod. 6. 7. 10 (Loeb Classical Library translation).

105. See SHA, *Vitae Max. et Balb.* 13. 5, for operations against the Carpi, and Zon. 12. 8, for proposed eastern expedition against Ardashir, but contrast Herod. 7. 8. 41.

106. In 241, Shapur destroyed Hatra (present-day al-Hadr) in punishment of the city's defiance of his father in 229 and 238; see Southern, *Roman Empire*, 235.

107. See Potter, *Roman Empire at Bay*, 229–232.

108. See ibid., 232–236, for the partisan literary tradition on Gordian III and Philip. For the sources on the expedition, see Dodgeon and Lieu, *Roman Eastern Frontier*, 34–48.

109. See Potter, *Roman Empire at Bay*, 229–230. Timesitheus died at an uncertain date in 243, after the victory at Rhesaena, during a campaign timed to avoid the heat of summer.

110. Amm. Marcel. 23. 5. 7 and Zos. I. 19. 1, for a centotaph to the emperor at Zaita, near Circesium. Zaita is nearly 250 miles (400 kilometers) north of Misiche (Persian Mizik).

111. *RGDS* ll. 6–9 = Dodgeon and Lieu, *Roman Eastern Frontier*, 35–36. Misiche (Persian Mizik) is located near present-day Fallujah, 40 miles (64 kilometers) northwest of Baghdad. Shapur thus joined battle several days' march north of Ctesiphon.

112. *RGDS* ll 9–10 = Dodgeon and Lieu, *Roman Eastern Frontier*, 45. See C. Köner, *Philippus Arabs: Ein Soldatenkaiser in der Tradition des antoninisch-severischen Prinzipats* (Berlin, 2002), 120–134, for the partisan accounts on the treaty. The price of 500,000 aurei (then struck at fifty to the Roman pound) might have been a notational sum, and the payment was rendered, in part, in base silver antoniniani (double denarii). The annual imperial military budget in 235 was 438,000,000 denarii. The sum was thus equivalent to nearly 3 percent of the military budget and perhaps just over 5 percent of the payrolls; see Harl, *Coinage in the Roman Economy*, 217–221.

113. See ibid., 129 and 133–135, for the debasement of the silver coinage.

114. See Dodgeon and Lieu, *Roman Eastern Frontier*, 47–48, and cf. discussion by Southern, *Roman Empire*, 359 n. 10, for the appointment of M. Julius Priscus, older brother of Philip, as *corrector*. Priscus's exactions drove the provincials in rebellion, declaring as their emperor M. Fulvius Rufus Jotapianus, a scion of the royal family of Commagene; see Köner, *Philippus Arabs*, 274–282. He most likely sought to win over the legions of the Upper Euphrates and northern Syria. Priscus first contained, and then crushed the rebellion.

115. See Winter, *Die Sasanidischen-römischen Friedenverträge*, 89–103; there were no territorial cessions by Philip, and the status of Armenia was not redefined.

116. *RGDS* ll. 10–19 = Dodgeon and Lieu, *Roman Eastern Frontier*, 50. Antioch, capital of Roman Syria, and Dura are listed as cities captured during Shapur's second campaign. See Amm. Marcel. 23. 5. 3 and Lib., *Or.* 24. 38, who date the capture of Antioch to early in the reign of Valerian and Gallienus, most likely in 253. See discussion by M. Rostovzeff, "*Res gestae divi Saporis* and Dura," *Berytus* 8 (1943): 23–37, and Baldus, *Uranius Antoninus*, 252–255. See *Oracula Sibyllina* 13. 11. 125–126, dating the capture to the reign of Trebonianus Gallus, either in 252 or 253. See discussion by Potter, *Roman Empire at Bay*, 248–250. Dura-Europos fell in 256 or early 257; see D. J. MacDonald, "The Dating the Fall of Dura Europos," *Historia* 35 (1986): 45–68.

117. See *RGDS* ll. 10–19 = Dodgeon and Lieu, *Roman Eastern Frontier*, 50, and see Potter, *Roman Empire at Bay*, 248–250, for discussion of sources and capture of Antioch in 253.

118. *RGDS* ll.19–37 = Dodgeon and Lieu, *Roman Eastern Frontier*, 57–58. The Antiochia and Seleucia in this list are likely Antiochia ad Cragum and Seleucia ad Calycandum, respectively. For the Classical sources, see ibid., 59–65, and see Southern, *Roman Empire*, 78–80 and 236–240.

119. See Zos. I. 36. 1–2, for Shapur treacherously seizing the emperor during negotiations. Lactantius (*De Mort. Persec.* 5) delights in reporting that Valerian was humiliated by being used as the shah's stepping stool while mounting his horse. The story is suspect, for Lactantius could well be reporting a story circulated among Christians who detested Valerian as a persecutor. For the date of Valerian's capture in the late summer of 260, see Harl, *Civic Coins and Civic Politics*, 108–109.

120. See Pat. Patr., *FHG* IV, 193, frag. 3; Syn., I, 716. Zon. 12. 23, and SHA, *Vita Val.* 4. 4 = Dodgeon and Lieu, *Roman Eastern Frontier*, 65–67. Neither Callistus nor Macrianus is called Praetorian Prefect; they were likely fiscal and logistical officers rather than field commanders. See H. Mattingly, "The Coinage of Macrianus II and Quietus," *Numismatic Chronicle* 5, no. 16 (1936): 53–61, and Harl, *Civic Coins and Civic Politics*, 159 n. 29 and 200 n. 77, for recognition of the emperors in Syria, Egypt, and several cities in Asia Minor.

121. See H. Ingholt, "Varia Tadmorea," in *Palmyre: Bilan et perspectives. Colloque de Strasbourg, 18–20 octobre 1973* (Strasbourg, 1976), 101–137, for descent of Odenathus. See Harl, *Civic Coins and Civic Politics*, 93 and 200–201 n. 83 and 86, for the rank of Odenathus. See also R. Stoneman, *Palmyra and Its Empire: Zenobia's Revolt against Rome* (Ann Arbor, 1994), 101–137.

122. SHA, *Trig Tyr.* 15. 1–5 and 18. 1. 3, and Zos. I. 39. 1 = Dodgeon and Lieu, *Roman Eastern Frontier*, 74–75. See also de Blois, *Talanta* 6 (1975): 7–23.

123. See Southern, *Roman Empire*, 240–244. These were Shapur's sons, Hormizd I (r. 272–273), Bahram I (r. 273–276), and his grandson Bahram II (r. 276–293).

124. See John Eadie, "The Transformation of the Eastern Frontier, 260–305," in *Shifting Frontiers in Late Antiquity*, ed. R. W. Mathisen and H. S. Sivan (Brookfield, VT, 1996), 72–79. For iconography on coins appealing to the army, see Alaric Watson, *Aurelian and the Third Century* (London; New York, 1999), 169–182. In 272, Aurelian raised two legions for his war against Zenobia and Vaballathus, the legions I Illyricorum and IV Martia, which were afterward stationed in Syria Phoenicia and Arabia Petraea, respectively. Probus (276–282) raised the three legions (I–III Isaurae). See Parker, "Legions of Diocletian and Constantine," 175–177.

125. See Winter, *Die Sasanidischen-römischen Friedenverträge*, 134, noting that there was no treaty between Rome and Persia between 244 and 299.

126. See Dodgeon and Lieu, *Roman Eastern Frontier*, 112–116, for sources on the expedition of Carus in 282–283. Carus succeeded to an expedition already planned by Probus (SHA, *Vita Prob.* 20. 1). See Aur. Vict., *De Caess.* 38. 2–4, and cf. Sidonius Apollinaris, *Carmina* 23. 91–96, for an initial campaign into Armenia. Carus might have marched across Mesopotamia, crossed into Adiabene, and marched down the Tigris to take Shah Bahram II by surprise, following the route of Alexander the Great in 331 BCE; see Southern, *Roman Empire*, 241–242.

127 See *ILS* 600, styling Carus *Persicus Maximus*; cf. *RIC* V. 2, 137, no. 18–26 and 145, nos. 95–98, for coins celebrating victory. For Carus = death, see SHA, *Vita Cari* 8. 3–7; Oro., *Ad Paganos* 7. 24. 4; Jordanes, *Rom.* 294 38. 6–9; Sync. I, 724; and Zon. 12. 30. 2.

128. Aur. Vict., *De Caess.* 39. 1; Aur. Vict., *Epit.* 39. 1; Eutrop. 9. 19; and Zon. 12. 30. 3. See Potter, *Roman Empire at Bay*, 294–298, and Southern, *Roman Empire*, 134–137.

129. See Dodgeon and Lieu, *Roman Eastern Frontier*, 124–131, for sources. Shah Narses likely invaded Armenia from bases in Media Atropatene and then invaded Roman Mesopotamia from the northeast via the Bitlis Pass.

130. See T. D. Barnes, *Constantine and Eusebius* (Cambridge, MA: Harvard University Press, 1981), 17, and Potter, *Empire at Bay*, 292–293. Diocletian was putting down the rebellion of L. Domitius Domitinaus in Egypt (294–297); Maximianus was campaigning in Mauretania; Constantius I Chlorus had just recovered Britain from the usurper Allectus (293–296).

131. Barnes, *Constantine and Eusebius*, 18; he argues that the harem was captured at Ctesiphon, but the sources locate the capture in Armenia.

132. See Dodgeon and Lieu, *Roman Eastern Frontier*, 131–134, for sources on treaty in 299. See analysis by Winter, *Die Sasanidischen-römischen Friedenverträge*, 169–170, who dates the treaty to 298.

133. See Cornelius C. Vermeule, *Roman Imperial Art in Greece and Asia Minor* (Cambridge, MA: Harvard University Press, 1968), 336–350, and M. S.

P. Rothman, "The Thematic Organization of the Panel Reliefs of the Arch of Galerius," *American Journal of Archaeology* 81 (1977): 19–40.

134. See Parker, "Legions of Diocletian and Constantine," 175–177; these were the legions IV Italica, VI Hispana, I Illyricorum, IV Martia, I, II, and III Isaura, I and II Armeniaca, and II Brittannica.

135. See Parker, "Legions of Diocletian and Constantine," 180–186. Diocletian added the legions I Iovia, I Martia, I Maximiana, I Noricorum, I Pontica, II Flavia Constantia, II Herculia, III Diocletiana, III Herculia, IV Parthica, V Iovia, V Parthica, VI Herculia, and VI Parthia. Constantius I Chlorus (r. 305–306) raised three legions deployed against the Romano-British emperor Allectus in 296: I Flavia Gallicana Constantia, I Flavia Martis, and XII Victrix; all units attested on the *Notitia Digntatum*. Three other legions might have been raised during the Tetrarchy. The legions I and II Armenica, which garrisoned the upper Euphrates in the fourth century, might have antedated the reign of Diocletian, or perhaps they were raised with the reorganization of the eastern frontier after the victory of Galerius over Shah Narses. The legion II Brittannica, attested on the *Notitia Dignitatum*, might have been raised by the Romano-British emperor Carausius (r. 287–293).

136. For the eastern frontier, see Eadie, in *Shifting Frontiers*, 72–79, and cf. survey of sites in David Kennedy and Derrick Riley, *Rome's Desert Frontier from the Air* (Austin, 1990). For the size of the imperial army under Diocletian, see R. MacMullen, "How Big Was the Roman Imperial Army?" *Klio* 62 (1980): 451–460. For military costs, see Harl, *Coinage in the Roman Economy*, 217 and 223; the soldiers were paid in silver clad fiduciary coins (*nummi*).

137. Zos. II. 34. 1–2, for the creation of field armies. The structure of command is surmised from the *Notitia Dignitatum* listing military units in the early fifth century.

138. See A. H. M. Jones, *The Later Roman Empire, 284–602* (Norman, 1964), 607–686; *contra* Luttwak, *Grand Strategy*, 127–190, whose view on a defense in depth is based on the premise of field armies operating as a mobile reserve for a defensive frontier. Yet, neither literary nor documentary sources articulate or assume such a defensive strategy.

139. See Southern, *Roman Empire*, 246–278, and Potter, *Empire at Bay*, 333–337.

140. See R. N. Frye, "The Political History of Iran under the Sasanians," in *Cambridge History of Iran* III. 1:136–137, who campaigned early in his reign to secure Himyar on the southwestern Arabian shore.

141. See John Mathews, *The Roman Empire of Ammianus* (Ithaca, NY, 1989), 135–136. The philosopher Metrodorus incited Constantine to war because Sassanid officials had confiscated gifts for the emperor; see Cedrenus I, 516–517 (Bonn edition). A version of the story was known to Ammianus Marcellinus. The story shifted the blame of the eastern war from Julian to Constantine.

142. See Amm. Marcel. XIV. 12; Aur. Vic. 41. 20; and Zos. I. 39. 2. Narses was defeated at Nasara.

143. See Potter, *Roman Empire at Bay*, 467–483, and, for sources, Dodgeon and Lieu, *Roman Eastern Frontier*, 164–230.

144. See Harl, *Journal of Historical Society* VII, no. 2 (June 2007): 219–220, and *contra* Lendon, *Soldiers and Ghosts*, 290–300, and P. Athanassadi-Fowden, *Julian and Hellenism: An Intellectual Biography* (Oxford, 1981), 192–194, arguing that Julian based his strategy and movements on the campaigns of Alexander the Great. They mistake inspiration for strategic imitation. Julian followed the route of Cyrus the Younger in 401 BCE rather than that of Alexander the Great in 331 BCE.

145. See Amm. Marcel. XXIII. 3. 1; Julian departed Carrhae on March 21 or 22, 363. For strategic surprise, see R. T. Ridley, "Julian's Persian Expedition," *Historia* 22 (1973): 317–330, and W. E. Kaegi Jr., "Constantius's and Julian's Strategies of Strategic Surprise against the Persians," *Athenaeum* N.S. 59 (1981): 209–213.

146. See Matthews, *Roman Empire of Ammianus*, 158–159.

147. See A Ferrill, *Fall of the Roman Empire: The Military Explanation* (London, 1986), 54–56, for Julian's deficiencies as commander, but contrast. Kagan, *Eye of Command*, 53–54.

148. See Matthews, *Roman Empire of Ammianus*, 156, especially on the trials at Constantinople in 362.

149. For the sources on the treaty of 363, see G. Greatrex and S. N. C. Lieu, *The Roman Eastern Frontier and the Persian Wars Part II: A.D. 363–630* (London; New York, 2002), 1–9.

150. See R. C. Blockley, "The Division of Armenia between Romans and Persians at the End of the Fourth Century A.D.," *Historia* 36: 222–234; the date still uncertain. See sources in Greatrex and Lieu, *Roman Eastern Frontier*, 28–30.

151. See N. Lenski, *Failure of Empire*, 307–319 and 355–368, for the losses sustained by the Eastern field army in 363 and 378, and 167–185, for the weak Roman position in Armenia in 378. See Ferrill, *Fall of Roman Empire*, 64–68, for low morale so that emperors avoided decisive battle in the fifth and early sixth centuries.

152. See Frye, *Cambridge History of Iran* III. 1:146–148. Hephthalites (called either Hoa-tun or Yanda in Chinese sources) were a Tocharian-speaking people who settled along the upper Jaxartes (Syr Darya) by the opening of the fifth century. Procopius describes them as Caucasoids (*Bell. Pers.* 1. 3. 2–4) so they likely assimilated many early Tocharian and Sogdian speakers. The Huns spoke an Altaic, likely Turkic, language; they too assimilated many tribes of eastern Iranian or Germanic origin. Romans and Persians had previously faced no serious threat from nomads; Rome and Persia enrolled Sarmatians and Choniates, respectively, as allies.

153. See Otto J. Maenchen-Helfen, *The World of the Huns: Studies in Their History and Culture*, ed. Max Knight (Berkeley, 1973), 1–17 and 297–386, for origins of Huns.

154. See Peter Heather, "The Huns and the End of the Roman Empire in the West," *English Historical Review* 110 (1995): 1–41.

155. See Josh. Styl., *Chron.* 18 = Greatrex and Lieu, *Roman Eastern Frontier*, 60. See R. C . Blockley, *East Roman Foreign Policy: Formation and Conduct from Diocletian to Anastasius* (Leeds, 1992), 83.

156. See Denis Sinor, "The Establishment and Dissolution of the Türk Empire," in *The Cambridge History of Early Inner Asia*, ed. Denis Sinor (Cambridge: Cambridge University Press, 1990), 285–305.

157. Proc., *Bell. Pers.* I. 2. 1–10, and cf. Agathias, *Hist.* IV. 26. 3–7; see Blockley, *East Roman Foreign Policy*, 51–52.

158. Proc., *Bell. Pers.* I. 11. 1–25.

159. See R. C. Blockley, "Subsidies and Diplomacy: Rome and Persia in Late Antiquity," *Phoenix* 39 (1985): 62–74, with analysis of the sources.

160. See Canepa, *Two Eyes of the Earth*, 154–223.

161. See Blockley, *East Roman Foreign Policy*, 87–96, and, for sources, Greatrex and Lieu, *Roman Eastern Frontier*, 62–82. Only the Persians claimed the payments as a subsidy to defend the Dariel and Derbent passes.

162. See D. Braund, *Georgia in Antiquity* (Oxford, 1994), 268–314.

163. See Blockley, *East Roman Foreign Policy*, 61.

164. See Isaac, *Limits of Empire*, 235–249.

165. See Blockley, *East Roman Foreign Policy*, 87–96, and, for sources, Greatrex and Lieu, *Roman Eastern Frontier*, 62–82.

166. See Greatrex and Lieu, *Roman Eastern Frontier*, 82–101, for sources of Persian War of 526–532. See also J. A. S. Evans, *The Age of Justinian: The Circumstances of Imperial Power* (London; New York: 1996), 114–119.

167. See Josh. Styl., *Chron.* 90 and Zach., *HE* 7. 6 = Greatrex and Lieu, *Roman Eastern Frontier*, 74–76, for building of Daras by Anastasius. See Proc., *De Aedificiis* II. 1. 14–21, for the strengthening by Justinian. See also B. Croke and J. Crow, "Procopius and Dara," *Journal of Roman Studies* 73 (1983): 143–159. Daras was less than 11 miles (18 kilometers) from Nisibis, less than a day's march.

168. Proc., *Bell. Pers.* I. 26. 3.

169. See Greatrex and Lieu, *Roman Eastern Frontier*, 104–106, for sources on the sack of Antioch. The name of the city built by Khusrau I translates: "Better than Antioch has Khusrau built this city." It was popularly known as Rumagan, "city of the Rhoumaioi (Romans)," later Arabic Rumiyya.

170. See Michael F. Hendy, *Studies in the Byzantine Monetary Economy, c. 300–1450* (Cambridge, 1985), 260–261. Reported sums of plunder taken by Khusrau total 1,730 pounds of gold.

171. See Proc., *Bell Pers.* I. 2. 6–10 and Agathias, *Hist.*, IV. 26. 4–7.

172. See Greatrex and Lieu, *Roman Eastern Frontier*, 82–102 and 123–125, for sources on the treaties between Justinian and Khusrau I. For analysis of the payments, see Harl, *Coinage in the Roman Economy*, 311–312. The total

payment over fifty years would have been 1.5 million solidi, or 20,833²/₃ pounds of gold.

173. See Michael Whitby, *The Emperor Maurice and Historian: Theophylact Simocatta on Persian and Balkan Warfare* (Oxford, 1988) 250–276, and, for sources, Greatrex and Lieu, *Roman Eastern Frontier*, 135–166.

174. See Whitby, *The Emperor Maurice*, 297–310. The Roman contingent was commanded by John Mystacon and Narses; a strong Armenian cavalry detachment served under Prince Muael II Mamikonian. For the appeal of Khusrau II to "two eyes of the earth," see Theo. Sim. 4. 11. 2–.3 = M. and M. Whitby, trans., *The History of Theophylact Simocatta* (Oxford, 1986), 117–118.

175. For treaty, see Theo. Sim. 5. 15. 2 = Greatrex and Lieu, *Roman Eastern Frontier*, 174–175.

176. See Kaegi, *Heraclius*, 37–49, for the usurpation of Phocas. The sources are hostile to Phocas; see the judicious reassessment by David M. Olster, *Phocas: The Politics of Usurpation in the Seventh Century: Rhetoric and Revolution in Byzantium* (Amsterdam, 1993).

177. See Canepa, *Two Eyes of the Earth*, 127, for Khusrau avenging his patron Maurice Tiberius. Later legend in Syriac sources alleged that Khusrau had married a daughter of Maurice Tiberius to legitimize his claim to the Roman Empire. For territorial aspirations of Khusrau II, see Pourshariati, *Sasanian Empire*, 140–142, and Kaegi, *Heraclius*, 49–57.

178. See Kaegi, *Heraclius*, 58–151, for the narrative of events in 610–626; for sources, see Greatrex and Lieu, *Roman Eastern Frontier*, 182–202. See also Clive Foss, "The Persians in Asia Minor and the End of Antiquity," *English Historical Review* 90 (1975): 721–743, for the Persian policy of devastation of Asia Minor (in contrast to the occupation and administration of Syria and Egypt). For compromise of Sassanid power by the emergence of powerful princely generals in the war, see Pourshariati, *Sasanian Empire*, 142–160.

179. See Kaegi, *Heraclius*, 131–147, citing sources on the siege. See also Averil Cameron, "The Theotokos in Sixth Century Byzantium," *Journal of Theological Studies* N.S. 29 (1978): 78–108, for the veneration of the Hodegetria.

180. See Kaegi, *Heraclius*, 156–191, for Heraclius's offensives in 626–628. For sources, see Greatrex and Lieu, *Roman Eastern Frontier*, 205–228.

Chapter 4

1. After almost a century of use, as represented in books such as Carl Stephenson, *Mediaeval Feudalism* (Ithaca, NY: Great Seal Books, 1942), and F. L. Ganshof, *Qu'est-ce que la féodalité* (Brussels: Lebègue, 1944; and trans. Philip Grierson, London: Longman Greens, 1952), the term first became questioned by E. A. R. Brown, "The Tyranny of a Construct: Feudalism and Historians of Medieval Europe," *American*

Historical Review 79 (1974): 1063–1088, and more extensively by
Susan Reynolds, *Fiefs and Vassals: The Medieval Evidence Reinterpreted*
(Oxford: Oxford University Press, 1994).

2. W. C. Sellar and R. J. Yeatman, *1066 and All That: A Memorable History of England, comprising all the parts you can remember, including 103 Good Things, 5 Bad Kings and 2 Genuine Dates* (London: Methuen, 1930).

3. Stephen Morillo, "Hastings: An Unusual Battle," *Haskins Society Journal* 2 (1990): 96–103.

4. Michael E. Jones, *The End of Roman Britain* (Ithaca, NY: Cornell University Press, 1996), covers the whole period well, but see P. J. Casey, *Carausius and Allectus: The British Usurpers* (London: Routledge, 2005) for Carausius's revolt.

5. For a discussion of all these invasions, including the Romans', see Kelly DeVries, "The Sea as a Defense for the British Isles from 55 BCE to 1066 CE," in *L'acqua nell alto medioevo LV Settimana* (Spoleto: Centro Italiano di Studi sull' Alto Medievo, 2008), I:319–356.

6. Frank M. Stenton's volume, *Anglo-Saxon England*, vol. 2, *Oxford History of England*, 3rd ed. (Oxford: Clarendon Press, 1971), is still the best study of the period, especially for the political history, but Robin Fleming's *Britain after Rome: The Fall and Rise, 400 to 1070* (London: Penguin, 2011), is the most recent. Correlative histories of France for the period include Edward James, *The Origins of France: From Clovis to the Capetians, 500–1000* (London: Macmillan, 1982) and, chronologically later, Elizabeth M. Hallam and Judith Everard, *Capetian France, 987–1328*, 2nd ed. (Harlow: Longman, 2001).

7. The seminal biography of William the Conqueror remains David C. Douglas, *William the Conqueror* (Berkeley and Los Angeles: University of California Press, 1964), despite others that have appeared since then. On Philip I, see Hallam and Everard.

8. See Warren Hollister, *Henry I* (New Haven, CT: Yale University Press, 2003) and Robert Bartlett, *England under the Norman and Angevin Kings, 1075–1225* (Oxford: Clarendon Press, 2000).

9. Jim Bradbury, *Stephen and Mathilda: The Civil War of 1139–53* (Stroud: Alan Sutton, 1996).

10. W. L. Warren, *Henry II* (New Haven, CT: Yale University Press, 2000), and John Hosler, *Henry II: A Medieval Soldier at War, 1147–1189* (Leiden: Brill, 2007). The best biography on Philip Augustus, in any language, is John W. Baldwin, *The Government of Philip Augustus: Foundations of French Royal Power in the Middle Ages* (Berkeley and Los Angeles: University of California Press, 1986).

11. Most English historians see Richard as the great warrior-king and a great general, although it is difficult to agree when the results seem so contrary. The best biography of the Lionheart is John Gillingham, *Richard I* (New

Haven, CT: Yale University Press, 1999), but see also his collected essays *Richard Coeur de Lion: Kingship, Chivalry and War in the Twelfth Century* (London: The Hambledon Press, 1994), which contains his seminal "Richard I and the Science of War in the Middle Ages," first published in 1984. For Philip, see Baldwin *The Government of Philip Augustus*.

12. For Philip, again see Baldwin *The Government of Philip Augustus*. The best biography of John remains W. L. Warren, *King John* (Berkeley and Los Angeles: University of California Press, 1961). The very important battle of Bouvines is discussed at length, but I think quite poorly, by Georges Duby, *The Legend of Bouvines: War, Religion and Culture in the Middle Ages*, trans. Catherine Tihanyi (Berkeley and Los Angeles: University of California Press, 1990).

13. Neither a single authoritative biography of Henry III nor a study of the Treaty of Paris has been written. Saint Louis is equally lacking in a biography that discusses his dealings with England—although that may indicate the relative unimportance of England to France, especially with the ease at getting Henry to acquiesce to his wishes. Otherwise, Jacques Le Goff's *Saint Louis*, trans. Gareth Evan Gollrad (Notre Dame, IN: Notre Dame University Press, 2009) will do.

14. The standard biography is that of Michael Prestwich, *Edward I* (London: Guild Publishing, 1988). The wars of Edward against the Scots and Welsh have overshadowed his dealings with the French in works such as Prestwich's *War, Politics and Finance under Edward I* (London: Faber and Faber, 1972), although it is apparent from Bryce and Mary Lyon, eds., *The Wardrobe Book of 1296–1297: A Financial and Logistical Record of Edward I's 1297 Autumn Campaign in Flanders against Philip IV of France* (Brussels: Palais des Académies/Paleis der Academiën, 2004), that his plans for attacking France were significant.

15. Seymour Phillips, *Edward II: The Chameleon* (New Haven, CT: Yale University Press, 2000).

16. The best single-volume history of the Hundred Years War continues to be Edouard Perroy, *The Hundred Years War*, trans. W. B. Wells (New York: Oxford University Press, 1951), although eventually it will be replaced by Jonathan Sumption's volumes of *The Hundred Years War*, which now number three and have covered the war to the end of the fourteenth century (*Trial by Battle; Trial by Fire; Divided Houses* [Philadelphia: University of Pennsylvania Press, 1991, 1999, 2009]). The first two of these cover the period from 1337 to 1360. On Edward III's pre-Brétigny campaigns, see Clifford J. Rogers, *War Cruel and Sharp: English Strategy under Edward III, 1327–1360* (Woodbridge: The Boydell Press, 2000).

17. Sumption, vol. 3. On the Bishop of Norwich's campaign, see Kelly DeVries, "The Reasons for the Bishop of Norwich's Attack on Flanders in 1383," *Fourteenth Century England* 3 (2004): 155–165; and on the Nicopolis Crusade, see Aziz Suryal Atiya, *The Crusade of Nicopolis* (London: Methuen, 1934).

18. On Henry V's campaigns, see Richard Ager Newhall, *The English Conquest of Normandy, 1416–1424: A Study in Fifteenth Century Warfare* (New Haven, CT: Yale University Press, 1924) and E. F. Jacob, *Henry V and the Invasion of France* (London: Hodder and Stoughton, 1947), which despite their ages have yet to be surpassed. And, on Joan of Arc, Kelly DeVries, *Joan of Arc: A Military Leader* (Stroud: Sutton Publishing, 1999).

19. The end of the Hundred Years War has been poorly represented by modern historians. For the moment, the best work is Juliet Barker, *Conquest: The English Kingdom of France, 1417–1450* (London: Little, Brown, 2009).

20. Kelly DeVries, *The Norwegian Invasion of England in 1066* (Woodbridge: The Boydell Press, 1999).

21. Philippe Contamine, *War in the Middle Ages*, trans. Michael Jones (Oxford: Basil Blackwell, 1984), 49–50. Philip was no friend to either, having defeated Robert's father at the battle of Cassel in 1071 and having supported Henry's brother, Robert, in their fight over Normandy.

22. David Bates, *William the Conqueror* (Stroud: Tempus, 2001), 79–81.

23. John Gillingham, "The Meetings of the Kings of France and England, 1066–1204," in *Normandy and Its Neighbours, 900–1250: Essays for David Bates*, ed. David Crouch and Kathleen Thompson (Turnhout: Brepols, 2012), 19.

24. Frank Barlow, *The Feudal Kingdom of England, 1042–1216*, 5th ed. (Harlow: Pearson Education, 1999), 168.

25. Warren, *Henry II*, 42. Although Henry is thought to have done homage to Louis VII in 1156 and in 1169, John Gillingham has shown that this was not the case: John Gillingham, "Doing Homage to the King of France," in *Henry II: New Interpretations*, ed. Chistopher Harper-Bill and Nicholas Vincent (Woodbrige: Boydell, 2007), 63–84.

26. Gillingham, "The Meetings of the Kings of France and England," 31–32.

27. Prestwich, *Edward I*, 321–323.

28. Craig Taylor, "The Salic Law and the Valois Succession to the French Crown," *French History* 15 (2001): 358–377.

29. An analysis and text of the treaty can be found in Eugène Cosneau, ed., *Les grandes traités de la guerre de cent ans* (Paris: Alphone Picard, 1889), 33–68.

30. Gillingham, *Richard I*, 269–320, and Warren, *King John*, 51–99, 217–224.

31. Gillingham, *Richard I*, 52–100.

32. Donald J. Kagay and L. Andrew Villalon, *The Battle of Nájera* (Leiden: Brill, forthcoming).

33. David Green, *Edward the Black Prince: Power in Medieval Europe* (Harlow: Pearson Longman, 2007).

34. Eleanor C. Lodge, *Gascony under English Rule* (London: Methuen, 1926), and M. G. A. Vale, *English Gascony, 1399–1453: A Study of War, Government and Politics during the Later Stages of the Hundred Years' War* (Oxford: Oxford University Press, 1970).

35. R. R. Davies, *Domination and Conquest: The Experience of Ireland, Scotland and Wales, 1100–1300* (Cambridge: Cambridge University Press, 1990), and John Sadler, *Border Fury: England and Scotland at War, 1296–1568* (Harlow, UK: Pearson Education, 2006).

36. Elizabeth Bonner, "Scotland's 'Auld Alliance' with France, 1295–1560," *History* 84 (1999): 5–30.

37. The articles collected in David Rollason and Michael Prestwich, eds., *The Battle of Neville's Cross, 1346* (Stamford: Shaun Tyas, 1998), are for the most part excellent. But see also Kelly DeVries, *Infantry Warfare in the Early Fourteenth Century: Discipline, Tactics, and Technology* (Woodbridge: The Boydell Press, 1996), 176–187.

38. A. A. M. Duncan, "Honi soit qui mal y pense: David II and Edward III, 1346–52," *Scottish Historical Review* 67 (1988): 113–141.

39. Anthony Goodman and Anthony Tuck, eds., *War and Border Societies in the Middle Ages* (London: Taylor and Francis, 1992).

40. Annie I. Dunlop, *Scots Abroad in the Fifteenth Century* (London: The Historical Association, 1942).

41. Davies, *Domination and Conquest*.

42. Kelly DeVries, "Owain Glyndŵr's Way of War," in *Owain Glyndŵr: A Case Book*, ed. Michael Livingston and John Bollard (Exeter: University of Exeter Press, 2013), 435–450. The standard biography for Owain Glyn Dŵr remains R. R. Davies, *The Revolt of Owain Glyn Dŵr* (Oxford: Oxford University Press, 1995), but Livingston and Bollard's casebook includes all the original sources—in the original languages and translations—and accompanying articles should facilitate more study.

43. The tablets edited and translated so far can be accessed on the website *Vindolanda Tablets Online*: http://vindolanda.csad.ox.ac.uk/.

44. Barri Jones and David J. Mattingly, *An Atlas of Roman Britain*, 2nd ed. (Oxford: Oxbow, 2007).

45. *Domesday Book: A Complete Translation* (London: Penguin Books, 2002).

46. Eileen Power's *The Wool Trade in English Medieval History* (Oxford: Oxford University Press, 1941) remains the single best study on this.

47. Ibid., 15–25.

48. Steven A. Epstein, *Wage and Labor Guilds in Medieval Europe* (Chapel Hill: University of North Carolina Press, 1991).

49. David Nicholas, *The Metamorphosis of a Medieval City: Ghent in the Age of the Arteveldes, 1302–1390* (Lincoln: University of Nebraska Press, 1987).

50. Henry Stephen Lucas, *The Low Countries and the Hundred Years' War, 1326–1347* (Ann Arbor: University of Michigan Press, 1929), and Kelly DeVries, "Contemporary Views of Edward III's Failure at the Siege of Tournai, 1340," *Nottingham Medieval Studies* 39 (1995): 70–105.

51. Kelly DeVries, "The Rebellions of the Southern Low Countries' Towns during the Fourteenth and Fifteenth Centuries," in *Power and the City in*

the *Netherlandic World*, ed. Wayne te Brake and Wim Kibler (Leiden: Brill, 2006), 27–44.

52. Wim Blockmans and Walter Prevenier, *The Promised Lands: The Low Countries Under Burgundian Rule, 1369–1530*, ed. Edward Peters, trans. Elizabeth Fackelman (Philadelphia: University of Pennsylvania Press, 1999).

53. Power, *The Wool Trade*, 43–45. The initial tax was 7s. 6d. per sack. The increased tax was 40s.

54. Ibid., 49–54.

55. Critics of Edward's post-Crécy moves include Alfred H. Burne, *The Crecy War: A Military History of the Hundred Years War from 1337 to the Peace of Bretigny, 1360* (London: Eyre and Spottiswoode, 1955), 204–207. On the battle of Crécy, see Michael Livingston and Kelly DeVries, eds., *The Battle of Crécy: A Casebook* (Liverpool: Liverpool University Press, 2016).

56. Kelly DeVries, "Hunger, Flemish Participation and the Flight of Philip VI: Contemporary Accounts of the Siege of Calais, 1346–47," *Studies in Medieval and Renaissance History* n.s 12 (1991): 129–181.

57. The quote comes from Henri Pirenne's *Economic and Social History of Medieval Europe*, trans. I. E. Clegg (New York: Harcourt Brace Jovanovich, 1936), 153.

58. Vale, *English Gascony*, 13–15, and E. M. Carus-Wilson, "The Effects of the Acquisition and of the Loss of Gascony on the English Wine Trade," *Historical Research* 21 (1947): 145–154.

59. Kelly DeVries, "The Sea as a Defense for the British Isles from 55 BCE to 1066 CE," in *L'acqua nell alto medioevo LV Settimana* (Spoleto: Centro Italiano di Studi sull' Alto Medioevo, 2008), I:319–356.

60. Ian Friel, *The Good Ship: Ships, Shipbuilding and Technology in England, 1200–1520* (Baltimore, MD: Johns Hopkins University Press, 1995) and N. A. M. Rodger, *The Safeguard of the Sea: A Naval History of Britain, 660–1649* (New York: W. W. Norton, 1997).

61. Jim Bradbury, *The Battle of Hastings* (Stroud: Sutton Publishing, 1998). The story of the papal *vexillum* is only recorded ca. 1140 by Orderic Vitalis and is not accepted by all historians.

62. On England's role in all of the Crusades, see Christopher Tyerman, *England and the Crusades, 1095–1588* (Chicago: University of Chicago Press, 1988).

63. Frank Barlow, *Thomas Becket* (Berkeley and Los Angeles: University of California Press, 1986).

64. Niccolò Capponi, "The Italian Interest in the Battle of Crécy," in *The Battle of Crécy: A Casebook*, ed. Michael Livingston and Kelly DeVries (Liverpool: University of Liverpool Press, 2016).

65. Kelly DeVries and Niccolò Capponi, "The Genoese Crossbowmen," in *The Battle of Crécy: A Casebook*, ed. Michael Livingston and Kelly DeVries (Liverpool: University of Liverpool Press, 2016).

66. More historical work needs to be done on French piracy during the Middle Ages, especially considering the amount of activity that took place during

the relatively peaceful period of 1280–1330, as found by Thomas K. Heebøl-Holm in *Ports, Piracy and Maritime War: Piracy in the English Channel and the Atlantic, c.1280–c. 1330* (Leiden: Brill, 2013).

67. On the French civil war, see Bertrand Schnerb, *Les Armagnacs et les Bourguignons: La maudite guerre* (Paris: Libraire Académique Perrin, 1988).

68. Margaret L. Kekewich, *The Good King: René of Anjou and Fifteenth Century Europe* (London: Palgrave Macmillan, 2008).

Chapter 5

1. Frederic C. Lane, *Venice: A Maritime Republic* (Baltimore, MD: 1973), 18–19.

2. Steven A. Epstein, *Genoa and the Genoese, 958–1528* (Chapel Hill, 1996), 138, 213–214.

3. Lane, *Venice*, 45, 49, 76–77, 122–134, 197.

4. Michel Balard, *Les Latins en Orient, XIᵉ–XVᵉ siècle* (Paris, 2006), 341.

5. The fundamental authorities on the Venetian and Genoese colonies are still Freddy Thiriet, *La Romanie Vénitienne au Moyen Age: Le développement et l'exploitation du domaine colonial vénitien (XIIᵉ-XVᵉ siècles)*, vol. 183, Bibliothèque des Écoles Françaises d'Athènes et de Rome (Paris, 1959), and Michel Balard, *La Romanie Génoise (XIIᵉ–début du XVᵉ siècle)*, 2 vols., bk 235, Bibliothèque des Écoles Françaises d'Athènes et de Rome (Paris, 1978); also published as *Atti della Società Ligure di Storia Patria*, Nuova Serie, 18, fasc. 1–2.

6. Epstein, *Genoa*, 325–326.

7. David Jacoby, "Mercanti genovesi e veneziani e le loro merci nel Levante crociate," in *Genova, Venezia, il Levante nei secoli XII–XIV*, ed. Gherardo Ortalli and Dino Puncuh (Genoa, 2001) (*Atti della Società Ligure di Storia Patria*, Nuova Serie, 41, fasc. 1), 223–224.

8. Geo Pistarino, "Miraggio di Terrasanta," in Geo Pistarino, *Genovesi d'Oriente* (Genova, 1990), 28.

9. Epstein, *Genoa*, 31–32.

10. Lane, *Venice*, 32; Balard, *Les Latins*, 129–130.

11. Hans Eberhard Mayer, *The Crusades*, 2nd ed. (Oxford, 1990), 75–76.

12. Balard, *Les Latins*, 131–134.

13. Gerald W. Day, *Genoa's Response to Byzantium 1155–1204: Commercial Expansion and Factionalism in a Medieval City* (Urbana; Chicago, 1988), 18–19.

14. Balard, *Les Latins*, 143–134.

15. Thiriet, *La Romanie Vénitienne*, 40–41.

16. Ibid., 41–42.

17. Day, *Genoa's Response to Byzantium*, 23.

18. Epstein, *Genoa*, 72–73.

19. Day, *Genoa's Response to Byzantium*, 24–25.

20. Epstein, *Genoa*, 78–79, 82–83; Balard, *La Romanie Génoise*, I, 25.

21. Ibid., I:28–29.

22. Ibid., I:30.

23. Thiriet, *La Romanie Vénitienne*, 51–52.

24. Ibid., 55.

25. Day, *Genoa's Response to Byzantium*, 30–31.

26. Ibid., 32.

27. Ibid., 31.

28. Ibid., 33, 35, 62–63.

29. Lane, *Venice*, 42.

30. Ibid., 43; Thiriet, *La Romanie Vénitienne*, 64, 96–97.

31. Lane, *Venice*, 43.

32. Thiriet, *La Romanie Vénitienne*, 78–91.

33. Ibid., 75–76.

34. Ibid., 87–88; Epstein, *Genoa*, 103–104.

35. Balard, *La Romanie Génoise*, I:39.

36. Ibid., 40–42; Epstein, *Genoa*, 97–98, 109–110.

37. Pistarino, "Miraggio di Terrasanta," 47–50.

38. Philip Argenti, *The Occupation of Chios by the Genoese and Their Administration of the Island 1346–1566*, 2 vols. (Cambridge, 1958), I: 9–10; Epstein, *Genoa*, 146; Lane, *Venice*, 73, 75.

39. Argenti, *The Occupation of Chios*, I:21–25.

40. Lane, *Venice*, 76–77; but for Settepozzi, see Balard, *La Romanie Génoise*, 47–48; Sandra Origone, *Bisanzio e Genova* (Genoa, 1992), 128.

41. Thiriet, *La Romanie Vénitienne*, 150.

42. Ibid., 149–150; Balard, *Les Latins*, 235.

43. Thiriet, *La Romanie Vénitienne*, 151–152; Origone, *Bisanzio e Genova*, 132.

44. Balard, *La Romanie Génoise*, I:47–55; Origone, *Bisanzio e Genova*, 128–133.

45. Marie Nystazopoulou Pélékdis, "Venise et la Mer Noire du XIᵉ au XVᵉ siècle," in *Venezia e il Levante fino al secolo XV*, ed. Agostino Pertusi, 3 vols. (Florence, 1973), I:ii, 553.

46. Balard, *La Romanie Génoise*, I:114–118.

47. Ibid., 58.

48. Pélékdis, "Venise et la Mer Noire," 563.

49. Silvia Schein, "From 'Milites Christi' to 'Mali Christiani': The Italian Communes in Western Historical Literature," in *I Comuni italiani nel Regno Crociato di Gerusalemme*, ed. Gabriella Airaldi and Benjamin Z. Kedar (Genoa, 1986), 679–689.

50. Balard, *Les Latins*, 264–266.

51. Alum was an important mineral, used in dying cloth and treating leather, among other things.

52. Lane, *Venice*, 83–84; Balard, *La Romanie Génoise*, I:58–61; Epstein, *Genoa*, 182–183.

53. Thiriet, *La Romanie Vénitienne*, 154–155.

54. Ibid., 179–209. See also: Geo Pistarino, "Politica ed economia del Mediterraneo nell'età della Meloria," in *Genova, Pisa e il Mediterraneo tra Due e Trecento. Per il VII centario della Battaglia della Meloria*, Atti della Società Ligure di Storia Patria, Nuova Serie, 24, fasc. 2 (Genoa, 1984), 23–50; Michel Balard, "Génois et Pisans en Orient (fin du XIIIe - début du XIVe siècle) Balard, Michel. (1989) (fin du XIIIe–début du XIVe siècle)."

55. Balard, *La Romanie Génoise*, 67.

56. Ibid.; Epstein, *Genoa*, 198.

57. Origone, *Bisanzio e Genova*, 130–139; Balard, *La Romanie Génoise*, I:61–68.

58. Argenti, *The Occupation of Chios*, I:60–65, 100.

59. Pélékdis, "Venise et la Mer Noire."

60. Thiriet, *La Romanie Vénitienne*, 160–162.

61. Serghej Karpov, "Venezia e Genova: rivalità e collaborazione a Trebisonda e Tana, secoli XIII-XV," in *Genova, Venezia, il Levante*, ed. Ortalli and Puncuh, 263.

62. Lane, *Venice*, 175.

63. Karpov, "Venezia e Genova," 258.

64. Giovanna Petti Balbi, *Simon Boccanegra e la Genova del '300* (Genoa, 1991), 346.

65. Karpov, "Venezia e Genova," 270–272; Balard, *La Romanie Génoise*, I:75–76; Lane, *Genoa*, 175.

66. Giorgio T. Dennis, "Problemi storici concernenti i rapporti tra Venezia, i suoi domini diretti e le signorie feudali nelle isole greche," in *Venezia e il Levante*, ed. Pertusi, I:i, 224–232.

67. Thiriet, *La Romanie Vénitienne*, 161–165.

68. Argenti, *The Occupation of Chios*, I:91–95.

69. Thiriet, *La Romanie Vénitienne*, 167.

70. Balard, *La Romanie Génoise*, I:78–79.

71. Geo Pistarino, "Dal declino sul mare di Levante tra cristiani ed islamici alla conquista del Mar Nero," in Pistarino, *Genovesi d'Oriente*, 127.

72. Karpov, "Venezia e Genova," 260.

73. Lane, *Venice*, 175–176.

74. Balard, *La Romanie Génoise*, I:61; Thiriet, *La Romanie Vénitienne*, 170–171; Lane, *Venice*, 176.

75. Ibid., 178–179; Epstein, *Genoa*, 220–221.

76. Lane, *Venice*, 179; Epstein, *Genoa*, 221.

77. Balard, *La Romanie Génoise*, I:150–162, 455–461.

78. Ibid., *La Romanie Génoise*, 143–150; Serban Papacostea, "Un tournant de la politique génoise en Mer Noire au XIVe siècle: l'ouverture des routes continentales en direction de l'Europe Centrale', in *Oriente e Occidente tra Medioevo ed Età moderna. Studi in onore di Geo Pistarino*, ed. Laura Balletto, 2 vols. (Genoa, 1997), II:939–947.

79. Peter Edbury, "Cyprus and Genoa: The Origins of the War of 1373–1374," in Peter Edbury, *Kingdoms of the Crusaders: From Jerusalem to Cyprus* (Aldershot,

UK: 1999), article XIV; "The Aftermath of Defeat: Lusignan Cyprus and the Genoese, 1374–1382," in Edbury, article XV; Jean Richard, "Chypre du protectorat à la domination vénitienne," in *Venezia e il Levante*, ed. Pertusi, I:ii, 658–663; Michel Balard, "La lotta contro Genova," in *Storia di Venezia, dalle origini alla caduta della Serenissima*, ed. Girolamo Arnaldi, Giorgio Cracco; and Alberto Tenenti, III, *La formazione dello stato patrizio* (Rome, 1997), 114.

80. Thiriet, *La Romanie Vénitienne*, 171, 173, 176–177.
81. Epstein, *Genoa*, 237–238; Francesco Surdich, *Genova e Venezia fra Tre e Quattrocento* (Genoa, 1970), 26–37.
82. Edbury, "The Aftermath of Defeat," 3.
83. Ibid.," 8.
84. Lane, *Venice*, 191–196; Epstein, *Genoa*, 238–241; Balard, *La Romanie Génoise*, I:91; Thiriet, *La Romanie Vénitienne*, 178.
85. Surdich, *Genova e Venezia*, 49–141. The Venetian fleet sent against Genoa in 1431, which defeated the Genoese off Portofino, was sent because Genoa was at that time under the lordship of Filippo Maria Visconti, duke of Milan, with whom Venice was at war, not because of any escalation in the fighting.
86. Thiriet, *La Romanie Vénitienne*, 381–383.

Chapter 6

1. Jane Burbank and Frederick Cooper, *Empires in World History: Power and the Politics of Difference* (Princeton, NJ: Princeton University Press, 2010), 2–3, 12–15.
2. Slogan based on *Iliad*, Book 5: 428–30, and Ovid, *Heroides*, 13:84; attributed to Matthias Corvinus, king of Hungary, on hearing of the marriage of Maximilian of Austria with Mary of Burgundy in 1477.
3. V. Saletta, *Il viaggio di Carlo V in Italia* (Rome, 1981), 322–323.
4. Oberösterreichisches Landesarchiv, Linz (Austria), *Khevenhüller Briefbücher* 4/311–12, Hans Khevenhüller to Rudolf II, July 13, 1588.
5. Instituto de Valencia de Don Juan, Madrid [hereafter IVdeDJ] 82/444, duke of Sessa to don Baltasar de Zúñiga, September 28, 1600; Archives Générales du Royaume/Algemeen Rijksarchief, Brussels, *Secrétairerie d'État et de Guerre* [hereafter, AGRB *SEG*] 183/170v–171, Zúñiga to Juan de Ciriza, April 7, 1619, copy; J. H. Elliott, *The Count-Duke of Olivares: The Statesman in an Age of Decline* (New Haven, CT: Yale University Press, 1986), 236, count-duke of Olivares to count of Gondomar, July 3, 1625.
6. Peter Marshall first identified and described "sub-imperialism" in his studies of British India in the eighteenth century. He noted the propensity of British merchants and administrators in Bombay, Madras, and Calcutta to do exactly what they wanted, regardless of the orders received from London. The same may be observed in all large early modern European empires.
7. F. Bronner, "La Unión de Armas en el Perú. Aspectos político-legales," *Anuario de estudios americanos* 24 (1967): 1133–1171, quotations on pp. 1138

and 1141 n. 31, Viceroy Chinchón to a councilor of Castile, March 14, 1628, and to Philip IV, May 18, 1629.

8. J. H. Elliott, *The Revolt of the Catalans: A Study in the Decline of Spain* (Cambridge: Cambridge University Press, 1963), 374–375, Olivares to Santa Coloma, viceroy of Catalonia, October 7, 1639.

9. P. S. Allen, *Opus epistolarum Des. Erasmi* (Oxford, 1906), 9:254, Erasmus to Bernard Boerio, 11 April 11, 1531.

10. R. Brown, ed., *Calendar of State Papers and Manuscripts Relating to English Affairs Existing in the Archives and Collections of Venice*, 38 vols. (London, 1864–1947), 3: 86, Antonio Giustinian's report to the Senate after his French embassy, September 7, 1520.

11. Duchess of Berwick and Alba, *Documentos escogidos del Archivo de la Casa de Alba* (Madrid, 1891), 284–286, Philip to Cardinal Granvelle, July 10, 1581, holograph; J. I. Tellechea Idígoras, *Felipe II y el Papado*, 2 vols. (Madrid, 2004–2006), 2:112, Philip II to Pope Gregory XIII, August 10, 1580, holograph.

12. J. Guillén Tato, *Museo Naval: Colección de documentos y manuscritos inéditos compilados por Fernández de Navarrete* (Nendeln, 1971), 18/146–160, "Relación"; Bishop Ribeiro Gaio quoted, along with other similar contemporaneous proposals, in C. R. Boxer, "Portuguese and Spanish Projects for the Conquest of Southeast Asia, 1580–1600," in Boxer, *Portuguese Conquest and Commerce in Southern Asia, 1500–1750* (London, 1985), chap. 3; P. E. H. Hair, *To Defend your Empire and the Faith: Advice Offered to Philip, King of Spain and Portugal, c. 1590* (Liverpool, 1990), the project of Manoel de Andrada Castel Blanco.

13. F. Braudel, *La Méditerranée et le monde méditerranéen à l'époque de Philippe II* (Paris, 1949), 320–321, (the opening of a section entitled "Les empires du XVIe siècle et l'espace"). Braudel once told me [the author] that he preferred "Distance: Public Enemy Number 1" as the translation of "L'espace: ennemi numéro 1" (*La Méditerranée*, 2 vols. (Paris, 1967), 1:326) to that of the English edition: "Distance, the First Enemy": F. Braudel, *The Mediterranean and the Mediterranean World in the Age of Philip II*, 2 vols. (London, 1972–1973), 1:355.

14. Biblioteca del Real Monasterio de San Lorenzo de El Escorial, Spain, *Ms* I. III. 30/122v, "Raggionamento" of Philip II for his son; E. Poullet and C. Piot, eds., *Correspondance du Cardinal de Granvelle 1565–1586* [hereafter *CCG*], 12 vols. (Brussels, 1877–1896), 4:558, Granvelle to Morillon, May 11, 1573, quoting with approval Don Pedro de Toledo, viceroy of Naples 1532–1553. Braudel, *The Mediterranean*, 1: 372–4; and G. Parker, *The Grand Strategy of Philip II* (New Haven, CT: Yale University Press, 1998), chap 2, provide copious examples.

15. Braudel, *The Mediterranean*, 1:372; Universiteitsbibliotheek, Leiden, Manuscript Department [hereafter UB], *Hs Pap* 3/3 Alonso de Laloo to

Count Hornes, August 31, 1566; Parker, *Grand Strategy*, 49, quoting Leonardo Donà; L. Firpo, ed., *Relazioni di ambasciatori veneti al Senato, tratte dalle migliori edizioni disponibili e ordinate cronologicamente,* 14 vols. (Turin, 1965–1996), 8:670, Final Relation of Donà, January 1574.

16. Lauren Benton, *A Search for Sovereignty: Law and Geography in European Empires 1400–1900* (Cambridge: Cambridge University Press, 2010), 2.

17. See J. C. Devos, "La poste au service des diplomates espagnols accrédités auprès des cours d'Angleterre et de France (1555–1598)," *Bulletin de la commission royale d'histoire* 103 (1938): 205–267; and C. Alcázar Molina, "La política postal española en el siglo XVI en tiempo de Carlos V,' in *Carlos V (1500–1558): Homenaje de la Universidad de Granada* (Granada, 1958), 219–232 (the contract of 1516 is discussed at pp. 227–229).

18. See duke of Berwick and Alba, *Epistolario del III duque de Alba*, 3 vols. (Madrid, 1952), 1:647–649 and 654, Alba to Margaret of Parma, June 16 and July 10, 1567, for the "Spanish Road" courier chain; and *Epistolario*, 3:121–123, Alba to Philip II, May 24, 1572, for the decision to send duplicates.

19. British Library, *Additional Ms* [hereafter BL *Addl.*] 28,264/26–27, Philip to Emanuel Philibert, August 9, 1557, holograph postscript; *Colección de documentos inéditos para la historia de España* [hereafter *CODOIN*], 112 vols. (Madrid, 1842–1895), 98:483, Philip to the count of Luna, August 8, 1563; *CODOIN*, 35:61, Philip to Alba, August 2, 1580, holograph postscript; Archivo General de Simancas [hereafter AGS] *Estado K* 1448/197, Philip to Don Bernardino de Mendoza, July 28, 1588.

20. Brunetti and E. Vitale, ed., *La corrispondenza da Madrid dell' ambasciatore Leonardo Donà (1570–1573),* ed. M., 2 vols. (Venice-Rome, 1963), 2:493, letter to Venice of June 18, 1572; G. Ugolini, "Le comunicazioni postali spagnole nell'Italia del XVI secolo," *Ricerche storiche* 23 (1993): 283–373, at p. 321.

21. B. Watts, "Friction in Future War," in *Brassey's Mershon American Defense Annual 1996–7,* ed. A. R. Millett and W. A. Murray (Washington, DC: Brassey's, 1996), 58–94, at p. 91; B. Jablonsky, *The Owl of Minerva Flies at Twilight: Doctrinal Change and Continuity in the Revolution in Military Affairs* (Carlisle, PA: Strategic Studies Institute, 1994), 33–36.

22. AGS *Estado K* 1490/50, Philip II to Emmanuel Philibert of Savoy, July 26, 1557, holograph; Archivo de la Casa de los Duques de Alba, Madrid, 5/69, Philip II to Alba, August 7, 1567, holograph.

23. J. Calvar Gross, J. I. González-Aller Hierro, M. de Dueñas Fontán, and M. del C. Mérida Valverde, eds., *La batalla del Mar Océano* [hereafter *BMO*], 3 vols. (Madrid, 1988–1993), 3:1274 and 1225, Philip II to the marquis of Santa Cruz, October 10 and 21, 1587, italics added.

24. *CCG*, 11:272, Granvelle to Margaret of Parma, September 21, 1584; Biblioteca Casanatense, Rome, *Ms* 2417/39, Juan de Silva to Esteban de Ibarra, August 13, 1589.

25. A. Bustamante García, "La arquitectura de Felipe II," in *Felipe II y el arte de su tiempo* (Madrid: Fundación Argentaria, 1998), 491–512 at p. 492.

26. R. McNamara with B. VanDeMark, *In Retrospect* (New York: Times Books, 1995), xvii.

27. Hispanic Society of America, New York, [hereafter HSA] *Altamira* 1/I/4, Vázquez to Philip II, and reply, undated but 1578.

28. C. Douais, *Dépêches de M. de Fourquevaux, ambassadeur du roi Charles IX en Espagne, 1565–72*, 3 vols. (Paris, 1896–1904) 1:191, Fourquevaux to Charles IX, March 15, 1567; UB Leiden *Hs Pap* 3/2 Alonso de Laloo to Count Hornes, Segovia August 3, 1566; BL *Egerton Ms.* 1820/340, Arthur Hopton to Secretary of State Coke, April 6, 1634, NS; P. M. Kennedy, *The Rise and Fall of the Great Powers* (New York: Random House, 1987), 515.

29. *CODOIN*, 75:190–1, Alba to Secretary of State Gabriel de Zayas, February 12, 1573; C. Álvarez-Nogal and C. Chamley, "Debt Policy under Constraints: Philip II, the Cortes, and Genoese Bankers," *Economic History Review* 67 (2014): 192–213, at p. 192.

30. *Actas de las Cortes de Castilla*, 17 vols. (Madrid, 1861–1891), 16:166–167, Juan Vázquez de Salazar to Philip II, April 28, 1593; ibid., 12:456, procurator of Seville, May 19, 1593; and ibid., 16:170, procurator of Burgos, summarized by Juan Vázquez de Salazar, May 6, 1593.

31. IVdeDJ 51/1, Vázquez to Philip II, and rescript, February 8, 1591.

32. BL *Addl.* 28,378/69–73v, 75–76 and 128–131, marquis of Poza to don Cristóbal de Moura, and rescript, June 9 and 13 and July 28/31, 1596; M. Drelichman and H.-J. Voth, *Lending to the Borrower from Hell: Debt, Taxes and Default in the Reign of Philip II* (Princeton, NJ: Princeton University Press, 2014).

33. BL *Addl.* 28,378/41–8v, rescript of Moura to Poza, May 15, 1596.

34. J. S. Brewer, J. Gairdner, and R. H. Brodie, eds., *Letters and Papers, Foreign and Domestic, of the Reign of Henry VIII*, 21 vols. (London, 1872–1920), 4:937–938, Dr. Edward Lee to Henry VIII, April 15, 1526; K. M. Setton, *The Papacy and the Levant, 1204–1571*, 4 vols. (Philadelphia: American Philosphical Society, 1984), 3:242, Doge and Senate to the Venetian ambassador in Rome, June 21, 1526.

35. AGS *Estado* 98/274–5, Memorial of Francisco Duarte, sent to Philip II, undated but completed before June 1553, when Duarte left the Netherlands.

36. HSA *Altamira* 18/IV/3c, Fray Diego de Yepes to Philip II, July 1, 1597; and 12/I/1, # 13, Yepes to Moura, May 27, 1598.

37. M. J. Rodríguez Salgado, " 'Ni cerrando ni abriendo la puerta.' Las negociaciones de paz entre Felipe II y Isabel I, 1594–98," in *Hacer historia desde Simancas. Homenaje a José Luis Rodríguez de Diego*, ed. A. Marcos Martín (Valladolid, 2011), 633–660, pp. 645 and 656, Philip II to Archduke Albert, Governor-General of the Spanish Netherlands, July 29, 1596 and April 13, 1598.

38. H. Kamen, *Spain in the Later Seventeenth Century 1665–1700* (London: Longman, 1980), 57.

39. Biblioteca de Zabálburu, Madrid [hereafter BZ] 144/61, Vázquez to Philip II, and reply, May 31, 1575, italics added.

40. J. C. Galende Díaz and M. Salamanca López, *Epistolario de la Emperatriz María de Austria. Textos inéditos de la Casa de Alba* (Madrid, 2004), 238–241, Empress María to Philip II, February 13, 1572.

41. *CCG*, I, 314–318, Granvelle to Philip II, May 19, 1566; AGS *Estado* 2843/7, consulta of the Council of State, September 5, 1577, opinions of the duke of Alba and Cardinal Quiroga.

42. AGS *Estado* 1297/42, count of Fuentes to Philip III, November 5, 1608.

43. Archivo Histórico Nacional, Madrid [hereafter AHN] *Estado libro* 714, unfol., *consulta* of the Council of State, October 19, 1629; Bibliothèque Royale/Koninklijke Bibliotheek, Brussels, *Ms.* 16147–16148/139–140, marquis of Aytona to the count-duke of Olivares, December 29, 1633; AGRB *SEG* 332/75, count of Oñate to the Cardinal-Infante, August 8, 1634.

44. B. Kervijn de Lettenhove, *Relations politiques des Pays-Bas et de l'Angleterre sous le règne de Philippe II*, 11 vols. (Brussels, 1882–1900), 7:397, Thomas Wilson to Francis Walsingham, December 27, 1574.

45. P. Levi, *The Drowned and the Saved* (New York: Summit, 1989), 48.

46. AHN *Inquisición Libro* 284/107 (old fos 96–97), Quiroga to Philip II and rescript, April 21, 1578; BL *Addl.* 28,262/558–559, Antonio Pérez to Philip II, and rescript, undated but October 1578.

47. BZ 145/76, Mateo Vázquez to Philip II, and rescript, November 10, 1588; AGS *Estado* 2851, unfol., "Lo que se platicó en el Consejo de Estado a 12 de noviembre 1588," and consulta of November 26, 1588, with holograph royal rescript.

48. *BMO*, 1:62–64, Philip II to Alba, September 14, 1571; AGS *Estado* 165/2–3, Philip II to Archduke Albert, viceroy of Portugal, September 14, 1587 (message for Santa Cruz), italics added.

49. IVdeDJ 53/3/56 and 144/36, Vázquez to Philip II and reply, May 13 and December 11, 1574.

50. Elliott, *Count Duke*, 378–379, Olivares questions on June 17, 1629 and Philip's replies, italics added.

51. M. Fernández Álvarez, *Corpus documental Carlos V*, 5 vols. (Salamanca, 1974–1981), 2:104, Philip IV to don Gabriel Trejo Paniagua, 1629; C. Seco Serrano, *Cartas de Sor María de Jesús de Ágreda*, 2 vols. (Madrid, 1958), 2:42 and 48, Philip IV to Sor María, January 11 and March 19, 1656.

52. G. Canestrini and A. Desjardins, *Négociations diplomatiques de la France avec la Toscane* (Paris, 1872), 4:737, Filippo Cavriana to the Tuscan government, Paris, November 22, 1587.

53. Firpo *Relazioni,* 10:198, Relation of Pietro Bassadonna, May 26, 1653, beginning "Correva l'anno 1647 ..."

54. G. Álvarez, F. C. Ceballos, and C. Quinteiro, "The Role of Inbreeding in the Extinction of a European Royal Dynasty," *PLoS ONE* 4(4): e5174, doi:10.1371/journal.pone.0005174, provide further detail, and explain how they calculated each coefficient.

55. J. I. Tellechea Idígoras, *El Papado y Felipe II. Colección de Breves Pontificios,* 3 vols. (Madrid, 1999–2002), 1:199–202, Pius V to Philip II, December 20, 1568, holograph.

56. AGRB *SEG* 195/64, Philip IV to Infanta Isabella, his regent in the Netherlands, August 9, 1626. See G. Parker, *Global Crisis: War, Climate Change and Catastrophe in the Seventeenth Century* (New Haven; London: Yale University Press, 2013), chap. 9, for details of the synergy between climate change, war, and rebellion in the monarchy of Philip IV.

57. Seco Serrano, *Cartas,* 1:28, Philip IV to Sor María, July 20, 1645, holograph.

58. A. Leman, *Richelieu et Olivarès: leurs négociations secretes de 1636 à 1642* (Lille, 1932), charts the numerous peace offers by the two statesmen—each one [peace offer] abandoned as soon as they gained the upper hand.

59. J. H. Elliott and J. F. de la Peña, *Memoriales y cartas del conde-duque de Olivares,* 2 vols. (Madrid, 1978–1981), 2:279, Olivares to Antonio Carnero, August 8, 1644; T. Monkhouse, *State Papers Collected by Edward, Earl of Clarendon,* 3 vols. (Oxford, 1767–1786), 3:16, Sir Edward Hyde to Secretary of State Nicholas, Madrid, April 14, 1650 NS; J. Alcalá-Zamora y Queipo de Llano, "Razón de Estado y geoestrategia en la política italiana de Carlos II: Florencia y los presidios, 1677–81," *Boletín de la Real Academia de la Historia* 173 (1976): 297–358, at p. 341, quoting the marques of Los Vélez, viceroy of Naples, to Charles II, November 11, 1678.

Chapter 7

1. Gabriel Piterberg introduces the idea of the Ottoman state as a "discursively contested field." The same rationale can be applied to western actors, notably the Habsburgs. See Gabriel Piterberg, *An Ottoman Tragedy: History and Historiography at Play* (Berkeley: University of California Press, 2003), 163–183.

2. For example, considering the conflicts on the frontier in Eastern Europe and Southern Europe in terms of opposed faiths minimizes—or hides—the attempts at compromise that also existed. See Cemal Kafadar, *Between Two Worlds: The Construction of the Ottoman State* (Berkeley: University of California Press, 1995), and Robert Bartlett and Angus MacKay, eds., *Medieval Frontier Societies* (Oxford: Clarendon Press, 1989).

3. This view was perhaps first expressed in the *Arthasastra* (The Art of Politics) of Kautilya, a work of the third century BCE, not dissimilar to Sun Tzu's earlier *Art of War.* However, Kautilya made a fundamental observation that applies readily to the situation of both Suleiman and Charles V. He wrote,

"A state with immediately proximate territory is the natural enemy...
. Encircling him on all sides, with territory immediately next to his is
the constituent called the enemy. In the same manner, one with territory
separated by one (other territory) is the constituent called the ally." See Roger
Boesche, "Kautilya's Arthasastra on War and Diplomacy in Ancient India,"
The Journal of Military History 67(1) (January 2003): 9–37, see pp. 18–20.

4. Geoffrey Parker, *The Grand Strategy of Philip II* (New Haven, CT: Yale
University Press, 1998), 78–80.

5. Charles V would eventually be the heir to his mother, Juana, who was the
immediate heir to the Spanish crowns, as daughter of Ferdinand of Aragón
and Isabella of Castile. The arrangement was that they should be joint
monarchs, but Charles quickly marginalized his severely disturbed mother.

6. Sultan Selim I died in 1520. He had campaigned with great success on the
eastern and southern Ottoman frontier, latterly against the Mamluk rulers
of Egypt. He had massively enlarged the Ottoman domain—almost tripled
it in size. He established the Ottoman presence in the Arabian Peninsula
and became the *Servant of the Holy Cities of Mecca and Medina*; he proclaimed
himself Caliph. Thereafter he took the titles *King of the Two Lands (Europe
and Asia), of the Two Oceans (The Mediterranean and the Indian Ocean), Conqueror
of the Two Armies (European and Safavid), and Servant of the Two Holy Shrines
(Mecca and Medina)*. These were extravagant claims of status, but the *Servant
of the Two Shrines* had specific duties in respect to the Haj and of increasing
the domain of Islam. He had bequeathed these imperial ambitions to his
son, Suleiman I. Emperor Maximilian I could not construct the same kind of
territorial power as Selim, being limited to his Austrian patrimony and his
Burgundian lands, by right of his wife. The preoccupation of all dynasties
was the future succession to the management of the family patrimony and,
hopefully, its increase. Many families died out through infant mortality, and
the politics of marriage making was an art at which Maximilian excelled;
it was the basis of his own success, and he used it to bring power by
inheritance.

7. Yona Pinson, "Imperial Ideology in the Triumphal Entry into Lille of Charles
V and the Crown Prince (1549)," *Assaph: Studies in Art History* 6: 212.

8. His great-grandfather Mehmed II, who had taken Constantinople in 1453,
established his position as *sultan I rum* after the conquest.

9. Gülru Necipoglu, "Süleyman the Magnificent and the Representation of
Power in the context of Ottoman-Hapsburg-Papal Rivalry," *The Art Bulletin*
71, no. 3 (1989): 401–427.

10. This appears in the later account of Osman Agha de Temechvar, *Prisonnier des
Infideles: un soldat ottoman dans l'Empire des Habsbourg* (Paris: Sindbad, 1998).

11. The primary tax on Christians and Jews was the *jizya*. Non-Muslims were
deemed to belong to their own community (*millet*), whose leaders dealt with
the state authorities on behalf of the community.

12. See Maria Goloubeva, *The Glorification of Emperor Leopold I in Image, Spectacle and Text* (Mainz: Von Zabern, 2000), 12–41.

13. Leslie P. Peirce, *The Imperial Harem: Women and Sovereignty in the Ottoman Empire* (New York: Oxford University Press, 1993).

14. Gábor Ágoston, "Information, Ideology, and Limits of Imperial Policy: Ottoman Grand Strategy in the Context of Ottoman-Habsburg Rivalry," in *The Early Modern Ottomans: Remapping the Empire*, ed. Virginia H. Aksan and Daniel Goffman (Cambridge; New York: Cambridge University Press, 2007), 75–103.

15. The Crusades in the east—Nicopolis in 1396 and Varna 1444—did not have Habsburg participation.

16. For the Ottomans as operating a "fiscal-military state," see K. Karaman and S. Pamuk, "Ottoman State Finances in European Perspective, 1500–1914," *The Journal of Economic History* 70, no. 3 (September 2010): 593–629.

17. See James D. Tracy, *Emperor Charles V, Impresario of War* (Cambridge: Cambridge University Press, 2002), 22. He is citing Wim Blockmans, "The Emperor's Subjects," in *Charles V, 1500–1558, and His Time*, ed. Hugo Soly (Antwerp: Mercatorfonds, 1999), 199, 234.

18. See Rhoads Murphey, *Ottoman Warfare 1500–1700* (London: UCL Press, 1999), Chap. 3, on military manpower and military spending, 35–64.

19. One traditional model was the attack on Styria and the town of Graz by raiders in 1480 and 1481.

20. Hakan T. Karateke, "On the Tranquillity and Repose of the Sultan: The Construction of a Topos," in *The Ottoman World*, ed. Christine Woodhead (London: Routledge, 2012), 116–129.

21. Gabor Ágoston, *Guns for the Sultan: Military Power and the Weapons Industry in the Ottoman Empire* (Cambridge: Cambridge University Press, 2005), 135–138.

22. Gabor Ágoston, "Habsburgs and Ottomans: Defence, Military Change, and Shifts of Power," *Turkish Studies Association Bulletin* 22, no. 1 (Spring 1998): 126–141.

23. Michael Hochedlinger, *Austria's Wars of Emergence: 1683–1797* (Harlow: Pearson Education, 2003), 84–92.

24. Ferenc Szakály, "Nándorfeáhérvár [Belgrade], 1521: The End of the Medieval Hungarian Kingdom," in *Hungarian-Ottoman Military and Diplomatic Relations in the Age of Suleyman the Magnificent*, ed. Géza David and Pál Fodor (Budapest: Hungarian Academy of Sciences, Institute of History, 1994), 68–69.

25. The exact status of the princes of Transylvania was in dispute. The Habsburgs asserted their suzerain rights, as did the Ottoman sultan. The sultan formally approved both Bethlen and Rákóczi.

26. Günhan Böreçki, "A Contribution to the Military Revolution Debate: The Janissaries Use of Volley-Fire during the Long Ottoman-Habsburg War

of 1593–1606 and the Problem of Origins," *Acta Orientalia Academiae Scientarium Hungaricae* 59, no. 4 (2006): 407–438.

27. On the Köprülü family policy of waging wars of territorial expansion as a panacea for the empire's internal problems, see Brian Davies, *Warfare, State and Society on the Black Sea Steppe, 1500–1700* (London: Routledge, 2007), 156–167. In 1681, the conclusion of the war with Russia with the Treaty of Bakhchisarai required the Ottomans and the Tatars to maintain peace on the Ukrainian front for a period of twenty years.

28. Fazil Ahmet Köprulu bore the title of *gazi* as a mark of honor, meaning "victorious." Even as late as the republican Turkey, Ataturk was accorded the title of *gazi* in 1921. Linda Darling remarks sensibly that "[i]t was however, only one thread in the complex identity of the Ottomans. Although the Ottomans forged new identities over time, forgetting the old, the process of forgetting and remaking did not obliterate those older identities but absorbed them, creating a more complex and ambiguous whole." See Linda T. Darling, "Reformulating the *Gazi* Narrative: When Was the Ottoman State a *Gazi* State?" *Turcica* 43 (2011): 13–53 see p. 51.

29. Andrew Wheatcroft, *The Enemy at the Gate: Habsburgs, Ottomans and the Battle for Europe* (London: The Bodley Head, 2008), 164–168.

30. Kenneth M. Setton, *Western Hostility to Islam and Prophecies of Turkish Doom* (Philadelphia: American Philosophical Society, 1992).

31. Charles Ingrao and Yasir Ilmaz, "Ottoman vs. Habsburg: Motives and Priorities," in *Empires and Peninsulas: Southeastern Europe between Karlowitz and the Peace of Adrianople 1699–1826*, ed. Plamen Mitev (Berlin: Lit Verlag, 2010), 5–17.

32. Caroline Finkel, *Osman's Dream: The Story of the Ottoman Empire 1300–1923* (London: John Murray, 2005), 289, citing Silahdar Tar'rihi.

33. The liberation of Vienna (1683); the capture of Buda (1686) and the second battle of Mohacs (1687) by Charles of Lorraine; the capture of Belgrade (1688) by Max Emmanuel of Bavaria; Louis of Baden, "Türkenlouis", and the battle of Slankamen (1691); and, finally, Prince Eugene of Savoy dealing the final blow at the battle of Zenta (1697).

34. On the reasons for Ottoman vitality, see Karen Barkey, *Empire of Difference: The Ottomans in Comparative Perspective* (Cambridge: Cambridge University Press, 2008).

35. On Tverda, see the UNESCO World Heritage proposal, http://whc.unesco. org/pg.cfm?cid=326&l=fr&id=161&&action=doc; on Brod, see the local site http://www.tzgsb.hr/pg008.htm; for Petrovaradin, a history at http://www. veljkomilkovic.com/OtvrdjaviEng.htm.

36. See Hochedlinger, *Austria's Wars*, 308–309. The reasonable enough explanation he gives is that the sultan "might enter [a] war on the Prussian side."

37. For example, Act 3, Scene 8:

> My tongue is almost paralysed Through not being able to order their reward:
> First you'll be beheaded, Then you'll be hanged, Then impaled On red hot
> spikes, Then burned, Then manacled And drowned; Finally flayed alive.

38. The Austrians annexed Bosnia-Herzogovina in 1908, fearing that in the
Balkan Wars an enemy like Serbia might overrun and annex this "Ottoman"
territory.

Chapter 8

1. Stalled militarily outside the capital and unable to mobilize more support
within France, Henri is supposed to have commented on his pragmatic
acceptance of Catholicism, "Paris is worth a mass."
2. Supposedly a vast conspiracy to assassinate King Charles II, subvert
Parliament, and return England to Catholic rule, the plot was actually
a hoax, concocted by Titus Oates. See John Kenyon, *The Popish Plot*
(New York: St. Martin's Press, 1972).
3. By this measure, Louis XIV revoked the Edict of Nantes, officially expelled
France's Protestant population, and effectually imposed Catholicism as the
state religion.
4. The fundamentals of the carrying trade involved (1) the importation of raw
materials and their re-export as manufactured goods, or (2) the import and
re-export of raw materials *or* finished goods on behalf of second and third
parties. In either case, reshipment benefited not only the port that received
and re-exported the various products, but also the country (and the specific
company) whose ships carried that commerce.
5. See P. Coronelli, *Partie Occidentale du Canada ou de la Nouvelle France* (map,
Paris, 1688).
6. For English fears of Dutch claims to "universal monarchy" through trade
(and the later mapping of this fear onto French trade and military-territorial
expansion), see Steven C. A. Pincus, *Protestantism and Patriotism: Ideologies
and the Making of English Foreign Policy, 1650–1668* (Cambridge: Cambridge
University Press, 1996).
7. Edward Vallance, *The Glorious Revolution: 1688–Britain's Fight for Liberty*
(New York: Pegasus, 2007); Steven C. A. Pincus, *1688: The First Modern
Revolution* (New Haven, CT: Yale University Press, 2011).
8. Also known as the War of the Grand Alliance or the War of the League of
Augsburg.
9. Starting in 1686, the League of Augsburg featured the Dutch, Austria, and
the Elector Palatine, opposing French expansion along the Rhine. It became
the Grand Alliance with the accession of William's British dominions in
1689. For a fuller record of Louis XIV's political and territorial ambitions,

and his many military campaigns, see John A. Lynn, *The Wars of Louis XIV, 1667–1714* (Harlow, UK: Pearson, 1999).

10. La Salle's first expedition on the Mississippi River occurred in 1673. After navigating the full length of the river in 1682, he claimed the entire watershed for France. Colonization began in earnest around the turn of the eighteenth century.

11. A comparison of relative naval strengths might have suggested Dutch command and a Dutch majority in the fleet at Beachy Head, but this was not the case. Dutch naval strategy in general tended not to rely on large numbers of heavy warships, and the Anglo-Dutch alliance as it emerged in 1688–1691 called for English precedence, both in number of ships and in command.

12. For a well-argued thesis on state finance and national economies of scale as foundations for a modern navy, see Jonathan Dull, *The Age of the Ship of the Line: The British and French Navies, 1650–1815* (Lincoln: University of Nebraska Press, 2009). For its relationship to U.S. naval policy, see *Dull's American Naval History, 1607–1865: Overcoming the Colonial Legacy* (Lincoln: University of Nebraska Press, 2012).

13. Peter Silver, *Our Savage Neighbors: How Indian War Transformed Early America* (New York: W. W. Norton, 2008). See also Richard White, *The Middle Ground: Indians, Empires and Republics in the Great Lakes Region, 1650–1815* (Cambridge: Cambridge University Press, 1991); Daniel Richter, *Facing East from Indian Country* (Cambridge, MA: Harvard University Press, 2001).

14. See Alan Gallay, *The Indian Slave Trade: The Rise of the English Empire in the American South, 1670–1717* (New Haven, CT: Yale University Press, 2003).

15. The Act of Union of 1707 formally joined England and Scotland, creating the United Kingdom of Great Britain. Though England remained the main political unit, its people, domains, and empire are best described as *British*.

16. The Quebec expedition involved some 6,000 sailors and 7,500 troops, most of the latter being colonials building on their success in Nova Scotia. Navigation problems at the mouth of the St. Lawrence ultimately doomed the campaign, but it was nonetheless the largest deployment of the Royal Navy to North America up to that time.

17. Named for *Jacobus*, the Latin form of James, Jacobites represented the Catholic male-line succession from Brtain's James II, including his son, James Edward Francis Stuart (1688–1766) and grandson, Charles Edward Stuart (1720–1788). Jacobitism was relatively widespread across the British Isles, for reasons varying from Irish Catholic and Scottish dynastic sympathies to opposition politics in England. Jacobite leaders often found support and homes in exile in France and Spain, and were often identified in pro-Hanoverian circles with Catholic Absolutist tendencies.

18. See David Chandler, *Marlborough as Military Commander* (Stroud, UK: Scribner, 1973, reprinted 1997, 2003); J. R. Jones, *Marlborough* (Cambridge: Cambridge University Press, 1993).

19. After the War of the Quadruple Alliance (1718–1720), the Duchy of Savoy exchanged Sicily to Austria in part for elevation to royal dignity. Rulers in Turin thereafter, until the Italian War of Independence in 1859, were known by the title of *king of Sardinia*.

20. Known as the *Assiento*, Spanish concessions were supposed to open the Spanish Main for thirty years to slaves transported on British ships, and 500 tons (effectively one ship) per year of other trade goods. Unregulated British trade, however, soon allowed for a much larger set of smuggling operations. Article XV of the Anglo-French agreement at Utrecht, meanwhile, placed the Six Nations Iroquois and their notional dependents under notional British protection—"notional" in both cases because this was only the British understanding of a vaguely worded provision. The French throughout the colonial period seem with some consistency to have regarded Native peoples as independent nations.

21. The Mississippi Company was originally formed in 1684, after La Salle's expeditions, and renamed the *Compagnie d'Occident* in 1717. Now under John Law's direction, it absorbed rival trading interests in France by 1719 to become the *Compagnie Perpetuelle des Indes*, with a monopoly on France's oceanic trade.

22. Newfoundland itself passed to British control by the Treaty of Utrecht in 1713, but both France and Spain continued to claim the surrounding waters and portions of sheltered islands for drying cod. Transatlantic voyages for fishing around the Grand Banks proved helpful as a means of training sailors for the French navy, but the trade in cod—much more than Canada's furs— was also valuable as a source of income for the French government.

23. Jon Parmenter and Mark Power Robison, "Perils and Possibilities of Wartime Neutrality on the Edges of Empire: Iroquois and Acadians between the French and British in North America, 1744–60," *Diplomatic History* 31, no. 2 (April 2007): 167–206; John Grenier, *The Far Reaches of Empire: War in Nova Scotia, 1710–1760* (Norman: University of Oklahoma Press, 2008).

24. Grenier, *Far Reaches of Empire*, chap. 3, calls this the *Mi'kmaq-Maliseet War*, but it is also known as Dummer's War and Father Râle's War.

25. See Jeremy Black, *Walpole in Power* (London: Sutton, 2001). For a much more extensive overall biography, see J. H. Plumb, *Sir Robert Walpole*, 2 vols. (London: Lane, 1956).

26. See Arthur McAndless Wilson, *French Foreign Policy during the Administration of Cardinal Fleury* (Cambridge, MA: Harvard University Press, 1936).

27. From 1714–1760, the Whig party as a whole was in the political ascendant, with only a relatively small minority of professed Tories and a few avowed Jacobites in Parliament. Not all Whigs, however, agreed with the "Old Corps" power structure—allies of Walpole and eventually the duke of Newcastle—so the party developed a powerful opposition wing.

28. For the Anglo-French break, see Jeremy Black, *The Collapse of the Anglo-French Alliance, 1727–1731* (New York: St. Martin's Press, 1987). For the Polish Succession, see John Sutton, *The King's Honour and the King's Cardinal: War of the Polish Succession* (Lexington: University Press of Kentucky, 1980). Stanislaus ruled Poland under Swedish auspices from 1704 to 1709, and his daughter, Marie Leszczynska, married Louis XV in 1725. Naples-Sicily became an Austrian domain in 1720 after the War of the Quadruple Alliance. Historically linked to Spain, however, the Kingdom of Naples was easily retaken in 1734 by Charles VII (r. 1734–1759), the future Carlos III of Spain (r. 1759–1788).

29. Under the Treaty of Utrecht, the islands of St. Vincent, St. Lucia, Dominica, and Tobago were to remain not only "neutral" but also uninhabited by colonists from either empire. French settlements on St. Lucia appeared at least from 1730, and on Dominica by 1734.

30. Led by escaped Akan warriors, the Stono Rebellion of 1739–1740 was the largest slave rising in British colonial America. Its known connection to Fort Mosé (Florida)—a base for escaped slaves just outside St. Augustine—also made the Stono Rebellion into one of the major proximate causes of the War of Jenkins's Ear (1739–1748). For race relations in late colonial Carolina overall, see Robert Olwell, *Masters, Slaves and Subjects: The Culture of Power in the South Carolina Low Country, 1740–1790* (Ithaca, NY: Cornell University Press, 1998).

31. The Convention of the Pardo, concluded at the end of 1738, seemed to promise a scaling-down of demands on both sides. Neither government ratified the agreement, however, and abuses continued on both sides.

32. For a close reading of the background to the 1739 war, see Philip Woodfine, *Britannia's Glories: The Walpole Ministry and the 1739 War with Spain* (Woodbridge, UK: Royal Historical Society, 1998).

33. Through much of the colonial era, China was a major importer of silver, and from the late seventeenth century its major supplier was Spanish America. Understandably, the annual ship tasked with carrying the silver from Acapulco, via Manila to Canton, was regarded as the richest possible prize on any of the world's oceans—albeit one of the least accessible. For Anson's voyage, see Glyn Williams, *The Prize of All the Oceans* (New York: Viking, 2000).

34. For Frederick's part, see Dennis Showalter, *Wars of Frederick the Great* (New York: Longman, 1996), 38–89. For the larger war, see Reed Browning, *War of the Austrian Succession* (New York: St. Martin's Press, 1993); M. S. Anderson, *War of the Austrian Succession* (New York: Longman, 1995).

35. French ground forces supporting the rising included only Scottish and Irish regiments in the French service. French warships intending to stage

diversionary operations never made contact with the Royal Navy, which deployed vastly superior forces in the Channel.

36. *Gallican* is the Roman province roughly corresponding to modern France. Pundits might also point to the Spanish province of Galacia (or the Kingdom of Wales, taken from the same root), but *anti-gallicanism* was often specifically anti-French. Anti-Gallican social clubs after 1745 waged a rhetorical war against French trade through pamphlets, public speeches, and occasional petty vandalism. Well-connected members also spoke against France in the House of Commons and produced propagandistic maps; Admiralty courts in the fall of 1756 registered a 450-ton ship from Deptford with the name *Anti-gallican*—a privateer the size of a small fifth-rate frigate carrying 208 crewmen, 30 cannon, and 16 swivel guns.

37. For more on Newcastle, see Reed Browning, *The Duke of Newcastle* (New Haven, CT: Yale University Press, 1975).

38. The "free trade" clause in an Anglo-Dutch treaty of 1678 formed the basis of Dutch hopes to trade with France during the Seven Years War. The British answer, made possible only by the vast supremacy of the Royal Navy, was "The Rule of the War of 1756." It stated that a neutral country (the Dutch) could not access the markets of a belligerent power (France) that were closed in peacetime—such trade, said British jurists, was tantamount to aiding the enemy and, therefore, unbecoming of a neutral. See Alice Carter, *The Dutch Republic in Europe in the Seven Years' War* (Coral Gables, FL: University of Miami Press, 1971).

39. Dupleix's taking of Madras, India, in 1746 was in the context of the First Carnatic War (1745–1748). His independent campaigns in 1749–1754 are called the Second Carnatic War, and Anglo-French hostilities in India connected to the Seven Years War are called the Third Carnatic War (1756–1761).

40. Whitehall, 7 March 1748/9 OS *London Gazette* no. 8829 (4–7 March 1748/ 9), 2–3; repeated in each edition of the *London Gazette* nos. 8830–37 (7 March 1748/9 to 4 April 1749). Further announcements about settlers for Nova Scotia appear in *London Gazette* nos. 8838–39 and 8843. The settlers' arrival was reported in an item from Whitehall, 15 August 1749 OS, *London Gazette*, no. 8875 (12–15 August 1749), p. 1. More generally, see T. R. Clayton, "The Duke of Newcastle, the Earl of Halifax, and the American Origins of the Seven Years' War," *The Historical Journal* 24, no. 3 (September 1981): 571–603.

41. By 1750, New Brunswick held three forts: Beauséjour and Gaspéreau on the isthmus of Chignecto, and a third at the mouth of the St. John River. The major expense in Maritime Canada, however, was the refortification of Louisbourg, returned in 1748. The British destroyed all three New Brunswick forts in 1755 and took Louisbourg in 1758.

42. Expansion of Fort Toulouse may have consumed up to half of Louisiana's defense budget for the year 1751. Louisiana also covered some costs for a major upgrade to Fort Chartres (Kaskaskia, Illinois) in 1753–1756.

43. Though the original proposal in 1750 only called for one fort, there were a total of four by 1754: Presqu'Île, Venango, Fort LeBoeuf, and Fort Duquesne. These covered further French settlements going up the Ohio River.

44. J. F. Bosher, *The Canada Merchants, 1713–1763* (Oxford: Clarendon Press, 1987).

45. For the full scope of cabinet intrigues, see J. C. D. Clark, *The Dynamics of Change: The Crisis of the 1750s and English Party Systems* (Cambridge: Cambridge University Press, 1982).

46. For the geographic range of the Seven Years War, even in its origins, see Daniel Baugh, *The Global Seven Years' War, 1754–1763: Britain and France in a Great Power Contest* (New York: Longman, 2011), chaps. 3–6; Mark Danley and Patrick Speelman, eds., *The Seven Years' War: Global Views* (Leiden: Brill, 2012), Introduction.

47. By far the best treatment of British naval operations is Daniel Baugh, *Global Seven Years' War*. From a policy perspective, see also Alfred Thayer Mahan, *The Influence of Sea Power upon History* (New York: Little Brown, 1892); Julian S. Corbett, *England in the Seven Years' War: A Study in Combined Operations* (2 vols., London: Longman, 1907). For the French side, see Jonathan Dull, *The French Navy in the Seven Years' War* (Lincoln: University of Nebraska Press, 2005).

48. By far the best summary of the war on the British side is Fred Anderson, *Crucible of War: The Seven Years' War and the Fate of Empire in British North America, 1754–1766* (New York: Knopf, 2000). See also Matthew C. Ward, *Breaking the Backcountry: The Seven Years' War in Virginia and Pennsylvania, 1754–1765* (Pittsburgh: University of Pittsburg Press, 2003). For the French side, see the classic Guy Frégault, *Canada: The War of the Conquest* (Toronto: Oxford University Press, 1969).

49. See Ian K. Steele, *Betrayals: Fort William Henry and the "Massacre"* (Oxford: Oxford University Press, 1990).

50. For one excellent example of confusion in French counsels, see Lawrence Jay Oliva, *Misalliance: A Study of French Policy in Russia during the Seven Years' War* (New York: New York University Press, 1964).

51. At the death of George II, his grandson George III ascended the British throne in October 1760. He was the first native-born British monarch since 1714. Arguably the first proper English monarch since Elizabeth I, his accession caused major realignments between Whig and Tory parties, generating instability in Parliament and the Cabinet until Lord North's ministry starting in 1770.

52. In response to unfair taxation, colonists raided the British tax ship *Gaspée* in 1772, and the Boston Tea Party was a response to British legislation in

favor of the East India Company. Fed up with these petty acts of resistance, Parliament by 1774 simply resolved to force the colonists into a subordinate political position vis-à-vis the mother country. In Britain these measures were known as the Coercive Acts; the colonists called them the Intolerable Acts.

Chapter 9

1. Huw Davies, *Wellington's Wars: The Making of a Military Genius* (New Haven; London: Yale University Press, 2012), 79.
2. Paul Schroeder, *The Transformation of European Politics, 1763–1848* (Oxford: Clarendon Press, 1994), 37.
3. Christopher Hall, *British Strategy in the Napoleonic War* (Manchester: Manchester University Press, 1992), 87; Davies, *Wellington's Wars*, 79–80.
4. Davies, *Wellington's Wars*, 80.
5. Piers Mackesy, *Statesmen at War: The Strategy of Overthrow, 1798–99* (London: Longman, 1974), 3; Davies, *Wellington's Wars*, 80.
6. Hall, *British Strategy*, 97; Davies, *Wellington's Wars*, 84–86.
7. Although this appears to be a trifling number, despite the heavy demands of the war in Iberia, the British shipped 120,000 muskets to Sweden and Russia before the end of 1812. In February 1813, the first shipment of arms sailed for Russia, carrying 50,000 stands of arms. Without the arms and ammunition required to confront the enemy, there might not have been a coalition for the British to create. Shipments in the spring and summer of 1813 amounted to over 100,000 muskets for the Prussians, 100,000 muskets for the Russians, as well as 116 guns and 1,200 tons of ammunition and shells. In the summer of 1813, the Swedes received 40,000 muskets. In November 1813 Castlereagh reported that nearly 1,000,000 muskets had been sent to Iberia and Central Europe. During the course of 1813, the British provided the following supplies to the Russian, Prussian and Swedish governments: 218 pieces of ordnance complete with carriages and the necessary stores for the field, rounds of ammunition, and "a suitable quantity" of gunpowder, shot, shells, and caissons; 124,119 stands of arms with 18,231,000 musket cartridges; 23,000 barrels of powder and flints; 34,443 swords, sabers, and lances; 624 drums, trumpets, bugles, and cavalry standards; 150,000 uniforms complete with great-coats, cloaks, pelisses, and overalls; 187,000 yards of cloth of various colors; 175,796 boots and shoes "with a proportionate quantity of leather;" 114,000 blankets; 58,800 linen shirts and pants; 87,190 pairs of gaiters; 69,624 pairs of stockings/socks; 90,000 "sets of accoutrements" 63,457 knapsacks; 14,820 saddles with blankets; 22,000 forage caps; 14,000 stocks and clasps; 140,600 shoe-brushes, combs, and black-balls; 3,000 gloves and bracers; 20,000 great-coat straps, brushes, pickers, and sponges; 5,000 flannel shirts, gowns, caps,

and trousers; 14,000 haversacks and canteens; 702 pounds of biscuit and flour; 691,360 pounds of beef and pork; 28,625 gallons of brandy and rum; and "marquees, tents, forage carts, and necessary camp equipment; surgical instrument cases, medicines, and all necessary hospital stores." John Sherwig, *Guineas and Gunpowder: British Foreign Aid in the Wars with France, 1793–1815* (Cambridge, MA: Harvard University Press, 1969), 287; Charles Stewart, *Narrative of the War in Germany and France in 1813 and 1814* (London: Henry Colburn and Richard Bentley, 1830), 366.

8. Brian Arthur, *How Britain Won the War of 1812: The Royal Navy's Blockades of the United States, 1812–1815* (Woodbridge: Boydell Press, 2011), 57. The British government's gross tax income in 1813 was £70,300,000, which equates to $5,038,412,390.86 in 2011 using a conversion based on the GDP Deflator. In 2011, the relative value of £1,333,334 from 1813 was equal to $95,560,263.82, while that of £666,666 was $47,780,060.24 using a conversion based on the GDP Deflator.

9. In 2011, the relative value of £500,000 from 1813 was equal to $35,835,081.02 using a conversion based on the GDP Deflator.

10. In 2011, the relative value of £2,500,000 from 1813 was equal to $179,175,405.08 using a conversion based on the GDP Deflator.

11. In 2011, the relative value of £1,000,000 from 1813 was equal to $71,670,162.03 using a conversion based on the GDP Deflator.

12. David G. Chandler, *The Campaigns of Napoleon: The Mind and Method of History's Greatest Soldier* (New York: Macmillan, 1966), 866–867; 869–870. For a discussion of the problems of the Grande Armée of 1813, see 867–869.

13. This came on the heels of poor harvests in both 1809 and 1810, causing average wheat prices to rise by 18.6 percent between 1810 and 1811, reaching unprecedented levels in 1812. Bread prices in London rose more than 15 percent between 1810 and 1812. Arthur, *How Britain Won the War of 1812*, 56.

14. British exports and re-exports to the West Indies and South America between 1807 and 1809 increased by more than 380 percent and imports by almost 280 percent until these levels fell by 31 percent and 64.5 percent, respectively, during the crisis of 1810–1811. Overall, between 1807 and 1814, total British exports rose by 28.7 percent and imports by 29.2 percent. Arthur, *How Britain Won the War of 1812*, 57.

15. Conversely, Napoleon licensed the export of French and German wheat to Britain. Arthur, *How Britain Won the War of 1812*, 56.

16. The British took French Guiana in January 1809, followed by Martinique in April; and Senegal in Africa in July. In 1810, the British gained France's last possession in America, Guadeloupe, and then its remaining African colonies, Isle-de-France (Mauritius) and Réunion. That same year, the island of Java nominally passed to France through the annexation of its mother country, Holland; but the British took this island as well in September 1811.

17. Kevin D. McCranie, "Britain's Royal Navy and the Defeat of Napoleon," unpublished manuscript, 5.

18. In 1813, London made the following subsidy payments: Austria: £700,000; Prussia: £650,039; Portugal: £2,486,436; Russia: £1,058,436 including arms valued at £400,936; Sicily: £440,000; Spain: £877,200; and Sweden: £1,334,992. In 1814, London made the following subsidy payments: Austria: £939,523; Denmark: £121,917; Hanover: £525,000; Prussia: £1,438,643 (includes £401,371 paid in Federative Paper); Portugal: £1,345,082; Russia: £2,708,834 (includes £783,000 paid in Federative Paper); Sicily: £316,666; Spain: £1,820,932; and Sweden: £800,000. In 1815, London made the following subsidy payments: Austria: £1,654,921; Hanover: £270,940; Prussia: £2,156,513 (includes £469,728 paid in Federative Paper); Portugal: £54,915; Russia: £2,000,033 (includes £888,922 paid in Federative Paper); Sicily: £33,333; Spain: £147,295; Sweden: £608,048; and £1,723,727 to minor powers. Sherwig, *Guineas and Gunpowder*, 287; Stewart, *Narrative*, 367–368.

19. McCranie, "Britain's Royal Navy and the Defeat of Napoleon," 5–7.

Chapter 10

1. Roger L. Williams, *Napoleon III and the Stoeffel Affair* (Wortland, WY: High Plains, 1993), 21–47; Geoffrey Wawro, *The Franco-Prussian War* (Cambridge: Cambridge University Press, 2003), 41–52.

2. Graf Alfred von Waldersee, *Denkwürdigkeiten*, 3 vols. (Berlin: Deutsche Verlags-Anstalt, 1922). See vol. 1 for insights from Waldersee's Paris sojourn, informed by the long reports he submitted at the time.

3. Wilfried Radewahn, "Europäische Fragen und Konfliktzonen im Kalkül der französischen Aussenpolitik vor dem Krieg von 1870," in *Europa vor dem Krieg von 1870*, ed. Eberhard Kolb (Munich: Peter Lang AG, 1987), 33–64.

4. Geoffrey Wawro, *The Austro-Prussian War* (Cambridge: Cambridge University Press, 1996), 276–277; Gordon Craig, *The Politics of the Prussian Army 1640–1945* (Oxford: Oxford University Press, 1955), 202–203; Lothar Gall, *Bismarck: The White Revolutionary*, 2 vols., vol. 1 (New York: Harper Collins, 1986), 301.

5. Wawro, *The Austro-Prussian War*, 277; Heinrich Friedjung, *The Struggle for Supremacy in Germany 1859–1866*, trans. A. J. P. Taylor (1897; repr., London: Macmillan, 1935), 302.

6. Wawro, *The Franco-Prussian War*, 17.

7. Otto Pflanze, *The Period of Unification 1815–1871, vol. 1 of Bismarck and the Development of Germany*, 3 vols. (Princeton, NJ: Princeton University Press, 1990), 300–301.

8. Wawro, *The Franco-Prussian War*, 19.

9. W. E. Mosse, *The European Powers and the German Question 1848–71* (Cambridge: Cambridge University Press, 1958), 260–270.

10. Wawro, *The Franco-Prussian War*, 20.

11. Wolfgang Schivelbusch, *The Culture of Defeat* (New York: Metropolitan, 2001), 122.
12. Michael Howard, *The Franco-Prussian War* (1961; repr., London: Methuen, 1979), 17, 37.
13. Wawro, *The Franco-Prussian War*, 46, 50–56.
14. Pflanze, *The Period of Unification*, 89.
15. Wawro, *The Franco-Prussian War*, 18.
16. Ibid., 32–38.
17. Eberhard Kolb, *Der Weg aus dem Krieg* (Munich: Oldenbourg, 1989), 58–64, 77–82.
18. Wawro, *The Franco-Prussian War*, 305.
19. Paul Kennedy, *The Rise and Fall of the Great Powers* (London: Random House, 1988), 149, 154, 171, 199, 200–201, 203, 243.
20. David G. Herrmann, *The Arming of Europe and the Making of the First World War* (Princeton, NJ: Princeton University Press, 1996), *passim*.
21. James Joll and Gordon Martel, *The Origins of the First World War*, 3rd ed. (London: Pearson Longman, 2006), 87–137.
22. Annika Mombauer, *Helmuth von Moltke and the Origins of the First World War* (Cambridge: Cambridge University Press, 2001), 17–25; Isabel V. Hull, *The Entourage of Kaiser Wilhelm II 1888–1918* (Cambridge: Cambridge University Press, 1982), 208–235.
23. Eugen Weber, *Peasants into Frenchmen* (Stanford, CA: Stanford University Press, 1976), *passim*; Wawro, *The Franco-Prussian War*, 311.
24. Herrmann, *The Arming of Europe*, 171–172.
25. Leonard V. Smith, Stéphane Audoin-Rouzeau, and Annette Becker, *France and the Great War 1914–1918* (Cambridge: Cambridge University Press, 2003), 24.
26. Robert A. Doughty, *Pyrrhic Victory: French Strategy and Operations in the Great War* (Cambridge, MA: Harvard University Press, 2005), 12; Terence Zuber, *Inventing the Schlieffen Plan* (Oxford: Oxford University Press, 2002), 110.
27. Jere Clemens King, *Generals and Politicians* (Berkeley: University of California Press, 1951), 12–14.
28. Smith, Audoin-Rouzeau, and Becker, *France and the Great War*, 16–24; Holger Herwig, *The Marne, 1914* (New York: Random House, 2009), 57–61.
29. Herwig, *Marne*, 219.
30. Holger H. Herwig, *The First World War* (London: Arnold, 1997), 98–106.

Chapter 11

1. See Kathleen Burk, *Old World, New World: Great Britain and America from the Beginning* (New York: Atlantic Monthly Press, 2008), chap. 5.
2. One example is Frank Costigliola, *Awkward Dominion: American Political, Economic, and Cultural Relations with Europe, 1919–1933* (Ithaca, NY: Cornell University Press, 1988).

3. Robin J. Moore, "Imperial India, 1858–1914," in *The Oxford History of the British Empire: The Nineteenth Century,* ed. Andrew Porter (Oxford: Oxford University Press, 1999), 427; B. R. Mitchell, *British Historical Statistics* (Cambridge: Cambridge University Press, 1988), 104.

4. Richard W. Steward, ed., *American Military History*, vol. I (Center for Military History, 2005).

5. US Bureau of the Census, *Historical Statistics of the United States: Colonial Times to 1957* (Washington, DC: US Department of Commerce, 1960), 7; Mitchell, *British Historical Statistics*, 11–13.

6. Kathleen Burk, *Britain, America, and the Sinews of War 1914–1918* (Boston: George Allen & Unwin, 1985), 45–48, 130–131.

7. For a list of the stations, and a map showing just where they were on principal steamer routes, see A. N. Porter, ed., *Atlas of British Overseas Expansion* (London: Routledge, 1991), 145–147. Examples included Malta, Ascension Island, and Buenos Aires; Glen O'Hara, *Britain and the Sea since 1600* (Basingstoke, UK: Palgrave Macmillan, 2010), 33–36.

8. Walter LaFeber, *The Cambridge History of American Foreign Relations*, vol. II, *The American Search for Opportunity, 1865–1913* (Cambridge: Cambridge University Press, 1993), 114–116; Paul Kennedy, *The Rise and Fall of British Naval Mastery* (London: Macmillan, 1983), 183.

9. Burk, *Old World, New World*, 193–194.

10. Jefferson to William Duane, August 4, 1812, Paul Leicester Ford, ed., *The Writings of Thomas Jefferson*, 10 vols. (New York: G. P. Putnam's Sons, 1893), IX, 365–367, quotation on 366.

11. Carl Benn, *The War of 1812* (Oxford: Osprey Publishing, 2002), 78–80; John K. Mahon, *The War of 1812* (Da Capo Press, n.d.; reprint Gainesville: University Press of Florida, 1972), 141–143. York was to be attacked and burned again three months later; ibid., 155.

12. Lord Bathurst to Major-General Robert Ross, 1814, War Office Despatches, British Archives, described as such and quoted in Henry Adams, *History of the United States of America during the Administrations of Thomas Jefferson and James Madison*, 2 vols., first published in 1889–1891 (New York: Library of America, 1986), vol. II, 997–998, 1000.

13. Sir Alexander Cochrane to Sir George Prevost, July 18, 1814, 684, 221; and Orders of Vice-Admiral Cochrane, July 1814, C. 684, 204, both MSS, Canadian Archives.

14. An Officer Who Served in the Expedition [G. R. Gleig], *A Narrative of the Campaigns of the British Army at Washington and New Orleans under Generals Ross, Pakenham, and Lambert, in the Years 1814 and 1815; With Some Account of the Countries Visited* (London: John Murray, 1821), 131.

15. Kenneth Bourne, *Britain and the Balance of Power in North America 1815–1908* (Berkeley: University of California Press, 1967), 75–78; R. W. Mowat, *The Diplomatic Relations of Great Britain and the United States* (London: Edward

Arnold, 1925), 117–123; Bradford Perkins, *The Cambridge History of American Foreign Relations*, vol. I, *The Creation of a Republican Empire, 1776–1865* (Cambridge: Cambridge University Press, 1993), 180–185.

16. See, for example Francis M. Carroll, *A Good and Wise Measure: The Search for the Canadian-American Boundary, 1783–1842* (Toronto: University of Toronto Press, 2001); Frederick Merk, *The Oregon Question: Essays in Anglo-American Diplomacy and Politics* (Cambridge, MA: Harvard University Press, 1967); Barry Gough, *Fortune's River: The Collision of Empires in Northwest America* (Madeira Park, BC: Harbour Publishing, 2007); E. C. Coleman, *The Pig War: The Most Perfect War in History* (Stroud: The History Press, 2009).

17. Burk, *Old World, New World*, 265, and ref. 192; Howard Jones, *To the Webster-Ashburton Treaty* (Chapel Hill: University of North Carolina Press, 1977), *passim*; Bourne, *Balance of Power*, 70 for Ashburton quotation.

18. Although there might be some competition from the surveying expedition of George Mason and Jeremiah Dixon, who surveyed the boundary between Pennsylvania and Maryland (1763–1768).

19. Gordon S. Wood, *Empire of Liberty: A History of the Early Republic, 1789–1815* (Oxford: Oxford University Press, 2009), 376–382.

20. The 54 degrees, 40 minutes parallel had been fixed in the Convention of 1824 as the line dividing the claims of the United States from those of Russia.

21. Burk, *Old World, New World*, 265–268; M. M. Quaife, ed., *The Diary of James K. Polk during His Presidency, 1845–1849, Now First Printed from the Original Manuscript in the Collections of the Chicago Historical Society*, 4 vols. (Chicago: A. C. McClurg, 1910), vol. I, 249.

22. Thomas Jefferson to James Monroe, October 24, 1823, Ford, *Writings of Thomas Jefferson*, vol. X, 277–278.

23. Canning to Rush, Private and Confidential, August 20, 1823, enclosed in Rush to Adams, August 23, 1823, no. 325, Despatches from Ministers to Great Britain, 1791–1906, Record Group 59 (State Department Papers), US National Archives, Washington, DC, Microfilm Series 30, Roll 25 (hereafter M30/25, etc.); Burk, *Old World, New World*, 250–252.

24. Charles Francis Adams, ed., *Memoirs of John Quincy Adams: Comprising Portions of His Diary from 1795 to 1848*, 12 vols. (Philadelphia: J. B. Lippincott, 1874–1877), VI, 177–179.

25. J. F. Watts and Fred L. Israel, eds., *Presidential Documents: The Speeches, Proclamations, and Policies That Have Shaped the Nation from Washington to Clinton* (London: Routledge, 2000), 55–56.

26. The ur-text is John Gallagher and Ronald Robinson, "The Imperialism of Free Trade," *Economic History Review*, Second Series, 6, no. 1 (1953): 1–15. According to Jürgen Osterhammel, informal empire implies more than economic asymmetry or cultural dependency, but rests on three pillars: (1) legal privilege for foreigners, (2) a free trade regime imposed

from outside, and (3) the deployment of instruments of intervention such as the gunboat and the "imperial" consul. Jürgen Osterhammel, "Britain and China, 1842–1914," in Andrew Porter, ed., *The Nineteenth Century*, 148–149. The one exception was British Guiana, which was created out of three Dutch possessions, Berbice, Demerara, and Essequibo, which were taken from the Dutch during the Napoleonic Wars.

27. Quoted in Wendy Hinde, *George Canning* (London: Collins, 1973), 345.

28. Emily S. Rosenberg, "Anglo-American Economic Rivalry in Brazil during World War I," *Diplomatic History* 2, no. 2 (Spring 1978): 131; Alan Knight, "Britain and Latin America," in Porter, ed., *The Nineteenth Century*, 122–145.

29. From a speech by James Stephen Hogg advocating an isthmian canal, given in Philadelphia on July 2, 1894. Robert C. Cotner, ed., *Addresses and State Papers of James Stephen Hogg* (Austin: University of Texas Press, 1951), 374, cited by Edward P. Crapol, *America for Americans: Economic Nationalism and Anglophobia in the Late Nineteenth Century* (Westport, CT: Greenwood Press, 1973), 219.

30. For a narrative and analysis of the whole dispute, see Burk, *Old World, New World*, 396–410.

31. Richard Olney to Thomas Bayard, No. 222, July 20, 1895, Diplomatic Instructions of the State Department 1801–1906, Department of State Papers, Record Group 59, US National Archives, fols. 306–316, Microfilm M77/90.

32. LaFeber, *The American Search for Opportunity*, 126.

33. Salisbury to Pauncefote, November 26, 1895, no. 15, Cmmd Paper United States, no. 1, and Salisbury to Pauncefote, November 26, 1895, no. 16, ibid. For President Cleveland's Annual Message, see Watts and Israel, eds., *Presidential Documents*, 181–184.

34. Zara S. Steiner, *The Foreign Office and Foreign Policy, 1898–1914* (Cambridge: Cambridge University Press, 1969), 24; T. G. Otte, "A Question of Leadership: Lord Salisbury, the Unionist Cabinet and Foreign Policy Making, 1895–1900," *Contemporary British History* 14, no. 4 (Winter 2000): 4–9.

35. The vehicle was the *Naval Defence Act of March 1889*, which mandated that "the establishment [of battleships] should be on such a scale that [the Royal Navy] should be at least equal to the strength of any two other countries," which meant those of France and Russia; as it happened, the Italian navy was bigger than the Russian, but no one anticipated an Anglo-Italian naval war. *House of Commons Debates*, 3rd Series, 1171; Jon Tetsuro Sumida, *In Defence of Naval Supremacy: Finance, Technology, and British Naval Power, 1889–1904* (London: Routledge, 1993), 13.

36. German announcement quoted by Lord Selborne, the First Lord of the Admiralty, in his Memorandum of February 26, 1904, CAB23/22, Cabinet Papers, (London; Kew: UK National Archives, 1904).

37. Admiral Sir John Fisher, quoted in A. J. Marder, *From the Dreadnought to Scapa Flow: The Royal Navy in the Fisher Era 1904–1919*, vol. I: *The Road to War, 1904–1914* (London: Oxford University Press, 1961), 4; Burk, *Old World, New World*, 433–435.

38. Karl E. Meyer, "The Opium War's Secret History," *New York Times*, June 26, 1997.

39. James Chambers, *Palmerston: "The People's Darling"* (London: John Murray, 2004), 194–196.

40. Peter Ward Fay, *The Opium War, 1840–1842: Barbarians in the Celestial Empire in the Early Part of the Nineteenth Century* (Chapel Hill: University of North Carolina Press, 1998).

41. Ping Chia Kuo, "Caleb Cushing and the Treaty of Wanghia, 1844," *Journal of Modern History* 5, no. 1 (March 1933): 34–54.

42. Earl Swisher, *China's Management of the American Barbarians* (New Haven, CT: Yale University Press, 1951), 46.

43. Justus D. Doenecke and Mark A. Stoler, *Debating Franklin D. Roosevelt's Foreign Policies, 1933–1945* (Lanham, MD: Rowman & Littlefield, 2005), 54–55.

44. George C. Herring, *From Colony to Superpower: U.S. Foreign Relations since 1776* (Oxford: Oxford University Press, 2008), 212–213.

45. From the journal of Townsend Harris, as quoted in Oliver Statler, *Shimoda Story* (New York: Random House, 1969), 77.

46. This was the lowering of the import duty on cottons and woollens from 20 percent to 5 percent. The whole episode was described by Consul General Townsend Harris in a despatch to the US State Department and in his journal: Townsend Harris to Sec State, no. 20, July 31, 1858, Despatches from U.S. Ministers to Japan, 1855–1906, RG 59, M133/1; Harris to Sec State, no. 28, September 1, 1858, M133/2; and Statler, *Shimoda Story*, 547–552.

47. Harris to Cass, No. 8, February 22, 1860, M133/3.

48. W. E. Adams, *Our American Cousins: Personal Impressions of the People and Institutions of the United States* (London: Walter Scott, 1883), 357.

49. From "The Adventure of the Noble Bachelor," first published in *Strand* magazine in 1892. Sir Arthur Conan Doyle, *Sherlock Holmes: His Adventures, Memoirs, Return, His Last Bow and The Case-Book: The Complete Short Stories* (London: John Murray, 1928), 246.

50. The plan was the work of officers from the Naval War College and the Office of Naval Intelligence and had been drawn up before Roosevelt was in office. John A. S. Grenville and George Berkeley Young, *Politics, Strategy, and American Diplomacy: Studies in Foreign Policy, 1873–1917* (New Haven, CT: Yale University Press, 1966), 272–282. The real concern of many American naval officers was the growing hostility of Japan toward the United States.

51. "Philippines through the Centuries," www.rms-gs.de/phileng/history/kap02.html, accessed August 18, 2016.

52. Bradford Perkins, *The Great Rapprochement: England and the United States, 1895–1914* (London: Gollancz, 1968), 44–45.

53. Ibid., 46.

54. Nothing the Germans could say checked the growth of this legend, which received sustenance from an erroneous account published the following year in Henry Cabot Lodge's *Our War with Spain.*

55. John Julius Norwich, *The Middle Sea: A History of the Mediterranean* (London: Vintage, 2007), 544–545. The Cabinet had approved the maneuver, although Parliament was left in the dark.

56. Afaf Lutfi al-Sayyid-Marsot, "The British Occupation of Egypt from 1882," in Porter, *Nineteenth Century*, 654–655.

57. Burk, *Old World, New World*, 432.

58. The amount of fighting the Americans engaged in was relatively small. Had the war continued until 1919, as both the British and the Americans expected, actual rather than potential American power on the ground would probably have been defining.

59. Bruce Kuniholm, *The Origins of the Cold War in the Near East: Great Power Conflict and Diplomacy in Iran, Turkey, and Greece* (Princeton, NJ: Princeton University Press, 1994 ed.), www.mtholyoke.edu/acad/intrel/petroleum/kuniholm.htm, accessed August 18, 2016.

60. Roosevelt to Churchill, March 3, 1944 and Churchill to Roosevelt, March 4, 1944, US Department of State, *Foreign Relations of the United States, 1944*, vol. III, 100–103.

61. Steventon to Black, February 4, 1916, D/12/3/1, and Spring Rice to Grey, January 28, 1916, sent on to Lloyd George, February 18, 1915, D/12/1/23, David Lloyd George Papers, House of Lords Record Office, London.

62. Burk, *Sinews of War*, 40–41.

63. For example, Ibid., 41–42.

64. Stephen Roskill, *Naval Policy between the Wars*, vol. I, *The Period of Anglo-American Antagonism 1919–1929* (New York: Walker, 1968), 300–330; B. J. C. McKercher, " 'The Deep and Latent Distrust': The British Official Mind and the United States, 1919–1939," in *Anglo-American Relations in the 1920s*, ed. B. J. C. McKercher (London: Macmillan, 1991), 223; Phillips Payson O'Brien, *British and American Naval Power: Politics and Policy, 1900–1936* (Westport, CT: Praeger, 1998), 181.

65. John R. Ferris, "The Symbol and Substance of Seapower: Great Britain, the United States, and the One-Power Standard, 1919–1921," in McKercher, *Anglo-American Relations in the 1920s*, 57–61; O'Brien, *British and American Naval Power*, 162.

66. Ibid., 198–199. Few of the ships were built.

67. US Bureau of the Census, *Historical Statistics of the United States*, 736.

68. "British Army Estimates Published," *The Barrier Miner*, February 20, 1920, http://trove.nla.gov.au/ndp/del/article/45545678 for 1920–1921,

accessed August 18, 2016; "Army Estimates, 1938," 332, H. C. Deb, March 10, 1938, cols. 2133–2255.

69. Burk, *Old World, New World*, 475–477.

Chapter 12

1. For an overall examination of the origins of World War I, see Richard F. Hamilton and Holger H. Herwig, eds. (Cambridge: Macmillan, 2003).

2. See Chapter 10 by Geoffrey Warrow in this volume for the emergence and course of the Anglo-German rivalry in the prewar period.

3. Winston S. Churchill, *The World Crisis* (Toronto, 1931), 101.

4. Margaret MacMillan, *The War That Ended Peace, The Road to 1914* (New York: Random House, 2013). For the latter view, see Niall Ferguson's comments in the *Guardian*, January 29, 2014, http://theguardian.com/world/2014/jan/30/britain-first-world-war-biggest-error-niall-ferguson, accessed February 1, 2014.

5. For the dangerous currents running not only throughout the German elites but throughout German society itself, see particularly MacGregor Knox's *To the Threshold of Power, 1922/33: Origins and Dynamics of the Fascist and Socialist National Socialist Dictatorships*, vol. 1 (Cambridge: Cambridge University Press, 2007), esp. chaps. 1 and 2.

6. For the origins and course of that rivalry, see Paul M. Kennedy, *The Rise of Anglo-German Antagonism, 1860–1914* (London: Allen & Unwin, 1987), as well as the Chapter 11 in this volume by Kathleen M. Burk on the British and American empires.

7. For Bismarck's period as the guarantor of peace in Europe, see Marcus Jones, "Bismarkian Strategic Policy, 1871–1890," in *Successful Strategies, Triumphing in War and Peace from Antiquity to the Present*, ed. Williamson Murray and Richard Hart Sinnreich (Cambridge: Cambridge University Press, 2014).

8. Carl von Clausewitz, *On War*, trans. and eds. Michael Howard and Peter Paret (Princeton, NJ: Princeton University Press, 1976), 88.

9. After World War II, one of the leading German panzer generals, Leo Geyr von Schweppenburg, wrote the British military pundit B. H. Liddell Hart the following note about his experience at the *Kriegsakademie* shortly before World War I: "You will be horrified to hear that I have never read Clausewitz or Delbrück or Haushofer. The opinion on Clausewitz in our general staff was that of a theoretician to be read by professors." King's College Archives, London, 9/24/61, 32.

10. For an excellent examination of the role of "military necessity" in German military thinking through the end of World War I, see Isabel V. Hull, *Absolute Destruction, Military Culture, and the Practices of War in Imperial Germany* (Ithaca, NY: Cornell University Press, 2005).

11. Significantly, throughout Prusso-German military operations during the Franco-Prussian War, Bismarck had ensured that German troops remained at a distance from the Belgian frontier. Interestingly, the Germans did not

possess the number of troops that the Schlieffen Plan required until the desperate efforts to increase the army's size in 1912. Holger H. Herwig, *The First World War: Germany and Austria Hungary, 1914–1918* (London: Bloomsbury, 2009), 49.

12. During the Franco-Prussian War (July 19, 1870–May 10, 1871), Bismarck had kept German military operations well away from Belgium.

13. As one commentator has noted, "[w]ithout clear guidance on strategy and foreign policy, it was difficult for [German] officials to choose a policy." Avner Offer, *The First World War: An Agrarian Interpretation* (Oxford: Clarendon Press, 1989).

14. Barbara Tuchman, *The Guns of August* (New York: Macmillan, 1962), 79–82.

15. And, of course, there would have been no Western Front.

16. Quoted in Richard Hough, *Dreadnought: A History of the Modern Battleship* (Penzance, Cornwall, UK: Periscope, 2003), 47.

17. Roy Jenkins, *Churchill, A Biography* (New York: Farrar, Straus & Giroux, 2001), 155.

18. The agreement allowed the British to concentrate their main battle fleet in bases on the shores of the British Isles, while the French concentrated their fleet in the Mediterranean. However, it also meant that the British were under a moral, if not political, obligation to protect the northern coast of France from attack by the German High Seas Fleet.

19. Llewellyn Woodward, *Great Britain and the War of 1914–1918* (Boston: Methuen, 1967), 21. Woodward's comprehensive examination still remains far and away the best study of the politics and strategic decision-making in Britain during the conflict.

20. Woodward, *Great Britain and the War of 1914–1918*, 19–20.

21. Two of those ministers did withdraw their resignations, including Sir John Simon, who would later serve as one of the arch-appeasers in Neville Chamberlain's cabinet in the late 1930s.

22. MacMillan, *The War That Ended Peace*, 627.

23. For an analysis as well as account of these hostilities, see Alan Kramer, *German Atrocities: A History of Denial* (New Haven, CT: Yale University Press, 2001).

24. For the *Wehrmacht's* behavior in World War II, see particularly Christian Streit, *Keine Kamaraden, Die Wehrmacht und die sowjetischen Kriegsgefangenen, 1941–1945* (Stuttgart, 1978).

25. The problem in terms of the post–World War I period was the fact that Allied propaganda exaggerated the extent of the German atrocities to include discussions of German troops supposedly spitting babies on their bayonets.

26. For the origin and course of those staff talks, see Samuel Williamson, *The Politics of Grand Strategy: Britain and France Prepare for War, 1904–1914* (Cambridge, MA: Harvard University Press, 1969).

27. For the Battle of the Marne and operations leading up to it, see Holger H. Herwig, *The Marne, 1914: The Opening of World War I and the Battle That Changed the World* (New York: Random House, 2011).

28. For the price paid by the British army for the fighting in Flanders in 1914, see Anthony Farrar-Hockley, *Death of an Army* (New York: W. Morrow, 1968)

29. For the extent of that incompetence, see particularly Max Hastings, *Catastrophe 1914* (New York: Knopf, 2013).

30. See again Niall Ferguson's comments, cited in note 4, about how avoiding the war would have prevented incompetent British generalship and untrained armies from coming up against far more skillful Germans.

31. In the largest sense, as in the case of the American Civil War, the embattled armies confronted the combination of the two great revolutions of the late eighteenth and early nineteenth centuries, namely, the French and industrial revolutions. The former enabled the modern state to maximize the mobilization of its population and resources, while the latter provided the state with massive support in weaponry and ammunition. For a further discussion of these issues, see Williamson Murray and MacGregor Knox, "Thinking about Revolutions in Warfare," in *The Dynamics of Military Revolution, 1300–2050,* ed. MacGregor Knox and Williamson Murray (Cambridge: Cambridge University Press, 2001).

32. For a discussion of the problems involved in the complex adaptations that took place in World War I, see Williamson Murray, *Military Adaptation in War, For Fear of Change* (Cambridge: Cambridge University Press, 2011), particularly chap. 3.

33. Isabel Hull is particularly good on this point; see her *Absolute Destruction*, 215–217.

34. This made neither strategic nor tactical sense. On the one hand, it was one more piece of evidence that the Allies were able to use in the United States about German frightfulness, while tactically the winds on the Western Front blew from west to east, which gave the Allies a considerable advantage in the gas warfare that was to characterize the remainder of the war. For the best work on the effects of gas war on the fighting on the Western Front, see Albert Palazzo, *Seeking Victory on the Western Front: The British Army and Chemical Warfare in World War I* (Lincoln: University of Nebraska Press, 2000).

35. For the French effort, see Robert A. Doughty, *Pyrrhic Victory: French Strategy and Operations in the Great War* (Cambridge, MA: Harvard University Press, 2008).

36. Quoted in Martin Gilbert, *Winston S. Churchill*, vol. III, *The Challenge of War, 1914–1916* (Boston: Houghton Mifflin, 1971), 226.

37. For Churchill's considerable role in the development of the tank, see J. P. Harris, *Men, Ideas, and Tanks: British Military Thought and Armored Forces, 1903–1939* (Manchester, UK: Manchester University Press, 1995).

38. That, of course, reflected Clausewitz's, as well as Thucydides', grim descriptions of the impact of friction and chance on military operations at every level.

39. The nature of the logistical difficulties is suggested by the difficulties their successors discovered in planning and executing Operation BARBAROSSA, Germany's invasion of the Soviet Union in 1941.

40. Quoted in Alistair Horne, *The Price of Glory, Verdun 1916* (New York: St. Martin's Press, 1963), 34.

41. By far and away the best account of the Somme Battle from the British perspective is Robin Prior and Trevor Wilson, *The Somme* (New Haven, CT: Yale University Press, 2005).

42. For an excellent study of how much the Battle of the Somme hurt the Germans, see Christopher Duffy, *Through German Eyes, The British and the Somme 1916* (London: Weidenfeld and Nicolson, 2006). See also Jack Sheldon, *The German Army on the Somme, 1914–1916* (London: Pen and Sword, 2005).

43. Erich Ludendorff, *Ludendorff's Own Story: August 1914–November 1918*, vol. 1 (New York: Harper, 1919), 24.

44. Ibid., 313, 316, 321.

45. For the development of German tactics on the Western Front, see particularly G. C. Wynne, *If Germany Attacks: The Battle of Depth in the West* (London: Faber & Faber, 1940); Timothy Lupfer, *The Dynamic of Doctrine: The Changes in German Tactical Doctrine during the First World War* (Leavenworth, KS: Combat Studies Institute, 1881); and Shelford Bidwell and Dominick Graham, *Fire Power: British Army Weapons and Theories of War, 1904–1945* (London: Pen and Sword, 1982).

46. For Haig's disinterest in tactics, see Timothy Travers, *The Killing Ground: The British Army, the Western Front, and the Emergence of Modern War, 1900–1918* (London: Allen & Unwin, 1987), chap. 5.

47. In this regard, J. P. Harris's *Douglas Haig and the First World War* (Cambridge: Cambridge University Press, 2009) has drawn a far more nuanced picture of the field marshal, which is that much more damning because its criticisms rest on a solid foundation of thorough research on what actually happened.

48. Here, in the German case, the General Staff system provided a second feedback loop to the army. Moreover, that feedback loop consisted of many of the brightest officers in the army who could emphasize important tactical information that was of immediate importance. In the British case, two of the foremost historians of the Western Front noted about British tactical successes in the first half of 1917: "It is a sorry comment on the dissemination of information by the higher [British] commands on the Western Front that the methods used to achieve success by one commander might be completely unknown to another." Robin Prior and Trevor Wilson, *Passchendaele, The Untold Story* (New Haven, CT: Yale University Press, 1996).

49. Throughout the Civil War, the British had objected to the conduct of the blockade of the Confederacy by Union naval forces, but the Foreign Office

had filed the American justifications away and now was delighted to use them in response to American complaints about the Royal Navy's blockade of Germany.

50. For the difficulties the blockade caused in Anglo-American relations, see Woodward, *Great Britain and the War of 1914–1918*, chap. 13.

51. See Offer's *The First World War* for an outstanding examination of the background to the blockade both in terms of (1) prewar British planning and debate over the possibility of blockading Germany, as well as (2) the increasing impact on the world economy of the global agricultural revolution taking place in the United States, Canada, Australia, and Argentina, and (3) its impact on German vulnerability to a blockade.

52. This was particularly true of its impact on the gas war that the Germans had so casually introduced in April 1915 on the basis of "military necessity." Without access to rubber, German and Austrian gas masks were enormously inferior to those that the Allied armies on the Western Front possessed. By 1916 the Germans had exhausted their supplies of tires for vehicular movement.

53. In the period immediately before the war, the scientist Fritz Haber, ironically Jewish, developed the processes that allowed the creation of ammonia, essential to the production of fertilizer and munitions. Up to 1914, the Germans imported nitrates from Chile for fertilizer and munitions production. The Haber process allowed Germany to produce munitions in sufficient quantity during the war, but fertilizer almost disappeared from German farms because of insufficient production of ammonia, with an obvious impact on agricultural production.

54. Hull, *Absolute Destruction*, 296.

55. Holger H. Herwig, *The Politics of Frustration, The United States in German Naval Planning, 1889–1941* (Boston: Little, Brown, 1976), 122.

56. Ironically, that destruction would considerably impede the advance of German troops in Operation MICHAEL in the spring of 1918.

57. Surely one of the most disastrous strategic decisions made by the Germans.

58. Quoted in Woodward, *Great Britain and the War of 1914–1918*, 240.

59. For a careful and insightful discussion, see Wilson and Prior, *Passschendaele.*

60. For a clear discussion of the political crisis in London at the end of 1916, see Woodward, *Great Britain and the War of 1914–1918,* chap. 18.

61. A thorough discussion of this appears in Prior and Wilson, *Passchendaele,* particularly chap. 19.

62. For the Treaty of Brest Litovsk, see particularly John W. Wheeler Bennett, *Brest-Litovsk, the Forgotten Peace, March 1918* (London: Macmillan, 1971).

63. Reichsarchiv, *Der Weltkrieg: 1814–1918,* vol. 14, *Die KriegFührung an der Westfront im Jahre 1918* (Berlin, 1944), 760.

64. Crown Prince Rupprecht, *Mein Kriegstagebuch,* vol. 2, ed. by Eugen von Frauenholz (Munich, 1929), 372.

65. For the course of these offensives as well as the lack of any clear strategic or operational conceptions behind them, see the outstanding work by David Zabecki, *The German 1918 Offensives, A Case Study in the Operational Level of War* (Abington: Routledge, 2006).

66. The German front lines in the west expanded from 390 kilometers to 510 kilometers, with those additional 120 kilometers having virtually no defensive systems; Harris, *Haig*, 485.

67. In effect, the Germans doubled the casualties suffered over the course of the previous major offensives on the Western Front.

68. For the British army's major contribution to the winning of the war, see J. P. Harris, *Amiens to the Armistice: The BEF in the Hundred Days Campaign, 8 August–11 November 1918* (London: Brassey's, 2003). See also Gary Sheffield, *Forgotten Victory: The First World War—Myths and Realities* (London: Headline, 2002).

69. Not all historians would accept that claim. A noted Yale historian has recently claimed that the Germans possessed 100,000 completely fresh troops available in the east to throw into the battle in the west in November 1918. That is sheer and utter nonsense. First of all, there were no fresh troops in the east, while 100,000 troops would have made no difference on the Western Front. Moreover, Germany's main allies, including Austria-Hungry, had collapsed, and Allied armies were rapidly approaching the Reich's frontiers from the south.

70. Quoted in Herwig, *The First World War*, 425.

71. For a clear discussion of the final collapse, see Knox, *To the Threshold of Power*, 157–159.

72. For a clear discussion of the close connection between the rise of a virulent anti-Semitism and the "stab in the back legend," see particularly Knox, *To the Threshold of Power*, 198–201.

73. For an examination of the complexities of the making of peace in Paris in 1919, see Williamson Murray, "Versailles: The Peace without a Chance," in *The Making of Peace: Rulers, States, and the Aftermath of War*, ed. Williamson Murray and James Lacey (Cambridge: Cambridge University Press, 2009).

74. The *Economist,* a journal that usually possesses a historical sensibility, commented that "[t]he final crime [was] the Treaty of Versailles, whose harsh terms would ensure a second world war." *The Economist*, millennium edition, January 2000.

75. Harold Nicholson's *Peacemaking 1919* (New York: MIT Press Journals, 1965) still is worth reading for the difficulties the peacemakers confronted.

76. Only American relief efforts prevented mass starvation in the occupied areas.

77. John Maynard Keynes, *The Economic Consequences of the Peace* (London: Macmillan, 1919).

78. For a wonderful examination of this effort, see Holger H. Herwig, "Clio Deceived, Patriotic Self-Censorship in Germany after the Great War," *International Security* 12, no. 2 (Fall 1987): 5–44.

79. Ironically, this effort played a considerable role in the self-delusion under which so many Germans fell and contributed considerably to Nazi propaganda in the run-up to the next war (1939–1945).

80. The American historian Sidney Fay would be singled out for special treatment: his history of the outbreak of the war, reflecting the pro-German bias of his German supporters, was reissued in 2010.

81. Among the British works that still stand up as great literature are Frederick Manning, *The Middle Parts of Fortune* (London, 1929, republished in a number of editions, 2007, 2013, 2014); Robert Graves, *Goodbye to All That: An Autobiography* (London, 1929); Siegfried Sassoon, *Memoirs of a Fox-Hunting Man* (London, 1928); *Memoirs of an Infantry Officer* (London, 1930); and *The War Poems of Siegfried Sassoon* (London, 2014); Wilfred Owen, *The Collected Poems of Wilfred Owen* (London, 1965). For a perspective on the woman's side of war, see Vera Brittain, *Testament of Youth* (London, 1930).

82. A new and much improved translation of the former was published recently as Ernst Jünger, *Storm of Steel*, translated by Michael Hoffman (London: Penguin, 2004). See also Ernst Jünger, *Copse 125: A Chronicle from the Trench Warfare of 1918* (London, 2003). Jünger is considered one of the great figures in German literature.

83. Most of the other works of literature were depictions of the conflict depicting heroic German youth fighting off the endless numbers of Allied armies. Not surprisingly, Erich Maria Remarque's *All Quiet on the Western Front* was atypical of German war literature.

84. For the Treasury's role in limiting defense spending, see G. C. Peden, *British Rearmament and the Treasury, 1932–1939* (Edinburg: Scottish Academic Press, 1973); see also Williamson Murray, *The Change in the European Balance of Power, 1938–1939* (Princeton, NJ: Princeton University Press, 1984), chap. 2.

85. For Hitler's discussions with his military leaders, see "Aufzeichnung Liebmann," *Vierteljahrshefte für Zeitgeschicte* 2, no. 4 (October 1954): 434–435.

86. Even in the face of Nazism's virulent militaristic propaganda, a considerable number of *Germans* swallowed the *Führer*'s statements about only wanting peace, which infuriated Hitler and Goebbels to no end in the late 1930s.

87. Gerhard L. Weinberg, *The Foreign Policy of Hitler's Germany, Diplomatic Revolution in Europe, 1933–36* (Chicago: University of Chicago Press, 1970), 281.

88. The Oxford Union was the university's debating society. Martin Gilbert, *Winston S. Churchill*, vol. 5, *1922–1939* (London: Heinemann, 1976), 454.

89. Gilbert, *Winston S. Churchill*, vol. 5, 550.

90. For a clear discussion of the strategic and economic issues involved in German rearmament, see Wilhelm Deist, *The Wehrmacht and German Rearmament* (London: Macmillan, 1981).

91. For the financial and economic difficulties that German rearmament efforts confronted during the 1930s, see Adam Tooze, *The Wages of Destruction, The Making and Breaking of the Nazi War Economy* (London: Allen Lane, 2006), chaps. 1–9. See also Murray, *The Change in the European Balance of Power*, chap. 21.

92. In this regard, the miserable performance of Britain's Labour Party is worth mentioning. While continuously demanding that Britain take a strong stand against fascism throughout the 1930s, the party voted against every single bill dealing with defense spending.

93. For the nature of Mussolini's foreign policy, see Knox's *To the Threshold of Power* and *Mussolini Unleashed, 1939–1941: Politics and Strategy in Fascist Italy's Last War* (Cambridge: Cambridge University Press, 1986).

94. Robert Paul Shay Jr., *British Rearmament in the Thirties* (Princeton, NJ: Princeton University Press, 1977), 44.

95. It was in Spain that the Germans discovered that the famed 88-mm anti-aircraft gun would make a wonderful anti-tank gun as well.

96. *Akten zur deutschen aus wärtigen Politik (ADAP)*, Series D, vol. 1, Doc. 19, "Niederschrift über die Besprechung in der Reichskanzlei am 5. November 1937 von 16,15–20,30 Uhr," 10.11.37.

97. British National Archives (BNA) CAB 23/88, Cab 20 (37), Meeting of the Cabinet, 5.5.37, 180.

98. In this regard, see my chapter in the forthcoming volume being edited by Peter Mansoor, The Ohio State University, and myself: *"Grand Strategy and Alliances."*

99. Martin Gilbert and Richard Gott, *The Appeasers* (New York, 1967), 52.

100. BNA, PREM 1/276, Chamberlain to Halifax.

101. Documents on British Foreign Policy (DBFP) 3rd Series, vol. 2, Doc. 590, 6.8.38., letter from Henderson to Halifax. The historian Louis Namier summed up Henderson in the following terms: "Conceited, vain, self-opionated [*sic*], rigidly adhering to his preconceived ideas, he poured out telegrams, dispatches, and letters in unbelievable numbers and of formidable length, repeating a hundred times the same ill-founded views and ideas. Obtuse enough to be a menace, and not stupid enough to be innocuous, he proved *un homme néfaste*—important, because he echoed and reinforced Chamberlain's opinions and policy." L. B. Namier, *In the Nazi Era* (New York: Macmillan, 1952), 162.

102. BNA, CAB 23/90A Cab 49 (37), meeting of the Cabinet, 22.9.37, 373.

103. See Table I-5, "Military Expenditures of Major European Powers, 1935–1938," in Murray, *The Change in the European Balance of Power*, 20.

104. BNA CAB 53/37, COS 698 (Revise), CID, COS Sub-Committee, "Military Implications of German Aggression against Czechoslovakia," 28.3.38, 145–146.

105. For Germany's economic difficulties, see particularly Tooze, *Wages of Destruction*, as well as Murray, *The Change in the European Balance of Power*, chap. 1.

106. There were apparently two sessions, one to discuss the strategic situation, the other the economic difficulties of Germany's surging rearmament programs. We have the notes from the first, but not the second. For the minutes of the discussion, see *ADAP*, Series D, vol. 1, Doc. 19, "Niederschrift über die Besprechung in der Reichskanzlei am 5. November 1937 von 16,15–20,30 Uhr," 10.11.37.

107. Gordon Brooke-Shepherd, *The Anschluss* (Philadelphia, 1963), 11–12.

108. For the course and outcome of the Fritsch-Blomberg crisis, see Harold Deutsch, *Hitler and His Generals* (Minneapolis: University of Minnesota Press, 1974).

109. For the course of the Czech crisis over the summer of 1938, see Murray, *The Change in the European Balance of Power*, chap. 5.

110. *ADAP*, Series D, vol. 2, Doc. 221, 30.5.38, "Der Oberste Befehlshaber der Wehrmacht an die Oberbefehlshaber des Heeres, der Marine und der Luftwaffe, Weisung für Plan Grün."

111. For the military and strategic aspects of the Czech crisis, see Murray, *The Change in the European Balance of Power*, chap. 7.

112. For Beck's various memoranda arguing against a war, see Bundesarchiv/ Militärarchiv, Beck Nachlass: "Betrachtungen zur gegen wärtigen mil. Politischen Lage," 5.5.38; Bemerkungen zu den Ausführungen des Führers am 28.5.38," 29.5.38; and "der Chef des Generalstabes des Heeres, An den Herrn Oberbefehlshaber des Heeres," 15.7.38."

113. Telford Taylor, *Munich* (Garden City, NY: Doubleday, 1979), 695.

114. For the diplomatic and political events see Taylor, *Munich*.

115. BNA CAB 23/94, Notes on a Meeting of Ministers, 30.8.38, 294–296.

116. Upon his return home from the conference, Chamberlain made the infamous remark that he had brought back from Munich "peace in our time."

117. BNA CAB 53/41, COS 773, COS Committee, "The Czechoslovak Crisis," 24.9.38.

118. For an analysis of the overall military situation had war broken out, and for a discussion of the Czech arms the Germans seized in March 1939 when they occupied the remainder of Czechoslovakia, see Murray, *The Change in the European Balance of Power*, chaps. 7 and 8.

119. Ibid., 271–273.

120. For a discussion of the complex debates that took place in the cabinet over the winter of 1938–1939, see Murray, *The Change in the European Balance of Power*, 274–278.

121. National Archives and Records Service (NARS), Captured German microfilm T-1022/3048/PG33272, Reichsverteidigungsausschuss, 15.12.38.

122. Jost Dülffer, *Weimar, Hitler und die Marine: Reichspolitik und Flottenbau, 1920–1939* (Dusseldorf, 1973), 504.

123. BNA CAB 23/98, Cab 11 (39), Meeting of the Cabinet, 15.3.39, 7–8.

124. Hansard, *Parliamentary Debates*, er., vol. 345, House of Commons (London, 1939), cols. 437–440.

125. Winston S. Churchill, *The Second World War*, vol. 1, *The Gathering Storm* (Boston: Houghton Mifflin, 1948), 347.

126. Alan Bullock, *Hitler: A Study in Tyranny* (London: Penguin, 1964), 445.

127. *ADAP*, Series D, vol. 6, Doc. 149, 3.4.39, "Weisung des chefs des Oberkommandos der Wehrmacht."

128. *ADAP*, series D, vol. 6, Doc 716, 24.7.39, "Vermerk über die Unterrechnung mit Sir Horace Wilson am 18., 3:15 Uhr bis 4:30 Uhr Nachmittags und am 21.7. von 13:00 Uhr bis 13:30 Uhr, mit Sir Joseph Ball am 20.7. 17:30 Uhr Uhr bis 19:30 Uhr und Mr. Hudson am 20.7. 17:30 Uhr bis 18:30 Uhr Nachmittags (Alle Unterredungen auf Aufforderung der englishen Herrn mit Wissen des Botschafters von Dirksen)."

129. BNA FO 371/22990, C 10359/16/18, Henderson to Halifax, 24.7.39.

130. That said, one must recognize that there was little chance that the Western Powers could have reached an agreement with Stalin and his crew of murderous ideologues. In the end, Hitler could offer Stalin peace and the opportunity to watch the capitalist powers destroy themselves. Of course, he did not calculate the sudden and disastrous defeat of the French Army in May 1940. For Soviet foreign policy during this period, see Adam Ulam, *Expansion and Coexistence: History of Soviet Foreign Policy, 1917–1967* (New York: Praeger, 1971).

131. Although there was obviously going to be a long period before the British military began to realize the increased targets for armaments production.

132. This also influenced the views of British political leaders. Halifax told French leaders in mid-May 1939 that "it should be remembered that the position of France and Great Britain is quite different than it was six months ago. They had embarked upon a policy that was both decisive and firm and which had had great influence upon the psychology of the whole world. . . . Our industrial output, particularly in the area of aircraft, had grown faster than at one time we had dared to expect. The general effect of this was to place our partnership in a position of evident strength." *DBFP*, 3rd Ser., vol. 5, Doc 570, 20.5.39, "Extract from Record of Conversation between the Secretary of State and MM. Daladier and Bonnet at the ministry of war, in Paris."

133. For the extraordinary support that the Czech arms meant for the Germans, not only militarily, but economically as well, see Jon Kimche, *The Unfought Battle* (New York: Stein and Day, 1968), 29; Deist et al., *Das Deutsche reich und der Zweite Weltkrieg*, vol. 1, 332; and *ADAP*, Series D, vol. 6, Doc 659, 12.7.39, "Das auswärtige Amt an den Chef des Oberkommandos

der Wehrmacht, and Doc. 703, 22.7.39, "Aufzeichnung des Leiters der wirtschaftspolitischen Abteilung." For an evaluation of Waffen SS on the Czech weapons it had used during the 1940 campaign, see NARS, T-175/104/2626133ff.

134. For a discussion of these weaknesses, see Murray, *The Change in the European Balance of Power*, chaps. 1 and 10.

135. Ibid., chart 12 and 327–329.

136. Ibid., charts 9, 10, and 11; and 326–329.

137. Ibid., 329–331.

138. NARS T-77/775, OKW files: "Denkschrift und Richtlinien über die Führung des Krieges im Westen," Berlin, 9.10.39.

139. Oil was, of course, the major vulnerability.

140. H. R. Trevor-Roper, ed., *Blitzkrieg to Defeat, Hitler's War Directives* (New York: Holt Rinehart and Winston, 1965), Directive No. 6 for the Conduct of the War, 9.10.39, 13.

141. Williamson Murray, "Modern Mechanized War," in *The Cambridge Illustrated History of War*, ed. Geoffrey Parker (Cambridge), 304.

142. For a discussion of these issues, see Williamson Murray, *Military Adaptation in War, For Fear of Change* (Cambridge: Cambridge University Press, 2011).

143. BNA, CAB 2/8, CID Minutes of the 360th Meeting held on 22.6.39, 232.

144. BNA, CAB 55/18, JP 470, 12.7.39., CID, Joint Planning Committee: "The attitude of Italy in war and the problem of French support to Poland," 3.

145. Réunion du Conseil Suprême Interallié qui s'est tenu à Brighton, 22.9.39. Fondation Nationale des Sciences Politique.

146. For Mussolini's eagerness to enter the war on Germany's side, see MacGregor Knox, *Mussolini Unleashed* (Cambridge: Cambridge University Press, 1982), chap. 1.

147. BNA CAB 2/9, CID, Minutes of the 368th meeting held on July 24, 1939, 74.

148. For the extent of those disasters, as well as a clear examination of the factors contributing to the gross incompetence of the Italian military, see Knox, *Mussolini Unleashed.*

149. Quoted in NARS T-311/234/43, OKH Genst. D. H., Abt. Fremde Heere West, 18.7.40, "Auswertung von franz. Beutematerial," "Der Oberbefehlshaber Gamelin an Oberst Fyda, polnisher Militär-attaché in Paris," September 1939.

150. BNA CAB 65/1 WM (39), War Cabinet 20 (39), 19.9.39.

151. The convoluted and extensive arguments within the cabinet and government are discussed in Murray, *The Change in the European Balance of Power*, 341–347. Included in the discussion is Churchill's devastating critique of the chiefs of staff memorandum of late December 1939.

152. BNA CAB 85/16, M.R. (J) (40) (s) 2, 11.4.40, Allied Military Committee, "The Major Strategy of the War, Note by the French Delegation."

153. See, among others, Roland Frieser, *Blitzkrieg Legend, The German Campaign in the West* (Washington, DC, United States Naval Institute Press, 2013); and Williamson Murray and Allan R. Millett, *A War to Be Won; Fighting the Second World War* (Cambridge, MA: Harvard University Press, 2001).

154. With the possible exception of Abraham Lincoln.

155. Quoted in Henry Pelling, *Britain and the Second World War* (London: Collins, 1970), 87.

156. R. V. Jones, *The Wizard War: British Scientific Intelligence, 1939–1945* (New York: Coward, McCann & Geoghegan, 1978), 102–105.

157. Basil Collier, *The Defence of the United Kingdom* (London: H. M. Stationery Office, 1995).

158. For British and German production and loss figures throughout the war, see Williamson Murray, *Luftwaffe* (Baltimore, MD: Nautical and Aviation, 1985).

159. Chef WFA, 30.6.40, "Die Weiterführung des Krieges gegen England," *International Military Tribune: Trial of Major War Criminals*, vol. 28 (Washington, DC, 1948), 301–303.

160. Quoted in Air Ministry, *The Rise and Fall of the German Air Force, 1933–1945* (New York: St. Martin's Press, 1983), 75.

161. For a discussion of the issues surrounding SEA LION, see Williamson Murray and Allan R. Millett, *A War to Be Won, Fighting the Second World War* (Cambridge, MA: Harvard University Press, 2000).

162. Aileen Clayton, *The Enemy Is Listening* (London: Hutchinson, 1980), 49.

163. Part of the explanation for the German failure to recognize the fact that the British were integrating radar into a system of air defense was the fact that they were only using it in a GCI (ground control intercept) mode in which each radar controlled and guided a single fighter. It would not be until 1943 that the Germans would create a systemic approach to air defense based on the integration of radar into the overall control of German fighters. By then it was too late.

164. Francis K. Mason, *Battle over Britain: A History of German Air Assaults on Great Britain, 1917–1918 and July–December 1940 and the Development of Britain's Air Defenses between the World Wars* (Garden City, NY: Doubleday, 1969), Appendix K, OKL, 16.7.40, Operations Staff IC.

165. Horst Boog, Jürgen Förster, Joachim Hoffman, Ernst Klink, Rolf-Dieter Muller, and Gerd Ueberschär, *Das Deutsche Reich und der Zweite Weltkrieg*, vol. 4, *Der Angriff auf die Sowiet Union* (Stuttgart, 1984).

166. Quoted in Richard Muller, *The German Air War in Russia* (Baltimore, MD: Nautical and Aviation, 1992), x.

167. Not only did German intelligence get everything wrong in its estimates of the capacity of the Soviet Union to resist an invasion, but from 1942 on, Soviet deception operations misled German intelligence as to the location and intent of every major operation the Red Army would launch over the

course of the remainder of the war. In this regard, see especially David
M. Glantz, *Soviet Military Deception in the Second World War (Soviet Military
Theory and Practice)* (London: F. Cass, 1989).

168. Roosevelt confronted major problems in facing down America's isolationists.
For an outstanding study of Roosevelt's strategic course in the run up to war,
see David Kaiser, *No End Save Victory: How Roosevelt Led the Nation into War*
(New York: Basic Books, 2014).

169. By May 1941, the British had developed most of the tactics and technology
necessary to defeat the U-boat menace. The problem would be that it
would take another two years to produce the ships, technological aides, and
weapons systems and train the anti-submarine force to a sufficiently high
level to crush the U-boat force. See Murray, *Military Adaptation in War*,
189–193.

170. John Terraine, *The Right of the Line: The Royal Air Force in the European War,
1939–1945* (London: Hodder and Stoughton, 1985), 259.

171. Ibid., 295.

172. See the comments in Josef Goebbels's diary: Josef Goebbels, *The Goebbels
Diaries, 1942–1943,* trans. and ed. Louis Lochner (New York, 1948), 154–155,
186. Given the belief among the Nazi leadership and especially Adolph Hitler
that the defeat in 1918 had largely resulted from a collapse of morale on the
home front, reports of morale problems as a result of the strategic bombing
of German cities were worrisome. See also Ian Kershaw, *Der Hitler-Mythos:
Volksmeinung und Propaganda im Dritten Reich* (Munich: Deutsche Verlags-
Anstalt, 1980).

173. For the impact on the Luftwaffe, see Williamson Murray, *Luftwaffe*
(Baltimore, MD: Nautical and Aviation, 1985), and for the best examination
of the V-2 program, its enormous cost, and lack of effectiveness, see Michael
Neufeld, *The Rocket and the Reich: Peenemünde and the Coming of the Ballistic Era*
(Washington, DC: Smithsonian, 1994).

174. Heimatsverteidigungs Programm 1943, "Besprechung beim Reichsmarshall
am 7.10.43, Obersalzburg, Fortsetzung," Albert Simpson Historical
Research Center: K 113.312–2, vol. 3.

175. Adam Tooze, *The Wages of Destruction, The Making and Breaking of the Nazi
Economy* (New York: Viking, 2007), 597–598

176. I am much indebted to Professor Phillips O'Brien of the University of
Glasgow for this point.

177. There was considerable irony in these numbers because airmen before the war
had argued that air warfare would avoid the terrible attrition of the trenches.
Ironically, the air war in World War II concentrated the attrition among the
officers and NCOs, in other words, the better educated.

178. Murray, *Luftwaffe,* chaps. 6–7.

179. For Zuckerman's contributions, see Solly Zuckerman, *From Apes to Warlords: The Autobiography (1904–1946) of Solly Zuckerman* (London: Collins, 1976). For Jones see Jones, *The Wizard War: British Scientific Intelligence, 1939–1945*.

180. For Winn's contribution to the winning of the war, see particularly Patrick Beesley, *Very Special Intelligence: The Story of the Admiralty's Operational Intelligence Centre, 1939–1945* (Garden City, NY: Doubleday, 1977).

Chapter 13

1. This chapter represents the thoughts and opinions of the author and not necessarily those of the US Government, the US Department of Defense, the US Navy Department, or the US Naval War College.

2. S. C. M. Paine, *The Sino-Japanese War of 1894–1895: Perceptions, Power, and Primacy* (Cambridge: Cambridge University Press, 2003), 62–63.

3. S. C. M. Paine, *Imperial Rivals: China, Russia, and Their Disputed Frontier* (Armonk, NY: M. E. Sharpe, 1996), 29–35.

4. This section is a distillation of China's traditional approach to foreign policy in ibid., 23–32, and the discussions of specific minority groups in Bruce A. Elleman and S. C. M. Paine, *Modern China: Continuity and Change 1644 to the Present* (Boston: Prentice Hall, 2010), 136–137, 155–156, 246–247, 346.

5. Evelyn S. Rawski, *The Last Emperors: A Social History of Qing Institutions* (Berkeley: University of California Press, 1998), 199–263.

6. Paine, *Sino-Japanese War*, 223, 235.

7. Mark Mancall, *Russia and China: Their Diplomatic Relations to 1728* (Cambridge, MA: Harvard University Press, 1971), 111–162; Peter C. Perdue, *China Marches West: The Qing Conquest of Central Eurasia* (Cambridge, MA: Harvard University Press, 2005), 133–297.

8. Bruce A. Elleman and S. C. M. Paine, *Modern China*, 47–49.

9. Ibid., 55–56, 103–105.

10. Bruce A. Elleman, *Modern Chinese Warfare, 1795–1989* (London: Routledge, 2001), 35–56.

11. Table 10.1, "Self-strengthening Projects," and Paine, *Modern China*, 166.

12. For the details, see Paine, *Imperial Rivals*, 114, and Part II in general.

13. John P. LeDonne, *The Grand Strategy of the Russian Empire 1650–1831* (Oxford: Oxford University Press, 2004), 74–81; S. C. M. Paine, *Imperial Rivals*, 114–117.

14. Vasilii O. Kliuchevskii, *Курс Русской истории* [*The Course of Russian History*], part 1, vol. 1 (1904; rpr., Moscow: Издательство "Мысль," 1987), 50.

15. Paine, *Imperial Rivals*, 250–253; Mark Harrison, "Soviet Economic Growth since 1928: The Alternate Statistics of G. I. Khanin," *Europe-Asia Studies* 45, no. 1 (1993): 141–167; Mark Adomanis, "Russia Is

Roughly Where the United States Was in the 1950s," *Forbes* (April 26, 2013), http://www.forbes.com/ sites/markadomanis/2013/04/26/economically-russia-is-roughly-where-the-united-states-was-in-the-1950s/?&_suid=14032752150670853851 6454864293, accessed June 20, 2014.

16. Alfred J. Rieber, *Merchants and Entrepreneurs in Imperial Russia* (Chapel Hill: University of North Carolina Press, 1982), 3–23; Paine, *Sino-Japanese War*, 72–74.

17. Nicholas V. Riasanovsky, *A History of Russia*, 5th ed. (New York: Oxford University Press, 1993), 265–271; John P. LeDonne, *Grand Strategy of the Russian Empire*, 93–99, 161, 168–176.

18. S. C. M. Paine, *The Wars for Asia 1911–1949* (Cambridge: Cambridge University Press, 2012), 88–89.

19. Paine, *Imperial Rivals*, 87–95.

20. Ibid., 49–97.

21. Table 7.3, "Opening of Treaty Ports (1843–94)," and Table 12.1, "Opening of Treaty Ports (1895–1911)," in Elleman and Paine, *Modern China*, 126, 205.

22. This section is a distillation of S. C. M. Paine, *The Sino-Japanese War*, 77–106.

23. Elleman and Paine, *Modern China*, 222–234.

24. S. C. M. Paine, "Japanese Puppet-State Building in Manchukuo," in *Nation Building, State Building, and Economic Development*, ed. S. C. M. Paine (Armonk, NY: M. E. Sharpe, 2010), 66–82.

25. O. Borisov, *Советский Союз и маньчжурская революционная база 1945–1949* {*The Soviet Union and the Manchurian Revolutionary Base 1945–1949*} (Moscow: Издательство "Мысль," 1975), 49, 53–54, 56.

26. Paine, *Wars for Asia*, 123–170.

27. Riasanovsky, *A History of Russia*, 369–380, 398, 408–415, 422–434.

28. William C. Fuller Jr., *Strategy and Power in Russia 1600–1914* (New York: Free Press, 1992), 394–451.

29. Riasanovsky, *A History of Russia*, 477–478.

30. Paine, *Wars for Asia*, 77–90.

31. Robert Conquest, *Harvest of Sorrow* (Oxford: Oxford University Press, 1986), *passim*.

32. Bruce A. Elleman, *Diplomacy and Deception: The Secret History of Sino-Soviet Diplomatic Relations, 1917–1927* (Armonk, NY: M. E. Sharpe, 1997), *passim*; Paine, *Imperial Rivals*, 320–332.

33. Paine, *Wars for Asia*, 50–57, 70–76, 86–88.

34. This section is a distillation of Paine, *Wars for Asia, passim*.

35. There are a few series of books written on the basis of Russian and Eastern European archives documenting this process. See, in particular,

the Harvard Cold War Studies Book Series edited by Mark Kramer and published by Lexington Press; the New Cold War History series edited by Odd Arne Westad and published by the University of North Carolina, Chapel Hill; and the Cold War International History Project at the Wilson Center.

36. Winston Churchill, "The Sinews of Peace" speech, given at Westminster College, Fulton, Missouri, March 5, 1946, http://history1900s.about.com/od/churchillwinston/a/Iron-Curtain.htm, accessed June 19, 2014.

37. Paine, *Wars for Asia*, 223–270.

38. Ibid., 152–154, 230–233, 237, 245–246.

39. Ibid., *Wars for Asia*, 259.

40. Yang Jisheng, *Tombstone: The Great Chinese Famine 1958–1962*, Edward Friedman, ed., Stacy Mosher and Jian Guo, eds. and trans. (New York: Farrar, Straus, and Giroux, 2012), *passim*.

41. Elleman and Paine, *Modern China*, 378–387; Nicholas Khoo, *Collateral Damage: Sino-Soviet Rivalry and the Termination of the Sino-Vietnamese Alliance* (New York: Columbia University Press, 2011), 56–57; Ilya Gaiduk, *The Soviet Union and the Vietnam War* (Chicago: Ivan R. Dee, 1996), 225; Henry Kissinger, *Diplomacy* (New York: Simon & Schuster, 1994), 723.

42. Kissinger, *Diplomacy*, 721–726.

43. Jonathan Haslam, *Russia's Cold War: From the October Revolution to the Fall of the Wall* (New Haven, CT: Yale University Press, 2011), 270–271; Quintin V. S. Bach, *Soviet Aid to the Third Word: The Facts and Figures* (Sussex, UK: Book Guild, 2003); Stephen G. Brooks and William C. Wohlforth, "Economic Constraints and the Turn towards Superpower Cooperation in the 1980s," in *The Last Decade of the Cold War: From Conflict Escalation to Conflict Transformation* (London: Frank Cass, 2005), 88–90; Andrei Grachev, *Gorbachev's Gamble: Soviet Foreign Policy and the End of the Cold War* (Cambridge: Polity, 2008), 22–24.

44. Grachev, *Gorbachev's Gamble*, 69, 109, 116, 161, 167, 182, 199, 204–207.

45. Owen F. Humpage and Michael Shenk, "Economic Growth Trends: Bifurcation?" Federal Reserve Bank of Cleveland, May 9, 2008, www.clevelandfed.org/research/trends/2008/0508/01intmar.cfm, accessed June 18, 2014.

46. Francis Fukuyama popularized the phrase in his article, "The End of History?" *National Interest* no. 16 (Summer 1989): 3–18.

47. Wang Zheng, *Never Forget National Humiliation* (New York: Columbia University Press, 2012).

48. Margarita Estévez-Abe, *Welfare and Capitalism in Postwar Japan* (Cambridge: Cambridge University Press, 2008), 16, 79–81, 99–100, 284.

Chapter 14

1. For the Teutonic Knights' conquest of East Prussia, see Hans Delbrück, *History of the Art of War*, vol. 3, *Medieval Warfare* (Lincoln: University of Nebraska Press, 1982), 377–383; and for the history of the Order in general, H. W. Koch, *A History of Prussia* (New York: Dorset Press, 1978), 1–22.

2. For Grunwald, see Delbrück, *History of the Art of War*, 523–526.

3. The US Army War College currently teaches "strategic landpower" as one of the five "operational domains," along with air, sea, space, and cyber. See, for example, Lukas Milevski, "Fortissimus Inter Pares: The Utility of Landpower in Grand Strategy," *Parameters* 42, no. 2 (Summer 2012): 6–15, as well as William T. Johnsen, *Redefining Land Power for the 21st Century* (Carlisle, PA: Strategic Studies Institute, 1998), 5–15.

4. Michael Stürmer, *The German Empire: A Short History* (New York: Modern Library, 2000), 12–13.

5. Robert B. Strassler, ed., *The Landmark Thucydides: A Comprehensive Guide to the Peloponnesian War* (New York: The Free Press, 1996), 1–23 (16).

6. For the partitions, see Norman Davies, *God's Playground, a History of Poland: The Origins to 1795* (New York: Columbia University Press, 1984), 520–542. See also Vejas Gabriel Liulevicius, *The German Myth of the East: 1800 to the Present* (Oxford: Oxford University Press, 2009), 40–43.

7. Alex Storozynski, *The Peasant Prince: Thaddeus Kosciuszko and the Age of Revolution* (New York: St. Martin's, 2010).

8. Davies, *God's Playground*, 542.

9. For a survey of the Polish minority in Prussia, see Volker R. Berghahn, *Imperial Germany, 1871–1914* (Providence, RI: Berghahn Books, 1994), 110–118.

10. The best one-volume work on the process is Dennis Showalter, *The Wars of German Unification* (London: Arnold, 2004).

11. Orlando Figes, *The Crimean War: A History* (New York: Henry Holt, 2011).

12. The *zemstvo* was for the peasantry and the landowners. *Encyclopaedia Britannica Online Academic Edition* (Encyclopedia Britannica, 2014). http://www.britannica.com/EBchecked/topic/656413/zemstvo. Accessed September 9, 2014.

13. W. E. Mosse, *Alexander II and the Modernization of Russia* (London: Tauris, 1992).

14. For Russia's post–Crimean War *recueillement*, the first of several in the period under discussion, see Barbara Jelavich, *St. Petersburg and Moscow: Tsarist and Soviet Foreign Policy, 1814–1974* (Bloomington: Indiana University Press, 1974), 133–134, 172–174.

15. "La Russie ne boude pas, mais se recueille." Ibid., 134.

16. Erich Eyck, *Bismarck and the German Empire* (New York: Norton, 1950), 68–72.

17. Quoted in Otto Pflanze, *Bismarck and the Development of Germany: The Period of Unification, 1815–1871* (Princeton, NJ: Princeton University Press, 1963), 186. Pflanze hastens to add, "Undoubtedly this was written in an exuberant moment. At no time did Bismarck ever officially advocate or follow a policy of extermination against a national minority."

18. But see Edgar Feuchtwanger, *Bismarck* (London: Routledge, 2002), a principal theme of which is Bismarck's willingness to cut a deal with Napoleon III, a figure who was abhorrent to most conservatives, as long as it was in the interest of Prussia.

19. Eyck, *Bismarck and the German Empire*, 69.

20. Jelavich, *St. Petersburg and Moscow*, 172.

21. For Bismarck as the skilled practitioner of balance of power politics, see the classic account by George F. Kennan, *The Decline of Bismarck's European Order: Franco-Russian Relations 1875–1890* (Princeton, NJ: Princeton University Press, 1981). For the "white revolutionary," see Lothar Gall, *Bismarck: Der weisse Revolutionär*, 2 vols. (Frankfurt am Main: Propylaen, 1980).

22. Henry Kissinger, *Diplomacy* (New York: Simon & Schuster, 1994), 164–165.

23. "Their majesties mutually promise, should the interests of their States diverge in respect to special questions, to take counsel together in order that these divergences may not be able to prevail over the considerations of a higher order which preoccupy them." From the Austro-Russian "Schönbrunn" Agreement, May 25, 1873, one component of the Three Emperors' League. Reprinted in Ralph R. Menning, ed., *The Art of the Possible: Documents on Great Power Diplomacy, 1814–1914* (New York: McGraw Hill, 1996), 177.

24. Bismarck was a man, after all, who in the course of his career (1) ignored the Prussian constitution; (2) forged documents to provoke other powers into war; (3) seized the Hanoverian treasury after deposing King George V and used the money as a slush fund to pay off journalists inclined to support his political positions; and (4) once stated that some states were "too great to be bound by the text of a treaty"—all duly noted by his biographers. For the quotation, see Eyck, *Bismarck and the German Empire*, 65–66.

25. W. E. Gladstone, *Bulgarian Horrors and the Question of the East* (New York: Lovell, Adam, Wesson, 1876). For the crisis in general, see Barbara Jelavich, *History of the Balkans*, vol. 2, *Eighteenth and Nineteenth Centuries* (Cambridge: Cambridge University Press, 1983), 352–361.

26. John D. Treadway, *The Falcon and the Eagle: Montengro and Austria-Hungary, 1908–1914* (West Lafayette, IN: Purdue University Press, 1983), 14.

27. For a solid analytical account of the Russo-Turkish War, see *The Art of War: William McElwee, From Waterloo to Mons* (Bloomington: Indiana University Press, 1974), 184–207.

28. The Anglo-Ottoman Cyprus Convention of June 4, 1878 ("His Imperial Majesty the Sultan further consents to assign the island of Cyprus to be occupied and administered by England") is reprinted in Menning, *Documents on Great Power Diplomacy*, 190–192. See also Barbara Jelavich, *The Ottoman Empire, the Great Powers, and the Straits Question, 1870–1887* (Bloomington: Indiana University Press, 1973), 112–117.

29. Quoted in Eyck, *Bismarck and the German Empire*, 262.

30. Alexander II's letter is sometimes known as the *Ohrfeigenbrief*, the "clip around the ear." See William Mulligan, *The Origins of the First World War* (Cambridge: Cambridge University Press, 2010), 29. "Les craintes qui me préoccupent et dont les conséquences pourraient devenir désastreuses pour nos deux pays." See Eyck, *Bismarck and the German Empire*, 263.

31. "Realpolitik Turns on Itself," in Kissinger, *Diplomacy*, 137–167.

32. "Wicked problem" is a notion developed originally by systems analysts, but now appearing more and more widely in discussions of strategy. "Wicked problems" are tangled, internally contradictory, and impervious to conventional solutions (as opposed to normal, or "tame" ones). See, for example, Kenneth J. Menkhaus, "State Fragility as a Wicked Problem," *Prism* 1, no. 2 (March 2010): 85–100.

33. For the clauses of the Dual Alliance, see Menning, *Documents of Great Power Diplomacy*, 197–199.

34. Eyck, *Bismarck and the German Empire*, 34.

35. Ibid., 264.

36. The clauses are reprinted in Menning, *Documents of Great Power Diplomacy*, 222–224.

37. For discussion of the incredibly complicated Bulgarian Unification crisis, including diplomatic intrigue, coups, and kidnappings, see Jelavich, *History of the Balkans*, 366–373. For the pertinent documents, see Menning, *Documents of Great Power Diplomacy*, 199–201.

38. Katkov in the Moscow *Vedomostei*, March 17/19 1887, reprinted in Menning, *Documents of Great Power Diplomacy*, 227.

39. Quoted in Feuchtwanger, *Bismarck*, 193.

40. Or "treaty providing security for one's rear," Michal Balfour, *The Kaiser and His Times* (New York: Norton, 1972), 107.

41. Caprivi's memorandum of May 22, 1890, is reprinted in Menning, *Documents of Great Power Diplomacy*, 241–243. See also the article by G. Gooch, "Bismarck's Legacy," *Foreign Affairs* 30, no. 4 (July 1952): 517–530, on the difficulty of basing foreign policy purely on *raison d'état*.

42. The Franco-Russian Treaty is reprinted in Menning, *Documents of Great Power Diplomacy*, 245–247.

43. The Franco-Russian Treaty, in ibid., 245–247.

44. For a discussion of the Buchlau conference, replete with what was discussed, what was not, and the mutually contradictory claims of these two "ambitious career diplomats," see Kenneth I. Dailey, "Alexander Isvolsky and the Buchlau Conference," *Russian Review* 10, no. 1 (January 1951): 55–63.

45. Kiderlen to Pourtalès, March 21, 1909, reprinted in Menning, *Documents of Great Power Diplomacy*, 341.

46. Five-Power Memorandum to the Serb Government, March 30th, 1909, reprinted in ibid., 342–343.

47. Quoted in Friedrich von Rabenau, *Seeckt: Aus seinem Leben, 1918–1936* (Leipzig: von Hase und Koehler Verlag, 1940), 316.

48. For German-Soviet military cooperation in the interwar era, see Manfred Zeidler, *Reichswehr und Rote Armee, 1920–1933: Wege und Stationen einer ungewöhnlichen Zusammenarbeit* (München: Oldenbourg, 1993). About thirty members of the German *Reichswehr* worked at Kazan, and some 200 pilots and observers at Lipetsk.

49. Robert Conquest is still the leading scholar on Stalin, industrialization, and the Purges. See *Harvest of Sorrow: Soviet Collectivization and the Terror-Famine* (Oxford: Oxford University Press, 1986) and *Stalin: Breaker of Nations* (New York: Penguin, 1991). The first "glasnost" era biography of Stalin offered a great deal of new material, none of it likely to rehabilitate him. See Dmitri Volgokonov, *Stalin: Triumph and Tragedy* (New York: Grove Weidenfeld, 1991). For a primary source account by a young American taking part in "socialist construction," see John Scott, *Behind the Urals* (Bloomington: Indiana University Press, 1989).

50. For Locarno, see Jonathan Wright, "Stresemann and Locarno," *Contemporary European History* 4, no. 2 (July 1995): 109–131. For the "eastern Locarno" problem (i.e., the Weimar Republic's refusal to accept the Versailles territorial settlement with Poland), see Christian Höltje, *Die Weimarer Republik und das Ostlocarno-Problem, 1919–1934* (Würzburg: Holzner-Verlag, 1958).

51. General Henry Pownall, director of Military Operations and Military Intelligence in the British War Office from 1938 to 1939. Quoted in Gerhard L. Weinberg, *The Foreign Policy of Hitler's Germany: Starting World War II, 1937–1939* (Atlantic Highlands, NJ: Humanities Press, 1994), 555. For a lucid discussion of the Anglo-French Guarantee to Poland, see also M. H. Bell, *The Origins of the Second World War in Europe* (London: Longman, 1986), 252–256.

52. Weinberg, *Foreign Policy of Hitler's Germany*, 568–570.

53. For the causes and circumstances of Litvinov's departure, see Volgokonov, *Stalin*, 346–349, as well as Weinberg, *Foreign Policy of Hitler's Germany*, 570–573.

54. For the text of the Nazi-Soviet Pact, as well as the Secret Additional Protocol, see *Documents on German Foreign Policy*, Series D, vol. 7 (Washington, DC: US Government Printing Office, 1956), 245–247.

55. Quoted in Conquest, *Stalin: Breaker of Nations*, 221. Ribbentrop wanted a preamble referencing "the friendly character of Soviet-German relations." Stalin rejected it: "The Soviet government could not honestly assure the Soviet people that there were friendly relations with Germany, given that for six years the Nazi government has been pouring bucketloads of mud on the Soviet government." Volgokonov, *Stalin*, 355.

56. Dmitri Volgokonov, "A Soviet Version," in *World War II: Roots and Causes*, ed. Keith Eubank (Lexington, MA: D. C. Heath, 1992), 271–272. See also the account by Dr. Paul Schmidt, an interpreter attached to the Ribbentrop mission to Moscow, *Hitler's Interpreter: The Secret History of German Diplomacy, 1935–1945* (New York: Macmillan, 1951), 135–141, as well as Michael Bloch, *Ribbentrop: A Biography* (New York: Crown, 1992), 246–250.

57. Weinberg, *Foreign Policy of Hitler's Germany*, 610.

58. Quoted in Donald W. Treadgold, *Twentieth Century Russia* (Hopewell, NJ: Houghton Mifflin, 1981), 314.

59. Quoted in Conquest, *Stalin: Breaker of Nations*, 221.

60. Volgokonov, "A Soviet Version," 271.

61. "Unsere Kriege kurtz und *vives* seyn müssen, massen es uns nicht konveniret die Sachen in die Länge zu ziehen, weil ein langwieriger Krieg ohnvermerkt Unsere admirable Disciplin fallen machen, und das Land depeupliren, Unsere Resources aber erschöpfen würde." Hugo von Freytag-Loringhoven, *Feldherrngrösse: Von Denken und Haldeln bevorragender Heerführer* (Berlin: E. S. Mittler, 1922), 56.

62. For World War I in the East, see Norman Stone, *The Eastern Front, 1914–1917* (New York: Scribner's, 1975), and Holger Herwig, *The First World War: Germany and Austria-Hungary, 1914–1918* (New York: Bloomsburg Academic, 2009). For Tannenberg, see Dennis Showalter, *Tannenberg: Clash of Empires* (Washington, DC: Brassey's, 2004).

63. For Warsaw and Lodz, see Robert M. Citino, *The German Way of War: From the Thirty Years' War to the Third Reich* (Lawrence: University Press of Kansas, 2005), 230–234.

64. Richard L. DiNardo, *Breakthrough: The Gorlice-Tarnow Campaign, 1915* (Santa Barbara, CA: Praeger, 2010).

65. Timothy C. Dowling, *The Brusilov Offensive* (Bloomington: Indiana University Press, 2008).

66. For the battle of Riga, see Robert M. Citino, *Quest for Decisive Victory: From Stalemate to Blitzkrieg in Europe, 1899–1940* (Lawrence: University Press of Kansas, 2002), 167–171.

67. See John W. Wheeler-Bennett, *Brest-Litovsk: The Forgotten Peace, March 1918* (New York: Norton, 1971).

68. Conquest, *Stalin: Breaker of Nations*, 224.

69. Quoted in M. K. Dziewanowski, *A History of Soviet Russia* (Englewood Cliffs, NJ: Prentice Hall, 1989), 246–247.

70. Conquest, *Stalin: Breaker of Nations*, 224.

71. For the Soviet war on Finland, see Gordon F. Sander, *The Hundred Day Winter War: Finland's Gallant Stand against the Soviet Army* (Lawrence: University Press of Kansas, 2013).

72. Quoted in Volgokonov, *Stalin*, 401.

73. Quoted in Conquest, *Stalin: Breaker of Nations*, 235.

74. For the opening of the German campaign in the Soviet Union, see the meticulously researched work by David Stahel, *Operation Barbarossa and Germany's Defeat in the East* (Cambridge: Cambridge University Press, 2009)

75. For the German drive, and then eventually creep, toward Moscow, see David Stahel, *Operation Typhoon: Hitler's March on Moscow, October 1941* (Cambridge: Cambridge University Press, 2013). For the Soviet counteroffensive, see Andrew Nagorski, *The Greatest Battle: Stalin, Hitler, and the Desperate Struggle for Moscow That Changed the Course of World War II* (New York: Simon & Schuster, 2007).

76. Timothy Snyder, *Bloodlands: Europe between Hitler and Stalin* (New York: Basic Books, 2010).

77. "Panslavism was in fact a fad; its influence in foreign policy was not long-lasting." Jelavich, *History of the Balkans*, 354.

78. Robert Kaplan, *The Revenge of Geography: What the Map Tells Us about Coming Conflicts and the Battle against Fate* (New York: Random House, 2012).

79. For the reunification of Germany as a problem of international politics and diplomacy, see Philip Zelikow and Condoleeza Rice, *Germany Unified and Transformed: A Study in Statecraft* (Cambridge, MA: Harvard University Press, 1997).

80. John Lukacs, *The Legacy of the Second World War* (New Haven, CT: Yale University Press, 2010), 188.

81. Gerhard L. Weinberg, "The Nazi Soviet Pacts: A Half-Century Later," *Foreign Affairs* 68, no. 4 (Fall 1989): 175–189, quotation on189.

Chapter 15

1. Hoshi Toru to Ōkuma Shigenobu, June 17, 1897, *Nihon Gaiko Bunsho* (Japanese Diplomatic Documents), U.S.–Hawai`i Annexation, vol. 22, 978; Junesay Iddittie, *The Life of Marquis Shigenobu Okuma: A Biographical Study in the Rise of Democratic Japan* (The Hokuseido Press, 1940), 298; John J. Stephan, *Hawai'i under the Rising Sun* (Honolulu: University of Hawai'i Press, 1984), 18–19. Hoshi Toru was the senior Japanese official in North America and held the diplomatic rank of Minister to Washington.

2. William Michael Morgan, *Pacific Gibraltar: U.S.-Japanese Rivalry over the Annexation of Hawaii, 1885–1898* (Annapolis, MD: Naval Institute Press, 2011), 196–197.

3. Ibid., 198–217; Morgan, "Anti-Japanese Origins of the Hawaiian Annexation Treaty of 1897," *Diplomatic History* 6, no. 1 (Winter 1982): 23–44.

4. Angus Maddison, *Historical Statistics of the World Economy, 1–2008 AD*, http://ggdc.net/maddison/ Historical_Statistics/horizontal-file_02_2010.xls. Accessed January 25, 2014.

5. Akira Iriye, "Imperialism in East Asia," in *Modern East Asia: Essays in Interpretation*, ed. James B. Crowley (New York: Harcourt, Brace, & World, 1970), 135–136.

6. Ibid., 135.

7. Nobutaka Ike, *Japan's Decision for War: Records of the 1941 Policy Conferences* (Stanford, CA: Stanford University Press, 1967), xix.

8. Walter LaFeber, *The Clash: A History of U.S.-Japan Relations* (New York: W. W. Norton, 1997), 51–52.

9. W. G. Beasley, *Japanese Imperialism, 1894–1945* (Oxford: Clarendon Press, 1987), 211–212.

10. Ibid., 76.

11. James B. Crowley, "Military Foreign Policies," in *Japan's Foreign Policy, 1868–1941: A Research Guide*, ed. James W. Morley (New York: Columbia University Press, 1974), 18–19.

12. Beasley, *Japanese Imperialism*, 82.

13. Yamagata's protégé, Lieutenant Colonel Tanaka Giichi, a future prime minister, played a lead role in drafting Yamagata's proposal. Crowley, "Military Policies," 24.

14. Ibid., 25.

15. Ibid., 25–28. The *genro* were a handful of very senior military and civilian officers who had played key roles in the early Meiji period and therefore served as informal but highly influential advisors to the throne and the cabinet. All elderly men in the World War I period, all but one was dead by 1924.

16. Beasley, *Japanese Imperialism*, 108–109.

17. These insular possessions were in the Carolines, Marshalls, and Marianas. After the war, Japan received a League of Nations mandate to rule these islands. See Frank W. Ikle, "Japan's Policies Toward Germany," in *Japan's Foreign Policy, 1868–1941: A Research Guide*, ed. James W. Morley (New York: Columbia University Press, 1974), 293–294.

18. Beasley, *Japanese Imperialism*, 112–115. The fullest treatment is Noriko Kawamura, *Turbulence in the Pacific: Japanese-U.S. Relations during World War I* (Westport, CT: Praeger, 2000), 23–31, and Chap. 2, which is devoted to the American response to the "Twenty-One Demands."

19. Kawamura, *Turbulence*, 44–45, 49–51.

20. Ian Gow, *Military Intervention in Pre-war Japanese Politics: Admiral Kato Kanji and the "Washington System"* (London: RoutledgeCurzon, 2004). This is a detailed, insightful portrait of a pivotal leader.

21. LaFeber, *The Clash*, 174–175; Michael A. Barnhart, *Japan Prepares for Total War: The Search for Economic Security, 1919–1941* (Ithaca, NY: Cornell University Press, 1987), 66–67.

22. Barnhart, *Japan Prepares*, 103–104.

23. Barnhart, *Japan Prepares*, 257.

24. The standard work on Ishiwara is Mark R. Peattie, *Ishiwara Kanji and Japan's Confrontation with the West* (Princeton, NJ: Princeton University Press, 1975).

25. Eri Hotta, *Japan 1941: Countdown to Infamy* (New York: Alfred Knopf, 2013), 177.

26. Rana Mitter, *Forgotten Ally: China's World War II, 1937–1945* (Boston; New York: Houghton Mifflin Harcourt, 2013); S. C. M. Paine, *The Wars for Asia, 1911–1949* (Cambridge: Cambridge University Press, 2012).

27. Quoted in Justus Doenecke and Mark Stoler, *Debating Franklin D. Roosevelt's Foreign Policies, 1933–1945* (Lanham, MD: Rowman & Littlefield, 2005), 45.

28. For the Imperial Conference of September 6, 1941, officials prepared likely questions and answers. To the question of whether war with the United States was inevitable, the answer was: ". . . the policy of the Unites States is based on the idea of preserving the status quo; in order to dominate the world and defend democracy, it aims to prevent our Empire from rising and developing in East Asia . . . the policies of Japan and the United States are mutually incompatible; it is historically inevitable that the conflict . . . will lead to war." Nobutaka Ike, *Japan's Decision for War: Records of the 1941 Policy Conferences* (Stanford, CA: Stanford University Press, 1967), 152.

29. Hotta, *Japan 1941*, 140.

30. Ibid., 144.

31. Robert J. C. Butow, *Tojo and the Coming of the War* (Palo Alto, CA: Stanford University Press, 1961), 418, 419, 420. Emphasis in the original text.

32. William R. Braisted, "The Evolution of the Unites States Navy's Strategic Assessments in the Pacific, 1919–31," in *The Washington Conference, 1921–22: Naval Rivalry, East Asian Stability, and the Road to Pearl Harbor*, ed. Erik Goldstein and John Maurer (Essex, UK: Frank Cass, 1994), 102–123.

33. Nobutaka Ike, *Japan's Decision for War: Records of the 1941 Policy Conferences* (Stanford, CA: Stanford University Press, 1967), 12.

34. Ike, *Records of the 1941 Policy Conferences*, 129.

35. Ibid., 5–13, quote from 6.

36. Ibid., 5–13, quotes from 12.

37. Ibid., 76–77.

38. Ibid., 107–108.

39. Ibid., 112–113. Though an attack of some sort against the Soviets was briefly discussed at later dates, it was never seriously considered.

40. Ibid., 129–130. The Liaison Conference was held September 3, 1941.

41. Ibid., 130.

42. Ibid., 136.

43. Ibid., 136.

44. Ibid., 139–140.

45. Beasley, *Japanese Imperialism*, 228–230; Barnhart, *Japan Prepares*, Table 9.1, 166.

46. Ike, *Records of the 1941 Policy Conferences*, 148. Suzuki spoke on September 6, 1941.

47. Barnhart, *Japan Prepares*, Table 7.2, 146; Table 13.2, 261.

48. Sidney Pash ably reviews the literature in *The Currents of War: A New History of American-Japanese Relations, 1899–1941* (Lexington: University of Kentucky Press, 2014), 198–206.

49. Hotta, *Japan 1941*, 155, 159.

50. Ike, *Records of the 1941 Policy Conferences*, 124–125.

51. Hotta, *Japan 1941*, 170–171.

52. Pash, *Currents of War*, 227, 231.

Chapter 16

1. *Wartime Production Achievement and the Reconversion Outlook: Report of the Chairman*, War Production Board (Washington, DC: US Government Printing Office, 1945), 106.

2. George Kennan, "The Long Telegram," sent to George Marshall, dated February 22, 1946, photocopy at the Truman Presidential Library, Harry S. Truman Administration File, Elsey Papers, http://www.trumanlibrary.org/ whistlestop/study_collections/coldwar/documents/pdf/6-6.pdf, 5. This was the framework for the later article Kennan wrote for *Foreign Affairs*, "The Sources of Soviet Conduct" (July 1947), http://www.foreignaffairs.com/articles/ 23331/x/the-sources-of-soviet-conduct.

3. Kennan, "Long Telegram," 5.

4. Before leaving their part of northern Azerbaijan, Moscow negotiated oil concessions with Iran, but the Iranians reneged on the deal after the Soviets departed.

5. For additional details on Soviet pressure on Turkey and Iran, see Vladislav M. Zubok, *A Failed Empire: The Soviet Union in the Cold War from Stalin to Gorbachev* (Chapel Hill: University of North Carolina Press, 2007), 40–48.

6. Robert Ferrell, *Off the Record: The Private Papers of Harry S. Truman* (New York: Harper and Row, 1980), 80.

7. For additional details on Truman's efforts to apply pressure, see Deborah W. Larson, *Origins of Containment: A Psychological Explanation* (Princeton, NJ: Princeton University Press, 1985), 279–283.

8. Nikita Khrushchev, quoted in *New York Times,* September 18, 1955, 19.

9. Mikhail Gorbachev, *Gorbachev: On My Country and the World* (New York: Columbia University Press: 2000), 65.

10. For a comparative analysis on how different US administrations implemented containment, see John Lewis Gaddis, *Strategies of Containment: A Critical Appraisal of American Policy during the Cold War*, rev. ed. (Oxford: Oxford University Press, 2005).

11. National Security Council, *NSC 68—A Report to the National Security Council*, April 14, 1950, 4.

12. Kennan, "Long Telegram," 15.

13. For details on the biological program, see Ken Alibek and Stephen Handelman, *Biohazard: The Chilling True Story of the Largest Covert Biological Weapons Program in the World—Told From the Inside by the Man Who Ran It* (New York: Delta, 2000).

14. Alexandr Fursenko and Timothy Naftali, "Soviet Intelligence and the Cuban Missile Crisis," *Intelligence and the Cuban Missile Crisis*, ed. James G. Blight and David A. Welch (London: Frank Cass, 1998), 66–67.

15. Ibid., 66.

16. Alexander Statiev, *Soviet Counterintelligence in the Western Border Lands* (Cambridge: Cambridge University Press, 2013), 330.

17. Fursenko and Naftali, "Soviet Intelligence and the Cuban Missile Crisis," 75.

18. For a detailed account of the dual-track decision and the Soviet failure to anticipate NATO's response, see Raymond L. Garthoff, *Détente and Confrontation: U.S.-Soviet Relations from Nixon to Reagan* (Washington, DC: Brookings Institution, 1994), 935–976.

19. Later, in the twilight of the Cold War, the superpowers agreed to dismantle their intermediate-range nuclear forces with the Intermediate-Range Nuclear Forces Treaty in 1987.

20. President George Washington declared in his Farewell Address, "It is our true policy to steer clear of permanent alliances with any portion of the foreign world." President Thomas Jefferson later stated during his inaugural pledge, "Peace, commerce, and honest friendship with all nations, entangling alliances with none."

21. For detailed accounts of the impact RAND Corporation analysts had on nuclear strategy, see Gregg Herken, *Counsels of War* (New York: Alfred A. Knopf, 1985); and Fred Kaplan, *The Wizards of Armageddon* (New York: Simon & Schuster, 1983.

22. NSC 162/2 stated that US security required a "strong military posture, with emphasis on the capability of inflicting massive retaliatory damage by offensive striking power." NSC 162/2, "Basic National Security Policy," October 30, 1953, 5.

23. See Richard K. Betts, *Nuclear Blackmail and Nuclear Balance* (Washington, DC: Brookings Institution, 1987), 123–129.

24. See Lou Cannon, *President Reagan: The Role of a Lifetime* (New York: PublicAffairs, 1991), 276–277.

25. President Reagan, "Address to the Nation on Defense and National Security," March 23, 1983, http://www.reagan.utexas.edu/archives/speeches/1983/32383d.htm.

26. For a firsthand account of this summit and President Reagan's refusal to consider SDI as a bargaining chip, see Ken Adelman, *Reagan at Reykjavik: Forty-Eight Hours That Ended the Cold War* (New York: Broadside Books, 2014).

27. The Air-Land Doctrine also provided a template (of sorts) for the Pentagon's more recent development of the Air-Sea Concept.

28. For comprehensive accounts of this dimension of the US-Soviet rivalry, see Peter Rodman, *More Precious Than Peace: Fighting and Winning the Cold War in the Third World* (New York: Scribner's, 1994); and Odd Arne Westad, *The Global Cold War: Third World Interventions and the Making of Our Times* (Cambridge: Cambridge University Press, 2007).

29. Quoted in Douglas Rivero, *The Detente Deception: Soviet and Western Bloc Competition and the Subversion of Cold War Peace* (Lanham, MD: University Press of America, 2013), 81.

30. Strobe Talbott, ed. *Khrushchev Remembers* (Boston: Little, Brown, 1970), 461.

31. John L. Gaddis, *We Now Know: Rethinking Cold War History* (Oxford: Oxford University Press, 1997), 169.

32. Bradford A. Lee, "American Grand Strategy and the Unfolding of the Cold War," in *Successful Strategies: Triumphing in War and Peace from Antiquity to the Present*, eds. Williamson Murray and Richard Hart Sinnreich (Cambridge: Cambridge University Press, 2014), 376.

33. Henry A. Kissinger, *Nuclear Weapons and Foreign Policy* (New York: W.W. Norton, abr. ed., 1957), 199.

34. Ibid.

35. *Address of the President of the United States*, March 12, 1947, http://www.trumanlibrary.org/whistlestop/study_collections/doctrine/large/documents/pdfs/5-9.pdf, 4.

36. See Matthew Ouimet, *The Rise and Fall of the Brezhnev Doctrine in Soviet Foreign Policy* (Chapel Hill: University of North Carolina Press, 2003).

37. For an assessment of the Politburo's internal debate on the Polish crisis, see Zubok, *Failed Empire*, 265–270.

38. Kennan, "The Sources of Soviet Conduct."

39. President Reagan's distaste for containment as a means to preserve the status quo was evident long before he became president. When asked in 1977 about his idea of US policy toward the Soviet Union, Reagan responded, "We win and they lose." See Richmond Allen, "The Man Who Won the Cold War," *Digest on Public Policy* No. 1 (Hoover Institute: 2000). http://www.hoover.org/research/man-who-won-cold-war, accessed August 18, 2016.

40. For a detailed account of the conceptual genesis and bureaucratic maneuvering that led to NSDD-75, see Thomas Mahnken, "The Reagan

Administration's Strategy Toward the Soviet Union," in *Successful Strategies*, 403–431.

41. For an account of US efforts to turn the tables on Soviet espionage, see Gus W. Weiss, *Duping the Soviets: The Farewell Dossier* (The Center for Strategic Intelligence, 1996), 121–126.

42. Artemy Kalinovsky, *A Long Goodbye from Afghanistan* (Cambridge, MA: Harvard University Press, 2011), 100.

43. Zubok, *Failed Empire*, 322.

44. See Michael Dobbs, *One Minute to Midnight: Kennedy, Khrushchev, and Castro on the Brink of Nuclear War* (New York: First Vintage Books Edition, 2009), 85–91.

45. For details, see James C. Oskins and Michael H. Maggelet, *Broken Arrow: The Declassified History of U.S. Nuclear Weapons Accidents* (Raleigh, NC: Lulu. com, 2008).

46. Gorbachev, *Gorbachev: On My Country and the World*, 57.

47. Ibid.

INDEX

Diocletian, 106, 132–36, 567n130, 568n135
Disraeli, Benjamin, 365–66, 457
Dixon, Jeremiah, 600n18
The Domesday Book (William), 171
Dominica, 277–78, 592n29
Domitian, 121
Domitianus, L. Domitius, 112, 567n130
Donggan Rebellion, 420, 421
Drake, Francis, 243
Dreyfus affair, 26–27, 339, 340, 341
Dual (Franco-Russian) Alliance of 1892/1894, 357
Dulles, John Foster, 534
Dupleix, Joseph François, 280, 593n39
Dutch Republic, 211, 226–28, 233
Duverney, Joseph Paris, 281

Ebert, Friedrich, 387
Edessa, Greece, 110, 117, 124–25, 131, 562n77
Edict of Fontainebleau, 269, 589n3
Edict of Nantes, 268, 589n3
Edward I, 160, 164, 173, 176, 178
Edward II (Black Prince), 160, 161, 166–67
Edward III, 156, 160–61, 165, 166, 168–69, 173, 174, 177, 180–81
Egypt
  Cold War, 531
  Genoa *vs.* Venice, 185, 190, 198, 203
  Rome-Byzantium *vs.* Persia, 112, 148, 556n28, 567n130
  Suez Canal, 365–66, 418
  US *vs.* UK, 364–66
Eight Trigrams rebellion, 421
Eighty Years War (1568–1648), 31, 269
Eisenhower, Dwight D., 412–13, 521, 523
Eleanor of Aquitaine, 158, 164, 166, 268
Elisabeth of Valois, 241
Elizabeth I, 211, 225
Enduring rivalries

allies in, 40–42
balance of power in, 3, 17
belligerence, 2
bullying, 2
characteristics, 2–6
commercial, 5
competition *vs.* rivalry, 5
debt loads, 26–27
development of, 3, 17–21, 18t, 49–50
domestic politics in, 3
domino theory of risk avoidance, 27–28
edge of power/edge of empire, 3
fear, honor, and interest in, 8–11
geopolitical imperative, ideology *vs.*, 36
global system shocks, 4, 11–17, 13–14t
ideology in, 7, 33–37
imperial overstretch, 24–26
information assessment in, 42–46, 50
maintenance of, 21–22
militarization in definition of, 5
money-victory relationship, 28–32, 454nn17–19, 546nn20–22
positional concerns in, 7
power asymmetries, 46–47
powers, growth trajectories of, 22–28, 23–24f
power shifts in, 3–4
preference, perception changes, 4
prestige motivations in, 7–9
proximity in, 12–15
root causes of, 6–11, 47, 48–49t
space between, 20–21
states/empires, reach of, 37–40
strategic commonalities, 4
subsidy treaties, 29–30
successive conflict effects, 4
system of rivalries, 16–17
time frames in analysis of, 5
war as result of, 4
Engelbrecht, Helmuth, 496
England *vs.* France. *see also* French Wars (1792–1815); New World rivalry
  Agincourt, battle of, 156, 178

England *vs.* France (*Cont.*)

Godwinson, Harold, 163
Goebbels, Joseph, 397, 610n86
Gorbachev, Mikhail, 441, 516, 520,
    529–30, 536–39
Gorchakov, A. M., 453, 454, 456, 457
Gordian III, 129–31, 562n77, 563n93
Göring, Hermann, 408, 411
Gourmont, Remy de, 339
Grand Alliance (League of Augsburg),
    270, 272, 273, 275, 589n9
Grandmaison, Louis, 341–42
Great Britain. *see also* England *vs.*
    France; French Wars (1792–1815)
    alliance making, pre-WWI, 8
    Anglo-Japanese Alliance, 358, 369
    conquest of by Hapsburgs,
        219, 228–29
    Continental System economic
        impacts, 312–13, 596nn13–14
    growth trajectory of, 23–24f, 23–25
    in India, 347
    military strategy, WWII, 94–95
    Napoleon's blockade of, 28–29,
        299–300, 312, 317, 596nn13–14
    prestige motivations in, 8–9
    public debt refinancing, 275–76
    rivalries, maintenance of, 22
    smuggling, illegal trade, 313–14,
        596nn16
    states/empires, reach of, 38
    subsidy payments, French Wars, 308,
        310, 314, 318, 597nn18
    subsidy treaties, 29–30
    taxation, 1813, 310, 596nn8–11
Great Depression, 389–90, 429–30,
    435–36, 481, 492
Greece *vs.* Persia, 38, 53–55, 58–60. *see
    also* Athens *vs.* Sparta
Gregory XIII, 215
Grenada, 538
Grey, E., 8–9
Grey, Edward, 374
Gunpowder Plot 1605, 269
Gustavus Adolphus, 253

Haber, Fritz, 608n53
Hadrian, 123–24, 152, 561nn62–63

Haig, Douglas, 381, 383–85
Halder, Franz, 410
Hamaguchi Osachi, 492, 494
Hamilcar Barca, 85, 87, 89–90
Hannibal, 81, 85, 86, 90–98
Hannibalianus, 136
Hapsburgs *vs.* Europe. *see also* Ottomans
    vs. Hapsburgs
    agency, structure, 230–33
    anti-Hapsburg alliances, 224–25
    Catalan revolt, 214, 226
    communications network, 217–18
    compliance bribes, 213–14
    Constitutions, 214
    Decree of Bankruptcy, 222
    development of, 18t
    diplomatic network, 218
    distance issues, 216–18
    domino theory, 227–30
    England, conquest of, 219, 228–29
    expansion strategies, 209–10
    financial issues, 222–24, 232
    Granada, war of, 225
    historical background, 210–13
    ideology in, 33, 215, 225,
        228–30, 233
    imperial overstretch, 222, 226–27
    incest, intermarriage within, 210,
        211, 231–32
    information assessment in, 42–44,
        219–21
    mental instability, 231–32
    money-victory relationship, 30–31
    papal support, 215–16
    Pavia, battle of, 224
    peace negotiations, 225–26
    Peace of Breda (1668), 231
    Peace of Nijmegen (1678), 231
    Peace of Rijswik (1697), 231
    Peace of the Pyrenees (1659), 231
    Portugal, 216, 226–27, 277
    problems, variety/complexity
        of, 221–24
    reputation maintenance, 227–30
    root causes of, 48t
    states/empires, reach of, 37–38
    sub-imperialism, 213–16, 580n6

success breeding failure
paradox, 224–27
systemic shocks as cause of, 13*t*
Treaty of Utrecht (1713), 214,
231, 274, 275, 277, 591n20,
592n11, 592n29
Union of Arms, 213–14
War of Spanish Succession, 214, 273
Hara Takashi, 490
Hara Yoshimichi, 503
Hardrada, Harald (Háráldr Hárðárði), 162
Harl, K., 37
Harley, Robert, 274
Harris, Townsend, 362
Hay, John, 485
Heaven-Earth Society rebellion, 421
Henderson, Nevile, 393–94, 399,
611n101
Henri of Navarre, 268, 589n3
Henry I, 158, 163, 164, 166
Henry II, 158–59, 164, 166–67, 176,
177, 268, 574n25
Henry III, 160, 164, 573n13
Henry IV, 161, 170, 176
Henry V, 156, 161–62, 169
Henry VI, 162, 178
Henry VIII, 268
Hephthalites, 106–7, 139, 140, 144,
145, 569n152
Heraclius, 147–50, 153
Herodian, 129, 130
Herodotus, 558n42
Hindenburg, Paul von, 378, 382
Hinsley, Harry, 413
Hiranuma Kiichiro, 495
Hitler, Adolf, 390–402, 404, 408–10,
434, 436, 466–69, 473, 610n86,
613n130
Hoare, Samuel, 405
Hong Kong, 360, 363, 364
Hormizd III, 140
Hormizd IV, 146
Hoshino Naoki, 503
Hughes, Charles Evans, 490
Hundred Years War, 24, 156, 161, 165,
167–70, 173, 175, 177, 178, 268,
573n16, 574n19

Hungary
Cold War, 533
Germany *vs.* France, 335
Ottomans *vs.* Hapsburgs, 242,
244–52, 255, 260–61

Ibrahim Pasha, 241–42, 246
Ideology
in China's rivalries, 35, 419
in Cold War, 35
in Crusades, 36
in enduring rivalries, 7, 33–37
in England *vs.* France, 268–70,
589nn1–3
in Genoa *vs.* Venice, 197–98
geopolitical imperative *vs.*, 36–37
in Hapsburgs *vs.* Europe, 33
in Ottomans *vs.* Hapsburgs, 235,
239–40, 242, 258, 585n2
in Rome-Byzantium *vs.* Persia,
107–8, 153
in US *vs.* Japan, 34, 479, 482, 494,
499–502
Imperial overstretch
Cold War, 540–41
enduring rivalries, 24–26
Hapsburgs *vs.* Europe, 222, 226–27
WWII, 24–26, 39
Inca Empire, 211
India, 347, 357
Indochina, 419, 499–500, 502–4
Industrial Revolution, 418,
421, 427–29
Innocent XI, 260
Inoue Junnosuke, 495
Inoue Nissho, 495
Intermediate-Range Nuclear Forces
Treaty (1987), 629
Interwar Years, 388–90
Inukai Tsuyoshi, 492
Ireland, 271
Ishii Kikujiro, 489
Ishiwara Kanji, 492–97
Ishtemi, 140
Islam, 4, 15, 150, 153. *see also*
Ottomans *vs.* Hapsburgs
Islamic State, 27–28, 35

Max Emmanuel of Bavaria, 588n33

Maximianus, 133, 567n130

Maximilian I, 236, 242, 586n6

Maximilian II, 247

Maximinus, 130

Maximinus II Daia, 135

Maximus, Fabius, 92, 94

McKinley, William, 480

McNamara, Robert, 221

Megarian Decree, 72–73,
551n48, 552n50

Megarians, 62–65, 68–73, 551n48

Mehmed II, 205, 236, 254, 586n8

Mehmed III, 247–48, 251

Mehmed IV, 255, 260

Memoire raisonné (Marquis de
Choiseul), 285

The Merchants of Death
(Engelbrecht), 496

Mesopotamia
caravan cities in, 110–11
Ctesiphon, 107, 112, 115–17, 119,
124–27, 129–38, 146, 149,
565n111
Roman fortifications, 128, 131
Roman invasion of, 116–17, 121
Rome-Byzantium *vs.* Persia,
110–12, 116–17, 121–29, 131,
133, 136–37, 142–47, 561n63,
567n126, 567n129
strategic importance of, 110–12, 117
US *vs.* UK, 366–68, 602n58

Messenia, 54, 60, 62–64, 69,
73–75, 78

Metrodorus, 568n141

Miao succession, 421

Midway Islands, 346

Mithridates I, 107

Mithridates II, 107, 116

Mithridates VI Eupator, 114–16

Molotov, V. I., 468–69, 473

Moltke, Helmut von the Elder, 323,
324, 328, 331, 334–36

Moltke, Helmut von the Younger, 343,
373, 376

Monroe Doctrine, 355, 356

Montecuccoli, Raimundo, 252,
253, 257

Montenegro, 456

Montfort, Philip de, 194

Montmartel, Jean Paris, 281

Montreux Convention (1936), 515

Morgan, W., 34, 44

Morgenthau, Henry, 496

Muael II Mamikonian, 571n174

Muhammad (Prophet), 153

Mujahedeen, 531

Munich Agreement, 398–400, 468,
612n116

Murad III, 247

Murad IV, 255

Murray, W., 8

Mussolini, Benito, 391, 405

Mystacon, John, 571n174

Napoleonic Wars. *see* French Wars
(1792–1815)

Narses (Shah), 111, 133, 135–36,
567n129, 571n174

Nasser, Gamal Abdel, 528

National Convention (1792–1795), 299

NATO, 436–37, 518–21,
524–25, 533–35

Nature and Causes of the Wealth of Nations
(Smith), 284

Naval Defence Act of March 1889,
357–58, 601n35

Naval power
in England *vs.* France, 175,
271–74, 276, 277, 282–83,
285–86, 590n11
Kriegsmarine (U boats), 377, 381–82,
393, 409, 412, 413, 616n169
in New World rivalry, 271–74, 276,
277, 282–83, 285–86, 348–49,
590n11, 601n35
in US *vs.* Japan, 486–87, 491,
493–94, 502–3
in US *vs.* UK, 348–49, 354, 355,
357–59, 369, 601n35
in WWI, 373–74, 378, 381–82,
605n18, 607n49, 608n51

in WWII, 375, 377–78, 381, 403–4,
    408–10, 412, 497
Nazi-Soviet Pact, 469–70, 472–73, 476
Nelson, Horatio, 299, 348
Nero, 120–22
Netherlands
    Anglo-Dutch alliance,
        269–71, 590n11
    Treaty of Rastatt (1714), 274
    War of the First Coalition
        (1792–1797), 292–96
    WWII, 398–400
Netherlands East Indies, 505
Neurath, Constantine von, 395
New World rivalry
    Affaire du Canada (1761), 285
    American Revolutionary War, 285,
        286, 292, 297
    Anglo-French alliance, 277–78,
        592nn28–29
    Anglo-Spanish war, 278
    arms exports to, 281, 285
    Assiento, 277, 591n20
    Canada-American border, 350–53
    Cape Finisterre, 278–79
    Caribbean, 278, 592n31
    Cartagena expedition, 278
    Charles Town, 273
    cod trade, 275–76, 591n22
    colonial claims, 275–76
    Convention of the Pardo,
        278, 592n31
    Crown Point fort, 276
    financial policy in, 280, 283–85
    First League of Armed
        Neutrality, 297
    fort-building, 280–81, 594nn41–43
    Fort Carillon, 283
    Fort Duquesne, 283
    Fort Frontenac, 283
    Fort Toulouse/Fort Chartres,
        281, 594n42
    Fort William Henry, 283
    free trade, 280, 593n38
    Kourou expedition, 285
    Latin America, 354–59, 600n26

Louisbourg, 278, 283
Louisiana, 276
Louisiana Purchase, 298
Malouines expedition, 285
Mississippi Company, 275, 591n21
Mississippi River expedition, 590n10
Natchez War of 1729–1731, 276
naval power in, 271–74, 276,
    277, 282–83, 285–86, 348–49,
    590n11, 601n35
Newfoundland, 275–76, 591n22
Niagara fort, 276, 283
nonconfrontation, 275–79
Nova Scotia, 281
Oregon Territory, 353–54
Plains of Abraham, 282
Portobello expedition, 278
Quebec expedition, 273–74,
    283, 590n16
Seven Years War, 279–84, 291
silver trade, 278, 592n33
slave revolts, 278, 592n30
smuggling, 277, 285, 591n20
St. Augustine, 273, 278
St. Lawrence waterway, 276
taxation, 272, 285, 594n52
"The Rule of the War of 1756,"
    280, 593n38
War of Jenkins's Ear, 278
War of the Austrian Succession, 278
Nian rebellion, 421
Nicholas I, 452, 456
Nicholas II, 378
Nicias, 75, 76
Nicolas V, 236
Nicopolis Crusade, 161
Niel, Adolphe, 323
Niger, Pescennius, 125
Nine Power Treaty, 490
Nine Years War (1688–1697), 270
Nixon, Richard, 439, 514, 533
Nye, Gerald, 496

Octavian, 118–19
Odenathus, Septimius, 129,
    131–32, 563n92

Okada Keisuke, 495
Ollivier, Emile, 323
Olney, Richard, 356
Olney Doctrine, 356–57
One-power naval standard, 369
Open Door Policy, 484–85, 493, 498, 499
Operation URGENT FURY, 538
Opium Wars of 1839–1842, 359–60,
    424–26, 444
Orhan, 236
The Origins of the World War (Fay), 496
Orobazus, 116
Orodes II, 117–18
Oroses I, 122–24, 151–52
Osman, 236
Osterhammel, J., 600n26
Ottomans *vs.* Hapsburgs. *see also*
    Hapsburgs *vs.* Europe
  battleground logistics,
    248–51, 261–62
  battleground tactical
    execution, 252–54
  Battle of Lepanto, 243
  Battle of St. Gotthard, 257–58
  Belgrade, 245, 250–51, 588n33
  Bosnia-Herzogovina, 589n38
  Buda, 239, 245, 247, 249,
    260–61, 588n33
  Constantinople, 14t, 236, 237, 244,
    247, 249, 261
  development of, 18t,
    237–38, 254–55
  as discursively contested field,
    235, 585n1
  Eger, 250, 251
  empire creation, 239–41
  enemies in proximate
    territory, 585n3
  families, origins of, 235–36
  financing of, 242–44, 251
  gazi, 245, 255, 588n28
  government structure, 244
  Granada, war of, 225
  helmets of Caesar, 238
  Holy League, 260–61
  Hungary, 242, 244–52, 255, 260–61

  ideology in, 235, 239–40, 242,
    258, 585n2
  information assessment in, 44
  information control in, 238–39
  janissaries, 240, 243–44, 250, 253
  Long War (1593–1606), 240,
    251–52, 257
  Malta, 243
  military recruitment, 240
  Mohacs, 245, 588n33
  objectives, 241–42, 262–63
  Oradea, 255–56
  Peace of Karlowitz (1699), 261
  Peace of Passarowitz (1718), 261
  Peace of Vasvár (1664), 257–58
  Petrovaradin, 262–63
  power by inheritance, 586n6
  proximity in, 12, 237, 262
  raiders, attacks by, 239, 243,
    252, 587n19
  root causes of, 48t, 214, 236
  royal titles, identities, 238, 239,
    586n6, 588n28
  Sava River, 263–64
  Slankamen, battle of, 588n33
  systemic shocks as cause of, 14t
  taxation, 239, 586n11
  Transylvania, 245, 247, 249, 252,
    255–58, 587n25
  Treaty of Bakhchisarai
    (1681), 588n27
  Truce of Edirne (1547), 249
  Truce of Zsitvatorok (1606),
    240, 251–52
  Tunis, 238, 241, 243
  Vienna, 245–48, 250,
    258–59, 588n33
  war making, 242–45
  women, 240–41
  Zenta, battle of, 588n33
Owain Glyn Dŵr, 170, 177, 575n42
Oxford Union, 610n88

Pacific War, 497–502, 627n28
Pacorus, 117
Paetus, Junius Caesennius, 121

Rome *vs.* Carthage (*Cont.*)
  Sardinia, 89, 90, 96
  Second Punic War, 19, 83–85,
    89–97, 151
  Sicily, 82–83, 87, 96
  Spain, 89–91
  Syracuse, 95–96
  systemic shocks as cause of, 13*t*, 15
  thinking, modes of, 86, 91–94
  Third Punic War, 10, 97–100
  Treaty of Lutatius, 89
  Truceless War, 89, 99
  Zama, battle of, 97
Roosevelt, Franklin D., 36, 359, 361,
    408, 410, 496, 497, 506–7, 514,
    529, 616n168
Ross, Robert, 351–52
Rudolf II, 243
Rupprecht, Crown Prince of
    Bavaria, 385
Rusk, Dean, 539
Russell & Company, 359
Russia. *see also* French Wars
    (1792–1815); Sino-Russo-Japanese
    relations
  Alexander II reforms, 453
  alliance making, pre-WWI, 8
  balance of power, 3
  Bolshevik revolution, 382, 430–32,
    434, 469
  in China, 424, 432, 438
  civil wars in, 430
  collectivization in, 431, 466–67
  communism in, 437–42
  communist parties
    establishment, 432
  Communist Party, 431, 437
  Derbent Pass, 110, 112, 139, 141,
    143, 555n20, 570n161
  economic conditions, 423, 520
  empire strategy, 422–25, 427,
    431–32, 445
  February Revolution 1917, 472
  First Five-Year Plan, 466
  foreign policy, 424, 432, 434
  geopolitical imperative, ideology
    vs., 36–37

  global system shocks, 4
  Gorbachev's reforms, 538–39
  growth trajectory of, 23*f*
  October Revolution 1918, 472
  prestige motivations, 9
  Red Army, 437
  serfs, emancipation of, 428, 453
  Sino-Soviet split, 439
  Sweden *vs.* Russia, 282
  as threat to Great Britain, 357
  Trans-Siberian Railway, 425, 427,
    431, 489
  Treaty of Brest Litovsk (1918), 384,
    430, 472
  Tsarist period, 422–25, 430
  in WWI, 378, 379, 382,
    430, 434–35
Russia *vs.* Germany
  Alexander II's letter to Wilhelm I,
    458, 622n30
  Anglo French Guarantee (1939), 468
  anti-Turkish rebellions, 456
  Balkans, 457–58, 461–65
  Bessarabia, 469, 473
  Bosnian Crisis of 1908–1909 (First
    Balkan Crisis), 463–65, 623n44
  Buchlau conference, 464, 623n44
  Congress of Berlin (1878),
    457–59, 622n30
  development of, 449–51, 474–75,
    620n3, 625n77
  Five Power Memorandum
    (1909), 464
  France, 454–56, 462, 467
  Franco-Russian Treaty (1894), 462
  German Confederation, 454–55
  German-Soviet military cooperation,
    465–66, 623n48
  Italy, 461
  Little Entente treaties, 467
  military strategies, 471–74
  minorities, extermination of,
    453, 621n17
  motivations, 465, 473–77
  Nazi-Soviet Pact, 469–70,
    472–73, 476
  Panslavism, 458, 460, 475, 625n77

War of the Grand Alliance/War of the
League of Augsburg, 31, 270,
272, 589n8
War of the Polish Succession, 279
War of the Quadruple Alliance, 274,
277, 591n19, 592n28
Wars of Religion (1562–1598), 269
Wars of the Fronde (1648–1653), 269
Wars of the Roses, 177
Washington, George, 286, 629n20
Washington System, 489–94, 501
Watanabe Jotaro, 495
Wawro, G., 8, 26–27, 40
Webster-Ashburton Treaty of 1842, 353
White Lotus Sect rebellion, 421
Wilhelm I, 328, 331, 458
Wilhelm II, 21, 337–39, 341, 343,
372–75, 380, 461–62
William I, 268
William III (William of Orange),
270–72, 279
William II Rufus, 158
William the Conqueror, 12, 157–58,
162–64, 175, 176, 572n7
Wilson, Horace, 401
Wilson, Woodrow, 361, 367, 381, 514
Winn, Rodger, 413
Wittigis, 144
Wohlthat, Helmuth, 401
World War I
alliances in, 42, 264, 374,
378–79, 381
artillery warfare, 383
attrition, year of, 378–82
Battle of Flanders, 383–84
Battle of Tannenberg, 472
Battle of the Marne, 375, 376
Belgium, 373–76, 383, 605n21
British Expeditionary Force (BEF),
373, 375–77, 381, 383
British people, conscription of, 381
civilian casualties, 375, 377, 605n25
communications, 381, 607n48
compromise peace 1917, 382–83
Dardanelles campaign, 378
declarations of war, 375–76

defense-in-depth tactics, 380
desertion, 385
development of, 18t, 21
Entente Cordiale, 374
events, public perceptions of, 389,
610nn80–83
financing of, 348
Gallipoli campaign, 378
gas warfare, 377, 606n34, 608n52
General Staff system, 381, 607n48
German atrocities, 375, 387, 605n25
German foreign policy,
372–73, 605n13
Germany, borders of, 387–89
Germany, defeat of, 385–86
Germany, food shortages in,
381, 608n53
Haber process, 608n53
historical literature, 389,
610nn80–83
Kitchener armies, 378
Kriegsakademie, 372, 604n9
Kriegsmarine (U boats),
377, 381–82
MICHAEL Offensive, 385, 609n66
military casualties, 376, 384, 385
military necessity *vs.* alliance
support, 386–87
naval power in, 373–74, 378,
381–82, 605n18, 607n49, 608n51
Nivelle offensive, 382
Operation ALBERICH, 382, 385, 387
Passchendaele, 382, 384
power asymmetries as
propaganda, 46–47
prelude to, 371–75, 604n9,
605n13, 605n21
preparations, level of, 19–20
root causes of, 8–9, 496
Russia in, 378, 379, 382,
430, 434–35
Sino-Russo-Japanese relations,
429–30, 435–36
Somme Battle, 379, 380
strategic issues, 376–78, 383–84,
386–87, 606n31

submarine warfare, 372, 377, 604n9
successive conflict effects, 4
systemic shocks as cause of, 4, 14t
Treaty of London (1893), 374
Treaty of Versailles, 387–89,
466, 609n74
Verdun, battle of, 379, 380
Western Front, 377, 378, 380–86,
609n67, 609n69
World War II
air warfare, 408–13, 616n177
alliances in, 42, 402
Allied military operations,
405–7, 410–12
Anglo French Guarantee
(1939), 468
Anglo-German Naval Agreement
(1935), 393
appeasement policy, 393–402, 405,
407, 414
attrition, battle of, 412
Austria, 278, 387, 396
Ball-Wilson negotiations, 401–2
Battle of Britain, 409–10
British bombing campaign, 410–12
British military production, 391–94,
399–400, 408, 611n91
civilian expertise, 408, 412–13
Czechoslovakia, 387, 396–401, 468
declarations of war, 402–4, 473
deterrence effects on, 444–45
Fall Weiss (Case White), 401
geopolitical imperative, ideology
vs., 36–37
German economic situation,
397–406
German military operations, 404–5,
410, 412, 615n167
German morale problems, 411,
616n172
German planning sessions, 395–96,
612n106
German rearmament program,
390–96, 400, 402, 466–67, 611n95
Germany, Allied blockade of, 375,
377–78, 381, 403–4, 408

goals, motivations, 9, 368, 390, 393,
396, 404, 407
Hitler's rise, 390–402, 610n86,
613n130
imperial overstretch, 24–26, 39
Italy, 391–92, 394, 405,
429–30, 468
Kriegsmarine (U boats), 393, 409,
412, 413, 616n169
military casualties, 412
Munich Agreement, 398–400, 468,
612n116
naval power in, 375, 377–78, 381,
403–4, 408–10, 412, 497
Nazi propaganda, 389, 397, 610n79
Netherlands, 398–400
Non-Aggression Pact, Soviet
Union, 402
Norwegian leads, 406
Operation BARBAROSSA, 378,
473–74, 607n39
Operation OVERLORD, 410
Operation Sea Lion, 94
Operation SEA LION, 409
opponents, understanding of,
409–10, 413, 414
Pact of Steel (1939), 468
Poland, 400–2, 405, 406, 465–72,
476–77, 621n17
radar in air defense, 408, 615n163
reparations claims, 389, 610n79
Romania, 400–1
root causes of, 3, 9, 465–67
Ruhr, 388, 403, 404, 411–12
Saar, 406
Soviet foreign policy, 402, 613n130
Soviet Union invasion, 410, 473–74,
615n167
Spain, 392, 611n95
strategic assessments, 397–99, 402,
409–10, 413–14, 613n132
strategic balance, 403–13, 615n163,
615n167, 616n172, 616n177
threat lethality effects, 445
United States, 407–8, 410, 412
V-2 rocket, 411